THE HISTORY OF THE
PENGUIN
INTERNATIONAL RFC

Sponsored by HSBC

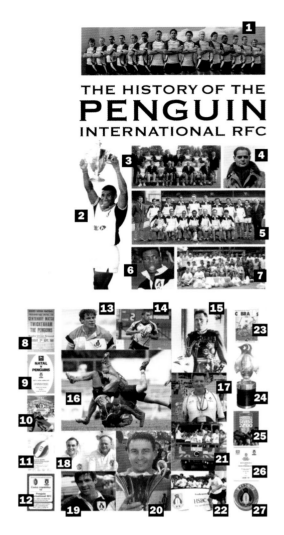

THE HISTORY OF THE PENGUIN INTERNATIONAL RFC

The History of the Penguin International RFC was written, photographed and designed by Dick Tyson and edited by Alan Wright.

First published in 2012 exclusively for The Penguin International Rugby Football Club by JJG Publishing, Sparrow Hall, Hindringham, Norfolk NR21 0DP.

A CIP catalogue record for this book is available from the British Library.
ISBN 978 1 899163 99 1

Typeset in ITC Franklin Gothic and Copperplate.

Printed in China through Colourcraft Ltd., Hong Kong.

www.penguinrugby.com

THE HISTORY OF THE
PENGUIN
INTERNATIONAL RFC

WRITTEN & DESIGNED BY
DICK TYSON

EDITED BY
ALAN WRIGHT

WITH AN INTRODUCTION BY
WILLIE JOHN McBRIDE

THIS BOOK IS DEDICATED TO THE MEMORY OF TONY MASON

AUTHOR'S ACKNOWLEDGEMENTS

I have based most of this book on a series of meetings and recorded conversations which Penguins Life President Alan Wright and I have had over the past few years, and on information garnered from the many Penguin RFC files that Alan opened in the past and has archived in London and Buckinghamshire (I would say in passing that it is very fortunate that Alan retained all of these files. Of course, these were not intended for posterity - they are mainly working files for matches, tours and administration - but they have made the job of this historian very much easier).

Alan and I have also endeavoured to contact as many Penguin Members as possible so as to utilise their recollections in this book. Most of the quotations within come from these conversations, files and recollections from individual Members - as well as from Alan's own writings.

I will add here that it has been an absolute pleasure working on the history of the PIRFC with this most knowledgeable, amusing and generous man - not only because we have at last realised a published history of this great Club, but also because the project has brought Alan and I together as close friends.

A number of other prominent Penguins have helped me by providing anecdotes, documents and photographs. Foremost among these are: Craig Brown (PIRFC Chief Executive Officer), Bill Calcraft (PIRFC Senior Vice-President), Vincent Bramhall (PIRFC Club Secretary), David Townsend (PIRFC Senior Vice-President), Derek Wyatt (PIRFC Advisory Board) and Doris Mason, widow of the Club's co-founder, Tony Mason. Alan would also like to take this opportunity to record his special thanks to Tisa Bateman, with whom he has worked closely over the past 25 years for the advancement of the Club. We thank you all very much for your help.

I have also quoted extensively from match reports written by the following people: Peter Bills, Craig Brown, Ian Bullerwell, Bill Calcraft, Tor Chittinand, Mike Cormack, Robin De Morgan, Al Ginepra, David Hallett, Lawrence Heyn, Tony Jarman, Neville Leck, Sean Lineen, Tony Mason, T.P. McLean, Andy Prior, Pedro Ribeiro, Ron Steel, Abby Wills and Alan Wright.

I must also thank my great friend Dave Urwin for reading and correcting the proofs so diligently, and especially for knocking my grammar into shape. I will take this opportunity to say that if there *are* any errors left in this book they are my fault, not his.

Many thanks to the following individuals and organisations who have made invaluable contributions to this book:
Ian Anderson, Dudley Ankerson, Maria Appleby, John Bailey, Richard Bennett, Gregg Botterman, John Breen, Ian Bullerwell, Dr. Hugh Burry, Tony Carpenter, Carlo Casagrande, Cathay Pacific Airways, Mike Cordell, Robin De Morgan, Ben Dormer, John Frame, Getty Images for the photographs of Douglas Bader on the front cover and on page 111; Willie John McBride on page 6; Fergus Slattery on page 81; Andrew Harriman on page 167; Waisale Serevi on page 210; Dudley Wood on page 217 and the 1999 Russell-Cargill Cup winning side on page 225, Howard Graham, Jeremy Greenwood, John Grove and Grove Industries, HSBC, Frank Hadden, Tony Hanks, Derek Harris, Dennis Hearn, Crawford Henderson, Stephen Herring, Steve Hill, Chris Horder, Valerie Hornett, Robin Hutton, Sheila Jarman, Gordon Keddie at Gala RFC, James K. Kincaid, Krokodyl (for the British Embassy, Paris photograph on page 292), Jill Logan, Mark MacWhite, John McKittrick, Derek Morgan, Giles Morgan, Martin Offiah and Harper Collins for kindly granting permission to quote passages from *Offiah - My Autobiography,* Wolfgang Österling, Phil Pask, Enzo Paolini, Nick Penny, David Powell, Sir William Purves, Mick Quinn, Chris Rea, Flo Rossigneux, Paul Selway-Swift, Sidcup RFC, Iain Sinclair, Tim Stevens, Paul Stimpson (Sports Editor, Cambridge News), Peter Sutherland, Bridget and Colin Thomas, Hugh Thomas, Dr. Kareen Thorne (Cambridge University RUFC Archivist), Tsunami Sports, Two Up Front (for the HSBC/PICA photographs on page 341), Lynne Tyson, Tom Wacker, Phil West, Mike Williams, Abby Wills, Rebecca Worth, Gregory Wright, Patrick Wright and John Zimnoch.

Please note that the Clubs, Counties and Countries referred to after the players names in the Penguin RFC squads throughout this book are correct for the year in which they appear. Of course, many players went on to play for other Clubs or representative teams after appearing for the Penguins - so a comprehensive list of all Penguin players and their Club/County/Country is given in the Appendices.

CONTENTS

HSBC is proud of its long term investment in rugby and is committed to help develop and grow the sport at all levels of the game around the world.

At the heart of all of their sponsorships, HSBC commits to helping develop the grassroots level of the sport and the HSBC Penguins are a key part of this. They are aligned with the bank's sponsorships to enable and encourage youngsters around the world to play rugby, often for the first time, and create a legacy through coach education and the delivery of kit.

The values of rugby echo those of the bank – sportsmanship, teamwork, fair play, respect, courage and integrity. A particular focus for HSBC is to invest in developing rugby markets, which reflects the bank's own strategy of realising the potential of emerging markets around the world.

Giles Morgan
Global Head of Sponsorship & Events,
HSBC Holdings plc

INTRODUCTION

I am very pleased to be writing this introduction to the history of the Penguin International RFC - the world's premier touring club. As you know, I am no stranger to touring myself, having toured with the Lions no fewer than five times - in 1962, 1966, 1968, 1971 and 1974. Looking back to those days, I remember that one of the best things about touring was to witness young men learning about the ethos of rugby football. About the setting of standards. About teamwork. About tolerance. About building character. About bringing human beings together for a common cause - a fine purpose. All the good things you try to teach men. Those values that you could take from the rugby field into your day at work - because, in the end, it is all the same thing.

It is a great shame, but so much of that has gone today, because many people seem to have forgotten why we played this great game for so long. It certainly wasn't for money, but unfortunately everything today seems to be about making a profit. Yet that is, in many ways, incompatible with the whole raison d'être of rugby football.

The Penguin International Rugby Football Club has demonstrated that, in a sport where it seems increasingly that everything *is* about profit, an amateur club can still attract the world's greatest players to turn out for them for the honour and the pleasure of it - and to attempt to win trophies. But what is even more encouraging is that it is those same players and their coaches, through the HSBC Penguin International Coaching Academy and the Penguin International Rugby Football Trust, that are ploughing a huge amount of time and effort back into the sport - by teaching rugby football and its ethos of loyalty, teamwork, friendship, courtesy and comradeship to boys, girls, women, men and aspiring coaches all over the world.

Bearing all of this in mind, it is interesting to look back in this book at the Penguin teams of the past. Unfortunately I never did play for the Penguins - I just had too many commitments with my club, Ballymena, and also with Ulster, Ireland and the British Lions (not to mention my full-time job with the bank). But many of my good friends and former team-mates *have* pulled on a Penguin jersey - Ray McLoughlin, Fergus Slattery, Ken Kennedy, Mick Molloy, Ollie Campbell, John O'Driscoll, Roger Wilkinson, Andy Ripley, Tony Neary, Ian McLauchlan, Alistair McHarg, Clive Rees... the list goes on and on. They were all truly great players who had one thing in common. They recognised something excellent in the spirit of this great club. In other words, they were all proud to be Penguins.

I do hope that this book will bring pleasure to rugby-lovers all over the world. I am sure the club, with its excellent committee and its long-standing alliance with HSBC, will continue to prosper.

Willie John McBride MBE Ballymena, Ulster, Ireland and the British & Irish Lions

In the future, there will be no markets left waiting to emerge.

By 2050, 19 of the 30 largest economies will be in countries we now call 'emerging'*. HSBC's international network can help you discover new markets wherever they emerge next. There's a new world out there.

There's more on trade at
www.hsbc.com/inthefuture

Issued by HSBC Bank plc.   AC22967   *Source: HSBC 'The world in 2050'

FOREWORD

The game of rugby football owes a very considerable debt to Alan Wright and Tony Mason for their foresight in the late 1950s in forming the Penguins out of Sidcup FC, and for their efforts in creating the Club it is today. From those relatively humble beginnings, and with a dedication par excellence, the Club has grown to be the premier rugby touring club anywhere in the world.

This book is a fitting tribute to both Alan and Tony but it also illustrates the best aspects of the game of rugby football. Despite the high profile that the professional game has now achieved on a world stage, the amateur game still flourishes for most players. The Penguins' values, which are so eloquently set out by Willie John McBride in the introduction, epitomise all that is good in the game and the Penguins have been exemplary ambassadors of those values in over 70 countries.

Rugby is not just about an 80-minute game played between two teams and one of the most exciting developments of the Penguins' history was the formation of the HSBC Penguin International Coaching Academy and the Penguin International Rugby Football Trust about 10 years ago.

There are many in the world who are not fortunate enough to have had an early exposure to rugby and the values and ethos of the game. The Coaching Academy goes from strength to strength and, primarily through coaching the coaches in countries where rugby is not a primary sport, the enjoyment of the game has been brought to many and the advancement of the quality of play in those countries has been noticeable.

I was very proud, several years ago, to be asked to become President of the Penguins, following a very distinguished line of former Presidents. Alan and Tony spent an enormous amount of time and effort on the development of the Penguins. Their efforts have, over the years, been supported by many enthusiastic and dedicated individuals who have helped to create the Club, Academy and Trust that exist today. I would like to take this opportunity to thank all of them for the work they have done, and in many cases continue to do, for the Penguins.

This book is a fitting tribute to the Penguins and all those who have been involved since its formation more than 50 years ago. I hope very much that you will enjoy reading it.

Richard Bennett President, PIRFC

PREFACE

I would first like to pay tribute to my dear friend, the late Tony Mason.

Commencing in 1949, our friendship extended over 54 years. From the outset we shared a driven enthusiasm for Rugby Union. Tony was completely dedicated to rugby. He was a perceptive selector, with an unerring eye for players' skills. His enthusiasm and energy knew no bounds - playing squash until nearly 80; executing his 'have boots, will travel' motto by playing alongside his grandson in our team in India, aged 72, and being the first father to play in the same team as his son at Twickenham, in 1967.

Communication with one another was mainly conducted at the telephone, and it is no overstatement to mention that we spoke almost daily for some 45 years, agreeing policy matters for the advancement of the Club. On our early tours, his devoted wife Doris acted as physio/nurse and was a universally respected and loved confidante to our young players.

The Penguins have remained an amateur club and our intention from the outset was to 'put something back into the game', our principal objective being to foster, by coaching and playing, the development, goodwill and cameraderie of Rugby Union throughout the world. This aspiration has been fulfilled by universal selection, worldwide travel, and a Committee drawn from 16 nations.

The Committee was comprised of the two founders for the first 17 years, with our first Treasurer, John Morgan, being appointed in 1977. In 1976 the Committee was enlarged when Sir Peter Yarranton and Derek Morgan joined us, both of whom played for England and later became Presidents of the Rugby Football Union. Our extensive friendships in the Southern Hemisphere have enabled us to have an all-year-round fixture list, a position established for the Club by Bill Calcraft (Australia, past Captain of Oxford University), Craig Brown (Waikato, New Zealand Maoris) and John and Richard Breen (Baravi Exiles, Fiji). I must say that it has given me very great pleasure to observe the international mix of our teams over the years.

The Club is proud to have been invited back to each and every country in which it has played, and clearly this speaks for itself. Moreover, the Editor of *The International Rugby Almanack* stated 'If there was a vote by players the world over for the most popular club the result would be the Penguin RFC. The Penguins really ought to be adopted by the Lord's Taverners as their worldwide ambassadors.'

Our worldwide friendships have been made not only through extensive travel but as a result, in the early amateur days, of the playing party being generally invited to be house guests in the countries in which we played, which cemented personal relationships.

In 1996 I was very pleased to arrange a wonderful sponsorship partnership with HSBC, the world's leading international bank. This has enabled our touring programmes to continue and, more significantly, our worldwide

coaching at grass-roots level. The coaching policy begun in 1959 culminated in the formation of the HSBC Penguin International Coaching Academy - the son is nearly as big as the father!

I was fortunate enough to have been introduced to Dick Tyson, the author of this book, at Sidcup on the day we played them to celebrate their 125th anniversary. Dick is a specialist Rugby Union writer and illustrator, and the author of many successful books, the most popular being *London's Oldest Rugby Clubs*.

I am confident, after 53 years, that the Club will continue to have international success with the benefit of its excellent committee drawn from 15 nations and the first-class leadership provided by Craig Brown (CEO) and Richard Bennett, our experienced and knowledgeable President.

The acorn planted by Tony Mason and myself has become an oak tree, and I trust this book will bring pleasure to rugby lovers throughout the world.

A.G.L. Wright Life President, PIRFC

GROVE

Penguin Intern
RFC

THE
SMAR
CHOIC

Grove Industries are proud sponsors of HSBC Penguins Leisurewear

Grove Industries, founded in 1983, operates apparel, sourcing and manufacturing operations on an international scale and is also famous worldwide for its high-quality knitted and woven ladies fashions. Its products are manufactured in China, Hong Kong and Macau. Other locations include India, Mauritius and Sri Lanka.

www.**grove**ind.com

*The Penguin International RFC squad at the Golden Anniversary Match at Twickenham -
Penguin International RFC (50 years old) v Commons & Lords RFC (25 years old).*

THE PENGUINS - AN OVERVIEW

Penguins owe everything to their alma mater, Sidcup FC - as it was known when formed in 1883 by Captain Edward Blanks. It was amazing that it started - as Sidcup, at that time, was a pleasant little village in Kent with a population of less than 1500. Sidcup owed its subsequent rapid growth to the building of its railway station in 1865.

Tony Mason and Alan Wright, the founders of the Penguins, met at Sidcup FC in 1949 and their harmonious and happy friendship endured for 54 years. There was an element of destiny in their association as Tony was born on 6th March 1918 and Alan on 7th March 1930. Those interested in astrology will note they were both Pisceans. On a more pragmatic basis, however, their friendship was assisted by their total love and devotion to the game of Rugby Union football; their playing together, both at home and on tour; their membership of the Club's selection committee for many years; and both being commissioned in the army (Tony in the Royal Engineers and Alan in the Royal Artillery). Additionally, their characters were entirely complementary and both were experienced Captains and Club Administrators.

Tony had a great sense of adventure and touring was 'in his blood'. In fact, he and Alan toured in Germany together in 1957, only two years before the inception of the Penguins. A touring side was Tony's idea and rapidly metamorphosed into the formation of the Penguin RFC. From the outset they shared the responsibilities on the basis of Tony undertaking fixtures and selection, and Alan the administration. However, there was a constant cross-fertilisation of these roles. Alan considers Tony was the *primus inter pares* during the early years, as it was his charisma, gregarious nature and enthusiasm that sparked the interest of the many great players who happily represented the Club. Quoting from *The International Rugby Almanack*: 'Tony had the uncanny knack, some call it talent, of selecting players from around the world before their own international selectors were aware of their abilities... '.

Alan overcame the difficulties of a Club that did not own a ground or a clubhouse by providing the Club with headquarters in St. James's, London. His main concern was to ensure that the Penguin Club was organised in a form and manner acceptable to Kent County RFU and the RFU for membership, and he persuaded the great Field Marshal Sir Claude Auchlineck GCB, CGIE, CSI, DSO, OBE, LLD (popularly known as "The Auk") to become the Club's first President.

The founders' ethos was to become good ambassadors for amateur rugby worldwide, both on and off the field. They created a special niche in Rugby Union through touring to countries where the game was growing in popularity,

Penguins' alma mater - Sidcup Football Club.

Field Marshal Sir Claude Auchinleck, the Penguins' first President.

Neale House, 62 St. James's Street. Penguins RFC HQ, 1959 - 1992.

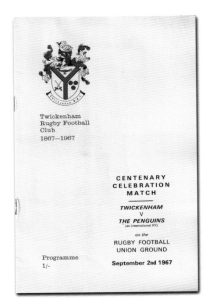

*The Twickenham Centenary Match
programme.*

*The registered logo of
the Penguin International RFC.*

and providing coaching whenever the opportunity arose. Tony decided that the Club's motto should be *on court le ballon à la main*. This policy proved successful until the advent of professionalism coupled with squad coaching.

The Club continued to grow, with tours all over the world, thus satisfying the founders' ambitions for adventure and fulfilling Tony's adage that players were attracted to glamorous destinations, which undoubtedly helped his selection policy.

The Club went from strength to strength until 1994 when Tony fell ill during the tour to Sweden and Denmark. It quickly became apparent that he was seriously ill. By 1996 Alan considered that the Club was at a crossroads, faced with the looming crisis of the game becoming professional and the radical changes that would quickly follow, doubtless affecting the finances of an amateur club and its touring/selection policies. Accordingly, in that year Alan made an approach to the Chairman of the great banking house of HSBC to ascertain whether the Bank would consider sponsorship. Fortunately the Penguins were well known to HSBC as a result of the Club's fine performances in the Hong Kong Sevens in 1987 and '88, and winning of the Malaysian International Tens in the years 1993 and '94. The Chairman of HSBC, Sir William Purves CBE DSO, approved this association and authorised Paul Selway-Swift, Deputy Chairman of HSBC Investment Bank, to regularise the arrangement.

Nick Martin (Harlequins and England) told the founders that the players loved and appreciated the egalitarian spirit within the Club. The late Sir Peter Yarranton described this spirit as 'magic' - one of his favourite words..

As from 1996, in his role of Chief Executive and then as Chairman, Alan initiated a major reformation of the Club's structure, with the help of his colleagues, so that as an amateur club it could nevertheless continue to live in the new world of the professional game. These changes embraced the registration of the Club's logo; the inclusion of the word 'International' in the Club's name; the enlargement of the Club's committee to include further representatives from over-seas and Oxbridge; and the establishment of the Club's educational charity. Andrew Thornhill QC advised the Club on the formation of the educational registered charity, which under his chairmanship has been a great success.

The most significant feature of this programme, however, was the formation of the HSBC Penguin International Coaching Academy in company with Craig Brown (Waikato, London Scottish, Watsonians and New Zealand Maoris). Under Craig's skilful direction the Coaching Academy has achieved worldwide recognition, including the honour of accompanying the British & Irish Lions tour to South Africa in 2009 by arrangement with HSBC, SARU and the Lions committee.

Although approaching 70 years of age, Alan went back to tour management and formed a splendid working relationship with Craig Brown, the Penguins most capped player, who was deservedly appointed, in quick succession, Director of Rugby, Deputy Chairman and, finally, Chief Executive Officer of the Club in 2010.

Alan has often said that the reformation of the Club's amateur committee has created a powerful body with considerable business skills and experience combined with professional knowledge that would be fully capable of running a large company.

The sponsorship established by Alan with HSBC is based on co-operation and reciprocity. The arrangement has 'fitted like a glove' through their mutually agreed international policy of advancing rugby and worldwide education through sport. The Club is proud to be a member of the HSBC family who have assisted the Club with friendship, help and hospitality in countries all over the world from Chile to Canada and the Czech Republic to China!

HSBC is recognised universally as the paramount patron of Rugby Union. Their investment in our great sport includes sponsorship of the HSBC Sevens World Series; the HSBC Asian Five Nations; the British & Irish Lions Tour to South Africa in 2009 and the forthcoming tour to Australia in 2013; and, one of the Penguins' favourite tournaments, the HSBC COBRA Invitational Rugby Tens.

The Club wishes to acknowledge the harmonious working relationship it has had in the past with Toby Forman and William Parry, and in recent years with Giles Morgan, Group Head of Sponsorship, who has astutely directed and administered this huge investment by HSBC in our great sport which has given so much joy and pleasure to millions of rugby lovers all over the world.

The Club is universally recognised as the world's premier touring club and the most travelled sports club in the world - an amazing achievement!

Dick Tyson August, 2012

The 'son' is almost as tall as the 'father'!
HSBC Penguin International Coaching
Academy coaches Ben Fisher,
Neil Young and Alex Edmonstone with
Jonah Lomu in Dubai, 2010.

HSBC ◆X◆
The world's local bank

Alan Wright has always considered
that the Club's sponsorship
arrangement with HSBC 'fits like a glove'.

Alan Wright and the author,
Dick Tyson, at the
Penguins v Commons & Lords RFC
match at Twickenham Stadium
in May, 2009.

THE FOUNDERS

TONY MASON & ALAN WRIGHT

Anthony Richard (Tony) Mason was born in South London on 6th March, 1918 *(writes Alan Wright)*. He was educated at Eltham College in South-East London. The College is a renowned rugby school, and from an early age Tony played rugby for the College, latterly in the 1st XV.

On leaving College in 1935, Tony became a surveyor for the London County Council (later known as the Greater London Council). He also joined his local rugby club, Sidcup FC. Tony would go on to play for Sidcup for the following 28 years (1935 - 1963) always in the 1st XV. According to the *Sidcup Football Club (RFU) Centenary History, 1883 - 1983*: *In 1935 a young all-round player, full of great energy and enthusiasm, who was destined to make an invaluable contribution to both the Rugby and Cricket clubs, came upon the scene - he was Anthony R. Mason.*

Eltham College is situated in Mottingham, South-East London. The modern campus is centred on an 18th-century mansion house (above) which is surrounded by 42 acres of playing fields. It has high academic standards and a reputation for sporting excellence. Notable Old Elthamians include: Professor Bill Deakin, psychiatrist; Professor Stephen Dunnett, neuroscientist; Nick Ferrari, radio broadcaster; Jamie Harris, Newport Gwent Dragons rugby player; Jim Knight, MP for South Dorset; Mervyn Peake, author, and Bryan Sykes, human geneticist.

The Sidcup 1st XV, 1936 - 37. Tony Mason is standing, second from the left.

Dick Hills, a contemporary of Tony's who played for the Old Askeans RFC, wrote the following affectionate appraisal of Tony's prowess on the field of play: *If you occasionally managed to penetrate the infantry and heavy artillery of the Sidcup 1st XV there was always 'Sidcup's Secret Weapon' at the back, Tony Mason, whose motto was 'Ils ne passeront pas.'*

Alan and Tony pictured together in Sidcup colours in the early '60s.

He was the only full-back I knew who could kick immaculately into touch while the ball was still in your hands.

Tony met his future wife Doris in the clubhouse in 1938, when she was helping to prepare the rugby teas and suppers. He was 20, Doris was 18.

At the outbreak of the Second World War Tony volunteered to join the Army. He served for the duration as a Lieutenant in the Royal Engineers.

Tony and Doris married in 1942, and lived on Main Road, Sidcup, just

According to Tony, this was one of the proudest moments of his life. He is pictured at Twickenham with his son, Mike, on the occasion of Twickenham RFC's Centenary Match against the Penguins in 1967. Tony was 49 years old at the time.

Tony Mason in 1947.

around the corner from the entrance to Sidcup FC in Sydney Road (for a long time they were the Club Members that lived closest to the ground). They had two children: son, Michael, and daughter, Penny - plus four grandchildren and seven great-grandchildren.

Over the years Tony amassed a large collection of badges. This one is from the Harlequins 10s Tournament of 2000.

Tony Mason worked for the LCC as an in-house Surveyor, but pretty much hated his job. He maximised his holidays to play in, or to manage, rugby matches and tours with the clubs he loved so much - Sidcup RFC and the Penguins.

Mike Mason took after his father and played rugby for Old Elthamians, Clifton and Kent as stand-off half and place-kicker. Doris recalls that at the age of eight, Mike would run the line at Sidcup - 'he had no choice!'

I first met Tony when I joined Sidcup RFC at the beginning of the 1949 - 50 season as a 19-year-old. Tony was 31 years old at the time, but despite the 12-year age difference we hit it off immediately. Tony played full-back but had a preference for stand-off half. He was a place-kicker of supreme ability. Tony also played with great distinction for the Kent County XV.

Doris Mason is the Club's First Lady and has been a Penguin enthusiast from the very beginning, providing assistance and support to Tony throughout his rugby career. Accompanying many of the worldwide tours, Doris was popular with the players both as a friend and an administering angel to the walking wounded.

Tony's 'AM' monogramed cufflinks - from the earliest days of the Penguins.

Tony was a great driving force, skilfully guiding the Club in the expansion of its worldwide programme. He was the first person I ever met who was totally immersed in Rugby Union - he adored the game, it was his life. Doris always said (with her tongue firmly in her cheek) that Tony's loves were, in order: 'One: Rugby. Two: Children. Three: Boxer dogs. Four: Me!'

Doris and Tony's homes were veritable shrines to the Penguins, full of photographs, ornaments and Penguin memorabilia from every country visited. They made lasting and true friends all over the world.

One of Tony's main strengths was his ability to spot young players who were good footballers. He would often say to me: 'We only want good footballers in the Penguins!' He was also a great selector and manager and established a very fine reputation around the world as an administrator and organiser. He used to say in the 'team talks': *Do the simple things well*. Essential advice when handling a team by invitation which had to play with little or no practice beforehand. With the advent of squad coaching this became even more necessary.

Tony and Doris in Kenya, 1983. The couple toured together all over the world with the Penguins.

The high point in Tony's rugby career was to be appointed Captain of Sidcup's 1st XV for the season 1956-57. He loved the amateur game and was a volunteer Steward at Twickenham for many years. He liked to be present at the international matches and at the Middlesex Sevens. This also gave him the chance to mingle with the players and officials, which helped us considerably with regard to inside information on up-and-coming selection prospects!

He managed every Penguins match from 1959 - 1997, including many

Tony was a Steward at Twickenham Stadium for many years - enabling him to make many invaluable contacts at the Rugby Union.

Doris Mason's house in Bristol: full of Penguins memorabilia!

Statuette of Tony and Doris.

Tony - always had his boots in the car, and he was always ready to play!

Alan Wright and Doris Mason reminisce about Tony in Bristol - August, 2008.

Sunday games to celebrate anniversaries, or the opening of grounds and Clubs. It is ironic, with hindsight, that these were mainly played in aid of Cancer Relief - a charity he always supported.

Tony disliked committees and minutes, leaving these to me, and he detested the idea of professionalism and the prospect of Rugby Union football becoming a business.

I suppose what I will always remember about Tony is that we just couldn't stop him playing! He played as often as he could. Tony's motto was 'Have boots, will travel.' The Penguin team at Twickenham in 1967 was Managed by Tony at the age of 49! His son, Michael, played stand-off half. It created a record as the first father-and-son combination to play in the same team at 'Headquarters'. Tony converted a try and Michael dropped a goal. To cap this, on our 1990 tour to India, Tony, at the age of 72, took to the field for a time, in company with his grandson, Andrew.

He was blessed with a great sense of humour, and kept himself fit, seldom drinking and never smoking. I was hard pressed to get him to take a drink even when we had an occasion to celebrate, such as winning a tournament or an international match, and then it would be something like a small sherry. He once mentioned to me that he had said to his boss towards the time of his retirement 'If you don't interfere with my rugby, I won't interfere with your business!' He played squash well into his seventies, which is why it was such a shock when he became ill in 1994. I visited him from time to time to keep him up to date with the Club's

continuing progress. He dealt with his illness in a supremely brave manner.

At our 40th Anniversary Dinner in 1999 I played a gentle joke on Tony by announcing an award to the 'Best Young Player' of the Club. I said that this young player was a great tackler and very good under the high ball, whereupon I presented Tony with a beautifully crafted silver Penguin bearing the following engravings:

Front:

Presented by A.G.L. Wright to A.R. Mason

in recognition of his outstanding achievements worldwide

in the advancement of Rugby Union Football

40th Anniversary PIRFC Dinner - Dorchester Hotel - 21st May 1999

Back:

This PENGUIN records the founding of the

Penguin International Rugby Football Club by Tony Mason and Alan Wright

and commemorates their 50 years of friendship

It gave me great pleasure that Tony was able to sit with me at Twickenham in 1999 and 2000 and see the Penguins win the Middlesex Sevens on both occasions. The last match he attended was in 2002 when we played British Universities at Iffley Road, Oxford.

Having declined several proposals from me that he should become President of the Club, I was very pleased when, finally, Tony accepted my recommendation in 2001 that the Committee appoint him to the office of Life President. Tony therefore became the first holder of this office. In the Spring of 2003, Kent County RFU honoured us both by appointing us Vice-Presidents in recognition of our worldwide service to Rugby Union.

In commemorating the Penguins' foundation, I am delighted that this history book will be dedicated to my best friend and co-founder, Tony Mason. It was with no little sadness that I gave the eulogy at Tony's funeral. However, I was pleased, with the help of Robert Horner (past President of the RFU; Kent Rugby Union; V-P Penguin International RFC) to arrange for Tony's achievements to be honoured through Robert kindly agreeing to utilise his special powers of dispensation to arrange the scattering of Tony's ashes at Twickenham. This was carried out by his son, Michael, in the presence of his family and myself, along the East touchline.

Tony will always be remembered for his huge contribution to Rugby Union. He died on 27th July 2003 after a courageous nine-year battle with cancer. He was 85 years of age. Tony was my greatest friend and I can do no better than to echo the sentiments of Doris Mason: 'We had lots of very happy times. That's what you're left with, really, memories. This book will refresh them.'

Alan Wright Co-Founder & Life President

The magnificent silver Penguin statue that Alan presented to Tony Mason at the Dorchester on 21st May, 1999.

The quintessential amateur - packed and at the airport, ready to tour! Doris: 'I don't think Tony would have liked present-day professional rugby. Watching it, maybe - but not the out-and-out professionalism.'

Alan was educated at the City of London School which, at that time, was situated on the Victoria Embankment, London. The school has many notable former pupils. They include:
Kingsley Amis, author;
Herbert Asquith, British Prime Minister 1908 - 1916, Mike Brearley, Captain of the England Cricket XI 1977 - 1981 and Denis Norden, writer and broadcaster.

Alan Wright was born in London on 7th March 1930. He was educated at Upton College (Bexleyheath), Mount Pleasant School (Christchurch), The City of London School and London University (College of Estate Management). Always a keen sportsman, Alan achieved his first sporting ambition by becoming an opening batsman for the City of London School. His sporting interests also included boxing, judo, swimming, water-skiing and golf.

Alan's sporting life changed in 1949 when he was accepted for membership of Sidcup FC and was fortunate enough to be coached in his first season (playing no.7) by Frank Woodward, a Welsh schoolboy international who later became the President of Sidcup. Alan's friendship with Tony Mason was cemented by playing with him in the 1st XV, together with Tony Jarman who later became a Penguin Committee member.

In the early 1950s Alan was called up for National Service during which time he was commissioned after attending Mons Officer Cadet School. During his army service, Alan was fortunate enough to Captain three teams, including the

Alan (holding the ball) Captained the Sidcup 'A' XV between 1960 - 1965. In the 1964 - 65 season the team were unbeaten - becoming the first 'invincible' Sidcup XV for over 50 years.

Colchester Garrison XV. Volunteering for the Territorial Army, he served in a regiment of the Royal Artillery in company with other Sidcup players.

After leaving the Army, Alan had an outstandingly successful business career, becoming first a partner and then, at a very early stage in his life, the senior partner in a firm of Chartered Surveyors. He also served as managing

director and chairman of many private and public investment companies including Murrayfield Real Estate, which at one stage owned the land upon which the famous Stadium was built.

Alan was dedicated to Sidcup FC and, after leaving the Army, proceeded for the remainder of his playing career to Captain junior sides to assist the Club in the advancement of young players. At this point it is perhaps best to quote from Sidcup Football Club's 'A Centenary History (1983)' which records, in 1949: *Amongst those who joined the Club was a well-groomed young man, A.G.L. Wright, who by 1968 had set up a remarkable record.* In 1960 it mentions: *The star of Alan Wright who had joined back in 1949 was now to shine for a record period of eight years.*

The History goes on to say: *Alan Wright was a keen student of tactics who led his side from wing forward. In the year 1964-65 the "A" XV had the first unbeaten season in the Club's history since 1908. Their playing record read P 26, W 24, D 2, points for 749, against 102. At one period they had an unbeaten run of over sixty matches.* The History concludes: *However, the most outstanding long-term achievement went to Alan Wright, who was skipper of a side for eight consecutive years, during which his overall record for the period reads: P 210, W 186, D 10, L 14, points for 5,022, against 836 (including two unbeaten seasons). The highlight being 1966-67: P 29, W 29, points for 1038, against 74 - an all-time Club record* (at this time a try was worth only three points).

All of the foregoing was taking place side-by-side with the inauguration of the Penguin Club where Alan was also an early member of the touring parties.

Alan married Lesley in 1957 and they have three children - one daughter (Kitty) and two sons (Gregory and Patrick).

In the Spring of 1957, Sidcup had its first overseas tour after the War to Germany, leaving Victoria Station on a Thursday at midday. Alan had only just got married two days previously but was nevertheless on the boat train platform! He ultimately made three tours to Germany, including managing the Penguins in 2001 when they met and defeated the German National XV.

In 1978, Alan became a Governor in the Dulwich Foundation and served first as an *Estate's Governor of the College of God's Gift* and subsequently, until his retirement in 2000, as a Governor of Dulwich College - after which he was made an Honorary Member of the Alleynian Club in recognition of his long and distinguished service.

Perhaps Alan's most treasured possession is a framed photograph of the 1967 Penguin team at Twickenham given to him by Tony Mason in 1984. The accompanying card reads: 'From Royce to Rolls, to celebrate 25 years of partnership and friendship, Best wishes, Tony'.

Sidcup FC's A Centenary History.

Trophy presented to Alan by his team mates, 'Al's Boys'. The plaque reads: SIDCUP FOOTBALL CLUB. A SMALL TRIBUTE TO A MEMORABLE SKIPPER FROM 'ALS' BOYS 1964 - 65 RECORD: PLAYED 26; WON 24; DRAWN 2; LOST 0; FOR 749; AG 102

The framed photograph of the 1967 Penguin team at Twickenham, given to Alan by Tony in 1984, together with its accompanying compliments card.

Special presentations that Alan holds dear to his heart - Top: 1989 Silver Penguin. Middle: 2004 Silver Salver. Bottom: 2003 PIRFC Golden Jubilee Plaque presented by the Hong Kong Rugby Football Union.

Two highly valued presentations made to Alan were, in 1989, a silver penguin engraved with the words:

'ON COURT LE BALLON A LA MAIN'
Presented to Alan G.L. Wright From his many friends of The Penguin Rugby Football Club in appreciation of his kindness, generosity and friendship

and in 2004, a silver salver bearing the words:

Presented to
Alan G.L. Wright by his many friends within the Penguin International Rugby Football Cub in appreciation of his untiring contribution to the club from its inception and to mark the commencement of The Alan Wright Rugby Scholarship 1959 - 2004

Both these awards were carefully and secretly arranged by Derek Harris (a friend, brother Gunner and Committee member) and the substantial Scholarship Foundation fund received contributions from no fewer than 293 members.

Alan is a Fellow of the Royal Institute of Chartered Surveyors, and a Freeman of the City of London having been a Liveryman of the Worshipful Company of the Gold and Silver Wyre Drawers for some 50 years. He has been a member of the MCC for over 40 years; is a Life member of Kent County CC; and was fortunate enough to be invited to be a playing member of the Invalids CC, the well-known touring club where membership was originally limited to service-men wounded in the First World War. He is a member of the Carlton Club, the RAC and The Berkshire GC, and was also a Governor of Dulwich College for many years.

Alan has been dedicated to the Penguins for 53 years, serving as Honorary Secretary for some 37 years and thereafter as CEO, Chairman and President. In rugby he achieved his lifetime ambitions of Captaining a team that won every match in the season, playing at Twickenham and, finally, Captaining the Penguins at Twickenham in the Club's 50th year in their Golden Anniversary match against the Commons & Lords RFC.

Alan has been an enthusiast for the Middlesex Seven-a-Sides from 1946 onwards and it undoubtedly gave him particular pleasure to see the Club win this great tournament back to back in 1999 and 2000.

Having meticulously organised and chaired the Club's 50th Anniversary Dinner, Alan, always a strategist, decided on reaching his ninth decade to retire from the Presidency. This decision was reached by him in the best interest of the Club and a wish to see younger men hold office. He was delighted to be elected Life President, following in the footsteps of Tony Mason, and will undoubtedly continue to assist the Club as an *ex officio* member of the Executive Committee.

Dick Tyson
Author

 **ALAN WRIGHT**

Proud moments: Alan Wright has played for the Penguins in two matches at Twickenham Stadium: At the age of 37 against Twickenham RFC in 1967 (far left), and later, at the age of 79, as Captain against the Commons & Lords RFC 42 years later in 2009 (left).

*For many years Alan had a number of debenture seats in the East Stand at Twickenham and rarely missed an international match.
His party would usually meet up in one of Alan's favourite pubs for brunch or lunch before setting off to take their seats.*

Alan at his London home.

ARCHIE HENDRICKSES
(Streatham-Croydon, Rosslyn Park,
Barbarians and England Trialist)
captains Penguins at Twickenham Stadium
in September 1967

1958 - 1969

THE EARLY YEARS

Alan Wright: 'Tony Mason and I first became friends at Sidcup RFC in the late '40s, prior to our founding the Penguins in 1959.

The highlights of the Club's first eleven years were:

♦ Joining the Rugby Football Union via membership of the Kent County Rugby Union;

♦ The appointment of our first President, the distinguished and much-loved Field Marshal Sir Claude Auchinleck (affectionately known by the troops as "The Auk");

♦ Playing at Twickenham Stadium for the first time;

♦ The Penguin Rugby Football Club becoming "international" by virtue of our first intercontinental tour to Zambia in 1968.'

*Colonel Frank Douglas Prentice.
Captain of England and
the British Lions before becoming
Secretary of the Rugby Union.*

1958

Although the Club was founded in 1959, the Penguins story really begins a year earlier in 1958. This was the year in which Tony Mason, who had been a playing member of Sidcup Football Club since 1935, first applied to the Secretary of the Rugby Union for the Union's permission to take Sidcup FC on an Easter tour to Berlin.

The Secretary, Colonel Frank Douglas Prentice, was a former Leicester Tigers and Barbarians player who had gone on to Captain both England and the British Lions before taking up his position with the Rugby Union in 1947.

When the Colonel (who was considered conservative even by some of his fellow Rugby Union Committee men) learned by inquiry that the tour was to take place in *East* Berlin (which, of course, at that time was behind the Iron Curtain and under Communist control) all hell broke loose - as Tony discovered when he later telephoned Colonel Prentice to check as to whether the Club had been given permission to tour. Tony told Alan: 'He nearly blew a gasket! He said

The Sidcup FC 1st XV of 1950 - 51, photographed in front of the old pavilion at Crescent Farm, Sidcup. Tony Mason sits second from the right. The team was full of characters including 'Dodo' Watts (1st XV Captain, holding the ball). "Dodo" was a Captain in the Royal West Kent Regiment which took part in fierce fighting against the Japanese in Kohema during World War II. It was 'Dodo' who had the task of interviewing Alan Wright before Sidcup accepted him as a member.

Colonel F.D. Prentice

Colonel Frank Douglas (Doug) Prentice was born in 1898 in Leicester and died 3rd October, 1962 in Paddington.

He was appointed Secretary of the Rugby Union in 1947, retiring due to ill-health in 1962.

Educated at Wyggeston Grammar School, Leicestershire.

Clubs and County: Westleigh RFC (now Leicester Lions RFC), Leicester RFC (1923 - 31), Barbarians FC

and the Leicestershire County RU (1925 - 31).

Won three England caps playing at number 8 in 1928 - a Grand Slam winning year.

England v Scotland, v Ireland and v France.

Captained the British Lions Tour of Australia and New Zealand in 1930 (he was the last Englishman to lead

the Lions until Bill Beaumont took the side to South Africa 50 years later).

Managed the British Tour of the Argentine in 1936.

Served on the Rugby Union Selection Committee from 1932 to 1947. Served in World War One from 1917

with the Royal Artillery. Served in World War Two between 1940 - 45 with RASC as Lieutenant Colonel.

Suceeded as Secretary of the Rugby Union by Robin Prescott in the 1963 - 64 season.

to me: "Do you know where you're going?" I said: "Berlin, Sir." He said: "Berlin my hat! It's behind the Iron Curtain!".'

By Tony's own admission, the Colonel really 'put the frighteners' on him - to such an extent that it wouldn't be until 1964 (well after Colonel Prentice's retirement in 1962) that the Penguins would finally apply to join the Rugby Union.

So in effect the Penguin International Rugby Football Club that we know today really owes its existence to Colonel Prentice's abhorrence of Communism and his refusal to let Sidcup FC tour behind the Iron Curtain in Easter, 1958 (or, as Alan Wright later said: 'We really ought to thank Joe Stalin for the foundation of the Club!)'.

The decision to ban the tour caused a great deal of disappointment amongst the intended tour party, and Tony was determined somehow to make amends to the players.

1959 CHRONICLE

May - Denmark, Sweden and
Holland Tour.
Captained by Tony Mason (England).
Penguins won two matches
in Copenhagen, Denmark.
Penguins beat Malmo RFC in Sweden.
Penguins won one match
in Amsterdam, Holland.

P..p..p...Pick up a ... Penguin

Friendly penguins! Penguin biscuits
were first introduced by William
MacDonald & Sons in 1932.
Top to bottom: The old wrapper,
a Royal Doulton ceramic penguin
and an ad from the early days.

1959

Tony Mason had been very close friends with a fellow Sidcup player, namely Alan Wright, ever since Alan had first joined the Club in the 1948 - 49 season. In early 1959 (with the help of Terry O'Connor, the then Rugby Football correspondent of the *Daily Mail*) Tony and Alan got together and organised an invitational touring side. The squad was to include mainly Sidcup men, together with a number of players from Westcombe Park, Old Dunstonians, Blackheath and Rosslyn Park who were also up for an end-of-season excursion.

As the squad's first tour was to be to Scandinavia, a name fitting for a cold climate was sought for the new Club. Alan explains: 'Tony chose the name "Penguins" after staying up all night, engrossed in his grandson's copy of *A Zoo Book of Animals*. In the morning he 'phoned me and said: 'What about calling the Club "Penguins"?' I liked it. We agreed that Penguins had the great benefit of being a friendly name, as opposed to all the "Pirates", "Buccaneers", "Vandals" and similar war-like names that other *clubs by invitation* had adopted. We were the first and only club by invitation to have a friendly name - and it helped us.'

Tony was also rather fond of a definition of the word that he later found: *Penguins: Nice, clean, friendly birds - but will bite savagely when molested.* Tony himself later said of the name: 'It gives the Club a friendly image. At the time when the Club was formed, penguins were popular. There were Penguin cakes, Penguin biscuits and Penguin books!'

Alan: 'As I say, I've always liked the name "Penguins". Tony chose the name and executed the whole thing - it was his work and his idea, and I agreed with it totally.'

From the outset Tony and Alan adopted complementary roles in the Club. Tony became the main Selector, Tour Manager and Fixture Secretary, and Alan took on the administrative role of Honorary Club Secretary - whilst also joining Tony in selecting the teams.

The two friends also decided to adopt a policy of open rugby football - running with the ball to attack from almost any position. It was also decided that, quite apart from the general enjoyment continental tours give to the tourists themselves, the Penguin Rugby Football Club would offer to provide (whenever invited) coaching help to newly-formed clubs and to schoolboys.

So it was that in May, 1959, Tony Mason co-selected and managed the very first Penguin Rugby Football Club Invitational Touring Side to Denmark, Sweden and Holland as the Tour Manager. Tony also Captained the Penguins in the four matches played.

It was an unfortunate year for Alan as he was strongly advised on medical grounds to take a break from business, which in effect prevented him from accompanying the Penguins' first tour. He took a month's sabbatical, his longest-ever holiday, and visited New Zealand where he had the pleasure of watching the Lions' second test match against New Zealand - surely a classic "busman's holiday".

The first two Penguin RFC matches were played in Copenhagen, and both were won by over 40 points (in one of these matches the Danish team was led by Jorgen Larsen - a man who would greet Tony Mason again 35 years later when Penguins once again visited Copenhagen in 1994).

After Denmark the Penguins went on to Sweden for a match against Malmo RFC (the game was won by over 60 points). It was at this match that Tony first played against Wolfgang Österling, an influential member of Malmo RFC. Wolfgang was so impressed with the Penguins' style of running rugby that when he and his friends founded their own club three years later in Trelleborg he named it *The Pingvin Rugby Club*, after the Penguins. The two Penguin Clubs subsequently developed a strong bond of friendship, and have kept in close contact ever since.

On their way home through Holland the Penguins played another game in Amsterdam and won it by over 40 points. Thus the tour was completed with four wins out of four and the scoring of over 200 points. But it wasn't just the winning and points-scoring that grabbed the attention of their hosts on this tour. It was the Penguins' cheerful willingness to share their expertise.

Tony would later (in 1998) remark of this tour: 'In 1959, rugby in Denmark and Sweden was in the early stages of development. The game in Denmark had been founded and kept going by a remarkable man called Eigil Lund - one of the head officers of the Mounted Police in Copenhagen - who had a great love of rugby. Rugby was so backward in Denmark in 1959 that the tour became an instructional and missionary one. After each game we would pick two teams, mixing Danish players with Penguins, and we would coach the Danes as we played.'

Alan adds: 'Yes, we commenced our coaching activity on an ad-hoc but well-thought-out basis from the very beginning - so our history of coaching goes back to this very first tour in 1959. We said from the outset that the Penguins would offer to provide coaching help to any clubs that wanted it, and we began to put this into practice after one of those first matches in Copenhagen. Tony said to the opposition: "OK. Your forwards and our forwards change shirts". So we played "half English and half Danish" versus "half Danish and half English"! We were trying to spread, in a small way, the Corinthian spirit of rugby.'

The Penguins didn't go on tour in 1960, but they did return to see their friends in Denmark at the end of the 1960 - 61 season.

The first-ever Penguin Invitational Rugby Football Club tour took in Denmark, Sweden and Holland. At the end of the tour the Danish Rugby Union President told the party that they were: '...the finest rugby ambassadors ever to come to Denmark.'

Danish RU pin badge from the Tony Mason collection.

The Penguins' first strip consisted of white jerseys, white shorts (the players had to supply their own) and the player's own club socks. Alan cheerfully admits that in these earliest days the jerseys were often borrowed from Sidcup RFC, who also played in white.

1961 CHRONICLE

May - Denmark Tour.
Captained by Tony Mason.
Penguins won all four matches.

Another fine Danish RU pin badge from the Tony Mason collection.

The Pingvin Rugby Club of Trelleborg was founded in October, 1962. Pingvins will celebrate their Golden Jubilee in 2012 with a match against the originals!

1961

In 1961 the Penguins went back to Denmark with Tony Mason both managing the tour and Captaining the team, as he had done two years earlier. The Penguin players were once again drawn mainly from London Clubs, and included a fair sprinkling of Sidcup RFC players.

Tony Mason later wrote of this tour: 'The Club returned to Denmark to play four matches, all of which were won handsomely. Friendships were cemented, with one player returning to marry his Danish girlfriend and take her back to New Zealand with him!'

Of these early Penguin tours Alan recalls: 'Well, the tours of '59, '61, '63 and '64 were all into Europe, and they were all very much organised and managed by Tony. We made a lot of friends. We played fifteen-a-side matches and stayed for three weeks at a time. All the travelling was done by ferry, train and coach, and, as amateurs, each player paid his own way. The Club had no funds at this stage and we certainly couldn't afford aeroplanes. These tours created the foundation of our friendships with many of the smaller European nations, which remain to this day.'

The Penguins didn't tour in 1962, but another event took place this year which would profoundly effect the Club's future - the retirement of Colonel Doug Prentice from the Rugby Union due to ill-health. His retirement paved the way for the appointment of Robin Prescott as the new Secretary. Robin subsequently became a good friend of both Tony and Alan and was very helpful to, and supportive of, the Penguins in their early years.

1962 was also the year that Wolfgang Österling became a founder of the Pingvin Rugby Club of Trelleborg, Sweden - naming it after the Penguin RFC.

The Pingvin Rugby Club of Trelleborg, South Sweden

The brainchild of Wolfgang Österling, formerly a player with the Malmo Rugby Club, the Pingvin Rugby Club was founded in Trelleborg, South Sweden, on the 18th October, 1962. The Club's name was directly inspired by Wolfgang's association with the Penguin Rugby Football Club which started when he was a player with the Malmo Club that played Penguins in 1959 (and also by the fact that, coincidentaly at that time a couple of penguins were living in his local park!).

The Pingvin Rugby Club was only the fifth rugby football club to be founded in Sweden. Pingvins struggled in their early years, running only one XV. The Club played in the Swedish Championship series for the first time in 1963. Pingvin's home ground was Järavallen at that time - a very windy, open pitch only 30 metres from the beach.

In 1970 the Club obtained their first club rooms in Algatan town centre, and by 1973 membership had increased sufficiently to run a 2nd XV. This was followed soon after by the formation of Junior and Colts sides.

At the beginning of the 1980s, bigger club rooms were obtained in a cellar on Valldammsgatan. During this time a new arena was also secured at Pilevallen, where the Pingvins have played ever since.

1963

In 1963 the Penguins went to France to play four matches. Another match was then played in Geneva, Switzerland. All of the matches on this tour were won.

Niggie Mee, a Harlequin Football Club player who also played for Sidcup and Bedford Athletic, was the Tour Captain. Niggie was a prop forward and a well-known character in the game at that time. As a matter of interest, Niggie was often referred to as 'Nigger' Mee. According to Bob Ingledew, the former President of Bedford Athletic and one of Niggie's oldest friends, this was because a certain Harlequin official couldn't spell his name and gave him the name 'Nigger' instead.

Alan recalls: 'I remember an evening match taking place in Beckenham in 1963 when Tony and I were playing for a Combined Clubs side against a Combined French University side. The score was 0 - 0 at half-time. After the break Tony kicked a penalty from the half-way line (he would have been 45 years old at this time) and the French just collapsed. We beat them by twenty or thirty points to nil. The kick destroyed the opposition's morale. After that they knew they couldn't transgress in their own half! Tony was a fantastic place-kicker in those days, even with the old leather ball that gathered so much weight when wet.'

1963 CHRONICLE

May - France and Switzerland Tour. Captained by Niggie Mee (England). Penguins played four matches in France and one in Switzerland. All were won.

The third Penguin tour was to France and Switzerland.

Wolfgang Österling (left) in August, 1986. He holds a Penguin that was presented to the Pingvins by Tony Mason to commemorate the opening of the new Pingvin clubhouse.

In 1983 the Pingvin Rugby Club started its first ladies XV.

The Club's first independent clubhouse was built at Pilevallen in the late '80s. A stand was later added, which was subsequently named *Wolfgang Österling's Stand*, after the Club's founder, Chairman and Honorary President.

To date (2012), the Pingvin Rugby Club senior squad have won eleven Swedish Championships. The senior Ladies squad have won two Swedish Womens' Championships and Pingvin Youth squads have won two U19 Swedish Championships as well as several Swedish Youth Team Championships. Many Pingvin RFC members have played for the Swedish National Team and the Pingvin Rugby Club are now one of the largest clubs in Sweden.

In 2012 the Penguins will celebrate their old friends the Pingvin RFCs' Golden Jubilee in style with a combined HSBC Penguin/King Penguin Coaching and playing tour.

1964 CHRONICLE

August - Denmark and Sweden Tour. Captained by Tony Mason (England). Penguins played two matches in Copenhagen, Denmark, and three matches in Stockholm, Sweden. All five matches were won.

Penguins beat Pingvins RC 33 - 5 in Trelleborg, Sweden

1st December - Tony Mason and Alan Wright officially apply for the Penguin RFC to become members of the Rugby Union

28th - 31st December - Belgium Tour. Captained by Tony Mason (England). Penguins beat Anderlecht 48 - 11 in Brussels
Penguins beat Kituro 37 - 3 in Brussels
Penguins beat Sporting Club Administration le Bruxelles (SCAB) 16 - 0 in Brussels
Penguins beat Brussels University 26 - 0 in Brussels

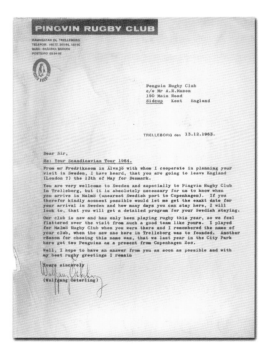

The original letter from Wolfgang Österling to Tony Mason, in which he explains why he named his new club the Pingvin Rugby Club and invites the Penguins to play in Trelleborg.

1964

1964 was unusual because it was the first time that the Penguins undertook two tours abroad in the same year, and it was also the first time they had toured during the UK rugby season.

The first of these tours took place in late summer. Tony again managed the tour and Captained the squad. The tour included the Penguin's third visit to Denmark and their second to Sweden. They played two matches in Copenhagen and three matches in Stockholm. All of these matches were won comfortably.

And then, after a request from Wolfgang Österling, a special match was added to the end of this tour, taking place in Trelleborg against the Penguins' newly-formed namesakes, the Pingvin Rugby Club (or, as Eigil Lund called them at the time, "The Chicks Club"!). The match took place on 28th August, 1964, and the original Penguins won by 33 points to 5.

Since the retirement of Colonel Prentice and the appointment of Robin Prescott to the position of Rugby Union Secretary at the end of 1962, Tony and Alan had been intending to apply to the Union to become a member club.

Then one day Alan was reading his copy of the *Rugby Union Handbook* when he discovered, to his horror, that the organisers/players of tours that had not received the approval of the Rugby Union could be suspended for life from playing Rugby Union football. Alan told Tony that the Club could also be running foul of RFU Bye-Laws relating to overseas tours. Because of the tenor of his earlier conversation with Colonel Prentice, Tony did not wish to make a formal application to the Rugby Union for membership at that time. Accordingly, it was only after the Colonel's retirement that Tony and Alan applied to the Rugby Union for the Club's admission to membership.

In October, 1964, Alan duly applied to Robin Prescott for the Penguin Rugby Football Club to become affiliated to the Rugby Union. He included, with the application, a record of all the fixtures that the Club had arranged for both 1963 and '64. Robin Prescott wrote back on November 10th, agreeing in principle with the application, and suggested that as both Alan and Tony lived in Kent it might be expedient for the Penguin RFC to join the Kent Rugby Union. This was because it would be the Kent County Rugby Union, as the Club's Constituent Body, that would have to support the Penguins in any request the Club made to become members of the Rugby Union.

Alan takes up the story: 'So Tony and I duly went to Twickenham, and we met Robin Prescott at exactly twelve noon on December 1st, 1964. He received us warmly and said that he appreciated our activities and thought that the Club would be beneficial to the best interests of Rugby Union football abroad - and that we fully deserved to become members. But the main procedure was, of course, through our County, Kent. In passing - Robin took us to lunch at The London

Apprentice - a wonderful pub at Isleworth overlooking the Thames, which, coincidentally, became my preferred venue for many years for entertaining my friends on international match days'.

Joining the Rugby Union made Tony Mason and Alan Wright very proud - their new Club was now official. With this in mind, Alan became determined to make sure that the Penguin RFC was set up in a business-like manner from the outset. On 15th December, 1964, Alan wrote the following letter to Tony: *I have been glad to share in the effort to join us in the Rugby Union, and I am pleased to be Secretary of the Club, but I would like to make it quite clear to you, as I want to tell everyone else, that the whole show really belongs to you and it would all be nothing without all the efforts that you have put into it over the years. Finally, I enclose a cheque for £25 which is a small gift from me to the Club so that we start off with some funds. We shall obviously have to regularize our membership arrangements so that we have a small income each year to pay our subscriptions to Kent and the Rugby Union, etc.*

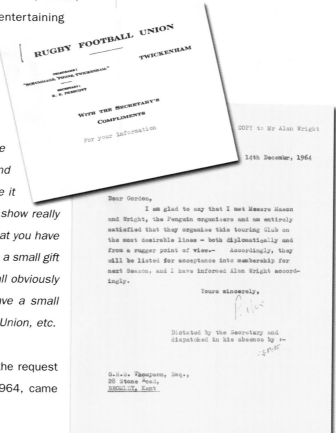

Over the years, the Club has undertaken many tours at the request of the Rugby Football Union. The first of these, to Belgium in 1964, came about soon after Tony and Alan's meeting with Robin Prescott.

Alan takes up the story: 'Not long after having been accepted into the Rugby Union (but without actually formally becoming members - the Penguins had to wait until 1965 to be admitted) Robin Prescott telephoned to advise me that he'd had a letter of complaint from the Belgium Rugby Union because a famous university college rugby football team had let them down over a tour at the last moment (for the second time), and could we stand in? I confirmed that the RFU could rely on us to undertake this match and, indeed, a short tour to Belgium.'

Normally Penguin tours were arranged to take place at the end of the season, but this, the second tour of 1964, was hastily arranged to take place between Christmas and the New Year. As Tony said at the time: 'Alan and I went into action through telex and telegrams and we were able to rearrange all of the fixtures by December 10th.' The Penguins travelled to Brussels on Sunday, 27th December, and returned to England on Friday, 1st January, 1965. The touring party consisted of 26 players and two spectators.

Above and left: Correspondence between Robin Prescott, his Committee and Alan Wright regarding the Penguins' acceptance into the Rugby Union.

A catholic range of London-based Clubs contributed to the Penguin squad in the winter of 1964. Top to bottom: Blackheath, London New Zealand, Old Elthamians, London Scottish, Rosslyn Park, Saracens, Sidcup, Westcombe Park.

Each member of the Penguins party were given a copy of the following information and instructions from Tony before leaving for Belgium:

Penguin RFC Tour to Brussels. Sunday 27th December 1964 - 1st January 1965. Fare £7/4/-. Hotel 15/- bed and breakfast. Total: approximately £11. Kit - All white, own socks. We like the party to wear blazers and dark grey slacks with a club tie if possible. Penguin ties are available at 8/6d.

We will play three games but if there are enough players we may play a fourth. Each player will get at least two games and some may get three - the lucky lads! We are going on this tour as ambassadors to help salvage the good name of British Club Rugby which has become somewhat tarnished in the eyes of the Belgian Rugby Union due to recent unfortunate happenings.

This was the first Penguin tour for which at least a partial line-up of the squad was recorded. And the man who compiled the list, T.P. McLean of the *Daily Herald*, even included a few interesting details about the tour party - especially those players with an antipodean background. He wrote:

M.C. Cormack - record points scorer of Ranfurly Shield Rugby, Auckland, and Blackheath FC; M. Grace of Combined Australian Universities (centre or full-back); Don Galbraith, formerly of Northcote Seniors; B. Slade of Invercargill Pirates; Chris Spence of Gisborne (no.8); Peter Bell of Blackheath FC and Bay of Plenty RFC (a future England international wing-forward who would go on to win four caps in 1968); C. Hacking and L. Bailey - two Southlanders who have both won County Caps; John Heggadon of Saracens FC (RFU) and Kent County RU (lock) and Bradman Bengka-Coker of Old Elthamians. Of Benka-Coker, McLean writes: He is a full-blooded negro from Sierra Leone whose father, who is a cricket fanatic, named one son Ponsford and the other Bradman (as a matter of interest, both of the rugby-loving Benka-Coker brothers attended Eltham College, the same school that Tony Mason attended, and both played for Old Elthamians, Rosslyn Park FC and Surrey County).

The Penguin party comprised six men from Blackheath, six from Sidcup, three each from London New Zealand and Old Alleynians, two each from London Scottish, Rosslyn Park and Westcombe Park and one each from Saracens and Old Elthamians. Eight players had won County Caps, 13 were regular 1st XV players and the others were from second or third XVs and possesed, according to Tony Mason: 'maturity and experience' or 'youth and promise'. Tony Mason later wrote a full report of the tour for the Rugby Union:

Monday, 28th December. Played Anderlecht under floodlights. The ground was covered in a foot of snow, the areas of the marking lines were solid

The original mustard yellow Penguin tie. Only 8/6d.

ice, and the temperature was 16 degrees below freezing point. The Belgians insisted on playing. The cold was intense, but the Penguins, being Penguins, won by 48 to 11.

Tuesday, 29th December. We were given a reception by the Martini Company at 6pm and we played Kituro RFC under floodlights. Kituro is Teddy Lacroix's own club. (Teddy was the Secretary of the Federation Belge de Rugby in Brussels at this time). Kituro Rugby Football Club (founded 1961) had been named after a mountain in the Congo and was made up of 120 members, all under the age of 25. The snow had compacted to six inches depth and a hard fall meant crashing on to rock-hard ice. The Pengiuns won 37 - 3 against, as Cormack put it, 'rather more clueful opposition'.

Wednesday, 30th December. Sporting Club Administration le Bruxelles (SCAB Rugby Club) under floodlights. Result 16 - 0 to us. At 8pm (the first three matches were played at this hour, incidentally) the snow had melted because of rain - but beneath two inches of water and slush lay solid, frozen ground. One of our Englishman refused to play because the conditions were so dangerous. The Belgians, tremendously keen, insisted on playing, and with a 16-stone centre and a brilliant Penguin, Paddy Mahon, we all capitalised on the unwillingness of the Penguins to expire on a foreign strand.

Thursday, 31st December. Finally came the University of Brussels, who we beat 26 - 0 in an afternoon game. (Alan, who played in this match, recalls: 'I was amazed that we even started. The pitch was all-white to begin with. So they flattened the snow and marked out the touchlines and other markings with red paint!').

On the morning of this day we were received in the Lord Mayor's Parlour in the Town Hall at Brussels.

Alan Wright: 'Peter Bell, of Blackheath and England, was one of our early playing members and a stalwart Penguin. In my view he was, for many years, the only forward whose presence on a pitch could change a pack that was going backwards in adversity to one that was going forward as the conquerers!'

A great friend of the Penguins: Robin Prescott in the early 1960s.

Robin Prescott, Secretary of the Rugby Union

Robert Edward Prescott (nicknamed 'Robin') was born 5th April, 1913, and died 18th May, 1975.

He was the son of Ernest Prescott, who himself had served as the 23rd President of the Rugby Union between 1925 and 1933.

Robin had been elected as a Vice-President of the Rugby Union in 1962 - 63 season but resigned in order to take up the professional appointment of Rugby Union Secretary. This decision forestalled the first possible example of a son following his father as President of the Rugby Union.

Robin was educated at Marlborough College (Captain 1931) and Trinity College, Oxford University (1932).

Clubs and County: Harlequin FC (Captain 1939), The Army, Combined Services, Guildford RFC (Captain 1946 - 48), Barbarians, Middlesex County (Captain 1939). He won six England Caps playing as a front-row forward.

Robin served in World War Two with The Royal Artillery in Central Mediterranean Forces.

Mike Cormack played for Blackheath and Auckland where he was a member of the Gallaher Shield winning team in 1966. Mike later became President of Auckland RFC 1987 - 88.

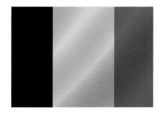

The unbeaten tour of winter 1964 smoothed the waters with the Belgium Rugby Union and made the Penguins even more friends in Europe.

Welcome early publicity, generated by the 1964 Belgium tour. Unfortunately, the proposed televised match against Racing Club de France never happened.

Tony finished his report with a note of thanks to the Rugby Union - and to Robin Prescott in particular: *It now only remains for me to thank you on behalf of the Penguins for making this tour possible by giving us the opportunity. We all enjoyed it and if any other opportunity for tours of this kind should arise, then we shall be very pleased.*

New Zealander Mike Cormack, the Blackheath and Auckland star who was probably the best-known name on the Penguins' team sheet at this time, later wrote of the trip: *We left on Boxing Day, 1964, taking the ferry both ways to Belgium. The team stayed at the Hotel De Touriste, in what is euphemistically called the 'entertainment' part of Brussels, and played four games on the same pitch in Brussels without losing. The pitch was a foot deep in fresh snow for the first game and minus seven degrees - quite a nice surface actually.*

The snow had largely disappeared for the second game, leaving frozen ground - not nearly as nice.

By the third game the ice was melting - leaving sharp shards and water. Very uncomfortable.

The final game began in snow but ended in good old mud, which we Kiwis are used to. All except the last match were played in the evening at around 8pm. The after-match started late and lasted into the next morning!

Tony Mason later summed up the Belgium tour in his own inimitable style: *Four games were played in four days, the temperature being minus nine degrees centegrade with ten inches of snow on the pitch. Conditions were so appalling that no game would have been contemplated in England - but being so aptly named we played and won the four games comfortably. All of the matches were played under floodlights. Our greatest achievement here was to convince an All Black trialist full-back to run with the ball in his own 25. When he returned home he was a convert to attacking rugby - but it was rumoured that he was shot by the New Zealand selectors for subversive activities!'*

Alan: 'There is another point I should make whilst we are concerned with the activities of the Club during the '60s, '70s and '80s. This is in regard to the many matches we played in the Home Counties on Sundays, usually for the benefit of the Cancer Relief Charity - which we made our charity of choice. They were special matches in which our opponents would be celebrating the opening of a new clubhouse, new ground or an anniversary - something of that nature.

'In those days we were always able to select a team of well-known players from first-class clubs, playing mainly in the Home Counties. This helped to maximise the attendance and, of course, the charitable donations. Unfortunately, this part of our programme was curtailed by the commencement of professionalism and the introduction of leagues.'

1965

Alan: 'From the outset I assumed responsibility for the majority of the Club's administration.

'On 1st February, 1965, I decided to write to Field Marshal Sir Claude Auchinleck, who, as General Auchinleck, was known world-wide as "The Auk" (at this time Sir Claude was the Chairman of the company of which I was the Managing Director). He had been Commander-in-Chief of the Eighth Army and he had won the first battle of El Alamein - being the first English General to stop Rommel and his *Afrika Korps*.

Insignia of the Eighth Army (left) and Afrika Corps (right).

'We had become good friends by the time I asked him if he would do the Penguins the great honour of becoming the Club's first President. He accepted. I'll mince no words in saying this - it gave us very considerable status in the world at large to have such an eminent soldier take this office for a newly-formed Club. It gave us *gravitas*.'

The Penguins embarked on a ten-day tour of Berlin, Hannover and Brussels on 21st May at 9.30am from Victoria Station, London. The touring party consisted of 26 players, one referee and two spectators (two more players flew out at a later date). Travel for the majority was by means of a train to Dover, a boat to Ostend and a coach to Berlin. The fares were £15/10/- per head. As usual, the party was managed by Tony Mason, but this time the team would be Captained by Archie Hendrickses - a well-known Streatham-Croydon RFC player who had been an England trialist.

Tony and Alan were particularly pleased about having organised this tour. It meant that they had at last managed to get a Rugby Union-approved tour over to Berlin - after all the trials and tribulations of being refused consent in 1958!

Once again, Tony wrote a comprehensive report of the tour for the Rugby Union. From it we learn that the Penguin RFC colours for this tour were, once again, all-white, combined with the player's own Club socks. We also learn that during their six-day-long stay in Berlin the players' accommodation was in the Berlin Police Barracks. With his tongue firmly in his cheek, Tony wrote in his tour notes to the players: *This means we must behave ourselves to a certain extent and must not wreck the joint!*

The Penguins had organised four fixtures in Germany: three in Berlin and one in Hannover. There was then a day set-aside for sightseeing in Cologne before the Club played a fixture in Brussels on the way back home.

Tony wrote in his report: *three matches were played in Berlin, on public parks that had excellent pitches and changing accommodation. They were: Berlin Police (won 42 - 11), Berliner Sport-Verein 1892 (won 62 - 3) and a Combined team from Turn-und Sport-Verein Siemensstadt (won 29 - 5 in pouring rain).*

1965 CHRONICLE

February - Field Marshall Sir Claude Auchinleck becomes the first President of the Penguin RFC.

May - Germany and Belgium Tour. Captained by Archie Hendrickses (South Africa). Penguins beat Berlin Police 42 - 11 Penguins beat Berliner Sport-Verein 1892 62 - 3 Penguins beat a Combined XV from Turn-und Sport-Verein Siemensstadt 29 - 5 Penguins beat Germania-List 29 - 7 in Hannover, Germany Penguins beat a Combined Brussels XV 26 - 3 in Brussels, Belgium

Field Marshal Sir Claude Auchinleck became the first President of the Penguin RFC in February, 1965.

Penguins played three matches in Berlin and one in Hannover during the German leg of their 1965 tour. During the course of their stay in the Berlin Police barracks, the Penguins' players were issued with Police whistles and told that if they got into trouble at any Berlin nightclub they only needed to whistle and the police would come along and get them out!

SPORT-CLUB
GERMANIA-LIST
VON 1900 E.V.
HANNOVER

*Germania-List amenities
and fixture booklet.*

The hospitality in Berlin was very good under the circumstances. Having no clubhouses of their own rather handicapped the Clubs, and local restaurants were used. The first game we had our meals were paid for and we bought the beer. The second and third games, we bought the meals and had our beer paid for.

After playing the three matches in Berlin the Penguins departed on the morning of Thursday, 27th May and arrived in Hannover that afternoon in time to play Germania-List in the evening.

Tony: *The match against Germania-List in Hannover was very good, the Penguins winning by 29 - 9. The game attracted about 200 spectators to their own Club ground and pavilion. Although the score against us contained two dropped*

Field Marshal Sir Claude Auchinleck - The first Penguin President

Field Marshal Sir Claude Auchinleck, GCB, CGIE, CSI, DSO, OBE, LLD.

Born 21st June, 1884 in Aldershot. Died 23rd March, 1981 in Casablanca.

Educated at Wellington College and at the Royal Military Academy, Sandhurst.

'The Auk,' as the Commander-in-Chief of the 8th Army, was Britain's first General to defeat Rommel's Afrika Korps in the first battle at El Alamein, and the only Field Marshal to be appointed on two occasions as Commander-in-Chief of the Indian Army.

In 1904 he joined the 62nd Punjab Regiment. He learnt Punjabi and was able to speak fluently with his soldiers. This familiarity engendered a lasting mutual respect.

During the First World War he served in Egypt, Palestine and Mesopotamia. He was Mentioned in Despatches and received the Distinguished Service Order in 1917 for his service in Mesopotamia.

Between the wars, Auchinleck served in India. He was both a student and an instructor in the Staff College at Quetta, and also attended the Imperial Defence College.

In 1929 he was appointed to command the 1st battalion, 1st Punjab Regiment.

In 1933, he took command of the Peshawar Brigade, which was active in the pacification of adjacent tribal areas. Auchinleck was again Mentioned in Despatches and received the CSI and CB for his skill in managing the operation.

In 1938, with war looming, Major-General Auchinleck was appointed to chair a committee to consider the modernisation, composition and re-equipment of the British Indian Army.

Upon the outbreak of the Second World War Auchinleck was summoned to the United Kingdom to command IV Corps.

In May, 1940, Auchinleck took over command of the Anglo-French ground forces in Norway - a military operation that was doomed to fail. After the fall of Norway he briefly commanded V Corps before becoming General Officer Commander-in-Chief, Southern Command.

In July 1941, following the see-saw of Allied and Axis successes and reverses in North Africa, Auchinleck was appointed Commander-in-Chief, Middle East Command.

goals and a penalty, the standard in Hannover was much higher than it had been in Berlin and there was a better all-round knowledge of the game there.

Germania-List, having their own clubhouse, were really able to entertain us. We were greeted with tea and biscuits before the game, a meal after the game, and breakfast in the clubhouse the next day. The beer flowed fast and free. We were made very welcome.

The party then went to Cologne for a day before leaving for Brussels and playing a Combined Brussels Club XV that afternoon.

Tony continues*: In Brussels we played a Brussels select XV raised from different Clubs. We won the game 26 - 3 (the match was played after a heavy*

Germania-List Sports Club pin badge from the Tony Mason collection.

It was at El Alamein that Auchinleck stopped the German/Italian advance in the First Battle of El Alamein.

Like his foe, Rommel, Auchinleck was subjected to constant political interference.

Churchill was desperate for some sort of British victory before the planned Allied landings in North Africa.

He badgered Auchinleck immediately after the Eighth Army had all but exhausted itself after the first battle of El Alamein. Churchill flew to Cairo in early August 1942 and replaced Auchinleck as Commander-in-Chief.

In 1943 Auchinleck was once again appointed Commander-in-Chief of the Indian Army and continued in the post until after the end of the war.

In 1946 he was promoted to Field Marshal but he refused to accept a peerage, lest he be thought associated with the Partition, a policy that he thought was fundamentally dishonourable.

He resigned as Commander-in-Chief and retired in 1947. In 1948 Sir Claude returned to Britain.

Although perceived as being a somewhat dour character, he was known as a generous and welcoming host.

Despite being a General for longer than almost any other soldier, he was never pompous, and hated all forms of display and affectation. Above all, he was a soldier of the utmost integrity, whose reputation, unlike that of many Allied officers, has grown with passing years.

In retirement, Sir Claude moved to Marrakech, where he lived quietly in a modest flat for many years, taking his morning coffee at the La Rennaisance Café in the new part of the city, where he was known by all simply as *le Marechal.*

Sir Claude died on 23rd March, 1981, at the age of 96. He was buried in Ben M'Sik European Cemetery, Casablanca, in the Commonwealth War Graves Commission plot.

A memorial plaque to Sir Claude was later erected in the crypt of St Paul's Cathedral.

Rather amusingly, the St Paul's tour guides still relate that when plaques for the other great WW2 military leaders were being installed in 1979, no one in the establishment had been in contact with Sir Claude for many years.

Cathedral officials telephoned the last number in Marrakech that they had on their records to enquire the date of his death, only to be told: 'Auchinleck here - but I won't be keeping you much longer!'

ON COURT LE BALLON A LA MAIN

Tony adopted the French phrase:
'On court le ballon à la main'
during the course of the
1964 German/Belgium tour.

cloudburst). A snack was served after the game and a few beers consumed in the clubhouse. It was a pleasant evening.

The tour was a great success both rugby-wise and socially.

The party left for Ostend on Sunday, 30th May at 10.30am, arriving in plenty of time for the 3pm boat back to Dover.

It was during this tour to Germany and Belgium that the Penguin Rugby Football Club adopted the motto: *On court le ballon à la main* – 'They run with the ball in their hands'. Alan explains: 'Why is our motto in French? It was Tony's idea. He went to Eltham College - he was well educated and could more than get by in French. So - I suppose he thought having the motto in French made it look more "traditional". So we had it in French!'

At the end of 1965 the Penguins had played 29 matches. All had been won, with a points difference of well over 1000 for, and only 132 against.

PENGUINS GERMAN RUGBY TOUR

Forwards		Outsides	
Archie Hendricksen	(Rosslyn Park)	Terry Elman	(Old Emmanuel)
Len DeLuca	(Ealing)	Mike Thatcher	(Wasps)
Colin Kinnear	(London Scottish)	Mike Grace	(Rosslyn Park)
Mike McLaughlin	" "	Mike Williams	(Ealing)
Barry Jones	(Beckenham)	Barry Welsh	(London N. Zealand)
John Wharton	" "	Lou Spratt	" "
John Hoare	" "	Tom Wakeford	(Met. Police)
Howard Harris	(Old Reigatians)	Bob Brooks	(Blackheath)
Ben Lohan	(Wimbledon)	Jim Bunyan	(London Irish)
Martin Farrell	(Old Alleynians)	Tony Mason	(Sidcup)
Joe Armstrong	(London Irish)	Alan Forster	(Old Alleynians)
Cautley Tatham	(Clifton)	Doug Harvey	(Wasps)
Tony Ball	(Sidcup)	Nick Dickenson	(Rosslyn Park)
Bob Wilson	(London N. Zealand)		
Reg Pierce	(London Irish)		

Referee   Peter Eveleigh (Old Askeans)

Spectators   Tony Hedge and Bill Moore.

NOTE   The Rugby Union is perturbed at the increasing amount of hooliganism on tours. Any damage incurred will be paid for by the individual and not the Club.

We have a good reputation on the Continent and we intend to keep it. See that we do, both on and off the field.

Our contact addresses are:-

WOLFRAM SCHRANKENMULLER
1, BERLIN 49,
BRIESINGSTRASSE 15.

HEINER EHLERS
HANNOVER
AM LISTHOLZE
ABENDRUH 64.

HOTEL DES TOURISTES
11, RUE DU MARCHE
BRUSSELS 1.

Right: The first typed teamsheet
included in the Penguin RFC files.
It lists the names and Clubs of the
28 players who went on tour in 1965,
plus the referee and two spectators
who accompanied them.

1966

In March, 1966, Penguins played their first-ever match in England, against a Combined XV from Bridgwater, Taunton and Weston-super-Mare - and lost.

This result - the Club's first-ever defeat - brought an abrupt end to the Penguins' 29-match, six-year winning streak. Tony Mason was very disappointed by the result (he later called the match, which was played in Bridgwater, Somerset, 'a fiasco').

The May/June tour to Portugal was Captained by Joe Armstrong and managed by Tony Mason. Colours for this tour were, once again, all-white.

It was the first time that the Penguins had travelled abroad by plane - the fare was £28 per person. They flew out for this 14-day tour on the evening of Saturday, 21st May, and arrived in Lisbon early on Sunday Morning. The Penguins stayed at the famous Benfica Stadium for the duration of the tour. They were very well looked after at the Stadium and found the whole experience extremely impressive.

The host union required the Club to play five matches in the first eight days, and then, as Tony Mason put it, there would be: 'six days of pleasing yourself on holiday.' The players' wives and fiancees had been accepted on this trip, as Tony and Alan realised that a two-week rugby tour would also have to double as a main summer holiday for most of the players.

Long-standing Honorary Vice-President of the Penguins, Pedro Ribeiro (Past President, Portuguese RU), who was playing for the Portuguese Club Tecnico in the early summer of 1966, recalls: 'I remember Penguins playing two games, both at the University Stadium in Lisbon. The first match was against Agronomia (who the Penguins would play again 44 years later in 2010 to celebrate Agronomia's 75th Anniversary) and Penguins won by a good score' (60 - 3).

'The second game was played against my own Club - Tecnico - and to the surprise of everybody, we won by 9 points to 6. I was on the winning side!

'I remember that Antonio Pina Cabral, a small man who was alongside me at centre three-quarter, put a tremendous tackle in on one of the Penguins' big locks at the very beginning of the game. This tackle galvanised the whole team, and we put on a very brave display, tackling everything that moved. We scored one try (worth three points at that time) and two penalties.'

The tour results were as follows: First match - Penguins beat Agronomia RFC 60 - 3, second match - Penguins lost to Tecnico RFC 6 - 9, third match - Penguins lost 0 - 13, fourth match - Penguins won 22 - 3, fifth match - Penguins drew with Benfica RFC 11 - 11.

1966 CHRONICLE

March - Penguins lost to a Combined XV from Bridgwater, Taunton and Weston-super-Mare in Bridgwater, England.

21st May - 5th June - Portugal Tour. Captained by Joe Armstrong (England).
Penguins beat Agronomia 60 - 3
Penguins lost to Tecnico 6 - 9
Penguins lost third match 0 - 13
Penguins won fourth match 22 - 3
Penguins drew with Benfica RFC 11 - 11

Penguins played five matches during their 14-day tour of Portugal in May. Of these, two matches were lost and one drawn - much to Tony Mason's disappointment, as he had hoped for a much better performance from the team.

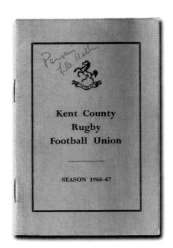

By this time the Club had become affiliated to the Kent Rugby Union and the Rugby Football Union.

With regard to results, it was a very unhappy tour for Tony Mason. The Club's first defeat at Bridgwater in March, closely followed by the two losses and a draw in Portugal, were bitter blows to Tony, who always hoped and expected that the Penguins would play well.

But it wasn't long before his *joie de vivre* returned after these setbacks - indeed, the following year would bring with it one of the happiest moments of Tony's life in the shape of a very special fixture at the home of Rugby Football.

Penguin RFC place mat from the mid-'60s incorporating the Club's new slogan.

1967

1967 was the turning of the tide. Indeed, it was a busy and remarkable year for the Club, and included a match which both Tony Mason and Alan Wright believed (rightly, as it happened) would be a signature event for the Penguins - namely the invitation to play at Twickenham Stadium against Twickenham Rugby Football Club to celebrate that Club's Centenary.

The match, and the media coverage it would undoubtedly bring, was also a catalyst for Tony and Alan to lavish some serious thought on the Penguin Rugby Football Club's colours and regalia.

Up until this year the two men had used a variety of different drawings and photographs of penguins to represent the Club on its stationery. But both Tony and Alan now decided that it was time to formalize the design - and also to choose a new, striking colour scheme for the Club's playing kit.

It was Tony who first had the brilliant idea of putting the rugby ball inside

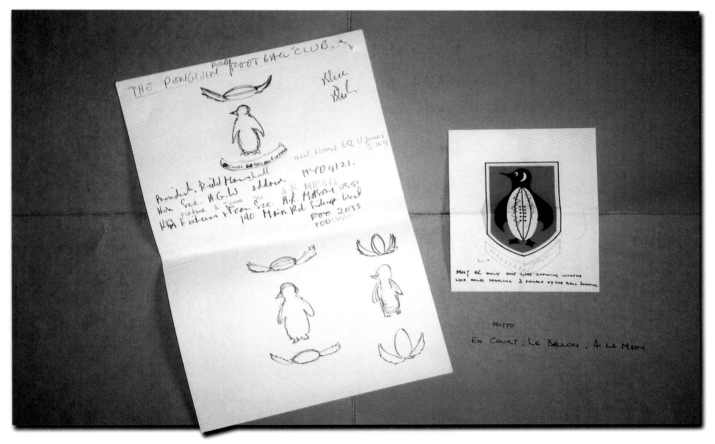

the body of the penguin in the Club logo. His new design made its first appearance later that year when Penguins wore the new motif on their jerseys for the first time in the Twickenham match. The Club also changed their all-white colours for this important game to those that they still wear variations of to this day - black, white and gold. The backs of the players' jerseys were entirely black (save for the numerals) and the gold stockings were chosen to represent a penguin's feet.

Tony Mason's original designs for the Club logo.

The Club tie - an early design swatch.

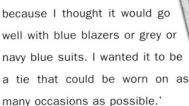

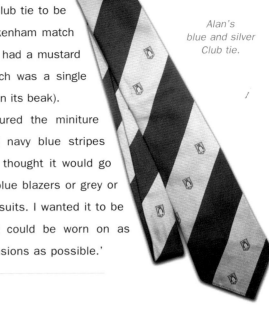

Alan's blue and silver Club tie.

Alan designed a new Club tie to be worn before and after the Twickenham match (up until 1967 the Penguins tie had a mustard coloured background, upon which was a single penguin balancing a rugby ball on its beak).

Alan explains: 'I featured the miniture Penguin logos with silver and navy blue stripes because I thought it would go well with blue blazers or grey or navy blue suits. I wanted it to be a tie that could be worn on as many occasions as possible.'

The earliest Penguin Rugby Football Club team photograph, taken in Somerset before the annual Combined Bridgwater, Taunton and Weston-super-Mare match. Back row: P. Sibley, R. Britton, J. Thorne, P. Bell, J. Heggadon, G. Keith, P. Jenkins, V. Marriott, R. Goody (touch judge). Seated: K. Wilson, G. Davies, A. Hendrickses, A. Mason, C. D'Arcy, J. Mawbey. On ground: J. Hiles, the Penguin Mascot, B. Cull.

While Tony and Alan were engaged in this branding exercise, the Club played their first match of the year - and the second of what was to become an annual early-Spring game in Somerset - against the Combined XV from Bridgwater, Taunton and Weston-super-Mare.

Penguins won this exciting, open, running game by 20 points to 15, thereby avenging the Club's first-ever defeat in the corresponding fixture in 1966.

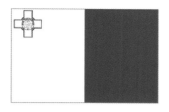

A month after beating the Bridgwater, Taunton and Weston-super-Mare Combined XV, the Penguins made a successful tour of Malta between 5th - 15th May inclusive. The Club was accommodated on the island by the British Army and the Royal Air Force. The Penguin colours for the tour were, once again, all white.

Alan recalls: 'I went on the Maltese tour, and it's a tour I remember reasonably well. At the time Malta was fully under the sway of the British Military. We played an Army team, an RAF team and a Malta XV. It was a tour probably arranged at relatively short notice, but it was, once again, typical of our tours - everybody paying their own way (the fare was £34 per head) and we all stayed with the Army or Air Force, or we were billetted with families.

'We were the first English rugby footall club to play on the island. Our two best results were wins over a Combined Services XV by 14 - 0 and a Malta XV by 34 - 0 (in Valletta). We did lose the final match, however - by 3 points to 11 against Royal Air Force Malta.'

The Penguins' first mascot made its appearance in early 1967.

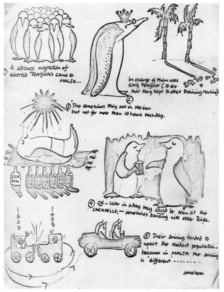

The story of the Maltese Tour, as sketched by a talented Penguin cartoonist.

Penguins squad:

Tony Mason (Sidcup, Joint Tour Manager and Captain), Alan Wright (Joint Tour Manager), George Green, Mike McKerrow (all Sidcup), John Wharton and Tony Whitton (Beckenham), Peter Cook, Martin Farrall and David Hawkes (Richmond), Brian Chappel, Bill Hackett, Phil Siddars and Peter Statt (Sutton), R. Brooks and R. Gerrard (Stafford), Dave Harn, Bob Hart and John Kent (Old Freemens), Randy Bowen and Terry Lewis (Esher), Keith Johnson (Wasps), Hugh Gill (Bromley), Mike Massey (Kersal), Trever Goslin (Southern), D. Chapman (Eastbourne), S. Tomlin (Penzance & Newlyn) and Alan Raines (Weston-super-Mare).

Dr. Hugh Cameron Burry

Hugh: 'It was only a very short time after I arrived in London in 1966 that I encountered Tony Mason. He rang me to enquire whether I would like to play for the Club in the West Country. He said he would meet me at Marble Arch and we would travel down together. What he didn't say was that he was going to drive with his head and shoulders over the back of the seat upon which he was driving, making continuous eye contact with me and only subjecting the road ahead to an occasional cursory glance when he thought somebody was slow getting out of our way! He gave me a detailed account of the state of rugby in Britain including what he thought were the failings of the game as a whole and it was clear that he knew a great deal about his chosen subject. I had no difficulty diagnosing a case of fulminating rugby mania. In the presence of this fever of enthusiasm I knew that I was comparatively sane although my friends would have said that a doctor in his mid-30s with defective eye sight and numerous battle scars would have to be mad to continue to put his body on the line in such a violent game. I was unable to convince Tony that I was no longer capable of playing 80 minutes of competitive rugby and he persuaded me that the mere fact that his squad contained an All Black, no matter how unfit or unskilled, would induce a degree of awe amongst the opponents and I would not have to actually do anything other than stand round looking threatening.

'I was keen to penetrate the phenomenon of English "rugger" having developed a healthy respect from my experience playing against the 1959 Lions. Tony did me the honour of selecting me for other games in the future, including the 1967 match played at Twickenham to celebrate the centenary of the Twickenham Rugby Club's foundation. I think Tony tended to select his squad with the idea of having a team that would be capable of competing with the opponents and perhaps get close to beating them - although it was rather "infra dig" to thrash any group who were attempting to have a happy anniversary.

'The main objective was to have an exciting game, with plenty of action and points being scored with older players having the opportunity from time to time of doing heroic acts which they had fantasised for years after being pushed out of the game by social or physical pressures. A nice feature of that game was that Tony was accompanied onto the field by his son, Michael. It was a good touch to see father and son able to combine in a team playing such a physically demanding game.'

Hugh Burry was born in Christchurch, New Zealand, on 29th October 1930. Educated at Christ's College, Christchurch. HS/HP, Christchurch Hospital 1955 - 1956. General practice 1957 - 1964. Medical Registrar, Christchurch Hospital 1965. Specialised in Rheumatology and Physiotherapy, Guy's Hospital, London 1968 - 1976. Specialised in Rheumatology and Rehabilitation Medicine in Wellington and Christchurch, New Zealand 1976 - 2000.

Hugh played at no.8 for New Brighton, Guy's Hospital, Canterbury and New Zealand (11 matches, 24 points). His first big sporting breakthrough came when he played for Canterbury against the touring Springboks in 1956. He played not only in Canterbury's 9 - 6 win, but also for New Zealand Universities when they, too, beat the South Africans. Frequently unavailable because of his medical practice, Hugh's vintage year came in 1959 when he formed a magnificent loose forward trio for Canterbury with Kel Tremain and John Graham. They starred in Canterbury's comfortable win over the British Lions in 1959 and Burry also played when Canterbury beat the All Blacks on their return home from Australia in 1957. He had the distinction of four times being in winning lineups against international rugby's greatest teams.

Hugh subsequently spent a considerable time in Britain advancing his medical career. He was involved in sports medicine from its infancy and on his return to New Zealand had a lengthy spell as Chairman of the New Zealand Union's medical advisory committee.

On 2nd September, 1967, the Penguins played the most important, high-profile match of their eight-year history.

Alan: 'There is a story behind how this match came about. Over the years I had said to Tony time and time again: "Why do you continue being an RFU Steward at Twickenham? I have stand seats and you could come along, have a nice lunch and then sit and watch the match in comfort." The Stewards were all unpaid volunteers, and one day Tony said: "Alan - I love being a Steward. I make all sorts of contacts with the players and other people." He then told me that it was through being an RFU Steward that he had met Tom Caygill (the Club Captain of the Twickenham Rugby Football Club who was also an RFU Steward) in early 1967. Tom had said to Tony: "We've been offered Twickenham Stadium for our Centenary Match. And we really want to play a team with a special reputation."

So Tony suggested to him that the Penguin RFC should provide that opposition, and he agreed.'

Above: Tony and Mike Mason. This was the first time a father and son had ever played together at Twickenham Stadium.

Of course, Tony immediately began to select a squad for this once-in-a-lifetime occasion with all of his customary enthusiasm and energy.

Alan recalls: 'With

regard to picking the team for this match: Tony had the cheek, he had the charm, and he had no hesitation in using his friendships (particularly amongst the 1st-class London Clubs) to invite some very good players to represent us. He had many excellent contacts amongst the players, and, of course, he prided himself in trying to select men he would describe as "footballers". He would always say: "I only want footballers!"

'We thought of this game as a signature match for the Penguins because it was going to really put us on the map for the first time. We were very aware that it would get us wide-spread coverage in the national press!'

Tony selected Alan to play at blind-side wing-forward in the match. Alan says: 'Well, they did let me play, and I trained for a whole year to play in the match - because I was 37 years old at the time.'

Tony picked his son Michael (Sidcup, Clifton and Kent) to play at stand-off half, and he picked himself to play at full-back (Tony was 49 years-old at this time, but supremely fit). In so doing he brought about the one and only occasion that a father and son have played together in the same team at "Headquarters".

The Penguin XV at Twickenham, Saturday, 2nd September, 1967.
Back row: D. Harn, G.J. Keith, H. Burry, W.M. Patterson, A.M. Davies, V.J. Harding, A.L. Horton, J. Thorne, A. Hancock, H. Owen (Touch Judge), T. Elmer.
Sitting: P. Cook, C.R. Jacobs, A.G. Wright, A.J. Hendrickses (Captain), A.R. Mason, M.A. Mason, R. Jones.
This wonderful squad contained many famous internationals, including England winger Andy Hancock (back row, third from right). Two years earlier, in 1965, Hancock had scored one of the greatest tries ever seen at Twickenham - a last-minute, 95 yard run against Scotland in a game known to this day as 'Hancock's Match'.

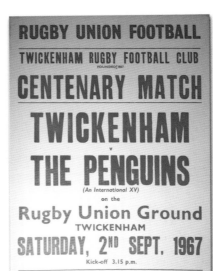

RUGBY UNION FOOTBALL

TWICKENHAM RUGBY FOOTBALL CLUB
FOUNDED 1867

CENTENARY MATCH

TWICKENHAM
v
THE PENGUINS

(An International XV)

on the

Rugby Union Ground
TWICKENHAM

SATURDAY, 2ND SEPT. 1967

Kick-off 3.15 p.m.

STAND TICKETS (Unreserved) Lower West	- -	10/-
(Unreserved) Lower East	- -	5/-
Admission to Ground and Enclosure	- -	2/6
CAR PARK 2/6

Tickets may be obtained in advance from: The Secretary, L. Townsend, The Glen,
St. Albans Gdns., Teddington, Middx., or any member of the Committee prior to the
day or at the Ground on the day of the Match

*The Penguins' match poster
and action photographs from the day.*

Entrance on the day was by the West Gate and the West Car Park was opened. Spectators had access to the whole ground. Ticket prices were: Ground Entrance 2/6d, Lower West Stand 10/-, Lower East Stand 5/-. The Rugby Union opened a bar, and food and beverages were provided for the players and officials after the match.

Because of time constraints it proved impossible for Tony to arrange a pre-match training session, so he asked his squad to meet in the players' dressing rooms in the West Stand at 2.00pm on the day of the match. This was to allow the Penguins' Captain, Archie Hendrickses, a chance to talk tactics, line-out drill and scrum-calls before the players got changed for the match. It must rank as one of the shortest pre-match tactical talks of all time at Twickenham. Kick-off was at 3.15pm.

The following report of the game appeared in the *The Sidcup and Kentish Times* the following week:

Twickenham RFC v Penguins RFC - A Special Centenary Match at Twickenham Stadium on Saturday, 2nd September.

In the opening match of the season at Twickenham Rugby Union head-quarters on Saturday the star-studded Penguin XV, containing nine internationals, beat Twickenham 16 - 9 in a match to celebrate Twickenham's 100th anniversary.

The Penguins took the lead through a penalty by Jones, but within twenty minutes found themselves well down as Twickenham produced three excellent scores through a 50 yard penalty by Mulhull, followed by tries from Gayle and Burke.

Penguins (who were formed nine years ago by two players from the Sidcup club, Tony Mason and Alan Wright) found themselves with defeat staring them in the face until the last 15 minutes when some scintillating play took them into a comfortable lead.

Keith ran over for an excellent try, converted by Jones, whereupon Michael Mason, formerly of the Old Elthamians, dropped an excellent goal, having, incidentally, hit the bar from 40 yards with a previous attempt.

Finally Hancock, the England winger, also formerly a Sidcup player, scored an excellent try from a first-class three-quarter movement which was converted by Tony Mason.

Twickenham, who have been in training since May, are to be congratulated for holding their opponents to such a close game. The standard at this time of the season was impressive and gave the spectators considerable pleasure.

The day was unique in that it was the first time that a father and son combination, Tony and Michael Mason, have played in the same team in a match at Twickenham. At full-back and fly-half they played with equal distinction (both scored) and it is doubtful whether such a combination has ever been seen before.

The Guardian's match report.

SUNDAY TIMES
SEPT 3rd '67

☆ ☆ ☆

RUGBY UNION

Old birds with sharp beaks

By Robin Marlar, Twickenham

Twickenham .... 9 pts	Penguins .... 16 pts

WHAT A DAY for the old 'uns. While Bill Alley kept Somerset afloat this morning with his wit and skill, Tony Mason, another 48-year-old, was getting ready to turn out for the same Penguins XV as his son Michael in the Twickenham club's centenary match. At full-back and fly-half they played with equal distinction. Has such a combination ever been seen before?

It was a fun match, but the standard of play was impressive, and if the Penguins won handsomely in the end by two goals, a dropped goal and a penalty goal against two tries and a penalty goal, they were six points behind Twickenham until 15 minutes from the end.

Age wasn't the only link with Lord's. Fred Price was umpiring there for the last time, a great 'keeper and character, who once lost his teeth in an explosive appeal: " Stand back, stand back I've lost me 'ampsteads " is likely to be his immortal cry.

At about the same time Ted Killick was captain and hooker for Twickenham and on one occasion he lost his glass eye in a scrum on a muddy pitch. Whether he yelled out, like a good Cockney, for his lost mince, history does not relate, but the game was certainly held up while the eye was found, wiped and put back in its rightful place.

Tony Mason founded the Penguins with Alan Wright, another well-preserved pillar of Sidcup, eight years ago. A touring side, they began in Scandinavia and since then have travelled all over Europe, reaching as far south as Malta. Their plumage is very smart; black on the neck and wings with a white front and yellow stockings. It being a dry day all the Penguins kept their white rumps, too, and there was no need for them to make progress with their egg by

running on their heels with the ball between their toes.

In fact both sides handled well, though some of the older and clumsier Penguins were apt to put it on the floor. Against distinguished three-quarters Twickenham held firm by producing tackling of the highest class. Gayle, their centre, brought down Hancock, Keith and Crook in full flight. As he scored a try with a classic gallop on the wing his transfer fee would certainly have doubled in these 70 minutes had this been a game of Soccer.

The contest opened with a testing punt to brother Mason, standing close to his own goal. He came away with it cannily and then saw Jones kick his 15 into the lead with a penalty goal. Mulhall, the Twickenham full-back, countered this with a beauty from wide on the 10-yard line, and then Burke scored a try from a Penguin clearance, and Gayle got his after Erb had started the move on the left wing. Twickenham kept their lead 9-3, and wags already had the Penguins on the taxidermist's couch ready for stuffing. However, Keith ran over and Jones converted the try, whereupon Mason's son dropped a goal from close range, having hit the bar earlier from 40 yards. Then Hancock ran in close to the posts and father Mason applied the *coup de grâce* with his conversion.

A thoroughly pleasant opening to a highly promising season.

Twickenham: M. Mulhall; R. Erb, D. Gayle, J. Saunders, C. Black; R. Bignell, R. Gray; T. Caygill (capt.), A. Reeves, N. Gunne, J. Bailey, R. Pearce, J. Burke, D. Lewis, D. Trevena.
Penguins: A. R. Mason (Sidcup); A. W. Hancock (Northampton & England), G. J. Keith (Wasps), W. M. Paterson (Wasps & England), P. W. Cook (Richmond & England); M. A. Mason (Clifton), R. Jones (Penarth); C. R. Jacobs (Northampton & England), J. D. Thorne (Bristol & England), A. L. Horton (Blackheath & England), V. S. J. Harding (Harlequins & England), A. M. Davis (Bedford & England), A. G. L. Wright (Sidcup), H. Burry (New Zealand), A. J. Hendrickse (capt.) (Rosslyn Park).
Referee: M. H. R. King (London Soc.).

RUGBY PROSPECTS

Chance to run with the ball

By U. A. TITLEY
Rugby Correspondent

A week ago the Penguins, a nomadic club founded by two Sidcup enthusiasts on avowedly Barbarian lines, opened the season at Twickenham against the Twickenham club, who are celebrating their centenary. The Penguin motto is *On court le ballon à la main* and on the occasion both sides did just that, reserving the touchlines for dire necessity.

That was a fine start, and it was even more encouraging that the England team to tour Canada should have followed the same lines in the trial match against Midland and Home Counties at Northampton earlier this week. It can be done, as these two matches proved, and the health of the game can best be guaranteed by the attendance of multitudes who will demand such fare at international as well as club level.

Today's second of three England trial matches will be played against the South of England at Exeter. They will do well to show the same enterprising spirit as in the first, and it is a fair bet that that engaging character, D. Rutherford, who broke an arm in New Zealand and who is now among the opposition, will show them the way.

Rivalry renewed

With the present firm going there is no excuse for anything else, and as a French team, the Racing Club de France, are visiting Richmond this afternoon, the crowd at the Athletic Ground will expect some lively, positive skipping around. This happy liaison will be further enhanced by the presence of a distinguished Frenchman, Admiral Noël, to whom both teams will be presented.

Blackheath, another club dedicated to " all out attacking Rugby ", will be at home at the Rectory Field to Old, Merchant Taylors'. May they live up to their tenets. Wasps and Saracens at Sudbury will be a renewal of vigorous rivalry, other metropolitan matches of promise in the metropolitan area being those between Rosslyn Park and U.A.U. at Roehampton and Streatham/Croydon and Old Alleynians at Thornton Heath.

London Scottish will be in Cornwall playing Penzance and Newlyn, and London Irish, who deserve better luck than they had last season, go to Bedford. At Cardiff there will be an all-Welsh affair with London Welsh as guests. Much is expected of the coach whom Cardiff have appointed in what somebody is said to have called a professional approach to an amateur game, a delicious, and perhaps unconscious, contradiction in terms.

More national press reports of the Twickenham Centenary Match, written by two of the most respected sports journalists in the business - Robin Marler and Uel Titley.

The Twickenham match was an unqualified success for the Penguin Rugby Football Club. As well as winning the game, the Club had, almost overnight, developed a reputation in rugby circles as an exciting, well organised invitational side that carried with it the Rugby Union stamp of approval.

On a more personal note, the Club founders were also well pleased with the outcome of the match - especially with the way that they themselves had performed in it. Both men had been slightly nervous of appearing in such illustrious company at Twickenham and were worried that they might 'let the side down'. That they didn't was made clear in a letter that Tony sent to Alan five days after the event (as Alan says: 'This is the one letter from Tony that I always held dear'). In it Tony writes to his best friend and co-founder:

Dear Well Preserved Pillar of Sidcup -

I thought I would let you know that I was very proud of you and the rest of the boys on Saturday. I reckon you all did the Penguins proud and I was thrilled to bits with the whole show and the way everything went.

I would like to thank you for all the help in marketing such a successful day and I hope you got as big a kick out of it as me. Our fears about letting the side down were unfounded as I think you compared favourably with the rest of the pack and we can walk with our heads held high.

Thanks once more and best wishes for the coming season. From another well preserved pillar of Sidcup,

Tony

Penguins squad:

A. Hendrickses (Rosslyn Park, Barbarians and England Trialist, Captain), H.C. Bury (Guy's Hospital and New Zealand), P.W. Cook (Richmond and England), A.M. Davis (Harlequins and England), T. Elmer, A.W. Hancock (Northampton and England), V.S.J. Harding (Saracens and England), D. Harn (Old Freemens), A.L. Horton (Blackheath and England), C.R. Jacobs (Northampton and England), R. Jones (Glamorgan Wanderers), G.J. Keith (Wasps and Scotland), A.R. Mason (Sidcup and Kent County, M.A. Mason (Clifton and Kent), H. Owen (Sidcup), W.M. Patterson (Wasps and England), J.D. Thorne (Bristol and England), A.G.L. Wright (Sidcup).

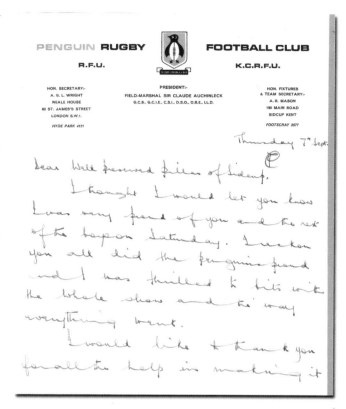

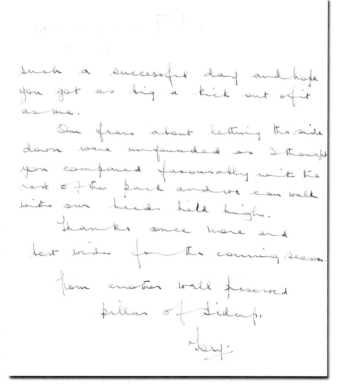

Next up for the Penguins was another high-profile match, this time against the Argentinian Club, Belgrano Athletic - one of the most successful teams in the Unión de Rugby de Buenos Aires. The Club was on tour in England at the time and had expressed an interest in playing against a Penguin side laced with internationals.

Alan: 'On Sunday, 1st October at 4pm we unusually staged, at Sidcup, a 'home' match against the champion club of Argentina, the Belgrano Athletic Club from Buenos Aires. We turned out a very good side and we were so Corinthian in our spirit then that we decided not to take a penalty in front of the posts that would have drawn the match. That, in the end, cost us the game. We lost to Belgrano by 23 points to 26.'

Alan and Tony put a great deal of time and effort into the organisation and marketing of this match, which Sidcup FC very kindly agreed to host. Their efforts were rewarded when an enormous crowd turned up to witness a very close and entertaining clash.

The following is a contemporary newspaper report of the game: *This was a match and a half that left probably the largest crowd ever to have watched a rugby match at Crescent Farm, Sidcup (estimated at over 1,200) gasping with delight and excitement.*

On a very blustery afternoon, Penguins kicked off with the wind behind them and quickly went into the lead with a try from Jolliffe converted by Allen. Before half-time Jolliffe and D'Arcy had scored two further first-class tries from exciting three-quarter movements and Allen added two penalty goals.

Belgrano's only reply to this was a penalty goal from Rosat which made the score 17 - 3 to the Penguins. At this point it was quite discernible why Belgrano are the champion club of the Argentine because of their well-drilled line-out work and their excellent tackling. The crowd had enjoyed the Argentinians' incessant chatter and the spirit in which they played the game.

The second half opened with the Penguins playing against the wind - but nevertheless, in true Barbarian fashion they continued to keep the game open from the outset and scored a further excellent try through Taylor, the Welsh open-side, making the score 20 - 3.

Belgrano's disappointment was only temporary for, at this stage, a trans-formation came over the game when Jurado, an Argentinian international and an excellent centre, made a fine straight break and scored a try. This was unconverted, as were four further tries scored by Forrester, Martin, Iparraguirre and J.C.

SIDCUP FOOTBALL CLUB

R.F.U. FOUNDED 1883

President : F. R. WOODWARD

Hon. Secretary	Hon. Match Secretary :	Hon. Treasurer
E. H. OWEN	G. F. CLIFFORD.	H. P. M. ORGAN
4B. THE COVERT	23. THE GROVE.	THORVERTON.
PETTS WOOD.	NORTH CRAY.	LEESONS HILL.
KENT.	KENT.	CHISLEHURST.
MM 27205	01-300 0201	MM 21862

A.G.L. Wright, Esq.,
Neal House,
S.W.1.
25th September, 1967.

Dear Alan,

Thank you for your letter of 21st September re Penguins V Belgrano.

Further to our many verbal and telephone conversations I confirm :

1. **Bar** The bar will be adequately stocked and manned.

2. **Tea** A hot tea will be supplied at a cost of 2/6 per head for 30 players, 2 linesmen, 1 referee and 28 other persons on the Belgrano party, plus 4 extra for yourself, Tony etc. A total of 65 for which the Penguins will be financially responsible.

Hot sausage rolls and cups of tea will be available for spectators - but only a limited number. However, hot pies will be available over the bar.

3. **Suppers** I should be grateful if you would lay on, with Doris Mason, arrangements for suppers as you think fit.

4. If you get a vast crowd it occurs to me that car parking could be a problem. In this event, providing the 2nd pitch is very firm, we could allow organised car parking on this pitch. But this decision will have to be taken on the day.

5. I will organise the groundsman re hot water, corner flags etc. and I will see to his payment.

6. The touchlines are already roped off as much as possible and suitable notices posted.

I think all your points are covered and I shall be praying for fine weather.

Regards,

If Penguins could be said to have a home in England, it is probably at Sidcup RFC's ground at Crescent Farm, Sidcup in Kent.
Above, a letter from Sidcup RFC to Alan Wright, finalising arrangements for the Belgrano match.

Anderson which made the score 20 - 18 with something like ten minutes to play.

At this stage the crowd were absolutely beside themselves with excitement and once again the Penguins went further ahead with an excellent penalty goal from Allen - making the score 23 - 18.

Time was now running out and Forrester, fielding a high kick, punted to the line and beat Jolliffe and the full-back to ground the ball for a try. Gradin converted from the touchline and made the scores level at 23 points each. Badia, the Argentinian full-back, shortly afterwards and to the delight of his side, kicked a fine penalty almost from the touchline to give Belgrano the lead for the first time in the match with only four minutes left to play.

Shortly afterwards the Penguins were awarded a penalty in front of the posts which, had they taken it, would have drawn the game. They disdained to do this in favour of a short kick in an attempt to score a try which would give them the opportunity to win the game outright. In a desperate final two minutes Belgrano kept their line intact and won what was probably the most thrilling match that will be seen this year at Crescent Farm.

The whole game was played at a fast pace and in a fine spirit. The Penguins never closed the game up at any time, even when they had their large lead, and this no doubt very much contributed to the success of the afternoon.

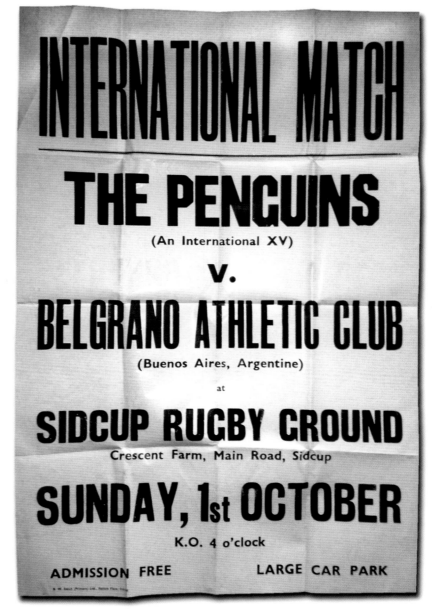

The Penguins had several hundred posters printed to publicise the Belgrano match. They were displayed in many shop windows in Sidcup and the surrounding area during the month of September, 1967.

Penguins squad:

A.J. Hendrickses (Rosslyn Park and England Trialist, Captain,), C.J. Allen (Richmond and Scotland Trialist), R. Britton (Rosslyn Park and Oxford University), F.J.R. Craig (Richmond and Ireland Trialist), C. D'Arcy (Saracens and Middlesex), A.M. Davis (Harlequins and England), J.R.W. Harvey (Richmond and England Trialist), R.K.L. Jolliffe (Richmond and England Trialist), V.J. Lewis (Rosslyn Park and Surrey), W.H. Raybould (London Welsh and Wales), B.I. Rees (London Welsh and Wales), D.M.B. Skinner (Rosslyn Park and Hertfordshire), J. Taylor (London Welsh and Wales), P.J. Thorne (Blackheath and England Trialist), F.B. Wrench (Harlequins and England).

1968 CHRONICLE

7th January - Combined Penguin and Sidcup XV play Petersham RFC (Australia) at Crescent Farm, Sidcup.

6th March - Penguins beat a Combined XV from Bridgwater, Taunton and Weston-super-Mare 12 - 5 in Bridgwater, England.

Spring - Zambia Tour. Captained by Bill Redwood (England). Penguins played and won four club matches and two international matches: Penguins beat Zambia in Kitwe Penguins beat Zambia in Lusaka

Deserved win for Penguins

BRIDGWATER, TAUNTON AND WESTON XV 5 pts., THE PENGUINS 12 pts.

Although the Combined XV scored the only try in this flood-lit match at Bridgwater, on Wednesday, they could hardly claim that victory did not go to a much superior team.

With any luck, the Penguins, given an early boost with three penalty goals from full-back **Mike Mason** (Clifton) in the first 23 minutes, could have swelled their total with several tries before the Combined XV broke away to score four minutes from no-side.

As it was, the only addition to the Penguins' total came in the second half when centre **Roger Abell** (Bath) dropped a goal following a long spell of pressure.

Although without a recognised scrum-half, **David Stevens** (Blackheath) had to switch from the back row when Simon Clarke (Bath) withdrew from the team, the Penguins were much more impressive for the greater part of the game. When the passes finally came the way of left wing **Graham McClymont** (Rosslyn Park), whose last appearance at Taunton Road was for the Australian tourists Petersham, he proved a constant threat.

But the Combined XV also had a danger man in their left wing, Doug Hazzard. One of his dashes down the wing enabled Robin Jones to link up and sent hooker Alan Raines over for the late try, which was converted by full-back **Roy Gummer**.

THRICE FAILED

It was Gummer's first success-ful place kick, for he failed with three penalties, one from a reasonably easy position, in quick succession soon after half-time.

Outside-half Ian Wright (St. Luke's), hooker Bob Vickery (Somerset Police) and No. 8 David Harn (Old Freemens) were also in fine form for the Penguins.

But with limited and often slow possession the young Combined XV half-back pairing of Mike Berry and Brendon Andrews could make little impression, the result being that the threequarters had very limited opportunities.

Gummer, however, put in some useful work at full-back while Jim Strong, Laurie Ross and Robin Jones were the outstanding forwards.

The Penguins won the third match in the series when they beat the Combined Bridgwater, Taunton and Weston-super-Mare XV 12 - 5 in March.

1968

On 7th January Penguins played another match at Crescent Farm, Sidcup, when they combined with Sidcup RFC to play a touring Australian side, Petersham Rugby Club from Sydney. Alan: 'Tony arranged this match. It was quite an informal affair, but Petersham were very happy to play us. The match was won by us, but sometimes in our early years scores were not recorded for posterity.'

Two months later, on Wednesday, 6th March, Penguins travelled to Bridgwater for the third year in a row to play the Combined XV from Bridgwater, Taunton and Weston-super-Mare. Although the home team scored the only try of the game, the Penguins were in a different class for much of the match, and won comfortably by 12 points to 5. Mike Mason, Tony Mason's son, scored nine of the Penguins' 12 points from penalties.

Penguins squad:

A. Mason (Sidcup, Captain and Team Manager), R. Abell (Bath), B. Battishall (Rosslyn Park), A. Baxter (St. Luke's College), I. Exeter (Blackheath), D. Harn (Old Freemens), M. Mason (Clifton), M. Mason (Harlequins), G. McClymont (Rosslyn Park and Petersham), R. Orledge (Bath), P. Sibley (Bath), D. Stevens (Blackheath), R. Vickery (Somerset Police), R. Williams (Harlequins), I. Wright (St. Luke's College).

Souvenir copper Penguins badge from Zambia.

The Zambia tour was another trip undertaken at the request of the Rugby Union. Alan recalls: 'In 1968 there was another very significant turning-point in our history. One day I received a telephone call from Robin Prescott at the Rugby Football Union.

'Robin said that the Zambian Rugby Union were very unhappy with the RFU. He explained that Zambia (previously known as Northern Rhodesia before its independence in 1963) had, up until that time, been affiliated to the South African Rugby Board. He went on to say that the Zambian Rugby Union were claiming that Twickenham had ignored them since they had been affiliated to the Rugby Union, and he asked me if Tony and I would take a strong Penguins team there and play them and spread some good-will? I said: "Any financial help?" Robin said: "Regretfully we cannot help you."

'Well, the Club went to Zambia for three weeks and played six matches in all - two against the Zambian national team and four against really good Zambian Clubs (the Clubs were mainly comprised of South Africans holding fairly senior positions in the copper mines and other industries).

'The Club had no funds and a tour so far away from England presented real problems in terms of finance. We would only be able to overcome this by

arranging to fly to Lusaka via Paris using a French airline, and through our hosts agreeing to accommodate our players in their homes. This latter policy was adopted for many years and we liked it very much because great friendships were made between the touring party and hosts all over the world.'

Alan recalls that during this flight, when they were flying over the Sahara Desert at about 4am the pilot announced over the plane's inter-com that because of very strong headwinds the aircraft was running out of fuel. Fortunately most of the touring party were asleep at the time! In the event, they had to divert to Luanda to refuel.

There were no fewer than three Penguin 'firsts' on this tour: It was the first time that the Club had ever toured outside Europe; the first time that Alan and Tony took on separate responsibilities on a tour that they were both on; and the first time ever that the Penguins introduced a formal selection committee.

Penguins XV for the match against Kitwe on the 1968 Zambia Tour (note that the team are once again wearing Sidcup FC jerseys).
Back row: Tony Mason, Glenn Robertson, Martin Webber, John Frame, Derek Morgan, Colin Payne, Steve Geary, Nick Martin, Dave Wrench, Referee, Alan Wright.
Front row: Clive Webber, Bob Frame, Colin Page, Bill Redwood, Harry Rae, John Lockwood, Bob Keddie.

Alan: 'At times, when we toured together, Tony liked me to be joint-manager. When we reached Zambia (which, of course, was a top-notch, serious tour) I said to him: "This is not a good system, Pop. We need one leader, otherwise we'll find chaps coming to me to say 'can I slope off?' and I say 'No', and they come to you and you may say 'Yes'. So you be the leader. I'll run the admin, the PR and the liaison with the alickadoos - ie, follow the army: *Chain of Command.*" It was clearly preferable to follow the army and have a chain of command in order to avoid duplication of decision.'

Alan did continue to sit in on selection, however. He explains: 'There was a keenness amongst the players to be selected for the two "test" matches versus Zambia. Accordingly, I proposed to Tony that we have a formal Selection Committee of five, including players from England, Scotland and Wales, thus ensuring impartiality. We were, after all, a London club, and this in practice worked very successfully.

Another fine metal/enamel badge from Tony Mason's collection. This one is a Northern Rhodesia FC pin from the Zambia tour.

Derek Morgan of Newbridge RFC and England. Derek went on tour to Zambia twice with the Penguins - in 1968 and 1972.

This unique Zambia Rugby Union commemorative plaque is fashioned from one of the ingots produced in the Zambian copper mines. It was presented to the Penguin RFC at the end of the tour.

'We had a very strong side. As our Captain we appointed Bill Redwood, who was the England scrum-half. We also included Ian Robertson, who was the Scottish stand-off half, John Frame, the thrusting Scottish international centre, and Colin Payne, an England lock who played for the Harlequin Football Club.'

The Penguins were unbeaten on this tour - and won both international matches against Zambia, one of which was played in Kitwe and the other in the capital, Lusaka. Regarding the match in Lusaka, Alan recalls: 'It so happens that I broadcast that second match against Zambia sitting on the top of the stadium in Lusaka. I think it was broadcast into Rhodesia at the time, which probably helped, in the end, to our receiving other African invitations.' Certainly the tour was highly successful and made the Penguins a lot of friends - and the Club was welcomed back to Zambia (and, indeed, Rhodesia) just four years later.

A particular feature of the Zambia tour was the fact that, quite without the Penguins knowing, the Rothmans Tobacco Company were so much in favour of seeing a good side from England playing Zambia that they very kindly put several cars at the Club's disposal for the entire tour. This was organised by one of their officers, Barney Barnard (Barney was a South African who had represented Transvaal and many Clubs in Zambia between the years of 1960 and 1969). Alan: 'We picked Barney to play in one match. Strangely enough, he stayed with me in London a year later in 1969, and then I saw him again 39 years after that - in Malaysia in 2008!'

Also present on this tour was Derek Morgan, the England number 8 who would later go on to become President of the Rugby Football Union and a Member of the Penguin Committee. He remembers this about his invitation to go away with the Penguins, and of the tour itself: 'I was first approached by Tony Mason at a post-International Dinner with an invitation to join this Penguins tour to Zambia. Well, my philosophy has always been "have boots will travel" which I had developed when I was single. My wife concurred in spite of two toddlers and a third on the way!

'Africa was new territory for me. We had a very good team - Tony Mason, Alan Wright, Geoff Cornford and Doris Mason organising us off the field, and Bill Redwood organising us on the field! I remember various details of the tour very well. Accommodation was often with families. My first accommodation was with Dai Jones! In Lusaka the Central Sports Club was a real 'colonial watering hole' where the head barman was called "Tennis"!

'Nchanga, Ndola, Kitwe and the most beautiful ground at Luanshya with (reputedly) the tallest goal posts in the world. Beautiful turf regularly watered from the mine into which it drained, only to be pumped up again to maintain the grass. And barbecues with no doubts about the weather! Three days in a game reserve was the highlight of the tour. The plane had to circle while some elephants were driven off the runway. An evening cruise on the Zambezi watching the most glorious sunset and then the river with perfect mackerel markings trailing from our stern.

Colin Payne and Ian Robertson giving commentary on the wildlife: "It's not real, it's a cardboard cut-out, look - there's a man pulling the strings to make it's ears flap!" and much, much more.'

Alan: 'I remember that although the boat had been stocked with alcohol we drank the boat dry in about half an hour! But it was an amateur tour, and it was the weekend. We wanted the boys to relax.' Derek Morgan is quick to point out: 'Tony and Alan always maintained that rugby had to come first on tours. Rigorous training took place on all non-match days and practise was taken extremely seriously. In the event, all the matches were won by playing in an attractive manner against stern opposition.' The blue-print for this tour became the pattern for future 15-a-side tours.

Scotland's John Frame recalls: 'A lasting memory (he will be pleased) is of Ian Robertson's negotiations with a trader of the local gypsy clan at the Victoria Falls. I don't remember the exchange rate but the currency was "kwacha" - which sounds like a duck with a problem. Ian was keen to buy a mask of such hideous features that it could only have been carved in Zambia - or maybe Yorkshire. The man wanted five kwacha but Robbo knew about barter and wished to prove it. We left, to give free rein to his money-market skills. Some time later he returned to the bus. '"How did you do, Robbo?" we asked, remembering that the trader had started at five kwacha. "Bloody brilliant" he replied. "I beat the bastard up to 20 kwacha before he gave in. What a plonker..." He still has that mask at home. It keeps the children from the fire in winter and his dog from the flower bed in summer. And *he* knows he got a bargain.'

Finally - no account of the Zambia tour would be complete without mention of the following incident. Alan explains: 'You must remember that in 1968 I was 38 years old and Tony was 50. At one of the Zambia international matches he was supposed to be introduced to the President of Zambia and I couldn't find him anywhere. Eventually someone noticed that he was about four pitches down, playing at full-back. He had been invited to play for them! As I have said before, he carried his boots with him everywhere!'

Penguins squad:

A. Mason (Tour Manager), A. Wright (Tour Manager, Admin), G. Cornford, D. Mason. B. Redwood (Bristol and England, Captain), B. Barnard (Transvaal), J. Frame (Gala and Scotland), S. Geary (Newbridge and Welsh Trials), B. Keddie (Scotland), J. Lockwood (Saracens and Kent County), N. Martin (Harlequins and England), D. Morgan (Newbridge and England), C. Page, C. Payne (Harlequins and England), H. Rae (London Irish, Ulster and Ireland), G. Robertson (Northampton and England trialist), I. Robertson (Watsonians, London Scottish and Scotland), C. Webber (Bridgwater), M. Webber (Newport), D. Wrench (Harlequins and England).

Doris and Tony Mason plus some of the Penguins' playing squad visit a copper mine during the 1968 tour.

Alan Wright: 'For years the managers of the big mines in the Copperbelt had a rivalry to see who could erect the highest rugby posts on their grounds. You'd be amazed at how tall some of these were. There was never any doubt about whether or not a penalty or a dropped goal had gone over the bar!'

Typical Tony - always ready to play!

1969 CHRONICLE

25th February - Penguins beat a Combined XV from Bridgwater, Taunton and Weston-super-Mare 28 - 12 in Bridgwater, England.

16th March - Penguins beat Sidcup at Crescent Farm, Sidcup.

May/June - Denmark and Germany Tour. Captained by David Powell (England). Penguins beat Hamburg Police, then won two matches in Denmark before returning to Germany to play St. Pauli RFC.

AYRES SNAPS UP FOUR TRIES

Combined XV 12pts,
Penguins 28pts

FOUR tries from David Ayres, the 22-year-old Bridgwater wing three-quarter, was not enough to save the Combined Taunton and Bridgwater team from defeat against the powerful Penguins last night.

Although handicapped when scrum half Billy Hullin, one of six internationals in the side, was forced to make a premature retirement with an arm injury, the Penguins got off to a flying start.

British Lions, John O'Shea and Derek Morgan, both crossed within eight minutes, the first of these tries being converted by Brian Page.

Then Northampton wings, Glen Robertson, and Derek Prout, followed suit to give the Penguins a 14-point lead before casual play by Robertson allowed Ayres to make the first reply.

Before half-time Page dropped a goal from near the touchline and Ayres was over again.

Prout soon broke away from the half-way line for Page to convert and then another swift counter from Page and Robertson produced a try for Hamish Keith.

Robertson completed the scoring, but the only reply in this period once again came from Ayres.

Match report of the Somerset game.

1969

The previous two years had really put the Penguin Rugby Football Club on the map. Thanks in part to the 1967 Twickenham match the Club had begun to build a reputation in the UK (particularly amongst players with the top London Clubs) as being one of the most fashionable and exciting invitational sides around. And with the success of the 1968 Zambia tour, the Penguins had also cemented their special relationship with the Rugby Union.

In contrast to 1967 and 1968, however, 1969 was a rather quiet year for the Penguins, with only two matches being played in the UK (the annual Somerset match and a match against Sidcup RFC). The Club also undertook another short overseas tour - across the English Channel to Denmark and Germany.

The first match of the year took place on Wednesday, 26th February. It was the fourth annual game in Somerset against the Bridgwater, Taunton and Weston-super-Mare Combined XV. The Penguins fielded a very powerful side for this match, including two British Lions - no.8 Derek Morgan (Newbridge and England, Captain) and prop John O'Shea (Cardiff and Wales) - as well as six other internationals. Tony Mason's son Michael also played in this match at stand-off half. The contest ended in a comfortable 28 - 12 victory for the Penguins.

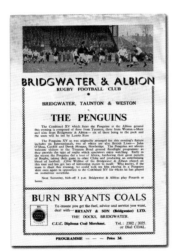

Bridgwater, Taunton and Western-Super-Mare programme.

Penguins squad:

Tony Mason (Match Manager), D. Morgan (Newbridge, England and the British Lions, Captain), G. Evans (Newbridge and Welsh Schools), S. Geary (Newbridge and Welsh Trials), A. Hendrickses (Rosslyn Park and England Trials), B. Hullin (Cardiff and Wales), G.J. Keith (Wasps and Scotland), J. Lockwood (Saracens and Kent County), M. Mason (Clifton and Kent County), M. Mason (Northampton and England Trials), J. O'Shea (Cardiff, Wales and the British Lions), B. Page (England Trials), D. Prout (Northampton and England), G. Robertson (Northampton and England Trials), J. Uzzell (Cardiff and Wales), D. Wrench (Harlequins and England).

On Sunday, 16th March, Tony and Alan took a strong side to play their old friends at Sidcup RFC. All of the proceeds from this match went to the National Society for Cancer Relief. The Penguins included five British Lions in their XV - Derek Morgan, Keith Savage, Gordon Connell, Ken Kennedy and Rodger Arneil - plus nine other internationals and two trialists. Penguins won the match comfortably.

Penguins squad:

D. Morgan (Newbridge, England and the British Lions, Captain), B. Page (Northampton and England Trialist), R. Arneil (Edinburgh Academicals, Scotland and the British & Irish Lions), H. Burry (New Zealand), G.C. Connell (London Scottish, Scotland and the British & Irish Lions), J. Frame (Gala and Scotland), K. Kennedy (London Irish and the British & Irish Lions), M. Malloy (London Irish and Ireland), A. McHarg (London Scottish and Scotland), J. Moroney (London Irish and Ireland), C. Payne (Harlequins and England), G. Robertson (Northampton and England Trialist), I. Robertson (Watsonians and Scotland), K. Savage (Northampton, England and the British & Irish Lions), D. Wrench (Harlequins and England).

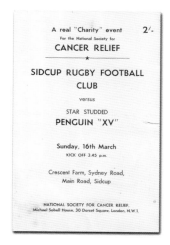

Sidcup v Penguins programme.

Penguins also toured Denmark for the third time and visited Germany twice between Friday, 30th May and Monday, 9th June under the Captaincy of Northampton's England and British Lion prop forward David 'Piggy' Powell.

David recalls: 'We met at King's Cross, caught a coach to Harwich and travelled over by ferry. Each player paid £22 for the tour and we had to find our own white jerseys and shorts!

'We took a strong team which included three other Northampton Saints, a few Welsh lads and a couple of players each from Wasps and Blackheath. We played a match in Hamburg then two matches in Denmark before travelling back to Germany to play the top German Team, St. Pauli RFC. I remember that we won all four matches comfortably.'

Specifically, the matches were against the Hamburg Police in Hamburg on Saturday, 31st May, then two matches were played in Copenhagen followed by the last game against St. Pauli RFC on 7th June - which again took place in Hamburg.

David continues: 'There was, however, a peculiar incident which took place in that last game against the Germans. The German player against whom I was propping took exception to the fact that I was outplaying him. He was a huge lad, much bigger than me, but I had a better technique. At the end of the match, and much to my surprise, he squared up to me and said: "Right - you and me, we fight now!" Well, Peter Duffy, a great friend of mine and my fellow prop on the tour, saw what was going on and flattened him - which quickly put an end to the stupidity! What was really amusing was that the rest of the St. Pauli RFC players started clapping Peter for doing it. It turned out that my opponent wasn't a very popular man, even with his own team mates. But rugby being rugby, of course, we all ended up in the bar together later that evening, the very best of friends!'

Alan: 'Yes, the Club has always had very good relations with the Germans and it was a happy, winning tour with a happy mix of players from famous - and not so famous - clubs.'

Northampton, England and British Lion prop forward David 'Piggy' Powell.

Penguins squad:

Tony Mason (Manager). David Powell (Northampton, Captain), Keith Allen (Northampton), C. Bacon (Blackheath), Gordon Barrett (Bridgwater), Alan Brown (Sidcup), Dave Chapman (Eastbourne), Tony Davies (Bromley), John Devenport (Wasps), Peter Duffy (Northampton), Alan Johnson (Eastbourne), Bobby Jones (Glamorgan Wanderers), Mike McKenon (Sidcup), Mike Newsom (Blackheath), Terry O'Gorman (Glamorgan Wanderers), Barry Oldham (Northampton), Nigel Parker (Oxford), Malcolm Pigg (Oxford), Alan Raines (Wasps), Mike Ray (Sidcup), Chris Sanham (Sidcup), Ray Tapper (Oxford), Bob Wylie (Old Freemens).

As a direct result of friendships made during the Zambia tour the previous year, in late summer Alan and Tony assisted in the liaison of a tour by the Central Sports Club of Lusaka, Zambia, when that Club toured England between 6th - 25th September. The tour was managed by Barney Barnard (the Rothmans employee who had played for the Penguins during the Zambia tour the previous year). During the tour CSC played against many friends of the Penguins (including Sidcup, Hampstead, Bridgwater, Weston-super-Mare, Minehead, Torquay, Beckenham and Askeans) before flying off home via Italy, where they stopped off and played the Roma Club.

Alan Wright was delighted to assist in the organisation of the Lusaka Central Sports Club's tour of England in September 1969.

The Foundation of the Rugby Football Union

Edwin Ash

Edward Holmes

Algernon Rutter

Frederick Stokes

Arthur Guillemard

By about 1870 it had become clear that Rugby was being played to a variety of rules, not only in London but country-wide. In December, 1870, Edwin H. Ash, the Secretary of the Richmond Football Club, wrote a letter to the newspapers which stated: 'Those who play the Rugby-type game should meet to form a code of practice, as various clubs play to rules which differ from others, which makes the game difficult to play.'

With this thought in mind, 32 members of London and suburban football clubs gathered together on the evening of 26th January, 1871, in the Pall Mall Restaurant at 9-10 Haymarket, London, 'to codify the rules of the game and to provide a central governing body.' It was at this meeting, presided over by Edward Carleton Holmes (the Captain of Richmond Football Club) that the Rugby Football Union was founded.

The 21 original member clubs enrolled that evening were: Addison, Belsize Park, Blackheath, Civil Service, Clapham Rovers, Flamingoes, Gipsies, Guy's Hospital, Harlequins, King's College Hospital, Lausanne, Law, Marlborough Nomads, Mohicans, Queen's House, Ravenscourt Park, Richmond, St Paul's School, Wellington College, West Kent and Wimbledon Hornets. Each club payed an entrance fee and annual subscription of 5/- (25p). They drafted a set of bye-laws and elected a President, a Secretary and a Committee of thirteen. The Union was to have one general meeting a year every October, to which each member club was entitled to send two of its members.

The Union officers entrusted to draft the new laws of the game were: President: Algernon Rutter (Richmond); Honorary Secretary and Treasurer: Edwin Ash (Richmond). The Committee consisted of: Reginald Birkett (Clapham Rovers), Frederick Currey (Marlborough Nomads), W.F. Eaton (Ravenscourt Park), A.J. English (Wellington College), J.H. Ewart (Guy's Hospital), Arthur George Guillemard (West Kent), F. Hartley (Flamingoes), Edward Carleton Holmes (Richmond), R. Leigh (The Law Club), Sir John Henry Luscombe (Gypsies), L.J. Maton (Wimbledon Hornets), E. Rutter (Richmond) and Frederick Stokes (Blackheath).

Barely two months later, in the first-ever international match, Frederick Stokes of Blackheath Captained England against Scotland - and his team included Luscombe, Birkett, and Guillemard, all of whom were members of that first ever Rugby Union Committee.

RHODESIA V PENGUINS
Salisbury, Rhodesia in March 1973

1970 - 1979

WORLDWIDE RECOGNITION

Alan Wright:
'We adopt a policy of "Reinforcing Success"
(an infantry maxim of World War One).
'Highlights of our second decade include tours to:
♦ Africa - Rhodesia/South Africa/Zambia (second tour);
♦ The Americas - USA/Bermuda;
♦ Asia - Soviet Union (USSR)/Sri Lanka.'

1970 CHRONICLE

11th March - Penguins beat a Combined XV from Bridgwater, Taunton and Weston-super-Mare 30 - 6 in Bridgwater, England

8th - 30th May - California Tour. Captained by Colin MacFadyean (England)
Penguins beat Southern California Colleges 23 - 8
Penguins lost to Northern California All-Stars 15 - 27 in San Francisco
Penguins beat San Francisco Rugby Club 32 - 0 in San Francisco
Penguins beat Combined Bay Area Touring Side and Olympic Club 12 - 3 in San Jose
Penguins beat Peninsular Ramblers 14 - 6 in San Jose
Penguins lost to Combined Southern University All-Stars 8 - 13 in Los Angeles
Penguins lost to Combined California Universities Touring Side 11 - 21 in Los Angeles

September - Penguins played Bedford Athletic to celebrate the opening of their new clubhouse. Penguins beat Bedford Athletic 32 - 9.

The annual West Country match was won easily, by 30 points to 6.

New horizons!

1970

Penguins played a total of nine matches in 1970 - their annual fixture in the West Country against the combined Bridgwater, Taunton and Weston-super-Mare XV in March, seven matches on tour to California in May and a special match against Bedford Athletic RUFC to celebrate the opening of that Club's new ground in September.

Closer to home, it was also in 1970 that Tony was elected on to his first County Rugby Committee - that of the Sussex County Rugby Union - whereupon he became a Sussex RU Selector. Alan wrote a congratulatory letter to Tony at the time. In the letter he also remarked: *Your election on to the Sussex Committee is, in my view, very important and now really removes the necessity to seek support for getting you on to the Kent County Rugby Union Council.* Tony, who had, of course, represented the Kent County Union as a player, had been interested in becoming a member of the Kent Committee for a number of years.

The Penguins' season started on the 11th March with the fifth in their series of annual matches against the Combined XV of Bridgwater, Taunton and Weston-super-Mare. The Penguins team for this fixture included no fewer than five Welsh internationals, one Scottish international and many international trialists. The match resulted in a comfortable win for the Penguins by 30 points to 6.

Penguins squad:

Tony Mason (Match Manager), M. Davies (Neath and Welsh Trialist), C. Evans (Newbridge and Wales), G. Evans (Newbridge and Gwent), A. Finlayson (Cardiff), S. Geary (Newbridge and Welsh Trialist), P. Hayward (Gloucester and English Trialist), G. Hodgson (Neath and Wales), A. Hughes (Newbridge), W. Lauder (Neath and Scotland), H. Norris (Cardiff, Wales and British Lions), T. Rees (Newport and Wales), J. White (Bristol), A. Williams (Cardiff), C.H.F. Williams (London Welsh and Welsh Trialist), M. Wiltshire (Bridgend and Wales).

One of Tony's USARU badges.

Penguins were the first British sporting team to visit California for 14 years, and only the second rugby football team ever to make the trip (the only previous visitors being an Oxford and Cambridge Combined Universities side). The tour was Captained by England's Colin MacFadyean.

Alan: '1970 opened new horizons for us, because we agreed to visit the United States. We had arranged a very good fixture list which included playing the combined Northern and Southern California Rugby Unions, who were going to unite for the very first time into one team to play us in the Olympic Stadium in Los Angeles.

'To cut a long story short - when we got to California we found that the anti-Vietnam War campaign had reached its height, that there were student riots, that television had ceased to function and that most of the professors in the universities had gone on strike.

'The upshot of all this was that the Americans, who had hired the Olympic Stadium in Los Angeles for the big match of Penguins v Combined Northern and Southern Californian Rugby Unions, decided to claim on insurance and cancel the match. Then all of our matches had to be rearranged and... well, we did our best in very difficult circumstances.'

The fixtures were hastily re-arranged on an ad-hoc basis. This was very much to the disadvantage of the Penguins, as the matches were then spread unevenly. There was only one match in the first five days, meaning that the remaining six fixtures had to take place in under two weeks. This heavy schedule in the latter days brought with it a lot of injuries, and the Penguins' strength was seriously depleted for the final two games of the tour.

Alan continues: 'We had selected a very strong side with several Welsh internationals in the team, including Derek Quinnell. We also had Colin MacFadyean, who had twice Captained England. He was a centre playing for Moseley at the time. Colin was originally in the party as the Vice-Captain, but he took over the Captaincy when Ray McLoughlin dropped out of the tour at the last moment.'

Regarding the opposition they faced in California, Alan has this to say: 'Most of the good American rugby players were men who had just failed to become professional American footballers. They had been taught Rugby Union football whilst studying at the Ivy League and other Universities. These institutions used the game as practice for the American football season.

'We had one very unusual incident on this tour. We were at a match against two clubs - "BATS", the Bay Area Touring Side, which was the strongest side in the United States, combined with the Olympic Club. The match was played in the Santa Clara Football Stadium, a big stadium that had an athletics track and a concrete kerb around the perimeter. When we got there somebody had thrown bits of foam rubber over this kerb. I asked the referee if I could have a meeting with him, the Captains and the officials, and I pointed out that if the field wasn't shortened away from this kerb somebody would surely have his face thrown on to the concrete and suffer severe facial or other injuries - and that, therefore, preventative measures should be taken. The American Captain looked

*Colin MacFadyean,
Penguins' Captain in the USA.*

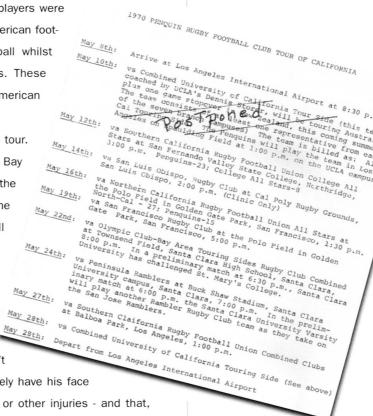

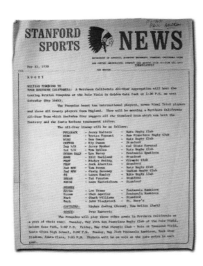

*11th May edition of the
Stanford University Sports Magazine
featuring the Penguins' match against
the Northern California All-Stars.*

*Mary and John Morgan
at the airport with their duty-free.
John had only lately become the
Penguin RFC's first Treasurer when
this picture was taken.
John had also been the London
Counties Auditor and was a member
of the Old Askeans Club.*

straight at me and said: "Are you limeys chicken?" In the event, we played the match on a limited but safe pitch. The match was publicised as USA v Great Britain.'

Al Ginepra, Secretary of the Southern California Rugby Football Union, later listed his star Penguins players of the tour. He wrote: *Not only did they run well, but the Penguins' passing, dummying, side-stepping, etc. were superlative. Particularly impressive in their three Los Angeles matches was the ability of the forwards to pass the ball around. Hooker Mark Robinson lost not one of his own heads, and took over half of his opposing hooker's ball. Best open-field coverage was provided by no.7 from the Wasps, John Devenport. Assuredly, the best scrum-half ever seen in Los Angeles is Welshman Martyn Davies, the Neath Captain. Glasgow's David Dearden played like an American footballer, as did Llanelli's bruiser, Derek Quinnell and Irish speedster Ray Flannery.*

Ginepra also had this to say about Tony and Alan: *Tony Mason and Alan Wright are sportsmen non-pariel. When the first match was postponed by campus disorders, they adjusted with charm and ease. At all times, both were thoroughly agreeable, helpful and fun. Someday these United States of America will have rugby ambassadors such as Tony Mason and Alan Wright - and 'The Game' will be appreciated by over 200 million people.*

Away from the rugby, the Penguins were royally entertained. The squad visited Disneyland, Anaheim Stadium to watch a California Angels baseball game, Hollywood and, of course, Sunset Strip.

Tony later wrote about this tour in his report to the Rugby Union: *The Californians seem to have the finest facilities in the world for sport and are exceptional and natural athletes. Additionally, the Americans are able to field forwards of exceptional size (without loss of mobility) and backs of considerable pace and power.*

Tony also added a rather humorous footnote, for Robin Prescott's eyes only: *Needless to say everyone had a fantastic time in a fantastic country. God help us if they take the game up seriously!*

Alan: 'Bearing in mind the strength of our touring party, it's amazing that we didn't win every match - but c'est la vie! We left America with a very good impression. They were very kind to us. When we stayed in San Francisco we stayed at, and were all made honorary members of, the prestigious Olympic Club.'

It was at the end of the American tour that Tony Mason started having second thoughts about the Penguin re-branding that he and Alan Wright had instigated in 1967. Since that famous match at Twickenham, Penguin teams had begun to wear black and white jerseys with a Penguin badge on the left breast for their bigger matches and tours. These Penguin-badged jerseys were eye-catching and very popular - and soon became highly sought-after momentos by opposition teams, spectators and, indeed, many of the Penguin players themselves. These badged shirts were very expensive, and the Club still had very little money, so it was no surprise when a clearly exasperated Tony Mason wrote later of this trend: *We are considering changing our jerseys to a less attractive design. Unfortunately souvenir hunters in America have removed a total of ten jerseys from our two sets, which really means that we have got to replace both now.*

Tony didn't know it at the time, but this was a problem that would never, ever go away!

The full results of the tour were: On the 12th May - Penguins beat Southern California Colleges XV 23 - 8 in Los Angeles; 16th May - Penguins lost to Northern California All-Stars 15 - 27 in San Francisco; 19th May - Penguins beat San Francisco Rugby Club 32 - 0 in San Francisco; 22nd May - Penguins beat Combined Bay Area Touring Side and Olympic Club 12 - 3 in San Jose; 24th May - Penguins beat Peninsular Ramblers 14 - 6 in San Jose; 27th May - Penguins lost to Combined Southern University All-Stars 8 - 13 in Los Angeles; 28th May - Penguins lost to Combined California Universities Touring Side 11 - 21 in Los Angeles. The Penguins played seven matches, won four and lost three.

Programmes from the Penguins' matches against San Francisco Rugby Club and The Northern California Rugby Union All-Stars.

Penguins squad:

Tony Mason (Tour Manager), Alan Wright (Tour Manager, Admin), John Morgan (Committee). Colin McFadyean (Moseley, England and British and Irish Lions, Captain), John Allen (Leicester and Midlands), Tony Bucknall (Richmond and England), Gerry Culliton (Wanderers and Ireland), Martyn Davies (Neath and Wales trialist), David Dearden (Glasgow), John Devenport (Wasps), Cyril Evans (Newbridge and Wales trialist), Alex Finlayson (Cardiff and Wales 'B'), Ray Flannery (Ireland), Jim Flynn (Wanderers, Leinster and Ireland), Kevin Flynn (Wanderers, Leinster and Ireland), John Hennigan (Blackheath), Brian Keen (Moseley and England), Kevin McGowan (Glamorgan Wanderers and Leinster), Terry O'Gorman (Glamorgan Wanderers), Brian Page (Bedford and England trialist), Derek Quinnell (Llanelli and Wales U21), Alan Raines (Wasps and Middlesex), Peter Rees (Newport and Wales), Mark Robinson (Bath), Bob Rowell (Leicester and England), Stack Stevens (Penzance and Newlyn, England), Max Wiltshire (Bridgend and Wales).

Another enamel badge from Tony Mason's collection.

On 5th September Penguins played a special UK match as part of the celebrations associated with the opening of Bedford Athletic RUFC's new clubhouse.

Tony Mason included five full internationals in his XV - Andrew Hurst (Wasps and England), Geoff Windsor-Lewis (Oxford University and Wales), Clive Ashby (Wasps and England), William Treadwell (Wasps and England) and Peter Yarranton (Wasps and England). The Penguins won this exciting match by 32 points to 9.

5th September - A UK-based match against Bedford Athletic RUFC.

BEDFORD ATHLETIC R.U.F.C.

v.

THE PENGUINS

Saturday 5th. September, 1970.

K.O. 3-00 p.m.

To commemorate the opening of the Clubhouse
at Putnoe Woods.

Official opening by Mr. R. Jacobs. 2-00 p.m.

Bedford Athletic match programme.

The following is an extract from a letter written by Tony Mason to RFU Secretary Robin Prescott on 16th September: *Quite recently, as you probably know, I had a cry of help from Bedford Athletic Rugby Club to raise a side for the opening ceremony of their new ground and clubhouse - and at short notice I was able to raise a team of a standard which I understand provided the home side with an enjoyable game of a good standard.*

Alan was later to say of this match: 'The team that we selected to play against Bedford Athletic was a very fine side, and it was with no little pleasure that we included Geoff Windsor-Lewis - Secretary of the Barbarian Football Club and a good friend and golfing partner.'

Penguins squad:

Tony Mason (Match Manager), A. Hendrickses (Rosslyn Park and England Trialist, Captain), C. Ashby (Wasps and England), C. Bale (Harlequins and Surrey), S. Corstorphine (London Scottish and Hampshire), F. Hawkins (Wasps and England Trialist), A. Hurst (Wasps and England), K. Jones (Harlequins and Surrey), W. Petch (Harlequins and Middlesex), T. Powell (Sidcup and Kent), P. Stafford (Rosslyn Park and Oxford University), W. Treadwell (Wasps and England), J. Turner (Blackheath and Kent), G. Windsor-Lewis (Oxford University and Wales), J. Wright (Harlequins and Hertfordshire), P. Yarranton (Wasps and England).

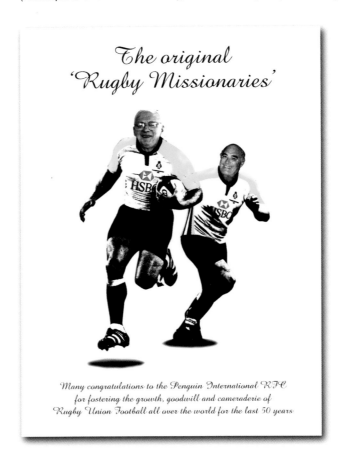

The original 'Rugby Missionaries'

Many congratulations to the Penguin International RFC for fostering the growth, goodwill and cameraderie of Rugby Union Football all over the world for the last 50 years

Peter Yarranton, one of the Penguins' players in the 1970 Bedford Athletic match (and later himself a Penguin President), coined the phrase 'Rugby Missionaries' when referring to Tony Mason and Alan Wright. 39 years later Dick Tyson brought the phrase back to life on a special card (right) to mark the occasion of the Club's Golden Anniversary in 2009.

1971

The Penguins didn't tour in 1971. Alan explains: 'After a very successful 1970, it is my recollection that we must have had to "soft-peddle" in 1971 owing, partly, to Tony being ill - but also in view of the fact that we were planning (with some excitement!) our second tour to Zambia - which would take place in 1972.'

Buenos Aires Hindu Club badge.

The Penguins were pleased to play two 'home' matches in 1971, however. The first of these was played on Sunday, 28th February, and featured a combined Sidcup and Penguins side which played in what was Penguins' second match against a Premiership Club from Argentina - the Hindu Rugby Club from Buenos Aires. It was won by 23 points to 11 and the side included six Sidcup players.

Sidcup/Penguins squad:

Tony Mason (Match Manager), P. Bell (Blackheath and England), B.J. Bennett (Sidcup), K. Bushell (Sidcup), P. Dixon (Harlequins), A.L. Horton (Blackheath and England), K. Issacs (Sidcup), S. James (Richmond), R.R. Keddie (London Scottish and Scotland), E. Kirton (Harlequins and New Zealand), M.F. Mills (Sidcup), K. Morris (Sidcup), C. Ralston (Richmond), K. Savage (Harlequins, Northampton, England and the British Lions), G. Williams (Sidcup), R.M. Williams (Blackheath).

Seven months later, on Sunday 10th October, Penguins played a match against a Kent County Rugby Union selection - again on Sidcup RFC's ground at Crescent Farm. Tony Mason selected a very strong side to play in this match (from which the proceeds - a magnificent £131 - went to the Lillian Board Cancer Clinic Fund). The squad included no fewer than 14 full internationals - two of whom were also British Lions. The match was won by Penguins.

Penguins squad:

Tony Mason (Match Manager), P. Bell (Blackheath and England), A. Bucknall (Richmond and England), H. Burry (Guy's Hospital and New Zealand), A. Davies (Harlequins and England), M. Davies (Neath, Wales 'B', and Welsh Replacement), J. Frame (Gala and Scotland), A. Hancock (Northampton and England), G. Hodgson (Neath and Wales), H. Keith (Wasps and Scotland), K. Kennedy (London Irish, Ireland and the British & Irish Lions), W. Lauder (Neath and Scotland), J. Loyd (Bridgend and Wales), A. McHarg (London Scottish and Scotland), K. Savage (London Scottish, England and the British & Irish Lions), I. Wright (Northampton and England).

1971 CHRONICLE

28th February - Sidcup/Penguins beat Hindu RFC 23 - 11 at Crescent Farm, Sidcup.

10th October - Penguins beat Kent County Rugby Union XV at Crescent Farm, Sidcup.

Sidcup/Penguins RFC v Hindu RFC match programme.

1972 CHRONICLE

11th - 28th August - *Zambia Tour.*
Captained by Derek Morgan (England).
Penguins beat Zambia in Mufilira
Penguins beat Lechwe in Ndola
Penguins beat Zambia in Ndola
Penguins beat Zambia in Kitwe
Penguins beat Diggers in Kitwe
Penguins beat Midlands in Lusaka

Below: A signed squad photograph of the 1972 Penguins.

1972

August 1972 brought with it the Penguins' second visit to Zambia. The Club had made a successful tour there only four years earlier (in 1968) and took great pleasure in revisiting the many friends that they had made at that time.

Derek Morgan Captained the tour (Derek was, of course, the former England number 8 who would later become President of the Rugby Football Union and a Member of the Penguin Committee. He had been on the 1968 Penguins tour to Zambia as one of the players). The Club selected a very strong squad for the 1972 tour, including twelve full internationals - four from England, three each from Scotland and Wales and two from Ireland.

Penguins played the Zambian national side three times, and also played three Club sides - Lechwe, The Diggers and Midlands. At this time Zambia had some very strong Clubs in the 'Copperbelt' towns because the copper mining companies employed many top-class rugby players from South African and they all had wonderful rugby grounds and facilities.

Derek Morgan has fond memories of this, his second time in Zambia: 'Well, four years later there I was, back again - this time as Captain!

'Bill Redwood was now working in Zambia, and when he told his wife I was coming to stay she left home!

'I thought that the country had suffered somewhat in the intervening

Diggers cigarette card.

years. Independance was all very well, but... Their rugby *had* improved, however, and we were fortunate to again depart unbeaten. The final game against the National XV was a very close affair.

'Off the field there was the usual variety of incidents to brighten the hard slog of training (although even sightseeing wasn't completely exempt - I remember running up three steps and then down two steps until the climb from river level to the very top of the Victoria Falls was completed. Not by all..!).

'And then Peter Bell and Robin Challis borrowed a motor boat. They surfaced after five days. The boat remains hidden.

'And there was plenty of drama at the airport when we were departing. The Deputy Chief Constable came to see us off - possibly to be certain that we had all gone! Dave Wrench picked up his uniform cap from the table, put it on, and was promptly arrested by the two soldiers on duty for disrespect to the national badge. The Deputy Chief Constable could not intervene. The Minister for Sport was called. He entered, looked at Wrench and immediately stood down the sentries. He and Dave then had a chat about Leeds University - where they had both been students. The Minister had first recognised Dave because he had been wearing his Leeds University tie!'

Gala and Scotland's hard-hitting centre John Frame also has many fond memories of the 1972 Zambia tour: 'For me, the Penguins on tour will always be a memory of Tony Mason, the indefatigable, kindly and inspired founder, with one Alan Wright, of the greatest touring side since... ever. And Doris Mason, of course. It's funny, but I remember Doris for her motherly approach to her boys' welfare - especially when she'd dispense liquid cement to settle our delicate little man tummies when we were struck down with whatever Zambian ex-pats were suffering from at that time.

'Everyone was pleased to see us. Red carpet stuff. And the rugby was competitive enough to make a real game of it until around the 60 minute takeover mark. The beer was good, and there were lots of swimming pools. With barbecues. No expense was spared, partly because tourists were not that common and the ex-pat community was small and up for novelty. That was us - novel. Kenneth Kaunda was implementing his "Zambianisation" policy, because of which my mate Ben Hodder, a mine manager in Kitwe, was leaving after 30 years of raising his family there. To this day I still have a big lump of copper inscribed with his name, commemorating my visit to stay in his house, eat his food, drink his drink and generally show my all-consuming appreciation in whatever way I could. But an "eat

PENGUINS TOUR PROGRAMME 1972

	August			August	
Friday	11th	ARRIVE LUSAKA	Sunday	20th	FREE
Saturday	12th	v. ZAMBIA at Mufulira	Monday	21st	v. DIGGERS at Diggers, Kitwe
Sunday	13th	FREE	Tuesday	22nd	TO NGOMA via LUSAKA
Monday	14th	v. LECHWE at Ndola Ndola/Roan v. Kitwe	Wednesday	23rd	FREE
			Thursday	24th	TO LIVINGSTONE
Tuesday	15th	FREE	Friday	25th	FREE
Wednesday	16th	TO ROAN	Saturday	26th	v. MIDLANDS at Lusaka
Thursday	17th	v. ZAMBIA at Roan	Sunday	27th	FREE
Friday	18th	TO KITWE	Monday	28th	LEAVE FOR LONDON
Saturday	19th	v. ZAMBIA at Kitwe Playing Fields			

The itinerary of the 1972 Penguins Tour of Zambia, which took place between the 11th - 28th August 1972.
All of the matches were won, but Derek Morgan, who had previously toured the country with the Club in 1968, later said: '...we were fortunate to again depart unbeaten.'

'Maybe Victoria did, but not me...'
John Frame at the Victoria Falls in 1972.

John Frame

John Frame was born in Edinburgh on 8th October, 1946.

He was educated at Inverness Royal Academy, New Park School, St. Andrews, Trinity College, Glenalmond and Edinburgh University.

Profession:

Accountant 1965 - 1968, Broker 1968 - 2000.

Married in 1974 to Sue.

Four children.

Served the Scottish Community Foundation 2000 - 2004 and The Sportsman's Charity 2004 - 2009 (a charity started by John in 1983).

John now runs *Alchemy Charity Advisors*.

Awarded the MBE for services to Sport and Youth in 2000.

Played rugby for London Scottish Schoolboys, Edinburgh University, Highland, Gala, Barbarians and Scotland 1968 - 73 (23 Caps).

drink and be merry" attitude prevailed, which suited us players really well. Kindness prevailed. Last days of summer feeling. There were a lot of Scots in Zambia, which resulted in fuelled singing of "Wull ye no come back again…"(ask a silly question!) etc, and much worldly advice to their fellow compatriots. Thanks to all of you Presbyterian ex-pats. You will not be forgotten.

'Then there were the game parks. I had with me a camera and took lots of pictures of animals in the wild. But they had camouflaged themselves as trees by the time Boots had done their best. So you'll have to take my word for it that I was there!'

Penguins squad:

Tony Mason (Tour Manager), Geoff Cornford (Assistant Tour Manager), Dave Chapman (Physiotherapist), Alan Johnson (Baggage Manager), Peter Dickinson (Referee).

Derek Morgan (Newbridge and England, Captain), John Allen (Leicester and Midlands), Brian Anthony (Newbridge), Peter Bell (Blackheath and England), Robin Challis (London Scottish and London Counties), Haydn Davies (Neath and Wales), James Flynn (Dublin Wanderers), John Frame (Gala and Scotland), Ronald Hannaford (Bristol and England), Ronald Hannah (West of Scotland and Scotland), Grahame Hodgson (Neath and Wales), Dennis Hughes (Newbridge and Wales), Michael Hunter (Glasgow High School FP and Glasgow), Wilson Lauder (Neath and Scotland), Arthur McMaster (Ballymena and Ireland), Douglas Neave (Watsonians and Edinburgh), Iain Pattison (West of Scotland and Glasgow), Colin Payne (West of Scotland and England), Maurice Trapp (Harlequins), Robert Wilkinson (Bedford and England reserve), Michael Williams (Blackheath and Kent), Ian Wright (Northampton and England).

1973

Alan: '1973 was a great year. We had become well known in Central Africa by visiting Zambia twice (in 1968 and 1972) and playing well.

'As a result of this we received an invitation from the Rhodesian Rugby Union to visit them. And they told us that they would pay our expenses, on the basis that we would forego any share of the gate. It meant that they would pay our air fares and provide an undertaking to furnish us with accommodation - mainly in people's homes. So this was the first time that we had ever embarked on a tour where the home unions assisted us financially.

'The tour was arranged so that the Penguins would play four matches in Rhodesia and then two matches in South Africa to increase the gate money.'

Tony and Alan picked a formidable squad for the six match tour that included 14 internationals, two of whom were also British Lions: Ireland's Fergus Slattery and Chris Rea from Scotland.

1973 CHRONICLE

15th March - June 4th - Rhodesia and South Africa Tour. Captained by Fergus Slattery (Ireland).

Rhodesia:
Penguins beat Goshawks 53 - 27 in Gwelo
Penguins lost to Mashonaland 6 - 15 in Salisbury
Penguins beat Rhodesia 'B' 37 - 9 in Hartsfield
Penguins beat Rhodesia 23 - 10 in Salisbury

South Africa:
Penguins lost to Southern Universities 10 - 26 at Newlands
Penguins beat Natal 27 - 12 in Pietermaritzburg

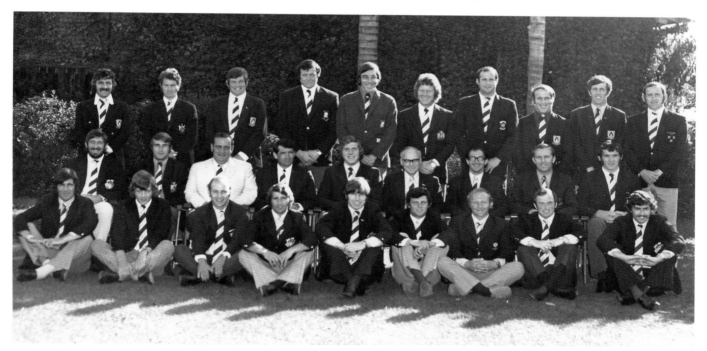

Alan continues: 'The first part of the tour was also notable because, for the first time, we had a coach. We knew we would be playing some matches at altitude and we were aware that even men who consider themselves to be absolutely fit would struggle in the second halves of these matches. We had taken with us Hugh Burry - who was an All Black. He had played for the Penguins before, in the West Country and at Twickenham in 1967, and he was a director of Sports Medicine at Guy's Hospital. He really put our players through it in Rhodesia.'

The first match against Goshawks in Gwelo was won easily by 53 - 27. The squad then travelled on by coach to the Police Club, Salisbury, to play Mashonaland, in what the Penguins expected to be a much tougher challenge.

Above: The 1973 Penguins.
Below: The Rhodesia Tour Programme.

Coach Hugh Burry's memories of the 1973 Rhodesia/SA Tour

After witnessing the very laid back attitude displayed in the 1967 Twickenham encounter, I was considerably startled and even disconcerted to hear Tony say that he was scheming a trip to South Africa and Rhodesia in 1973. I had toured there with the 1960 All Blacks and remembered very vividly the strength, speed, agility, stamina and determination displayed by the teams we had encountered. The thought of confronting these people with the average Penguin selection was quite disturbing, but Tony said that he was well on the way to assembling a really strong team which should be the equivalent of a sort of British Lions 'A' side.

It was at this time that I came to realise that Tony had, as his action man, Alan Wright - who apart from sharing Tony's enthusiasm for rugby was equipped with the organisational skills sufficient to enable him to have a brilliant business career. Not only that, but Tony assured Alan that the Penguins were going to get modern and have a coach.

I started to relax a little when I realised that Tony was not going to ask me to play but that I would be there to coach the team. It was still a daunting project, however, because I was well aware that coaching in Britain at this time was regarded by most players (and probably all referees) as being merely an exercise in teaching players to cheat more effectively! I had, however, experienced a good deal of success in galvanising Guy's Hospital RFC and the London Welsh RFC to embrace the notion that the game was all about getting more players to where the ball was quicker than your opponents. This, of course, demanded excellent physical fitness, intelligence and organisation.

Nevertheless, the general attitude of the group to "training" was one of suspicion, turning to dismay when our first session took two hours under the burning Jo'burg sun! By the time they lost their first game (most had been at a nightclub the night before) they came to heel when Alan turned on them and said they were a disgrace and had let down Tony Mason and the image of British rugby. I was then able to crack the whip a bit! They could see towards the end that what I was trying to do was increase their enjoyment of the game which was what we were really there to do - and not to just drink gallons of booze. After all, we had a very strong team which included some very very good players.

The Penguins soon realised that by playing the excellent rugby that they were capable of producing they would have a much more satisfying tour. Some of the rugby played by the Penguins, particularly in the game against Natal, would have been a credit to any Lions' selection. Personally I was sad when the tour came to an end because so much potential was being revealed and there seemed to be so much more that we might achieve. On the whole I believe that the squad did enjoy the experience, even including the episode when they were offered to the denizens of a lion reserve. I was surprised that they did not feel insulted when the lions failed to show any interest in them!

Apart from anything else, these memories will give me an opportunity for correctly presenting the circumstances of the 'Great Lion Hunt' (see page 78). As Alan had put it, it seems that, like the Duke of Plaza Toro, I was leading my regiment from behind 'because I found it less exciting'! But in fact I was right up there and leading the run - and in a position to confirm that the material stuck to Watts' jersey after he had being lying on his back doing sit-ups was indeed lion turd! I confess this discovery did mildly disquiet me and when I stabbed myself in the lower leg jumping over a barricade of thorn bush which had obviously been put up to protect the vegetable patch from the lions, I had an uneasy feeling that the smell of my blood would be hanging heavy in the air and could excite the nostrils of a hungry lion! You will therefore have no difficulty in believing that I led the troops back to our base and was first into the swimming pool as I understood that lions were not very strong swimmers!

Penguin cartoons from the Rhodesia Tour Programme.

"I don't mind the rugby but it's the black tie and stiff shirt that get me."

AND WHAT'S MORE I SAW YOU PECKING IN THE SCRUM

DO YOU HAVE TO PRACTICE WITH THE CHILDREN

Dr. Hugh Burry. Hugh played for the Penguins many times, most notably in the 1967 Twickenham match. He was also the Penguins' coach on the 1973 Rhodesia Tour. Before the tour, Tony Mason said to Alan: 'We're going to get modern and have a coach.' to which Alan replied: 'The players won't like that!' During the course of the tour, however, (and especially when playing at altitude) the players came to appreciate Hugh's clever conditioning exercises.

They were right. It was written of the Mashona XV before the match:

The Marshona players have geared themselves to a high pitch for this game and they will obviously be a sterner challenge for the visitors than Goshawks. Motivation is always hard when playing for an invitation side, and that's something Mashonaland - with 13 Old Hararians players - are not short of.

The match was won by Mashonaland 15 - 6, and the general consensus among the tourists was that they had, perhaps, underestimated the strength of the Rhodesian representative side and gone into the match a little over-confident.

Chris Rea recalls: 'I think that Tony and Alan did a brilliant job in their selections. They struck a marvelous balance between the social and the serious. Mind you, after the unexpected loss to Mashonaland, Alan Wright assembled us all in a garden and gave us a dressing down - pointing out that rugby always comes first, that the the tour was not a 'jolly' and that we had a responsibility to uphold the spirit and the traditions of the Penguin Rugby Football Club. He also pointed out to us the huge amount of work Tony had put in to make this tour a success.'

The next match took place at Hartsfield, home of Matabeleland rugby,

SCOTTISH UNION PENALIZES STARS FOR BEING IN BBC TEAM

By NEVILLE LECK

INTERNATIONALS Chris Ray, right, and Ian Robertson, two of the backs in the star-studded Penguins team to play Southern Universities at Newlands to-morrow, are in the curious position of being allowed to play anywhere in the world except their own country.

Also, they may not play for a Scottish team.

It's all because they are full-time sports commentators with the BBC.

The notoriously conservative Scottish Rugby Football Union considers this enough to brand them as professionals.

But the ban is not permanent yet.

"As far as I know the matter is still under review. But as things are at present we can have no ties with Scottish rugby." Ray, a centre in the British Lions team which triumphed in New Zealand in 1971, told me after the Penguins had practised at Newlands yesterday that he went into radio as a commentator

and journalist immediately he returned from the New Zealand tour, and Robertson just before that.

"We both knew when we took on the job that it would mean working Saturdays and that this would be the end of top-class rugby for us in Britain." Ray added.

Cape Times article on two of the Penguins' stars, Ian Robertson and Chis Rea.

where the Penguins took on Rhodesia 'B'. Ian Robertson and Willie Oakes, the half-back combination that had spurred the tourists to victory over Goshawks, were both recalled to the Penguins XV for the match. Outside them in the backs were Chris Rea and Ian Muchie, with Martin Cooper and Wally McMaster on the wings. The changes worked well, and Rhodesia 'B' were well beaten 37 - 9.

The Penguins were still training hard every day, and Chris Rea remembers one amusing incident very clearly: 'One day Hugh Burry sent a few of the boys out on a cross-country training run. Among them were Noel 'Jumbo' Dwyer, a big front-row forward who played for Landsdowne, and Wally McMaster, the speedy Irish international wing-threequarter from the Balleymena Club. Wally McMaster, incidentally, never tired of telling everyone: 'I am the fastest man on the planet!' Well, 'Jumbo' had forgotten to take his running shoes

Jumbo Dwyer and Wally McMaster.

Penguins rattle Rhodesia

PENGUINS 23, RHODESIA 10

SALISBURY. — Penguins ended their four-match rugby tour of Rhodesia with a handsome 23—10 victory over the national side at the police grounds here on Saturday — a victory that handed out all the lessons of basic rugby.

With complete control, Penguins were able to pressure the Rhodesians into mistakes — and they obliged with some shocking lapses in handling and tackling. National coach Ian McIntosh was not disappointed with his team's performance. He said after the match: "We were forced into mistakes by the constant pressure Penguins applied". — (Sapa.)

Rhodesia match report.

with him on the tour, so he went out in his boots - which, of course, tended to make him even slower than he usually was. However, half-way through the run, Wally was very unexpectedly overtaken by Jumbo - who was himself being pursued by a lion!' (Also see Hugh Burry's own account of the Penguins' training on the page before last).

Alan: 'Our principal match in Rhodesia was against the Rhodesia National XV, who had three Springboks in their side at the time. The match took place on the Police Ground (as it was called in those days) in Salisbury. We beat Rhodesia 23 - 10, playing very well.'

After the match Ian McIntosh, the Rhodesian National Coach, said: 'We were forced into mistakes by the constant pressure Penguins applied.'

Above and below:
Action from the Rhodesia Tour.

Alan continues: 'Three days after beating Rhodesia we went to South Africa. We played in Newlands at sea-level in the mud, and lost to the Southern Universities XV - an excellent combined Stellenbosch and Cape Town Universities side.'

Neville Leck, a South African journalist who attended the game, wrote in his match report: *Southern Universities did more than merely accept Fergus Slattery's pre-match challenge to play open rugby at Newlands yesterday. They threw it back at Slattery's obviously surprised Penguins with so much interest, the British tourists were 19 - 0 down and well on the way to their 26 - 10 defeat before they really knew what had hit them. And afterward Slattery admitted: 'No, we didn't expect them to run as much as they did - and certainly not as well.'*

The score was 19 - 0 at half-time, thanks to Southern Universities' Ian McCallum scoring a try, and kicking two conversions and a penalty, plus two tries from Hennie de Vos.

After an ear-bashing the Penguins came back a dramatically changed team. For long periods in the second half it was the tourists, rather than the students, who had the obviously delighted crowd standing most often. With forwards like Slattery, flank Wilson Lauder, big David Watt and prop Frank Jackson working like Trojans, they at last began to win some usable possession - and then we saw some handling that at times was reminiscent of French rugby at its best.

Their fight-back failed to bring them victory, but with men like the big and deceptive Welshman Alex Finlayson, elusive fly-half Ian Robertson and thrustful wing Billy Steele all running dangerously, they certainly gave the students some headaches and were a little unlucky not to get at least two more tries than the two that they did get.

Still, those tries, scored by Steele and Slattery, were both gems, notably Slattery's. The ball seemed fixed to his boot by a piece of elastic as he dribbled it some 40 yards at full pace before scoring.

Lauder goaled the second try while the students' second-half points came from a slick try by Potgeiter after a scissors move-ment and a second penalty from McCallum.

THE ARGUS, MONDAY MAY 28 1973   31

THE PENGUINS forwards scrummed against those of London Counties at Newlands B ground today in preparation for their match against Southern Universities on Wednesday. Ken Kennedy (Counties pack leader) is on the extreme left; Fergus Slattery, the Penguins captain is seen adjusting a players' back, and in the white shirt is Dr Hugh Burry, the Penguins coach, who toured South Africa as a No 8 forward with the All Blacks in 1960. (Report, page 30.)

Above: Training before the first match in South Africa against the Southern Universities XV (a combination of Stellenbosch and Cape Town Universities). Below: Winger Fransois Wahl of Southern Universities makes another break in the Universities' 26 - 10 victory over the Penguins at Newlands.

Danie Craven

Daniël Hartman Craven was born in October, 1910, and died on the 4th January, 1993.

He was more famously known as 'Danie' or 'Doc' Craven. He was, perhaps, South Africa's best (and best-known) rugby administrator. Educated at Lindley High School and Stellenbosch University, he played for Western Province, Eastern Province, Northern Transvaal and won 16 Caps for South Africa.

During the 1930s he was one of the world's leading scrum-halves. After the war he became Springboks Coach between 1949 - 1956. Under his guidance the Springboks played 23 tests and won 17.

Craven became the President of the South African Rugby Board (SARB) in 1956. He was also a member of the International Rugby Board and was its Chairman on several occasions. The last part of Craven's chairmanship of the SARB occurred during the South Africa's most tumultuous years. Rugby had become a symbol of Afrikaner power. In the 1970s and '80s, the outlawed African National Congress, allied with overseas anti-apartheid movements, succeeded in getting South Africa isolated from sporting contact with the rest of the world.

In 1988, in a bid to return to global competition, Craven met leaders of the African National Congress and brokered a deal to form a rugby association fielding an integrated team for foreign tournaments.

Although the deal did not lead to an immediate end of the sporting isolation, it paved the way for the formation of the South African Rugby Football Union (SARFU) in 1992. Craven served as its first Chairman for a year, until his death in 1993. The South African *Craven Week Schools Rugby Competition* is named after him, as is the *Danie Craven Stadium* and the *Danie Craven Rugby Museum* in Stellenbosch.

Tony and Alan were proud to be numbered amongst Danie's friends. He always had a good word to say about the Penguins.

This statue of Danie Craven and his dog Bliksem is at Coetzenburg in Stellenbosch. Rather amusingly, 'Bliksem' is Afrikaans for 'Bugger'!

It was at Newlands that the Penguin touring party encountered Danie Craven, the number one figure, post-war, in South African rugby.

Alan: 'Danie Craven made a speech afterwards and described our performance by calling us the best rugby footballing side that he'd seen come from England since the end of the Second World War. He invited us to come back to South Africa at any time we chose.'

Alan continues: 'The final match of the tour was when we played Natal at Maritzburg. We won the match comfortably - although it had been a rather physical contest in which the referee only just managed to retain control.'

Ron Steel, a journalist at the game, wrote of the contest: *Fergus Slattery's tourists dazzled 8,000 spectators at Woodburn Stadium, Maritzburg, yesterday. Brilliantly led by the Irish international flank forward, the Penguins whipped Natal at their own free-running game. A snappy backline, in which centre Finlayson was outstanding, punched huge holes in the Natal defence. Scrum-half Oakes was nippy and wing McMaster a powerful runner, and their forwards were a devastating unit.*

Natal dominated the first 20 minutes, however, moving their backs at every opportunity. Full-back Swanby was always a danger when joining the backs and Thorne, the former All Blacks' centre, was also prominent at times.

Penguins held a 6 - 3 lead at half-time and soon increased it to 12 - 3. But then a spirited Natal fight-back eventually levelled the scores at 12 - 12. But after the penalty by Skewis that had put Natal back on even terms, the Penguins, looking the fitter side, pulled away with full-back Ensor landing a penalty. Minutes later Penguins were awarded a penalty try and then came two late drop goals in quick succession.'

Alan has the last word: 'The Club played some wonderful rugby on that tour under the Captaincy of Fergus Slattery, who holds the tour very dear in his heart and often talks of it.

'All-in-all that tour stood us in very good stead.'

The Natal Programme.

Penguins squad:

Tony Mason (Tour Manager), Alan Wright (Tour Manager, Admin), Hugh Burry (Coach). J.F. Slattery (Blackrock College, Ireland and British Lions, Captain), J. Allen (Leicester), W.F. Anderson (Orrell and England), M.J. Cooper (Moseley and England), Q. Dunlop (West of Scotland and Scotland), N.J. Dwyer (Landsdowne and Ireland Trialist), A.H. Ensor (Wanderers), A. Finlayson (Cardiff), J. Flynn (Wanderers and Ireland Trialist), J. Jarrett (England Trialist), R.R. Keddie (Watsonians and Scotland), W. Lauder (Neath and Scotland), M. Leadbetter (Broughton Park and England), M. Lovett (London Scottish and Scotland Trialist), N.A. McEwan (Gala and Scotland), A.W. McMaster (Ballymena and Ireland), I. Murchie (West of Scotland), B.F. Ninnes (Coventry and England), W. Oakes (Instonians and Ireland Trialist), C.W.W. Rea (London Scottish, West of Scotland, Scotland and British Lions), I. Robertson (Watsonians and Scotland), W.C.C. Steele (Langholm, RAF, Bedford and Scotland), J. White (Bristol), D. Wyatt (Bristol and England).

Fergus Slattery in the colours of the British Lions. Slattery toured with the Lions to New Zealand in 1971 and South Africa in 1974.

Fergus Slattery

John Fergus Slattery was born February 12th, 1949, in Dún Laoghaire, Ireland. Educated at Blackrock College and University College, Dublin. Profession: Property Consultant.

Clubs: Blackrock College RFC, University College Dublin RFC, Leinster, Irish Wolfhounds, Public School Wanderers, Barbarians (including the famous 23 - 11 victory against the All Blacks at Cardiff Arms Park in 1973), French Barbarians, South African Quaquas Barbarians.

International Ireland: 1970 - 74. 61 caps, 18 as Captain. Tours: Australia 1979, South Africa 1981.

British and Irish Lions: 1971 New Zealand, 1974 South Africa. Inducted into the International Rugby Hall of Fame in 2007.

Fergus Slattery is a past Captain and an Honorary Vice-President of the Penguin International RFC.

1974 CHRONICLE

May 7th - 26th - Bermuda Tour.
Captained by Jim Flynn (Ireland).
Penguins beat Renegades RFC 34 - 4
Penguins beat Bermuda XV 63 - 3
Penguins beat Bermuda Police 57 - 7
Penguins beat Bermuda Athletic
Association RFC 54 - 0
Penguins beat Teachers RFC 15 - 4
Penguins beat Bermuda XV 40 - 3

September - Penguins beat Jersey
in St. Helier

September - Penguins beat Palmerston
in Dublin.

*Above: The 1974 Penguin RFC
membership Card.
Below: The ultimate tour destination?*

1974

One of Tony's favourite sayings was: 'Glamorous places attract good players.' So the Penguins had made every effort to visit such places: Zambia, California, Rhodesia, South Africa... and then, in 1974, the Penguins toured Bermuda for the first time.

This first Bermuda tour proved so successful amongst the players that both Tony and Alan were convinced afterwards that it had further enhanced the Penguin Rugby Football Club's growing reputation as a serious, adventurous but friendly Club, and had helped a lot with future selection.

Tony and Alan had no problems selling such a wonderful destination to their selected players (the tour cost each player just under £100) and were able to take an exceptionally strong team under the Captaincy of Jim Flynn, a Dublin Wanderer and an Irish trialist.

*Bermuda
Rugby Union
pin badge.*

Alan takes up the story: 'Bermuda is very close to the hearts of the Penguins. We stayed in people's homes and we made very good friendships out there. We played all the local Clubs. We were made Members of the Police Club so that we were always able to take meals with the Bermuda Police at any time we chose - so as not to be too heavy a burden on our hosts or their wives.'

*Bermuda
Police RFC
badge.*

Mrs Jill Logan is the widow of John Logan, who at the time was the President of the Bermudian Rugby Union and organised the Bermuda end of the tour (and the three subsequent tours of 1978, 1982 and 1986). She says of the 1974 tour: 'The 1974 Penguins tour was much the largest and most important incoming tour we had ever undertaken, and it was a great help to John to have the vastly experienced Tony Mason at the other end. As usual in those days all the visitors were put up by private individuals, and finding beds for 36 people for three weeks was asking quite a lot of our small rugby-playing population. But "old faithfuls" and hitherto unknown rugby supporters came through splendidly - and with their assistance we were able to accommodate all of the tourists comfortably. John secured the last two beds on the morning they arrived!'

Alan continues: 'This was the first of our four successful tours to Bermuda. In many ways we felt that we helped to put Bermuda on the rugby map - because prior to our going, the tourists that Bermuda had had up until that time were mainly the Ivy League Universities.

STANDING *(left to right)* W. McCracken, D. Chapman, Q. Jackson, B. Morgan, L. McDermott, A. S. Fraser, M. Pett, J. Dale, J. Shipsides, S. Outerbridge, S. Leibowitz, I. Barnes, D. Lunn, P. Shufflebottom, D. Hurdle, J. Brady, C. Garde, P. Yarranton, C. McKenzie, R. Clegg, P. Agnew, C. Thorburn, R. Lewis, C. Harvey
SEATED: L. Jones, D. W. Morgan, M. A. Quinn, T. W. Smith, R. Dunn, J. Flynn, A. Mason, A. J. Findlayson, M. Carter, G. Crothers, M. Hunter
FRONT: J. Price, S. McCallum, A. A. Black, M. Thompson, J. Lansbury, D. Griffiths, K. Jamieson, C. Sparks, G. Bentley, B. Sherry, B. Mewitt, P. Davies

They would go there at Easter time, boys and girls, for a bit of whoopee and rugby. But our tours to Bermuda were serious tours, full of good sportsmanship, and the Bermudians liked us. They had a lot of ex-pats there who had played high-class rugby and they could play to a good standard.'

The Penguins played six matches on the tour, winning all of them comfortably. The first match against Bermuda, played on Sunday, 12th May, resulted in the biggest win of all, by 63 points to 3. Most of the damage was done in the final 14 minutes of the match, when a super-fit Penguins side scored 34 points against their tiring opponents.

There was plenty of time for rest and recreation on the tour, too. Jill Logan remembers: 'On Wednesday, 8th May, Bacardi International, who were well known for entertaining distinguished visiting sporting groups, were certainly favourably impressed by one aspect of rugby. The game was new to them, but we had persuaded them that the Penguins would be suitable recipients of their hospitality. The venue was a fairly formal cocktail party at the Company's offices on Pitts Bay Road on a large marble platform overlooking the fountains and the harbour (a notable feature of these parties is that only the many varieties of Bacardi Rum or soft drinks are served). Halfway through the party we noticed little ripples of excitement among our hosts. They were thrilled! They were having to send down into the cellars for reinforcements. They had never before held a party of this kind where their guests had drunk so deeply into their reserves! The party ended most amicably, with the hosts delighted at the record amounts put away by their guests, and the guests firmly convinced that Bacardi and ginger was the drink of the tour.

'I also remember sailing out to Paradise Lake on a big catamaran. It was a really hot afternoon and the fellows couldn't wait to get in the water... including Graham Crothers, who jumped in with the others and came up shouting to be rescued - he'd forgotten he couldn't swim! On another occasion, we were all sitting on the top deck of one of the tour boats when someone's bill-fold blew overboard. Roger Clegg dived off the rail and picked it up almost as soon as it hit the water!'

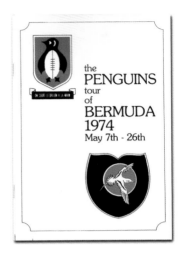

Bermuda Tour Programme.

Bermuda Royal Gazette match report -
Penguins 34 - Renegades 4.

Lyn Jones makes a break against Bermuda in Penguins' overwhelming 63 - 3 win.

*Bermuda Royal Gazette match report
of the Penguins v Bermuda match
on 12th May.
The visitors won by 63 points to 3.*

TRAINING AND COACHING

We will not have time for any fancy stuff so we will stick to the simple basics, do them well and cut out mistakes.

FORWARDS

Scrum like hell all the time, 8 man shove on their ball. We must be first to the loose ball, it is essential that we back each other up and there is always a man up to take the pass. Make sure you can give the pass properly and make sure there is someone who can take it properly. No wild stuff, better die with it and set up another phase rather than let it run loose. At all kick-offs, drop outs, penalty kicks forwards take up scrum formation.

Line out;   Will be a clean catch and hold. There will be no tapping back, especially in our 25.

BACKS.

Quick passing to the wings and backing up in support. Fly half does the loop. The blind side winger comes in between fly half and scrum. Long ball missing out a centre. Outside centre runs wide and his winger runs straight and fast inside him to take the pass. Full back picks his moment to join the line anywhere.

REMEMBER;

We all run with the ball whenever we can, we do it safely and not wildly. One of the best places to attack from is our own 25 but we do not commit suicide.

Above all make sure you are supremely fit.

If you can get these points in your minds before we get there it will help the coach in the short time at his disposal to lick us into shape.

*Tony Mason's helpful instructions to
Penguin players going on tour.*

Jill Logan has the last word about the feelings that the tourists engendered in their Bermudian hosts: 'One of the hostesses boasted that she was inundated with flowers because her guest presented her with a floral offering every day to apologise for the night before!

'But the proof of the pudding was that we had no trouble finding beds for the subsequent Penguin tours, when hosts usually asked for the same players that had stayed with them previously, and, as usual, many friendships were formed and continued in later years. They were so well-behaved on tour that no rumours reached me. We were always glad to have them back.'

Penguins squad (with original programme annotations!): Tony Mason (Tour Manager), Alan Wright (Tour Manager, Admin), Geoff Cornford (Liaison Manager - President of Sussex County Rugby Union, Wasps, Crowborough and Sussex), Dave Chapman (Physiotherapist and extra forward - Wasps, Eastbourne, Kent and Surrey). Doris Mason (Queen Sewing Bee!!), Lois Cornford (Chief Nurse and Home Comforts!!)

Jim Flynn (Dublin Wanderers and Ireland Trialist, Captain and Coach), Paddy Agnew (CIYMS, Ulster and Ireland), Ian Barnes (Hawick and Scotland), Ally Black (Boroughmuir, British Police and Scotland Trialist), Joe Bradey (Wanderers and Leinster), Roger Clegg (Bangor, Ulster and Ireland), Graham Crothers (North of Ireland and Ulster), Alex Finlayson (Cardiff, British Police, Barbarians and Wales), Steve Fraser (Highland and Scotland Trialist), David Griffiths (Wasps and Waterloo), Mike Hunter (Glasgow High School FP and Scotland), Lyn Jones (Cardiff and Wales), John Lansbury (Sale, Barbarians and England Trialist), Phil Llewellyn (Swansea, Glamorgan, Barbarians and Wales), Struan McCallum (Jordanhill and Scotland Reserve), Doug Morgan (Stewarts-Melville, Edinburgh District, Barbarians and Scotland), Mickey Quinn (Lansdowne and Ireland), Brendan Sherry (Terenure College and Ireland), John Shipsides (Wilmslow, Cambridge University, Cheshire and England Trialist), Peter Shufflebottom (Wilmslow and Cheshire), Conor Sparks (Terenure College and Ireland Reserve), Charles Thorburn (London Scottish, Middlesex, Barbarians and Scotland Trialist), Peter Yarranton (Wasps, RAF, Combined Services, Middlesex, Barbarians and England).

1974 also brought with it the Penguins' first visit to Jersey. The Club played a match to celebrate the opening of a new ground and pavilion for the Jersey Rugby Football Club in St. Helier. The match was won by Penguins.

Alan: 'We have an affinity with Jersey. We took a strong side and we won the match. We were Captained by John Frame, one of our favourite players - a big, outstanding centre for Gala and Scotland. Of course, John had already toured with us twice before - to Zambia in 1968 and to Zambia again in 1972.'

The Penguins made their first trip to St. Helier in 1974.
They would return again four years later at the invitation of Jersey RFC.

Penguins played the Irish club Palmerston RFC in September to celebrate their 75th Anniversary. The game took place at Milltown Road, Dublin and the Penguins selected a good side.

Hugh Burry recalls: 'The 1974 match to celebrate the anniversary of Palmerston RFC was quite a serious encounter but I remember that they crumbled in the second half and we won convincingly. One amusing incident in that match was when I scooped up a loose ball and saw that I had a clear run in to the try line as long as I could "out sprint" the defenders. I was aware of arms flailing round and clutching at me as I took off and felt surprised because I didn't think there were any defenders in the location. That was correct - it turned out that the arms and legs flailing out were my team mates trying to grab me and strip the ball off me so they could score the try! You probably think I am romancing, but as it happens the incident was recorded for posterity in a photograph published next day in the *Irish Times*!'

Penguins squad: Tony Mason (Team Manager).
Paddy Agnew (CIYMS and Ireland), Ian Barnes (Hawick and Scotland), Peter Bell (Blackheath and England), Neil Bennett (Bedford), Ally Black (Boroughmuir and Scotland 'B'), Arthur Brown (Gala and Scotland), Hugh Burry (Guy's Hospital and New Zealand), Roger Clegg (Bangor and Ireland), Martyn Davies (Neath and Wales 'B'), Tony Ensor (Wanderers and Ireland), Drew Gill (Gala and Scotland), Barry Ninnes (Coventry and England), Billy Steele (London Scottish and Scotland), John Watkins (Gloucester and England), J. White (Bristol).

GROUND:
MILLTOWN ROAD,
CLONSKEAGH,
DUBLIN 6.
PHONE: 97 31 26

PLEASE DO NOT
ADDRESS
CORRESPONDENCE
TO THE CLUB
GROUNDS.

FOUNDED 1899

PALMERSTON FOOTBALL CLUB

Hon. Treasurer:
D. POLLARD
68 Johnstown Grove,
Dun Laoghaire,
Co. Dublin.
Phone: 85 30 56

41,Landscape Gardens,
Churchtown,
Dublin, 14.

Hon. Secretary:
W. D. MERREY,
"Haroldville"
17, Strandville Ave.,
Clontarf, Dublin 3.
Phones: Home 33 67 91
Office 42 9 21

3rd October 1974

Mr. Tony Mason,
190, Main Road,
Sidcup,
Kent,
England.

Dear Tony,

The Penguins came to see us for an all too brief weekend and have gone.

They have left us grateful for many things. First, for the attractiveness of the football that your team played and which won the admiration of the largest crowd seen at our Club for years. Then, off the field one could not ask for greater ambassadors for the game.

The Penguins have on their first visit to Ireland created a very special place for themselves. We hope that this will be the first of many trips to Ireland. Thank you once again for the marvellous organisation you put into the trip.

Your idea that the Penguins might open our new ground is indeed an excellent one and for my own part I would love to see you play over here again. Please keep in touch.

I look forward to meeting you again. Please give my regards to Doris.

Yours sincerely

John

John M. V. Butterly.
Secretary,
Rugby Authority, Palmerston F.C.

Palmerston RFC's Secretary John Butterly wrote this delightful thank-you letter to Tony Mason a few days after the match. Since the merger with De La Salle RFC in 1985 the Club has been known as De La Salle Palmerston RFC.

1975 CHRONICLE

Spring - Portugal Tour.
Captained by Ally Black (Scotland).
Penguins beat Direito 38 - 18
Penguins beat Tecnico 42 - 6
Penguins v CDUL
Penguins v Benfica

Ireland Tour.
Captained by Martyn Davies (Wales).

Penguins were based at the Benfica Stadium in Lisbon during the May 1966 Portuguese tour, and all of the matches were played in Lisbon.
The full match itinerary was:
18th May v Direito (Law Students)
20th May v Tecnico (Engineering Students)
22nd May v CDUL (Lisbon University)
24th May v Benfica RFC.

A proposed tour of South Africa was cancelled this year.

1975

Alan: 'In 1975 the Penguins toured Portugal for the second time - successfully and happily' (the first Penguin tour to Portugal had taken place nine years earlier in 1966). Once again the squad (Captained by Ally Black of Boroughmuir and Scotland 'B') was put up at the Benfica Club in Lisbon. Tony Mason managed this tour. It cost £55 per player.

Pedro Ribeiro, long-standing Honorary Vice-President of the Penguins, says of the trip: 'In 1975 I was in my first term as President of the Portugal Rugby Union and I was in charge of the organisation of the tour at that end.

'Searching through my records I have managed to find the first two match results: Penguins 38 - Direito RFC 18, and Penguins 42 - Tecnico RFC 6.

Alan: 'You may recall that we had made great friends of Danie Craven (the patriarch of South African rugby) in 1973 during our Rhodesia/South Africa Tour. He had been very generous in his appreciation of our style of play and Club management.

'Tony and I had remained friends with him, and in 1975 the three of us met at Twickenham. After a discussion, which took place on the terraces, he confirmed that he would be pleased to assist the Club in arranging a second tour to South Africa in 1976. A provisional programme of matches was agreed which appeared to suit the South African Rugby Board and ourselves. Subsequently, the Rugby Football Union approved our application to tour, but we were not, at that stage, able to confirm the six fixtures - and, accordingly, the reservation made by the RFU was that they wished to approve the fixtures.

'Only a few weeks before we were due to fly to South Africa the South African Rugby Board sent a representative to the RFU at Twickenham with their proposed fixture list. This did the Penguins a great honour, as it was comprised of the six strongest provincial teams in South Africa - being all usual British & Irish Lions fixtures. The Rugby Union, however, decided that they did not consider that this fixture list was appropriate to a Club side - which, doubtless, was a fair and reasonable decision, as it would have meant us taking on the likes of Transvaal and Orange Free State (although we had, indeed, defeated Natal in 1973!). Up to this time we had believed that the fixture list would only contain two provincial fixtures. Accordingly the tour did not take place. We were sad that it didn't take place, but the RFU have been so kind to us over so many years - and I think they were correct in the decision they arrived at at that time. In conclusion, it is conceivable that because of the pressures between Whitehall and the RFU relative to the question of Apartheid, that this could also have been an influencing factor in regard to the proposed tour.'

Tony Mason also took the Club, Captained by Martyn Davies of Neath and Wales 'B', to Ireland later in the year. Unhappily no record was retained of this match.

1976

Alan: 'In March, 1976, we went to Scotland to play Gala in Galashiels for their Centenary celebrations. Ian 'Mighty Mouse' McLauchlan Captained the Penguins team. It was an open, free-flowing and very exciting match.'

Tony and Alan picked a formidable XV for this game, including seven full Scottish internationals, two England internationals plus one international each from Australia and South Africa. The home team won by 16 points to 8.

1976 CHRONICLE

6th March - Penguins lost to Gala 8 - 16 at Netherdale, Galashiels, Scotland. Captained by Ian McLaughlan (Scotland).

Gala pin badge from Tony Mason's collection.

Above and left: Gala RFC programme cover and the two teams for the Club's Centenary Celebration Match.

Penguins squad: Tony Mason (Tour Manager, Players), Alan Wright (Tour Manager, Admin). I. McLauchlan (Jordanhill and Scotland, Captain), D. Bell (Watsonians and Scotland), A.A. Black (Heriot's FP), A.B. Carmichael (West of Scotland and Scotland), R. Davies (Oxford University and Australia), L.G. Dick (Jordanhill and Scotland), Q. Dunlop (West of Scotland and Scotland), D. Hare (Leicester, North and England), N.A. McEwen (Highland and Scotland), D. Mackay (Highland), D. McDonald (Oxford and South Africa), T. McNab (Glasgow HSFP), D.W. Morgan (Stewart's-Melville and Scotland), C. Payne (Northern and England), C. Sparks (Terenure).

Gala RFC

Gala RFC was founded in 1875 and presently play in Scottish Premier One at Netherdale, Nether Road, Galashiels.

Since producing their first international player in 1890, Gala have provided Scotland with 46 players, the latest being tight-head prop Geoff Cross in 2011. Perhaps Gala's finest hour in Scottish Rugby history came in March, 1971, when on two successive Saturdays six Gala men appeared in the Scottish XV which twice beat England - Arthur Brown, John Frame, Jock Turner, Duncan Paterson, Peter Brown and Nairn McEwan.

Over the years our friends at this great Club have provided many fine players to the Penguins.

1977 CHRONICLE

August - USSR Tour. Captained by
Bob Wilkinson (England).
Penguins beat Czechoslovakia 44 - 13
Penguins beat Poland 16 - 10
Penguins beat Romania 20 - 9
Penguins beat USSR 'B' 50 - 15
Penguins beat USSR 25 - 13
Penguins won the Eastern European
Inter-Nations Championship

2nd October - Penguins played
an Old Elthamians Invitational side
in aid of The Cancer Relief Charity

*1977 Tour badges from
Tony Mason's extensive collection.*

1977

1977 was one of the Penguins' most significant years and was indeed a highlight in the Club's history - for it was in this year that the Rugby Union were invited by the Soviet Ministry of Sport to send an England team to the Soviet Union to play in a special fifteen-a-side tournament to celebrate the 60th Anniversary of the Russian Revolution.

Alan takes up the story: 'The Rugby Union, you will not be surprised to learn, declined to send an England team. However, Derek Morgan was a member of the Rugby Union Tours Fixtures Committee, and I'm pretty confident that I'm using the same words here as he said to the Committee: "Well, what about a club representing the West taking up this invitation? I'd like to suggest the Penguins."

'The Rugby Union Committee agreed, and Bob Weighill, who was the Secretary of the Union at the time, came on the 'phone to me. He explained the situation and informed me that the Rugby Union Tours Committee had agreed that the Penguins would be given the opportunity to take on the tour and play.

'We were representing the Rugby Football Union. Once again I asked if the Rugby Union would help with the finances of this tour, and once again the answer was negative. But the Russians *did* agree to look after us once we got to the Soviet Union - with accommodation and internal transport.

'In fact I had a long and difficult negotiation with the Soviet Ministry of Sport - not a happy one. They often sent me telegrams, which I dreaded receiving, ending with the words: *With fraternal sportsman's greetings* - having told me that we couldn't do this and we couldn't do that! The telegrams were always very terse and direct.

'The tour was due to take place in Latvia. Then, out of the blue, about three weeks before we were due to leave, I got a telegram advising me that the tournament had now been switched to Tbilisi in Georgia. They were switching it hundreds of miles! And so I tried to re-book on Aeroflot, who simply said: "We can't help you - no tickets."

'I sent a telegram to the Soviet Ministry of Sport who sent me back a message telling me to sort it out, and that Aeroflot wasn't under their direct control.

*The squad pose in front of their Aeroflot
plane before setting off for the USSR.*

I didn't know what to do, really. So I 'phoned the Foreign Office and I asked to speak to the "Russian Desk". The Foreign Office official said to me: "There's only one way to deal with this! Just tell them to sort out Aeroflot otherwise you're not going - and they can have the tournament without you!'

'So this time I sent a tough telegram to the Soviet Ministry of Sport, and lo and behold, co-operation arrived from Aeroflot. Well, they told us that we would have to fly first to Moscow and then on to Tbilisi - there was no direct flight. Then the Ministry of Sport also told us that they couldn't make any practice facilities available to us. And then, what was worse... well, after I'd done all of these negotiations, I received another very terse confirmation stating that they would only issue visas for the players, a referee and one official. And that was it. So I said to Tony: "Well, Pop, you go, I'll have to stay."

'There were some little incidents on the tour that Tony told me about in detail when he got back, almost word-for-word. For example, when the squad got to Moscow, they were put in a State Hotel. When the boys went down in the lift in the morning an aged crone would press into each player's hand two sheets of toilet paper - to last the whole day! Such was life in the Soviet Union.

The Eastern European Inter-Nations Championship Tournament programme.

'They had to stay in Moscow for two days. So Tony took all of the players to a public park where they practised in the snow - so the team did get a bit of practice in before they got to Tbilisi.

'There was another very sensible thing that Tony did before the squad flew out. He told all the players to try to buy as many pairs of jeans as they possibly could and take them

with them to the Soviet Union in their luggage. The players sold these jeans for about £110 a pair and made themselves some useful pocket money. A Tuborg or Carlsberg beer in the Soviet Union at the time was four or five pounds a bottle, but Russian champagne was only 15/- for a large bottle!

'In the end Tony got together a wonderful team that would have been quite good enough for a Junior Lions Tour. It was a very strong side which featured a great pack. We had fifteen internationals in the touring party, which was Captained by the England second-row, Bob Wilkinson. We won every match.

'The toughest game was, of course, against Romania (who at that time had a strong national team that, in two years time, would give Wales a fright by losing by just one point in Cardiff). We were aided by the fact that during this match a Romanian player was sent off!

Penguins 25 points, USSR 13 points. An action picture from the final tie. Penguins' players, from the left: Dugald Macdonald (Scotland), Mike Fitzpatrick (Ireland), Maurice Colclough (England), Mark Keyworth (England), Jacko Page (England) and Mickey Quinn (Ireland). Tony sent a letter to all of the Penguin players before the tour began. In it he wrote: 'We will be representing the Western World and their way of rugby life against the Iron Curtain countries so it is a great, prestigious tour, and we are honoured to be taking part. We must be super fit. Make no mistake - these countries are flexing their muscles on us so we must be sure our muscles are flexible and harder.'

Derek Wyatt leads a rush during the match against the USSR in Tbilisi.

Tony Mason poses on the balcony of his hotel room in Moscow during the first days of the Soviet Tour.

'We got a lot of good publicity off the back of this tour. Winning the tournament was a bit of a sensation, really! When he got back I managed to get Tony on to Radio London - talking about the fact that a London Club had gone behind the Iron Curtain to the Soviet Union and won this prestigious tournament.'

After the tour, Alan wrote the following press statement outlining the Penguins' wonderful feat: *The Penguins accepted an invitation from the Soviet Central Sports Committee to play in this unique and arduous tournament, comprising five fixtures in nine days!*

In traditional Russian style each player was presented with a bunch of flowers before the first match against Czechoslovakia and although out-of-season form might have been expected, the Penguins played well as a team and won 44 - 13, scoring eight tries (Wyatt 3, Williams 2). This immediately lifted the morale of the whole party.

Two days later Penguins struggled to beat Poland by 16 - 10, having made eight changes from the team that beat the Czechs. Williams scored the only two tries of the match.

The third match caused the party the gravest concern, in view of

Romania's display against France during the previous season. From an early stage of the game the opposition displayed a pattern of late-tackling, which culminated in the Romanian full-back being sent off by the referee. The Penguins' strong and mobile pack retained control throughout and this resulted in an excellent 20 - 9 win, the Penguins scoring three tries through Wyatt, Evans and Ninnes. Quinn kicked two penalty goals. The Romanian response was three penalty kicks.

The next match, against the USSR 'B' XV, gave the Penguins the opportunity to display the pre-determined moves that they had practised and provided a decisive win by 50 - 15, Campbell distinguishing himself by scoring 20 of the points (a drop goal, three penalties and five conversions).

Ollie Campbell

*Clockwise from top left:
the Penguins receive flowers from Russian children before the first match;
a line-out in the USSR match;
awaiting kick-off against the USSR;
sightseeing;
Ollie Campbell watches Mickey Quinn kick a penalty against Poland;
Roger Quittendon and Mickey Quinn.*

Top: The victorious Penguin team get together for a photograph after winning the final tie in the The Eastern European Inter-Nations Championship Tournament.
Above: Man of the Tournament - Northampton Saints and England's star scrum-half, Jacko Page.

The last match of the Tournament, against the host nation, was another fast and physical match, played in extreme heat. The Soviet Union showed themselves to be a well-trained team with large and very mobile forwards.

This match determined the fate of the Tournament, for had the USSR won, then three teams would have tied for first place. However, the Penguins were unflagging in their efforts and ran out eventual winners 25 - 13, Wyatt scoring a try and a drop goal, with another try from Williams and Quinn kicking four penalties and a conversion.

At the end of the Tournament the crowd in the Olympic Stadium gave the Penguins a standing ovation when Tony Mason was presented with the winners' trophy and Jacko Page was presented with the 'Man of the Tournament' award.

Roger Quittenton, the well-known English international referee, accompanied the party. In addition to refereeing some of the games, Roger was also invited to lecture to referees from other countries. His contribution was much appreciated by the Russian Officials who made a special presentation to him.

The top scorer was Mickey Quinn with 42 points, all from kicks. Gareth Williams scored seven tries and Derek Wyatt scored five tries and a drop goal.

The 1977 USSR Tour was also noteable in that it brought together Dugald Macdonald and Tony Mason. Dugald was, at the time, Captain of Oxford University, and it gave the two men the opportunity to discuss the possibility of the Penguins playing a fixture against Oxford University sometime in the future.

Although nothing came of the discussions at the time, the seeds were sown and not forgotten. A few years later Derek Wyatt (who was also a player on this tour and himself an Oxford Blue) raised the subject again at the University - this time with the happy result that Penguins did eventually appear on the Oxford University fixture list for the first time nine years later in 1986.

Penguins squad: A.R. Mason (Manager), R. Quittendon (Tournament Referee, Sussex Society). R. Wilkinson (Bedford, England and British Lions, Captain), P. Agnew (CIYMS and Ireland), S. Blake-Knox (Bangor and Ireland), O. Campbell (Old Belvedere and Ireland), M. Colclough (Angouleme, Rosslyn Park and England), M. Davies (Neath), G. Evans (Coventry and England), R. Finn (University College Dublin and Ireland), M. Fitzpatrick (Wanderers), N. French (Wasps), R. Greaves (Moseley), M. Howells (Aberavon), V. Jenkins (Bridgend), P. Keith-Roach (Rosslyn Park), M. Keyworth (Swansea and England), D. Macdonald (Oxford University and Scotland), N. Martin (Harlequins and England), B. Ninnes (Coventry and England), J. Page (Northampton and England), M. Quinn (Lansdowne and Ireland), G. Rees (Aberavon), G. Williams (Bridgend and Wales), D. Wyatt (Bedford and England).

Alan adds a postscript: 'This wonderful team would have been capable of playing any one of the home countries!'

On Sunday, 2nd October, the Penguins played an Old Elthamians Invitational XV at the Old Boys' ground in Chislehurst in aid of The Cancer Relief Charity.

Old Elthamians RFC are, of course, the Old Boys' Club of Tony Mason's school, and they were very pleased that Tony was able to bring along more or less the same team that had won the Eastern European Inter-Nations Championship in Tbilisi only the month before.

Penguins won the match comfortably.

Above: Letter from the RRF, received after the tour. Translated, it reads:
Dear Sir - Greetings.
The Russian Rugby Federation thanks the Penguin Rugby Club for taking part in the International Tour in Russia.
We hope the sporting contact will continue in the future.
General Secretary B. Petrenchuk.

Right: Alan Wright's Press Release regarding the Penguins v Old Elthamians Invitational XV match of Sunday, 2nd October.
The Penguins' squad that took part in the match is recorded at the base.

1978 CHRONICLE

5th - 21st May - Bermuda Tour.
Captained by John Frame (Scotland).
Penguins beat Bermuda Police 72 - 9
Penguins beat Renegades RFC 45 - 9
Penguins beat Bermuda 44 - 0
Penguins beat Mariners RFC 50 - 4
Penguins beat Teachers RFC 33 - 6

1978 Bermuda Tour Programme.

1978

The Penguins toured Bermuda between 5th - 21st May. This was Penguins' second tour to Bermuda, the first having been four years earlier, in 1974. Thanks to rampant inflation, the players had to pay £176 each for this tour, against just under £100 pounds per person for the first one.

Alan Wright: '1978 was a highly successful "Bermuda year". Very pleasant. A happy time.

'Bermudian tours, where we were able to take very strong sides, helped us to cement the Penguin RFC amongst the first-class clubs as far as selection was concerned.'

Once again, all of the Club's players and officials were hosted in private homes. This arrangement prompted Tony to write in the pre-tour fact-sheet (which was sent out to each individual player): *...this will mean you are expected to behave like a human being and a gentleman - they can be synonymous - it may be a strain but you WILL pull through.* Of course, they did pull through, and many lasting friendships were made!

All of the rugby played on this tour took place at the National Sports Club, Middle Road in Devonshire. The NSC was also the main tour headquarters. Temporary membership had been afforded to the touring party at the NSC, as well as at the Bermuda Police Recreation Club and the Mariners Club.

The 1978 Penguin RFC squad.

The matches themselves were won comfortably. The 'Blue Machine', as the Bermudian Police RFC are known, were blown away as the Penguins scored 72 points - although the Police did score a try after an interception.

Renegades RFC scored nine points against the Club in the second match of the series, but a superbly fit Penguin XV managed to run in eight tries in a big 45 points to 9 victory.

Penguins included no fewer than twelve internationals in their XV for the 'Test Match' against Bermuda. The game was played in 75-degree heat and the islanders had no answer to their visitors' superior fitness and skill. The Penguins ran in nine tries to win 44 - 0.

Mariners RFC, at the time known as the 'Cinderellas' of Bermudian rugby because the club hadn't won a match for two seasons, were next up. Although they fought hard, they hardly ever got to the ball! They were well beaten, 50 - 4.

Irish international Willy Duggan, who happened to be on honeymoon in Bermuda at the time, turned out for the Penguins' final tour opponents, Teachers RFC, but he couldn't prevent Penguins from registering their fifth straight win of

Bermuda Rugby Union plaque.

the tour by 33 points to 6.

This result meant that the Penguins had won all five of their matches handsomely, and that they had scored 244 points, with only 28 points being scored against them.

After the tour, Alan, in a letter to John Kane, President of the Bermuda Rugby Football Union, wrote: *The matches were played in an excellent spirit and our players very much enjoyed taking part and the off-field friendships that were made after the games.*

Officials of the Bermuda Rugby Union and Penguin RFC.
Penguin Committee men:
2nd left - John Morgan,
3rd left - Tony Mason,
6th left - John Frame,
7th left - Alan Wright,
8th left - Peter Yarranton,
9th left - Geoff Cornford.
John Kane, the founder of the present-day Bermuda Classic event, stands fourth from the left next to Tony Mason.

Penguins squad:

Tony Mason (Manager), Alan Wright (Hon. Secretary), John Morgan (Treasurer), Dave Chapman (Physiotherapist), Geoff Cornford (Player Liaison), Peter Yarranton (Public Relations), Jeff Kellehan (Referee, Wales).

John Frame (Gala, Edinburgh 'A' and Scotland, Captain), Paddy Agnew (Bangor and Ireland), Peter Bell (Blackheath and England), Steve Blake-Knox (North of Ireland FC, Belfast and Ireland), Roger Blyth (Swansea and Wales), John Cantrell (University College Dublin and Ireland), Roger Clegg (Bangor and Ireland), Martin Cooper (Moseley), Alex Findlayson (Cardiff), Mike Fitzpatrick (Wanderers), Bill Gammell (Edinburgh Wanderers and Scotland), Nigel Gaymond (Bristol), Bert Greaves (Moseley and England Trialist), Morton Howells (Aberavon), Keith Hughes (London Welsh and Wales, Tour Doctor), Mark Keyworth (Swansea and England), Dugald Macdonald (Toulouse), Wallace McMaster (Ballymena and Ireland), John Moloney (St. Mary's College, Dublin), Jacko Page (Northampton and England), Roger Powell (Llanelli and Gloucestershire), Micky Quinn (Lansdowne and Ireland), Tony Rodgers (Bedford and England Trialist), Duncan Wilson (Boroughmuir and Scotland 'B').

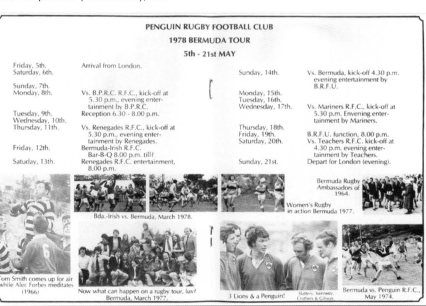

Bermuda Tour itinerary as detailed in the Tour Programme.

After returning from Bermuda at the end of May, Alan Wright began lengthy negotiations with the Secretary of the Argentinian Rugby Union to set up a Penguins tour of Argentina. This tour finally came to fruition two years later in August, 1980.

Kit Gutteridge (12) fights for possession

Visiting Penguins demolish Bermuda rugby squad

The visiting Penguins Rugby Club, playing with 12 full internationals, whipped a spirited Bermuda squad at National Sports Club yesterday by 44 points to nil to win the second such encounted in four years.

With the temperature at about 75 degrees, the game tended to be slower than much of the rugby played this season. In the end it was the superior fitness and skill of the visitors that prevailed.

At half time the score had stood at 10-0 with the possibility of a close finish.

Bermuda, led by captain Roy Dunn, elected to play with short line outs and exert continual pressure on the Penguins centres. The Bermuda forwards were determined to stall the speed of players such as Keith Hughes, John Frame and Bill Gammell.

It was John Moloney who opened the scoring with a try from a set scrum. He dummied the defence only yards from the line. Roger Blyth kicked a fine conversion.

Then 22 minutes later, after being under severe pressure, Frame was forced to make a long pass across centre field. Gammell collected the ball and put Blyth over for the try.

Just before half time Bermuda had the opportunity to score from three penalties but were unable to find the uprights. Mark Carter, the Renegades player who made such an impact in the club game against the visitors, had the first try after David Doyle had kicked forward to just in front of the Penguins' posts. A penalty in the ruck gave Carter the chance but the ball went wide.

In injury time in the first half Donald McDonald was twice penalised for offside in the line-outs and Brian Mewitt missed both kicks.

At the beginning of the second half, Martin Cooper showed how it is done with two penalties from offences by Bermuda in the set scrum.

Following that Gammell got the first of his two tries after a Moloney pass put him easily over in the corner.

The Penguins were still having to work hard for possession in the loose and their next try found the ball moving amongst their backs with amazing speed to elude Bermuda. Hughes started the movement by passing to Cooper, who made a 25-yard break. Then McDonald dummied and passed back to Cooper, who had Hughes on the outside and the score went to 24-0 after Blyth kicked the conversion.

With 12 minutes to go still had plenty of life. Jeff Baker just failed with a penalty kick and Stuart Outerbridge made a 75-yard dash up the centre of the field after he broke away from his own line. He kicked forward and Gammell just beat Tony Roache to the ball and touched it down.

In the last nine minutes Bermuda conceded 18 points.

Gammell had a fine fifty-yard run down the touch line to score in the corner. Moments later Peter Bell, who had replaced Mark Keyworth in the pack, put Roger Powell over for another try.

The Penguins completed their scoring with an easy try from Mike Gibson which Blyth converted before scoring the final try himself with the aid of Cooper and Steve Blake-Knox.

Penguins' next outing is against Mariners on Wednesday at 5.30 p.m. at National Sports Club.

*Press report of the Bermuda v Penguins 'Test Match'
which took place at the National Sports Club
on Sunday, 14th May.*

*Mementos from the tour:
Bermuda Police RFC plaque
and a ticket to
the Police Club Disco
for the evening of
Monday, 8th May.*

THE PENGUINS
BERMUDIAN NIGHT
TONIGHT
DISCO, RAFFLE, SUPPER
ADMISSION $2·50, DRINKS 60¢
7·30 pm for 8 pm
POLICE CLUB. PROSPECT.

Broom Road, Teddington, Middx
TW11 9NU
01-977 8821

Lensbury Club

5th June 1978

Mr. A.G.L. Wright
Honorary Secretary
Penguin Rugby Football Club
Neale House
62 St. James's Street
London
SW1A 1LY

My dear Alan,

BERMUDA TOUR 1978

Thank you for the copy of your thank you letter to John Kane which prompts me to write this note to you with a copy to Tony Mason and to Bob Weighill.

This year's tour by Penguins again served to underline to me the superb organisation and tour discipline of the Club. In congratulating Tony for bringing such amicable and talented ambassadors of rugby together from all over Great Britain I would also like to say, officially as a member of the Rugby Football Union Committee, that the manner in which the tour party, both individually and collectively, conducted itself on and off the field was in the highest tradition of rugby football in every sense.

To underline this, Mary also confirms that it was the happiest and most well mannered group she could possibly wish to have accompanied.

Well done and congratulations.

Yours sincerely

PETER G. YARRANTON
General Manager

CC ARM
T. Morgan

*A letter from Peter Yarranton to Alan Wright, congratulating the Penguins on
staging yet another magnificent tour.*

1979

1979 was another very special year for the Club. The RFU received a notification from the Sri Lankan Rugby Union that it was their Centenary season. Once again Bob Weighill suggested to the Penguins that the Club might like to tour on their behalf.

The Club also played four 'home' matches in England this year, all of which were against very worthy opponents - Worthing, Jersey, the Kent County Rugby Union and Askeans. All were won - which made 1979 an 'unbeaten' season.

In passing - it was also this year that Alan Wright first started to urge Tony Mason to become the President of the Penguin RFC. But as Alan says: 'He didn't want to. Neither of us wanted to. I suppose we never thought we would grow old!'

The 1979 'season' began for the Penguins on Sunday, 11th March, with a trip to the south coast. The Club had been invited to play Worthing RFC to celebrate the official opening of their new clubhouse and ground at Angmering. The clubhouse was officially opened before the game kicked off by R.E.G. 'Dickie' Jeeps CBE, Chairman of the Sports Council and a past President of the Rugby Football Union. Tony and Alan selected a powerful Penguins squad to mark the occasion - including eleven full international players. Penguins won this very entertaining match.

After the game Tony Mason wrote, on behalf of Alan and himself, to all of the Penguins players involved: *We would like to thank you all for turning out for the game at Worthing. It was much appreciated by us and very much by the locals who were highly delighted with the game. You all played in the true tradition and spirit of the Penguin style and produced a game which did the occasion proud.*

1979 CHRONICLE

11th March - Penguins beat Worthing. Captained by Jacko Page (England).

17th July - 4th August - Sri Lanka Tour. Captained by Mick Quinn (Ireland). Penguins beat Defence Services Invitation XV 40 - 3 Penguins beat SLRFU President's XV 49 - 6 Penguins beat Up-Country 74 - 3 Penguins beat SLRFU President's Colts XV 47 - 3 Penguins beat SLRFU President's XV 53 - 4 Penguins beat SLRFU Colts XV 30 - 0

2nd September - Penguins beat Jersey 24 - 10. Captained by Jacko Page (England).

23rd September - Penguins beat Kent County Rugby Union in the KCRU Centenary Match. Captained by Hugh Burry (New Zealand)

7th October - Penguins beat Askeans in the Askean RFC's 50th Anniversary Celebratory Match.

Penguins squad:

Tony Mason (Match Manager), J. Page (Northampton and England, Captain), P. Bell (Blackheath and England), R. Blyth (Swansea and Wales), P. Curtis (Rosslyn Park and Sussex), H. Davies (Cardiff and England U19), H. de Goede (Cardiff and Canada), W. Dickinson (Richmond and England Trialist), K. Kennedy (London Irish, Ireland and British Lions), M. Keyworth (Swansea and England), N. Martin (Harlequins and England), D. Mather (London Scottish and Western Province), G. Rees (London Welsh and British Universities), A. Richards (Wasps and England Trialist), R. Shackleton (Richmond and England), A. Short (London Scottish and Sussex), M. Taylor (Wasps and New Zealand), P. Warfield (Rosslyn Park, Sussex and England), G. Williams (Bridgend and Wales 'B'), D. Wyatt (Bath and England).

WORTHING R. F. C. (Royal Blue with Chocolate and Gold Hoops)			PENGUIN R. F. C. INTERNATIONAL XV (White and Black)	
		Referee: J. T. PRINCE (Sussex Society)		
15. J. FORREST		Full Back	15. R. BLYTH	(Swansea and Wales)
14. P. BAKER	(Sussex)	Right Wing	14. A. RICHARDS	(Wasps and England Trials)
13. S. BAKER		Centre	13. M. TAYLOR	(Wasps and New Zealand)
12. N. SMITH		Centre	12. R. SHACKLETON	(Richmond and England)
11. D. N. BARNES	(Sussex) Capt.	Left Wing	11. D. WYATT	(Bath and England)
10. A. SCRIMGOUR		Stand Off	10. H. DAVIES	(Cardiff and England (U.19 Group))
9. P. FRAMPTON		Scrum Half	9. J. PAGE	(Northampton and England)
1. R. DOWLER		Prop	1. D. MATHER	(L. Scottish & W.Province (S.Africa))
2. A. WALTERS		Hooker	2. K. KENNEDY	(L. Irish and Ireland)
3. S. CHATWICK		Prop	3. W. DICKINSON	(Richmond & England Trials)
4. M. MEADWAY		Lock	4. N. MARTIN	(Harlequins and England)
5. T. HUTTON		Lock	5. H. de GOEDE	(Cardiff and Canada)
6. C. COULSON	(Sussex)	Flanker	6. M. KEYWORTH	(Swansea and England)
7. L. COOMBE	(Sussex)	Flanker	7. G. WILLIAMS	(Bridgend and Wales B)
8. S. STONER	(Sussex)	No. 8	8. P. BELL	(Blackheath and England)
		KICK-OFF 3.00 p.m.		
Replacements:			*Replacements:*	
P. RITSON	(Sussex)	*Touch Judges:*	P. WARFIELD	(Rosslyn Park, Sussex & England)
J. CARD		P. McGOVERN (Sussex Society)	A. SHORT	(L. Scottish and Sussex)
A. BATTY		P. M. JONES	P. CURTIS	(Rosslyn Park and Sussex)
F. ROBERTS		(Worthing R.F.C.)	G. REES	(L. Welsh and British Univs.)

The two teams: Worthing RFC v Penguin RFC.

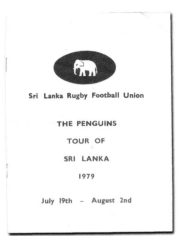

Sri Lanka Rugby Football Union

THE PENGUINS

TOUR OF

SRI LANKA

1979

July 19th - August 2nd

Date & Time	Ground	Match
19th July 4-45 p.m.	Longden Place	Penguins Vs Defence Services
22nd July 4-30 p.m.	Talduwa	Penguins Vs President's XV
25th July 4-30 p.m.	Darawella	Penguins Vs Upcountry
28th July 4-30 p.m.	Nittawela (Kandy)	Penguins Vs President's Colts XV
31st July 4-45 p.m.	Longden Place	Penguins Vs President's XV
2nd August 4-30 p.m.	Longden Place	Penguins Vs President's XV

Top: 1979 Tour programme.
Above: The Sri Lanka Tour itinerary.

But undoubtedly, the main event of 1979 was the Sri Lanka tour, with the Penguin Rugby Football Club yet again breaking new ground. This would be the fourth time that the Penguins had been asked to field a side to represent the Rugby Union - the previous occasions being the Belgium tour of 1964, the Zambia tour in 1968 and the USSR 60th Anniversary Tournament of 1977.

Alan takes up the story: 'Bob Weighill, the Rugby Union Secretary, 'phoned to say that the Sri Lankan Rugby Union had asked England to send a team over to celebrate their Centenary, but that this wasn't really on. Would we like to go on their behalf and play the games and join in the celebrations? Well, it was a great honour to be asked and we were happy to do it.

'So. We were guests of the Sri Lanka Rugby Union and they particularly asked us to take a young party. In the event, no fewer than twelve of the party were under 23 years old.'

In a Sri Lankan newspaper interview, given just before the first match, an extremely confident Tony Mason said of the Penguins selection: *This is the youngest tour party ever to represent the Penguin Club. We have come here to play attractive rugby. Our strength is everywhere, we have no weakness.*

The Penguins squad was indeed formidable, and included no fewer than seven internationals: Mickey Quinn (stand-off half/full back), Stephen Blake-Knox (winger), Martin Cooper (stand-off half), John Cantrell (hooker), Bobby McGrath (scrum-half), Peter Warfield (centre) and Peter Bell (wing-forward). In addition, the squad also included six Scottish U23 players and an England Colt. Paul Ackford,

The Sri Lanka President's XV line up with the Penguins. Penguins players, back row: Andy Raynor, Kevin Douglas, Dave Aitcheson, Peter Warfield, Bosco Morrissey, Roger Powell, Dave Graham, Charlie Ralston, Dougie Dye, Peter Enevolson.
Penguins players and officials, front row: Bobby McGrath, Peter Bell, Tony Mason, John Cantrell, Rob Brotherston.

who was at the time a 21-year-old student playing for Rosslyn Park, was also selected to tour but had to drop out at the last minute.

Alan: 'Mickey Quinn, the Irish international who played full-back, centre and stand-off half for Ireland, was our excellent Captain. He's quite an extraordinary personality. He has one of the most expansive, happy personalities that one could encounter in a man. The unsuspecting might think that he was often inebriated - but he doesn't drink at all. He is a teetotaller.

'One of our "star" players, Martin Cooper, fell down a six-inch step on the first day and had to have his foot put in plaster, and so didn't play at all! Despite this, the squad knitted together very well and played some excellent rugby, which pleased the very sizeable crowds which we attracted.'

Lawrence Heyn, Sports Editor of the Sri Lankan newspaper *Sun and Weekend* wrote of the tour at the time: *Sri Lanka's rather modest rugby brew was spiced in British flavour when the Penguin RFC from the United Kingdom made a three-week tour here.*

The Penguins soared through a triumphant six-match tour with enormous victory margins in each of their games.

Statistically, the Penguins scored 293 points on tour while conceding only 19 points to their opponents. In a tally of 55 tries there were 32 conversions with the remaining nine points coming from a drop goal and two penalties.

In retrospect, the names of two outstanding young players spring to mind. The little Scot John Munroe Barrie was undoubtedly the tour's big success. His nippiness at the base of the scrum and tireless supporting play won him tremendous acclamation in the local press. Harlequins' Kevin Douglas too played his role as flank-forward to perfection and his fitness and avaricious appetite for tries was stunning.

However, the skipper, Michael Quinn, remained the 'brains' of the Penguins. Quinn, with nine caps for Ireland, was forced through necessity to occupy the fly-half's berth for all six games (his relief Martin Cooper came a cropper on the night of the teams arrival and was a write-off for the tour).

The Penguins opened their tour against the Combined Defence Services XV, a team made up of players from the Sri Lankan Army, Navy and Air Force. In 80 minutes the latent power of the tourists was exhibited as the Penguins barely exerted themselves in picking up 40 points while yielding only a single penalty to the Services.

In Colombo, Talduwa, Darrawella and Kandy the Penguins had try-orgies.

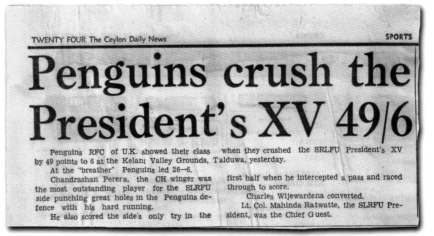

Penguins coast to a 40-3 win

The Penguins RFC of UK opened their tour of Sri Lanka with a facile 40 points to 3 win over the Defence Services at Longden Place yesterday.

Sri Lankan press cuttings report on the Penguins' winning progress throughout the tour.

TWENTY FOUR The Ceylon Daily News   SPORTS

Penguins crush the President's XV 49/6

Penguins RFC of U.K. showed their class by 49 points to 6 at the Kelani Valley Grounds, Talduwa, yesterday.

At the "breather" Penguins led 26—6.

Chandrashan Perera, the CH winger was the most outstanding player for the SLRFU side punching great holes in the Penguins defence with his hard running.

He also scored the side's only try in the first half when he intercepted a pass and raced through to score.

Charles Wijewardena converted.

Lt. Col. Mahinda Ratwatte, the SLRFU President, was the Chief Guest.

Pictures from Mickey Quinn's
Sri Lanka Tour album.

Left: Some of the Penguin RFC team
pose informally.

Above, top to bottom: Alan Wright
and Tony Mason in the crowd;

Mickey and Tony discuss tactics;

Doris Mason with the Tour Mascot;

Tony presents the Penguins team to
Sri Lankan Rugby Union officials.

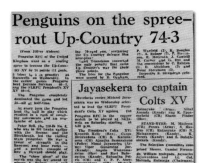

Penguins on the spree— rout Up-Country 74-3

(From Jiffey Ableen)

Penguins RFC at the United Kingdom went on a rousing spree to trounce the Up-Country XV 74 points (11 goals, 2 tries, 1p. 2 a penalty) at Darrawella on Wednesday. In the earlier games Penguins beat Defence Services 46—2 and the SLRFU President's XV 49—6.

The Penguins completely dominated the game and led 34—all at half-time.

At every turn the Penguins kept the ball in play which resulted in a rash of sweeping movements and an avalanche of tries.

Peter Bell (fly, 310-lb No. 8, who was in Sri Lanka earlier with the Boscos and the Blackheath, led the visiting team yesterday. He was a tower of strength in the line-out and loose rucks — and a perfect example of how a forward should play.

The "show piece" of the match was the try scored by winger A. Rainer — a real sizzler, after a hectic seventy-yard run, scattering the Up-Country defence like nine-pins. Nihal Tennekoon converted the only penalty that came Up Country's way for the three points.

The tries for the Penguins were scored by D. Graham,

P. Warfield (3), R. Douglas (3), A. Rainer (3), P. Stevenson, R. McGrath, J. Cantrill M. Carter and G. Dee and the conversions by C. Ralston (3), M. Mitchinn (3) and Peter Stevenson (2).

Inspecthy S. Sivandran refereed.

Jayasekera to captain Colts XV

Burgheos centre Michael Jayasekera was on Wednesday selected to lead the SLRFU President's Colts XV against the Penguins RFC in the rugger match to be played at Nittawela on Saturday starting at 4.30 p.m.

The President's Colts XV: Kenneth Kelly (Hav.), Carga Sriwardena (CR) S. Karunasena (CH) Ajantha Samarakoon (Police) Nimal Jayaseriya (Army) Viper Gunaratne Jnr. (Kandy), Angelo Wickremaratne (Hav) and Ravi Balasuriya (Kandy), Rohantha Peiris (CH) and C. P. F. Abeygunaratne (CR) Michael Jayasekera, (Capt) and Daya

Ratnayake (Army) Nihal Ananda (Kandy) and K. Eppacchchela (CH), Shane Pinder (Hav).

STAND-BYES: M. Mathyas (CR) Perera (Army) S. Hasloon (CR) Ratnayake (CH) N Mahaganaru (Kandy), S. Perera (Kandy) and S. Bulathsinhala (Kandy).

The Selection Committee, comprised Messrs. Gamini Fernando, William Malepada, Jayantha Jayawardena and Lt. Col. Malinda Ratwatte (Chairman.)

More Sri Lankan press cuttings.

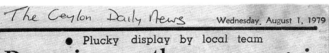

The Ceylon Daily News   Wednesday, August 1, 1979

● Plucky display by local team

Penguins on the spree again

What the local rugby players lacked in size and weight they made up by a determination to to fight against overwhelming odds before going down 4—53 to the Penguins of UK at Longden Place. yesterday.

The visitors who were up against Colombo's extreme heat as well, ran and passed with all the delight, and abandon we have come to expect from teams from Great Britain. They scored 5 goals (5 tries and a penalty) to the solitary try scored by the SLRFU President's XV.

The try scored by the hard-running Chandrashan Perera was as good as any scored by the visitors. Just before half time Chandrashan had to switch to the centre berth as Michael Jayasekera had to leave the field with an injury. Receiving a pass from fly-half Hafi Abdeen Chandrashan scattered the Penguins defence with a power-packed run down the left flank. When the Penguins defence moved in to squelch him, he kicked a "grubber" and burst through to collect and score amidst a thunderous cheer from the appreciative crowd.

The local "pack", too, played with a lot of determination and 'fire'. The Penguins were made to fight every inch of the way by this light-weight set of forwards. In tackling, too, they excelled . . . thus curtailing the visitors moves to a great extent. Angelo Wickremaratne in particular gave a fine display in this department and was a great spoiler as well for the Penguins.

The Penguins struggled to open their account in the first eleven minutes. Bosco Morrissey, the Penguins flanker touched down first. Mickey Quinn converted and Penguins took the lead at 6—0. From

then onwards they kept piling on the points at regular intervals but it was in the last ten minutes that they really hit a 'purple patch'. They unleashed a few moves which held the crowd spellbound with the ball changing hands through the entire team. Some of their moves were reminiscent of the London Welsh side that thrilled local fans a few years ago.

Referee Jagath Fernando also did a good job. There were

times when the Britishers questioned his decisions but Jagath struck firmly to them. Skipper Charles Wijewardena was a disappointment as he missed a "sitter" of a penalty right in front of the posts and also muffed some difficult ones.

Morrissey, John Douglas, John Cantrell Robby McGrath and Vince Cannon scored the tries. Skipper Mickel Quinn and Edward Rayner converted the kicks at goal

Mr. Nissanka Wijewardena, Chairman, Bank of Ceylon was the chief guest.

Down and out .... A Penguins player is "grassed." Bharatha Hegoda tries to pluck out the ball from the fallen player's hands while Chandrashan Perera moves in to collect the pass. An incident in the Penguins-President's XV rugger clash at Longden Place yesterday which the visitors won 53—4. — (Pictures by Jayantha Divisekera.)

Michael Jayasekera, the President's XV centre tries to dodge past a Penguins player in yesterday's rugger match.

The Penguins produced possibly their most exhilarating performance in Talduwa in the Kelani Valley, 50 kilometres outside of Colombo. Against a picturesque setting the Penguins spun out breath-taking moves amongst forwards and backs with clean handling and delightful control.

Up in the hills of Darrawella the Penguins found the cooler climate more to their liking as they ground out the tour's highest score of 74 - 3 against the Up-Country XV. Then, in the majestic city of Kandy, steeped in rich traditions of kings and glittering peraheras, the Penguins defeated a Sri Lanka RFU Colts XV.

Back in Colombo for the final two encounters with representative sides, the Penguins extended their winning vein with winning margins of 49 points and 30 points. Although the margins of victory might indicate a complete whitewash, Sri Lanka rugby was richer for the visit of the Penguins. There was a visible transformation of the players when at the tail-end of the tour they refused to take any more beatings without any resistance. As for the Penguins - they won the hearts of all Sri Lankans not only for their style of rugby, but also by their manner off the field. For them, the invitation is clear: Come again Penguins.

Alan sums up: 'It was a highly successful tour. We played most of our matches around the capital, Columbo, and one in Kandy, the traditional capital of Sri Lanka, which is about four hours drive from Columbo. The grounds were first-class in the main - with good turf and nice stands.

'All the games were won. I think we probably averaged something like forty points per match. The Sri Lankan sides tackled well, but I suppose the dominant feature was the height and weight of our forwards, together with the collective and individual skills of our backs.

'Showing the strength of belief in amateurism, each player and official on the Sri Lanka tour paid £325 (the Sri Lanka RU being responsible for all internal travel and accommodation). This was by far the highest amount that any Penguin tour had cost the players and officials to date.'

Penguins squad:

Tony Mason (Tour Manager), Alan Wright (Hon. Secretary), John Morgan (Assistant Tour Manager and Treasurer), Peter Bell (Coach), Dave Chapman (Physiotherapist), Jeff Kellehen (Referee) and Doris Mason (Nurse).

Michael Quinn (Landsdowne and Ireland, Captain), David Aitchison (Highland), Alan Barrie (Highland), Steve Blake-Knox (North of Ireland FC, Belfast and Ireland), Robert Brotherston (Highland), Don Budge (Stockwood Park), Vincent Cannon (Northampton), John Cantrell (University College Dublin and Ireland), Martin Cooper (Moseley), Paul Curtis (Rosslyn Park and Sussex), Kevin Douglas (Harlequins), Douglas Dye (Boroughmuir), Peter Enevoldson (Oxford University), Steve Fraser (Highland), David Graham (Highland), Morton Howells (Aberavon and Barbarians), Michael Kearney (Landsdowne), Robby McGrath (Wanderers and Ireland), Bosco Morrisey (Terenure and Ireland Trialist), Jamie Paton (Edinburgh Academicals), Roger Powell (Llanelli and England Trialist), Charles Ralston (Rosslyn Park), Andrew Rayner (Wasps and Hertfordshire), Peter Steven (Heriot's FP), Peter Warfield (Rosslyn Park, Sussex and England).

The Penguins scored a total of 293 points in their six tour matches. The Sri Lankan sides could only manage 19 points in reply.

PENGUINS LAUNCH THE CENTENARY

Report by
MAX HEWITT

THE Penguins international touring side to meet Jersey in the opening game of the centenary rugby season will be one of the strongest ever to visit the Island.

All the Penguins are either full internationals or international trialists and the only injury doubt at present is outside-half Huw Davies (Cardiff and England Under 23) who got a nasty knock recently when playing for his club on a short pre-season tour to South Africa.

But, just in case Davies is unfit England's Neil Bennett is travelling reserve.

The full team is:—
Wyatt (England); Blake-Knox (Ireland), Taylor (New Zealand), McMaster (Ireland), Richards (Wasps); Davies (Cardiff), Page (England); Clegg (Ireland), Roach (Rosslyn Park), Howells (Aberavon), Powell (Llanelli), Martin (England), Pomfrey (Bristol), Lambie (Scotland), Morrisey (Ireland).

The referee is Mr. Jeff Kelleher, of Wales.

The game is on Sunday, September 2, kick-off 3 p.m.

At the annual general meeting of the Hampshire Rugby Football Union, a proposition that "seeding" in the Hampshire KO competition be abolished, with the exception of the previous year's winners, was soundly defeated by 41 votes to eight.

This proposal would, on grounds of expense, have effectively excluded Channel Islands' clubs.

At the same meeting, David Bulstrode, chairman of the Jersey Rugby Council, was re-elected to a third term as a member of the Hampshire RFU Executive Committee after a contested election.

He will again serve on the County KO sub-committee and has also been delegated to redraft the rules of the Hampshire RFU, last revised in 1954.

Arrangements have now been completed for this season's junior competitions in Jersey. With the continued growth of rugby in the Island, the Sugden Cup has been divided into two divisions with Ian Macmillan, a former president of the Jersey Rugby Club, having donated a trophy for the Second Division. The divisions will comprise the following:

Division I. — Beeches OB, Jersey 3rd XV, Jersey 4th XV, St. Helier, United Banks.

Division II. — Beeches 2nd XV, Jersey Wanderers, Jersey Youth, Quennevais OB, United Banks 2nd XV.

It is encouraging to see Beeches 2nd XV and Quennevais OB entering for the first time. The two leading sides in each division will meet in the finals for the two cups.

By agreement between the clubs the competition will be run this year on the following basis:—

1. The matches will be arranged at the meetings of the Jersey Rugby Council.
2. The teams will be divided into two divisions.
3. In each division every team will play each other twice, two points being awarded for a win and one point for a draw.
4. In the event of two teams finishing equal there shall be a play-off, unless in the opinion of the Rugby Council this is impractical to arrange, in which case points for and against difference shall count.
5. The two top teams in each division shall meet to play for their respective cups.
6. No player may play for two clubs in the competition in the same season.
7. Clubs are expected to field teams of strength appropriate to the relative division. If it is claimed that unfair selection has been made, a hearing shall be held before the Rugby Council, who shall have the power to order a replay or forfeit the match.
8. In the finals only players who have appeared for that team in a minimum of four cup matches in the season will be eligible.
9. No players who has played six or more matches for Jersey 1st XV in the current season shall be eligible to play in the finals.
10. In the event of a final being drawn, ten minutes each way extra time shall be played. If the sides are still equal, the cup will be shared.
11. Should a team "scratch" any fixture, the match will be awarded to their opponents by a score of 24—0.
12. The captain of each side will be responsible for supplying to the chairman of the Rugby Council within seven days after each match the names of his team.
13. Any complaint or arbitration concerning the competition shall be referred to the Rugby Council, whose decision shall be final.

Geoff Richards (Wasps)

Jersey RFC plaque. This was Penguins' second trip to Jersey, the first having taken place five years earlier in 1974.

Penguins travelled to St. Helier in September to play in Jersey Rugby Club's Centenary Match. The squad included eight full internationals - and a young South African who was studying at Oxford University by the name of Nick Mallett (Mallett, of course, would later go on to play for Western Province and the Springboks, and coach the Boland Cavaliers RFC, Stade Français, South Africa and Italy).

The *Jersey Evening Post* wrote of this match, which took place on

TEAMS

Jersey R.F.C.		Penguins R.F.C.	
Red Jersey - White Shorts		White Jersey with Black Yoke - White Shorts - Yellow Socks.	
T. Mee (Capt.)	15	D. Wyatt	(Bath & England)
J. Jordan	14	S. Blake-Knox	(N.I.F.C. & Ireland)
L. Small	13	A. Raynor	(Wasps & Herts)
P. Noble	12	W. McMaster	(Ballymena & Ireland)
A. Clarke	11	T. Richards	(Wasps & England Trialist)
J. Taylor	10	N. Bennett	(London Welsh & England)
K. Barry	9	J. Page	(Northampton & England)
I. Anderson	1	R. Clegg	(Bangor & Ireland)
M. Lowe	2	M. Williams	(Blackheath & Kent)
E. Kenwright	3	M. Howells	(Aberavon & Barbarians)
R. Allan	4	R. Powell	(Llanelli & England Trialist)
D. Botrel	5	N. Mallett	(Richmond & Western Province) S.A.)
L. Gallafly	6	N. Pomphrey	(Bristol & England)
D. Liddiard	8	I. Lambie	(Watsonian & Scotland)
D. Burton	7	B. Morrisey	(Terenure & Ireland Trialist)
Replacements	J. Wells		
	D. Kelk		

Referee : J. Kelleher (Wales)
Touch Judge : D.J. Tranter
M.J. Engleman (C.I. Referees Society)

Jersey RFC v Penguin RFC team sheet.

Penguins' Morgan Howells about to be tackled by Jersey prop Ernie Cartwright.

Jersey open-side Dai Burton runs in for his try.

Penguins played Kent at Blackheath FC's Rectory Field.

2nd September: *Nearly 1,000 spectators saw a memorable 80 minutes of sparkling rugby football at St. Peter yesterday afternoon.*

Eight home country internationals, six county players or international trialists, plus a Western Province representative from South Africa made up one of the best teams to have played on Jersey soil since the international XVs brought to the island in the mid-sixties.

The quality of the Penguins' rugby matched the occasion. They won, as anticipated, but they had to pull out all the stops to do so in the face of some very determined Jersey tackling and counter-attacking play that certainly seemed to surprise the distinguished visitors. The final score was 24 - 10 to the Penguins, whose tries were scored by Nigel Pomphrey (2), Tony Richards and Roger Powell.

Alan recalls: 'This was our second time in Jersey - it was to celebrate their Centenary. We took a very strong side Captained by England's Jacko Page. They came very close to holding us in a close match.'

Penguins squad:

T. Mason (Match Manager), A.G.L. Wright (Hon Sec). J. Page (Northampton and England, Captain), N. Bennett (London Welsh and England), S. Blake-Knox (North of Ireland FC and Ireland), R. Clegg (Bangor and Ireland), M. Howells (Aberavon and Barbarians), I. Lambie (Watsonians and Scotland), N. Mallett (Richmond and Western Province S.A.), W. McMaster (Ballymena and Ireland), B. Morrisey (Terenure and Ireland Trialist), N. Pomphrey (Bristol and England), R. Powell (Llanelli and England Trialist), A. Rayner (Wasps and Hertfordshire), T. Richards (Wasps and England Trialist), M. Williams (Blackheath and Kent), D. Wyatt (Bath and England).

On Sunday, 23rd September Penguin's home County, the Kent County Rugby Football Union, did Tony Mason the great honour of asking him to select an International XV to play the Kent County side in their Centenary Season Celebration Match at The Rectory Field, home of Blackheath FC.

Kent agreed that this special international XV would play in Penguin RFC jerseys. The side was Captained by long-serving Penguin Hugh Burry (Guy's Hospital and New Zealand). Tony encountered many selection difficulties in the run-up to this match, but managed to select a strong side that knitted together in magnificent fashion and won very well. The quality of the rugby football was very high and some marvellous tries were scored.

Penguins squad:

Tony Mason (Match Manager). H. Burry (Guy's Hospital and New Zealand, Captain), P. Bell (Blackheath and England), A. Davies (Harlequins and England), M. Davies (Neath and Welsh Reserve), J. Frame (Gala and Scotland), A. Hancock (Northampton and England), G. Hodgson (Neath and Wales), H. Keith (Wasps and Scotland), K. Kennedy (London Irish, Ireland and British Lions), W. Lauder (Neath and Scotland), J. Lloyd (Bridgend and Wales), A. McHarg (London Scottish and Scotland), S. Reany (London Scottish and New Zealand Trialist), K. Savage (Harlequins, England and British Lions), I. Wright (Northampton and England).

On Sunday, 7th October, in their final game of the decade, the Penguins played Askeans RFC, the Club of John Morgan, the London Counties Auditor and the first Penguins' Honorary Treasurer. It was the Askeans' Golden Anniversary Celebratory Match and it was played in aid of The Cancer Relief Charity. The Penguins included two All Blacks at inside and outside-centre, and won the match in handsome style.

Askeans were the Penguins' final opponents of the '70s.

ALL BLACKS V PENGUINS
Hong Kong Sevens, Happy Valley, March 1987

1980 - 1989

LIFE IN THE FAST LANE

ALAN WRIGHT: 'HIGHLIGHTS OF OUR THIRD DECADE
INCLUDE TOURS TO:
♦ THE AMERICAS - BERMUDA (TWO)/BRAZIL/CHILE;
♦ AFRICA - KENYA (TWO);
♦ THE PRESTIGIOUS INVITATION TO APPEAR IN
THE HONG KONG SEVENS TOURNAMENT IN 1987 AND 1988
WHICH BROUGHT THE CLUB WORLDWIDE MEDIA COVERAGE.'

1980

1980 CHRONICLE

August - Argentina Tour.
Captained by Nick Martin (England).
Penguins beat La Plata 21 - 0
in La Plata
Penguins beat Córdoba Province
in Córdoba
Penguins beat C.A. Banco Nacion
in Buenos Aires

12th October - Lewes RFC
Golden Jubilee Match

Los Penguins en Córdoba

*Argentinian press cutting, welcoming
the Penguins to Córdoba.*

*Top: Tony Mason consults with
members of the Argentinian RU.
Bottom: Penguin players relaxing.*

Alan Wright: '1980 was our birthday year - we were 21!

'It was another special year, as we were to embark on only our second tour of a major rugby-playing nation - in this instance Argentina (having previously toured South Africa in 1973).

'The negotiations for this tour were both lengthy and intricate, commencing in 1978 with a meeting here in London with the Secretary of the Argentinian Rugby Union. The difficulties to be overcome included financial responsibility within Argentina, the proportion of air fares to be paid by the Penguins, and the requirement that our squad was to include a large element of capped players. The overall arrangement was the retention by the hosts of the gate money, on the basis that they pay for the visiting team's internal travel, subsistence and accommodation.

*From Tony
Mason's
badge
collection.*

'In May, closer to the start of the tour, it became necessary to arrange for it to be reorganised, postponed or cancelled because it had not been possible for the hosts to confirm the details of the itinerary including fixtures, practice, travel and hotel arrangements - the latter being essential for next-of-kin information.

'The tour was re-scheduled for August that year, all the necessary details having been confirmed. I was unable to go along as I had pre-paid for a family holiday at that time on the understanding that the tour would take place in May.

'Tony selected an exceptionally strong touring party under the captaincy of Nick Martin who played lock for Harlequins, Bedford and England. The squad included no fewer than 20 capped players from the four home Unions. This team played extremely well in winning the first three matches against powerful opposition - beating La Plata, Córdoba Province and C.A. Banco Nacion (Banco Nacion were at this time captained by the brilliant Argentinian fly half, Hugo Porta, who played 58 times for Los Pumas over 20 years, captaining them on 34 occasions).

'On the day before our match versus Banco Nacion, an international match between a World XV and Argentina was played in aid of charity following a huge flood. At the last minute, the World XV found their team depleted and after an appeal to the Club we helped them with players.

'Unfortunately, following the celebrations after the Banco match a national flag in the city centre, resembling a club flag, was aquired as a souvenir by a member of the touring party - acting impulsively and without malice aforethought. It was returned with apologies. However, in the light of this - and the inflammatory press coverage - our officials, Tony and Derek, obtained advice at high level, and acting on this advice the tour was terminated.'

The RFU subsequently requested the Club to provide them with a copy of the players' *Tour Guidelines* and indicated their satisfaction with this document.

At this time Argentina had a military government and, sadly, history records that the Falklands War commenced in April, 1982.

Happily, 21 years later sport prevailed over politics and the Penguins returned to Argentina, the tour having been arranged by the Penguins' Argentinian committee member, Luis Criscuolo - a former Argentine international. This was a most successful and popular tour managed by Alan Wright and Craig Brown and the Penguins remain unbeaten in Argentina.

Penguins squad: Tony Mason (Tour Manager), Derek Wyatt (Assistant Tour Manager, Oxford University, Bath and England). Nick Martin (Harlequins, Bedford and England, Captain), William Anderson (Dungannon, N. Ireland), John Berthinussen (Gala, Scotland 'B'), John Cantrell (Blackrock and Ireland), Gary Coakley (CIU), Mark Douglas (Llanelli and Wales), Colin Fisher (Waterloo and Scotland), Bill Gammell (Heriot's FP and Scotland), Ron Hakin (CIYMS and Ireland), Des Hanrahan (Blackrock and Ireland 'B'), John Horton (Bath and England), Neil Hutchins (Cardiff and Wales 'B'), David Irwin (Queen's University, Ireland and British & Irish Lions), Gregor Mackenzie (Highland and Scotland 'B'), Robby McGrath (Wanderers and Ireland), Alf McLennan (Wanderers and Ireland), Gerry McLoughlin (Shannon and Ireland), John Moran (Blackrock and Ireland Trial), Barry Ninnes (Coventry and England), John Palmer (Bath and England 'B'), Iain Paxton (Glenrothes, Scotland and British & Irish Lions), Gareth Roberts (Swansea and Wales), Conor Sparks (Blackrock and Ireland Reserve), Tony Swift (Swansea and England), Peter Warfield (Rosslyn Park, Sussex and England), Frank Wilson (CIYMS and Ireland).

On Sunday, 12th October, Penguins played a special match against the Sussex Club, Lewes RFC, at the Stanley Turner Ground, Lewes, to celebrate that Club's 50th Anniversary. Once again, not knowing that the Penguins would one day assemble a history, no record was made of the winning score! In passing - although the Club are proud to have remained unbeaten in all of their charity matches, the aim was always to take an attractive team to maximise donations, usually to The Cancer Relief Charity. As it said in the programme on the day of the match: *There will be a collection in aid of Cancer Relief during the game - so remember! You didn't have to pay to get in!*

Penguins squad:

Tony Mason (Match Manager). G. Birkett (Harlequins and Scotland), J. Doubleday (Bristol), K. Douglas (Saracens), G. Gilbert (Richmond), S. Gorvett (Bristol), A. Harrower (Saracens), B. Innes (Coventry and England), G. Pearce (Northampton and England), R. Pomphrey (Bristol), N. Preston (Richmond and England), G. Roberts (Swansea and Wales 'B'), T. Swift (Swansea), S. Thomas (Coventry), N. Vintner (Richmond), D. Wyatt (Bath and England).

Penguin beat La Plata selection 21-0 in debut

THE visiting English team, Penguin R.F.C. played their first match in Argentina yesterday at La Plata against a combined team made up of players from Universitario de La Plata, La Plata and Los Tilos under a continuous and copious rainfall and in spite of the very slippery ball the visitors were able to score four tries (one converted) and a penalty to win by 21-0.

Because of the poor conditions the match was not very interesting with the taller and heavier British forwards dominating play with most of the scrums and lineouts in their favour.

In the first half Palmer converted a try by Hanrahan and scored a penalty for Penguins to lead 9-0. In the second half tries were scored by Wyatt, Irwin and Sparks, none of them being converted.

• **TEAMS**
Penguin R.F.C.: Mackenzie, Countrell, McLoughlin, Martin, Hakin, Berthinussen, Hanrahan, Packstone, Douglas, Sparks, Gambelle, Hutchins, Wyatt, Coasjey, Palmer.

La Plata Combination: Varela, Villareal, P. Roan, Mercerat, J. Roan, Sagarra, Patat, Santander, Ballester, Cosentino, Alvarez, Rucci, Zaparat, Paniza, Gravanich.

The first match against La Plata was played in heavy rain. The visitors won convincingly.

The teams for the match against C.A. Banco Nacion Argentina.

Dirk presented to Alan Wright by the Argentinian Rugby Union.

Alan Wright made a significant administrative change to the running of the Club in October when it was decided that the Penguin RFC should, in future, have more regular (and more formal) Committee Meetings.

Alan explains: 'Like other clubs by invitation, the majority of Penguin Rugby Football Club business has always been done between us at the telephone, by letter or, more recently, by email. Regular Committee Meetings do take place, however, and the very first of these was held at The Stafford Hotel, London, on Tuesday, 21st October 1980.'

Those present at this meeting were: Alan Wright (Hon. Secretary), Tony Mason (Hon. Tour and Team Secretary) John Morgan (Hon. Treasurer) and Peter Yarranton (PRFC Committee Member). Tony, who hated any kind of rugby officialdom and formality, had this to say afterwards (probably with his tongue pretty firmly in his cheek): 'It was quite an historic occasion - and very enjoyable and productive. I look forward to the next one in the year 2001!'

It was also decided at this meeting that 'Penguin Honorary Members' would in future be known as 'Honorary Vice-Presidents and Vice-Presidents' - as they are still known to this day.

*The imposing entrance of
The Stafford Hotel in
St. James's Place, London.*

*The Agenda for the first-ever official
PRFC Committee Meeting (the
hand-written notes are Alan Wright's).
It took place at 7.45 pm on
21st October and was:
'Quite an historic occasion', according
to Tony Mason!*

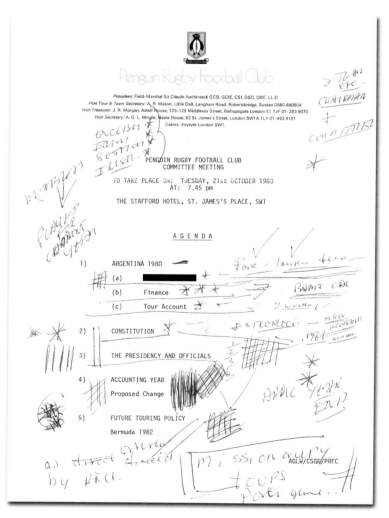

1981

The Penguins did not tour this year.

Sadly, the Club suffered its first major blow with the death of Field Marshal Sir Claude Auchinleck, Penguin's first President, on 23rd March. Sir Claude had first accepted the Presidency of the Penguins from Alan Wright 16 years earlier, in 1965.

Alan and Tony, together with Peter Yarranton, decided to keep the military tradition going by inviting the world-famous World War Two fighter ace Sir Douglas Bader to become the Club's new President.

Alan: 'We've had some distinguished Presidents - including three great airmen. And the greatest of them all, of course, was Douglas Bader. I asked him if he'd take on the Presidency, and he said: "I'll be your President, but I'd first like to know a bit more about the Club."

'So I invited him to lunch at The Connaught Hotel on a very very cold day late in 1981. I stood in the vestibule waiting for him to arrive. The taxi came. He got out of the cab, paid the driver, and the taxi started to drive off.

'I ran forward and said: "Excuse me, Sir, have you left your overcoat and your scarf in the taxi? Don't let him go!" He turned around to me, smiled and said: "I don't need an overcoat and scarf. When you've no ******* legs the blood goes round a ******* sight faster!"

'His love of rugby was apparent throughout the excellent lunch conversation. In fact, I was aware that he had been a brilliant centre for the Harlequins prior to his accident. It was common knowledge that he was on the verge of being selected for an England trial at that time. We were so glad that this wonderful gentleman decided to become our President.'

SIR DOUGLAS BADER

TELEPHONE:
01-584-0902

5, PETERSHAM MEWS
LONDON, SW7 5NR

A.G.L. Wright Esq.,
Neale House,
62 St. James's Street,
LONDON SW1A 1LY

9th February, 1982

Dear Mr. Wright,

Thank you for your letter of the 6th January.

You do me a great honour in asking me to be President of your Club. I shall be delighted to accept with one reservation, that you do not ask me to take part in any of your activities, except possibly a dinner in London, or something of that nature. I cannot agree to travel round the country, because in my advancing years it is getting to be a problem!

I know you will understand. If you still want me, then I shall be delighted, if not, I shall not complain.

Best wishes and again, thank you for inviting me to be your President.

Yours sincerely,

Douglas Bader

DOUGLAS BADER

Sir Douglas Bader formally accepted the Presidency of the Penguins in early 1982.
30 years later, as Alan Wright was reading a Christmas gift from Dick Tyson (a fine book by Ian Cooper entitled: 'Immortal Harlequin - The Story of Adrian Stoop'), Alan first discovered that in 1934 Bader had confided to his wife Thelma that the loss of his legs meant he could no longer bear to watch rugby football. The fact that Bader later accepted the Presidency of the Penguins speaks volumes about Alan's powers of persuasion - and also of Bader's appreciation of the Club's ethos.

1981 CHRONICLE

Penguins did not tour this year.

Death of Penguins' first President, Field Marshal Sir Claude Auchinleck. Sir Douglas Bader becomes Penguins' second President.

So what became of the Auk?

NEWS that the Queen is to visit Morocco in October calls to mind a memorable encounter reported by a friend of Mandrake who was there recently. Sitting in a favourite cafe on the Avenue Mohammed V in Marrakesh he became aware of a very tall, very old gentleman, eyeing him from a table in the corner. The old gentleman did not speak to him, but watched him warily for a while and then left.

Next day he was there again, and this time my friend heard him passing the time of day in French that had a strong English accent with a group of extremely deferential Moroccans.

It was a Monday, and it happened that my friend had with him a copy of the previous day's *Sunday Telegraph*, brought to him by a businessman who had arrived direct from London

overnight. When the old gentleman began eyeing him again, Mandrake's friend offered him the newspaper. The following conversation ensued:

Old gentleman: "Who are you, Sir?" Mandrake's friend gave him his name.

Old gent: "Are you a reporter, Sir?" "No Sir."

Old gent: "Do you know me, Sir?" "I regret Sir, that I do not."

Old gent: "My name, Sir, is Auchinleck. I will take your newspaper."

Mandrake's friend could not conceal his astonishment, and Field Marshal Sir Claude Auchinleck, aged 97, smiled

with satisfaction. "You thought I was dead," he said.

It transpires that the Field Marshal has lived in Marrakesh for almost 20 years. His Moroccan friends say that he has become more and more disaffected with the British Establishment, never having fully recovered from his dismay at having been removed by Churchill from his wartime Middle East command in favour of Montgomery.

Two British links remain, however. Once a year—on the Queen's birthday—a diplomat from our Embassy in Rabat calls on the Field Marshal and presents him with flowers. And the British garrison in Gibraltar maintains a series of corporal drivers, on six-month secondments, to drive the old soldier about Marrakesh in his rather battered car.

Field Marshals never retire, and so technically Sir Claude is still on the active list. He was ADC General to King George VI for several years, as well as having been Supreme Commander in India and one of the Viceroy's War Council.

It seems probable that if the Queen were to visit Marrakesh, where King Hassan of Morocco and his brother Moulay Abdullah have some of their grandest palaces, in the shadow of the Atlas mountains, she would wish to see her oldest Field Marshal.

Sir Claude's Moroccan friends are not sure how he would react. One of them told Mandrake's friend on the telephone the other day: "Of course, he wouldn't be disrespectful to your Queen, but he will not get dressed up for anything these days, and he won't wear a tie. . . . But if the Queen went along to the cafe, he'd be pleased to see her. . . ."

Sir Claude visits the cafe—which, in respect for his privacy, I forbear to name—every morning. He is known as *Monsieur Le Général*. But his Moroccan friends have only the vaguest idea as to his career as a soldier. In their eyes, his greatest distinction is that he knew de Gaulle.

Field Marshal Sir Claude Auchinleck, as Eighth Army men will remember him.

A clipping from the Sunday Telegraph telling the story of Field Marshal Sir Claude Auchinlech's latter days in Morocco.
This affectionate article was written in June, 1980, less than a year before the great man's death on 23rd March, 1981.

Sir Douglas Bader - The second Penguin President

Group Captain Sir Douglas Robert Steuart Bader CBE, DSO & Bar, DFC & Bar, FRAcS, DL.

Born 21st February, 1910, in St John's Wood, London. Died 5th September, 1982, in London.

Sir Douglas Bader was Britain's greatest RAF fighter ace during the Second World War.

He was educated at Temple Grove Prep School, Eastbourne, St. Edward's School, Oxford, and Cambridge University. Bader played both cricket and Rugby Union football to a very high standard during his educational years. He also played first-class Rugby Union football for the Harlequin FC, and at one time was widely tipped to win an England Cap. Bader joined the RAF in 1928. On December 14th, 1931, he lost both of his legs in a crash at Woodley Airfield whilst attempting a low-level aerobatic manoeuvre. Bader recovered and tried to stay in the RAF, but he was retired for medical reasons on 30th April, 1933.

Bader married Thelma Edwards on 5 October, 1933.

After the outbreak of war in 1939 Bader was re-assigned to the RAF, and posted to a fighter squadron in 1940. Bader soon scored his first kills over Dunkirk during the Battle of France. By August, 1941, he had claimed 22 German aircraft shot down, the fifth highest total for a pilot in the RAF. Later that same month Bader was forced to bail out over German-occupied France. He was captured and spent the rest of the war as a prisoner of war.

His captors treated Bader with great respect. When he had bailed out he had left behind his right prosthetic leg, trapped in the aircraft. General Adolf Galland, the famous German flying ace, offered the RAF safe passage to drop off a replacement. The British responded on 19 August, 1941, with 'Operation Leg'. An RAF bomber was allowed to drop a new prosthetic leg by parachute to St. Omer, a Luftwaffe base in France. Despite being treated well as a prisoner of war, Bader caused as much trouble as possible while he was kept in confinement. He even managed to escape in August 1942, only to be immediately recaptured. He was then sent to the infamous Colditz Castle.

When he was eventually liberated in April, 1945, Bader requested a return to action but his request was denied. After returning to England, Bader was given the honour of leading a victory fly-past of 300 aircraft over London in June, 1945, and was later promoted to Group Captain. He remained in the RAF until February, 1946, when he left to take up a job at the Royal Dutch/Shell petrochemical company. Despite this, Bader was still considered to be one of the most inspirational British heroes of the age. He had also become very active in charity fundraising, and in 1976 Bader was knighted for his services in helping other disabled people.

His workload was exhausting for a legless man with a heart condition, and, after a London Guildhall dinner honouring the 90th birthday of Sir Arthur 'Bomber' Harris, Bader died of a heart attack on 5 September, 1982, at the age of 72.

1982

Alan Wright: 'This was the Club's third tour to Bermuda. We played five matches under the Captaincy of Irish international John Cantrell, including a match against the Bermuda national side - who were, at that time, the Caribbean Champions.

'Bermuda - the National XV - played with great skill and determination in the main match of the tour, and deservedly achieved a 21-all draw (at this time only the second drawn match in our history) having scored the two best tries in the match and coming back from a nine point deficit.'

It is quite remarkable that up until the present Penguins have only ever drawn three matches in the entire history of the Club - the others being against Benfica in 1966 and Combined Services at the Twickenham Stoop in June, 2007.

Alan continues: 'Despite the disappointment of the drawn game, the tour was another great success. As I said, we had an Irishman as Captain - along with eight others! Tony and I liked to have Irishmen with us. If you have a small group of Irishmen in a group of 25 men they spread charm and bonhomie. They are the men who extend friendships more naturally than, perhaps, any of the rest of us.

'They were the players who would always express their thanks to the tea ladies in the pavilion for the way they were being looked after. They introduced a happy and humourous note to the touring party. These are small things that help to make good social contact - which has always been a vital part of our tours.

1982 CHRONICLE

2nd - 14th May - Bermuda Tour.
Captained by John Cantrell (Ireland).
Penguins beat Teachers RFC 52 - 13
Penguins beat Renegades RFC 38 - 6
Penguins draw with Bermuda 21 - 21
Penguins beat Mariners RFC 53 - 3
Penguins beat Bermuda Police 52 - 6

*Death of Sir Douglas Bader,
Penguins' second President,
after less than a year in office.*

Greetings

Thank you, on behalf of our Club, for your kindness in inviting us once again to be your guests and to play in Bermuda.

We hope that this will further strengthen friendships made in 1974 and 1978.

Congratulations on winning the Caribbean Championship once again.

DOUGLAS BADER
President — Penguin Rugby Football Club

*Sir Douglas Bader's message
to the Bermuda Rugby Union.*

The 1982 Penguin Touring Party.

Teachers RFC plaque.
Teachers was founded in 1967
by a quintet of English teachers
whose early opposition
was mainly provided by sailors
from visiting UK naval forces.
In 1982 Penguins beat them
by 52 points to 13 with tries from
John Mahoney (four), Bill Gammell
(two), Peter Hewitt (two), Peter Stiff
and Charles Ralston.

'We were keen to be good ambassadors because unfortunately in those days British rugby tourists had a reputation for misbehaviour abroad. The Penguin Rugby Football Club tried to be apart from that. We had fun, of course, but not by taking jokes too far, so as to offend others.'

On the eve of the tour the Bermudian press wrote of the tourists: *The Penguins have proved to be one of Bermuda's most exciting tour teams, with their brand of flowing and attacking rugby. Tomorrow, with the large number of internationals on show, a large crowd is expected to see if these 1982 Penguins are up to the standard of the previous Penguins tours. Judging by their lineup, they should be.*

The tour began with big two wins - against Teachers RFC (52 - 13) and Renegades RFC (38 - 6) before the drawn match against Bermuda. The Penguins squad got back to their normal high-scoring ways in the final two matches of the tour, however, when they beat Mariners 53 - 3 and the Bermuda Police 52 - 6. The final Tour record read: P. 5, W. 4, D. 1. Points for: 216, points against: 49.

Penguins squad:

Tony Mason (Tour Manager, Players), Alan Wright (Tour Manager, Admin), John Morgan (Treasurer), Peter Yarranton (Committee).

John Cantrell (Blackrock, Leinster and Ireland, Captain), David Brewster (Stewart-Melville and Scotland 'B'), Vince Cannon (Northampton, Barbarians and England replacement), Paul Dean (St. Mary's College, Leinster and Ireland), John Fraser (London Scottish, Surrey and Scotland Trialist), Bill Gammell (Heriot's FP, Edinburgh District and

The Royal Gazette, Monday, May 10, 1982   Page 17

SPORT 3

Impeccable Cotter shines as the Penguins are held at last

In one of the finest displays of rugby seen in Bermuda, the Island's national team recovered from a nine point deficit to share the honours with the unbeaten Penguins touring side at Nationals yesterday.

The game finished all square at 21-21, and the crowd thrilled to the action, which saw the Penguins harnessed for the first time in their three visits to Bermuda since 1974.

Penguins had 75 per cent of the possession, but the Bermuda side defended superbly and produced some fine attacking movements when the opportunities presented themselves.

In the end, it was Bermuda who scored the two best tries of the game, much to the delight of the large and partisan crowd.

The Penguins, as expected, dominated the line-outs with their big number eight John Mahoney, and with Bermuda opting for a big forward rather than a pure striker, the scrums also went the Penguins' way.

But that possession enabled Bermuda to put the pressure on as they hit the Penguins' back line with two players at a time.

Chris Ralston opened the Penguins' scoring with a penalty goal in the seventh minute, while John Jeffrey added to it two minutes, driving over from the base of

a scrum.

But in the 23rd minute, Bermuda outhalf Martin Cotter, who was to kick so impeccably later on, put Bermuda on the scoreboard with a 35 yard penalty.

The tourists increased their lead in the 29th minute when Bermuda were penalised for going over the top. Ralston scored with a penalty.

Then came one of the best tries in the game.

The ball came back from

some loose play to Mawhinney, who broke towards the backline. Drawing the opposition half-backs, he fed the ball to David Doyle.

Stuart Outerbridge, coming into the line from full back, drew the defence while the ball went to Ron Hall who went over in the corner.

A magnificent kick by Cotter got the conversion points from the touchline and suddenly Bermuda had

their backs up.

But two more Ralston penalties gave Penguins an 18-9 lead at the interval.

In the second half, Cotter kicked a beautiful penalty from inside his half, and four minutes later, he found the spot again to reduce the Penguins lead to 18-15.

Ralston gave the Penguins breathing space with another penalty kick in the 50th minute, but it was to be the last they would score.

Bermuda came forward in waves searching for the breakthrough, which came in the 73rd minute. Outerbridge went blind from a scrum and, jinking round the Penguins's defenders, passed to Board to go over in the corner.

Cotter, in magnificent form, kicked the points from the touchline to level the scores and give Bermuda a tremendous draw against opposition of the highest calibre.

Royal Gazette
report of
the 21 - 21
drawn match
with the
Bermuda
national XV.

Scotland), James Gossman (West of Scotland, Glasgow District and Scotland), Peter Hewitt (Heriot's FP, Scottish Schools, Edinburgh and Scotland), Jerry Holland (Wanderers and Ireland), Mark Howe (Bedford, England U23s), John Jeffrey (Kelso, Northumberland, English Universities and British Universities), Ronan Kearney (Wanderers, Leinster and Ireland), Frank Kennedy (St. Mary's College, Leinster and Ireland Trialist), Terry Kennedy (St. Mary's College, Leinster and Ireland), Alan Lawson (Heriot's FP, Middlesex and Scotland), Robbie McGrath (Wanderers, Connacht and Ireland), Gregor McKenzie (Highland, Barbarians and Scotland U23), Mark McWhite (Lansdowne and Irish Schoolboys), Rory Moroney (Landsdowne, Munster and Irish Trialist), Mike Rafter (Bristol, Gloucestershire and

England), Charles Ralston (Middlesex, South West Counties and England U23s), Alun Rees (Bath and England U16), Peter Stiff (Bristol, South West Counties and England U23s), Paul Stringfield (Rosslyn Park, Middlesex and Waikato U23s).

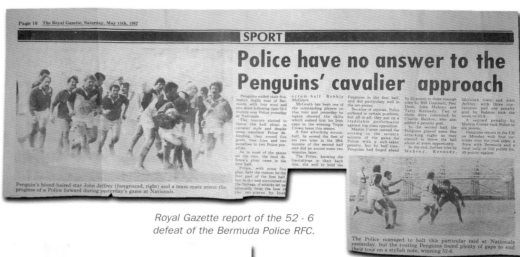

Royal Gazette report of the 52 - 6 defeat of the Bermuda Police RFC.

*Above left:
Penguins Tour Party Pen Pictures signed by the players and officials.*

Top: Penguins and Bermuda teams.

*Above: Penguins v Bermuda lineout,
Penguin players, L-R:
John Fraser (3), Jerry Holland,
David Brewster, Vince Cannon,
John Jeffrey (with ball), John Mahony.*

*Left: Penguins v Mariners,
Penguin players only, L-R:
Peter Hewitt (15), Charlie Ralston,
Frank Kennedy (13), John Fraser,
David Brewster (hands on hips),
Peter Stiff, Vince Cannon and
Mark Howe.*

Sadly, the great fighter ace Sir Douglas Bader, Penguin RFC's second President, died of a heart attack at the age of 72 on 5th September, after a short time in office.

1983 CHRONICLE

20th March - *Penguins beat Sidcup 42 - 22 in the Sidcup Football Club Centenary Match at Crescent Farm, Sidcup. Captained by Simon Halliday (England).*

July - *Kenya Tour. Captained by Vince Cannon (England). Penguins beat Kenya Rugby Football Union Chairman's XV 28 - 15 in Nairobi Penguins beat Mwamba 49 - 4 in Nairobi Penguins beat Scorpions 36 - 10 in Nakuru Penguins beat East Africa 41 - 3 in Nairobi Penguins beat Scorpions 39 - 3 in Mombasa Penguins beat Kenya 19 - 7 in Nairobi*

Sir Robert Lawrence becomes Penguins' third President.

Sir Robert Lawrence.

1983

In January 1983 Sir Robert Lawrence CBE, ERD accepted the Penguin Committee's invitation, made by Alan Wright, to become the Penguin Rugby Football Club's new President. He succeeded Sir Douglas Bader. The appointment of Sir Robert, an RE Colonel during the war, continued the Club's military tradition with regard to its Presidents.

Alan recalls: 'Bobby Lawrence had a great sense of humour. As a founder member of the Bloody Men RFC, he once boasted at a dinner that the Bloody Men had never lost a match. After a significant pause and much lifting of eyebrows, he added the words "...because they never played a match"!'

Tony Neary of Broughton Park, England and the British Lions (of whom it was written that he was: *the supreme English flanker of his generation*) also became a Member of the the Penguin Committee at this time. This meant that at the start of the 1983 season the Penguin Committee consisted of: Tony Mason (Chairman and Team Secretary), Alan Wright (Hon. Secretary), John Morgan (Hon. Treasurer), Peter Yarranton, Tony Neary and Derek Morgan.

On 20th March the Penguins took a very strong side along to Crescent Farm to play Sidcup Football Club in their Centenary match. The Penguins squad included ten full internationals and several other players who were on the brink of international selection - among them Simon Halliday (who Captained the side) and a promising young Oxford University stand-off half by the name of Stuart Barnes.

Because of their long association with Sidcup (indeed, both men were Vice-Presidents of the Club) Tony and Alan considered it to be a great honour to have been invited to bring a side. Sidcup, on their part, believed that it was they who should thank the Penguins, for 'the distinction and privilege of their visit'. The match itself was an exciting, free-flowing game, despite taking place in heavy rain.

Sir Robert Lawrence - The third Penguin President

Sir Robert Leslie Edward Lawrence CBE, ERD (OA) was born on 29th October, 1915, and died in 1984. Educated at Dulwich College from 1929 to 1934, he was appointed a prefect and played rugby football for the 2nd XV with some games for the 1st XV. At nineteen Lawrence started work with the London and North Eastern Railway as a traffic apprentice. He married Joyce Ricketts in 1940. They had one son and one daughter.

Sir Robert served throughout the war with the Royal Engineers in France, Norway, the Mediterranean and Germany, reaching the rank of Colonel and being twice mentioned in dispatches as well as being appointed OBE (Military) in 1944.

Alan Wright: 'There is a strange story about Bobbie Lawrence. He was serving in Norway in 1940 when the Germans invaded. Bobbie Lawrence was, at that time, the Communications Officer at Field Marshal Auchinleck's HQ. One night he received an order "For the C-in-C's Eyes Only". Bobbie said to me "I didn't know whether to wake him up - but I knew what it was. It was the order to evacuate immediately - to run for it before the Germans collared the lot of us!".

It was won by the Penguins by 44 points to 22.

Penguins squad:

Tony Mason (Match Manager), Alan Wright (Hon. Secretary).

V. Cannon (Northampton and England, Captain), T. Allchurch (Rosslyn Park and England 'B'), S. Barnes (Oxford University and England 'B'), P. Bell (Blackheath and England), K. Bushell (Harlequins and England 'B'), P. Curtis (Rosslyn Park and England U23), J. Fraser (London Scottish), J. Gadd (Glocester and England 'B'), S. Halliday (Bath and England 'B'), P. Keith-Roach (Rosslyn Park and England trialist), N. Martin (Bedford and England), W. McMaster (Ballymena and Ireland), J. Page (Northampton and England), N. Preston (Richmond and England), M. Rose (Coventry and England), P. Stringfield (Rosslyn Park), A. Swift (Swansea and England), R. Wilkinson (Bedford), P. D. Wyatt (Bath and England).

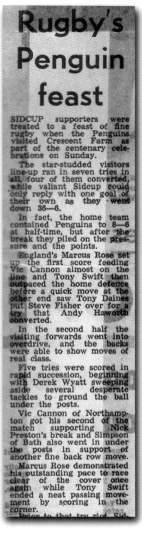

Rugby's Penguin feast

SIDCUP supporters were treated to a feast of fine rugby when the Penguins visited Crescent Farm as part of the centenary celebrations on Sunday.

The star-studded visitors line-up ran in seven tries in all, four of them converted, while valiant Sidcup could only reply with one goal of their own as they went down 36—6.

In fact, the home team contained Penguins to 8—6 at half-time, but after the break they piled on the pressure and the points.

England's Marcus Rose set up the first score feeding Vic Cannon almost on the line and Tony Swift then outpaced the home defence before a quick move at the other end saw Tony Daines put Steve Fisher over for a try that Andy Haworth converted.

In the second half the visiting forwards went into overdrive, and the backs were able to show moves of real class.

Five tries were scored in rapid succession, beginning with Derek Wyatt sweeping aside several desperate tackles to ground the ball under the posts.

Vic Cannon of Northampton got his second of the match supporting Nick Preston's break and Simpson of Bath also went in under the posts in support of another fine back row move.

Marcus Rose demonstrated his outstanding pace to race clear of the cover once again while Tony Swift ended a neat passing movement by scoring in the corner.

Sidcup match report from the Kentish Times of 24th March, 1983.

'So it was an irony when Bobbie became President of the Penguins following Auchinleck. because he and the Auk, our first President, had met this one time - during the the Nowegian Expedition.'

After the war Sir Robert returned to LNER and after nationalisation of the railways he became divisional manager of the London Midland Region in 1959, and Chairman and General Manager of the region from 1968 to 1971. In 1971 he also became a member of the British Railways Board and Chairman of BR Hovercraft Ltd., British Rail Engineering and BR Metro Ltd. But perhaps his most important appointment was that in 1972 to the Chairmanship of the British Rail Property Board which administers all of British Rail's massive holdings in land and property. Here he was in charge of a large programme of property development and investment, embarking on many schemes in conjunction with private developers.

Despite these commitments he always retained a great love for his old school, Dulwich College. He became a College Governor in 1970 and Chairman of the Finance and General Purposes Committee in 1982. Another of his great loves was rugby football, and rarely did he miss a 1st XV home match - and often he was present at away matches as well. He was also the Founder of Wembley RFC and President of the 'Bloody Men', the well-known rugby-watching Club.

I-DIRN

BOEING 727-200

In 1983 the Penguins made their first tour of Kenya. Penguins' Committee Member Peter Yarranton made the initial introductions between the Club and the Kenya Rugby Union. The Kenya RU were 'anxious to have a side over that would promote the game'.

Rugby had been played in Kenya since 1909, and East Africa had always been an esteemed calling post for touring sides. In the past the Union had hosted the British Lions in 1955 and 1962, the Springboks in 1961 and Wales in 1964.

The tour took place between 14th and 31st July, and the cost to each player and supporter was £355 per person. For the majority of the tour the party was, as usual, hosted in private homes.

Tony Mason wrote a full report on the tour which appeared in the October 1983 edition of *Rugby World* magazine. What follows are extracts from Tony's article, married with some personal notes which he made later:

The Penguins made their fourth visit to Africa recently, touring Kenya for the first time as guests of the Kenya Rugby Football Union. The party comprised eleven Englishmen, seven Irishmen, five Scots and two Welshmen. The Penguins were managed by Tony Mason.

The first match, played the day after arrival in Nairobi, was against the Kenya Rugby Football Union Chairman's Select XV. The match was played in fine weather and resulted in a win for the visitors by 28 points to 15.

The second match was against Kenya's champion Club, Mwamba, and was won by the Penguins 49 - 4. This turned out to be a superb game of rugby. The Kenya Times commented: '...the visitors played quite the best rugby seen in Kenya for years. The final score was hard on local pride but none could deny the superb quality of Penguin rugby yesterday.'

Mwamba RFC were the first Club we have played which was totally made up of black players. After the game they put on a show of Kenya tribal dancing in the Mwamba clubhouse. During a lull in proceedings a burly, nearly naked white figure, resplendent in a grass skirt and headress and carrying a war drum, took to the stage and proceeded to bring the house down with his own 'tribal dance'. Under the disguise was the 6'2", 16-stone frame of Wasps' prop, Martin Brooks. The locals thought this exhibition was terrific and were falling about laughing.

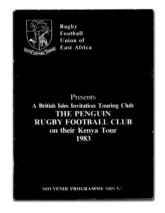

Rugby Football Union of East Africa

Presents
A British Isles Invitation Touring Club
THE PENGUIN
RUGBY FOOTBALL CLUB
on their Kenya Tour
1983

SOUVENIR PROGRAMME SHS 5/-

Top: The Penguins tour party line up in front of their transport to Kenya.
Above: The official East African RFU Souvenir Tour Programme.
Below: The full tour itinerary.

PROPOSED ITINERARY FOR THE 'PENGUINS' RFC
TOUR TO KENYA 1983

Weds 13th July 1983	Arrive JKA,time to be confirmed.Hosts to pick-up. Training session at RFUEA Ground 4.30p.m.,shower and change for 'Sundowner'at RFUEA at 6.30p.m
Thurs 14th July	Match versus Kenya Cup Winners 1983(or in event title tied,Nairobi Clubs XV) at RFUEA,kick-off 5.00p.m
Fri 15th July	Training session at RFUEA in the morning,training and coaching sessions at schools in the afternoon.
Sat 16th July	Match versus Kenya Chairman's XV at RFUEA,kick-off 4.30p.m . Dinner at the 'Carnivore' followed by Disco,approx 8.30p.m
Sun 17th July	Curry lunch at Nichol's Club,Nahawa,relax and enjoy facilities throughout the afternoon.
Mon 18th July	Meet at RFUEA at 08.00a.m for departure to Nara, Cottars Camp.
Tues 19th July	Cottars Camp game viewing etc.
Weds 20th July	Return to Naivasha for match versus Scorpions RFC, Naivasha Sports Club,kick-off 5.00p.m. Overnight stay in Naivasha,to be hosted by Oribis RFC
Thurs 21st July	Meet at Naivasha SC at 10.00a.m to return to Nairobi. Hosts to collect from RFUEA at approx 12.30p.m
Fri 22nd July	Training at RFUEA 10.00a.m.Coaching and training sessions for schools in the afternoon at approx 4.30p.m
Sat 23rd July	Match versus 'East African Select XV ('Tuskers') at RFUEA Ground,kick-off 4.30p.m Maharanjah Restaurant,Muinde Mbingu Street for curry and p/u followed by disco at Tanunga
Sun 24th July	Free day
Mon 25th July	Depart for Mombasa time to be confirmed Arrive Mombasa and transported to Nomads Camp,Diani Beach.
Tues 26th July	Free day
Weds 27th July	Match versus Scorpions RFC at Mombasa SC,kick-off 5.00p.m.
Thurs 28th July	Free day
Fri 29th July	Return to Nairobi,morning flight suggested to allow for training session at RFUEA in the afternoon.
Sat 30th July	Match versus Kenya XV at RFUEA,kick-off 4.30p.m
Sun 31st July	Bar-b-que lunch at the home of Mr.Norman Jarman, Riverside Drive,Kilaleshwa,12.30p.m until.........
Mon 1st August	Depart at some ungodly hour,hosts to ensure that their guests reach JKA at least one hour and a half before departure time(approx 1100p.m meeting at JKA)

Wasps FC's prop Martin Brookes brought down the house in Mwamba.

Tony and Doris Mason on tour in Kenya.

The party travelled to Nakuru for their next match, seeing much of the country on the way, including breathtaking views of the Rift Valley. We all purchased sheepskin hats for £1 each - which became the headgear of choice for the tour. On arrival in Nakuru we did a sharp training session. No sooner had we finished than the heavens opened and there were floods everywhere. It was just as well this happened as it delayed two players being taken to their host's farm. Whilst they were away the farm was raided by armed bandits and the houseboy and farmhouse were set on fire and severely burned.

The next day, after early rain, the match against the Scorpions was played in fine weather, and resulted in another good win for the Penguins 36 - 10.

On returning to Nairobi for their match against the East Africa XV, the Penguins put on another fine exhibition of power and running rugby to come out the winners by 41 points to 3.

The fifth game was played in the principal seaside resort of Mombasa and resulted in a win for the Penguins by 39 to 3 against the Scorpions.

The final match was played in Nairobi against the Kenya National XV. This was a very hard, very vigorous game, with the Penguins eventually running out the winners 19 - 7.

All of the home teams had a strong inclination to run their good ball and the games were played in a good spirit, with those in Nairobi attracting large crowds. The four matches played there were also broadcast.

The Penguins scored a total of 212 points with 42 against. Among the principal scorers were Arthur Emyr, who scored nine tries and a total of 42 points; Stuart Barnes, two tries and a total of 38 points; Mark Jermyn, five tries and 28 points; John Horton, four tries and 22 points, and Diamuid Leonard, Alan Armstrong and Dougie Dye all scoring three tries apiece.

The Penguins were received with great kindness and friendliness at all venues and at all times, and the players have voted it one of the happiest tours in the Club's history.

The *Kenya Weekly Review* wrote after the tour ended: *The Penguins lived up to their motto: 'They run with the ball in hand' by doing so at every opportunity - sometimes from seemingly impossible situations. The Kenyan sporting crowds unquestionably got their money's worth.*

Tony Mason said later of their hosts: 'The hospitality was superb and extremely generous. They consider their hospitality to be their 16th man - and they are right. We were greeted with friendliness and kindliness wherever we went.'

Top: Tony Mason at Nairobi Airport.
Above: The players and the alikadoos had plenty of free time in Mombasa to enjoy themselves.

Oketch to lead Kenya against Penguins

By ZACK OLUOCH

TOM Oketch, captain of the national Rugby club champions — Mwamba R.F.C. — has been selected to skipper the no-surprise national team which plays the visiting Penguins R.F.C. on Saturday at Ngong Road.

Oketch who has captained the national squad for the last three years, will play at his regular No. 8 position, according to the list of players released yesterday by Bill Okwiry, chairman of the Kenya Rugby Football Union selectors' sub-committee.

Dave Madara, the diminutive fly-half from Impala whose game has been getting better and better this season is the only new cap on the side, which will also have six reserves.

The squad has eight Mwamba, six Kenya Harlequin, five Impala and two Nondies players.

The starting line-up will be: Eric Ayodo, Danny

PENGUINS are said to favour the colder climes, but at Kenya's famous Salt Lick Lodge on Monday morning, following a game-viewing drive in which they encountered large herds of elephant and buffalo in the Hilton-owned game sanctuary adjoining the giant Tsavo West National Park, they were wallowing in the African sun and donned shirts only for the group picture taken by John de Villiers, Nairobi-bound following a short coast safari.

Kimoro (Impala), Jackson Omaido (Quins), Ben Mukuria, Pritt Nyandatt (Mwamba), Dave Madara, Nesbitt Wesonga (Impala), Tom Oketch (captain, Mwamba), Andrew Mwenesi (Impala), Max Muniafu (Mwamba), Dave Awimbo (Mwamba), Arthur Kibisu, Chris Onsotti (Quins), Evans Vitisia and John Gichinga (Mwamba).

Reserves are: Sam Ndegwa (Quins), Buba Muimi (Mwamba), Mike Evans, Chris Everad (Nondies), Cliff Mukulu and Paul Ngoga (Quins).

Meanwhile, Rugby focus turns on Mombasa this afternoon when Penguins R.F.C. take on Scorpions Invitation XV at the Mombasa Sports Club from 4.30 p.m.

This will be Penguins' fifth tour match and their second against Scorpions, whom they beat 36-10 last Wednesday in Nakuru. They are favoured to repeat the performance.

Penguins, who last Saturday underlined their superiority over

RUGBY

local sides by whipping a makeshift East Africa Select 41-3, seem destined to win all their six tour matches including the one against the national team on Saturday.

Scorpions, whose game against the visitors was described as very entertaining, have an advantage over the other teams in that they have been given two matches. And having been involved in one of those teams, they could well patch up all the loopholes that made them lose in Nakuru.

They have a formidable defence in Andy Price, whose game last Saturday showed some flaws, but is expected to be in top form for today's game, as will skipper Ian Wood.

If Dave Evans, whose kicking made all the difference in the Chairman's XV match recovers from the leg injury he suffered about ten days ago, then the visitors need to avoid making silly mistakes which would result in penalties.

To date, the visitors have a record of playing an open game, the sort that is common to Kenya. Kenyans have tried to play the same style, only that they have come out second best to Penguins.

Press report of the Penguins v Kenya match in Nairobi.

Above: Two squad photographs taken at the Salt Lick Lodge in Nairobi.

Penguins squad:

Tony Mason (Tour Manager), Geoff Cornford (Assistant Tour Manager), Peter Bell (Coach), David Chapman (Physiotherapist), John Morgan (Hon. Treasurer), Doris Mason (Nurse!).

Vince Cannon (Northampton and England Reserve, Captain), Paul Ackford (Rosslyn Park and England Trialist), Alan Armstrong (Jordanhill and Scotland 'B'), Stuart Barnes (Oxford University), Martin Brooks (Wasps and England U23), Matt D'Arcy (Terenure and Leinster), Dougie Dye (Boroughmuir, Heriot's FP, Dunfirmline, Scottish Schools and Zambia), Arthur Emyr (Swansea and Welsh Squad), Nigel Gaymond (Bath, Somerset and British Universities), John Hall (Bath and England U23), Simon Henderson (Rosslyn Park and England U23), John Horton (Bath and England), Mark Jermyn (Rosslyn Park and England Colts), Ian Kirk (London Scottish and Anglo-Scots), Alan Lawson (Heriot's FP, Barbarians and Scotland), Diarmuid Leonard (Lansdowne and Munster), Gerry Macklin (Cambridge University, England U23 and England Squad), Rory Maroney (Lansdowne and Munster), Roy Palmer (Collegians, Ulster and Ireland 'B'), David Pickering (Llanelli and Wales), Steve Smith (Ballymena and Ulster), Steve Snoddy (Bangor and Ulster President's XV), Rickie Stewart (Collegians, Ulster and Ireland 'B'), Steve Townsend (Wakefield, Yorkshire and England U23), Peter Whitelaw (Heriot's FP and Edinburgh District).

Penguin logo signed by the entire 1983 Penguin RFC touring party.

*Tony Neary pictured in 2009.
Tony played for Broughton Park,
Northern Division, England and the
British and Irish Lions.
He served on the Penguins' Committee
for 14 years between 1983 and 1997
and is still a Penguin International RFC
Vice-President.
He played for the Penguins
in the Golden Anniversary Match at
Twickenham in 2009.*

Tony Neary

Tony Neary was born on 25th November, 1948.

He attended De La Salle College in Salford and Liverpool University before qualifying as a solicitor.

He represented England at U18 Basketball as well as at Rugby Union Football.

An open-side wing-forward, he played his club rugby for Broughton Park RFC.

His international career began in 1971 and his 43 appearances for the England team was a record at the time

of his retirement. He Captained England in seven international matches between March, 1975,

and March, 1976. He finished on a high note in 1980, beating Scotland to help Bill Beaumont's

team win the Grand Slam for the first time since 1957.

Nigel Botherway of the *Guardian* newspaper once said of him: 'He set the template for future England No 7s.'

The wonderful website www.*sporting-heroes.net* has subsequently written of Tony Neary's England career:

In many ways Neary was a player ahead of his time; a merciless, supremely technical flank forward

with the ball handling skills of a back. Indeed, at a time when England tries were something of a rarity,

"Nearo" frequently augmented his faultless defensive work by chipping in with crucial scores.

The most notable of these was in England's logic-defying 16 - 10 away win over New Zealand in 1973.

Later that year the man from Salford was at it again with another against Australia at Twickenham,

a win that cemented a hat-trick of victories over the three southern hemisphere giants.

This often overlooked achievement was all the more remarkable given England's dire record in the Five Nations,

and one that even the great Welsh sides of the 1970s were unable to emulate.

Tony Neary also went on two tours with the British and Irish Lions - to South Africa in 1974 and to

New Zealand in 1977. He was also a member of the legendary North team which beat the New Zealand All Blacks

at Otley in 1979.

Tony joined the Penguin RFC Committee in early 1983 and served for over 14 years before retiring in 1997.

Both Tony and his two sons are Vice-Presidents of the Penguin International RFC.

The Dorchester in Park Lane, London.
It has become the venue of choice
for Penguin Grand Reunion Dinners
ever since this first one in 1984.

A letter to Tony Mason from the
Penguins' new President, Sir Robert
Lawrence. 'Bobbie', although unwell,
attended the Silver Anniversary Dinner
and gave a fine speech. Tragically he
passed away only a few months later.

1984

1984 marked the Penguin Rugby Football Club's Silver Anniversary season. Reaching this milestone was celebrated by holding a very special 25th Anniversary Dinner on the evening of 4th May at the Dorchester Hotel in Park Lane, London. The Silver Anniversary Dinner was attended by approximately 550 people.

Among the many distinguished guests were the Right Honourable Edward Heath, MBE, former Prime Minister; Dickie Jeeps, President of The Sports Council and past President of the Rugby Union (1976 - 77); G. F. Reidy, President of the Irish Rugby Union; A. Grimsdell, Honorary Treasurer of the Rugby Union and Air Commodore R.H.G. Weighill CBE, DFC, Secretary of the Rugby Union (who would, himself, later become President of the Penguin RFC).

It was in his speech at this dinner that Ted Heath MP (former leader of the Conservative Party and Prime Minister between 1970 - 74) and a 'Man of Kent' himself, made a good joke at Tony and Alan's expense. He said: 'I've supported Tony and Alan all these years because they were in my constituency in Kent, and I've always liked rugby. And what do they do? Bugger off and live in Sussex!'

As the Club had virtually no funds at this time, Tony had been concerned about the cost of this dinner before the event. Alan confirmed there and then that he would personally underwrite any loss incurred and would ensure that any surplus would be donated to club funds. The evening proved to be a great success, however, and these Special Penguin Anniversary and Grand Reunion Dinners have been held at five-yearly intervals ever since. Alan's undertaking remained for the next 25 years and happily always resulted in a substantial donation being paid into club funds.

The Club's
Silver Anniversary
fixture card,
1983 - 1984.

Three Knights on a very special night!
Left to right: Sir Edward Heath, Sir Robert Lawrence and Sir Peter Yarranton.

This page: The Penguin RFC Silver Anniversary Dinner at The Dorchester Hotel on 4th May, 1984.
Above: A personal note from Tony Mason to Alan Wright celebrating the Club's Anniversary.
Left: Tony Mason and Alan Wright.
Below, left: Three Old Askeans - John Morgan (Penguin RFC and Kent Rugby Union Treasurer), Sid Green (scriptwriter for Anthony Newley, Frankie Howerd and Morecambe and Wise) and Wilf Hawkins (President of the Askeans RFC).
Below, right: Sir Peter Yarranton makes his speech.
Bottom, left: Sir Robert Lawrence addresses the room.
Bottom, right: Alan Wright and Ted Heath.

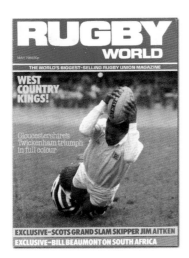

On the touring front, Tony Mason had been trying to mark the occasion of the Club's Silver Anniversary with a special tour. Initially he had hoped to take the Penguins to New Zealand for the last two weeks in June and the first week in July - but the high costs involved in taking thirty or so people half-way around the world meant that the trip had to be, very reluctantly, postponed.

Instead, Penguins gladly accepted an invitation from the Associacao Brasileira de Rugby to tour Brazil, and became the first-ever British rugby club to tour the country (although in 1936 a British team had played a Brazilian Select XV - and the touring side included Prince Alexander Obolenski, the scorer of perhaps the most famous try ever scored by an Englishman). It is also interesting to note that Brian Keen (who toured with the Penguins to California in 1970) won four caps for England in 1968 and four caps for Brazil in 1971.

Founder members Tony Mason (left) and Alan Wright, the driving force behind Penguin RFC.

The Boys from Tblisi . . . Penguins behind the iron curtain for a tournament in 1977. See caption below.

PENGUINS AT 25—STILL PUTTING ON THE STYLE!

SELECTION committees come and go. Continuity is frequently difficult to maintain and the new incumbents often wants either to redress the balance, as Derek Morgan did over Mike Slemen, or sweep clean like the Welsh selectors did in 1982.

Ponder then the overwhelming success of the Penguin RFC who since their foundation 25 years ago has maintained the basis of its two man committee of Tony Mason and Alan Wright only expanding it recently to include John Morgan, Peter Yarranton, Tony Neary and Nick Martin. Ponder too the fact that they have had the foresight to select thirty players before they were capped, including Maurice Colclough, Andy Ripley, Mike Gibson, Iain Paxton and Derek Quinnell.

The Penguins celebrate their Silver Anniversary with a first ever dinner at The Dorchester on 4 May. Nearly 600 players and guests will be in attendance to hear the likes of the Rt. Hon. Edward Heath MBE, MP., Peter Yarranton, Ian Robertson and Sid Green (the script writer to Morecombe and Wise). But, the assembled will also be paying tribute to Messrs Wright and Mason

The Penguins, English rugby's foremost touring side, celebrate their silver anniversary in May with a gala dinner at the Dorchester Hotel in London. DEREK WYATT, himself a vice president and playing member of the club, traces their history.

who have done more to spread the gospel throughout the world than anyone else.

Since 1959 when they began their escapades abroad they have averaged 6700 miles per tour. But their early matches were always in Europe and after the Penguins went inter-continental in 1968, their mileage has increased to 9250 miles a tour.

In the heady days in 1959 when the club accepted an invitation to visit Denmark, Sweden and Holland, the cost to the players was £15 a head. Last year's sojourn to Kenya troubled the players to the tune of £350 and this year's ambitious tour to Brazil will

probably be in the region of £450. Yet, as usual, players will be waiting for the invitations to drop on their mat. I asked Tony Mason who has seen every Penguin game and managed every tour abroad if he could explain the secret of the Penguins success:

"I have always believed it to be a players game. I try and select players who play an open, expansive game, after all our motto is 'On Court Le Ballon a la Main.' (They run with the ball in their hands). I watch many games and I have established a network of friends in Ireland, Wales and Scotland who let me know very quickly if there is a promising player on the horizon. Nothing excites me more than seeing fresh talent. I also look carefully at those players who have only been capped once or twice because they often have been a shade unlucky and I have been amazed at their ability which sadly was never given a chance to blossom. In turn these players who have missed out on a Lions or international tour have responded with dedication and enthusiasm such that I am pleased to note that we haven't lost abroad since 1975 though Bermuda earned a creditable draw in

RUGBY WORLD (May, 1984)—37

1982."

The Penguins mix their tours: it is not always Bermuda (!) although they are welcomed visitors there which is probably the most sought after destination for rugby in the world. They have toured USA 1970, Zambia twice (1968 & 1972) Rhodesia and South Africa (1973), Sri Lanka (1979), Argentina (1980) and most ambitious of all, Tbilisi, Georgia (1977) to play in the Eastern European Cup which included Poland, Czechoslovakia, Rumania and the USSR 'A' and 'B' XVs and which they won handsomely. Brazil beckons and South Korea and Taiwan could be on the itinerary for 1985 returning again to Bermuda in 1986.

The lack of publicity that the Penguins have received is simply because they rarely play at home. However, when they do, it is inevitably for a charity like Cancer Relief for whom they have raised over £1000 in the past few years. Typically, on 7th October, they will be taking an International XV to play Chipstead RFC to celebrate the centenary of the National Society for the Prevention of Cruelty to Children (NSPCC). They have graced Twickenham. In 1967 they helped Twickenham RFC celebrate its centenary; a match noted not just for the presence of Ron Jacobs, Mike Davies and Andy Hancock but for the unique fact that a father and a son played in the same team — namely Tony and Mike Mason.

Alan Wright the quiet administrator behind the scenes considers that the Penguins have made so many friends world-wide because "We haven't lost the fun element in rugby. To be sure we have had some narrow escapes on the field but the players have welcomed the responsibility to play the game their way. On tour they run the show and on

selection the manager and coach have always been in a minority."

The current president of the club is Sir Robert Lawrence, a notable Old Alleynian who has founded two rugby clubs — namely Wembley RFC and the Bloody Men RFC. The latter has achieved a notable reputation as the most famous spectators' club to follow England during the 5 Nations Championship.

As to the origin of the name Penguin, Tony Mason observed that it seemed rather obvious once they knew their were destined for Sweden. Ornithologists will delight in the fact that these birds have migrated so far northwards.

Enough then of the past quarter century, clubs must continue to develop and expand and already on the Penguins' agenda is a coaching and referee unit to go in advance of, or with,. or which would stay behind after, a tour.

As to the real reason for the Penguins success, apart from the passion Mason and Wright have for the game and for a life long friendship they have shared (yet they are chalk and cheese), it must be because the club was born out of the bowels of a junior rugby club, Sidcup, with no pretensions. Nor has it lost this infectious spirit which thankfully still resides in this marvellous game of ours below the International level. ■

Author Derek Wyatt in action for Oxford University in 1982.

M. Keyworth (Swansea and England), B. F. Ninnes (Coventry and England), D. M. Wyatt (Bedford and England), G. Williams (Bridgend and Wales), V. Jenkins (Bridgend and Wales), M. J. Colclough (Angouleme and England), M. P. Fitzpatrick (Lansdowne and Ireland), P. Keith-Roach (Rosslyn Park and England Reserve).

Front Row L to R:

J. J. Page (Northampton and England) — Man of the Tournament, M. A. M. Quinn (Lansdowne and Ireland), R. Finn (UCD and Ireland), M. Davies (Neath and Welsh Trial), N. French (Wasps and England Trial), D. A. Macdonald (Oxford University and South Africa), G. Rees (Aberavon and British Universities), S. E. F. Blake-Knox (Bangor and Ireland), M. Howells (Aberavon and Welsh Trial), S. O. Campbell (Old Belvedere and Ireland).

Back Row L to R:

R. Quittenton — referee, G. W. Evans (Coventry, England and British Lions), R. Greaves (Moseley and England Trial), N. O. Martin (Harlequins and England), A. R. Mason — Manager, R. M. Wilkinson — Captain (Bedford and England), P. J. Agnew (C.I.Y.M.S.),

38— RUGBY WORLD (May, 1984)

Top and above: This article about the Penguins' Silver Anniversary featured in the May, 1984 edition of Rugby World Magazine. The piece was written by Tony and Alan's very close friend, Penguin Committee Member Derek Wyatt.

The Club selected a very strong squad for the tour, ably Captained by Nick Martin of Bedford and England. Every member of the Penguins team had won international or district honours - the party included seven capped players, seven international 'B' team representatives and five players who had only recently represented England at U23 and Scotland at U21 levels.

Tony Mason's Associacao Brasileira de Rugby enamel badge.

Tony Mason said of the tour at the time: 'This is a very special tour to celebrate the Club's Silver Jubilee and also because the Brazilian Rugby Union have asked for help from the International Rugby Board. We are giving that help.

'We have offered to coach in their schools and their clubs and the offer has been gladly accepted. It is a soccer-mad country and to help them promote the game of rugby we must behave ourselves on and off the field and be good ambassadors at all times. They are looking for guidance and we hope to give them this by playing good, running and attractive rugby and showing them that the game can be enjoyed.'

The first eight days of the tour were spent in Rio de Janeiro where the Club played two games. The final twelve days were spent in São Paulo where seven more matches took place, including those against the Brazilian Club side SPAC (the São Paulo Athletic Club) plus the big 'Test Match' game against the Brazilian National XV, and the special match against fellow-tourists CURDA (Club Universitario de Asunción), who were probably the strongest Paraguayan Club side at that time.

Whilst in Rio de Janeiro the Penguins stayed at a hotel paid for by the Associacao Brasileira de Rugby. In São Paulo the whole party were hosted in private homes in time-honoured Penguin style.

C.U.R.D.A.

All of the matches on the tour were won comfortably. It is interesting to note that this was the first time in three years that a Brazil national XV had been assembled by the Associacao Brasileira de Rugby to play an international match.

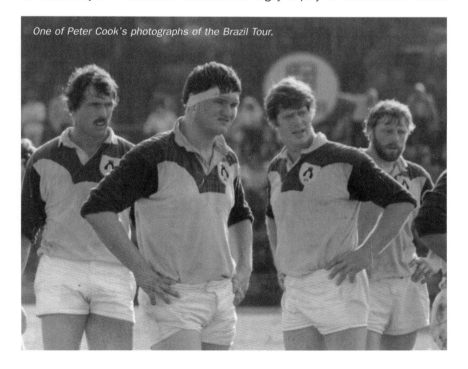

One of Peter Cook's photographs of the Brazil Tour.

The occasion of the 1984 Penguin RFC Tour marked the first time that a Brazilian national XV had been assembled to play against international opposition for over three years. Each Penguin player and official paid £450 (excluding insurance) towards the cost of the tour. The tourists thought that the general standard of play in Brazil was quite good, and that the Brazilian players were very enthusiastic - but that they were overwhelmed by the class of the Penguins. The coaching and experience which the Club endevoured to pass on to the Brazilians was absorbed enthusiastically, the results of which began to show in the final match against Brazil, which also proved to be the hardest. The Brazilian players later told the Penguins' officials that they had learnt more playing against the Penguins than they had in six years playing against local opposition. The match on 4th August against the Paraguay champion team, CURDA, was a good game against a side well organised and trained - but once again superior skill and experience was the over-riding factor. This game did, however, lead to the opinion amongst the tourists that rugby was slightly more advanced in Paraguay than in Brazil.

Above: This charming hand-carved and painted wooden plaque was made to commemorate the match between CURDA and the Penguins that took place on 4th August, 1984 in São Paulo. The Club Universitario de Asunción (CURDA) was founded in 1970 in Asunción, Paraguay.

Above: Top to bottom:
Presentation plaque;
Official Brazil Tour Programme;
Peter Cook, Mickey Quinn
and Nick Martin relax on the beach.

Chipstead RFC v Penguins RFC
match programme.

Alan Wright recalls: 'It was a very successful three-week tour. It was very much a 'missionary tour' to help Brazilian rugby grow. They were not one of the stronger South American sides. I remember Tony telling me when he got back that CURDA, the club side from Paraguay, so wanted to play us that they made a thousand mile round trip in order to play us in São Paulo.

'I remember that one of our players, Arthur Emyr, the Welsh international, eventually married a "Miss Brazil" after first meeting her over there during the course of this tour!'

The full results of the 1984 Brazil tour were:

Penguins beat Rio de Janeiro XV 84 - 10 in Rio de Janeiro; Penguins beat Niterói RFC 84 - 9 in Rio de Janeiro; Penguins beat São Paulo Athletic Club 61 - 3 in São Paulo; Penguins beat São Paulo Universities 114 - 9 in São Paulo; Penguins beat São Paulo University Medical School 76 - 0 in São Paulo; Penguins beat São Paulo Combined XV 59 - 3 in São Paulo; Penguins beat Alphaville Tennis Club 96 - 0 in São Paulo; Penguins beat Brazil 52 - 0 in São Paulo; Penguins beat CURDA of Paraguay 82 - 9 in São Paulo.

Penguins squad:

Tony Mason (Tour Manager), Derek Wyatt (Assistant Tour Manager), John Morgan (Hon. Treasurer), Laurie Prideaux (England Panel Referee).

Nick Martin (Bedford and England, Captain), Alan Armstrong (Jordanhill and Scotland 'B'), Steve Burnhill (Roundhay and England U23), David Cockburn (Boroughmuir and Scotland 'B'), Peter Cook (Nottingham and England 'B'), Matt D'Arcy (Terenure and Leinster), Arthur Emyr (Swansea and Wales 'B'), Stuart Evans (Swansea and Wales 'B'), Ian George (Northampton, Barbarians and England Bench), Mike Gibson (Lansdowne and Ireland), Mike Hall (Boroughmuir and Scotland U21), Paul Haycock (Terenure and Ireland 'B'), Ken Hepburn (Boroughmuir and Edinburgh District), Colin Hynd (Jed-Forest and Scotland U21), Geraint John (Llanelli, Wales 'B' and Wales Squad), Brian Moore (Nottingham and England U23), Rory Moroney (Lansdowne and Ireland), John Morrison (Loughborough University and England U23), David Pickering (Llanelli and Wales), Nick Preston (Richmond and England), Mickey Quinn (Lansdowne and Ireland), Marcus Rose (Cambridge University, Rosslyn Park and England), Mark Ryan (Lansdowne and Leinster), Steve Townsend (Wakefield and England U23), Peter Whitelaw (Heriot's FP and Edinburgh District).

On 7th October the Penguins took a very strong squad down to Surrey to help Chipstead RFC celebrate their 25th Anniversary. The side was Captained by Nick Martin, and included some wonderful players - Andy Ripley, Marcus Rose, Ian George, Peter Bell and Brian Moore all made an appearance for the visitors.

In a break from the tradition of always playing in aid of Cancer Relief, all proceeds of this particular match went to Chipstead RFC's charity of choice: The National Society for the Prevention of Cruelty to Children's Centenary Development Appeal. The final score was 70 points to 6 to the Penguins.

Chipstead RFC v Penguins RFC commemorative plaque.

Penguins squad:

Tony Mason (Match Manager). Nick Martin (Harlequins and England, Captain), Peter Bell (Blackheath and England), Vince Cannon (Northampton), Peter Cook (Nottingham and England 'B'), Paul Curtis (Harlequins and England 'B'), Huw Davies (Wasps and England), Arthur Emyr (Swansea and Wales 'B'), Ian George (London Welsh and England), M. Jermyn (Rosslyn Park), H. McHardy (Harlequins), Brian Moore (Nottingham and England 'B'), J. Moreland (Rosslyn Park), Andy Ripley (Rosslyn Park, England and British Lions), Marcus Rose (Harlequins and England), P. Taylor (Rosslyn Park), M. Underwood (Northampton).

Tragically, the Penguins lost their third President in the summer of 1984 with the death of Sir Robert Lawrence after a short illness. Sir Robert was succeeded as President by Douglas Harrison, Past President of the Rugby Football Union and a close friend of Tony Mason.

Douglas Harrison.

Douglas Harrison - The fourth Penguin President

Douglas Hamilton Harrison CBE was born 10th February, 1911. Died in 1985.

Douglas was a Dorset farmer by profession.

In Rugby football: Stanley House, Scotland (Captain), Harrow, Wimborne RUFC (Chairman),

Dorset and Wiltshire RFU (Honorary Secretary 1937-64).

Represented the Dorset and Wiltshire RFU from 1949 - 1966.

Served on the RFU Executive Committee from 1961.

Assisted with Secretarial duties at Twickenham during the illness of F.D. Prentice, 1962.

Chairman of the RFU Centenary Committee from 1965.

Elected RFU President 1966-67.

First President of the RFU School Section, 1969. First President Rugby Football Schools Union, 1970.

Member of the Four Home Unions Committee and a member of the International Board.

'Douggie' Harrison made a round-the-world tour on behalf of the Rugby Football Union in 1967.

The tour included Singapore, Australia, New Zealand, Fiji, Canada and New York.

As one of the most prodigious workers for the game in the 1960s, his special achievements were

the re-organisation of the game at schoolboy level and organising the 1971 Centenary celebrations

of the Rugby Football Union.

1985 CHRONICLE

27th April - Jed-Forest Centenary Year Sevens Competition at Riverside Park, Jedburgh.
Semi-finalists, Jed-Forest Sevens
(Penguins' first sevens tournament)

4th - 6th May - Jersey Tour. Captained by David Pickering (Wales). Penguins beat Jersey in St. Helier.

Death of Douglas Harrison, Penguins' fourth President.

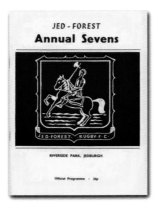

JED - FOREST
Annual Sevens

JED-FOREST RUGBY F.C.

RIVERSIDE PARK, JEDBURGH

Official Programme : 20p

Jed-Forest Sevens programme.

1985

In February the Penguins received an invitation from Jed-Forest RFC to enter a team in their Centenary Year Seven-a-Side Tournament on Saturday, 27th April. Tony Mason in particular was very keen to put out a good team in Jedburgh for this, the Penguins' first-ever foray into sevens rugby football.

The squad met up in Scotland on the Friday, played on Saturday, 27th April, and returned home on Sunday.

Alan: 'We did quite well and reached the semi-finals. I think one of the main reasons we were beaten was that Bill Gammell, the brilliant Scottish wing three-quarter, naturally turned out for his own club instead of playing for us!'

Tony Mason, in a letter to the Jed-Forest RFC Committee after the event, wrote: *...the Jed Sevens were thoroughly enjoyed by all the Penguins lads. We were most impressed by the friendliness shown to us by all the locals and we felt very much at home.*

Penguins squad:

Tony Mason (Tour Manager, Players), Alan Wright (Tour Manager, Admin). Chris Howard (Loughborough University, Captain), Alan Anderson (North Berwick), Peter Buckton (Liverpool), John Ellison (Cambridge University), Mark Howe (Bedford), Kevin Simms (Wasps and England), Simon Smith (Richmond). Reserves: Alan Armstrong (Sterling), Peter Whitelaw (Heriot's FP).

The Borders Sevens Circuit

The Borders Sevens Circuit is the name given to the Rugby Union Sevens Tournaments that are held annually in the Scottish Borders.
It is the oldest Sevens Circuit in the world with most of the competitions dating from the 19th century.
The ten most prestigious of these tournaments make up a league competition known as 'The Kings of the Sevens'. Competing teams gain points depending on how far they progress in each tournament. Winners gains ten points, runners-up seven points, semi-finalists five points and teams that are eliminated at the quarter-final stage gain three points.

The Border Sevens Circuit consists of:
April/May - Gala Sevens, Melrose Sevens, Hawick Sevens, Berwick Sevens, Peebles Sevens, Langholm Sevens, Earlston Sevens and Jed-Forest Sevens.
August - Selkirk Sevens and Kelso Sevens.

Alan Wright: 'Between 4th and 6th May, 1985, we also went to St. Helier in Jersey under the Captaincy of David Pickering, the Welsh international. It was our third time in Jersey, and this time we had been invited to take part in the celebration of the 40th anniversary of the island's liberation from German occupation in May, 1945.

'For these short visits we used to fly over, stay a night, and then come back - but we had good friendships with Jersey. It was all part of our policy in those days of accepting invitations to play clubs to open pavilions, open grounds, and play for charity.

'As you can see below, the Penguins squad was an exceptionally strong one, and included no fewer than seven internationals (Preston, Burnhill, Swift, Chilcott, Hakin, Davies and Pickering) as well as six other players who would very shortly go on to represent their countries. I think that Sole, Moore and Chilcott must have been quite a handful for the Jersey front-row!'

Penguins won the match comfortably by 70 points to 12.

Penguins squad:

Tony Mason (Tour Manager). David Pickering (Llannelli and Wales, Captain), Steve Burnhill (Loughborough), Gareth Chilcott (Bath), Peter Cook (Nottingham), Phil Davies (Llanelli), Ronnie Hakin (Bath), Simon Hodgkinson (Nottingham), Geraint John (Bridgend), Andy Martin (Cambridge University), Brian Moore (Nottingham), John Morrison (Loughborough), Mick Preston (Richmond), David Sole (Bath), Ricky Stewart (Newport), Tony Swift (Swansea).

Alan: 'I think that it was probably in this year that Tony had the nous to write to apply to the Hong Kong Rugby Union asking if Penguins could play in the Hong Kong Sevens. He got back a letter saying that they would put us on the reserve list. Of course, our chance to play didn't come up until about twelve days before the tournament took place, two years later, in 1987!'

Sadly, Penguins' President Dougie Harrison died this year, and, like Sir Douglas Bader and Sir Robert Lawrence before him, only a year after accepting the office.

Air Commodore Bob Weighill (who was, at this time, the RFU Secretary) was invited, following in the Club's military tradition, to become the fifth President of the Penguins in a letter written to him on the 5th November by Alan Wright. Bob accepted Alan's invitation, and took up his new office in February, 1986.

Above: Bob Weighill (centre) in his days as RFU Secretary.
RFU Assistant Secretary Don Rutherford is on the left and John Burgess, who was appointed England Coach in 1974, is on the right.
Below: The letter from Bob Weighill in which he accepted Tony and Alan's invitation to become the President of Penguins.
In the letter Weighill also mentions the new Penguins v Oxford University RUFC fixture - of which more in the next chapter.

1986 CHRONICLE

26th February - Penguins lost to Oxford University Past and Present 19 - 23 at Iffley Road, Oxford.

May - Tour to Bermuda. Captained by Mickey Quinn (Ireland). Penguins beat Teachers RFC 52 - 7 Penguins beat President's XV 38 - 3 Penguins beat Renegades RFC 51 - 3 Penguins beat Mariners RFC 25 - 3 Penguins beat Bermuda 44 - 7 Penguins beat Bermuda Police 45 - 9

1st October - Penguins lost to Cambridge University Past and Present 24 - 28 at Grange Road, Cambridge.

Air Commodore Bob Weighill becomes Penguins' fifth President.

The Penguins first played Oxford University Past and Present on Wednesday, 26th February, 1986. It would mark the start of a lasting friendship - not only with the OURFC Committee, but also with a man who played for the University on that day, Australian wing-forward Bill Calcraft.

1986

The Penguins played Oxford University Past and Present for the first time at 2.30 on the afternoon of Wednesday, 26th February at the University sports ground at Iffley Road, Oxford.

This prestigious fixture, which Tony and Alan had been hoping to arrange for some time, came about after Tony first discussed the possibility of an Oxford University/Penguins fixture with Dugald Macdonald during the Penguins' 1977 Tour of the USSR (Dugald was, at that time, the Captain of Oxford University RFC). Although Dugald didn't have time to set the wheels in motion at the time, Derek Wyatt, long-time Penguin Committee man and an Oxford Rugby Blue himself, did talk to Dr. Alan Taylor at St. Catherine's College about the possibility of arranging an annual Oxford University/Penguins fixture.

On 21st February, 1985, at Derek's suggestion, Tony penned a letter to Dr. Taylor to put the case for the Club. In it he wrote: *The Penguin RFC would very much like to play at Oxford University and we would envisage a Penguin side containing present internationals, past internationals, up-and-coming players and probably some youth players from the U21 or Colts teams. The side would contain players from all levels so that it would be an experience for both teams and would be a great help for young players to have the opportunity to visit Oxford.*

I am sure that if we can arrange a mutual date I visualise this fixture as a help to the University Captain in assessing his players for the following seasons Varsity match and if we are able to help in this way, we would be delighted to do so.

The OURFC Fixtures Secretary Mr. J.C.H. Anelay wrote back two weeks later, offering the Club a fixture with the University on Wednesday, 26th February, 1986 - leaving open the possibility (subsequently confirmed, of course) that it could well become an annual match.

Bill Calcraft

William Joseph Calcraft was born on 23rd May, 1959, in Sydney, Australia, and is proud to be one of four generations of Calcrafts who have attended The Scots College, the renowned Australian School in Sydney. He is currently a Managing Director of a London-based Renewable Energy Fund which invests and manages operating renewable energy assets, mostly wind farms and solar parks, all over Europe.

Bill played at flanker for The Scots College in Sydney and then at senior rugby for Sydney premiership-winning side Manly, New South Wales Waratahs, Oxford University RFC, the Barbarian Football Club and Australia. He played 21 times for Australia and made three overseas tours with the Wallabies - including the 1984 Grand Slam tour of the UK and the 1986 Bledisloe Cup winning tour of New Zealand (Captain of Oxford University, and on numerous occasions Captain of both New South Wales and Australia). For the past few years Bill has been turning out for the London Division club, Watford-based Fullerians RFC in their over 35s team. He feels well qualified for this age group and is currently preparing for next season. Bill: 'I came up to Oxford in 1986/'87. When I first came across the Penguin RFC I was playing for Oxford University Rugby Football Club, and we played a fixture against them. I knew nothing about the Penguins.

The news brought great pleasure to everyone involved with the Penguins. Tony Neary summed up the general feeling when he wrote in a letter to Alan at the time: *This is certainly a marvelous fixture to obtain and if it can be maintained on an annual basis, that would be a tremendous achievement.*

This inaugural match was a keenly contested affair. It ended in dramatic style when Welshman and Oxford Blues Captain Simon Griffin (in the face of some hearty booing!) directed the Blues fly-half Ashley Johnson to kick a last minute penalty goal to secure Oxford's one point lead and the match by 23 points to 19.

At the beginning of 1986 Alan also received a letter from Tony Mason with news on the progress of negotiations regarding another fixture which the two men were hoping to arrange. In it he wrote: *I am working on the Cambridge University game, and Mark Bailey has sent the ball rolling. I will follow up with Tony Rodgers this weekend...* (Mark Bailey is the former CURUFC, Wasps and England wing three-quarter, and Tony Rodgers was, at this time, the CURUFC Honorary Fixtures Secretary. Tony later became the Head Coach of CURUFC. Both men later became Penguins Vice-Presidents).

Alan Wright: 'So - we started playing Oxford University Past and Present in February, 1986, and Cambridge University Past and Present in October, 1986. Then, after professionalism came along, the matches were changed to the Penguins playing the University Blues.

'Originally we would turn out teams very often with six or seven current England international players. These matches used to be reported in the national press - *The Times* and the *Telegraph* in particular. But, of course, these days there are no reports of amateur matches at all in the national press - except occasionally for schools and armed forces rugby - and the Varsity Match itself.'

Ross Reynolds and Bill Calcraft on tour in New Zealand with Australia in 1986. The two men would play in the same Penguins team in the 1988 Hong Kong Sevens. Aussie scrum-half Nick Farr-Jones stands in the background.

That's when I first met Tony Mason and Alan Wright, and we had a very pleasant chat after the match. Little did I realise that within just a few months I'd be talking to them again. Tony rang me up and said "We've had an invitation to play in the Hong Kong Sevens and we'd like to invite you to come to Hong Kong with us and Captain the Penguins." Of course, I said yes. So, in 1987 I played no other role other than giving Tony my number and then coming along from Oxford - where I'd been studying away. It was Tony and Alan that put that first Hong Kong Sevens Penguin side together. I had a slight advantage over the rest of the squad in that I'd been out there at the Hong Kong Sevens the in 1986 with the Australian team. But in 1987 the Penguins' biggest advantage, of course, was an unknown teenager from Rosslyn Park called Martin Offiah! When the squad first met up we had absolutely no idea who anybody else was. On to the plane we got, and boom! - we were over there!'

Alan Wright: 'Bill Calcraft has had a very successful career as an astute banker and was an outstanding Captain (particularly at Sevens) and a first-class Sevens Squad Manager. He has been a dedicated member of the Penguins' Committee for 25 years and is now a Senior Vice-President of the Club. In recognition of his love for his alma mater, Bill has kindly presented "The Alan Wright Cup", to be played for annually by Oxford University RFC and PIRFC.'

The 1986 Penguin RFC Tourists in Bermuda. Sadly, this would be the last time that the Club would tour the island due to the imminent launch of the Golden Oldies Festival.

The Club toured Bermuda for the fourth time between 5th - 24th May, taking a powerful side which included Mick Quinn, Simon Hodgkinson, Tony Swift, Mike Hall, Mark Davies and the up-and-coming England 'B' hooker Brian Moore. Each player paid £370 towards the trip. As had become the norm, the party was hosted in private homes.

This would be the last time that the Penguins toured Bermuda. In 1988, two years after the Penguins left for home, John Kane of the Bermuda Rugby Union launched a new 'Golden Oldies' rugby festival called The Bermuda Classic - a tournament that has subsequently become one of the most successful Golden Oldies events in the worldwide rugby calendar.

The Golden Oldies started in 1988.

Alan Wright: '1986 marked our fourth and final visit to Bermuda. We had first been invited to tour the island twelve years before, and that first tour was so successful that they asked us to go back again every four years. Tony's view was still that, as they were touring with an amateur club, players liked to have some glamour - and that Bermuda provided that glamour. Wonderful hotels, sporting facilities, beaches and nice people. Remember - our customary position with regard to touring (as we were still a Club with little or no money) was that our players paid their own fares and that we were all accommodated in people's homes in the main. This provided and made us great friendships.

Above and right:
John Morgan's detailed match records. The results were:
Penguins 52 - Teachers 7
Penguins 38 - President's XV 3
Penguins 51 - Renegades 3
Penguins 25 - Mariners 3
Penguins 44 - Bermuda 7
Penguins 45 - Bermuda Police 9

'We played each of the clubs in Bermuda - they had four. The National team could put out a very good side. They had so many high-quality expatriates working there - some former Blues and men who had played first-class rugby both in England and Ireland. They were very happy tours. And this was the last one.'

Alan later wrote, in his synopsis of the tour: *The touring party returned at the end of May from their fourth tour of Bermuda where we were the guests of the Bermuda RFU. It was once again a very happy, enjoyable and successful tour, managed ably, as ever, by Tony Mason. Other members of the Committee who were present on the island included Peter Yarranton, who acted as Public Relations Officer and John Morgan, who kept very detailed records of all the matches and scores.*

The Club won all six matches played and scored 48 tries of which 27 were converted. The leading scorers were Tony Swift (30 points), Simon Hodgkinson, Gordon Forbes and Mike Hall (all scoring 24 points).

The touring party enjoyed many social engagements as guests of the individual Clubs and were formally received by His Excellency the Governor at a special reception held at Government House.

For the last match of the tour the Club invited Derek Hurdle, a member of the Teachers RFC (who first played against the Penguins for Bermuda in 1974) not only to play for the Penguins but also to Captain the side against the Bermuda Police RFC.

Penguins squad:

Tony Mason (Tour Manager), Alan Wright (Hon. Secretary/Admin), John Morgan (Hon. Treasurer) Peter Yarranton (Public Relations Officer), Ray Megson (Referee), Mike Lewis (Physiotherapist).

Mick Quinn (Lansdowne, Leinster and Ireland, Captain), Mark Davies (Swansea and Wales), Carl Dennehy (Ebbw Vale), Gordon Forbes (Watsonians), Dan Foughy (London Welsh), Doug Graham (Heriot's FP), Chris Gray (Edinburgh, Scotland), Mike Hall (Cardiff, Bridgend, Wales and British Lions), Les Hamilton (Haddington), Simon Hodgkinson (Moseley, Nottingham and England), Derek Hurdle (Teachers RFC and Bermuda), Colin Hynd (Jed-Forest), Graham Jenion (Sale), David Lines (Mariners), Collin MacDonald (Oxford University), Clive Miller (Watsonians), Brian Moore (Nottingham and England 'B'), Phil Orr (Old Wesley, Ireland and British & Irish Lions), Simon Page (London Welsh), Rickie Stewart (Newport), Tony Swift (Swansea, Bath and England), Brian Thomas (Ebbw Vale), Sandy Thomson (Kelso), John Ward (Nottingham), Colin Watkins (Ebbw Vale), Neil Weir (London Scottish), Peter Whitelaw (Heriot's FP).

RUGBY: Penguins 45, Police 9

Tourists wrap it up in style — but suffer from pitch

Report of the Bermuda Police match.

Team sheet for the match against the President's XV.

Simon Hodgkinson's post-tour letter to Tony and Doris Mason.

Brian Moore

Brian Moore (born 11th January, 1962 in Birmingham) won 64 caps as hooker for England between 1987 and 1995, and was a member of the Grand Slam winning sides of 1991, '92 and '95. He won five caps for the British & Irish Lions, and in 1991 he was voted *Rugby World Player of the Year*. He is a solicitor and a well-known Rugby TV comentator and newspaper columnist. Of the Penguins, he wrote in his autobiography: *The Penguins are widely known as the poor man's Barbarians, but for me they have been preferable because they have some of the status and the glamour of the Barbarians, but none of the bullshit. I have always held a soft spot for the Penguins.*

Passport photograph of future Harlequins and England hooker Brian Moore from the 1986 Bermuda Tour Supplement.

On Wednesday, 1st October, the Penguins played their first-ever fixture against Cambridge University Past and Present at Grange Road, Cambridge.

In a letter of thanks to Chris Taylor at Cambridge University, Tony Mason later wrote: *I thought the game was a most enjoyable one played in the right spirit by two good sides out to entertain with running rugby which was much appreciated by the players and spectators alike. I hope the University enjoyed it as much as we did, and thought it was worth the effort. The Club and the players were grateful for the privilege of playing at Cambridge on such a pleasant occasion.*

It is interesting to note that the Cambridge Past and Present team included no fewer than five internationals: Fran Clough, Kevin Simms, Steve Smith, Mark Bailey and Rob Andrew. The match itself produced a scintillating contest which culminated in each side scoring six tries. The home side prevailed 28 - 24.

Penguins squad:

Tony Mason (Match Manager).

Vince Cannon (Northampton, Captain), Andrew Harriman (Harlequins), J. Cullen (Richmond), M Gibson (London Irish and Ireland), C. Gray (Nottingham), Simon Hodgkinson (Moseley, Nottingham and England), M. Howe (Bedford), Ralph Knibbs (Bristol), R. Kurangi (NIFC and NZ Tour), Gary Pearce

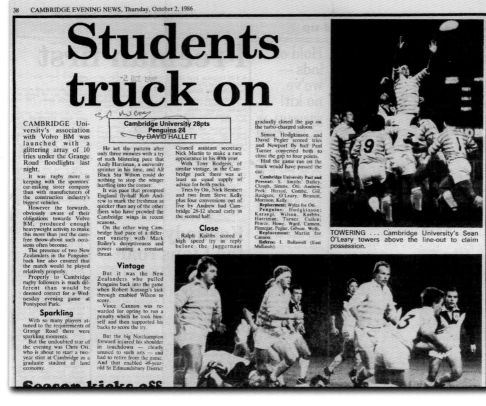

38   CAMBRIDGE EVENING NEWS, Thursday, October 2, 1986

Students truck on

Cambridge University 28pts
Penguins 24
By DAVID HALLETT

CAMBRIDGE University's association with Volvo BM was launched with a glittering array of 10 tries under the Grange Road floodlights last night.

It was rugby more in keeping with the sponsors' car-making sister company than with manufacturers of the construction industry's biggest vehicles.

However the forwards, obviously aware of their obligations towards Volvo BM, produced enough heavyweight activity to make this more than just the care-free throw-about such occasions often become.

The presence of two New Zealanders in the Penguins' back line also ensured that the match would be played relatively properly.

Properly to Cambridge rugby followers is much different than would be deemed correct for a Wednesday evening game at Pontypool Park.

Sparkling

With so many players attuned to the requirements of Grange Road there were sparkling moments.

But the undoubted star of the evening was Chris Oti, who is about to start a two-year stint at Cambridge as a graduate student of land economy.

He set the pattern after only three minutes with a try of such blistering pace that Andy Harriman, a university sprinter in his time, and All Black Stu Wilson could do nothing to stop the winger hurtling into the corner.

It was pace that prompted England fly-half Rob Andrew to mark the freshman as quicker than any of the other fliers who have prowled the Cambridge wings in recent seasons.

On the other wing Cambridge had pace of a different variety with Mark Bailey's deceptiveness and power causing a constant threat.

Vintage

But it was the New Zealanders who pulled Penguins back into the game when Robert Kurangi's kick through enabled Wilson to score.

Vince Cannon was rewarded for opting to run a penalty which he took himself and then supported his backs to score the try.

But the big Northampton forward injured his shoulder in touchdown — clearly unused to such arts — and had to retire from the game. And that enabled 40-year-old St Edmundsbury District

Council assistant secretary Nick Martin to make a rare appearance in his 40th year.

With Tony Rodgers, of similar vintage, in the Cambridge pack there was at least an equal supply of advice for both packs.

Tries by Oti, Nick Bennett and two from Steve Kelly plus four conversions out of five by Andrew had Cambridge 28-12 ahead early in the second half.

Close

Ralph Knibbs scored a high speed try in reply before the juggernaut gradually closed the gap on the turbo-charged saloon.

Simon Hodgkinson and David Pegler scored tries and Newport fly-half Paul Turner converted both to close the gap to four points.

Had the game run on the truck would have passed the car.

Cambridge University Past and Present: S. Smith; Bailey, Clough, Simms, Oti; Andrew, Peck; Herrod, Combe, Gill, Rodgers, O'Leary, Bennett, Morrison, Kelly.
Replacement: Wyles for Oti.
Penguins: Hodgkinson; Kurangi, Wilson, Knibbs, Harriman; Turner, Cullen; Pearce, Howe, Ward, Cannon, Pinnegar, Pegler, Gibson, Wells.
Replacement: Martin for Cannon.
Referee: J. Bullawell (East Midlands).

TOWERING . . . Cambridge University's Sean O'Leary towers above the line-out to claim possession.

Cambridge Evening News match report of the Cambridge University game.

(Northampton and England), D. Pegler (Wasps), Paul Turner (Newport), J. Ward (Nottingham), John Wells (Leicester), Stu Wilson (New Zealand).

Ian Bullerwell

Ian: 'My first encounter with Penguins was as a Referee who had been invited to referee Cambridge University Past and Present against the Penguins at Grange Road, Cambridge in the mid 1980s. Players of the calibre of Mark Bailey, Fran Clough, Kevin Simms and Rob Andrew were playing for Cambridge, whilst Penguins, Captained by Paul Turner, hosted many famous international players. The games were always keenly contested but a pleasure to referee.

Ian was a skilful and dedicated Selector and Manager of the Penguin teams that played Oxbridge XVs for many years.

'I retired from refereeing after the World Cup in 1991 and a year later took over as Chairman of Bedford Rugby Club. I remember receiving a call from Tony Mason one Tuesday morning asking for help. Penguins were playing the next evening against Cambridge University and were four players short. Could I help? I duly did and a long and very happy association with Penguins began. Tony invited me to assist him with the 1993 trip to Limerick for the International Sevens Tournament. The squad was Captained by Eric Peters, the Cambridge University and Scottish International, and whilst we had great fun, the team did not perform to anywhere near the level that was expected and we were eliminated in the quarter-finals. This I know was a great disappointment to Tony so Eric and I organised a whip round - and thanks to the generosity of the players involved we were able to present Tony with a lovely watch which we purchased in the Duty Free shop at the airport. For the first time in many a year he seemed lost for words, but Doris subsequently told me that he was extremely touched by the gesture and treasured the watch.

'For the past few years I have been responsible for organising teams to play Oxford and Cambridge Universities on a yearly basis, as well as accompanying teams in Singapore, Thailand, Italy and Paris. It has been great fun and has provided me with many happy memories. In my professional life as an insurance broker I have also organised the player insurance for the UK fixtures and also the international trips.

'My own rugby career started at Bedford Modern School in 1960, and on leaving school I joined the Bedford Club who at the time were running four sides. I managed to represent all four teams at one time or another, but in 1976 a back injury saw the end of my playing career. After a brief flirtation with coaching I decided that involvement on the pitch as a Referee was my preferred option - and thanks to the help and support of the East Midlands Society, combined with the encouragement of several senior Referees, I quickly climbed the ranks. In November, 1988, I achieved a personal ambition when I was appointed to England's Three Man International Panel and shortly afterwards I found myself refereeing my first major international at Cardiff Arms Park. The match between Wales and Romania was a game which will long live in my memory, not least for the fact that Romania won the game by 16 points to 9, the first time they had achieved a victory on Welsh soil. My refereeing career enabled me to travel the world and establish contacts with players and coaches which have been of benefit to me during my Penguin career.' (Ian did, in fact, referee and officiate as a touch judge for the International Referees Board on no fewer than nine occasions.)

Ian became the Penguins' first Chief Executive Officer in 2001 and gave exemplary service in this important post until 2003. He has been an outstanding Selector and Manager of Penguins teams to play Oxbridge matches and has helped to greatly advance the friendships between the Club and the Universities.

1987 CHRONICLE

5th March - *Penguins beat Oxford University Past and Present 60 - 42 at Iffley Road, Oxford.*

28th March - *Cathay Pacific/Hong Kong Bank Invitation Sevens, Hong Kong. Captained by Bill Calcraft (Australia). Penguins beat French Barbarians 22 - 0 Penguins beat Papua New Guinea 20 - 10 Penguins beat Western Samoa 20 - 4 Penguins lost to New Zealand 0 - 28 Semi-finalists, Hong Kong Sevens*

3rd May - *Cambridge Invitation Sevens Tournament Finalists*

21st October - *Penguins beat Cambridge University Past and Present 41 - 19 at Grange Road, Cambridge*

Oxford and Penguins pile up 102 points

By Victor Swain

Oxford University ... 42 pts Penguins ... 60

OXFORD UNIVERSITY and the Penguins broke all the conventions of the modern game by playing free-flowing, Barbarian-style rugby at Iffley Road yesterday with a flood of tries and amassing more than a 100 points between them.

The Penguins, nominally only an invitation touring side, have broken new ground this season by playing both Oxford and Cambridge Past and Present for the first time, their only home fixtures.

They stunned Oxford with their brilliant running and passing, opening big gaps in the defence. Almost before the students had got into the game, Martin Offiah, of Rosslyn Park, had scored a hat-trick of dazzling tries.

But to the University's credit, they recovered both their composure and determination and contributed to the freedom and gaiety of the game with a number of fine tries.

Tries galore

A calculator would have been a handy instrument to keep track of the score as the points came with a rush. Apart from Offiah's contribution, Penguins' first-half tries were scored by

Jones, Caskie, Court and Clive Rees.

The elusive John Galley, at outside-half, was at the heart of the Oxford revival, scoring two tries and kicking two penalties and four conversions.

Oxford's five other tries were added by Furnival (2), Maullin, Vessey and Chislett.

Apart from kicking eight conversions, Paul Turner crossed for one of the Penguins' second-half tries, the others being scored by Offiah, Court and Knibbs.

OXFORD UNIVERSITY—S. Vessey, A. Furnival, B. Mullin, A. Duthie, D. Woollar, J. Galley, S. Taylor, M. Rule, J. Chislett, N. Peacock, C. Crane, J. Beck, N. McBain, S. Griffin, C. MacDonald.

PENGUINS—L. Renwick (London Scottish), M. Offiah (Rosslyn Park), D. Caskie (London Scottish), R. Knibbs (Bristol), C. Rees (Reading), P. Turner, R. Stewart (Newport), M. Rennie (Rosslyn Park), A. Lynch (Redingensians), P. Essenhigh (Blackheath), V. Cannon (Northampton), D. Cronin (Bath), M. Court (Banbury), O. Jones (Neath), R. Cheval (Askeans).

Referee.—R. G. James (Leicester).

Daily Telegraph report of the 1987 Oxford v Penguins match.

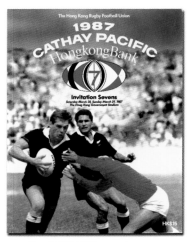

The 1987 HK7s programme.

1987

On 5th March the Penguins played the second of what would become annual matches against Oxford University Past & Present. This exciting match, in which over 100 points were scored, was won by the visitors by 60 points to 42. Tony Mason had selected a real 'flyer' from Rosslyn Park by the name of Martin Offiah. Offiah, a lightning-fast wing-threequarter who constantly threatened the Oxford defence, scored four tries. He impressed Tony so much that Tony was determined that, if he could arrange it, Martin would play for the Penguins again.

Tony summed up the match perfectly when he wrote a couple of days later: *It was a most exciting spectacle of rugby and a joy to watch.*

Penguins squad: Tony Mason (Match Manager). V. Cannon (Northampton, Captain), D. Caskie (London Scottish), R. Cheval (Old Askeans), M. Court (Banbury), D. Cronin (Bath), P. Essenhigh (Blackheath), A. Jones (Neath), R. Knibbs (Bristol), A. Lynch (Redingensians), M. Offiah (Rosslyn Park), C. Rees (London Welsh), M. Rennie (Rosslyn Park), L. Renwick (London Scottish), R. Stewart (Newport), P. Turner (Newport).

HK7 badge from Tony's collection.

Next up was a trip to the world-famous Hong Kong Sevens at the end of March. Alan explains: 'Well, 1987, when taken together with 1988, is the highlight of the decade. All the things that happened over the course of these two years brought about a huge change in the image of the Club.

'For the two years prior to this Tony had become friends with the Hong Kong Rugby Union with a view to seeking an invitation to play in the Hong Kong Sevens. At this time the national teams from Fiji, Australia, New Zealand and all over the world were taking part, but England wouldn't send a team.

'Well, we didn't know it at the time, but the Penguins had been made the number one reserve team for the 1987 tournament. And at the last minute - that is, nine or ten days before the event, and at about 4.30 in the morning - the Chairman of the Hong Kong Sevens, Brian Stevenson (who is, incidentally, still a great friend of mine and an Honorary Vice-President of the Club) came on the 'phone to Tony. Brian said: "The Malaysians have refused to play because the New Zealanders are picking some of their Caveliers who have played in South Africa. So, because of apartheid, they're out. And you're in!"

'So there we were, being given an opportunity to enter the Hong Kong Sevens tournament. But there was a drawback. There was only a short time to go before the tournament started! Tony 'phoned me at about 6am and said: "What do you think? We can play in the Hong Kong Sevens." And I said, "Well, I'd like time to reflect on it because we might make terrible 'Charlies' of ourselves!

The New Zealand Cavaliers trip to South Africa

The key event that opened the door to the Penguins' participation in the 1987 Hong Kong Sevens Tournament was the New Zealand 'Cavalier' tour of South Africa - a so-called unofficial venture that was, in fact, backed by key rugby figures in both New Zealand and South Africa.

This unusual event took place in April/May 1986, at a time when national teams were effectively banned from playing South Africa because of the Republic's apartheid policies.

All efforts to halt the tour were thwarted, and it went ahead as (secretely) planned, with South Africa winning the series 3 - 1 against what was virtually a full-strength All Black XV.

The International Rugby Football Board expressed its disapproval, but the Cavalier 'rebels' were let off very lightly, being banned for only two tests.

How the hell are we going to get a team together that can stand up to the likes of Fiji and New Zealand with so little time?" He and I had quite a long telephone conversation, in the course of which he said: "Well, look at it this way. If we don't say yes they may never ask us again!" We decided jointly to show confidence and accept.

'Tony remembered that Bill Calcraft, an Australian international number 7, had been the Captain of Oxford University Past and Present when we had played them in 1986 and had played very well against us. We asked him if he'd like to play, he agreed, and Tony made him our Captain.

'And then the great achievement in selection at this late stage was to ask Martin Offiah, who was playing for Rosslyn Park. He agreed to play. He'd had no real honours at that time except for playing for the Rosslyn Park 1st XV and the Surrey County RU. He was only 19 years old.

'With only three days to go before setting off for the tournament Tony got a 'phone call from Martin Offiah to say his mother had said he couldn't go. She said: "I don't want him larking about in Hong Kong when I'm paying for him to go to college to become a PT expert." He was our "flyer". It was a bit of a crisis. So Tony said: "What the hell shall we do?" I said (and these are my very words): "When you want to, you can charm the birds off the trees - you 'phone her and tell her you'll look after him." Anyway, Tony did 'phone her, he did charm her, and Martin did go. We also took with us on the trip two other great players who had played for us against Oxford earlier that month - Ralph Knibbs and Paul Turner.

'Off we went to Hong Kong (the tournament took place on Saturday, 27th and Sunday, 28th March). It was the first time we had played in a world-class Sevens tournament. I must add that the Hong Kong RU have given a blue-print to the world as to how to run Sevens tournaments. They run to perfection, administratively. We were very proud to play in it when we did.

Bill Calcraft at the HK7s.

Martin Offiah's autobiography,
Fast and Loose.

Martin Offiah and the Penguin RFC

Alan Wright on Martin Offiah's time with the Penguin RFC: 'Tony did Martin Offiah a big favour by

persuading his mother to let him come to Hong Kong. It changed Martin's life, really.

He has written openly about it in his autobiography. He has nice things to say about the Penguins.'

Bill Calcraft recalls: 'When we came back from the 1987 HK7s I was invited to Captain

the Barbarians on their Easter Tour. Three games in three days - Cardiff, Swansea and Penarth.

Martin Offiah had also been invited (Mickey Steele-Bodger had seen the television replays of Martin scoring his

tries for us in the HK7s). So Martin was on the wing and he scored three scorching tries against Cardiff.

I watched him carefully and he was catching the ball, running back, making tackles... I said to one of the officials,

"I tell you what, you should think about getting this young bloke signed up and involved in representative rugby."

You know, if things had stayed the same he would surely have been picked for England.

But within a week he'd gone to Rugby League.'

Alan: 'Martin became a Rugby League professional only three months later. Widnes RLFC saw his wonderful

performances for us, and for the Ba-Bas against Cardiff, and offered him £25,000 to play for them.

'So from being a young unknown wing three-quarter at Rosslyn Park in March, by May he was a fully-fledged

professional with Widnes! And he was no longer going to college - which was, of course, what his mother really wanted!'

What follows is an extract from: *Offiah - My Autobiography - Fast and Loose* by Martin Offiah,

which is reproduced curtesy of Collins Willow, an imprint of Harper Collins Publishers, London.

'One day I got a call from Tony Mason, who ran an invitation side, rather like the Barbarians, called the Penguins.

He asked me to play in a match against Oxford University, and within 15 minutes I'd scored three tries;

I collected a fourth before the final whistle. And because I'd done well for the Penguins, I was asked to go

to the Hong Kong Sevens with them, in a side that included Paul Turner, now player/coach at Bedford.

I almost missed out on the trip to Hong Kong because my mother refused to let me go - she believed that my

studies should come first and my rugby second. Tony Mason rang her and explained how important it was

for me to go, but mum still thought I'd be missing exams if I went, and only changed her mind after I'd got

permission for the trip from the principal of my college. As far as I was concerned, nothing was going to stop me:

I wasn't going to let anything put me off what I wanted to do. Ironically, I think I inherited that attitude from my

mum, because she's always been a strong-minded person. My dad is more of an intellectual: he writes for law

journals, magazines and newspapers and often sends us copies. They're always about the philosophical side of

life, whereas mum has always been more practical and down to earth.

'Anyway, I made it to Hong Kong and I loved it there. It was the first time I'd been abroad, apart from visiting my

mum and dad in Nigeria, and although I had played at the Middlesex Sevens the previous year, the Hong Kong

Sevens was the first occasion that I walked around the ground and people asked me for my autograph.

And although we were virtually unknown, we got into the semi-finals, where we played the All Blacks and

were up against players like Terry Wright, Frano Botica, Emosi Koloto, Zinzan Brooke and Mark Brooke-Cowden.'

The Penguins line up before their first match in Hong Kong.

'The first match was against the French Barbarians who had been the beaten finalists the previous year. I think we were odds-on for a hiding. But we put up a fantastic performance. Martin Offiah, our youngest player there, amazed the crowd by scoring three tries in the first half.'

Bill Calcraft takes up the story: 'We started playing, and, of course, we had this absolute star with us on the wing called Martin Offiah. Young, black, a quiet sort of guy who wasn't saying a lot. I had never heard of him. He was at Rosslyn Park and he had never been selected for anything other than Surrey County rugby. So we got out there, passed the ball to him and it was fairly evident that young Martin here was not only elusive, but rocket-fast. So as the Captain in this tournament my major tactical contribution was this: "When we secure the ball, we will shift it, efficiently, to that guy on the wing and see how he goes!"

'And Martin quickly became huge. He was just phenomenal, wasn't he? He was a huge favourite with the crowd. This is how cocky he was - he would get the ball and run and he would round people with sheer speed. But then he'd let them chase him - and then he'd slow-up so the opposing player would keep going,

Tony Mason who, according to Alan, '...pulled a wonderful side together from nowhere.'

Above: The Pre-final Ceremony.
Below: Martin Offiah wows the crowd.
All the superb HK7s photographs
in this book were taken by
Michael Schwartz, a long-standing
Vice-President of the Penguins.
At the time, Alan Wright wrote
of the pictures:
'The shots are really beautiful and
have given us very great pleasure.'

thinking he was going to catch him. And then Martin would just hit the gas again! And not only that, but he'd talk to them! He was talking to them as they were chasing him up the field! Which gave us quite a lot of confidence, really!'

Alan continues: 'Bill turned out to be a very good choice as Captain and under his direction the team became great favourites of the crowd that year.

'I think we were crowd-pleasers for five reasons:

1. The standard of our attacking play - because although we weren't a well-drilled unit and lacked practice, we excited the crowd.

2. When each of the matches were over our Captain Bill Calcraft lined our team up and he had them bow formally to the four sides of the ground - which absolutely set the crowd on fire. You see, we were virtually unknown in Hong Kong and I think it was a very modest thing to do - because we were having a lot of glory, winning our games. Yes, they loved us for that!

3. When the team walked out for the semi-final against the All Blacks they all did the 'Penguin Walk' which also went down very well!

4. Martin Offiah was the outstanding runner and crowd favourite in these Hong Kong Sevens. Indeed, we all hoped he would be voted the Player of the Tournament (in passing, it was also a great shame that he was never to win an England Cap - which, of course, was down to him later becoming a professional Rugby League player with first Widnes and then, later, with Wigan).

5. Everyone seemed to love our kit, particularly the children. It must have been the Penguins name and colours. The team were continually asked for souvenirs. If we could have opened a shop everything would have sold out in hours!'

Tony Mason and Martin Offiah.

Bill: 'We started playing some good rugby on that first day. It was very evident that we were the most successful and popular side from Europe that year by quite a way. In those days the Sevens were very much dominated by Fiji, Australia and New Zealand. Some other teams just seemed to be out for a good time (I must say that, having been to the HK7s before and since, the best thing to do is to turn up as late as possible, and keep a bit of your powder dry!).'

In the event the Club performed superbly. On day one the Club beat the French Barbarians by 22 points to nil, and Papua New Guinea by 20 points to 10, which entitled the Penguins to take their place in the quarter-finals. On day two the Penguins went on to beat Samoa by 20 points to 4, before losing 0 - 28 to the tournament favourites and eventual winners, the mighty New Zealand All Blacks, in the semi-final. The tournament attracted teams from 24 nations and a crowd of 28,000 assembled to watch the second day - a record attendance.

Bill Calcraft continues: 'There's a big ex-pat community in Hong Kong and they seemed to cotton on to us. There we were - we had this young winger who was quite sensational and we were having a bit of success. And the Penguin strip was very identifiable - and there were kids running around shouting for us! We played our role in the march-past, too, with the "Penguin Shuffle"! And we got all the way to the semi-final. Did we expect to get that far? I don't know.

PENGUINS team manager Tony Mason believes his side has always a chance in the tournament no matter what opposition they meet.

The British side made an impressive debut yesterday by qualifying for the Cup competition following wins over the French Barbarians, last year's losing finalist, and Papua New Guinea.

"Before we met the French Barbarians, we thought we had a chance. We have played very well considering that the team had little time to practise and the players only met each other for the first time on Tuesday," said Mason.

The team, a late inclusion in the tournament, is a combination of Welsh, English, Scottish and Australian players.

Martin Offiah, who played a prominent role in his team's victories, also agrees that his team has its chances despite the strength of the opposition.

"We're quietly confident about our chances," he said. A first-year sociology student, Offiah earned a standing ovation from the crowd as one of the most talented wingers seen yesterday. "I have done a bit of athletics but rugby has always been my background," said Offiah who has sprinted the 100 metres dash in just over 10 seconds.

News report after day one of the tournament.

Match action from the quarter-final against Western Samoa.

'We played the All Blacks in the last four of the tournament. And quite frankly they were clearly too good for us and we didn't really get too close to them. Those All Blacks were a wonderful group of players, and included legends of the game like Buck Shelford and Zinzan Brook. Remember - they were on their way to winning the first World Cup!

'But I have to say we did secure the first ball in that game, from a line-out, and all I wanted to see happen was a quick pass to Martin and see how he goes. Instead, we kicked the ball up the field! I couldn't believe my eyes. I thought: "What have we done?"'

Alan: 'Yes, we got into the semi-final against the All Blacks, who were a wonderful side and had been able to practise. And they beat us. With difficulty, but by a fair margin. But we left Hong Kong feeling as though we'd been winners in a way. We had taken a scratch team that had been put together a few days before the tournament. And to have got so far as to reach the semi-finals - and to play the All Blacks - we thought this was a very great honour for the Penguin Rugby Football Club.'

The History of the Hong Kong Sevens Tournament

The world's premier Rugby Sevens Tournament was born over pre-luncheon drinks at the venerable old Hong Kong Club on a misty spring day in 1975. Present were: A.D.C. 'Tokkie' Smith (Chairman of the Hong Kong Rugby Football Union), Duncan McTavish (HKFC Captain), Trevor Bedford OBE (Chaiman of several HK-based companies and a Director of HSBC) and Ian Gow (Rothmans Tobacco Company). It was Gow's idea, as Promotions Manager for his firm, to sponsor a new Rugby Tournament with top teams from throughout the world competing.

On March 28, 1976, less than a year after Tokkie Smith and Ian Gow shared a glass, clubs from Korea, Australia, New Zealand, Tonga, Japan, Sri Lanka, Malaysia and Fiji participated in the first Hong Kong Sevens Tournament.

It was an astonishing accomplishment; in less than 12 months, a team of talented, dedicated volunteers - together with the generous sponsorship of Cathay Pacific Airways - had created a sporting event that was to fire the imagination of the rugby world.

As the Tournament grew throughout the '70s and '80s in both supporter popularity and the number of participating teams (which had now progressed from club sides to representative teams) it moved from its original home in the Hong Kong Football Club to the Hong Kong Government Stadium.

By the beginning of the '90s, with demand for tickets having outstretched the capacity of the Stadium for over five years, it was time for a larger facility.

The Stadium that had been the Tournament's home for 12 years was re-built in 1994 and the 40,000-seat Hong Kong Stadium is its current venue.

Bill: 'The tournament was highly successful for us and people got behind the Penguins and we had a lot of fun. It was a great breakthrough for the Club.

'It really put the Penguins on the map, because in those years it was a stand-alone tournament - it was unique. It gave the Club a huge amount of exposure. I would add, in passing, that we played in the same heavy jerseys in which we would have played a game in the depths of winter in Oxford on a Tuesday night! But we've evolved since then. At the time the Penguins had no money!'

Alan: 'This was our first serious venture into the abbreviated game. We hadn't really played serious seven-a-side before. We were very excited about it. Well, it changed the face of the Penguin Rugby Football Club because it spread our name around the world. It was on television back home in England and it was shown live in lots of countries, so it cemented our burgeoning reputation. We became the "heroes from zero".

'So there you have it. As well as Bill Calcraft, Ralph Knibbs and Martin Offiah, the squad also included Mike Budd, Mike Kendrick, Nick O'Brien, Peter Steven and Owain Williams. And, of course, Paul Turner played at stand-off half. He was a big star in those days. Tony should be given a lot of credit for putting this side together from nowhere. They put up such a wonderful performance. He was so good at selection. As I've said before, he always said to me: "We want footballers." And he was right.

Above and below:
Semi-final action from the match
against the All Blacks.

'We were very, very popular visitors to Hong Kong, and they loved us. That's why we were invited back again next year. It was all very exciting.'

Tony Mason sent a copy of the following letter to each member of the squad after the tournament ended:

We would like to thank you for playing at such short notice for the Penguin Club in the Hong Kong Sevens. You all played extremely good Sevens Rugby and the crowd really appreciated the way you played and this was shown by the way they adopted the Club as their 'pet'. We became the personality team of the tournment and this was due to the way you played and behaved.

I know the Organisers were most grateful for our appearance in the Tournament and were even more delighted after we had beaten the French Barbarians by an excellent display of sevens technique.

There was plenty of time for a little R&R in Hong Kong! Top: Tony Mason with Penguins' photographer Michael Schwartz. Middle: Alan outside the Jumbo floating restaurant in Hong Kong harbour. Bottom: Patrick, Alan and Gregory Wright. Patrick and Gregory are both Penguin V-Ps.

I was very pleased for you that you settled so quickly into a team as it could so easily have been seven individuals trying to play.

Our thanks once more and we hope you enjoyed the trip. You looked very good on BBC TV's Rugby Special!

And in a letter to Brian Stevenson, from whom the invitation to take part in the Hong Kong Sevens originally came, Tony wrote: *It was a magnificent experience and one that I am sure will live in the minds of all who participated for the rest of their lives. I know that I myself will remember and treasure the spectacle of the march around the field on the Sunday and will never tire of relating my experience to people who will be willing to listen. The Penguin lads who took part I know will go back to their Clubs and for the rest of the season they will be 'ear bashing' their Clubmates with the thrill of the Sevens.*

Penguins squad:

Tony Mason (Tournament Manager), Alan Wright (Hon. Secretary), Michael Schwartz (Hon. Club Photographer). Bill Calcraft (Oxford University and Australia, Captain), Mike Budd (Bridgend, Cardiff, Crawshay's Welsh and Wales 'B'), Mike Kendrick (Sale, Lancashire and England U23), Ralph Knibbs (Bristol and England 'B'), Nick O'Brien (Cardiff), Martin Offiah (Rosslyn Park and Surrey County), Peter Steven (Heriot's FP and Scotland), Paul Turner (Newport and Wales 'B'), Owain Williams (Glamorgan Wanderers, Cardiff and Wales 'B').

Penguins and All Black players gather together after their semi-final.

On Sunday, 3rd May, Penguins took part in the 2nd Cambridge University Invitational Sevens at Grange Road, which featured other such successful sevens experts as the Co-optimists, Irish Wolfhounds and Crawshay's Welsh. 'Past and Present' squads from Oxford and Cambridge Universities also took part. A strong Penguins side were beaten in the final of the competition.

Penguins squad: Tony Mason (Match Manager). Vince Cannon (Northampton, Captain), Ralph Knibbs (Bristol and England 'B'), Nigel Melville (Headingley), Martin Offiah (Rosslyn Park), M. Ross (Wasps), Mickey Skinner (Harlequins), Ricky Stewart (Newport), Paul Turner (Newbridge and Wales).

The Penguins' second annual match against Cambridge University Past and Present took place under floodlights at 7.15pm on the evening of 21st October at Grange Road, Cambridge.

The Club, Captained by Vince Cannon (one of Penguins' longest-serving and most-capped players) won the match comfortably by 41 points to 19 - even though Cambridge included four England players in their back division, plus a young future Scotland international by the name of Rob Wainwright (who would go on to play for the Club in Hong Kong in 1988 and also Captain the Penguins in 1994).

This exciting, running match was sponsored by Volvo. Tony Mason later wrote to each Penguins player: *We would like to thank you all for turning out... and putting on a superb exhibition of attractive rugby. It was a joy to watch, a terrific team effort in wet conditions. I know the opposition hosts were taken by surprise by the superiority of our play, but I also know that they thoroughly enjoyed the game and appreciated our play.*

Northampton Saints lock Vince Cannon had first Captained Penguins on the 1983 Kenya Tour. Four years later he reprised the role during the Cambridge Sevens in May and in the match against Cambridge University Past and Present in October. Kettering-born Cannon was a fixture in the Saints team between 1973 and 1989, a period in which he racked up 438 appearances - easily the most for a second-row forward and the third highest in the history of the Saints.

Paul Selway-Swift

Paul had a long and distinguished career in banking, first as an international officer and finally as Deputy Chairman of HSBC Investment Bank. His successful playing years as a lock extended over a long period, first representing Allhallows School, Bath Schoolboys and the Hong Kong Bank in Beckenham - and subsequently in Asia where he played for the Hong Kong Football Club, the Hong Kong National XV in the Asian Tournaments, and against England in 1971. In England on home leave in 1969-70, he returned to Bath and played in all three sides (1st, 2nd and 3rd) in the one season. Finally, in India in 1973 he captained the famous Calcutta Football Club for two seasons.

On being appointed a Club Patron, and subsequently serving for many years as a Committee Member, Paul's enthusiasm, financial acumen and guidance have been a great help to the Club.

Paul Selway-Swift (7th from left, second row) shown on the occasion of the Hong Kong v England match which took place on 30th September, 1971. Paul is in famous company - including such great players as Peter Wheeler, Fran Cotton, Nigel Starmer-Smith, Budge Rogers and fellow-Penguin Tony Neary.

1988

THE TIMES THURSDAY MARCH 3 1988

A vintage display is one to savour

By David Hands

| Oxford Univ P and P.... | 18 |
| Penguins...................... | 26 |

Peter Robbins, the late England flanker to whose memory this fixture will be an annual tribute, would have enjoyed himself at Iffley Road yesterday, even though his old university was beaten by three goals and two tries to three goals.

It was a hard, competitive match and if Robbins would have shaken his head over some of the distribution of the backs, the play of the forwards from his old club, Moseley, and that of the New Zealander, Thompson, would have made his eyes sparkle. It was, indeed, the ball-winning capacity of the Penguins forwards which turned the scales against a student side containing 13 Blues of varying vintage.

Of the old boys, Barnes was playing his fifth game since his return after suffering a severe facial injury against Coventry last November.

It is not often that a prop forward from each side scores two tries but Ubogu did so at the start of each half, and Essenhigh matched his effort, though his second may qualify as one of the shorter runs of the season, since it came from a lineout on the Oxford line.

In stark contrast, the try which settled the match, after the Penguins had turned round leading 10-6, came from the visitors' own try-line. Hackney, the Loughborough wing who scored three times against Oxford in the Stanley's XV match in November, did well to tackle Vessey in the corner. When the

Penguins won the subsequent ruck, Buzza dummied delightfully to give Hackney just enough room to get round Polkinghorne and make 80 metres to the other end.

Ubogu, in support of Campbell, opened the scoring in a game which featured not one penalty kick at goal. But the Penguins settled, aided by Hackney's interception and crisp handling by Smith and Exeter before Essenhigh, with the hint of a dummy, opened their account. Thompson, with that drop of the shoulder characteristic of New Zealand flankers – he is from Auckland but playing with Abertillery this season – charged over to give the Penguins their interval lead.

Another interception gave Exeter his try but Oxford fought their way back into the match through Ubogu and McBain, who played a powerful game. Indeed they took a brief lead at 18-16, only for the experienced Penguins to finish in the style which their administrators clearly expect of them.

SCORERS: Oxford University: Tries: Ubogu (2), McBain. Conversions: Barnes (3). Penguins: Tries, Essenhigh (2), Thompson, Exeter, Hackney. Conversions: Howard (3).
OXFORD UNIVERSITY PAST AND PRESENT: R Egerton; A Duthie (rep: D Polkinghorne), M Brown, T O'Brien (Bedford), R Vessey (capt; S Barnes (Bath), D Kirk, V Ubogu; J Chislett, S Fergusson (rep: S Williams), S Griffin (Pontypridd), C Crane, W Campbell, A Cameron, N McBain.
PENGUINS: A Buzza (Loughborough University) (rep: R Davies, New College, Oxford); S Hackney (Loughborough University), T Exeter (Moseley), R Maclean (Gloucester), C Howard (Rugby); A Martin (Cardiff), R Stuart (Newport); G Smith (Moseley), C Barbor (Moseley), P Essenhigh (Rosslyn Park), R Thompson (Abertillery), V Cannon (Northampton, capt), L James (Glamorgan Wanderers), R Barr (Moseley), P Shillingford (Moseley).
Referee: D Leslie (Manchester).

The Times match report of the Oxford University Past and Present match which took place on Wednesday, 2nd March.

The Penguins' year began on 2nd March, when the squad travelled to Iffley Road in Oxford to play against Oxford University Past and Present in what had this winter become known as *The Peter Robbins Memorial Match*. Peter Robbins had played for Oxford University, Moseley, Coventry and England at wing-forward between the mid '50s and early '60s. He had died on 25th March, 1987, at just 54 years of age. As a special tribute to one of their finest players, Moseley RFC provided no fewer than five of the Penguins players on the day.

The match itself, against a very strong Oxford University side which included All Black Captain David Kirk and future England internationals Victor Ubogo and Stuart Barnes, was won 26 - 18. David Hands of *The Times* wrote of the match: *A vintage display is one to savour.*

Penguins squad:

Tony Mason (Match Manager). V. Cannon Northampton, Captain), C. Barbor (Moseley), R. Barr (Moseley), A. Buzza (Loughborough University), R. Davies (Oxford University), P. Essenhigh (Rosslyn Park), T. Exeter (Moseley), S. Hackney (Loughborough University), C. Howard (Rugby), L. James (Glamorgan Wanderers), A. Martin (Cardiff), R. McClean (Gloucester), P. Shillingford (Moseley), G. Smith (Moseley), R. Stewart (Newport), R. Thompson (Abertillery).

Tony Mason's Hong Kong RFU badge.

And then, less than three weeks after the Oxford University Past and Present fixture, a delighted Tony Mason and Alan Wright were packing their bags for Hong Kong again.

Alan Wright: 'Just like 1987, 1988 was one of the Club's real highlights because we were invited to return to the Hong Kong Sevens - which filled us all with great excitement.

'We again made Bill Calcraft the Captain. And we selected the most fantastic team. There were three All Blacks in our side, including David Kirk, the New Zealand Captain of the first World Cup-winning team; Craig Green, who played 39 times on the wing for New Zealand; and Wayne Smith, who subsequently went on to become an All Blacks coach. He was capped 35 times by the All Blacks and in this year was probably the most capped five-eighth to play for New Zealand.

'Wayne Smith and Craig Green had been playing in Italy and they were happy to accept an invitation on the basis that we were able to organise their return journey to New Zealand. David Kirk was at Oxford University at the time, and we had already met up with him earlier in March at Iffley Road.'

David Kirk, who had been the All Blacks' playmaker when they won the 1986 Hong Kong Sevens, relished the prospect of playing against his old team mates in the 1988 tournament. Talking a month before the Sevens began, he said: 'It will be quite an experience for me if we play the All Blacks. I have played many times for New Zealand but it will be the first time I've played against them. I've spoken to a number of the boys who are likely to play for the All Blacks and they're looking forward to it as much as me.'

Alan: 'We also selected Rob Wainwright, who had played a very fine match against us for Cambridge University the previous October, and happened to be Cambridge University's Heavyweight Boxing Champion. There is a story to be told about Rob's selection for the Hong Kong Sevens.

'What had happened was that we had originally picked the famous Scottish international back-row forward John Jeffrey for the tour. But John was in the Scotland team that beat England at Murrayfield that year - and after the post-match celebrations he had, allegedly, thrown the Calcutta Cup across Princes Street in Edinburgh after a drinking spree with England's Dean Richards.

'As a result of this I received a telex from the Secretary of the Scottish Rugby Union two days before we were due to leave for Hong Kong, saying: *John Jeffrey has been suspended and will not be allowed to play in the Hong Kong Sevens.* This was a great shame for the Penguins because we'd made a special arrangement with the Scottish Rugby Union for John to play for us. Scotland were playing in Australia a week after the Hong Kong Sevens in a Sydney Seven-a-Side rugby tournament and the SRU had given him special permission to come with us.

'Anyway. Tony and I remembered Rob Wainwright's performance against us in October and asked him if he'd like to come instead. He was 22 years old at the time.'

The letter from the Hong Kong Sevens Organising Committee inviting the Penguins to participate in the 1988 tournament.

Precious! Hong Kong Sevens tickets.

The 1988 Calcutta Cup Incident

After Scotland's 6 - 9 loss to England at Murrayfield in 1988 the Calcutta Cup was damaged by several drunken players - said to have included England number 8, Dean Richards, and Scotland flanker, John Jeffrey. They were alleged to have played football with the 110-year-old trophy along Princes Street in Edinburgh.

Jeffrey received a six-month ban from the Scottish Rugby Union, whilst Richards was given a one-match ban by the Rugby Union.

Jeffrey later said about the incident: 'I accept the suspension without complaint but I deny damaging the cup.'

He added later: 'When we took it away it wasn't damaged and when we brought it back it was.

I have to say we were responsible.'

The selection of Rob Wainwright for the 1988 HK7s

Alan Wright: 'Rob Wainwright had to be brought in at the very last minute in 1988 because John Jeffrey had been suspended by the Scottish Rugby Union as a result of his being involved in the Calcutta Cup incident with Dean Richards. Tony and I had a quick discussion and Rob's name came up. He was 22 years old at the time, playing rugby and studying at Cambridge University. We thought he'd played very well against us for the University that season. And we were flying on Wednesday! So we 'phoned Rob and put him in the team.' Rob was subsequently capped 37 times for Scotland (16 as Captain) between 1992 - 98 and once for the 1997 British Lions in South Africa. He subsequently Captained the Penguins in Sweden and Denmark in 1994.

When reflecting on John Jeffrey's late withdrawal from the squad, it is interesting to note part of a letter that Tony Mason wrote to Peter Duncan (Chairman of the Hong Kong Sevens Organising Committee) a couple of weeks before the Sevens started. It gives a wonderful insight into Tony's state of mind before the start of a big tournament. He wrote: *Only a couple of weeks to go and hopefully we will be in Hong Kong getting psyched up for the battles ahead. My worry starts now increasing as we get nearer the Monday 21st March departure date with fear and sweating everytime the phone rings over that weekend - fear that there is a cry-off. I just keep praying. The only time I go to church is that weekend!*

Photographs from the 1988 tournament. Left: The pre-final march past. Centre: Match action. The Penguins beat Papua New Guinea, Hong Kong and the French Barbarians to progress through to the semi-finals. Right: David Pickering.

Top: The 1988 HK7s Penguin RFC team. Above left: Everyone loved the Penguins - and these two supporters even dressed the part!
Above right: Autographs of the entire Penguins squad were in great demand during the course of the tournament.

This page: Action from the semi-final against the All Blacks, and the two teams pose for a photograph together after the match.

Alan: 'We also had John Bentley with us in Hong Kong, who, incidentally, has the special distinction of having played for Great Britain Rugby League and for the British Lions. So we had a heavyweight team and we really thought we might win it - although we'd had no practice. Once again we reached the semi-final, having beaten Papua New Guinea and Hong Kong on the first day and the French Barbarians the next day in the quarter-final. And then, for the second year running, who do we find that we're playing in the semi-final? The All Blacks!

'You could hear them tramping up and down inside their dressing room, chorusing out: "We ARE the All Blacks - They WERE the All Blacks - We ARE the All Blacks - They WERE the All Blacks" because, of course, we had three All Blacks in our team!'

The match against the All Blacks was a very physical affair. Rob Wainwright, who had received a knock in an earlier round, was forced to come on as substitute when David Kirk and Paul Turner both had to leave the field with leg injuries. But he played his part in a gallant performance which drew huge applause from the 28,000 capacity crowd. Despite this, the Club went down by 16 points to nil against their mighty opponents.

Alan continues: 'We failed to overcome this wonderfully gifted and well-trained All Blacks team and lost narrowly for the second year running. It felt like winning, not like being the beaten semi-finalists. To get to the semi-final of such a strong tournament, for the second year running, with a scratch team, was yet another landmark in our history. And it was the second time we'd appeared on worldwide TV playing in a big stadium - which really raised our profile once again.'

The Penguins' results were: Penguins beat Papua New Guinea 38 - 0, Penguins beat Hong Kong 14 - 0, Penguins beat French Barbarians 22 - 6. Semi-final: Penguins lost to New Zealand 0 - 16.

Penguins squad:

Tony Mason (Manager), Alan Wright (Hon. Secretary), John Morgan (Hon. Treasurer), Michael Schwartz (Hon. Photographer).

Bill Calcraft (New South Wales, Barbarians, Oxford University and Australia, Captain), John Bentley (Sale, North of England, Yorkshire and England 'B'), Craig Green (Treviso, Canterbury and New Zealand), David Kirk (South Island Universities, Otago Colts, Oxford University and New Zealand), David Pickering (Llanelli, Neath, Crawshay's Welsh, Barbarians and Wales), Ross Reynolds (Manly, New South Wales and Australia), Wayne Smith (Casali, Canterbury and New Zealand), Paul Turner (Newbridge, Crawshay's Welsh, Barbarians and Wales 'B'), Rob Wainwright (Cambridge University).

Inset, left: Penguins' Captain Bill Calcraft waves to the crowd after the match against the All Blacks.
Top: Alan and Greg Wright at the after-tournament party.
Above: After match drinks.
Below: David Kirk interview.

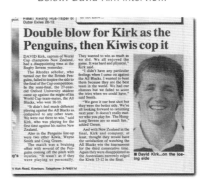

Double blow for Kirk as the Penguins, then Kiwis cop it

CURUFC VOLVO BM INVITATION SEVEN-A-SIDE TOURNAMENT

Grange Road
1 May 1988
10.00 a.m. to 5.00 p.m.

Admission by Programme only
Adults £1.00
Children and OAPs free

Penguins won the CURUFC 7s in May.

On 1st May, 1988, the Penguins won the Third Annual Cambridge University RUFC/Volvo BM Invitation Seven-a-Side Tournament which took place at Grange Road, Cambridge. Alan: 'We held the Shield until 2011, as it was never played for again (the trophy has subsequently been returned to Cambridge University). We were proud to win it when we did. We overcame our friends Crawshay's, the famous Welsh club-by-invitation side, in the final.'

Penguins overcame Captain Crawshay's VII in the final of the CURUFC Sevens.

The other sides taking part that day were The Luddites (from the north of England, who included Tony Underwood in their side), the Co-Optimists (from Scotland, including Gavin Hastings and Findlay Calder), Cambridge University (including Rupert Moon and Rob Wainwright), Oxford University (including Victor Ubogo), plus six Eastern Counties junior clubs - Cambridge, Ipswich, Norwich, Saffron Walden, Southend and Sudbury.

The results were: Pool 1: Penguins beat Saffron Walden RFC 48 - 0; Penguins beat Cambridge University Past and Present 14 - 4; Penguins beat the Co-Optimists 24 - 16. Penguins beat Crawshay's Welsh 18 - 12 in the final.

Penguins squad: Tony Mason (Match Manager). A. Woodhouse (Loughborough University, Captain), A. Buchanan-Smith (Loughborough University), A. Buzza (Loughborough University), C. Howard (Rugby), A. McDonald (Loughborough University), N. Preston (Richmond and England), C. Sheasby (Harlequins), P. Thornley (Leicester), S. Tubbs (Loughborough University).

In July long-serving Penguin player and Committee man Peter Yarranton was elected as Vice-President of the Rugby Football Union.

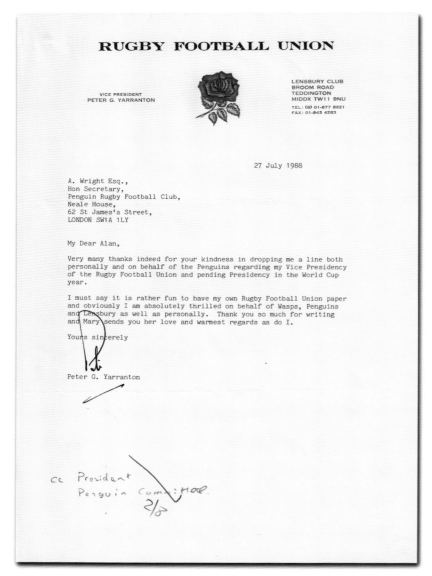

RUGBY FOOTBALL UNION

VICE PRESIDENT
PETER G. YARRANTON

LENSBURY CLUB
BROOM ROAD
TEDDINGTON
MIDDX TW11 9NU
TEL: (8) 01-977 8821
FAX: 01-943 4283

27 July 1988

A. Wright Esq.,
Hon Secretary,
Penguin Rugby Football Club,
Neale House,
62 St James's Street,
LONDON SW1A 1LY

My Dear Alan,

Very many thanks indeed for your kindness in dropping me a line both personally and on behalf of the Penguins regarding my Vice Presidency of the Rugby Football Union and pending Presidency in the World Cup year.

I must say it is rather fun to have my own Rugby Football Union paper and obviously I am absolutely thrilled on behalf of Wasps, Penguins and Lensbury as well as personally. Thank you so much for writing and Mary sends you her love and warmest regards as do I.

Yours sincerely

Peter G. Yarranton

cc President
Penguin Committee.
2/8

Left: A letter to Alan Wright from Peter Yarranton. It was written just after his appointment as Vice-President of the Rugby Union. He was to become President of the Union in 1991.

 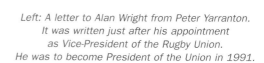

Newbridge badge from Tony's collection.

Alan Wright: 'On the 29th September 1988 we went to play Newbridge RFC as part of their Centenary year celebrations. Newbridge was the Welsh Club where Derek Morgan had played in his early days. This match unfortunately became possibly the most difficult selection problem we had ever encountered. At the very last moment we lost a large number of players in the team because of a Welsh Trial game that was arranged at very short notice.' Not surprisingly, the Penguins failed to win this match.

Penguins squad: Tony Mason (Match Manager), David Pickering (Neath and Wales, Captain), David Burnell (London Scottish and Scotland), Anthony Clement (Swansea and Wales), Damian Cronin (Bath and Scotland), Steve Hackney (Loughborough and English Students), Geraint John (Cardiff and Wales 'B'), Colin Laity (Neath and Barbarians), Audley Lumsden (Bath), John Orwin (Bedford and England), Allan Phillips (Cardiff and Wales), Charlie Richardson (London Scottish and Scotland 'B'), Ricky Stewart (London Irish and Ireland 'B'), Mike Teague (Gloucester and England), David Trick (Bath and England), Victor Ubogo (Oxford and English Students).

On the 19th October Penguins played Cambridge University Past and Present at Grange Road, Cambridge. Penguins had to make five late changes to their squad on the night, mainly due to several Clubs withdrawing players because of the new league system in England. Cambridge deservedly won this high-scoring encounter by 50 points to 25.

Penguins squad: Tony Mason (Match Manager).
C. Balding (Rugby), P. Brady (Harlequins), P. Burnell (London Scottish), A. Cruikshank (St. John's, Leatherhead and Trinity Hall), J. Hall (Haileybury School and St. John's College), P. Hopley (Wasps), C. Howard (Rugby), D. Kaye (Nottingham), A. Mitchell (London Scottish), J. Orwin (Bedford), M. Rennie (Rosslyn Park), L. Renwick (London Scottish), D. Richardson (Wasps), C. Sheasby (Harlequins), R. Stewart (London Irish), R. Taylor (Nottingham), H. Thomas (Glamorgan Wanderers).

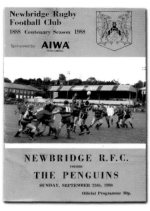

Penguins were beaten by Derek Morgan's old Club, Newbridge, in September.

Penguins also lost the annual Cambridge University game 50 - 25 in October.

Bailey leads strong charge against weakened Penguins

By Peter Bills

Cambridge P and P	50
Penguins	25

The difficulties of the Penguins in recruiting players for this kind of friendly encounter against Cambridge University Past and Present, at Grange Road last night, is inexplicably linked to the presence of league fixtures in all the clubs' programmes.

The side originally envisaged by Tony Mason, doyen of Penguins rugby, scarcely bore resemblance to the XV which took the field. Most senior clubs refuse point blank these days to release players about to be involved in league games.

Happily, Mark Bailey, in typically individualistic style, calmly drove a coach and horses through the best laid imaginations of selectors by appearing last night.

Bailey scored his side's first try after a somewhat frenetic start by scoring wide out on the left following Simms's neat side steps. Bailey's enthusiasm for the fray was apparent by his 70-yard weaving run for his team's second try and he then put in Hancock for the third. Martin converted the first.

Penguins' contribution to play, as pleasantly balmy as the night, was not inconsiderable. Twice, from severe deficits at 14-0 and 22-10, they produced scores which challenged Cambridge's ascendency.

Mitchell kicked a penalty goal either side of half-time, but could not convert an excellent try by Sheasby, who galloped away from 50 yards like a runaway race horse, his Cambridge pursuers resembling jockeys vainly attempting to arrest their errant mount.

But Penguins had their troubles containing Bailey. Early in the second half he put in Hancock for another try and then had a key role in tries by Davies and Stileman. Davies had taken the field at half-time, replacing Pembroke student, Townsend.

Kaye maintained Penguins' interest in proceedings with a crash-over try, and Mitchell added a third penalty.

Clough exposed the Penguins' tiring defence with a try under the posts as Cambridge continued to run possession from all phases. Smith also scored, from a kick ahead, Martyn converting the first.

Simms and Stileman scored late tries, Simms converting his own and Howard scored for Penguins, Mitchell converting.

SCORERS: Cambridge: Tries: Bailey (2), Hancock (2), Stileman (2), O'Leary, Davies, Clough, Smith, Simms. Conversions: Martin (2), Simms. Penguins: Tries: Sheasby, Kaye, Howard. Conversions: Mitchell (2). Penalty goals: Mitchell (3). CAMBRIDGE UNIVERSITY PAST AND PRESENT: A. Martin (Cardiff); M Bailey (Wasps), F Clough (Wasps), K Simms (Wasps), S Smith (Wasps), S Townsley (Solihull and Pembroke College; rep: H Davies, Wasps); M Hancock (Heversham GS and Hughes Hall); N Herrod (King Henry VIII; Coventry and Clare), B Gilchrist (Rosslyn Park), J Freeman (Leamington), W Stileman (Oxford Univ.), S O'Leary (Wasps), I Morrison (London Scottish), S Kelly (Wasps), N Bennett (Huntington). PENGUINS: D Richardson (Wasps); C Balding (Rugby), L Renwick (London Scottish), P Hopley (Wasps; rep: J Hall, Haileybury School and St John's College), C Howard (Rugby); A Mitchell (London Scottish), R Stewart (London Irish); P Burnell (London Scottish), R Taylor (Nottingham), M Rennie (Rosslyn Park), J Orwin (Bedford), D Kaye (Nottingham), P Brady (Harlequins; rep: A Cruickshank, St John's Leatherhead and Trinity Hall), C Sheasby (Harlequins), H Thomas (Glamorgan Wanderers). Referee: C J Harrison (East Midlands).

1989 CHRONICLE

2nd March - Penguins beat Oxford
University Past and Present 36 - 16
at Iffley Road, Oxford.

July - August - Kenya Tour.
Captained by Peter Stevens (Scotland).
Penguins beat Kenya Harlequins 54 - 3
Penguins beat Nondescripts 59 - 6
Penguins beat Chairman's XV 45 - 12
Penguins beat Scorpions 40 - 6
Penguins beat Nairobi University 61 - 10
Penguins beat
Kenya National XV 30 - 18

Dark Blues go crashing

NON-EXISTENT tackling and over generosity in the number of times they gave the ball away cost Oxford University their heaviest defeat of the season against Penguins at Iffley Road yesterday.

The visitors, largely made up of Welshmen and Scots, scored 18 points in each half as they ran in seven tries, four of which were converted. After being pedestrian for nearly an hour the Dark Blues replied with two goals and a try.

Brian Smith crossed over for Oxford's first try from a five metre scrum and he converted two touchdowns by David Cook when the Dark Blues ran the ball from tap penalties.

But they continued to give points away as

Oxford Univ 16, Penguins 36

fast as they scored them and Cook was one of the few players to emerge with credit.

Penguins fullback Andy Martin led the rout with a hat-trick of tries and four conversions and the other tries were scored by David Millard (2), Calvin Wyles and Michael Budd.

Oxford University: Cook, Kennedy (Bucknell 66 mins), Richards, Evans, Watson, Smith, Fell (Taylor 63 mins), Orr, Norwitz, Williams, Coleman, Wensley, Buckland, Reader, Egan.

Referee: Mr D. Thomas (Gloucester).

● Oxford University RFC's match at Rugby, scheduled for Saturday afternoon, has been brought forward to tomorrow night (7.15) because of the Five Nations Championship.

Penguins scored seven tries in their 36 - 16 win over Oxford University on 1st March.

1989

Penguins' first match of the year saw them run in no fewer than seven tries. David Millard scored two whilst Calvin Wyles and Michael Budd scored one each to beat Oxford University Past and Present 36 - 16 in the Peter Robbins Memorial Match at Iffley Road, Oxford. The Penguins team featured eight Welshmen, including an all-Bridgend back-row of Budd, Yardley and Williams.

Penguins squad: Tony Mason (Match Manager). Vince Cannon (Northampton, Captain), Michael Budd (Bridgend), David Butcher (London Scottish), Phil Cue (Bath), Simon Deer (Rosslyn Park), David Griffiths (Newport), Simon Henderson (Rosslyn Park), Lloyd Isaacs (Neath), Andy Martin (Bridgend), David Millard (London Scottish), Steve Powell (Neath), Owain Williams (Bridgend), Richard Wintle (Bridgend and Wales), Calvin Wyles (Rosslyn Park), Paul Yardley (Bridgend).

On Friday, 5th May, the Penguins celebrated their 30th anniversary with a Dinner and Grand Reunion at the Cafe Royal in Regent Street (The Dorchester, the Club's preferred venue, had decided to embark on a renovation programme at very short notice and had cancelled all bookings). This was the largest Dinner that the Club had ever organised, with over 750 attending. Among the many notable guests present on the night were Club President Air Commodore R.H.G. Weighill, the Right Honourable Sir Edward Heath, Mick Quinn, Chris Rea, Sir Denis Thatcher and Nigel Starmer-Smith.

Right: Letters from Captain Michael Pearey (Vice- President of the RFU), and Keith Rowlands (Secretary of the IRB). Just two of many thank-you letters the club received after the 30th Anniversary Dinner and Grand Reunion which took place at the Cafe Royal on 5th May, 1989.

Tony's Kenya Harlequins badge.

Alan Wright: 'In 1989 we went on our fifth tour of Africa, and our second time over to Kenya (the first Kenya Tour took place in 1983).'

The Penguins played all six matches of the tour in Nairobi, where the squad were accommodated in private houses by their hosts, the Kenya RFU. The party then flew on to Mombasa on 30th July where they relaxed for a few days at the Traveller's Beach Hotel, seven miles north of Mombasa. The party returned to London on 4th August.

The Penguins were Captained by Peter Steven of Heriot's FP and Scotland, and the squad included Peter Cook and John Morrison, the England 'B' forwards, as well as Troy Coker, the outstanding Oxford University and Australian flanker. The side also had twelve England and Scottish U21 and 'B' XV representatives, together with the half-back pairing of the Lansdowne Club, who were, at that time, the Irish Cupholders.

On Sunday, 16th July, in the first match of the tour, Penguins beat Kenya Harlequins (the 1988 Kenya Enterprise Cup Winners) by 54 points to 3. Two days later the Nondescripts RFC (Kenya Cup Winners of 1988) were beaten 59 - 6.

Simon Hodgkinson, at that time England's international full-back, had a fine game in the Club's third victory against the Kenyan RFU Chairman's XV. In a 45 - 12 win, Hodgkinson's tally of 21 points was made up of two tries, one penalty and five conversions. Next up, Penguins beat the Scorpions RFC (Kenya's free-running version of the Barbarians) by 40 points to 6.

Penguins, following what had become a tradition of having top-class referees on tour with them at this time, took the Scottish international referee Ray Megson along - to referee, and to give lectures to the Kenya Society of Referees.

But it so happened that he also refereed the Penguins' fifth game against Nairobi University - an eventful match about which Tony Mason later wrote: *We were very grateful that Mr. Megson was able to referee in three of our games - one of which, against Nairobi University, was a very physical encounter (they are not called 'The Mean Machine' for nothing - 'handbags at the ready!'). Nevertheless, the match was won handsomely, 61 - 10.*

The final game of the tour, against a strong Kenya National XV, was a much closer affair than the previous matches, but the Penguins still managed to prevail, the final score being 30 points to 18.

Penguins have toured Kenya twice - in 1983 and in 1989.

Tony Mason at Nairobi airport.

Jersey badges, top to bottom: Kenya Harlequins RFC, Nondescripts RFC and Scorpions RFC.

Penguins humiliate Cup holders Nondescripts 59-6

By Manoah Esipisu

THE visiting United Kingdom rugby side, Penguins, yesterday humiliated Enterprise Cup holders Nondescripts 59-6 at the Parklands Sports Club.

The match was a one-sided affair, with the visitors toying with their hosts, and making tries at their own pace.

Basically it was due to this total command of the game that Penguins got the only try for Nondies late in the second half. Prop O'Brien Conon and Derek Stark were running the ball in their own 22, making a build-up for another try, when by a simple miscalculation the fell (but with both men in cover).

There was Gwada Ogot lurking in the area to pick the loose ball and sprint unchecked for the touch-down under the posts. Carl Hartley made the conversion.

The Penguins were in the match from the other side, showed their own class by a considerable 27-0 lead at the interval over the Kenyan winners of the Enterprise knock-out

tournament whose junior side also claimed the Mwamba Cup.

The sheer brilliance of Derek Stark and David Stoddard saw them make two and one try respectively that were "something" in themselves. For those three tries later in the second half, it was a tinge of scheming rarely seen on the local scene. Dummies and pacing in full speed was Stoddard's forte, while for Stark it was the speed more than anything else that carried the day.

Yesterday, Penguins made ten tries and five conversions, for the overall 59-6 win. An unmatched display in the second half gave them 32 match points.

The tries came through Derek Stark (2), Henderson Crowford (2) and David Stoddard, Ogier, Glenn Taylor, Peter Steven and Fred Tubb all of whom made one try apiece. The man who made himself 'king' of Parklands was Fred Tubb whose massive kick enabled him stab home the conversions that followed the tries. He had five massive

conversions to his credit to the chagrin of the several hundred Nondies fans who braved the pulverising atmosphere created by the visitors.

Penguins' ball handling and running is a class higher than when last they were in the country several years ago. They were so precise that they left their hosts stunned at times on their way to making valuable tries.

Their dummies (made so often by O'Brien, Stoddard and Stevens) and ability to change the course of the ball, added to their faking ability and solid defence formation gave Nondies no chance at all to spring back into the game controlled superbly by Mark Riley.

The visitors won all scrums (defying the hefty Nondies pack) and grabbed all 'in' balls coming from the touch-lines.

Save for Gwada's flash of speed for the merited try (for which he had to dive in running for celebration purposes), Nondies were completely overwhelmed in their own back-yard.

In their opening match, the visiting Penguins annihilated Kenya Harlequins 54-3 at the Rugby Football Union of East Africa ground (home of Quins), in a match in which ironically it was Quins who had taken the lead with a 20th minute penalty convertion.

Penguins (both players and their manager) are expected to conduct a coaching session for willing Kenyan players today at 5:00 pm at the Impala Club before they face the Chairman's Select XV under the Impala Club floodlights in a match expected to kick-off at 6.30 pm tomorrow.

Alan Wright was unable to tour Kenya due to business commitments. He therefore arranged for copies of Kenyan newspaper match reports to be sent to his workplace in London by means of fax machines.

Mr. ALAN WRIGHT 1-491-1742

From Mark Riley.

SUNDAY NATION, JULY 23, 1989 31

Penguins lock forward Troy Coker lunges for a line-up ball against Scorpions Invitational XV yesterday. The British visitors used their set piece domination to great effect and won the match 40-6. — Picture by KENYA PHOTO

UK Penguins sting Scorpions

It was a very happy tour, and the Penguins amassed 52 tries (16 of which were scored by three wingers). Owain Williams was the top try-scorer with seven, and Simon Hodgkinson, the England full-back, was the highest points scorer with 64 points (three tries, six penalties and 17 conversions. The final tour statistics were: Played six, won six, points for 289, points against 55.

Tony Mason and Alan Wright received many letters from the players after this tour, complimenting them on their excellent organisation and thanking them for the wonderful memories.

The following letter from Crawford Henderson, an Oxford University sprinter who was one of the young Scottish players on the tour, is typical:

I was a bit apprehensive about the tour before we left England, in that it was to be my first tour, I would be with a whole bunch of players whom I had never met before and the Penguins had a highly reputed name in rugby circles. However, my worries proved totally ungrounded and I found eveyone in the tour party to be very outgoing and friendly - thus I had enormous fun off the pitch. It was a great way to experience Kenya (on Safari I was on the 'Irish Bus' and I haven't laughed so much in ages!). What with everything, I don't think I could have wished a better initiation to touring - thank you very much.

On the pitch, I have not enjoyed rugby so much since school, for it was not only great to be playing with some of the top players, but also a very welcome relief to play an open game (without that heavy emphasis on winning at all costs). The amount of ball that came out to the wings was much appreciated!

The results were: Penguins beat Kenya Harlequins 54 - 3, Penguins beat Nondescripts 59 - 6, Penguins beat Chairman's XV 45 - 12, Penguins beat Scorpions 40 - 6, Penguins beat Nairobi University 61 - 10, Penguins beat the Kenya National XV 30 - 18.

Penguins squad:

Tony Mason (Manager), John Morgan (Hon. Treasurer), Ray Megson (Referee), Doris Mason and Mary Morgan (Nurses!). Peter Steven (Heriot's FP and Scotland, Captain),

Colin Aitkins (Loughborough University and England U21), Troy Coker (Oxford University and Australia), Peter Cook (Nottingham and England 'B'), Greg Dilger (Lansdowne and Connacht), Neil Donovan (London Irish and Western Australia), Noel Downer (Lansdowne), Tim Exeter (London Scottish and Scotland 'B'), Crawford Henderson (London Scottish and Scotland U21), Simon Hodgkinson (Nottingham and England), Nick Killick (Harlequins and England U21), Phil Meadows (Heriot's FP and Devon), David Millard (London Scottish and Scotland 'B'), John Morrison (Bath and England 'B'), Connor O'Brien (Trinity College and Irish Universities), Peter Purcell (Lansdowne and Ireland), Charlie Quinn (Lansdowne and Leinster), John Robertson (Heriot's FP and Scotland U21), Derek Stark (Ayr and Scotland 'B'), David Stoddart (Heriot's FP and Scotland U21), Glen Taylor (Loughborough University and England U21), Gavin Thompson (Rosslyn Park and England U21), Seb Tubbs (Loughborough University and England U21), Richard Wareham (Loughborough University and England U21), Owain Williams (Bridgend and Wales 'B').

Some of Peter Cook's photographs from the highly successful Kenya Tour.
Above: On safari.
Left: The squad share a meal.

PENGUINS MIDDLESEX SEVENS WINNING SQUAD
The Lensbury Club, May 1999

1990 - 1999

WORLDWIDE SUCCESS
IN THE ABBREVIATED GAMES
(7S AND 10S)

ALAN WRIGHT: 'HIGHLIGHTS OF OUR FOURTH DECADE
INCLUDE SUCCESS IN:

♦ THE SCANDINAVIAN STOCKHOLM TENS;

♦ THE MALAYSIAN RUGBY UNION/COBRA INTERNATIONAL TENS;

♦ THE ITALIAN RUGBY UNION INTERNATIONAL SEVENS;

♦ THE NORDIC SEVENS;

♦ SPECIAL REUNION TOUR TO SWEDEN TO PLAY PINGVIN RFC

♦ THE MIDDLESEX SEVENS - BACK-TO-BACK WINNERS IN 1999
AND 2000 (UK TELEVISION COVERAGE).

♦ ON THE NON-PLAYING SIDE:
OUR CONCERN WITH TONY MASON'S HEALTH
"THE GRAND ALLIANCE" - SPONSORSHIP BY HSBC.'

1990 CHRONICLE

21st February - Penguins beat Cambridge University Past and Present 36 - 27 at Grange Road, Cambridge.

5th - 21st August - India Tour including the British Airways Calcutta Cup Centenary Tournament. Captained by Kevin Rafferty (Scotland). Penguins beat a Calcutta XV 68 - 0 Penguins beat a Calcutta/Bombay Select XV 58 - 6 Penguins beat Maharashtra State Police 68 - 0 Penguins beat Armenian IMOB 70 - 3 Penguins beat Wayfoong 43 - 0 **Winners, BA Calcutta Cup**

7th - 9th September - Belgium. Captained by Bill Calcraft (Australia). Penguins beat Boitsfort 23 - 15

Above: Cambridge lock Andy MacDonald stretches for the ball. Below: Richard Moon makes a break for Cambridge.

1990

The decade began with a 36 - 27 win at Grange Road in the annual Cambridge University Past and Present fixture on Wednesday, 21st February. This fixture was of special significance, and also a great honour for the Penguins, because it was the first of two very special Anniversary Matches arranged by the Cambridge Club in the 1989 - 90 season to celebrate 150 years of rugby football being played at the University (the other match would be against Captain Crawshay's Welsh XV the following month).

Cambridge University Past and Present put out a formidable XV which included a trio of Wasps and England backs - S. Smith, F. Clough and M. Bailey. The Penguins, not to be outdone, included Steve Bates (another Wasps and England Cap) at scrum-half and Jonathon Webb (Bath and England) at full-back plus seven England 'B' or U21 players together with six other internationals in a very strong combination.

Peter Bills of *The Times* wrote of the match: *If Cambridge University Past and Present envisaged a fairly gentle exercise as the backdrop to the more serious message of the evening - the University's appeal for £150,000 - they had clearly not told their visitors.*

The Penguins had a number of players with points to prove. Jonathan Webb, discarded by club and country, scored three tries in the first hour with some speedy and forceful running.

Three Oxford University RFC internationals performed manfully for the

Cambridge University
Rugby Union Football Club

150th ANNIVERSARY APPEAL

1839/40 – 1989/90

CURUFC, Grange Road, Cambridge CB3 9BN
Tel: 0223-354131 or 0223-870215

21st February Cambridge University Match Programme.

Penguins. Smith, especially, produced much of his goal-kicking rhythm, which could yet persuade Ireland to employ his talents at some stage of the match against France in Paris on Saturday week. Tony Underwood, the victim of a broken jaw in early December, was equally full of commitment.

Cambridge were swept aside after Martin's early penalty. A penalty try was awarded for a collapsed scrum and then Clarke stormed over for the next score. Smith converted the first and then beautifully goaled Webb's first try.

Webb's second try followed a drive in the loose by the Romanian Raducanu. Smith again landed a neat conversion.

Cambridge hit back with tries by Moon and Clough, Martin improving both. But Webb scuttled away for his third try and Barley's score put Penguins clear.

Penguins squad: Tony Mason (Match Manager).

D. Peglar (Wasps and England 'B', Captain), B. Barley (Wakefield and England), S. Bates (Wasps and England), B. Clarke (Saracens and England 'B'), P. De Glanville (Durham University and England U21), G. Hein (Oxford University and USA), D. James (Oxford University and USA), J. Olver (Harlequins and England Reserve), C. Raducanu (Boroughmuir and Romania), C. Sheasby (Harlequins and England 'B'), B. Smith (Oxford University, Murraha, Ireland and Australia), M. Speight (London Welsh and New Zealand), T. Underwood (Leicester and England 'B'), J. Webb (Bristol and England), R. Williams (London Welsh and New Zealand).

Alan Wright: 'In passing - Tony and I were both convinced that Jonathan Webb's outstanding display in this match, and the publicity that it received, earned him selection almost immediately back into the England team.'

Top: The Penguins squad before the final against Wayfoong. Tony Mason is wearing the no.18 jersey. He was 72 years old at the time! Above: Kevin Rafferty with the Cup.

The main tour of the year took place in August. And, for the fifth time in the Penguins' history to date, it came about as the result of an invitation to tour on behalf of the Rugby Football Union (the previous occasions, it will be remembered, were: Belgium in 1964, Zambia in 1968, the USSR in 1977 and Sri Lanka in 1979).

Alan Wright explains: 'Bob Weighill, Secretary of the RFU, 'phoned me to say this was a special year in India. He said: "The Indians are celebrating the Tercentenary of the City of Calcutta between the 5th and the 21st August. It also marks the gift of the Calcutta Cup to the Rugby Union. We can't send an England XV - would you go to play in the celebrations on our behalf?"

'So the Club, Captained by Kevin Rafferty of Heriot's FP, went to Calcutta and played in *The British Airways Calcutta Cup Centenary Tournament*. We won every match, and in so doing we were presented with a very handsome trophy - a replica of the Calcutta Cup - which was donated by British Airways.'

The full results were: Penguins beat a Calcutta XV 68 - 0, Penguins beat a Calcutta/Bombay Select XV 58 - 6, Penguins beat Maharashtra State Police 68 - 0, Penguins beat Armenian IMOB 70 - 3. Cup Final: Penguins beat Wayfoong 43 - 0.

Alan: 'It was a very good "missionary" tour. It was also notable that Tony incuded his grandson Andrew in the Penguins' touring party. Andrew had won a half-blue at Cambridge University playing Rugby League (although he was, at this time, playing Rugby Union football, of course). One of the great features of this tour was that Tony and his grandson played together in one match... Tony was 72 years old at the time! You see, he just couldn't resist these things!'

The victorious Penguins after the final. Tony Mason proudly holds the British Airways Replica Calcutta Cup.

Above: Tony thanks the hosts.

The 1990 Penguin Tourists in Calcutta.

Penguins squad: A. R. Mason (Manager). K. Rafferty (Heriot's FP, Captain), G. Aherne (Lansdowne), P. Cook (Nottingham), C. Egan (St. Mary's Collage), M. Freer (Nottingham), A. Griffiths (Moseley), D. Griffiths (Cardiff), S. Jardine (South Glamorgan Institute), A. Jenkins (Cardiff), J. Kennedy (St. Mary's College), W. Kilford (Nottingham), J. Luke (South Glamorgan Institute), A. Mason (St. John's College, Cambridge University), A. McRobbie (Heriot's FP), J. Murphy (Lansdowne), A. Nichol (Heriot's FP), J. O'Callaghan (Cambridge University), J. Robertson (Heriot's FP), K. Simms (Wasps and England), N. Simms (Cambridge University), T. Swan (Waterloo), D. Titcomb (Bristol), P. Whitelaw (Heriot's FP).

Just over two weeks after returning from India the Penguins were off again - this time to Belgium. The Club played a special match against Boitsfort Rugby Club to celebrate both the 40th Anniversary of the reign of the King of the Belgians and the 20th Anniversary of the Club. The Penguins won a surprisingly close match by 23 points to 15.

Alan: 'Bill Calcraft Captained this team. We'd had a good friendship with Belgium ever since our two previous trips there in 1964 and 1965.'

1991

Penguins beat Cambridge University Past and Present 62 - 22 in their annual match on the evening of 20th February at Grange Road, Cambridge.

The scoreline was a reflection of the fact that the Cambridge University Past and Present team relied heavily on being able to call upon a host of English internationals who had progressed from the University to Wasps in the 1980s - but with an important round of Cup rugby coming up on the Saturday directly following this match, none were available to play against the Penguins.

Penguins, on the other hand, had selected a squad fully expecting to be facing the usual Cambridge University back division of seasoned internationals.

David Hallett of the Cambridge Evening News wrote of the match: *From the start Cambridge were all at sea and it took just three minutes for Lindsay Renwick to score the first of the game's 17 tries.*

The Light Blues trailed 6 - 36 at half-time.

For a time in the second half it seemed they had discovered their sea legs, scoring a try and a goal to pull back to 16 - 36 before they finally admitted they were out of their depth and sank quietly.

1991 CHRONICLE

20th February - Penguins beat Cambridge University Past and Present 62 - 22 at Grange Road, Cambridge.

22nd - 27th May - Second Italian International Sevens Tournament, Catania, Sicily. Captained by David Millard (Scotland). Penguins beat Spain 36 - 0. Penguins beat Hong Kong 34 - 0 Penguins beat Western Samoa 36 - 0 Penguins beat Netherlands 20 - 16 Penguins beat Sicily Select 24 - 10 Penguins lost to Fiji 6 - 34 Finalists, Italian Rugby Union International Sevens

---

36 CAMBRIDGE EVENING NEWS, Thursday, February 21, 1991

DAVID HALLETT reports on a record night at Grange Road

Sport

Students fail to see funny side

HEARD the latest joke doing the rounds in Cambridge rugby circles?

What goes from nought to 60 in an hour? The scoreboard at Grange Road.

A joke is the only way to describe what happened at the university rugby ground last night when a super slick Penguins team ran in 13 tries against a Past and Present students team.

Record

Needless to say it was a Penguins' record on home territory although Britain's most-travelled rugby club did top 100 points against an Argentinian side in Brazil a few years back.

And it was — needless to say — the worst defeat suffered by a Past and Present Cambridge side. It would have been even more had Penguins kicked their goals.

They managed to convert only one of six second half tries although four others were in front of the posts — no

| Cambridge Univ P and P ....22 |
| Penguins....................62 |
| **By DAVID HALLETT** |

wonder the harassed scoreboard operator had the final score as 66.

Over recent seasons the Light Blues have built a formidable reputation with their past and present side. But that relied heavily on the host of English internationals who progressed from Cambridge to the Wasps club in the eighties.

With cup rugby on Saturday none were available last night, leaving the cupboard a little bare.

Penguins, on the other hand, picked their team expecting that they might be facing a back division of internationals.

The problems for Cambridge were compounded by the freeze which has prevented the students from training for more than a fortnight.

They clearly used the time to study and were not prepared either mentally or physically for the challenge that faced them.

That can be the only explanation for they way they folded in the face of the opposition's high-speed skills.

From the start Cambridge were all at sea and it took just three minutes for Lindsay Renwick to score the first of the game's 17 tries.

The Light Blues trailed 36-6 at half time.

For a time in the second half it seemed they had discovered their sea legs, scoring a try and goal to pull back to 16-36 before they finally admitted they were out of their depth and sank quietly.

What made it all the more galling was that four of the tries and four of the five conversions were scored by Oxford Blues.

Orchestrated

Bill Calcraft, an Australian former skipper at the other place, scored twice in the first half and Gary Hein, the American who loves scoring tries against Cambridge, touched down twice after the break while Kent Bray,

the Australian who orchestrated the whole show from fly half, kicked four goals.

If there was any consolation it came in the desire of outstanding Scottish centre Paul Rouse to secure a future place at Cambridge.

Scorers. Cambridge: Tries — Given, Reed, O'Callaghan, Pool-Jones. Conversions: Sutton (3).

Penguins: Tries — Calcraft (2), Hein (2), Renwick (2), Poole (2), Smith (2), Appleson, Philpot, Rouse. Conversions — Bray (4), Appleson.

Cambridge University Past and Present: Parton; Underwood, Reed, Robinson, Given; Sutton, Hancock; Foster, Mair, Freeman, O'Callaghan, Robertson, Jenkins, Bates, Pool-Jones.

Replacements: Johnson for Robinson, Ashworth for Mair.

Penguins: Appleson (London Scottish); Hein (Oxford University), Philpot (Coventry), Rouse (Dundee FP), Renwick (London Scottish); Bray (Harlequins), Kardooni (Leicester), Jones (Harlequins), Howe (Bedford), James (Harlequins), Pinnegar (Wasps), Poole (Leicester), Calcraft (London Welsh), Smith (Coventry) Clarke (Saracens).

Referee: B Marshall (Devon).

JIM O'CALLAGHAN ... scored a rare try.

What made it all the more galling was that four of the tries and four of the five conversions were scored by Oxford Blues.

Bill Calcraft, an Australian former skipper at the other place, scored twice in the first half and Gary Hein, the American who loves scoring tries against Cambridge, touched down twice after the break while Kent Bray, the Australian who orchestrated the whole show from fly-half, kicked four goals.

David Hallett's Cambridge Evening News match report from Thursday 21st February.

As usual, Tony Mason later penned a post-match thank-you letter to all the players who had turned out for the Penguins that evening. In it he wrote: *You all put on a marvellous exhibition of running rugby, and of how the game should be played. It was breathtaking to watch, with the speed and handling of the moves being incredible for a scratch side.*

The Cambridge players and officials were shellshocked after the game, and found it hard to believe that they had lost by such a score.

I hope you enjoyed playing as much as we enjoyed watching.

Penguins squad: Tony Mason (Match Manager). B. Calcraft (London Welsh, Captain), A. Appleson (London Scottish), K. Bray (Harlequins), B. Clarke (Saracens), G. Hein (Oxford University), M. Howe (Bedford), D. James (Harlequins), A. Jones (Harlequins), A. Kardooni (Leicester), A. Philpot (Coventry), C. Pinnegar (Wasps), J. Poole (Leicester), L. Renwick (London Scottish), A. Rouse (Dundee HSFP), B. Smith (Coventry).

May saw the Penguins make their first-ever visit to Italy, where they played in the second Sicilian International Invitation Sevens Tournament in Catania, Sicily. The Club was defeated in the final by Fiji, who played under the Captaincy of their world-famous sevens star, Waisale Serevi.

Alan recalls: 'In 1991 we were, for the first time, invited by the Federazione Italiana Rugby to play in the Italian Rugby Union International Sevens. And we were pleased to reach the final. We had a brilliant team which included Harlequins' and England's Nigerian Prince, the outstanding winger Andrew Harriman.

'Unfortunately we had a rather bad injury list. No excuses - that's what happens in rugby! We were fairly beaten in the final by a brilliant Fijian national team Captained by the wonderful Waisale Serevi. This was the first time we had encountered Serevi.'

Sean Lineen of Boroughmuir RFC and Scotland (the original 'Kilted Kiwi' who originally hailed from Auckland) was invited to play for the Penguins in the Sicilian Sevens, and he wrote a diary of his experiences for the July, 1991 edition of the Scottish magazine *Scottish Rugby*. The article, reproduced below in its entirety, gives a wonderful view of the tournament from a player's perspective:

Tony Mason, Manager of the Penguins, had brought together ten young men to participate in what is becoming more and more popular through the summer months - a sevens tournament in an exotic location. And Sicily, land of the Mafioso, was no exception.

One of the main benefits of going on a trip such as this, besides an opportunity to visit such a fantastic place, is the chance to meet people from around the rugby world, and enjoy yourself, give or take a few 15 minute spells of

1991 brought the Penguins' first visit to Italy.

2nd SICILY SEVEN
INTERNATIONAL RUGBY
TOURNAMENT
25 - 26 MAGGIO 1991 · ore 10-13 / 17-21
CATANIA - STADIO RUGBY S.M. GORETTI

intense pain on the rugby pitch.

Sicily has a local side, Catania, which competes in the Italian First Division, and with rugby now the fastest growing team sport in the country it was the chance to place sevens rugby on the map.

This tournament is into its second year and must rank behind only Hong Kong in playing strength. In our section were Spain, Hong Kong and Western Samoa, while other teams included a South African VII (disguised as a Sicily invitation team), Irish Wolfhounds, Argentina, Welsh Academicals, the United States of America and, of course, Fiji.

So, as we disembarked from the plane on the Wednesday afternoon it was a case of "do the best you can, but most of all enjoy yourself." An included bonus was the fact that Wednesday afternoon training was cancelled.

So after dropping our luggage off at our hotel we all headed for a dip in the sea - which lasted all of ten seconds as the water was as cold as the Meggetland showers.

The major coup for our team was establishing a tab at the hotel bar. This meant that whenever you needed a drink all you had to do was go up to the bar and place your order, followed by the two words "Penguins' tab".

Wednesday night was a chance to get to know one another to develop team spirit, and, indeed, after vast quantities of red wine not only were we going to win the tournament, but everyone was going to join someone else's club within our group!

Thursday afternoon brought us back to the main reason for being there. Rugby training is never easy, but to participate in 90 minutes of gruelling sevens training, in 90 degrees plus of heat, with a thumping hangover is something I wouldn't wish even on Grant Fox.

Thursday night was spent discussing tactics over a couple of beers at dinnertime. I can still see Neil Back's face as his tooth came out while eating a piece of brick-like bread!

On Friday morning two touch practice games had been arranged against Italy and Holland. The team played well enough against Italy, but alarm bells started to ring when Holland easily accounted for us by four tries to nil. This brought us back to earth with a crash and in the end ultimately put us back on the right track.

Friday afternoon was spent up at a resort called Taormina, which to me would rank as one of the loveliest towns I've ever seen. Built on the top of a mountain, it takes over 30 minutes to get to the top - but the views, shops, people and atmosphere make it a must for any tourist. That evening you could hardly walk along the pavements as they were jam-packed with tables and chairs and trendily dressed locals sipping their cappucinos and vino. Andy Harriman led the way in

The Penguins squad for the 1991 Sicily Sevens.
Back row: Tony Mason (Manager), Sean Lineen, Graham Drummond, Owain Williams, Kent Bray, Ian Dixon.
Front row: Harvey Thornicroft, David Millard, Neil Back, Andrew Harriman.

The backbone of a wonderful Penguins VII -
Top: Sean Lineen. Middle: Neil Back.
Bottom: Harvey Thornicroft.

Penguins were put to the sword in the final by an absolutely brilliant Fiji VII which was led by Waisale Serevi.

our fashion parade with his yellow long-sleeved Ralph Lauren polo shirt, while young Harvey Thorneycroft (a man with a future) decided he liked his red Fred Perry top so much that he left it on for the remainder of the tour.

Something good must have been in the red wine as our first day ended with great success. Having accounted for Spain 36 - 0, we then dispatched Hong Kong 34 - 0 and the much fancied Western Samoa 36 - 0.

Everyone played well, and I was especially pleased for Graham Drummond as he had missed selection for Scotland's North American tour.

In fact, the management were so delighted with our unexpected victories that they made the fatal mistake of taking us out to one of the finest seafood restaurants in the area. And did we feast! The best fish, tiger prawns and mussels were all consumed with great gusto. But unbeknown to anyone, one of the boys, who shall remain nameless, had ordered twelve lobsters as a second main course. As the waiters came down the stairs with these succulent dishes, I have to admit the management, Tony Mason and Tony Jarman, controlled themselves well. Needless to say everything in sight was devoured and we returned to our hotel around 1am. That was a day I'll remember for a long time.

Our legs were very stiff the next morning but luckily David Millard (studying to be an osteopath) had brought his bag with him and doubled up as a physio.

Our quarter-final was against Holland, our conquerors in the touch game on Friday. Revenge is sweet, even if it needed a last-minute try to secure victory. In the other half of the draw Fiji disposed of their arch-rivals Western Samoa, and looked very impressive. The match was rugby sevens at its best.

The atmosphere was now building up.

The two semis saw Fiji defeat a defiant Irish Wolfhounds side, while we managed to sneak past the Sicily select side 24 - 10, courtesy of three Andy Harriman tries.

Everyone anticipated a keenly contested final, including ourselves, but Fiji had other ideas. They moved into top gear and it seemed there were twenty of them on the field - even though we tackled our hearts out we never managed to secure possession and lost convincingly 34 - 6.

Jerseys were eagerly swapped, trophies collected and then everyone prepared for the night's entertainment. The banquet that evening was a roaring success. 16 teams together in one hall, singing incoherent songs and trying to outdo each other. It was a great sight to see a Samoan and a Fijian up on a table dancing together, as they are the fiercest of rivals.

It always amazes me why flights are booked for the early hours of the morning. Yes, we were up at 5.45am, having barely slept, and back to Catania Airport to catch a flight to Rome and then on to Heathrow.

But you can't complain really, having visited a beautiful island, made a

final, but most of all, having just made nine life-long friends.

Who did pay that bar tab anyway?

Alan Wright adds: 'I'm glad to say that we have played in the Italian Rugby Union International Sevens twice more since 1991 (in 1993 and 1994), and on each occasion we have won it.

'But finally, there's a wonderful story about this 1991 tour. Andrew Harriman was newly down from university and had started his own business, with which he kept in touch throughout the tour (one has to remember that these were amateur days). On the day we were leaving Italy, and to Tony's amazement, Harriman presented him with a telephone bill for something like £87.

'Well, Tony threw up his hands in horror (you have to bear in mind the fact that Penguins had had next to no funds for most of our existence and the players paid their own way). Tony, being a true amateur through and through, had started to protest when Harriman, in his perfect Cantabrigian English, said to him: "I say, Tony - if you want Rolls Royce players representing the Penguins, you've got to learn to pay Rolls Royce expenses." Which we managed to pay!'

Penguins squad:

Tony Mason (Manager). D. Millard (London Scottish, Captain), I. Armstrong (Wasps), N. Back (Leicester), K. Bray (Harlequins), I. Dixon (London Scottish), G. Drummond (Boroughmuir), A. Harriman (Harlequins and England), S. Lineen (Boroughmuir and Scotland), H. Thorneycroft (Northampton), O. Williams (Bridgend and Wales).

Harlequin FC's and England's exceptional wing three-quarter Andrew Harriman.

Andrew Harriman

Andrew Tuoyo Harriman. Born 13 July, 1964, in Lagos, Nigeria.

Educated at Radley College and Cambridge University. Cambridge Blue in both rugby and athletics in 1985.

Played on the wing for Cambridge University, Harlequins and England.

Harriman was known as one of the quickest and most exciting runners of his generation. In 1988 he won his first and only cap against the touring Australians (won 28-19 by England). He then played for England 'B' against the Emerging Australians, France and Italy. Harriman was an exceptional exponent of sevens rugby and appeared for the Harlequins in three Middlesex Sevens finals. In the 1991 event he scored seven tries in four matches.

He represented the Barbarians in the Hong Kong Sevens tournament in 1991, during which he scored memorable tries in the quarter-final against Australia and the semi-final against Fiji.

He also Captained England when they won the inaugural Rugby World Cup Sevens in 1993 - during which he famously outran the celebrated Australian winger, David Campese.

Andrew is now a London-based property developer.

1992 CHRONICLE

19th February - Penguins beat Cambridge University Past and Present 50 - 19 at Grange Road, Cambridge.

2nd May - Irish Rugby Football Union Aer Lingus International Sevens. Captained by Colin Laity (Wales). Penguins beat Limerick 12 - 8 Penguins beat Welsh President's VII 40 - 6 Penguins beat Munster 18 - 6 Penguins lost to France 12 - 16 *Semi-finalists, IRFU/Aer Lingus Sevens*

1st - 15th August - Indonesia, Singapore and Hong Kong Tour. Captained by Peter Cook (England). Penguins beat International Sports Club of Jakarta in Indonesia. Penguins beat Bucks Club in Singapore. Penguins beat Singapore National XV in Singapore. Penguins beat Hong Kong Wayfoong Invitational XV 36 - 7 in Hong Kong. Penguins beat Hong Kong President's XV 28 - 8 in Hong Kong.

The IRU International Sevens was hosted by the Munster Rugby Union in Limerick.

1992

The Penguins' year began at a chilly Grange Road in Cambridge on 19th February when the Cambridge University Past and Present side were comfortably beaten in the annual match. Alan later wrote: *This was a most exciting match which was very even at half-time, but was finally won by the Club 50 - 19 after a very competitive game.*

Penguins squad: Tony Mason (Match Manager).
David Millard (London Scottish and Scotland 'B', Captain), Warwick Bullock (Coventry and England U21), Justin Cassell (Saracens and England 'B'), Barry Crawley (Saracens), Stuart Davies (Rosslyn Park and England Students), Robert Dawson (London Welsh and Zimbabwe), Martin Gregory (Saracens), Garry Holmes (Wasps and England 'B'), Damien Hopley (Wasps and England Bench), Ian Hunter (Northampton and England), Mat Keenan (London Irish and Western Samoa), Jason Minshull (Coventry), Alec Snow (Heriot's FP, Edinburgh and England Students), John Steele (Northampton and England 'B'), Harvey Thorneycroft (Northampton, Barbarians and England 'B').

Next up was another prestigious sevens competition, the Irish Rugby Football Union Aer Lingus International Sevens. The tournament took place on 2nd May and was hosted by the Munster Rugby Union in Limerick. Penguins beat Limerick (12 - 8), the Welsh President's VII (40 - 6) and Munster (18 - 6) before eventually losing to France in the last seconds of the semi-final, by 12 points to 16.

Penguins squad: Tony Mason (Tour Manager), Ian Bullerwell (Assistant Manager). Colin Laity (Neath and Wales 'A', Captain), Gerry Ainscough (Leicester and England 'A'), Steve Hackney (Leicester and England 'A'), Stuart Jardine (Pontypool and England 'A'), Eric Peters (Cambridge University and England Students), David Pickering (Neath and Wales), John Quantrill (Rugby and England Students), Kurt Seecharran (Bristol University and England Students), Ed Thomas (Neath and Wales 'A').

The summer brought with it the news that Cathay Pacific had kindly agreed to sponsor the Penguin RFC in 1992 and 1993 - years which included two very successful tours that took in Indonesia, Singapore, Hong Kong and Malaysia.

ON A ROLL: Penguins arrive in Hongkong, seen as the toughest part of their tour.

Alan Wright: 'The Club was sponsored for the first time by Cathay Pacific Airways (through the good offices of Penguins' oldest Vice-President and a dear friend, the late Francis Nott) and played five matches during the August tour of the Far East. The Club was Captained by Peter Cook of Nottingham RFC and the tour took place between the 1st - 15th August. Each player paid £235 towards the cost of the trip.

'The first match was against the ISC (International Sports Club) in Jakarta. Tony had set his heart on playing in Indonesia and the boys flew over especially for the match. We then played two matches in Singapore - one against Singapore Rugby, the other against the Bucks Rugby Club.'

The Penguins won all three of these matches quite comfortably, racking up over 160 points in the process.

Alan continues: 'We then flew on to Hong Kong and played against two sides that were, essentially, Hong Kong 'A' (Wayfoong) and Hong Kong. The Penguins won these two matches as well.'

According to newspaper reports of the time, the

Penguin Rugby Football Club

Kent County R.F.U.   The Rugby Football Union   Sussex County Rugby Union.

President: Air-Commodore R.H.G. Weighill, C.B.E, D.F.C.

Committee:

Chairman & Team Secretary: A.R. Mason, Impennes, Collington Lane West, Bexhill on Sea, East Sussex TN39 3TA. Tel: 04243 4788
Hon Secretary: A.G.L. Wright, Neale House, 62 St. James's Street, London SW1A 1LY. Tel: 071-973 0700. Fax: 071-491 1742
Hon. Treasurer: J.R. Morgan, Little Pettings, Hodsoll Street, Wrotham, Kent TN15 7LH. Tel: 0732 822632
N.G. Martin, W.G.D. Morgan, P.G. Yarranton

FAR EAST TOUR
THURSDAY, 30TH JULY TO TUESDAY, 18TH AUGUST, 1992
JAKARTA - SINGAPORE - HONG KONG

DEPARTURE:	We will leave Heathrow on Thursday, 30th July on the 6.30 p.m. flight to Jakarta.
RETURN:	We will leave Hong Kong on Monday, 17th August on the 10.30 p.m. flight arriving Gatwick at 8.00 a.m.
ITINERARY:	The local rugby players will be hosting us at all venues.
	We stay in Jakarta from Friday, 31st July until Wednesday, 5th August when we depart for Singapore. We depart for Hong Kong on Tuesday, 11th August where we will stay until we depart for Gatwick on Monday, 17th August.
COST:	It will cost each player £235 starting from Heathrow. There will be other expenses that will crop up from time to time. Although we will be hosted and a lot of the entertainment will be laid on for us there will be times when you will have to buy a meal.
INSURANCE:	The Club will take out an all-in insurance to cover all the players.
INOCULATIONS:	Apply to your Doctor who will prescribe what is necessary. Do it now.
VISAS AND PASSPORT:	Passport only necessary. Check yours now.
CLOTHING:	The weather is expected to be hot and humid so only lightweight clothing is needed.
KIT:	We supply jerseys and socks but bring your own white shorts.
	You are advised to have long and short studs.
GENERAL:	We have an excellent reputation as ambassadors of good rugby and have always been invited to return. We aim to protect that reputation and we are going to enjoy ourselves but rugby comes first and we will train every day and aim to win our matches and enjoy ourselves even more.
	If you are prepared to work and play hard and carry out our philosophy you are welcome to join the team, if you only want to have a holiday we would rather you did not come. You have been asked because we feel you can uphold our traditions.

Please fill in the enclosed forms and return to me with your deposit, without delay, in the self addressed envelope enclosed.

TONY MASON
Chairman and Team Manager
(Tel: 04243-4788)

The 1992 Jakarta, Singapore and Hong Kong tour itinerary.

Penguins were made to battle for the first time on tour against a Wayfoong side that included several international and well-established club players. In steamy conditions Penguins ran in six tries to Wayfoong's one.

Penguins then ended the tour on a high with a four-try-to-one, 28 points to 8 points victory over the Hong Kong President's XV at the delightfully named Happy Valley Ground. Tony Mason said of this match: 'It was very difficult with the heat and humidity, and in the last ten minutes Hong Kong tackled extremely well. We thought that as the match wore on they would tire, but they kept fighting to the end. We would have scored a lot more tries if it were not for the Hong Kong XV's tackling.'

This tour is also notable in that it marked the first time that Craig Brown was selected to play for the Penguins.

Craig: 'I was playing for London Scottish, and one evening after training I was asked by Dave Millard if I was interested in going on a "Penguins tour". Well, I didn't know what "Penguins" was or were, but he gave me Tony Mason's number,

Craig Brown on tour with the Penguins.

Craig Brown

Craig Stuart Brown was born on 6th May, 1965, in Te Kuiti in the King Country, New Zealand.

He is currently the Project Director for Mott MacDonald in South Africa (and was chosen to re-design and supervise the planning of the Johannesburg to Durban railway). His hobbies are wine, touring and socialising.

Played for Taumarunui Athletic and Taumarunui High School, then Waikato and Auckland Universities (flanker/number 8). Craig was picked in the Waikato squad and played for the 'B' team. He was also a member (together with Gavin Hastings and four All Blacks) of the Auckland University team that won the Gallagher Shield in 1987.

Craig: 'I first moved over to the UK in 1991 to see the world. On arrival in London I asked Gavin Hastings where he thought I should play. It was no surprise when he said London Scottish! I played there for three seasons before taking a job in Glasgow in 1994. Whilst in Scotland I played for one season at GHK then for six seasons at Watsonians.'

Alan Wright: *Tony first picked Craig as a player. He's modest, knowledgable, not easily kidded and he's a big fella!*

He has a unique record in the Malaysian Tens. He was a player the first time Penguins won in 1993, the Captain in the second win in 1994 and the Tour Manager when Penguins won again in 2006, 2010 and 2011.

Craig has a great deal of input as to how our tours are run. He is first-class and very able. And as the leading light in the HSBC Penguin International Coaching Academy it was he who expanded it quite early on by cleverly saying: "Never mind coaching young blokes to play rugby, let's coach men to become coaches." And we've done that very successfully. Craig has become... well, I now call him "the hub of the wheel". He has been promoted by the Club in quick succession through the offices of Tour Manager, Players; Director of Rugby; Director of the HSBC Penguin International Coaching Academy; Vice Chairman and now, very deservedly, he is our Chief Executive Officer. He is a brilliant all-rounder and will continue to succeed in every matter in which he engages in life. We are so pleased, as our most capped player, that he has gone on to become such a formidable administrator, manager and selector - universally held in high regard in the Rugby world.

so I 'phoned. For a couple of days all I got was a fax machine! But that got sorted and I eventually spoke to Tony and he told me all about the tour, and said that I could come along, and that was brilliant.

'Regarding the trip - it took us about 24 hours to get to Jakarta - a bit over, maybe, by the time we did all the stops.

'We were met at the airport. There was a guy saying: "Penguins this way please, put your bags in the van and then everybody get on the bus." But the bus had no seats except for two big huge cane chairs. So Tony Mason and his wife Doris sat in the cane chairs and for the rest of us it was standing room only!

'The other interesting feature about this vehicle was that there was a wee gentleman at the front wearing a green jacket and a big green dicky bow. He was sporting a Carlsberg logo on his shirt, and he had a wee bar next to him at the front of the vehicle. He was pouring beers from a keg of Carlsberg under the table!

'So we got taken through the streets of Jakarta to a pub where we met the billets that we were staying with. Jakarta was great and we had the chance to look around.

'We had the first "meet" the next day because we had the first game against "ISC" - which is the International Sports Club of Jakarta. I remember we had to chase off a swarm of dragonflies which were the size of your hand from the field before we could start. And then there we were, into the first game. The match was played in extremely hot conditions - in the 30s and quite humid so that was a new experience for a lot of us. We won the match quite comfortably and then went to the first "after-match" with the locals and had a tremendous time. We then had one or two days to ourselves in Jakarta and we went out to an island for a night for a bit of R&R.

A swarm of dragonflies had to be chased off the field in Jakarta before the match could start.

An adventure!
Hong Kong, Singapore and Indonesia.

Below: The unbeaten Penguins squad celebrate the end of the 1992 tour.

Top: Hong Kong action.
Above: The victorious Penguins team.

'We moved on to Singapore where we played two matches. We played the Bucks in one match and a National XV in the other. It was three days between matches.

In Singapore we got billeted again - a very enjoyable experience. We had a chance to look around Singapore but we did train every day. The games were played in the late afternoon - again, very hot conditions, very dry pitches. We managed to win the games - not by huge scores but comfortably enough.

'We finished in Singapore and then moved back to Hong Kong, and got billeted in Hong Kong once again. In Hong Kong we played Hong Kong "A" (Wayfoong) and Hong Kong.

'Hong Kong "A" was played in the evening. A lot of the men playing for the Hong Kong team obviously came along after work.

Then there was the main game that we had been building up to, which was against the Hong Kong President's XV. We played them down at Happy Valley, and it was a pretty fiesty encounter, actually. Fairly even, I think we won by four tries to one. Yes, it was a pretty torrid game. But as soon as the final whistle went... you know, the usual rugby rules applied and we all had a good evening out.

No slip-ups for Penguins

By NAZVI CAREEM

RUGBY UNION

THE British Penguins were made to battle for the first time in their Asian tour, but still managed a 36-7 victory over a Wayfoong side at Hongkong's Hammer Hill Stadium last night.

On a steamy night at Choi Hung, the Penguins ran in six tries and made three conversions as they overcame brave tackling from the Hongkong side, which contained a host of international and established club players.

The tourists led 10-0 at half-time and they soon discovered that Wayfoong were not going to be as easily overrun as the Singaporeans and Indonesians were at the hands of the Penguins earlier this month. The Penguins totalled more than 160 points against those two.

The tourists' manager Tony Mason said of last night's game: "The humidity made handling the ball very difficult.

"It was not like the humidity we experienced in Indonesia or Singapore, where it would dry up quickly. The players just kept on sweating.

"But that does not take away from the splendid tackling of the Hongkong players. If they hadn't tackled as well as they did, we would have got a great many more tries."

The Penguins' last match of their tour will be their toughest when they meet a Hongkong President's XV tomorrow at Happy Valley.

Several of the President's side turned out for Wayfoong last night, while the rest kept a close eye on proceedings from the touchlines, as they trained under the guidance of Hongkong national coach George Simpkin.

The Penguins took the initiative and went 10-0 up through tries from Rosslyn Park player John Fowler and Irishman Ken Lawless.

Exhausted players from both sides had to take a drinks break mid-way through the first half.

Lawless scored another try in the second half, while Scotland's 1991 Hongkong Sevens representative Ron Kirkpatrick, Oliver Kiely and Richard Mynott scored a try each.

Mynott had two conversions, while full-back Aidan White added another.

Wayfoong's try came through Football Club forward Ashley Jones, who dived over from a five-metre penalty.

Justin Weston converted for Hongkong.

It was the first match in Hongkong played under the International Rugby Board's new rules, where a try is worth five points instead of four.

And the Penguins used another of the new rules to their advantage at one stage, when a quick throw behind the point where the ball went out resulted in a try, following a sweeping left-to-right movement.

Tomorrow's team will be selected from players who have been attending regular weekly training over the past couple of months, and is seen as a stepping stone for a place in Hongkong's squad for next month's Asian Rugby Football Championships in Seoul, South Korea.

Simpkin has stressed that the squad is not indicative of the one which will ultimately be going to Seoul.

Newspaper reports of the final two matches of the tour which took place in Hong Kong.

Ducking out . . . Penguins scrum-half Oliver Kiely is a picture of concentration as he rifles a pass from the scrum base to his backs. The Penguins beat the Hongkong President's XV 28-8 to remain unbeaten on tour.

Penguins retain unbeaten record

By NAZVI CAREEM

THE Penguins ended their Asian tour with a 100 per cent record after beating a Hongkong President's XV 28-8 at Happy Valley last night.

In the toughest and final match of their tour, the Penguins scored four tries against Hongkong's one for a comfortable, yet bruising victory.

The Penguins, who beat a Hongkong Wayfoong side on Thursday, leave for Britain tomorrow, having started their Asian tour earlier this month in Indonesia and Singapore.

Penguins manager Tony Mason was satisfied with the result and praised Hong-

kong's defensive qualities.

"It was very difficult with the heat and humidity, but in the last 10 minutes, Hongkong tackled extremely well," said Mason.

"We thought that as the match wore on, they would tire, but they kept fighting to the end. We would have scored more tries if it were not for the Hongkong tackling."

National coach George Simpkin was using the match as a trial for players hopeful of making the Hongkong side for next month's Asian Rugby Football Tournament in Seoul, South Korea.

And the local players started at a furious pace with Hongkong winning a penalty from 30 yards after only four minutes.

Steve Powley made no mistake from in front of the posts to give Hongkong a 3-0 lead.

Penguins found themselves in a similar position three minutes later, but Richard Mynott surprisingly put the effort wide.

Terry Cooper came on for Hongkong after 18 minutes to replace hooker Patrice Rollier, who had a head injury.

But three minutes later,

Mynott equalised with a 20-yard penalty.

Penguins went into an 11-3 half-time lead with an excellent try by Russell Adams after a dazzling run down the middle by Mike Hutton.

Cooper scored a try for Hongkong 10 minutes into the second half to reduce the deficit to 11-8.

But the Penguins then took control of the match with Gary Parker scoring their second try four minutes later.

They added two more tries through Craig Brown and Hutton.

Parker kicked over one penalty and also converted Brown's try.

'So that was that trip to Hong Kong - very good - a long trip home sitting there in the back of the plane after, obviously, quite a night out on that last night, but a tremendous experience. Getting back to the airport in Gatwick, having been on the road with these guys for two and a half weeks, it was hard saying goodbye to every-body - but that's what touring's all about. So we all said goodbye, and hoped, you know, some of us would meet up again. It was a tremendous experience.

'Reflecting on the trip, I decided that Penguins was a great institution that had provided me with a great opportunity. I'd met lots of people, and I thought, well, if I ever get picked again then I'd have to be available!'

> **"Reflecting on the trip, I decided that the Penguins was a great institution that had provided me with a great opportunity. I'd met lots of people, and I thought, well, if I ever get picked again then I'd have to be available."**
>
> *Craig Brown*

Penguins squad: Tony Mason (Manager), Peter Whitelaw (Assistant Manager, Coach and player), John Morgan (Hon. Treasurer).

Peter Cook (Nottingham and England, Captain), Russell Adams (Heriot's FP, Edinburgh Accademicals and Scotland Students), Kevin Barrie (Jed-Forest), Craig Brown (London Scottish and Waikato), Vinnie Cunningham (St. Mary's Dublin and Ireland), Bruce Davies (Queensland 'B', Cambridge University and Australia U21), John Fowler (Rosslyn Park and England Students), Andy Holder (Rosslyn Park and London Division), Mike Hutton (Richmond), John Kennedy (St. Mary's Dublin), Oliver Kiely (St. Mary's Dublin, Shannon and Munster), Ronnie Kilpatrick (Jed-Forest and Scotland 'B'), Kenny Lawless (Clontarf), Gordon Lawrie (Heriot's FP, Mussleburgh and Scotland U19), John Morrison (Bristol and England 'B'), Jamie Murphy (Greystones and Landsdowne), Richard Mynott (Swansea and Welsh Students), John Packo (Little Munster), Gary Parker (Melrose), Mark Regan (Bristol and England U21), Aidan White (St. Mary's Dublin), Peter Whitelaw (Heriot's FP and Gala).

Sir Peter Yarranton - The first Penguin RFC player to become President of the Rugby Union (1991-92).

Alan organised a special dinner for the Club Committee in October to mark Sir Peter Yarranton's Presidency of the Rugby Union. In taking up this position, Peter became the first Playing Member of Penguins to hold this high office.

Peter Whitelaw

Peter Whitelaw was a dedicated Penguins player for over a decade who also served on many Penguins tours as Assistant Manager and Coach. He is undoubtably one of the most popular and respected members of Heriot's Rugby Club - a great Club who over the years have provided many gifted players to the Penguins.

1993 CHRONICLE

13th and 14th February 26th Malaysian Rugby Union/COBRA Tens International Tournament, Kuala Lumpur, Malaysia. Captained by David Pickering (Wales).
Penguins beat Singapore 26 - 7
Penguins beat Spain 29 - 5
Penguins beat Durban Harlequins 19 - 0
Penguins beat Old Blues (California) 31 - 0
Penguins beat Papua New Guinea 26 - 12
Penguins beat Fiji (Fijian Army Rugby Club) 20 - 5
Winners, Malaysia RU/COBRA International Tens

22nd February - Penguins beat Cambridge University Past and Present 22 - 18 at Grange Road, Cambridge.

1st May - Irish Rugby Football Union Aer Lingus International Sevens. Captained by Eric Peters (Scotland).

22nd - 23rd May - Italian Rugby Union International Invitation Sevens. Captained by Chris Sheasby (England).
Penguins beat Welsh Water Buffaloes 42 - 5
Penguins beat Netherlands 42 - 7
Penguins beat USA 27 - 12
Penguins beat Zebre 41 - 5
Penguins beat Lupi 33 - 7
Penguins beat Italy 31 - 14
Winners, Italian RU International Sevens

1st - 12th August - Malaysia and Singapore. Captained by Peter Cook (England).
Penguins beat Singapore 91 - 0
Penguins beat Malaysia 40 - 16
Penguins beat Malaysia 24 - 7
Penguins beat Anchorman Invitation XV 44 - 15
Penguins beat Singapore 41 - 0
Penguins beat Combined Singapore Cricket Club/Bucks RFC 48 - 0

10th November - Penguins lost to Oxford University 14 - 52 at Iffley Road, Oxford.

18th November 1993 - Dubai Sevens. Captained by Phil Pask (England).
Penguins lost to New Zealand 17 - 21
Penguins lost to Crawshays 5 - 7
Penguins lost to Roma 7 - 12
Penguins lost to Netherlands 9 - 12

February, 1993 - Penguin RFC's first of many visits to the Malaysia RU/COBRA Tens.

1993

Alan Wright: '1993 was a very busy year for the Club, and it is another "highlight" year - because we were invited to take part in the Malaysian/Combined Old Boys' Rugby Association (more commonly called COBRA) Tens for the first time. In many ways it was a significant date in the history of the Penguins, because, from that day onwards, we've grown closer and closer to Malaysia and the Far East.

'We had been invited following an unfortunate incident involving a participating team the previous year - which had resulted in them being ushered to the airport and sent home.

'The Rugby Union suggested to Tony that we may be able to go there and "fly the flag!" The RU hoped that we would be good ambassadors in a Mohammedan country. And, indeed, so we were.

'The COBRA Tens (which is the world's number one tens tournament) had been going from the late 1960s. The Malaysians invented ten-a-sides in order to provide a game where the caucasian physique would not dominate so much as it does in XVs. So it's played identically to sevens except it's ten-a-side and ten minutes each way.

The Malaysia RU/COBRA Tens

Or, to give it its full title: 'The Malaysian Rugby Union - Combined Old Boys' Rugby Association Tens International Invitation Tournament'. The world's first ten-a-side rugby tournament was held in Malaysia in 1967. The tournament was the brainchild of a number of Combined Old Boys' Rugby Association (COBRA) members. The idea was to create a game that is fast and open but still retains much of the character of the XVs version. In its early years the COBRA Tens was mainly the domain of local clubs and several invited foreign teams, but in 1992 the Tens went fully international. That year Australian champions, Randwick of Sydney, defeated a very strong Marist St. Joseph of Samoa - and for the first time famous players like Lawrence Dallaglio, Phil Kearns and Olo Brown played on Malaysian soil.
Since this first appearance in 1993 the Penguins have played in the Tens many times and have become very close friends of COBRA.
Key COBRA men that Penguins have dealt with over the past 16 years include Zain Yusoff, Nazahudin Bar-Huran, Charlie Wong, Datak Krishnain Tan, Tommy Pereia, Boon Hoon Chee, Faizan Zain and, of course, House Captain Rory Teng - who keeps the refreshments flowing!

Above and right: Two more fine examples from Tony Mason's badge collection.

'The rules have varied. Now they're required to make you play five forwards, but on this particular occasion, the team putting the ball into the scrum could determine the number of forwards that packed down - between three and five.

'We'd not played tens before. We sat in the bar in the hotel where we had a film of the previous year's tens. We were trying to work out the difference in tactics between the sevens and tens. Tens is a very different game - it's more like a one-day cricket match, whereas sevens is like 20/twenty and XVs is like a three-day match.

'We had a fine side which was Captained and coached by David Pickering of Neath and Wales (who would later become the Chairman of the Six Nations Committee). It also included Damian Hopley of Wasps and England (who subsequently became the President of the Professional Player's Union). And we also had Tony Underwood from Leicester. Interestingly, it just so happened that while we were holding our team meeting on that first afternoon, there was a knock on the door and Tony got a telegram to tell him that he was playing for England the next Saturday!'

In what was an extremely strong competition, the Penguins won comfortably in the pool and knock-out stages.

Alan: 'In the final tie the Fijian national team was represented by their Army. No one gave us a chance. But our tackling and place-kicking was absolutely wonderful, and we beat them 20 - 5. It was a terrific win. I even managed to get Tony Mason to have a few drinks that night! And it really cemented our friendship with COBRA. They are the dominating force and energisers of Malaysian rugby. We have stayed firm friends with them ever since that time.'

Craig Brown recalls this of his first trip with the Penguins to the COBRA Tens in Malaysia: 'Tony Mason gave me a call, wanted to know if I was interested in going, which I was! Again, we were just told to meet at the airport at such-and-such a time, such-and-such a day, in a letter that arrived beforehand. We met up at the airport. I knew a couple of the players from London Scottish, didn't really know the rest. The team was captained by David Pickering from Wales, and included two Cambridge University Blues.

1993 Malaysia RU/COBRA Tens programme.

Above: Match action and rest and recreation in Malaysia.

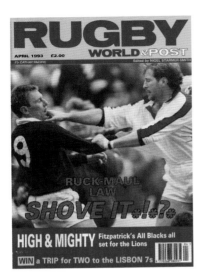

Above and below: Rugby World & Post and the COBRA Tens article.

'Anyway, it was a bit of the unknown, because none of us had ever played tens before. Away we went, flying from London to Kuala Lumpur. We arrived on Thursday night having left the Wednesday evening. We were met at the airport by our liason officer, Naza. He has become a good friend of the Club now - Nazahudin Bar-Huran. He took us to the hotel and explained all about life in Malaysia - the dos-and-don'ts and the protocols and a little bit about the Tournament.

'We stayed at the Crown Princess Hotel with all the other teams. The favourites were Fiji, represented by the Fijian Army squad - ten of their 13 players had played for Fiji so they were a very good side and allegedly had not been beaten at sevens, tens or fifteens for 10 years. The defending champions from the year before, Randwick, from Australia, were also there. They also had a very good team, with Ewan McKenzie and one other player who was in the Australian front-row at the time. They also boasted a host of other players who played for New South Wales/Australia.

'Day one arrived. I think the first game we had was against Singapore. We managed to win that comfortably enough - but it was unbelievably hot - 35 degrees out in the sun! David Pickering was quite smart. He structured the warm-ups each day so that we had a longer one to start with, a shorter one, and then for the last game of day one it was really just "Put your boots on, run down, stretch and on we go!". It all went well and we won all of our games on day one. When we arrived we soon found out that all of the locals understood how the Penguins worked - that is they knew that we all met for the first time at the airport. They didn't think that we'd actually win *any* games on day one... well, perhaps *one* of them. They certainly never imagined that we would make the top eight. They were of the opinion that we'd more than likely be in the bottom eight when it came to the business end of day two of the tournament.

'Anyway, we won our pool, which was great, as we hadn't really known what to expect.

'We then set about day two. Three games coming up. We beat Old Blues comfortably. Then our second game was against Papua New Guinea. We got stuck into them and there was some outstanding play by the likes of Damian Hopley, Martin Haag from Bath and others. We managed to win our way through to the final - it was unbelievable. The guys were laughing and joking about it and saying: "We're not that smart, are we? Because we have to play one extra game - and a longer game - at 15 minutes each way against the Fijians. Who nobody can get close to!"'

At the start of the final against Fiji the Penguins could only muster ten fit men, three of the squad having been injured. However, under the rules of the Tournament help could be sought, and Harry Charalambous and Michael Jorgensen of the Australian Club Randwick were kind enough to become Penguin substitutes.

Alan Wright: 'In the event, we were most appreciative of this very sports-manlike and friendly help when, with some six minutes to go, we were reduced to nine men - although we were leading at that stage by by 17 points to 5. Having lost a centre, Michael Jorgensen went onto the field and played extremely well in the last few minutes, in our colours.

'This Penguins side was a wonderful team and perhaps it's unfair to give any one player particular credit. However, in the final Martin Haag pretty much cleaned up at every lineout - both our ball and theirs. Our place kicking was superb, too - and of course we had tremendous gas in the three wingers, John Kerr, Crawford Henderson and Tony Underwood.'

Craig Brown continues: 'Our game plan was based on close tackling, good kicking and a strong line-out. We said, "Let's just not bother running the ball in all this heat, let's use the boot, get it down there and work from there." Anyway, we went well and we got to half-time having scored two tries to nil and we were leading. The boys were just enjoying it and getting stuck in, and everybody was very focused. And we ended up winning! I think it shocked a lot of people that we'd actually managed to win the tournament and beaten this crack Fijian team in the process. It was a tremendous feeling. We were absolutely exhausted at the end of it, to be honest, having played those three games in those very hot conditions. It was very hard, physical rugby.

'The boys had a pretty good night - Damian Hopley is a master on the piano so we all had a bit of a sing-song. We left for home the next day, back to the UK. It was brilliant. Obviously it was a great team to be part of, a great bunch of men. I think we achieved something quite special for Penguins Rugby in terms of tens, and that really set up the "Tens Love Affair" for the Penguins. We have played an awful lot of tens since that week in 1993 - and done pretty well!'

The tournament results were: Penguins beat Singapore 26 - 7; Penguins beat Spain 29 - 5; Penguins beat Durban Harlequins 19 - 0; Penguins beat Old Blues (USA) 31 - 0. Semi-final: Penguins beat Papua, New Guinea 26 - 12.

Final: Penguins beat Fiji (Fijian Army Rugby Club) 20 - 5. Penguin RFC were the winners of Hui Weng Choon Trophy.

David Pickering and Tony Mason with the Hui Weng Choon Trophy after their unexpected triumph at the 1993 Malaysia RU/COBRA Tens.

This tour produced one of the Club's finest and most prized testimonials. It came in the form of a letter (above) written by Stephen Hilditch to RFU Secretary Dudley Wood. Stephen was one of a number of well-known International Referees that were officiating at the 1993 COBRA Tens. In his reply to this letter, Dudley Wood wrote: I am very grateful for your letter concerning the Malaysian Tens Tournament, and particularly for your reference to the conduct and performance of the Penguin RFC. They certainly did us proud, as they did in India the previous year - and they can now call themselves champions of Malaysia and the Indian Sub-continent!

Penguins - Winners of the COBRA 10s.

Penguins squad: Tony Mason (Tour Manager, players) Alan Wright (Tour Manager, Admin).

David Pickering (Neath and Wales, Captain/Coach), Craig Brown (London Scottish and Waikato), Fanie du Toit (Oxford University and Western Province), Max Duthie (Cambridge University), Luc Evans (Treorchy, Bridgend and Wales), Martin Haag (Bath), Crawford Henderson (London Scottish and Scottish Students), Damian Hopley (Cambridge University, Wasps and England Bench), John Kerr (Haddington, Watsonians and Scotland 'B'), Eric Peters (Cambridge University and England Students), Justin Redrupp (Swansea, Newport and Wales U21), Rob Smith (Boroughmuir), Tony Underwood (Cambridge University and Leicester).

David Pickering

David Pickering was born on 16th December, 1960. He won 23 caps for Wales between 1983 and 1987 and Captained the national team on eight occasions. He played club rugby for Llanelli RFC and Neath RFC.

After the end of his playing career David went on to coach Neath RFC for five years before becoming Team Manager of the Wales 'A' team, and subsequently the Welsh national team.

He took over as Welsh team manager during the Graham Henry era of the late 1990s. His appointment in 1998 saw him in place as Wales went on an eleven-match unbeaten run which included their first win over South Africa.

He managed the team through the 1999 World Cup (which was hosted by Wales) before stepping down to be replaced by Alan Phillips in 2002.

David succeeded Glanmor Griffiths as Chairman of the WRU in 2003. Since then he has overseen two Grand Slam campaigns and a turnaround in financial terms from the troubles that saw the Celtic Warriors disbanded in 2004. David's tenure with the WRU has seen the Union reduce debts by up to £30 million.

He was elected to replace Frenchman Jacques Laurans as head of the Six Nations committee in May 2008. Pickering was elected for a three-year term, making him one of the most senior administrators in world rugby.

On Wednesday, 10th November, just over a week after their COBRA Tens triumph in Malaysia, the Penguins were back in England at a dark and cold Grange Road where Cambridge University Past and Present were beaten in a close match, by 22 points to 18.

Interestingly and coincidentally, Bedford RFC's Pavel Berwin (who played at stand-off half for the Penguins in this match) formerly played for the Russian National side. Pavel is the brother of Leonid Berwin, who was in the Soviet side that played against Penguins in the Eastern European Inter-Nations Championship

in Tblisi, Georgia, in 1977.

The Penguins side for this match also included the brilliant Dave Scully, the English fireman who was part of the England Sevens squad that won the 1993 Sevens World Cup.

Penguins squad: Tony Mason (Match Manager).
Peter Cook (Nottingham and England Bench, Captain), Paul Alston (Bedford), Brian Barley (Wakefield and England), Dave Barnett (Rosslyn Park), Pavel Berwin (Bedford and Russia), Spencer Bromley (Rugby and Northern Division), Dave Curry (Rosslyn Park and England Students), Neil Donovan (London Irish), Diccan Edwards (Wakefield), Nick Fielden (Northampton), John Fowler (Rosslyn Park and England Students), Crawford Henderson (London Scottish and Scottish Students), Ray Hennessey (London Irish), Graham Peacock (London Welsh), Mark Rennel (Bedford), Dave Scully (Wakefield).

On 1st May the Penguins took part in the Irish RFU Aer Lingus International Sevens. Tony Mason had two players drop out the day before flying out, and asked Ian Bullerwell to help. Ian brought in Paul Alston and Mark Rennell from Bedford, and also went along on the tour to assist Tony. The Penguins were Captained by Eric Peters and the squad also included Audley Lumsden from Bath. Penguins were expected to make the final of the tournament, but were knocked out in the quarter-finals after making several uncharacteristic mistakes.

Tony Jarman, a former 1st XV team mate of Tony Mason and Alan Wright at Sidcup and a Penguin enthusiast since the Club's foundation in 1959, accepted an invitation to join the Committee this year as Hon. Press and Public Relations Secretary. He also took over the Penguin International Ticket Service.

Following the Club's successful participation in the 1991 event when they lost to Fiji in the final, Penguins were invited by the Federazione Italiana Rugby to play in the fourth Italian Rugby Union International Invitation Sevens Tournament, held in Catania, Sicily on 22nd and 23rd May.

Previous winners included Fiji in 1991 and Namibia in 1992, at a time when the tournament was part of the preliminary rounds of the World Cup Sevens. In 1993 teams from as far apart as the Ukraine and the United States were taking part - the latter fielding one of the stronger sides.

Tony and Alan selected a very strong side, Captained by Chris Sheasby of Harlequins and England Sevens, and including Mark Thomas of the Welsh Sevens squad plus two other real flyers on the wing - Rugby's Spencer Bromley and Harlequins' Everton Davis.

Dave Scully, England Sevens World Cup Winner.

Glasgow-born back-row forward Eric Peters (Cambridge University RUFC, England Students and England U21) also played for Saracens, Bath, Harlequins, Fylde, Rotherham and Connacht. He chose to play international rugby for Scotland, for whom he won 29 caps at no.8.

Chris Sheasby - Harlequins and England Sevens.

The United States VII gave the Club one of their toughest games in the last of their pool matches, but apart from this the formidable Penguins VII won all of their other matches comfortably.

In the final against the Italian National VII, the Penguins dominated from the start. Mark Thomas scored from the kick-off, followed by Everton Davis (who scored twice) and Gary Parker to bring the score to 26 - 0 after five minutes of the second half. Penguins tired towards the end and let the Italians in for two tries before Chad Lion-Cachet, Captain of Oxford University at the time, delivered the final blow, crossing the Italian line to bring the final score to 31 - 14. It was a marvellous win and the Penguins' second major tournament triumph of the year.

The full results were: Pool games: Penguins beat Welsh Water Buffaloes 42 - 5, Penguins beat Netherlands 42 - 7, Penguins beat USA 27 - 12. Quarter-final: Penguins beat Zebre 41 - 5. Semi-final: Penguins beat Lupi 33 - 7. Final: Penguins beat Italy 31 - 14. Penguins became the 1993 Italian Rugby Union International Sevens Champions.

Penguins squad:

Tony Mason (Team Manager, players), Alan Wright (Team Manager, Admin), Tony Jarman (Hon. Press and PR Secretary). Chris Sheasby (Harlequins and England Sevens, Captain), Spencer Bromley (Rugby and Northern Division), Everton Davis (Harlequins and England 'B'), Nick Knowles (Northampton), Chad Lion-Cachet (Oxford University and South African Universities), Gary Parker (Melrose and Scottish Southern Districts), Phil Pask (Northampton and East Midlands), Andy Purves (Melrose and Scottish Southern Districts), Martyn Steffert (Northampton and New Zealand Universities), Mark Thomas (Rosslyn Park and Wales Sevens).

Between 1st and 12th August the Penguins were once again in the Far East - on their second Asia Tour, once again sponsored by Cathay Pacific Airways.

The first challenge was a three-match triangular tournament with Malaysia and Singapore U23s. The Penguins then played the Anchorman Invitation XV before playing two more matches in Singapore.

Page 62

RUGGER/Friendly

WANNA DANCE?: Penguins' Rob Subbiani (with ball) ready to side-step a Singaporean player during a friendly yesterday.

PENGUINS IN MEAN MOOD

IT was not their best but still Penguins of England thrashed Singapore 91-0 in a friendly at Padang Merbok yesterday. They could have even hit the century mark if they were sharper with their conversions.

Penguins, who led 34-0 at halftime, scored eight goals and five tries.

The Singaporeans, on Saturday, were beaten 24-0 by Malaysia.

Leading the cast for Penguins in their riot yesterday were winger Rob Subbiani and centre John Kennedy who executed five tries each.

What made it more interesting Subbiani and Kennedy executed most of their tries from delightful and speedy runs from their own half. The Singaporeans just could not do anything to stop them.

Penguins, with the services of Scotland and Wales internationals, simply proved that they were in a 'different dimension' altogether compared with Singapore.

The international in the side were Luc Evans (Wales), Mark Moncrieff (Scotland), Rodney Pow (Scotland) and under-21 internationals Ken O'Connell of Ireland and under-21 Scottish international David McGavin.

Penguins, who won the MRU-Cobra International 10s early this year, were obviously better in every department yesterday.

Ball-handling, forwards, backline, techniques, skills and you name it.

Penguins will play Malaysia at the same venue tomorrow. — **MUSTAPHA KAMARUDDIN**

The results of these six matches were:

1st to 5th August: Triangular tournament with Malaysia and Singapore U23: Penguins beat Singapore 91 - 0; Penguins beat Malaysia 40 - 16; Penguins beat Malaysia 24 - 7.

7th August: Penguins beat Anchorman Invitation XV 44 - 15.

10th to 12th August: Penguins beat Singapore 41 - 0; Penguins beat Combined Singapore Cricket Club/Bucks RFC 48 - 0.

Penguins squad:

Tony Mason (Tour Manager), Tony Jarman (Hon. PR and Press Secretary). Peter Whitelaw (Heriot's FP, Edinburgh District, Player/Coach). Peter Cook (Nottingham, Midland and Northern Divisions, Barbarians and England Reserve, Captain), Gary Abraham (Rosslyn Park), Paul Allen (Bedford), Keith Amos (Selkirk and South of Scotland), Kent Bray (Oxford University, Harlequins and New South Wales), Craig Brown (Watsonians and Scottish Exiles), Luc Evans (Bridgend, Bedford, Barbarians and Wales), John Kennedy (St. Mary's Dublin), Nick Knowles (Northampton), Dominic Malone (Bedford), Leigh Mansell (Bedford and East Midlands), David McGavin (Bedford and Scotland U21), Mark Moncrieff (Gala and Scotland Sevens), Jamie Murphy (Greystones), Ken O'Connell (Sundays Well, Munster, Ireland U21 and Ireland 'B'), Rodney Pow (Selkirk, South of Scotland and Scotland Sevens), Adam Reuben (Birmingham/Solihull), John Robertson (Heriot's FP, Edinburgh), Rowan Shepherd (Edinburgh Academicals and Scottish Students), Martyn Steffert (Northampton and Waikato), Peter Stevens (Heriot's FP, Edinburgh District and Scotland), Rob Subbiani (Bedford and Welsh Students), Chris Turnbull (Heriot's FP), Matthew Wright (Northampton and English Universities), Dominic Wyer-Roberts (Bedford).

On 10th November the Penguins travelled to Iffley Road, Oxford, to play Oxford University. The Penguins squad, which was managed by Tony Mason and Captained by Phil Pask of Northampton, included Spencer Bromley (Rugby), Craig Brown and Crawford Henderson (both London Scottish).

The Club's new Hon. Press and PR Secretary, Tony Jarman, wrote at the time: *It was a delight to renew acquaintance with the Varsity. However, a bare three weeks before their Twickenham appearance, they were too strong for a Penguins line-up which had been depleted by the Courage League calls of the Senior Clubs.* Oxford won 52 - 14.

RUGBY

CLOSE ENCOUNTER ... Stand-off Asmawi Bujang grapples for the ball with a Penguin player at padang merbuk yesterday. — Pic: JOHARI EMBI

Penguins coast to another win

MALAYSIA 16 PENGUINS 40

PENGUINS of England got their first good session of rugby after a three-day wait, with this emphatic win over the national team in the last match of the Sukom '98 Anniversary tournament.

Never mind the scoreline. Unlike the Singaporeans who went home humiliated 91-0 by this motley squad of players, the young Malaysians showed a lot promise and spirit.

Malaysia scored three penalties through Idris Che Long (3rd, 34th) and Fauzi Jamil (20th). Fauzi also made a try in late second half.

Winger Rob Subbiani was again in an uncompromising mood, scoring three tries and paving the way for his teammates in the others.

The visitors play the national team again tomorrow before winding up their tour here with a match against Anchorman on Saturday.

Above and far left: Newspaper reports of the Penguins' unbeaten tour of the Far East in August.

Another first - the Club travelled to Dubai in November.

Phil Pask Captained the Penguins at the Dubai Sevens Tournament.

On 18th November Tony Mason took a hastily assembled squad, Captained by Northampton's Phil Pask, to the Dubai Sevens as a late entry. Because of the domestic calendar it was only possible for the players to arrive in Dubai the night before the competition started. Sadly, this was not a tour in which fortune favoured the brave.

Alan: 'Unfortunately we didn't progress very well. The team that we sent to play in Dubai ran into no end of bad luck, with injuries coming out of their ears. It was rather sad, really - it was a good team and they lost by some very close scores. Oh well. C'est la vie - you win some, you lose some!'

The competition results were: Pool A: Penguins lost to New Zealand 17 - 21, Penguins lost to Crawshays Welsh 5 - 7, Penguins lost to Roma 7 - 12. Plate competition: Penguins lost to Netherlands 9 - 12.

Phil Pask

Phil Pask was born 14th March, 1960 and educated at the University of Birmingham (BA Physical Education, Graduate Certificate of Education), Queen Elizabeth School of Physiotherapy (Graduate Diploma in Physiotherapy) and the Manchester Metropolitan University (MSc. Physiotherapy and Sports Injury), ACPSM Gold Level.

Playing career: Birmingham University, Worksop RFC, East Midlands 1987 - 94, Notts, Lincs & Derbyshire 1988 - 89, Penguins 1993 - 97, Northampton Saints 1st XV 1986 - 95. England Sevens 1994.

Post playing: 1994 - 2003 Northampton Saints Physiotherapist. 1997 to date - England Rugby Physiotherapist, including World Cup winning side 2003 and 2007 Finalists. 2005 to date - British and Irish Lions Physiotherapist New Zealand and South Africa Tours.

Phil: 'My time with the Penguins as a player - and my association with them since - is one of those extraordinary things. I have been priviliged to play with, and become friends of, some remarkable people, including Wayne 'Buck' Shelford, Tim Rodber, Martin Johnson, Jason Leonard... the list goes on and on! I have also met some remarkable organisers along the way, like Alan Wright and Tony Mason. Remarkable rugby men who gave players like Harvey Thorneycroft, Paul Alston and myself from Northampton Saints the chance to play rugby worldwide in enviroments and competitions we would not normally experience.

'I have been privileged through my profession and my enthusiasm for the game to continue to work with some of the finest rugby players and people you could wish to meet. And through my work with England and the British Lions I am continually bumping into past and present Penguins. I was particularly pleased during the 2009 Lions to South Africa Tour to see the work done by Craig Brown and the HSBC Penguin Coaching Academy in conjunction with the SARU.

Being a Director of the Club, I still have a strong association with Northampton Saints - and I feel comfortable in the knowledge that other young players from the Club may be afforded the same opportunities as I through the continued work of the Penguin International Rugby Football Club.'

1994

'OUR GLORIOUS YEAR'

1994 was the Penguins' 'Glorious Year' in which the Penguins won every tournament they entered. The highlights of the year were undoubtedly the retention of the two major trophies won by the Club in 1993 - the Malaysian Rugby Union/COBRA Tens and the Federatzione Italiana International Sevens.

The return to Kuala Lumpur in January to defend the Malaysian/COBRA Tens title which Penguins won at the first attempt the previous year was, initially, frought with problems. No fewer than seven of the originally selected squad of thirteen were unable to travel due to international selection and league commitments. Nevertheless some excellent last-minute replacements were destined to prove highly effective.

Craig Brown recalls: 'As had happened the year before, we all received a letter of selection from Alan and Tony. We weren't told who else was going. We got to Heathrow to find that quite a few people had pulled out on the lead up to the trip.

'So there we were at the airport. I met all the players and Tony just walked up to me and asked me if I'd be the Captain. I was a bit surprised, actually, I hadn't thought about that at all. I was just looking forward to going on the trip and doing my bit for the Penguins and playing as hard as I could! Obviously I accepted - I thought it was a great honour. But it changed the whole character of the trip for me, because all of a sudden I had to think in a different way. I had to lead. Maybe I also put a bit more effort into getting to know the players on the way over!

'We left on a Wednesday night and we got into Kuala Lumpur at about 6pm on the Thursday. I remember that as we came through customs and immigration there were all these lights and camera crews. As Captain I had to give an interview, and I think Tony gave an interview as well. So that certainly got the players tuned in to what the whole trip was going to be about.

'We then made our way to the Crown Princess Hotel, where we were staying. After we had checked in I said: "Well guys, as your Captain I think we should all go for a walk and have a look around." Team bonding, basically!

'The next day, Friday, we had training scheduled. That first training was pretty bad to be honest - a few of the men were suffering from lack of sleep and jet-lag, so the training was pretty abysmal. So I told them that they should all go back and get some sleep, and that we'd go out again and train in the afternoon.

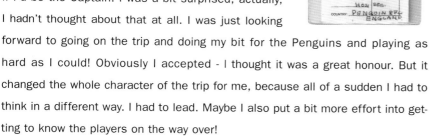

MRU/COBRA 1994 plaque.

1994 CHRONICLE

20th - 24th January - 27th Malaysian Rugby Union/COBRA Tens International Tournament, Kuala Lumpur, Malaysia. Captained by Craig Brown (New Zealand).
Penguins beat Singapore 50 - 0
Penguins beat Korea 26 - 0
Penguins lost to Ponsonby (New Zealand) 6 - 8
Penguins beat South Africa Violets 22 - 0
Penguins beat Kobe Steel 17 - 10
Penguins beat Western Samoa 21 - 17
Winners, Malaysia RU/COBRA International Tens

23rd February - Penguins lost to Cambridge University 18 - 30 at Grange Road, Cambridge.

13th May - Penguins 35th Anniversary Grand Reunion Dinner at the Dorchester Hotel.

20th - 28th August - Tour to Sweden and Denmark. Captained by Rob Wainwright (Scotland).

20th August - Scandinavian Stockholm Tens:
Penguins beat Stockholm Exiles 10 - 0
Penguins beat Fredriksburg 47 - 5
Penguins beat Ensköping 35 - 0
Penguins beat Pingvins 21 - 0
Penguins beat Frölunda 46 - 0
Penguins beat Riga Select 31 - 0
Penguins beat President's X 8 - 7
Winners, Scandinavian International Tens

23rd August - Penguins beat Sweden at Ensköping 62 - 20

25th August - Penguins beat Pingvin RC at Trellesborg 64 - 18

28th August - Nordic Sevens, Copenhagen:
Penguins beat Nordic Select 21 - 5
Penguins beat VEM Prenza (Moscow) 50 - 5.
Winners, Nordic Sevens

29th - 30th September - Fifth Italian Rugby Union International Invitation Sevens in Sicily. Captained by Craig Brown (New Zealand).
Penguins beat Sweden 40 - 0
Penguins lost to Naples Select 18 - 24
Penguins beat Roma Police 34 - 0
Penguins beat Sicily Select 35 - 7
Winners, Italian RU International Sevens

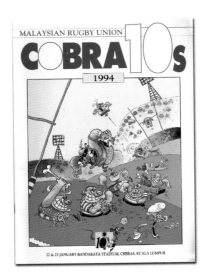

1994 Malaysian Rugby Union/ COBRA Tens Souvenir Tournament Programme.

Tony Mason presides over the traditional pre-tournament evening meal in Kuala Lumpur.

Ponsonby Rugby Football Club - 'A good one to lose!'

'We went back out later and it was a lot better. Everybody was a bit tired that Friday night, but well tuned-in, you know, because all the teams were arriving at the hotel. And you meet the odd person you know and everyone's looking and saying: "Who does he play for?" or "Where does he come from?" There's a buzz about the place. It's very exciting.

'So come Saturday, day one, there were three games in the pool we were in. We won the first game easily enough, the second one was a bit harder but then we went into the third one and we lost by two tries to one. This was against Ponsonby, a top New Zealand club team. It was close. Basically we sort of changed tactics a bit in this game. We thought that we'd have to match their big forwards so we went for a different style of play.'

Alan Wright takes up the story: 'We had a very good side, but we had lighter forwards. After the first two matches - against Singapore and Korea - we had already won promotion to the quarter-final. We were guaranteed to be in the last eight because in all of these tournaments it is the top two from each pool that go through - the teams that come second always play the winners from the other pool.

'We had the third match of our pool to play. I looked carefully at the card and if we were to win it we would be in the half of the draw with all the big forwards and if we lost it we'd be in the half with all the lighter, faster forwards.

'I whispered to Tony - and this is the only time I ever said this to him in all the years we knew each other: "Pop, this would be a good match to lose." He said: "Don't let anyone hear you say that!" Well, the match was against Ponsonby, the champion club of Auckland. We were leading them by six points to three when, by a sheer chance, the referee allowed a forward pass right under our noses and they beat us 8 - 6!'

At the time, however, Craig Brown knew nothing of Alan's comment. Craig: 'On reflection, finishing second in our pool actually put us into the side of the draw with all the smaller sized, quicker teams - which we were. Ponsonby went into the other side of the draw with the Canadian and American teams - who had huge forwards. So in some ways it worked out to our benefit. We made our way through the quarter-final and semi-final - close games with some great individual skill from people who scored very important tries when we needed them.'

Alan: 'So there we were in the half of the draw with our light, mobile forwards. And we were lighter and more mobile than all of our opponents.

'We had some 'hairy' matches to make the final, playing a very strong South African squad and Kobe Steel Rugby Club - a team which included many of the Japanese National side.'

Craig: 'We made it to the final and played against the Samoan National Ten. They had selected six internationals in their squad, including the formidable Junior Paramour. The team was a fluent and highly-drilled side who had reached the final without losing a game.

'They were typical Samoans - big lads who hit hard. I remember at one stage Gareth Rees got absolutely pole-axed in a tackle - and the look on his face, searching for breath as he lay on the ground, made me smile a bit! But he got up and carried on!

'It was a great performance. We somehow managed to win 21 - 17. It was a great effort all-round from everybody - we got some points on the board and then we had to really dig deep and defend.'

At the time Tony Jarman wrote of the final: *It brought together two sides of contrasting styles. In their 21 - 17 victory it was clear that Penguins had the edge at half-back with the Oxford University half-back pairing of Fanie du Toit and Gareth Rees performing brilliantly and delivering quick ball to the strong running and tackling outsides John Kerr, Jason Keytor, Crawford Henderson and Spencer Bromley. And it was Bromley's brilliant diagonal run to score in the second half that broke the Western Samoa's hearts.*

Alan: 'It was a most dramatic final against the Samoan national team. The score was 21 - 17 to us with three and a half minutes to go. They were camped in our 22 but they didn't score again. We held them out with first-class tackling. It was a wonderful win. So we had back-to-back wins in the Malaysian RU/COBRA Tens. We're very proud of that.'

Craig Brown celebrates what must rank as one of the Penguins' finest-ever victories.

Pictures from the MRU/COBRA Tens.

Craig Brown holds aloft the Hui Weng Choon Trophy after Penguins beat the mighty Western Samoans in the final.

Les Jackson

Alan: 'Les Jackson was a last-minute selection to play in the centre for us in the COBRA 10s. He was a Super-Heavyweight boxer who was a giant in stature and weight. Indeed, whilst playing for Wasps Vandals in England, no member of an opposing team had been able to stop him from scoring if he received the ball from less than 50 yards out. Les was so big that the entire COBRA Tens crowd stood and applauded everytime he appeared!'

Craig: 'Yes - it was huge. A year before, in 1993, they had no idea who the Penguins were, but understood that we were an 'invitation' club who all met at the airport on the way over. So they didn't even think we'd make the cup round - let alone win the thing. So to win it again, back-to-back in '94, was huge.'

Tony Mason had this to say about the Penguins' magnificent win: '...it was an epic, bruising game. We used exactly the same tactics that were successful last year against the Fijians, namely hassle, bustle, pressure and tackle them out of the game. My boys did just that. The Samoans did not like it as they had come to the final after having swamped a strong Ponsonby team 27 - 3 and were red-hot favourites. We gave a very gritty display and did not wilt under their aggression.'

The full results were: Pool games: Penguins beat Singapore 50 - 0, Penguins beat Korea 26 - 0, Penguins lost to Ponsonby 6 - 8. Quarter-final: Penguins beat South African Violets 22 - 0. Semi-final: Penguins beat Kobe Steel 17 - 10. Final: Penguins beat Western Samoa 21 - 17. Penguins won the Hui Weng Choon Trophy, back-to-back.

Craig: 'The Malaysian Rugby Union/COBRA Tens was a great result for the Club. It really got us into the swing of tens rugby. A couple of good wins like that and people are looking and thinking: "...well, these guys are doing something right when it comes to tens!" It was a fantastic tour. The Penguins had a great evening after winning, and we all headed home happy chappies on Monday night!'

Penguins squad:

Tony Mason (Chairman and Manager), Alan Wright (Hon. Secretary), Tony Jarman (Hon. Press and PR Secretary), Ken Russell (Vice-President).

Craig Brown (London Scottish, Captain), Spencer Bromley (Rugby), Stewart Burns (Blackheath), Bruce Donald (Northampton), Crawford Henderson (London Scottish), Les Jackson (Wasps), John Kerr (Watsonians), Jason Keyter (Harlequins), Andrew Metcalfe (Wakefield), Phil Pask (Northampton), Gareth Rees (Oxford University), Mark Sowerby (Wakefield), Fanie du Toit (Oxford University).

Post-tournament celebrations. 'The Penguins had a great evening after winning, and we all headed home happy chappies on Monday night!'

The Malaysian press reports on the Penguins' magnificent achievement on January 24th - the day after the final.

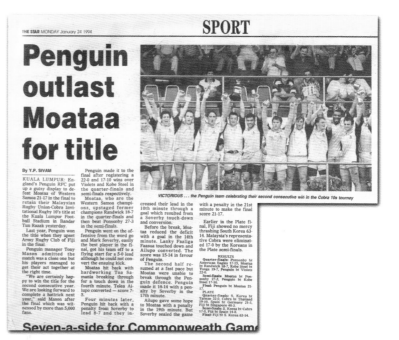

Page 82

The Malay Mail, Monday, January 24, 1994

Mail SPORT

RUGGER/ MRU-Cobra International 10s

Aussie Williams goes Japanese

FORMER Wallaby Ian Williams is looking forward to showing his skills again for champions Japan in the Asian Rugby Football Union (ARFU) championships in October in Kuala Lumpur.

The 30-year-old winger yesterday helped Kobe Steel RFC to a semifinals berth in the MRU-Cobra International Invitational 10s at KLFA Stadium yesterday.

Not many expected Kobe to reach the semifinals as they were up against the powerful Vava'u RFU of Tonga in the quarterfinals.

But Kobe stunned the Tongans 19-7 to meet eventual champions Penguins RFC of England in the semifinals.

Kobe were beaten 17-10 but not before a good fight.

Said Williams: "I would love to play for Japan and return to KL for the ARFU championships."

Williams entertained the fans with his delightful and tricky runs and should not have a problem making the Japanese team.

Williams made his debut for Japan in a Test match against Wales in October.

"As for the Cobra 10s, I am pleasantly surprised we managed to make the semifinals. We never aimed this high," said Williams, who played alongside Wallaby star David Campese in the World Cup.

CHAMPS AGAIN: Penguins RFC of England players show off their spoils after retaining the MRU-Cobra International 10s title yesterday.

WELL DONE, LADS

By MUSTAPHA KAMARUDDIN

IT was an evening to cherish for Penguins RFC of England's skipper Craig Brown and his band of men as they retained the MRU-Cobra International Invitational 10s at KLFA Stadium yesterday.

The Penguins tasted glory again after breaking the hearts of exciting Moataa

Penguins retain title with exciting win

RFC of Western Samoa with a hard-earned 21-17 win in the final.

"I am happy we managed to win the title for the second consecutive year. I must tell you it was tough down there.

"The Samoans were pretty good and luckily we managed to hold them back," said Brown, skippering the team the first time.

Space

Brown said their game-plan was to tackle a lot to break the tricky Samoans' rhythm.

"This proved fruitful as the Samoans did not have much space to do their normal running," said the 28-year-old Brown, a software engineer, who also has the credit of playing in New Zealand with Waikataa.

Brown said overall the competition was much tougher this time as there

GOING STRONG: A charging Craig Brown of the Penguins in the thick of action yesterday in the MRU-Cobra International 10s final against Moataa. Penguins won 21-17.

were several strong teams like Ponsonby RFC of New Zealand, the American Eagles and Violets.

Penguins scored a goal, a try and three penalties while Moataa replied

through two goals and a try.

One of the heroes for Penguins was Canadian international Garath Rees.

Rees, a last minute inclusion, contributed 16 points

from a try, three penalties and a conversion.

Penguins' other try was executed by Mark Somerby.

Penguins: Bruce Donald, Mark Somerby, Craig Brown, Phil Pask, Stephanus Du Toit, Garath Rees, John Kerr, Spencer Bromley, Jason Keyter, Crawford Henderson.

Substitute: Leslie Jackson.

Moataa: Faaliga Faasua, Herman Retzlaff, Asofa Penu, Fereti Faasua, Junior Paramore, Mose Galuvao, Anetelea Aiolupo, Toa Samania, Too Vaega, Tagiilima Vaeau.

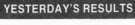

ALL TIED UP: Penguins' Garath Rees (in black) tackles a Moataa player in the final yesterday.   Picture: Khalid Redeza

YESTERDAY'S RESULTS

Cup Q-finals: Ponsonby bt American Eagles 17-15; Moataa bt Randwick 18-7; Kobe Steel bt tonga 19-7; Penguins bt Violets 22-0.

Semifinals: Moataa bt Ponsonby 27-3; Penguins bt Kobe Steel 17-10.

Final: Penguins bt Moataa 21-17.

Plate Q-finals: Korea bt Taiwan 22-0; Cobra bt Thailand 19-10; Spain bt Germany 21-3; Nabua bt Singapore 40-3.

Semifinals: Korea bt Cobra 19-10; Nabua bt Spain 14-8.

Final: Nabua bt Korea 63-14.

The annual match against Cambridge University Past and Present was played on Wednesday, 23rd February at Grange Road, Cambridge.

Penguins lost the match by 18 points to 30. The score may well have been closer but unfortunately three of the Club's players had been delayed until 30 minutes into the first half by a fire on the London to Cambridge railway line!

Penguins squad: Tony Mason (Chairman and Manager).

Bill Calcraft (Manly and Australia, Captain), Craig Brown (London Scottish), Stuart Burns (Blackheath), Fran Clough (Wasps), Neil Donovan (London Irish), Crawford Henderson (London Scottish), Mark Howe (Bedford), Ian Hunter (Northampton), Leigh Mansell (Bedford), Phil Pask (Northampton), Gareth Rees (Oxford University), Steve Shortland (Wasps), Charlie Simpson (Bedford), Brett Taylor (Northampton), Harvey Thorneycroft (Northampton).

On Friday, 13th May, Penguins celebrated their 35th anniversary with another Anniversary Dinner and Grand Reunion at the Dorchester Hotel.

Alan: 'I am a great fan of the Dorchester. It's not got the biggest room in London (Grosvenor House is much bigger, and so is the Hilton), but I think that going to the Dorchester gives the Club Dinner and Reunion a special "buzz". And in the main, the object of the evening is not to raise money, as most dinners are. The object is to have a reunion - to get together as many of our former players from Ireland, Scotland, Wales, and sometimes New Zealand, Fiji and Australia as possible.'

Over 550 people attended the 1994 event, including such luminaries as Club President (and former RFU President) Air Commodore Bob Weighill, Dudley Wood (Secretary of the Rugby Union), Sir Denis Thatcher (in his role of Life Vice-President of the London Society of Rugby Football Union Referees), Mickey Steele-Bodger from the Barbarian Football Club, Mickey Quinn (Lansdowne, Leinster and Ireland) and the Right Hon. Sir Edward Heath.

Alan tells the following amusing story about Sir Edward Heath and Lord Brockwell: 'Well, we've only had the one Prime Minister as a member of the Penguins - Sir Edward Heath. He has made speeches at our Grand Reunion Anniversary Dinners on the three occasions that he has attended (1984, 1989 and at this one in 1994) - and he was very witty and very popular.

I once mentioned to a friend, one of our great Honorary Vice-Presidents, Robin Butler (Lord Brockwell, one-time Cabinet Secretary and a President of Oxford University RFC), that "Ted Heath speaks very well and is very amusing". Robin responded with a humorous smile: "Well, Alan, he should be because I used to write his speeches."...Shades of "Yes Prime Minister"!'

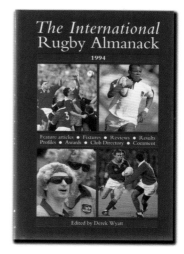

The International Rugby Almanack is a hardback book which first appeared on the bookshelves in 1994. It was edited by Derek Wyatt. In it he wrote, under the heading 'Ninety-Six Clubs plus Four Unusual Sides':
If there was a vote by players the world over for the most popular club, the result would be the Penguins RFC. The odd thing about this lot is, except for very rare occasions and usually for charity, they only play outside the UK.
As a consequence, few readers will have heard of them. Formed over 30 years ago by Tony Mason and Alan Wright, they have trod where very few rugby clubs, provincial sides or even international XVs have wanted to go.
Tony Mason has the uncanny knack, some call it talent, of selecting players from around the world before their own national selectors were aware of their abilities - Maurice Colclough and Ollie Campbell to the USSR in 1977, Stuart Evans to Brazil in 1984, Andy Nicol to Calcutta in 1990, David Millard, Gary Parker, Chris Sheasby and Eric Peters in 1992 and '93 to points everywhere. The Penguins really ought to be adopted by the Lord's Taverners as their world-wide ambassadors and Twickenham should reward them by giving them the last fixture of an incoming tour.

Robin Butler, Lord Brockwell.

Photographs from the Penguins' 35th Anniversary Dinner and Grand Reunion at the Dorchester in London.
Top row, left to right: Alan Wright, Dennis Thatcher, Tony Mason and John Morgan; Bob Weighill speaks; Alan Wright and Bob Weighill.
Main picture: Ted Heath makes his speech. Bottom row, left to right: Alan Wright, Chris Rea, Ian Robertson and Bob Weighill;
Mick Quinn speaks; Ian Robertson, Steve Smith, Tony Neary and Nick Martin.

The August 1994 Denmark and Sweden tour was remarkable inasmuch as it was the first tour that the Penguins undertook in which they played all of the recognised versions of rugby union football. In a nine-day period the Club played in the Stockholm Tens, then played two games of XVs (one against the Swedish national team and the other against the Pingvins Rugby Club in Trelleborg) and then completed the tour by winning in the Nordic Sevens Tournament in Copenhagen.

It was also a nostalgic occasion for Tony Mason and Alan Wright, who hadn't toured Sweden since 1964. Alan: 'This was Tony's last tour of Scandinavia. He was Tour Manager. The background of this tour was that I realised that we were both getting old (bearing in mind that I was 64 and Tony was 76 at this time). I said to him: "These great friends of ours in Sweden have a club that is nearly as old as ours. Don't you think, while we're both still alive, we ought to go and play them?" So the principal reason for going to Sweden and Denmark was to play the Pingvin Rugby Club (the only club in the world to be named after us) in Trelleborg, Sweden - because the men who founded it were still alive and we were very close to them.

'And then I said to Tony: "The only other tens competition that is worth playing in Europe is the Stockholm Tens - let's have a tilt at that while we're there." Then we arranged a match against the Swedish national team. Tony made Rob Wainwright Tour Captain. Rob is a delightful man, who had, of course, first played for us in the 1988 Hong Kong Sevens.

'Well, Scandinavia was a wonderful tour. Tony took a big gamble. We played all of these matches with no locks (we relied on having big no.8s in the second row for the Tens or the XVs matches). Our last port of call was to go on to Copenhagen and play in the Scandinavian Sevens.

'We started off by winning the Stockholm Tens. The other teams in the Stockholm Tens included our friends the Pingvins, plus Riga Select (the best players of Riga and Latvia), Warblers RFC (an invitational club first formed in Bahrain in 1981 and run along similar lines to the Penguins), one of Craig's former Clubs, London Scottish, and The President's X (a star-studded squad which was made up of five Bath and England players and ten top Swedish players who had been selected by the Swedish National Coach. The Bath players included the England Captain Phil De Glanville and his fellow England international, Jonathan Callard).

'The final was a very dramatic match against The President's X, in which we were winning until the last couple of minutes. We were leading 5 - 0, and with two minutes to go they scored under our posts and converted, and we were losing 5 - 7. There was a minute to go and we were awarded a penalty after

The Penguins once again found the time to visit their great friends - Wolfgang Österling of the Pingvins, and Eigil Lund, founder of the Danish Rugby Union.

Winners of the Stockholm Tens. Rob Wainwright holds the cup.

Plaque commemorating the Penguins v Sweden match of 23rd August.

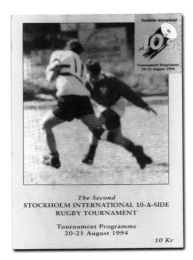

Stockholm Tens Tournament Programme.

Nordic Sevens Programme.

'The Battle of the Penguins' Programme.

Craig 'wrapped up' one of the opposition, thus preventing him from passing. The referee awarded us a penalty for non-release of the ball after a tackle! Luc Evans kicked it and we won by 8 points to 7!

'Incidentally - our team was very Gaelic. And England had beaten Scotland quite narrowly not too long before, so the boys really enjoyed this win against a team that included so many England internationals!'

Alan continues: 'We then played two XVs matches. First, we overcame the Swedish national team in Ensköping. The Swedes were strong in the forwards but not so organised in the backs. They performed well in the first half until persistent pressure from the Penguins broke their defence. In the second half it became clear that we had too strong a combination, and Penguins ran out winners by 62 points to 20.

'Two days later we had a wonderful game against the Pingvins Club, who had been League and Cup Champions of Sweden that year. Craig Brown was our Captain for this match. We were received with generosity and open arms.'

Tony Jarman later wrote of this happy occasion: *Wonderfully welcomed and feted for our three-day visit, a winning score of 64 - 18 seemed a churlish way to repay such hospitality - yet once again the style of our play won the hearts of our hosts, and the evening reception, attended by our President Bob Weighill (who made a special visit), proved that it is not always the score that matters.*

Alan Wright: 'Finally, we went to Copenhagen and we beat the champion club of Moscow in the final of the Nordic Sevens Tournament - so we had a wonderful, unbeaten tour.'

Scandinavian Tour Results:

Stockholm Tens - 20th and 21st August.

20th August: Penguins beat Stockholm Exiles 10 - 0, Penguins beat Fredriksburg Netherlands 47 - 5, Penguins beat Ensköping 35 - 0.

21st August: Penguins beat Pingvins 21 - 0, Penguins beat Frölunda 46 - 0, Semi-final: Penguins beat Riga Select 31 - 0.

Final: Penguins beat President's X 8 - 7.

XVs Matches:

23rd August - Penguins beat Sweden 62 - 20.

25th August - Penguins beat Pingvin RC Trelleborg 64 - 18.

Nordic Sevens Tournament, Copenhagen - 27th and 28th August.

Semi-final: Penguins beat Nordic Select 21 - 5.

Final: Penguins beat VEM Penza (Moscow) 50 - 5.

Penguins squad:

Air Commodore R. Weighill (President), Tony Mason (Chairman and Team Manager), Alan Wright (Hon. Secretary), Tony Jarman (Hon. PR and Press Secretary), Peter Whitelaw (Heriot's FP and Edinbugh District, Player/Coach), Jill Kerr (Physiotherapist).

Rob Wainwright (West Hartlepool, Army and Scotland, Captain), Russell Adam (Heriot's FP and Scotland U19 and U21), Spencer Bromley (Oxford University and Harlequins), Craig Brown (London Scottish, Scottish Exiles and Waikato), Paul Burke (London Irish and Ireland 'A'), Graham Dall (Heriot's FP and Scotland U19), Luc Evans (Treorchy and Wales), Brian Gabriel (Leicester and Midlands Division), Peter Garrett (Bedford and East Midlands), Charlie Gildea (Sundays Well and Munster), Fergus Henderson (Watsonians and Scotland U19 and U21), John Kerr (Watsonians and Scotland 'A'), Phil Lawlor (Bective Rangers, Leinster and Ireland), Dominic Malone (Bedford), Leigh Mansell (Bedford and East Midlands), Jamie Murphy (Greystones and Leinster U21), Cameron Murray (Hawick and Scotland U21), Ken O'Connell (Sundays Well, Munster and Ireland), David O'Mahoney (Cork Constitution and Munster), Rodney Pow (Selkirk and Scottish Southern Districts), Ivan Power (Greystones and Leinster), Matt Whiteley (Moseley and Midlands U21).

This charming penguin tapestry was presented to the Club after the Pingvin match.

Cruelly, in the midst of a happy and glorious year for the Penguin Rugby Football Club, Tony Mason fell ill. Alan recalls: 'This August Scandinavian tour really marks the turning point in the history of the Penguins.

'We hadn't long been in Stockholm when I realised that Tony was pretty ill. But he was too proud to take any medical treatment or to admit it. I took him aside quietly and said: "I'm with you, you've also got Rob Wainwright to help look after things. Why don't you just go and see a doctor while you're here? Take it easy." But he wouldn't. He just stuck at it and lived - breakfast, lunch and dinner - off vanilla ice-cream for the rest of the tour.

'And it really marked in our friendship the end of his ability to do all the things he'd done all his life - play squash with young people, be active... and I was very sad about it. But I loved him, so I couldn't do anything about it. I couldn't say to him, "go home, go to hospital". He wasn't a man, in view of my closeness to him, to whom I could say those kind of things.

'When we returned home, I motored Tony down to Sussex where we both lived at the time. His wife Doris came and collected him and I think I knew from that point that he had been very badly ill. At that time he didn't really know what it was. Shortly afterwards he was diagnosed as having myeloma, cancer of the bones. But that didn't stop him. It was really only in 1997 that he really had to throw in the towel.'

Within three weeks of returning home from the Scandinavian Tour, the Club faced the problem of raising a side to defend the title won at the Italian International Sevens the previous year. The matches were scheduled to take place in Sicily on 29th and 30th September, and with Courage League games scheduled in the UK for 1st October, it proved impossible to select any of the players that had been involved in the previous year's victory.

With typical ingenuity Tony Mason sought out Senior Clubs that had players awaiting completion of their registration periods.

So it was that Craig Brown was able to Captain a strong team in the Italian Sevens that included Crawford Henderson of London Scottish and Oxford University, and two Wasps players: Aaron James and Paul Volley.

Alan: 'Crawford Henderson really was, for a long time, a star winger for the Penguins. He was unlucky not to be capped by England. He had real speed - he was capable of running the 100 meters in 10.6 seconds.' Craig Brown recalls: 'Yes - Crawford was very quick - and his nickname on this tour was, indeed, "10.6"!'

The Swedish VII, who had been the Club's opponents in XVs a couple of weeks before, were well beaten in the first match. But then, in one of the strangest upsets to befall the Club in recent tournaments, the wheels fell off the Penguins' scoring machine and the Club lost to a Naples select team who had themselves been beaten by Sweden in the previous game. Luckily Penguins had scored more tries than the other teams and so progressed through to the next round.

The following day a young and fit Italian Police VII were well beaten, and the Penguins met the Sicily Select VII in the final. The home side led 7 - 0 until just before half-time, but the second-half was one-way traffic. Penguins ultimately ran out winners by 35 points to 7.

Craig Brown: 'I was the Captain on this tour, and it was an interesting tournament. We had a couple of close games on the way - a lot of it probably to do with the fact that a lot of the guys had come out of playing fifteens and within the space of two days had to turn around and get to be a sevens team - which is not always easy to do.

'One thing that always sticks in my mind was that all of the teams were being hosted in one hotel, and there were two major functions going on there. One was the fact that all of these rugby teams were there, of course, but the other was the "European Porno Queen" Conference! So also staying at our hotel were all of the male and females who... well, "get it together" for a living. And we had plenty of time to chat to them. It was most interesting. Of course, what do they *not* want to do on their day off? Yup, you've guessed it!'

Results of the Italian RU Sevens: Pool A: Penguins beat Sweden 40 - 0, Penguins lost to Naples Select 18 - 24. Semi-final: Penguins beat Roma Police 34 - 0. Final: Penguins beat Sicily Select 35 - 7.

Top: Aaron James.
Above: Paul Volley.

Penguins squad: Tony Mason (Chairman and Tour Manager), Alan Wright (Hon. Sec), Peter Whitelaw (Assistant Manager), Tony Jarman (Hon. Press and PR Manager). Craig Brown (Glasgow HSFP, Kelvinside and Waikato, Captain), Tim Ewington (London Irish and Northern Suburbs), Justin Grimmond (West Hartlepool and Manly), Crawford Henderson (London Scottish and Oxford University), Troy Jacques (West Hartlepool and Northern Suburbs), Aaron James (Wasps and Southland), Matt Jenson (West Hartlepool and Northern Suburbs), Ian Shand (Heriot's FP), Paul Volley (Wasps).

In December, 1994, Derek Wyatt and Roy Bish joined the Penguin Committee. Derek Wyatt - a long-standing Penguin stalwart - is a former Bedford, Bath, Oxford University, Barbarians and England three-quarter, and Roy Bish (Aberavon) has coached both Cardiff RFC and Oxford University.

And so ended a glorious year to remember, in which the Club won four International Tournaments - the Malaysia RU/COBRA Tens, the Scandinavian International Tens, the Nordic Sevens and the Italian International Sevens.

Alan Wright and Derek Wyatt together at Twickenham in 2009.

Derek Wyatt

Derek is the former MP for Sittingbourne & Sheppey. He was born 4th December, 1949 and educated at Westcliff County High School, Colchester Royal Grammar School, St Luke's College, Exeter, the Open University and at St. Catherine's College, Oxford. Derek Wyatt MP founded - and was the Chairman of - the British House of Commons all-party internet group from 1997 to 2007. He was on the Culture, Media and Sport Select Committee from 1997 to 2005 and the Public Accounts Committee in 2007 before becoming the Parliamentary Private Secretary to the Rt. Hon. Margaret Hodge MP, Minister for the Arts, and, unofficially, to Gerry Sutcliffe MP, Minister for Sport. In February, 2009, he became PPS to Lord Mark Mallock-Brown at the Foreign Office. He has chaired five all-party committees in the House of Commons.

Derek has played rugby for Bedford, Bath, Oxford University, the Barbarians and England. He was capped for England as a wing three-quarter, coming on as a replacement for David Duckham against Scotland at Murrayfield in February, 1976. He also played for England against the United States at Twickenham in October 1977, in a match for which full caps were not awarded. He scored four tries. He also played for Oxford University in the 1981 Varsity Match in which *Rothmans Rugby Yearbook* described him as 'the player of the day'. Derek has written five books on rugby and one on the cinema. He is a Fellow of the Royal Society of Arts, the Hon. Worshipful Company of Information Technologists, and the Industry and Parliamentary Trust. He is also a Freeman of the City of London. Derek first played for the Penguin RFC on the 1977 USSR tour. He has been a long-serving, dedicated and loyal Committee Member of the Penguins, and has provided much help and guidance with suggestions relating to tours and, of course, was instrumental in organising the very successful Penguins' Golden Anniversary Match at Twickenham in 2009.

1995 CHRONICLE

6th - 7th January - *Uruguay Sevens, Punta del Este. Captained by Craig Brown (New Zealand). Penguins lost to Rosario 14 - 49 Penguins beat Tonga 19 - 9 Penguins lost to Chile 14 - 24*

22nd February - *Penguins beat Oxford University 45 - 19 at Iffley Road, Oxford.*

2nd and 3rd September - *28th Malaysia Rugby Union/COBRA International Invitation Tournament, Kuala Lumpur, Malaysia. Captained by John Kerr (Scotland). Penguins beat Singapore 39 - 0 Penguins beat Taipei 43 - 0 Penguins beat Argentina 19 - 0 Penguins beat South Korea 12 - 7 Penguins lost to New Zealand Maori 12 - 14. Semi-finalists, Malaysia RU/COBRA International Tens*

Tony Mason in Punta del Este, Uruguay. He had to push himself to take charge of this tour.

1995

Alan Wright: 'In January, Tony Mason pushed his health to the very limit and took the Penguins to Uruguay.'

The Uruguay International Sevens Tournament coincided with Courage League fixtures, which ruled out selecting any players from English League Clubs. Tony Mason therefore turned his attention to selecting players from Scottish Clubs (who were playing friendly games that weekend) and from Oxford University.

Craig Brown: 'It was another interesting tournament. All of the games kicked off at about 4 o'clock in the afternoon, which meant that the last game on day one took place at about 2.30am. There were some big teams there - New Zealand, Fiji and a host of others. We had a team made up of five men from Scotland, two Oxford Blues and myself. Tony Mason had gone for speed - he'd picked four wingers and we were quite big in the forwards.

'We were drawn in a pool with a two South American teams and Tonga. We were doing rather well against one of the fancied Argentinian teams. At half-time we did our substitutions, but straight after half-time we had an injury.'

It was unfortunate that after making two replacements at half time, the Penguins' real 'flyer', Mark Moncrieff, was injured - meaning the Club had to play the second half with only six men against Rosario, after leading 14 - 8 at the break.

Craig continues: 'We did beat Tonga, however, in a good, physical game. So we went through into the "Silver Cup" competition.

'The next day didn't go well - I think we lost our first game. It was close, but that was it. But it was a good trip, and Uruguay is an interesting place to go to. We were very impressed when we were walking along the beaches and also with some of the nightlife. But you know, the guys did try hard - there was no problem there. Overall, a very enjoyable trip that gave a lot of guys who would never otherwise have got to Uruguay some very good memories!'

The results in Uruguay were: Penguins lost to Rosario (Argentina) 14 - 49, Penguins beat Tonga 19 - 9. Silver Cup: Penguins lost to Chile 14 - 24.

Penguins squad (pictured left): Back row: Tim Smithers (Rosslyn Park), Gareth Allison (Oxford University), Tony Mason (Tour Manager), Neil Martin (Oxford University), Ian Corcoran (Gala). Front row: Gary Parker (Melrose), Mark Moncrieff (Gala), Craig Brown (Watsonians, Captain), John Kerr (Watsonians), Fergus Henderson (Watsonians).

On 22nd February Penguins played Oxford University under floodlights on a very wet night at Iffley Road.

Penguin half-backs Tim Jensen and Tim Ewington played exceptionally well, but it was full-back Andy Tunningley of Saracens who stole the show - giving an immaculate display in the most exacting conditions. Penguins ran out worthy winners by 45 points to 19.

Penguins squad:
Tony Mason (Match Manager). Simon Brown (Harlequins), Stewart Burns (Blackheath), David Currie (Harlequins), Neil Donovan (London Irish), Max Duthie (Rosslyn Park), Tim Ewington (London Irish), John Green (Saracens), Aaron James (Wasps), Tim Jensen (Wasps), Jason Keyter (Bristol), Simon Mitchell (Harlequins), Dave Simms (Gloucester), Guy Spencer (Rosslyn Park), Andy Tunningley (Saracens), Richard West (Gloucester), Mike White (Wasps).

On 2nd and 3rd September the Penguins took part in the 28th Malaysia Rugby Union/COBRA Tens International Invitation Tournament in Kuala Lumpur. The Club were very keen to defend their title and to win the tournament for the third time in a row.

Alan: 'Tony Mason, despite his failing health, led the team in Malaysia where we had the young Scotsman John Kerr of Watsonians - a brilliant winger - leading the side. We liked John very much. We didn't win the Tens in Malaysia this time - we made the semi-final. We put up a good show, but we had a lot of injuries.'

Despite the balance of the side being somewhat less than ideal, the Penguins had an excellent first day and won their three pool matches without conceding a solitary point - beating Singapore 39 - 0, Taipei 43 - 0 and Argentina 19 - 0. Tony Mason was very impressed with one Penguins player in particular on day one, and said: 'I think that Tim Smithers from Rosslyn Park is of star quality with his three tries and his excellent tackling...'

Penguins met Korea in the quarter-final the next day, and in a close-fought affair eventually won through 12 - 7 after extra time. The semi-final brought them up against a very strong New Zealand Maori team. Tony said after the match: 'We lost in the semi-final to our old bogey-men, New Zealand. The boys fought all the way and only went down 12 - 14 in the last seconds, having been leading 12 - 0 with two and a half minutes to go.'

Tony Jarman wrote a report to the Penguin Committee Members at the conclusion of the tournament. In it, he said: *Sad to relate, our purple patch has come to an end. Penguins were beaten in the semi-final 12 - 14 by a very good New Zealand Maori side... This year the tournament included sides of a much stronger calibre and it was noticeable that Japan and New Zealand had arrived*

John Morgan (above), the first Treasurer of the Penguins, retired from the position in December 1995, after giving the Club great service for 23 years. John was succeeded as Hon. Treasurer by Dennis Hearn, Deputy CEO of Trusthouse Forte.

Stephen Herring

Stephen Herring, one of the UK's leading tax experts, joined the Penguins in 1995 as the Club's Honorary Accountant. Stephen was educated at William Hulme's Grammar School, Manchester and Manchester University.

Stephen: 'In the 1970s I was too slow and weak to command more than an occasional 1st team place as a forward and too tall and slow to be considered as a back. Much better at cricket, lacrosse, table tennis and chess; captaining the WHGS in the last two "sports".

I am now seen regularly at Bedford Blues, Old Trafford (Lancs CCC only), Northamptonshire CCC and, yes, at the Etihad Stadium in Manchester.'

Craig Brown became a New Zealand Maori in the final of the 1995 MRU/COBRA Tens when they asked him to bench for them as a result of a run of injuries. Not only did Craig come on at half-time, he scored the winning try in their victory in the final.

The MRU/COBRA Penguins squad.

three days early in order to acclimatise.

Although we lost to the final winners it is a pleasure to relate that the Maoris, having lost three players to injury before the final, asked Craig Brown, our Kiwi stalwart, if he would bench for them. Not only did he come on at half-time, but to the great joy of the Penguin party he scored the winning try.

The results were: Penguins beat Singapore 39 - 0; Penguins beat Taipei 43 - 0; Penguins beat Argentina 19 - 0; Penguins beat South Korea 12 - 7 AET. Semi-final: Penguins lost to New Zealand Maori 12 - 14.

Penguins squad (pictured left): Back row: Tony Mason (Team Manager), Jim Nayler (Orrell, Newcastle), Stuart Buchanan-Smith (London Scottish), Charlie Vyvyan (West Hartlepool, Sale), Iain Neary (Clifton), Craig Brown (Watsonians), Jos Baxendale (Sale and England). Front row: Tim Smithers (Rosslyn Park), Tim Jensen (Oxford University), Kern Yates (Wakefield), John Kerr (Watsonians, Captain), Paul Roblin (Rosslyn Park), Tim Ewington (West Hartlepool, London Irish), Arwel Thomas (Swansea, Bristol and Wales).

Richard and John Breen and the Baravi Exiles Rugby Club

1995 saw two of the PIRFC Fiji Committee Members and Selectors, Richard and John Breen, form a Club in Fiji called The Baravi Exiles RFC (nicknamed 'The Magicians'). The Baravi Exiles have subsequently become instrumental in selecting top-level Fijian players for the Penguin International RFC.

Richard Breen was born in 1971 and educated at Downside School (Captain 1st XV 1989) and University College, London. He played his rugby football at Mana RFC (Fiji) and with the Baravi Exiles. Richard founded the Club in 1995 and has served the Exiles as a player, selector, Chairman and Manager. He also managed and coached the Club at every HKFC Tens Tournament between 1996 - 2000. John Breen (Richard's father) was born in 1942 and educated at Newbridge College, OP Ireland and The College of Technology, Dublin. He played his rugby football at CYM Dublin, The College of Technology Dublin RFC, and Wimborne Minster RFC (Dorset). John is currently Club President and has also served the Baravi Exiles as Tour Manager, selector, assistant coach (and even as waterboy!). John: 'Baravi Exiles have benefitted enormously by being associated with the Penguins, and both Richard and I are extremely proud to be the Club's representatives for Fiji.'

Alan Wright adds: 'Penguins are deeply indebted to Richard and John for their work and selection on behalf of the Club.'

Left: Baravi Exiles (playing as the Guardforce Magicians) at the Hong Kong Tens in 1999. John and Richard Breen are standing, back left. In their short history, the Baravi Exiles have become one of the most successful Clubs in Fiji. Sometimes playing under different names (as a mark of respect to their generous sponsors) the Club has a marvellous record, especially with regard to the Hong Kong Football Club Tens Tournament:
1996: Winners (playing under the name of Mana Magicians) - Mana Magicians 25 v BB Aliens 17
1997: Finalists (playing under the name of Guardforce Magicians) - Guardforce Magicians 19 v Jade Aliens 39
1998: Winners (playing under the name of Guardforce Magicians) - Guardforce Magicians 26 v Australian Legends 21
1999: Winners (playing under the name of Guardforce Magicians) - Guardforce Magicians 38 v Qantas Australia Legends 10
2000: Winners (playing under the name of FPD Savills Magicians) - FPD Savills Magicians 24 v Clifford Chance Aliens 19

1996

On the evening of 6th March the Penguins, Captained by Paul Turner of Pontypool, Newbridge, Bedford and Wales, beat Cambridge University by 46 points to 38 in a marvellous game at Grange Road. Tony Jarman later wrote of this match: *The sheer daring of Paul Turner's play, entered into by all the team and their opponents, resulted in a spectacle of rugby which it is difficult to imagine being surpassed.*

Later on in March Penguins beat Oxford University by 46 points to 5 at Iffley Road - strangely the second time in a month that the Club had scored exactly 46 points against Varsity opposition!

Alan Wright: 'In 1996 our only visit abroad was to the Malaysian Rugby Union/COBRA Tens. It was our fourth year playing in this tournament. Despite the fact that the New Zealand Maoris were the favourites, closely followed by Argentina, the final was fought out between Samoa and Fiji, which was my own guess!' (Samoa eventually ran out winners 31 - 24).

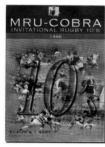

1996 Malaysian Rugby Union/COBRA Tournament Programme.

'Mainly due to selection difficulties because of the league system, we selected our youngest-ever team to leave England. We took no fewer than nine university students, and we had to make three late changes through injuries which left us with no wingers. Nevertheless, we put up a very good performance and made the final day, departing only after losing a close match against New Zealand.'

Tony Jarman wrote of this tour: *In this brave new age of professionalism it was always going to prove difficult to raise a side; add to this that the weekend was the first in the league championships in England, Wales and Scotland and the selection problems facing Tony Mason were obvious.*

1996 CHRONICLE

6th March - Penguins beat Cambridge University 46 - 38 at Grange Road, Cambridge.

March - Penguins beat Oxford University 46 - 5 at Iffley Road, Oxford.

August/September - 29th Malaysia Rugby Union/COBRA International Invitation Tournament, Kuala Lumpur, Malaysia. Captained by Craig Brown (New Zealand).
Penguins beat Singapore 57 - 5
Penguins beat Western Australia 28 - 5
Penguins lost to Argentina 0 - 15
Penguins lost to New Zealand Maori 10 - 25

November - The HSBC Sponsorship of Penguins begins.

Above: Random shots taken before and during the Tournament.
Left: Tony and the players do the famous 'Penguin Walk' during the march past.

Above: Penguin players and officials enjoying he post-tournament party.

Brent Pope.

The tournament took place at the Kelana Jaya Stadium in Petaling Jaya, Selangor, and the pool games were played on Saturday, August 31st. Penguins beat Singapore and Western Australia comfortably, but lost to a very strong Pumas team. Being one of the top two teams in their group the Club went forward into the final day, but were beaten by the New Zealand Maori by 10 points to 25.

Craig Brown, who Captained the touring party, recalls: 'Brent Pope came along on this tour. Tony Mason had been trying to get Brent to play for us for quite a while. He had played for Otago for years and he was an All Black Trialist. Then he went to Dublin to play over there at St. Mary's. The rest of us on that tour were all youngsters, really! Josh Lewsey was there as a 19 year-old. I recall that it was a very wet tournament - huge puddles on the field!'

Western Australia badge from Tony's collection.

Penguins squad: Tony Mason (Tour Manager), Alan Wright (Hon. Secretary), Tony Jarman (Hon. Press and PR Secretary).
Craig Brown (Watsonians, Captain), Rob Ashforth (Cambridge University), Danny Barrett (Bristol University), Quentin de Bruyn (Oxford University and Orange Free State), Russell Earnshaw (Cambridge University), Jonathan Garth (Wanderers), Jim Jenner (Bristol University), Tim Jensen (Blackheath), Josh Lewsey (Bristol University), Brent Pope (St. Mary's Dublin), David Proctor (Heriot's FP), Ben Ryan (Cambridge University) Ian Tucker (Sydney University, Oxford University and Blackheath).

The Penguin Rugby Football Club Executive Committee was formed this year. Its members were: Tony Mason - Chairman, Alan Wright - Hon. Secretary, Dennis Hearn - Hon. Treasurer Elect, Tony Jarman - Hon. Press and Public Relations Secretary, Phil d'A. Keith-Roach - Assistant Team and Fixture Secretary.

Brent Pope

Brent Pope was selected in the original 1987 New Zealand Rugby World Cup training squad, but had to withdraw before the tournament got underway due to an injury sustained in the final All Black trials.

Pope played nearly one hundred first-class games for Otago, winning a National First Division Championship title in 1991. He went to Ireland in 1991 where he played for both St. Mary's and Clontarf RFC.

Pope successfully coached both clubs to three separate National Division titles, three All Ireland Floodlit Cups, and two Leinster Senior Cups. Brent is still the only Leinster-based Coach to have ever won the AIB League First Division title with St Mary's RFC in 1999/2000. He also coached at Senior Provincial level with Leinster in 2000.

He has represented Canterbury, South Island, New Zealand Universities, Leinster, The Barbarians and the New Zealand XV as well as becoming Captain of the Penguins in 1997 and '98.

Brent has worked for RTÉ Sport for over a decade and has also appeared in many other television programmes.

Alan Wright: 'During 1996 I became very concerned that the advent of professional rugby, combined with Tony's ill health, might bring an end to all the work we had put in together over the previous 37 years.

Vernon Pugh.

'When Vernon Pugh, Chairman of the International Rugby Board, announced in August 1995 from the Ambassador Hotel in the heart of Paris: "Ladies and Gentlemen, we declare that the game of Rugby Union is now open", I felt he might just as well have added the words "for business" because indeed it was the day that a great amateur sport with huge traditions was transformed into a commercial business.

'My primary concerns were that professionalism would make selection very difficult, and that the costly insurance of players and the necessity of being able to provide expenses would be beyond our means as an amateur club. But above all that professionalism could bring with it a possible casting aside of the game's great tradition of friendship and sportsmanship.

'Sitting in the stand in Malaysia that year, I bemoaned the advent of this position to David Townsend and contemplated the prospect of approaching HSBC to ascertain whether they would consider becoming our principal sponsor. David encouraged me to make this request as we both appreciated that the Club had established a fine reputation in Asia by virtue of our high performances in the Hong Kong Sevens in 1987 and '88, and winning the Malaysia RU/COBRA Tens back to back in 1993 and '94. Additionally, knowing that the bank's motto was *the world's local bank*, I thought that perhaps we could do a lot for the grass roots of rugby and that at the same time we would be good ambassadors in countries throughout the world.

Sir William Purves.

'On 8 November 1996 I wrote to Sir William Purves who at that time was Chairman of HSBC, setting out this position in some careful detail. It was a "Red letter" day for the Club when I received a phone call some three days later from Sir William when he said definitively to me "the Bank will sponsor the Penguins through a Group Company". Later he telephoned me to confirm that the Group had a preference for the Club to be sponsored by HSBC Investment Bank and that I should arrange the details with Paul Selway-Swift, the Deputy Chairman, mentioning that Paul was a Rugby man and that he assumed we would arrive at a mutually fair and reasonable arrangement.

'Sponsorship therefore was realised early 1997 when I agreed the final arrangements with Paul Selway-Swift and planned that our first sponsored tour would be to the Czech Republic and Hungary. We had a very good friend in the Czech Rugby Football Union, namely Eduard Krutzner, who Tony first met in the Soviet Union in 1977 when he was coaching the Czechoslovakian rugby team and who subsequently became Secretary to the Czech RFU, and, finally, its President.'

HSBC ◆X◆
The world's local bank

HSBC is one of the oldest banks in the world. It is also the world's largest banking group and the world's sixth largest company. The Hongkong and Shanghai Banking Corporation was first established in Hong Kong in March, 1865.
Its founder was a Scotsman, Thomas Sutherland, who wanted a bank that operated on 'sound Scottish banking principles'. These days HSBC have around 7,200 offices in over 80 countries and territories around the world.
HSBC is also a long-term investor in Rugby Union football around the world. Its partnerships include the HSBC Sevens World Series, the British & Irish Lions, the HSBC Asian 5 Nations, the HSBC Asian Sevens Series and the HSBC Waratahs Super XV team.
Through HSBC's longstanding partnership with the Penguin International RFC and the formation of the HSBC Penguin International Coaching Academy, the Bank's commitment to grassroots development of the game has been realised across hundreds of local communities wordwide.

1997 CHRONICLE

31st January - Penguins lost to Oxford University 3 - 17 at Iffley Road, Oxford.

26th February - Penguins lost to Cambridge University 32 - 34 at Grange Road, Cambridge.

4th - 16th June - Czech Republic and Hungary.
Captained by Brent Pope (New Zealand).
4th - 11th June,
Czech Republic (Prague):
Penguins beat
Praga Sparta RFC 111 - 10
Penguins beat Czech Republic
National XV 55 - 28
Penguins beat Czech Republic
National U23 XV 51 - 26
11th - 16th June,
Hungary (Budapest and Kecskemét):
Penguins beat Budapest Exiles 105 - 14
Penguins beat
Nass Kecskeméti RFC 99 - 12

25th and 26th October -
Singapore Cricket Club
50th International Sevens Tournament.
Captained by Nick Penny (Scotland).
Penguins beat Kurumi (Japan) 53 - 0
Penguins beat
Loughborough University 17 - 5
Penguins lost to
Durban Harlequins 5 - 21
Penguins beat
Cambridge University 36 - 5
Penguins beat Petone (Wellington,
New Zealand) 26 - 19
Penguins beat Palmyra
(Australia) 42 - 19
**Winners, Singapore
International Sevens Ablitt Plate**

27th October - The Penguin RFC renamed The Penguin International RFC.

The first Penguin International Fixture Card featuring the logo of the Club's new sponsors.

1997

1997 marked a dramatic change in the way the Club would be run in future. It was the year that HSBC commenced their long-running sponsorship of the Penguin Rugby Football Club.

The year would also mark a change in the leadership of the playing side of the Club, due to Tony Mason's deteriorating health. And 1997 also brought with it the start of League Rugby Union Football in the UK - a change that would profoundly affect Penguin selection policies in the long term.

Thanks to their newly arranged sponsorship deal with HSBC Investment Banking the Club already had their next tour lined up and Tony Mason started to pick the team - although he was ill.

Alan: 'But then Tony picked up the 'phone to me and said: "I think I've come to the end of the road, Alan. I can't go to the Czech Republic and Hungary as Tour Manager." Fortunately, Tony had previously appointed a deputy to assist him, namely Phil Keith-Roach, a former Penguin player who was also a housemaster at Dulwich College and a past Captain at Rosslyn Park.

'I confirmed to Phil Keith-Roach that it was now his time to become Tour Manager. But within a short period of time he advised me that his own health was in decline and that he couldn't do it. He suggested that Hugh McHardy, a Chief Executive of Esher RFC (with whom Phil had worked in selecting a team for London Counties) should manage the tour. This was agreed after Hugh (who had played for the Penguins in the past) had a meeting with Tony.'

It is a matter of interest that although Tony was not up to managing the Czech Republic/Hungary Tour, at the very last minute he decided to tour as a spectator.

Meanwhile, on the playing front, 1997 was the first time that the Penguins played both Universities at the beginning of the year.

On this occasion Penguins lost both matches, being well beaten by Oxford University on 31st January, but only narrowly losing a real thriller at Grange Road to Cambridge by 32 points to 34.

One of the main reasons why both of the Penguins' Varsity matches were lost was because Tony was having great difficulty persuading the now fully-professional UK clubs to release players.

He wrote of the situation at the time: *...this season there was an understandable reluctance to release players, partly due to congestion and uncertainty with fixtures. The more enlightened of the senior club coaches realise that clubs like the Penguins can be useful to the professional clubs with overlapping squads where they are unable to keep their players match-fit. By allowing them to play for the Penguins they can keep them happy and ready for action. We hope we can continue to help the clubs - without interfering with their team preparations...*

The Penguin touring party arrived in Prague on 4th June to commence the first tour for which the Club had the sponsorship of HSBC. It is interesting to note that the Club had last played Czechoslovakia - a country that no longer exists, of course - exactly twenty years before, during the 1977 Russian Tour.

Alan Wright met Eduard Krutzner, the Secretary of the Czech Rugby Union, right at the beginning of that tour. The two struck up a great friendship almost as soon as they met, and have remained friends to this day.

Alan: 'Penguins had a wonderful Kiwi Captain for this tour in Brent Pope. Brent is now a famous figure in Ireland, where he broadcasts on rugby. He has also coached several Irish first-division Clubs to great success. The tour party was also noteable for including two youngsters with famous names in the world of rugby football: Charles Starmer-Smith, a 19-year-old scrum-half playing for the French Club Begles, whose father Nigel, the TV commentator, played for Oxford University, Harlequins and England. Also selected was Steve Martin from Neath RFC, whose father, Allan, won 34 caps for Wales and was also a British Lion.'

At this time the make-up of the Penguins' tour party broke a Club record in that it contained representation from no fewer than ten countries - namely Australia, Canada, the Czech Republic, England, France, Ireland, New Zealand, Scotland, South Africa and Wales. In light of this selection, perhaps it is not surprising that the Club's title officially became 'The Penguin International Rugby Football Club' a few months later in Singapore on 27th October.

In his Tour Report to the RFU, Alan Wright later wrote of the three-match Czech tour: *The matches against the Czech National XV and the Czech National U23 sides were played to a high standard of skill, tactical appreciation and*

The 1997 Penguins Tour Party to the Czech Republic.

Top: The Club's tour hotels.
Below: The Tour itinerary.

Programme:
Wednesday 4th June
■ *arrive at Prague Airport at 20.50 hrs.*
■ *departure by coach to the Hotel STÍRKA*

Thursday 5th June
■ *8.45 hrs. departure to the Praga R.F.C. ground for training by coach*
■ *13.30 hrs. lunch in Pub „Na Vlachovce"*
■ *19.00 hrs. Czech Rugby Union Dinner in wine restaurant „U Tří Grácií"*

Friday 6th June
■ *13.00 hrs. lunch in Pub „Na Vlachovde"*
■ *15.15 hrs. departure to the Praga R.F.C.*
■ *17.30 hrs. match PRAGA - SPARTA R.F.C. : PENGUIN R.F.C.*
■ *19.30 hrs. team Super in the Clubhouse*

Saturday 7th June
■ *9.45 hrs. departure to the Praga R.F.C. ground for training by coach*
■ *13.30 hrs. lunch in Pub „Na Vlachovce"*

Sunday 8th June
■ *12.00 hrs. lunch in Pub „Na Vlachovce"*
■ *13.15 hrs. departure to the ground of Tatra Smichov F.R.C. by coach*
■ *16.00 hrs. match CZECH REPUBLIC NATIONAL XV. : PENGUIN R.F.C.*
■ *20.00 hrs. team Super in the Pub „U Špirků"*

Monday 9th June
■ *free day*

Tuesday 10th June
■ *12.30 hrs. lunch in Pub „Na Vlachovce"*
■ *14.30 hrs. departure to the ground of Říčany R.F.C.*
■ *17.30 hrs. match CZECH REPUBLIC NATIONAL U-23 : PENGUIN R.F.C.*
■ *19.30 hrs team Super in the Clubhouse*
■ *21.30 hrs. return to the Hotel by coach*

Wednesday 11th June
■ *8.00 hrs. departure to Budapest by coach*

The Official Tour Programme and Presentation Plaque.

Above and right: The Czechs were very considerate hosts and looked after the Penguins extremely well during the course of the 12-day tour.

competitiveness. *The facilities in the Czech Republic are A1 and the clubhouses and grounds are delightful. The social events after these matches were held away from the grounds in very good venues.*

The results of the three matches played in Prague were: Penguins beat Praga Sparta RFC 111 - 10; Penguins beat the Czech Republic National XV 55 - 28 and Penguins beat the Czech Republic National U23 XV 51 - 26.

On Wednesday, 11th June the Penguins travelled eight hours by coach to Budapest in Hungary for the second leg of the tour.

In his RFU Tour Report, Alan wrote: *In Hungary the game has only been established for 17 years and the playing strength of the touring party outclassed that of the hosts. Therefore, this part of the tour was really of a 'missionary' nature.*

In this part of the tour Penguins played Budapest Exiles RFC (another huge win, by 105 points to 14) before going on to Kecskemét to play Nass Kecskeméti RFC. In this, the final match of the tour, the Penguins only just failed to score a hundred points for the third time in six matches - winning by 99 points to 12 (after this match had been going for 50 minutes the teams were mixed up in time-honoured 'Penguin missionary' fashion, and the final score was 109 - 39!).

It is interesting to note that Penguins did not attempt to kick penalty goals in the five tour matches.

Alan: 'It was a very successful tour. The Czech Rugby Union received us with open arms and their hospitality was thoughtful, considerate and really excellent in every way. And the Hungarian Rugby Union, despite a lack of funds, showed great kindness and generosity in the manner in which we were entertained after each match.

Above: Tony Mason hands out Penguin plaques and ties during the Czech Republic and Hungary Tour.

ČESKÁ RUGBYOVÁ UNIE

ČESTNÁ VSTUPENKA

na mezinárodní utkání

VÝBĚR ČESKÉ REPUBLIKY - PENGUIN R.F.C.
dne 8. 6. 1997 od 16.00 hodin
na hřišti RC Tatra Smíchov (Podbělohorská ulice, Praha 5)

Dennis Hearn, who was at this time Penguins' Honorary Treasurer and Statistician, wrote later in his record of the tour: *I look back on the rugby played with a real glow of happiness, at times it was truly magical and a living testament to a wonderful sport.*

Attached are the bare facts, impressive enough in themselves but one needs to record that these games were not just walkovers. All of our opponents played their hearts out to the last minute and many of them were highly skilled individuals. They had everything to lose and tried hard not to do so. The collective talent of our boys was just too great.

Penguins squad:

Tony Mason (Chairman), Alan Wright (Hon. Secretary), Hugh McHardy (Manager), Dennis Hearn (Hon. Treasurer and Tour Statistician), Tony Jarman (Hon. Press/PR Secretary), Phil Keith-Roach (Coach/Kit Master), Roy Bish (Liason Officer/Committee), Derek Wyatt (Committee), Geoffrey Warren (RFU Panel Referee).

Brent Pope (Canterbury, South Island, New Zealand Universities, Otago, New Zealand Barbarians, New Zealand XV, Clontarf and Leinster, Captain), Rob Ashforth (Cambridge University), Richard Butland (Bath), Andy Clark (Richmond, England Universities), Alan Edmunds (Neath and Wales), Simon Emms (Llandovery), Luc Evans (Swansea, Barbarians and Wales), Stuart Evans (Swansea and Wales), Neil Fletcher (Leicester), Gary French (Bath), Michael Higginson (Old Wesley), Marty Hyde (Cambridge University and Australian Universities), Andrew Jones (Llandovery), Steven Martin (Neath), Sean McCahill (Sundays Well and Ireland), Mario Meyer (Thanet Wanderers and Northern Transvaal), Niall Murphy (Sundays Well), Andrew Orugboh (Wasps), Andrew Rees (Resolven), Florent Rossigneux (Stade Français and French Barbarians), Ben Ryan (Cambridge University and West Hartlepool), Charles Starmer-Smith (Begles), Karl Svoboda (Oxford University and Canada), Aleric Turtle (Trinity College, Dublin), Ben Whetstone (Bedford), Scott Wolfe (Wasps).

Above and below: Match action from the 1997 Czech Republic and Hungary Tour.

David Townsend

Alan Wright writes: David attended Long Eaton Grammar School and Sheffield University. An ardent sportsman, he played rugby football for Long Eaton Grammar School, Sheffield University, Nottingham, the Singapore Cricket Club and HSBC. His career with HSBC as an International Banking Officer was undertaken in countries in the Far East from 1972 - 2000. He also served for a number of years on the organising committee of the Singapore Sevens.

David's enthusiasm for the Penguins was sparked by meeting Tony Mason and Alan Wright at the Hong Kong Sevens in 1987. Since becoming a committee member in 1996, David has played a significant role in the Club's expansion, encouraging Alan's approach to HSBC for sponsorship and subsequently joining him in liaison meetings with the bank (at one of which the HSBC Penguin Iinternational Coaching Academy was formed). He arranged for the Penguins to play, for the first time, in the Singapore Sevens Tournament in 1997, and assisted in securing the prestigious invitation from the Ministry of Sport to tour the People's Republic of China in 2000. David's outstanding diplomacy as the Club's Liaison Officer, and his local knowledge, have greatly contributed to tours in many parts of the world, including Germany, Argentina, Borneo, Malaysia, Singapore and Hong Kong. David was appointed a Senior Vice-President of the Club by the Committee in 2011.

In October Penguins were invited to Singapore to play in the Singapore Cricket Club 50th International Rugby Sevens Tournament. The invitation came about through long-standing Committee Member David Townsend having also been a Member of the Singapore Rugby Union's Sevens Committee.

Alan Wright remembers this as the tour that would change the face of the Club forever: 'This tour really began a new era for the Penguins. Professionalism was closing the door on us. It had made it almost impossible for us to pick a UK-based team to play fixtures away from England between September and May. And because of our very strong connections "down under" - with Craig Brown being a New Zealander and Bill Calcraft being an Australian - the situation began to open up the prospect of us being a truly international club.

The Penguins squad with the Singapore CC Sevens Plate.

'So I espoused internationalism to the Penguin Committee. And it was not too long after this that I proposed to the Committee that our name be changed to 'The Penguin International Rugby Football Club' to more fairly reflect what we did - that is, our tours, our selection and our Committee were now truly international. And I thought it gave gravitas to our title and our activity.

The birth of the Penguin International Rugby Football Club

The Club's title officially became 'The Penguin International Rugby Football Club' at an Executive Committee Meeting held in Singapore on 27th October, 1997. Reflecting the new international flavour of the Penguins, several new members joined the Committee this year. Among them were Bill Calcraft (Australia), Karl Svoboda (Canada), David Townsend (Hong Kong and the Far East), Brent Pope (New Zealand) and Fanie du Toit (Republic of South Africa).

'Returning to the Singapore Sevens Tournament, it is a very strong competition. With the help of Bill Calcraft, we picked a squad of which eight were Australians, playing for Australian Premiership teams in Sydney - including, of course, his own club, Manly RFC, and also Sydney University.'

The tournament was played out on the 25th and 26th October at the beautiful Padang ground in the centre of Singapore.

Bill Calcraft remembers: 'I managed the Penguin Sevens sides in '97 and '98. We had to pull in young players from Manly and other Sydney clubs. It was also the first time that I ever met Craig Brown!

'It was a really tough tournament - they were nearly all New Zealand and South African sides. It was then I realised that the game was changing rapidly. Instead of the more traditional sevens, where you had a few skillful forwards and a bit of speed here and there, these teams were coming out with all big men, and every one of them could run it in. It was changing the whole thing. We were combative, but we couldn't win the main tournament.

'But we learnt a lot from it. For instance - I had never been to a rugby match in hotter conditions. It had to be 40 degrees. And we were playing in our heavyweight 'Oxford' jerseys! Craig and I knew then that if we were going to ask these guys to put the effort in, that we would have to change that. Ever since then we've had great gear - the best in the world. You don't notice how heavy the old stuff is when you're playing on a winter evening in Oxford, do you?'

Alan: 'Interestingly, this Penguin side was the youngest ever to represent the Club. We were beaten by the Durban Harlequins in the main competition. They were a very strong South African team. But we did succeed in winning the Plate Competition by beating the Western Australian side Palmyra in the Plate final - I do believe it's the only time we've ever won a Plate!'

The Penguins played themselves into the Plate Final by keeping their heads against an uncompromising New Zealand side, Petone RFC. The final itself pitted the Penguins against the hard-tackling, take-no-prisoners style of Palmyra. The class of the Penguins prevailed and the Club ran in no fewer than six tries to win the Plate 42 - 19.

Nick Penny of Watsonians RFC, the former Scotland Sevens Captain who also Captained the Penguins in this tournament, has his own special memories of the trip: 'My memories of the Singapore CC 7s include: Meeting a great bunch of Aussies, including a very young Chris Malone and a great bloke called Nick Humphries. The Penguins seemed to have talked most of the Aussie U21 team into playing for us, which I was delighted about - a real bunch of mongrels!

'Meeting Bill Calcraft for the first time and realising that the Penguins were more than just three very enthusiastic, old posh boys - that is, Mason, Wright and Jarman!

Singapore Cricket Club International Sevens Tournament Programme.

The wonderful cartoonist Gren's (Grenfell Jones MBE) depiction of the beautiful Padang Sports Ground in the centre of Singapore.

Another from Tony Mason's enamel rugby badges collection.

The Penguins have strong friendships with Australia, New Zealand, Fiji and Samoa.

'Sweating more than I ever had before. And then, before the match, being presented with the heaviest cotton rugby jersey possible!

'Tough games throughout, but taking great pleasure in beating both Loughborough and Cambridge University.

'A hard-fought Plate semi-final against Petone RFC. And ultimately a comfortable win in the Plate Final against Palmyra. We went out with our foot to the floor in the first half and they were burst by half time.

'Celebrations, Penguin style, afterwards.

'Attending the "Aussie Legends Kangaroo Court" and making the fatal mistake of calling the Green and Gold Jersey the Green and Yellow Jersey. Cue me getting destroyed by a group of Aussies that included Mark Ella!

'Last but not least, a long flight home, sitting between Tony Mason and Alan Wright. The conversation during that flight was fascinating, and I found both men to be amazingly interesting, generous and funny. And more enthusiastic about what rugby should be about than anyone I had ever met!'

Alan Wright has the final word on the Singapore Cricket Club Sevens: 'One of the best things that happened on that tour was that we cemented our friendship with Australia. That, and our New Zealand connections, which spread to Fiji through Bill Calcraft and led to Samoa through Craig Brown, means that the Penguins now have strong friendships with four great rugby countries in the southern hemisphere.'

The full Ablitt Cup results were: Penguins beat Kurumi (Japan) 53 - 0; Penguins beat Loughborough University 17 - 5; Penguins lost to Durban Harlequins 5 - 21. The Ablitt Plate quarter-final: Penguins beat Cambridge University 36 - 5; Semi-final: Penguins beat Petone (Wellington, New Zealand) 26 - 19. Final: Penguins beat Palmyra (Australia) 42 - 19. Penguins were winners of the Ablitt Plate.

Penguins squad: Tony Mason (Chairman), Alan Wright (Hon. Secretary), Bill Calcraft (Coach), Tony Jarman (Hon. Press/PR Secretary).
Nick Penny (Watsonians, Edinburgh and Scotland Sevens, Captain), Dominic Byrne (Manly, AIS U21), Mark Challander (Sydney University), Neil Crooks (Gala and Scotland Sevens), Michael Griffin (Sydney University, AIS U21), Nick Humphries (Manly), Chris Malone (Manly, AIS U21 and Australia U21), Tim O'Brien (Manly, AIS U21), John Slater (Manly, AIS U21 and Australia U21), Nick Timmins (Manly).

Penguin stalwart and Committee Member Derek Wyatt was also in the news in 1997. Derek was not only elected as an MP to the House of Commons, but also appointed Chairman of the All-Party Parliamentary Rugby Union Committee.

1998

On 29th January Alan Wright hosted a Committee Dinner at The House of Commons in honour of, and to give thanks to, HSBC for their tremendous support of the Club in 1997. Among the guests that night were Sir William Purves and Paul Selway-Swift from HSBC, Bob Blizzard MP, Tony Mason, Sir Peter Yarranton and Bill Calcraft. The Dinner was arranged by long-standing Penguin Committee Member Derek Wyatt MP.

The Club's playing season got underway in February. Alan Wright: 'Uniquely, we played both Cambridge University and Oxford University within a 48-hour period.

'On 25th February we played Cambridge, winning a splendid match 63 - 52. We had the pleasure of Waisale Serevi playing with us, instead of against us, and he converted all of our tries in a most casual manner! Serevi was playing for Leicester Tigers at the time, and they very kindly made him available play for us. He was, and still is, quite brilliant. His team-mate, Marika Vunibaka, played on the wing and scored eight fantastic tries. This wonderful Penguin International team also included two brilliant young players from Dulwich College who would very soon go on to play for England - David Flatman and Andrew Sheridan.

And then, against Oxford on the 27th, the match was all-square with two minutes to go, but we went on to win a very evenly fought contest 36 - 29.'

In his report on these two matches, Tony Jarman wrote: *In perhaps one of the most audacious coups of our history, last week we took on the two Universities within three days - and won both matches.*

Although in playing detail the two games were very different, on both occasions we were able to field excellent selections - which is a very considerable compliment to the efforts of Tony Mason and Ian Bullerwell.

Against Cambridge University on Wednesday the game was played in ideal conditions for open, flowing rugby, and the game proved to be one of the most spectacular in the history of this fixture.

Although the University started strongly, scoring almost from the kick-off, we were fortunate in having Waisale Serevi at stand-off half - an excellent play-maker who set the tone in scoring our first try in his inimitable sevens-style, receiving the ball on the 22 and touching down under the posts without a hand being laid on him.

Honours were evenly divided until half-time, which was taken 33 - 42 to Penguins, further tries having been added by the Leicester pair Niall Malone and Marika Vunibaka.

In the second half the Club stretched away with a further five tries from Vunibaka, who demonstrated searing pace and poetry in motion on the left wing - a joy to watch.

1998 CHRONICLE

25th February - Penguins beat Cambridge University 63 - 52 at Grange Road, Cambridge.

27th February - Penguins beat Oxford University 36 - 29 at Iffley Road, Oxford.

27th May - 2nd June - Croatia Tour. Captained by Richard Kinsey (England). Penguins beat Croatia National XV 64 - 20 in Makarska.

18th June - 8th July - Brazil and Chile Tour. Captained by Brent Pope (New Zealand). 18th - 25th June, Brazil: Penguins beat São Paulo Athletic Club 104 - 5 Penguins beat Pasteur RFC 105 - 5 Penguins beat Bandeirantes 134 - 0 26th June - 8th July, Chile: Penguins beat Southern Chilean Selection 77 - 3 in Concepción Penguins beat Northern Chilean Selection 56 - 36 in Viña del Mar Penguins lost to Chile National XV 27 - 32 in Santiago.

7th - 8th November - Singapore Cricket Club 51st International Sevens Tournament. Captained by Craig Brown (New Zealand). Penguins beat Watembezi, Kenya 17 - 10 Penguins beat Singapore Cricket Club 42 - 0 Penguins beat Hammerheads (Papua New Guinea) 24 - 19 Penguins lost to Taradale 0 - 32

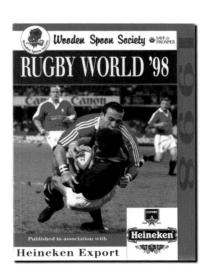

Tony Mason wrote an article for the 1998 Rugby World Annual entitled: 'Penguin Rugby Club - Life in the Fast Lane'. Tony Jarman later commented: 'He has written it in his inimitable low-key, humourous and modest fashion.'

*Rugby genius Waisale Serevi first
played for Penguin International RFC
on 25th February, 1998.*

*Thank-you letters to Alan Wright from
Andrew Sheridan and David Flatman
after the Cambridge University match.
At this time Alan was a Governor of
their school, Dulwich College.
It is a matter of interest that Alan
obtained the permission of both their
Headmaster and parents for the two
lads to play in the match.*

The match was also notable in that it was the first time that two school-boys had played for the Club; both David Flatman and Andrew Sheridan are in their final year at the all-conquering Dulwich College and they performed very well at loose-head and blind-side wing-forward respectively.

On the Friday evening at Oxford conditions were very different, the game being played in near gale-force winds. The style of rugby differed, too. Penguins fielded a very strong pack which was altogether too much for the University. Chris Horsman of Bath had an outstanding game at loose-head and was influential, together with Kevin Whitley and Neil Watkins, in pinning the University in their own 22 for much of the game. This assisted scrum-half Dann Bailey in having a rare old evening and scoring a hat-trick of tries. The University were to be congratulated on their persistence and they scored on four occasions from breakaways.

In the final quarter Oxford drew level at 29 - all, only to be overtaken in the final minutes by Penguins with a try from Kevin Whitley which was converted by Alistair Kennedy.

It is interesting to note that a future British Lion and England World Cup winning hooker by the name of Steve Walters played for the Penguins in this match. The young man in question is now better known as Steve Thompson!

25th February - Penguins v Cambridge University.
Penguins squad:
Ian Bullerwell (Match Manager), Tony Jarman (Hon. Press and PR Secretary).
Crawford Henderson (Rosslyn Park, Captain), Nigel Clark (Bedford), David Flatman (Dulwich College and England U19), Mark Fontaine (Northampton), Nick Humphries (Manly), Aaron James (Wasps), Niall Malone (Leicester and Ireland), Chris Mee (Rugby), Matt Powell (Saracens), Waisale Serevi (Leicester and Fiji), Mark Sharp (Tabard), Andrew Sheridan (Dulwich College and England U19), Steve Summers (Ely and Cambridge), Marika Vunibaka (Leicester and Fiji Sevens), Tim Withers (Rugby).

27th February - Penguins v Oxford University.
Penguins squad:
Ian Bullerwell (Match Manager), Tony Jarman (Hon. Press and PR Secretary).
Crawford Henderson (Rosslyn Park, Captain), Dan Bailey (Rugby), Steve Barnes (Northampton), Matt Davies (Rugby), Richard Francis (Neath), Chris Gubbins (Rugby), Chris Horsman (Bath), Nick Humphries (Manly), Alistair Kennedy (Rugby), Andy Parton (Henley), Steve Walters (Northampton), Ian Warbrick (London Scottish), Neil Watkins (Neath), Kevin Whitley (Moseley), Ben Wigley (Rugby).

The tour to Croatia in May and June was the first tour in the history of the Club that took place without Tony Mason being present. This was occasioned by both Tony and his wife Doris being seriously ill.

Alan Wright: 'In May and June we made our first visit to Croatia. Croatia were then in their sixth year of independence from the Yugoslavian Republic - they broke away and fought for their freedom.

'The tour came about through unusual circumstances, thanks to Bill Calcraft's introduction. Bill, who had, of course, been a member of our Committee for many years, was acting as a merchant banker raising a huge loan for Croatia.'

Bill Calcraft: 'In my investment banking job, I'd been working in what's called "the Emerging Markets". So I'd spent a few years in Croatia and I'd been heavily involved in one of their first-ever international bond transactions. Whilst there I'd also struck up a good relationship with a few people in the government. And I found the Croatians were big people and great sportsmen in a lot of areas.'

The Penguins tried their best to help the Croatian National XV qualify for the 1999 World Cup Finals.

Alan: 'During the negotiations Bill met the Prime Minister of Croatia. He mentioned that the Croatians had a rugby team and that they were trying to qualify for the 1999 Rugby World Cup, and had to play Italy. If they could beat the Italians by 14 points they would qualify (as it happened the Croatians lost to Italy and didn't succeed in getting into the last 24). They asked Bill, "Why don't you bring your team over and give us a strong game?" The Prime Minister arranged for the state airline to fly us there. They were very generous hosts. We stayed in a sea-side hotel in a town called Makarska that had a big athletics stadium where the match was played.'

The Penguins squad in Croatia.

Bill: 'We were hosted wonderfully well in Zagreb and Makarska by the Croat Government and the Croatian Rugby Union. The Deputy Prime Minister also helped the Club a lot.'

Alan: 'We took a wonderful team with the biggest pack ever put on the field by Penguins. It was a good game. The Croats were very well coached by a New Zealander and they had three All Blacks playing against us (including the Rugby League/Union star Frano Botica), who had dual nationality. Their forwards put up a fine performance against our very heavy pack, but we beat them rather handsomely by 64 points to 20.'

Bill: 'Yes - the Croats were big people, but we were bigger! We took a fantastic team out there.' Alan: 'We certainly gave tham a hard trial. And we very quickly became good friends with them.'

Roy Bish
and Hugh Thomas

Roy Bish (above left) was the Penguin Liaison Officer for the 1997 Czech Republic/Hungary tour and Assistant Manager on the 1998 Brazil/Chile tour. According to Hugh Thomas (above right, of Aberavon, Cambridge University, London Welsh, Newcastle Gosforth and Llanelli): 'Both Roy and I played for our home club, Aberavon. That was the beginning of our long friendship. Indeed, it was Roy who first introduced me to the great Penguins rugby fraternity (Hugh played for the Penguins in 1988).

In 1965 Roy became the first qualified coach to coach Cardiff RFC. The Cardiff team of that era became synonymous with a brand of 15-man attacking rugby that was the prototype for the successes at national level throughout the 1970s.

Roy was also Oxford University RFC's Coach when they beat South Africa 6 - 3 during the infamous "Apartheid Tour" of 1969.

He later coached Italy between 1975 - 77 where his influence put Italy on the road to joining the Six Nations Championship.

Roy died in 2006 at the age of 75.'

Alan Wright adds: "Roy Bish was loved and revered by countless Italian International rugby players.'

Living up to its new title, the Penguin International squad was drawn from no fewer than seven different nations, and included internationals from Wales, Scotland, Ireland, Australia and Argentina.

Bill: 'Touring for two weeks these days is quite hard now, what with professionalism. But a lot of players are still willing to go away for two or three days, and a lot of our squad had never been to Croatia. It is a spectacular country, especially down on the Dalmatian coast. So we were able to take a really first-class side. It was such a good experience that we went back again a year later!'

In a post-tour letter to Drago Lulic, the Croatian Rugby Union Selector, Alan Wright wrote: *Our Club considered it a great honour to be invited to Croatia to play your national team. It was an excellent match, played in a very good spirit, and we hoped that it would be of help to you in your preparation for the forthcoming international against Italy. We very much hoped that you would win this match, and the writer made a bet in your favour...*

We understand that you would perhaps like us to visit you again next year, and I can confirm that our Committee would be most pleased for the Club to play the Croatian National XV in Makarska in 1999.

Penguins did indeed return a year later in 1999, between 2nd - 7th June when they played the Croatia National XV again, and also a NATO XV.

Nick Penny, the Scottish Sevens Captain, later wrote of the 1998 tour: *...it was a pleasure to have played in the match and to have been involved in what was one of the most enjoyable tours I have ever been on. The team gelled immediately and to have met old friends (Mathew Wintle, Nick Humphries and Simon Fenn) and to have played with quality players such as Warrick Waugh and Matt Pini was a great experience for me...*

Penguins squad:

Alan Wright (CEO), Bill Calcraft (Tour Manager and Coach), Tony Jarman (Team Liaison and Hon. Press Secretary), Roy Bish (Committee Member and Tour Liaison Officer), Nigel Yates (RFU Panel Referee).

Richard Kinsey (Wasps and England 'A', Captain), Jan Bonney (London Scottish), Ian Buckett (Swansea and Wales), Paul Burke (Bristol and Ireland), Paul Cooke (Blackheath), Gary Cressman (Honourable Artillery Company), Luis Criscuolo (Coventry and Argentina), Brian Cusack (Bath and Ireland 'A'), Chad Eagle (Bristol), Simon Fenn (London Scottish), Paul Graham (Blackheath), Nick Humphries (Oxford University and Manly), Andy le Chavalier (Wasps), Grant McKelvey (Watsonians and Scotland), Nick Penny (Watsonians and Scotland Sevens), Matthew Pini (Richmond, Australia and Italy), Paul Sampson (Wasps and England), Warwick Waugh (Randwick, Australia), Matthew Wintle (Llanelli), Martin Wood (Wasps), Chris Wright (Harlequins).

It was in May, 1998, that Alan telephoned his great friend Peter Yarranton, who, as well as being a Penguin Committee Member of many years standing, was also on the Middlesex Sevens Committee. This call would set in motion events that would later result in one of the Penguin International Rugby Football Club's most glorious triumphs - although neither man knew it at the time.

Alan recalls the conversation: 'Peter picked up the phone and realised it was me. He asked: "How are you, Alan?" I said: "Peter, you must think I've got spots!" He said: "What are you talking about?" I said: "Well, there you are, on the Middlesex Sevens Committee. In the last two years the Army have played, the Barbarians have played - what about an invite for us?!!" He said; "You know, you're dead right - I hadn't thought of it. I'll talk to the Committee and try and get the Penguins an invitation."

'About two months later we were invited.'

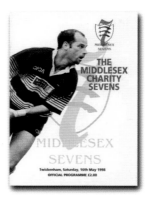

Peter Yarranton extended an invitation for the Penguins to take part in the 1999 Middlesex Sevens in May, 1998.

18th June - 8th July brought the Penguin International RFC's major tour of 1998 - to Brazil and Chile. This would be the Club's second tour of Brazil, the first having taken place fourteen years before, in 1984.

HSBC was keen for the Penguins to tour Brazil and Chile where the bank had many interests, and the Club was happy to oblige. Indeed, from the outset of their happy relationship with HSBC the Penguins had taken the view that if the Rugby Unions of countries where HSBC have an interest were happy to receive them, then they would, in turn, be very pleased to go and play in those countries.

The major tour of the year would take place in June/July to Brazil and Chile. It would be the Penguins' second time in Brazil, but their first visit to Chile.

Tony Mason did a lot of the preparatory work for this tour with regard to selection and liaison with the Club's hosts in Brazil and Chile. Sadly, he was unable to join the tour in the end, due to his wife Doris still being quite seriously ill. Alan Wright, who was unable to tour due to business commitments, wrote to Tony two weeks before the Club departed, sympathising with Tony's predicament: In this letter he says: *I do think you have taken the correct decision not to go to Brazil... You and I have done so much together that there was always going to be a time when we had to rely on our friends to run the show, and that time has come.*

So it was that the tour management was left in the very capable hands of Tony Jarman, Roy Bish, Craig Brown and the Penguin Team Captain, Brent Pope.

It was a long (19-day) tour, with three matches being played in each country. The three matches in Brazil were played at the São Paulo Athletic Club (SPAC) ground in São Paulo against local club sides. The Penguins ran up huge scores in these matches. And one win, the 134 - 0 victory over Bandeirantes RFC, comfortably beat the Club's previous biggest victory (the 111 - 10 win over Praga Sparta Rugby Football Club just the previous year).

The Brazil/Chile Tour Squad.

Craig Brown recalls: 'We were so dominant in these matches that we would mix up the teams at half time in true Penguin fashion. The Brazilian players enjoyed playing alongside our players and learnt a lot from the experience. And it was very sociable. Everybody was billetted with families, so Penguins were scattered to the four corners of São Paulo - which is a massive place! I remember landing there at six in the morning and it took us two hours to drive half-way across it!

'We then moved on to Chile. We flew to Santiago then drove all the way down to a place called Concepción where we were due to play a match against a Southern Chilean Selection XV. We beat them comfortably.

'When we left Concepción we had to drive all the way back up north to Viña del Mar, near Santiago. The day we did this was the same day that Argentina were playing England in the 1998 soccer World Cup. Well, we had Luis Criscuolo, an Argentinian player (now, of course, a Penguin Committee Member) with us on the bus, and he recruited everyone who wasn't English to support Argentina. The bus was split about 50:50 - you were either for England or you were against England! This journey turned out to be a 16-hour marathon. We just drove straight up Chile! And during this journey the boys had to come up with all sorts of things to entertain themselves.

'After this marathon trip we played the Northern Chilean Selection in Viña del Mar and beat them by 56 points to 36. But the really big match was to be last match of the tour - against the Chile National XV in Santiago.

'Before this match we had a couple of days on the beach where we organised some "beach olympics" by way of training. After this the Penguins squad travelled into Santiago and spent two days preparing for the match against Chile.'

The Chile National XV proved to be a tough match. Craig remembers: 'They were a very good team. We went into the lead early on - Graeme Ingles scored a try after about three minutes and it all seemed to be going well. But they fought back and in the end we lost by five points - the final score was 27 - 32. It was a fierce game and there were some "handbags"!'

Alan: 'In passing - we had tried to arrange the tour so that we played Chile first but we were unable to arrange the itinerary in this manner.'

The Federación de Rugby de Chile's national rugby union team is known as 'Los Condores' ('The Condors').

Penguins team before the match against Chile.

Craig: 'When you look at the players we had on that team who were youngsters - a lot of them went on to play international rugby. Marcus Di Rollo, Gordon Ross and Simon Taylor (who was only 19 years old at the time of the tour) went on to play for Scotland, and I think Barry Stewart already had a couple of Scottish caps at that stage. They all went on to big things!'

The results of the tour were:

Brazil: Penguins beat São Paulo Athletic Club 104 - 5, Penguins beat Pasteur RFC 105 - 5, Penguins beat Bandeirantes RFC 134 - 0.

Chile: Penguins beat Southern Chilean Selection 77 - 3, Penguins beat Northern Chilean Selection 56 - 36, Penguins lost to Chile 27 - 32.

Penguins squad:

Tony Jarman (Tour Manager and Hon. Press and PR Secretary), Roy Bish (Committee Member, Tour Liaison Officer and Coach), Eric Woodmason (RFU Panel Referee).

Brent Pope (Canterbury, South Island, New Zealand Universities, Otago, New Zealand Barbarians, New Zealand XV, Clontarf and Leinster, Captain), Nick Booth (Oxford University), Craig Brown (Watsonians), Sean Burn (London Irish), Steve Cottrell (Richmond), Luis Criscuolo (Walsall, Coventry and Argentina), Aaron Davis (Bedford), Marcus Di Rollo (Watsonians), Neil Dickson (Boroughmuir), Ian Gardner (Caerphilly), Tom Holloway (Newbury), Graeme Ingles (Watsonians), Scott Keith (Selection Paloise, Wellington), Andy le Chavalier (Wasps), Simon Miall (Newbury), Derek Patterson (Selkirk and Watsonians), David Proctor (Heriot's FP), Gordon Ross (Heriot's FP), Grant Ross (Stade Francais and France 'A'), Ben Ryan (Newbury), Iain Sinclair (Watsonians), Barry Stewart (Edinburgh Academicals), Simon Taylor (Heriot's FP), Martin Waite (Watsonians), Jason White (Watsonians and Caledonian Reds).

The following Committee minutes are dated 1st September, 1998:

Alan Wright reported to the Committee with no little sadness that Tony Mason had advised him on the 13/8/1998 that he now wished to take a sabbatical from his responsibilities within the club. This was due, in part, to Doris being ill. It was also at this time that the Committee decided that it would not be possible for any one Committee member henceforth to shoulder the same responsibilities and duties that had so ably been carried out by Tony Mason in the past, and the meeting confirmed that these duties - namely selection, fixtures and management - would, of necessity, have to be shared by members of the Committee in future. As Alan put it at the time: 'The acorn planted by the Founders of the Club 40 years ago, having grown into a mighty oak, now requires considerable husbandry.'

Penguin IRFC mentioned in Parliament by Derek Wyatt MP in June.

Whilst debating the subject of sport in the House of Commons, Derek Wyatt MP was quoted thus in Hansard on 5th June, 1998:
'...I mention a club that is not often referred to in dispatches, the Penguin International RFC, which is now in its 40th year. It is run by the same two stalwarts, Alan Wright and Tony Mason, who ran it when it was founded...
For most of its history the team has been run on a shoestring budget. It has survived the professional era thanks to the generous sponsorship of HSBC Investment Bank...
When it was not deemed politic the Penguins toured on behalf of the RFU places such as the Soviet Union in 1977.
They have played in or against teams from no fewer than 53 countries and have helped countless young people to further their international careers. They have been our greatest international sporting ambassadors, but few know anything about them...'

Tony Jarman holding the Russell Cargill Cup at Twickenham.

Alan: 'I will mention in passing that the 1998 Brazil/Chile Tour was a long tour of three weeks and Tony and I couldn't go (for the reasons already given). This being so, Tony Jarman was made the Tour Manager.

'Tony was a very dear friend - I nicknamed him 'Jam Pot' and I really liked him very much. With great sadness I made the oration - that's a pompous word - at his funeral. He was a man who had been in the Sidcup 1st XV at the same time as Tony Mason and I, and when he retired from being a Director of a very big engineering firm he volunteered to help with the Penguins, and in 1994 became a member of the Committee.'

Tony Jarman

Alan Wright writes: Tony Jarman was a Man of Kent and was educated at Sir Roger Manwood's School, Sandwich (1943 - 45). He had a most successful career as a civil engineer, becoming a director of the world-famous Matthew Hall Group of Companies.

Tony played for Sir Roger Manwood's School 1st XV and for Thanet Wanderers, and in 1948 joined Sidcup where he played in the 1st XV as prop and pack leader, playing alongside Tony Mason and the writer. He later became a referee for the Kent Society. In 1994, Tony became the third Sidcup member to join the Penguin Committee, becoming the Club's first PR/Media Secretary, Chairman of Selectors, Manager of the tours to Brazil/Chile in 1998 and Poland in 1999, and Administration Officer, Middlesex Sevens Finals 1999 and 2000.

Tony was dedicated to the Club and, of course, to rugby. He was noted for his cheerful enthusiasm and was much liked by all. He died in 2002, leaving his loving wife, Sheila, and devoted family.

Tony has been sadly missed by Penguins players and officials alike

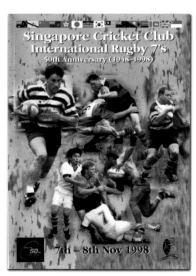

1998 Singapore Cricket Club International Sevens Programme.

Between 7th - 8th November the Penguins once again took part in the Singapore Cricket Club International Sevens. Craig Brown recalls: 'Our team consisted of some players from the UK, a few from Australia and a Kiwi.

'The Singapore Cricket Club Rugby Sevens is a tough tournament - they have a lot of very good teams there. The previous year Penguins had won the Plate, so this time we asked ourselves, "Do we want to aim for the Plate again, or do we want to go on to the next level?" Of course, we all decided that we wanted to go as far as we could.

'We had Peter Jorgenson playing for us, who's played for Australia at both Rugby Union and Rugby League, and a lot of up-and-coming young Aussies who were playing for Australia Sevens at that time. So we went for it - but once again we only managed to make the Plate! We did make the quarter-finals where we met the eventual winners, Taradale RFC from New Zealand - a very good outfit - and we lost. So it was a disappointing end, but a good effort.'

The results were as follows: Penguins beat Watembezi, Kenya 17 - 10; Penguins beat the Singapore Cricket Club 42 - 0; Penguins beat Hammerheads (Papua New Guinea) 24 - 19; Penguins lost to Taradale (New Zealand) 0 - 32.

Penguins squad:

Bill Calcraft (Tour Manager and Coach), Alan Wright (CEO), Ian Bullerwell (Tour Manager, Admin/ Hon. Fixture Secretary), Tony Jarman (Hon. Team Liaison and Press Secretary). Craig Brown (Watsonians and Waikato, Captain), Greg Bruwer (Wanderers Johannesberg and South African Barbarians), Dominic Byrne (Manly, AIS U21 and Australia U21), Luis Criscuolo (Coventry and Argentina), Peter Jorgenson (Penrith RL, Northampton and Australia), Craig Morgan (Cardiff), Tim O'Brien (Manly and AIS U21), Florencio Sequeira (Walsall and Argentina Sevens), John Slater (Manly, AIS U21 and Australia U21), M. Watson (Wanderers Johannesberg and Transvaal).

Peter Jorgenson is an Australian wing three-quarter who played both Union and League. He started with Randwick RFC in 1991. Whilst there he played two games for the Wallabies.
He switched codes in 1995 to play for Sydney Roosters before joining Penrith Panthers in 1997.
In 2002 he switched back to Union when he joined Northampton in the UK. He also played for Rotherham and Edinburgh before retiring in 2007.

Dudley Wood CBE

Dudley Ernest Wood was born on 18th May, 1930.

He was educated at Oxford University. Worked at ICI and was and was Overseas Manager for Petrochemicals.

He joined the RFU as Secretary in September 1986 and retired in 1996.

During Dudley's tenure as RFU Secretary, the RFU spent £60,000,000 increasing Twickenham Stadium's capacity from 65,000 spectators (of whom 18,000 were standing) to 75,000 all seated.

Dudley played at lock and at number 8. He won Oxford Blues in 1952/1953 and was invited to attend England trials. He played club rugby for Bedford, Rosslyn Park, Waterloo and finally Streatham-Croydon, where he played on into his late thirties.

Alan Wright writes: Dudley is a great man and he is a brilliant public speaker. I have persuaded him to be a principal speaker at all but one of our special Anniversary and Grand Reunion Dinners and his speeches have always been very well received. Much to his amusement I once coined the phrase that he is a *Master Craftsman of the Guild of Wordsmiths*!

Perhaps Dudley's most famous quote came was when he was asked for his views on the special relationship between the Welsh Rugby Union and the Rugby Football Union. He replied:

The relationship between the Welsh and the English is based on trust and understanding.
They don't trust us and we don't understand them.

Dudley is a great friend to many members of the Committe and the Club is proud that this extremely popular man is a PIRFC Honorary Vice-President.

1999 CHRONICLE

19th February - Penguins beat Oxford University 29 - 21 at Iffley Road, Oxford.

3rd March - Penguins beat Cambridge University 52 - 19 at Grange Road, Cambridge.

7th April - Penguins beat Moseley RFC 38 - 36 at The Reddings, Moseley, in Moseley RFC's 125th Anniversary Match.

21st May - Penguins' 40th Anniversary Grand Reunion Dinner at the Dorchester Hotel, London.

29th May - Middlesex Charity Sevens, Twickenham, London.
Captained by Waisale Serevi (Fiji).
Penguins beat Sale 47 - 0
Penguins beat Harlequins 28 - 12
Penguins beat
San Isidro (Argentina) 28 - 7
Penguins beat Saracens 40 - 35
Winners, Middlesex Charity Sevens

2nd - 7th June - Croatia Tour.
Captained by Richard Kinsey (England).
Penguins beat
Croatia National XV 36 - 10
Penguins beat NATO XV 98 - 3

18th - 24th June - Czech Republic Tour.
Captained by Brian Cusack (Ireland).
Penguins beat
Czech National XV 33 - 28
Penguins beat Czech Lions 65 - 10

24th - 28th June - Poland Tour.
Captained by Brian Cusack (Ireland).
Penguins beat
Poland National XV 48 - 18

3rd - 4th July - Thai Rugby Union's 1st International Sevens Tournament (Phuket). Captained by Cameron Pither (Australia).
Penguins beat Malaysia 37 - 0
Penguins beat Hong Kong 50 - 0
Penguins beat Belgium 24 - 5
Penguins beat Germany 56 - 0
Winners, Thai RU International Sevens

5th August - Penguin International Rugby Football Trust established

1999

PENGUINS UNBEATEN

Alan Wright: 'This was a glorious year for the Club and will remain in my memory, notably because although we went all over the world we remained undefeated, including playing for the first time, and winning, the Middlesex Sevens.

'It certainly was a very busy year and I was pleased to be able to go on all three tours. Unfortunately Tony Mason was seriously ill at this time. Although it was not my wish, bearing in mind I was almost 70, I decided to return to tour management and reorganise its direction. This was executed by sharing responsibilities and creating a new post of Tour Manager (Players), a role to which Craig Brown was eminently suited. Indeed, it was in the course of this year that Craig was invited to join the main committee, having been a member of the selection committee for some years.

The year started, as usual, with the annual matches against Oxford and Cambridge Universities, and a special match to celebrate the 125th Anniversary of the founding of Moseley RFC in 1873.

On 19th February Penguins beat Oxford University RFC 29 - 21 in a close match at Iffley Road. Penguins were Managed by Ian Bullerwell and Captained by Richard Kinsey of Rugby RFC. The squad included Paul Burke of Cardiff and Ireland and Paul Sampson of Wasps and England.

On 3rd March Penguins beat Cambridge University RUFC 52 - 19 at Grange Road. Again, the team was Managed by Ian Bullerwell and Captained by Richard Kinsey. A strong squad included Paul Burke of Cardiff and Ireland, Luis Criscuolo of Coventry and Argentina and Ian Buckett of London Welsh and Wales.

Alan: 'We returned to Croatia for the second year running at the invitation of the Croatian Rugby Union to play their national team and also the NATO Army XV.'

The major tour, sponsored by HSBC, was the invitation to return to the Czech Republic, combined with playing Poland's national team for the second time in the history of the Club, the first being in 1977.

Other significant events in 1999 included the 40th Anniversary Grand Reunion Dinner, at which Alan presented Tony with a personal gift of a magnificent silver Penguin trophy to mark 50 years of friendship and to record 40 years of working together since he and Tony Mason founded the Club in 1959.

The Club was honoured to be invited to play a special match on 7th April to celebrate Moseley FC's 125th Anniversary. A large number of very fine players from Moseley have represented the Club over the years and in an exciting and close encounter, Penguins beat the home club at The Reddings by a very small margin, the final score being 38 - 36.

Once again, the Penguins were Managed by Ian Bullerwell and Captained by Richard Kinsey. The team included six players from Wasps and three each from London Scottish and Rugby Lions. In passing, it is interesting to note that the Club won every match when captained by Richard Kinsey, the giant lock forward from Wasps who had also played for Queensland.

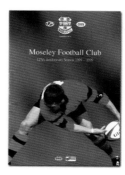

Moseley FC - beaten 38 - 36 in their 125th season by the Penguins.

On 21st May the Penguins held their 40th Anniversary Grand Reunion Dinner at the Dorchester Hotel in Park Lane, London. Once again the Club attracted an impressive list of distinguished guests. Among them were: His Excellency Mr. Andrija Kojakobic, Ambassador of Croatia, Mr. Ivo Silhavy of the Embassy of the Czech Republic, P.C. Trunkfield, President of the RFU, G.D.M. Brown, President of the Scottish RU, the Right Hon. Sir Tasker Watkins VC, CBE, DL, President of the Welsh RU, and W. Österling, President of the Pingvin RFC (Sweden).

The speakers were: The Rt. Hon. Sir Edward Heath, Dudley Wood, Sir Peter Yarranton, Bob Weighill and the great Cliff Morgan (Cardiff, Wales and the British and Irish Lions), who gave a wonderful speech about 'The Game We Love'.

During the course of the Dinner, Alan made a special, personal presentation to Tony Mason of a magnificent silver Penguin statuette. On the front of the base are the words: *Presented by A.G.L. Wright to A.R. Mason in recognition of his out-standing achievements worldwide in the advancement of Rugby Union Football.*

On the back are the words: *This Penguin records the founding of the Penguin International Rugby Football Club in 1959 by Tony Mason and Alan Wright and commemorates their 50 years of friendship.*

The magnificent silver Penguin that Alan presented to Tony Mason on 21st May, 1999. Alan began the presentation by kidding Tony that it was an award to him for being voted the Club's Young Player of the Year!

As a result of Alan's telephone call to Peter Yarranton in May, 1998, the Penguins duly received an invitation to be one of the guest teams at Twickenham at the 1999 Middlesex Sevens.

Alan: 'The first time I ever visited Twickenham was in 1946 - and it was to watch the Middlesex Sevens. St. Mary's Hospital won it. It was a competition I had always admired and I was delighted when the formal invitation arrived inviting us to play in the Final.

'This proved a great challenge to both the Club and especially to Bill Calcraft, our Director of Sevens and successful Captain of our team in the Hong Kong Sevens. I decided to call a special meeting of the selection committee in view of the difficulties that were apparent as a result of the game becoming professional.'

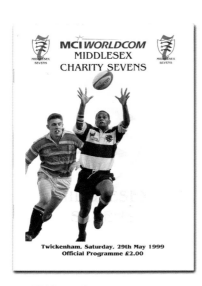

*Middlesex Sevens programme -
29th May, 1999.
It is interesting to note that the
1999 Middlesex Sevens Tournament
was only the third time in the history
of the competition that prize money
was offered to the winning teams.
The first two occasions
(1997 and 1998) were both won
by the Barbarians.*

Alan continues: 'The format of the Sevens had recently changed and instead of the competition being played on two successive weekends, with 12 places in the last 16 being fought over in the preliminary competitions held around London, the finalists would probably be all the Premiership/top clubs in England, together with specially invited guest Sevens from foreign countries.

'We appreciated that there would be very few players we could select from England, and that we would have to utilise our friendships worldwide to put a side together that would do justice to this great invitation. I suggested that the one player we needed to begin with was the peerless Waisale Serevi, but we didn't know where he was playing. Bill Calcraft, who knew Serevi from Hong Kong, took it upon himself to locate Serevi and invite him to play.'

Bill Calcraft: 'I knew he was a great player, a real superstar, and after a couple of calls I found him. You've got to be clever to get him, I can tell you! He's shy, modest and unassuming and he doesn't answer the telephone. The secret is to get his wife. Because when you get on well with his wife he comes to the phone!

'Serevi had played against us in Italy and had played for us against Cambridge University. He is certainly a genius, and when you work with him things can happen. The Committee had decided that although we were an amateur club we would follow the professional clubs' procedures by advising our squad that if we were fortunate enough to win any prize money, then half of this would be shared between the players. Serevi was pleased to have a straightforward agreement in this respect and was happy to have a bit of a say in who else would be selected, which, as far as I was concerned, was fine.

'Then Alan and I went out to the Hong Kong Sevens in early 1999, basically with the idea that, having just got Serevi organised, and knowing that he'd be out there with Fiji, we could see him and decide who else we could select for our side. We stayed way out on the Peak with David Townsend, which was very gracious of him, and we had a good time in Hong Kong. Alan, Serevi and I went a long way towards settling the squad.

'Naturally we included some Fijians and mixed it up with some very talented New Zealanders. I also managed to pull in Nick Humphries from the Manly Club in Sydney, and to top up the position, Ian Bullerwell stepped in and selected two excellent players from Bedford Blues.'

Alan: 'Our two players from the Blues were Jason Forster, who would subsequently became the manager of Henley RFC and who also played for Wales Sevens, and Darragh O'Mahony, who later played for Ireland and was a very intelligent, very fast winger. Funnily enough Darragh ended up the next year playing against us for the Saracens!

'We were also greatly helped by Gordon Tietjens, the New Zealand

Sevens Coach - he recommended to us two good players, Karl Izatt and Craig Newby (who went on to play for Leicester and the All Blacks). Not only did they come over and play in the Middlesex Sevens for us - they both toured with the Club to the Czech Republic and Poland, and were also included in the Sevens squad in Thailand.'

Bill: 'It was a fantastic effort, getting our squad together, and in the end we had a really good side!'

Alan: 'But then, at the very last minute, we lost our scrum-half and we couldn't find a good enough replacement anywhere. So I said: "Ask Serevi who he wants." He said: "Let my brother play." Now, his brother Meli had no reputation as an international player, but you didn't need to have the brains of Einstein to work out that they'd probably played together for most of their lives - scrum-half, stand-off half - can there be a stronger combination? So his brother was in. And he played very well.'

Bill: 'Well, the 1999 Middlesex Sevens tournament was pretty tough, playing all of these professional clubs. We got our wins, but it certainly wasn't plain sailing. But Serevi could pull things out of the hat like no other player in the world could do.'

Alan: 'We had a wonderful team. And the incredible thing about the day, having beaten Sale, Harlequins and San Isidro - the champion club of Argentina - when we reached the final we were losing 0 - 7, 7 - 14, 7 - 21, 14 - 28, I think, at half-time. And with a minute to go we were losing 28 - 35, when Serevi scored a miraculous try, which he converted to make the score 35 - 35. We won the sudden-death play-off with a brilliant try by Qua Qua.'

Bill: 'For the final tie against Saracens I remember moving a couple of the players around positionally, because I thought it would release some of our runners. But when you've got some of the world's best players you don't start telling them how to play Sevens! You just organise them so that the whole thing can run smoothly, really.

Penguin squad for the 1999 Middlesex Sevens:
Back row: Dan Qua Qua (Baravi Exiles and Fiji Sevens), Karl Izatt (Kia Toa and New Zealand Sevens), Sailosi Nawavu (Baravi Exiles, Fiji Sevens and Fiji), Ian Bullerwell (PIRFC Honorary Fixture Secretary), Takai Seru (Gordon's), Jason Forster (Bedford, Newport and Wales Sevens), Nick Humphries (Manly and Oxford University), David Peirce (Wasps - Honorary Physiotherapist).
Front row: Meli Serevi (Natulcake), Bill Calcraft (PIRFC Director of Sevens - Manly, Oxford University and Australia), Craig Newby (North Shore and New Zealand Sevens), Bob Weighill CBE, DFC, PIRFC President), Waisale Serevi (Mont de Marsan, Fiji Sevens and Fiji, Captain), Alan Wright (PIRFC Co-founder and Honorary CEO), Darragh O'Mahony (Bedford and Ireland), Tony Jarman (PIRFC Manager, Admin).

'What I will say about the final is this. The score at full-time was 35 - 35. Consider what happens then. You're in a five-minute-each-way, sudden-death situation, right? So the Saracens' French stand-off Alain Penaud started the play, and kicked the ball into touch. In Sevens that means that it's a free ball to the other side at the half-way mark, because he'd kicked it out on the full. I've often thought to myself - if you made that fatal mistake - you know, it's 35-all, there's the Russell-Cargill Cup to win and you've just handed over possession to the opposition - who is the last player in the world that you'd want to give the ball to and say - "Have a free-tap over there and see if you can get past us and score?" It's got to be Waisale Serevi - he's a genius!

'But that's exactly what happened. Well, I'll tell you right now - he and Dan Qua Qua, walking across, already had it sorted. Serevi tapped the ball, he's done a little shimmy and a step, Qua Qua's already at full-speed, Serevi's just shifted it two meters and Qua Qua's followed his own kick ahead to touch down under the posts! It was all over in five seconds.'

Alan: 'It was a wonderful occasion for the Club, providing only our second opportunity to play at Headquarters, the first being in 1967. It was of significance to us that the tournament was televised and reported fully in all the national newspapers.'

Bill: 'We won the handsome cash prize of £50,000 which, for an amateur club, was a very good input to our treasury at that time. I asked Alan to

The Middlesex Sevens

The Middlesex Sevens are held annually at Twickenham Stadium in London. Dr J.A. Russell-Cargill, a London-based Scot, instigated the competition in 1926.

The Sevens were held at the end of the rugby union season in May for the first 75 years of its existence.

The competition moved to August in 2001, due to a lack of players and stadium availability in May.

The tournament is a charitable event, now officially called the Middlesex Charity Sevens, with the current beneficiaries being The RFU Charitable Trust and the PRA Benevolent Fund.

The Middlesex Sevens has seen many notable great players take the field including Waisale Serevi, Eric Rush, Lawrence Dallaglio, Henry Paul, Robbie Paul, Clive Woodward, Will Carling, JPR Williams, Prince Alexander Obolensky, Va'aiga Tuigamala, Martin Offiah, Ben Gollings, Simon Amor, David Strettle, Josh Lewsey and Andy Ripley.

Traditionally the Middlesex Sevens has been an invitation tournament with entertainment derived from overseas and qualifying sides challenging the top teams in the Rugby Union.

In 2005 the tournament became a twelve-team competition with Guinness Premiership teams only participating. This attracted much criticism. Rugby League sides were no longer invited and there was further lack of diversity in terms of domestic and overseas teams. However, the 2008 tournament saw the return of invitation sides with the Ospreys, the Newport Gwent Dragons and the British Army all taking part.

IMAGES OF MIDDLESEX SEVENS '99

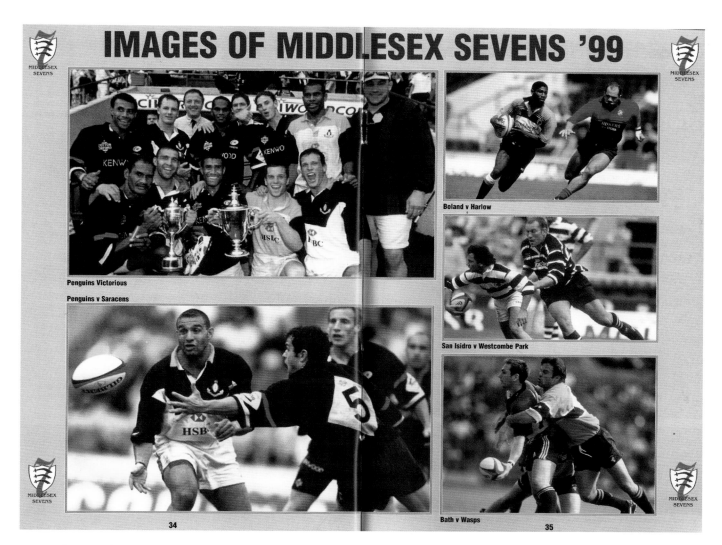

Penguins Victorious

Penguins v Saracens

Boland v Harlow

San Isidro v Westcombe Park

Bath v Wasps

34

35

ensure that our players' prize money was given to them quickly as I wanted to be certain that as they were professionals our promise to them was delivered without delay.'

Alan: 'Certainly, appearing so successfully on television in England excited quite a bit of interest in the Club, and winning a Blue Riband tournament raised our profile and reputation amongst the first-class players.

'At this time Tony Mason was very fragile, but he sat with me in the East Stand throughout the afternoon. I wanted him to have the very great pleasure of seeing us play for only the second time at Twickenham - and win!

'After the final Derek Mann presented us with the Russell-Cargill Cup. Derek was the Chairman of the Middlesex Committee and I must say that he's a

Pictures from the 1999 tournament in the Middlesex 7s 2000 programme.

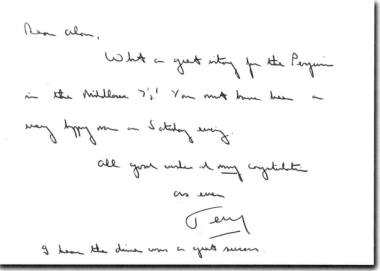

Tony Mason's congratulatory note to Alan regarding the Penguins' great win.

Geoff Windsor-Lewis, Honorary Secretary of the Barbarian FC (winners of the previous year's Russell-Cargill Cup) penned this very kind and thoughtful congratulatory letter to the Penguins soon after the tournament.

true gentleman in every sense of the word. He's one of the rare men in this world who epitomises the expression "To thine own self be true". He will stand up and be counted against anything if he has a strong belief. He doesn't give in to any cajoling. He was a wonderful President of the Middlesex RU, and he was very helpful to us. He is still, to this day, an Honorary Vice-President of the Penguins.

'We had a party back in the Lensbury Club in the evening where Serevi actually made a short speech. All-in-all we were very proud to have won the Middlesex Sevens. It was a wonderful day and the team we put together was a very good combination. Above all, it was such a very great honour to join the famous clubs in becoming winners of what has been, over the years, London's favourite rugby tournament.''

The full PIRFC results were: Penguins beat Sale 47 - 0; Penguins beat Harlequins 28 - 12; Penguins beat San Isidro (Argentina) 28 - 7. Final: Penguins beat Saracens 40 - 35 AET. Penguin International RFC were winners of the Russell-Cargill Cup.

Penguins squad: Bill Calcraft ((Director of Sevens), Bob Weighill (President), Tony Mason (Chairman), Alan Wright (CEO), Craig Brown (Selector), Ian Bullerwell (Selector), Tony Jarman (Admin/Liaison). Waisale Serevi (Mont de Marsan, Fiji Sevens and Fiji, Captain), Jason Forster (Bedford, Newport and Wales Sevens), Nick Humphries (Manly and Oxford University), Karl Izatt (Kia Toa and New Zealand Sevens), Sailosi Nawavu (Baravi Exiles, Fiji Sevens and Fiji), Craig Newby (North Shore and New Zealand Sevens), Darragh O'Mahony (Bedford and Ireland), Dan Qua Qua (Baravi Exiles and Fiji Sevens), Meli Serevi (Natulcake), Takai Seru (Gordon's).

Serevi's 1999 Twickenham...

Bill Calcraft: 'Here's a story! I had selected Waisale, who at the time was playing for Mont de Marsan in France, and had made travel arrangements for him to arrive in England the day before to join our one and only training session at the Lensbury Club where we were staying.

'On the Saturday morning we were all sitting in the sun with our kitbags, waiting for the coach to take us to Twickenham Stadium, when Waisale comes over to me and says: "Bill, just one thing, I think I would like to go back to France after the semi-final. Will that be alright?" I thought this was a bit tricky, so I went over to Alan Wright and told him what was happening.

Of course this made Alan very concerned and he said: "If he feels that way, we'll play the substitute."

I said: "Take it easy, Alan, I will talk to him again. If things don't go well, you can come over and be the heavy artillery."

I had another chat with Waisale, and it transpired that he had latterly become a little panicky about returning to his club which had reached the final of a league knock-out Cup, now due to be played the very next day, Sunday afternoon, in the south of France!'

...surprise - loyalty - heroism

Alan Wright: 'Presumably Waisale thought he would be at Twickenham for the afternoon and then return to France without difficulty, without considering the possibility that play, if we reached the final, would not end until the early evening, that an injury might be sustained, and that there could be transport difficulties. It was apparent he should have advised us that he could not play. Waisale undoubtedly considered that he was acting loyally by keeping his word to both clubs.

Also, he must have been concerned that our squad contained four fellow Fijians including his own brother brought in by him at the last moment. In the event, we reorganised his travel arrangements with an earlier flight and a taxi to take him to the airport immediately after the final, which we won due to Waisale's outstanding play, scoring a brilliant try to level the score at 35 - 35 and bring about a "sudden death" play off.' Bill: 'Fortunately, this story had a happy ending. The final at Twickenham was spectacular, and Waisale did indeed play for Mont de Marsan the following day. They won the Cup, with Waisale scoring 17 out of the 23 points. So Waisale was a hero two days running!'

Alan: 'No wonder the great R.C.C. (Clem) Thomas was moved to describe Waisale Serevi as "the greatest living footballer"!'

The Penguins stayed at the Hotel Biokovo during their time in Makarska.

The Penguins wanted to pay tribute to the NATO Peace Keeping Force in Croatia. The Club played a NATO XV in Makarska on the day of the ceasefire.

Alan Wright: 'Shortly after winning the Middlesex Sevens we made our second visit to Croatia - which was every bit as successful as the first.'

Bill Calcraft: 'In a nutshell, we were invited back again this year on the back of the relationships and the success of the first tour.

'This time I thought we could just step it up a little bit. I had actually played against the British Army a few times in Germany, and I know that rugby's a big game in the army. I was sitting in my office in London one afternoon, and in an idle moment I thought: You know what? Why don't we play SFOR - the Stabilisation Force. It's the NATO Stabilisation Force in Bosnia (the war was still on). It's made up of soldiers from many different countries - New Zealanders and all sorts. So I got on the 'phone and found my way in remarkably quick time - only three or four 'phone calls - to the senior officer in charge of rugby in Sarejavo. I spoke to the officer (he was a Colonel) and told him who we were, and that we were coming over to play, and would they be interested in a fixture? Well he was massively enthusiastic about the idea. They had about 5,000 players to choose from, Kiwis and Australians and so on and so forth.'

Alan: 'First of all we were entertained in Zagreb, the capital of Croatia, by the directors of the National Bank - thanks to Bill Calcraft's great friendship with all the powers-that-be in Croatia. Then we flew on very late at night to the coast where we had the strange experience of being kept on the ground in the plane for about two and a half hours with no explanation. And in the end I worked out that NATO were firing rockets over our heads into Serbia because the war was still going on in the Balkans!

'We had a happy time on this tour. We played two matches - one against the Croatian National Team and one against a NATO XV.

'The match against the Croatian National XV was quite unusual, inasmuch as the team contained a lot of men with dual nationalities - South Africans, New Zealanders and Australians. It was a closer encounter than that of the previous year - the measure of this was that both sides scored 10 points in the second half. However, Penguins won the game comfortably enough, 36 - 10.

'As for the NATO match - Bill was very keen for us to go into the battle zone and play the British Army. In the end I said to him: 'We can't do that - I'm not prepared to risk men's lives. It's too big a responsibility. If we took men who then wandered off into a minefield - because it was proposed that the match be played in a city that was surrounded by them - it would be a serious error to allow players to be endangered whilst in our care.'

Bill: 'That's right. I actually had it in my mind that we would play in the Sarajevo Olympic Stadium. But Alan was concerned about safety. We were told that it was pretty safe, but that there was still the odd sniper about! So I said to the Colonel: 'We'll be in Makarska - why don't you fly your players down to the

coast? So they flew their players down. They were a bit unlucky apparently because a lot of their New Zealand players left Sarejavo the week before the match. But they still put out a pretty good side.

'I spoke to some of them later. They said that they'd been picked out of the front-line, flown down to the coast and they'd been there for a week training! Unfortunately for our opponents we had a very good team which scored a large number of points. They found themselves in the position we were normally in, having had no opportunity to practice together.

'I also remember that we played that match, and later that night a cease-fire was announced and the war ended at midnight.'

The results of the two tour matches were: Penguins beat Croatia National XV 36 - 10; Penguins beat NATO XV 98 - 3.

Alan, in his thank-you letters to the Croatian dignitaries that had hosted the tour, wrote: *Thank you for the very generous hospitality you extended to us during our tour. Once again we were able to assemble a first-class professional side to visit Croatia. The side included players from eight different nationalities, several of whom have represented their countries at international rugby and all of whom are professionally contracted players.*

Again this year our players returned home with the greatest impressions of your country. We have greatly enjoyed our two visits to Croatia and look forward to welcoming the Croatian National XV in England when we have arranged for them to play matches against Cambridge University, British Police and the Penguins in early November.

Unfortunately, this last fixture had to be cancelled due to the Penguins being unable to raise a strong enough XV - the professional players' league commitments again being the problem. The Penguins did, however, hold a special lunch for the 30-strong Croatian Rugby Union on Friday, 5th November, at The London Apprentice in Isleworth.

Penguins squad:

Bill Calcraft (Tour Manager, Playing), Alan Wright (Chief Executive), Tony Jarman (Hon. Team and PR Secretary and Tour Manager, Admin), Chris Rees (London Society Referee), David Peirce (Hon. Physiotherapist). Richard Kinsey (Rugby Lions, Wasps, Queensland and Barbarians, Captain), Ian Buckett (London Welsh and Wales), Richard Butland (Richmond, Bath), Mark Challender (Oxford University), Ryan Constable (Saracens and Australia), Luis Criscoulo (Coventry, Barbarians and Argentina), Alwyn Davies (Rugby Lions), Mel Deane (London Irish), Kevin Dunn (Gloucester, Wasps), Caine Elisara (Stade Francaise and Holland), Matthew Gallagher (Coventry), Nick Humphries (Oxford University), Karl Izatt (Kia Toa and New Zealand Sevens), Andy le Chevalier (Wasps),

A letter from the Wasps' Physiotherapist David Peirce thanking Alan Wright for his invitation to tour with the Penguins in June. David had also acted as the Penguins' physio at the Middlesex Sevens in May.

Craig Newby (North Shore and New Zealand Sevens), Beade O'Conner (Oxford University), Derek Patterson (Glasgow Caledonians and Scotland), Floro Sequeira (Coventry and Argentina Sevens), Marc Watson (Wanderers and South Africa Sevens), Mark Weedon (Wasps), Kevin Wirachowski (Wasps and Canada), Chris Wright (Harlequins).

Programme for the 20th June International against the Czech Republic and the match against the Regional Select XV two days later.

Joel Stransky.

Less than two weeks later, on 18th June the Club departed for its main Tour to the Czech Republic and Poland. The tour was managed by Alan Wright (Czech Republic) and Tony Jarman (Poland) and Craig Brown was Tour Manager, Players, for the entire tour.

Craig recalls: 'We had two matches in Prague - one against the national team and one against a regional select team. After that our last game was in Sopot, near Gdansk in Poland, and we played their national team there. The Penguins squad was a good mixture of men, mainly out of the UK - we didn't have anybody travelling from the other side of the world for these matches. We went into Prague and we had a couple of days preparing for the game, because it was a big match. The Czech national team had three imported players - a hooker and a prop who played for Sale, and also Joel Stranski, the South African International stand-off who dropped the goal that won the '95 World Cup. He played for them as well.'

Alan: 'The hardest game of the tour was undoubtedly that against the Czech National XV. Joel Stransky was at stand-off half (he qualified for the national team because has a Czech grandfather). This match was extremely well publicised and, we understand, produced the biggest crowd to watch a rugby match in Prague since the end of the Second World War. There was a wonderful group of cheerleaders and an excellent brass band to add to the occasion.

'With time almost up the Penguins were trailing the Czech XV by 26 points to 28. Peter Macauly from Thanet Wanderers (the only player in the touring party from a junior club) scored a try. After its conversion the final whistle blew and we had won a very close match 33 - 28.'

Craig: 'It was a hugely intense and close game, in which we scored a try to win the match with only two minutes to go. Derek Lee, the Scotland full-back, played outstandingly well for us that day. He ran really well - he glides along and hits the gaps. It was Peter Macauly (the Thanet winger who has subsequently gone on to do some coaching for the Penguins) who got the winning try. It was a good team effort by everybody.

'Two days later we played against the Czech Lions, a regional select XV. This game was easier and we won comfortably by 65 points to 10. But it was still a pretty hard game, and the guys knew that they'd been in a match.

'The following morning we had the bus drive from Prague to Sopot, near Gdansk in Poland, which was meant to take eight hours but in the end took something like twelve. So it was a long day for everybody on the bus, and we only had two stops on the way! The Entertainments Committee did well keeping everbody amused on the bus for that long a time, and we got up to Sopot late at night.

'We had a couple of training sessions on the beach and then we went to play the game against the Polish national team in Gdansk.

Penguins were Captained by Brian Cusack in this match. Again, it was a pretty hard game, even though we won reasonably well. The collisions and the contacts were pretty fierce, and a few people got cuts and stitches and what-not. But overall, it was a great tour.'

The results were: Penguins beat Czech National XV 33 - 28; Penguins beat Czech Lions 65 - 10; Penguins beat Poland National XV 48 - 18.

The Penguins arrived in Sopot late at night after an arduous twelve-hour coach trip.

Penguins squad:

Alan Wright (Tour Manager, Czech Republic), Tony Jarman (Tour Manager, Poland), Craig Brown (Player/Tour Manager, Players) Doug Chapman (RFU Panel Referee), David Peirce (Hon. Physiotherapist).

Brian Cusack (Landsdowne and Richmond, Captain), Chris Cano (Bedford), Caine Elesara (Stade Francaise and Holland), Gary French (London Welsh), Stefan Goosen (Perthshire, Western Province RSA), Graham Inglis (Watsonians), Angus Innes (Cambridge University), Jon Ions (Wasps), David Jenkins (Harlequins and England U21), Scott Keith (Stade Francaise, Croatia), Andy le Chevalier (Wasps), Derek Lee (Edinburgh Reivers and Scotland), Cameron Little (Glasgow Hawks and Glasgow Districts), Peter Macauly (Thanet Wanderers and Kent), Nick Marsh (Oxford University Greyhounds), Darragh McElligott (Clontarf), Russ Morgan (Coventry), David Proctor (Heriot's FP), Scott Reid (Leicester), Peter Robertson (London Scottish), Florent Rossingeux (Wasps), Oliver Slack (Cambridge University), Ian Stent (Heriot's FP), Henry Tarr (Oxford University Greyhounds).

Alan: 'I had to leave the Summer tour and come back to England for two or three days whilst the team went on to Poland because I had a very unusual and critical negotiation to settle. Out of the blue we'd received an invitation to play in the first Thailand International Sevens, which was to be held in Phuket in early July. The invitation had come via a firm of Welsh travel agents. I did want us to go but it was complicated.

'In the end it was arranged. And we managed to take with us four of the wonderful team that had won the Middlesex Sevens. The whole squad knitted together and played sevens to a very high standard - particularly in the final, which

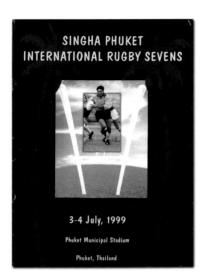

Programme for the first Thailand International Sevens competition which took place in Phuket on 3rd and 4th July.
Penguins won the Tournament by beating the German National Seven 56 - 0 in the final.

It was also in 1999 that Alan proposed that the tie he had originally designed back in 1967 be altered to include the Roman numerals 'XV' on the dark blue strip to denote that that the wearer was a Penguins player.
Prior to this innovation there was only one tie for both Vice-Presidents and Players.

pleased the large crowd *and* the Thai Rugby Union. And we won the tournament!'

The Penguins squad was led by Cameron Pither, the Australian Sevens Captain. The tour was managed by Alan Wright and the Tour Manager (Players) and Coach was Richard Kinsey. The Penguins played exceptionally well, conceding only one score during the whole course of the tournament. After three wins against Malaysia, Hong Kong and Belgium, Penguins beat the German VII in the final. Penguins' Saula Rabaka was named 'Player of the Tournament'.

The day after the tournament, Tor Chittinand wrote in the Sports Section of the Bangkok Post: *Penguins, representing England, made it four wins out of four over the weekend as they won the Singha Phuket International Rugby Sevens at Phuket Municipal Stadium yesterday. Roared on by an appreciative crowd of mainly foreigners, Penguins routed Germany 56 - 0 in the final.*

The English side produced an admirable effort and with three outstanding Fijian players in the team they always looked like finishing as winners of the tournament.

In the first half of the final, Penguins scored 24 points without reply. Then the best player of the tournament, Fijian Saula Rabaka, crossed for a try after the break and almost immediately Chris Wright got another to give the English side a commanding 34 - 0 lead.

By the end, the Germans had been totally overwhelmed by Penguins, who had beaten the Belgium team 24 - 5 in the semi-final.

Afterwards, Penguins Coach Richard Kinsey said: 'We are very pleased to win the tournament. Our team played very well throughout - although we were disappointed to concede a try to Belgium in the semi-final when we made a mistake by defending poorly.

'On Saturday we did not allow any points to be scored against us, so before the final I told my team not to let the Germans score and they managed to achieve that.

'The tournament was fantastic and we enjoyed staying in Phuket very much. The enthusiastic crowd also helped and they continued to watch despite the rain. The enthusiasm of players and spectators alike suggests that this tournament has the momentum to grow into a significant event on the international rugby calendar.'

Unfortunately, the following season's Thai International Sevens Tournament had to be cancelled due to the main sponsor running into commercial difficulties. The Penguins did return in 2001, however, to defend their title.

Penguins' results in Phuket were: Penguins beat Malaysia 37 - 0, Penguins beat Hong Kong 50 - 0, Penguins beat Belgium 24 - 5, Penguins beat Germany 56 - 0. Penguins were winners of the Thai Rugby Union Cup.

Penguins squad:

Alan Wright (Tour Manager), Bill Calcraft (Director of Sevens), Richard Kinsey (Tour Manager, Players, and Coach), Tony Jarman (Chairman, Selection Committee).
Cameron Pither (Australia Sevens, Captain), Fred Asselin (James Bay, Canada Sevens and Canada), Nick Humphries (Manly and Oxford University), Karl Izatt (Kia Toa and New Zealand Sevens), Norman Ligairi (Baravi Exiles and Fiji), Sailosi Nawavu (Baravi Exiles, Nadi RFC and Fiji), Craig Newby (North Shore and New Zealand Sevens), Saula Rabaka (Baravi Exiles and Fiji U23), John Ufton (Wasps), Chris Wright (Harlequins and London Counties).

A significant event in this year was the establishment of the Penguin International Rugby Football Trust, a registered charity with educational objectives primarily through the coaching of rugby union.

Alan Wright had the idea of forming a Trust as the Penguin Rugby Club was a non-profit-making body and he hoped that it could be strengthened by becoming a charitable trust. Alan discussed this with Andrew Thornhill, a long-established Penguin Vice-President, and, incidentally, one of the most eminent tax QCs in the UK. Andrew successfully handled the whole matter with the Charity Commissioners, becoming the Trust's first Chairman.

Alan: 'Really, it was all a question then (to use an expression I used at the time) of putting an acorn into the ground (exactly as Tony Mason and I did with Penguins fifty years ago) and seeing if an oak tree would start to grow. And it did!'

Andrew Thornhill QC - Chairman of The Penguin International Rugby Football Trust. Alan Wright writes: Andrew Thornhill QC has had a long and distinguished career at the Bar, taking silk in 1985. He has been a Recorder since 1997. He has also served for many years as a Governor and Chairman of the Governors at Clifton College, Bristol. His playing career extended from Clifton College Preparatory School to Corpus Christi College, Oxford, where as a dashing three-quarter he played in the College League XV from 1963 - 1965. His last match was in 2009 at Twickenham, playing for Penguin International RFC against the Commons & Lords RFC. Andrew has given great service and wise counsel to the Penguins as a committee member, Patron and, significantly, as the Chairman of the Trustees of Penguin International Rugby Football Trust - which, inter alia, administers The Alan Wright Rugby Scholarship.

The Penguin International Rugby Football Trust

The Penguin International Rugby Football Trust is a charity which was established on 5th August, 1999, and registered on 7th June, 2000 (it is registered with the UK Charity Commission under Charity No. 1081047).

The charity's objectives are educational, with particular reference to the worldwide provision of coaching for young persons in the skills of rugby football and, where appropriate, the provision of financial and other assistance for those youngsters.

The Trust supports the HSBC Penguin International Coaching Academy which organises structured rugby coaching programmes and coach-tutoring courses for youngsters in overseas countries where that expertise is not available locally. The Trust is also responsible for the administration of the Alan Wright Scholarship.

These charities are funded exclusively by donations.

Needless to say, donations from any personal and/or corporate sources will be most welcome at any time to enable the charity to continue its activities.

On 10th December Alan Wright hosted another Dinner at The House of Commons - the second this year. This Dinner was held to celebrate the great success of the HSBC Penguins tour of the Czech Republic and Poland earlier in the year. Amongst the guests were the Croatian and Polish Ambassadors, the Secretary of State to Bosnia and Hertzagovinia, Derek Wyatt MP (who also organised the very special venue) and Keith Harris (Chief Executive, HSBC Investment Bank plc). The Penguins' President, Bob Weighill, was also in attendance.

Below:
Penguin stalwart Derek Harris and Welsh rugby legend Phil Bennett.

1999 also saw Derek Harris join the Penguin Committee. Derek has subsequently served the Club in many capacities.

Derek P.C. Harris

Alan Wright writes: Derek was educated at Clayesmore School and played rugby at fly-half for the school and Dorset Schoolboys; thereafter he was a playing member of both Blackheath FC and Sidcup FC.

He had an distinguished career, having been 30 years in the tobacco industry; a director of Philip Morris UK; and Chairman of both Abdulla Ltd. of Bond Street and Melbourne Hart & Co. Ltd.

Derek was highly regarded throughout the world as a cigar specialist, and was Master of The Worshipful Company of Tobacco Pipe Makers & Tobacco Blenders in 1986. He was also a volunteer member of the Territorial Army, serving as an officer in the Royal Artillery.

Derek's outstanding charitable works involved 30 years as the General Commissioner of Taxes, and 12 years as National Director of the National Association of Boys' Clubs with responsibility for no fewer than 2,600 clubs in the UK.

He joined the Penguin Committee in 1999 and has served the Club in many capacities including Hon. Secretary of the International Ticket Bureau, Finance Officer on the tour to the People's Republic of China in 2000, and as a trustee of the Penguin charity.

Derek is a born leader, an excellent administrator, and a witty and highly regarded public speaker. He has made a most valuable contribution to the success of the Club.

Hang Kek Kang

Craig Brown writes: The late Hang Kek Kang (who sadly died in September, 2011) was asked to be the Penguins' Liaison Officer in Malaysia in the late 1990s and the Club Committee was delighted when he accepted. From that time Hang accompanied the Club on their every visit to Kuala Lumpur and, indeed, all the other tournaments that the Penguins played in Asia.

Hang formerly served as a Warrant Officer in the Bomb Squad of the Malaysian Army. He had lived in the UK and he did a lot of his army training in Great Britain.

The Penguins first met Hang in 1993 and were impressed by his enthusiasm, his contacts, his 'can-do' attitude and by his friendly and engaging personality. He had much experience in being a Liaison Officer over the years for many teams, including the New Zealand Sevens squad at the 1998 Commonwealth Games.

Hang was a valuable member of the Penguin International RFC Management Team and had a superb skill at managing all of those many essential jobs that make a major Penguin International RFC overseas tour run smoothly.

Hang was a very special friend of the Penguin International RFC and he will be sorely missed.

Hang Kek Kang and Penguins' Coach John McKittrick during the Malaysia Tour of 2006. Hang first joined the Penguins in the late '90s.

UALE MAI
Penguins' HSBC COBRA International Tens
winning Captain, Malaysia, September 2006

2000 - 2011

THE RIPPLES SPREAD

Alan Wright: 'Highlights of our fifth decade include:

♦ The establishment of the HSBC/Penguin International
Coaching Academy;

♦ The Academy being appointed to accompany
the British & Irish Lions Tour to South Africa;

♦ The Academy being invited to become coaches to
the Asia Five Nations Committee;

♦ Our most ambitious tour to date, which encompassed
twin continents and included the winning of
the European Grand Prix Sevens Tournament;

♦ Tours to the Americas (Argentina/Canada/Mexico/USA);

♦ Tours to Europe (France/Germany/Malta/Scotland);

♦ Sevens tournament (Thailand);

♦ Tens Tournaments (Borneo/Malaysia/Mexico);

♦ Our Golden Anniversary, which was celebrated
at Twickenham Stadium with a "Twin Anniversary"
Golden Oldies Match between the
Penguin International RFC (50 years old)
and the Commons/Lords RFC
(who were 25 years old - a happy coincidence!)

♦ Our "Blaze of Glory" when we win
the Singapore Cricket Club Sevens
and the HSBC COBRA International Tens'

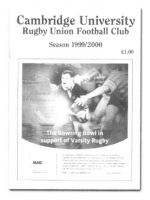

Cambridge University v Penguins match programme.

2000

The Penguins' new millennium playing campaign started at Counden Road in Coventry on 16th February, when Penguins, under Team Manager and Selector Ian Bullerwell and Captained by Paul Burke, the Cardiff and Ireland fly-half, beat Coventry RFC 36 - 26 in a very special match to celebrate the Coventry Club's 125th Anniversary. The Penguins' squad also contained Caine Elisara, the Dutch international, John Tait of Cardiff and Canada and no fewer than seven Bedford players. The Club considered it a very great honour to be asked to play in this famous and venerable Club's Anniversary fixture.

Programme notes and team sheet from the Coventry match.

Penguins beat Cambridge University 67 - 24 in an exciting, high-scoring encounter at Grange Road on 1st March in what would be the first of two games against the Light Blues that took place in 2000. Once again the Penguins were Managed by Ian Bullerwell and Captained by Paul Burke and included John Tait in the line-up.

On 8th May HSBC honoured the Penguins by hosting a Dinner at the Middle Temple, courtesy of Andrew Thornhill QC. Guests included the Chinese Ambassador and Martin Johnson - who was, at this time, the current England Captain.

On 14th May Penguins were invited to play a special ten-a-side match against Harlequins, the hosts, prior to the Middlesex Club Sevens Final at the Twickenham Stoop. Penguins beat Quins 33 - 10.

Alan Wright: 'Shortly after the Quins match came our visit to The People's Republic of China between the 29th May - 4th June.

'I arranged the tour with the Ministry of Sport of The People's Republic, and it was to be the first time that a European rugby club had ever toured China. Our sponsors were very pleased, of course, bearing in mind that China is the principal trading nation of HSBC.

'The tour was inspired in 1998 as a result of George Simpkin, former

coach to the Hong Kong Rugby Union, becoming the National Director of the Chinese RU. This culminated in David Townsend (who had, in the first instance, drawn my attention to the fact that the Chinese Army had adopted rugby union as a character-building compulsory sport) arranging a meeting in Hong Kong between Mr. Li Gaochao, the Secretary General of the Chinese Rugby Union, and I, during which it was agreed that we would be welcome tourists in 2000.

'The Penguins' ethos for this very special tour was to concentrate on the promotion of goodwill. To this end we took a first-class coach to assist the Chinese team and other young players in Shanghai, as well as Nigel Yates, one of England's top-six referees. It was agreed with the hosts that Nigel would referee the matches and also hold seminars throughout our stay.

'The touring party was advised with some care as to life in China - including "Dos and Don'ts" guidelines that the Bank very kindly drew up for us. And out of respect for our hosts we selected our normal-strength touring side which was drawn from eight countries.

'Originally the two "Test Matches" (as the Chinese called them) were to be played in Bejing. But at the last moment they changed the event to Shanghai - producing a few admin difficulties that I overcame (I had booked the original flights with SAS, and I appealed to them to cancel our bookings and return our money to our travel agent, but they simply passed the cheque on to Virgin Airlines and we flew Virgin. I thought this was a very magnanimous gesture by SAS as I considered that this change of destination would probably not be covered by our insurance policy).

'It was an exciting tour, treading new ground. Craig Brown and I worked very happily together once again. The Chinese received us in a very dignified, pleasant and helpful manner, and they were very efficient. We were fortunate that the Deputy Manager from the Ministry of Sport (whose responsibilities were, strangely enough, rugby and golf) was Susan Zhang Xuan, a talented lady who spoke very good English. She translated my speeches at dinners and other functions, including training sessions - particularly when we were coaching China's national team.

'We took a strong team, including Arwel Thomas, the Welsh stand-off half, and we also had with us player/coach Richard Kinsey from Wasps FC for the purposes of organising the coaching of the Chinese. In the end (because of injuries) he also played for us, and he scored a try in each match.

'The Chinese were coached by George Simpkin (a Kiwi who had previously coached Fiji as well as Hong Kong) and their forwards played just like New Zealanders. The Chinese are certainly not all little men! There is a Province where they have men who grow tall and are suitable as back-row forwards and locks.

'The first match was played on 1st June at the new Yucai Middle School Stadium in front of a large crowd. The result was a 75 - 22 win for the Penguins.

The Penguin RFC broke new ground in 2000 by becoming the first European rugby club ever to tour The People's Republic of China. Rugby football is a relatively new sport in the People's Republic. The first domestic club, the China Agricultural University Rugby Club, was only formed as recently as 1990. The Chinese National Rugby Team was founded in 1997 by the Chinese National Rugby Football Association.

At the last minute the Penguins' base was switched from Bejing to the Nikko Pudong Hotel, Shanghai.

Derek Harris, Tony Jarman and Alan Wright in Pudong.

Shanghai - the old city.

Above: The match against the Chinese National team in Shanghai.

No account of the tour would be complete without mention of the brilliant practical joke that the team played on Penguins' prop, Andy le Chevalier, in the latter stages of the final match. Andy, a very good-natured and non-violent man, was sent off by tour referee Nigel Yates for fighting. Andy, who had never been sent off before in his whole career, immediately sought out Alan Wright and the rest of the Penguin management to proclaim his innocence. It was only later that he was let in on the secret - before the match his team mates had got together with Nigel Yates to arrange the whole thing!

'The second match was played on a wonderful ground - at (but not in) the magnificent Shanghai Stadium. We coached the Chinese National team the day before, particularly in regard to their forward play, and come the match they led us for the first 25 minutes. For a moment or two I thought we'd over-coached them! However, the ultimate score was 88 - 20 in our favour.

'Both were hard matches but played in a very good spirit.'

The China tour finished with a grand Farewell Party on 4th June, 2000, at the Regal Shanghai East Asia Hotel, where special awards were presented to Mr. Hu Aiben (Vice-President of the Chinese Rugby Football Association), Mr. George Simpkin (National Director of Rugby) and Mike Lu (Captain of the Chinese National XV) among others. David Townsend, Penguins' Liaison Officer, was also presented with a surprise award for helping to initiate and organise the tour.

Alan: 'So all-in-all we left China with good memories, having had a happy time and creating lot of good-will. I presented the leading Chinese functionaries who attended the farewell dinner with ties and hats and a plaque. I made them all laugh, because the hats I gave them had been made in China, purchased by Tony Jarman in Dover, had Penguin hat-bands put on them elsewhere in the UK and then we took them all the way back to China to give them back as presents!'

It is, perhaps, some indication of the quality and depth of the coaching that China received from the Penguins that, only three days after the PIRFC tour ended, the Chinese national team played their first international against Hong Kong - and won 17 - 15. China then travelled on to Japan for the Asian Championships and won two of their three matches (against Thailand and Singapore) losing by only one point to Sri Lanka.

As Alan wrote later, in his tour report to HSBC: *The really pleasing aspect of the tour was that the members of the touring party conducted themselves, both on and off the field, as exemplary ambassadors for the Club, the UK, Ireland and in particular, HSBC, and I am in no doubt that our visit was 100% successful.*

In a letter to Alan dated 20th July, 2000, Penguins' Tour Captain Brian Cusack (the Landsdowne and Ireland 'A' lock-forward) wrote the following letter to Alan: *I am writing to thank you and congratulate you on a very successful tour to The People's Republic of China. The tour was an outstanding success and seemed to be thoroughly enjoyed by everyone. I felt the tour not only benefited both players and officials but also our hosts, who seemed genuinely pleased that we visited their country. They proved to be outstanding hosts and committed opponents.*

From your experiences of travelling you have realised that going to countries where there is an extreme language barrier can be to the detriment of the tour, but everything ran with the utmost smoothness.

From a personal point of view, it was a great honour to Captain a Penguins tour for the second time - and it is something which I am extremely proud of. I was delighted to play with and Captain a great bunch of guys. Thank you.

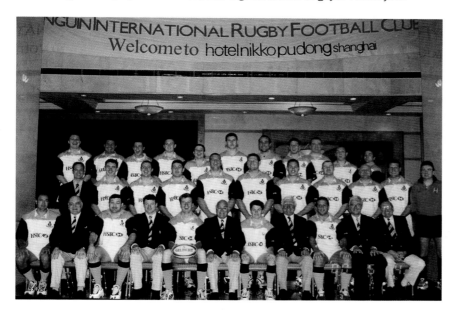

Penguins squad: Alan Wright (Tour Manager), Craig Brown (Tour Manager, Players), David Townsend (Liaison Officer), Tony Jarman (Hon. Press and PR), Derek Harris (Tour Treasurer), Hugh Thomas (Penguin Committee), Richard Kinsey (Coach to CRU), Nigel Yates (Referee), David Peirce (Hon. Physiotherapist).

Brian Cusack (Lansdowne, Captain), Paul Beal (Bedford), Nick Broughton (Bedford), Fergal Campion (St. Mary's), Luis Criscuolo (Argentina), Gordon Dickson (Watsonians), Chad Eagle (Bristol), Caine Elisara (Netherlands), Mike Friday (Wasps), Ben Harvey (Worcester), Graeme Inglis (Watsonians), Kevin James (Neath), Richard Kinsey (Wasps), Andy le Chevalier (Wasps), Dougal Macer (Wasps), Darragh McGilliott (Clontarf), David Moore (Clontarf), Florent Rossigneux (Bedford), Laurence Scrase (Wasps), Marko Stanojevic (Bristol), Ian Stent (Heriot's FP), Arwel Thomas (Swansea and Wales, Vice-Captain), Jon Ufton (Wasps), Chris Wright (Harlequins), Danny Zaltzman (Bedford).

PIRFC and CRFA officials at the farewell dinner at the end of the tour. Susan Zhang Xuan, the CRU's Tour Liaison Officer, holds her Panama hat.

A thank-you letter from the China Rugby Union to the Penguins. It was written by Susan Zhang Xuan.

Middlesex Sevens 2000 programme.

Alan: 'And now, of course, we come to one of the highlights of this decade - our return invitation to the Middlesex Sevens.

In the year 2000 the Middlesex Rugby Union had decided that the tournament would be played at the end of August as opposed to its traditional slot in May. Because of this reorganisation our position as defenders of the title remained doubtful for a while - but we *were* invited back.

'When this invitation was made the Middlesex Sevens Committee advised us that they were again providing us with worldwide expenses to be used on a discretionary basis of trust because they were looking for us to bring a team that would, hopefully, stand up to the Premiership sides - as we had the year before.

Pictured above is probably the greatest Sevens team of all time - the Penguin International squad for the 2000 Middlesex Sevens: Back row: I. Bullerwell (Selector), C. De Goldi (New Zealand Sevens), V. Delasu (Fiji, Fiji Sevens), R. Kinsey (Assistant Coach), C. Brown (Assistant Manager), C. Elisara (Netherlands), F. Asselin (Canada, Canada Sevens), S. Rokini (Fiji, Fiji Sevens), Julian Lamden (Treasurer). Front row: D. Qua Qua (Fiji, Fiji Sevens), B. Calcraft (Team Manager and Director of Sevens), W. Serevi (Fiji, Fiji Sevens, Captain), B. Weighill CBE, DFC (President), E. Rush (New Zealand, New Zealand Sevens), A. Wright (Chairman), C. Pither (Australia Sevens), T. Jarman (Liasion Manager).

'Now this time we really applied our knowledge, and the team we produced - which was subsequently acknowledged in the Twickenham programme as being "The Masters of Sevens" - was quite simply the best Sevens team that has ever trodden the turf at Twickenham up until that time.

'We had, for the first and only time in the history of rugby, Eric Rush, the number one Sevens expert from New Zealand, playing in the same team as the number one Sevens expert on the planet, Waisale Serevi. And we had the Captain of Australian Sevens, Cameron Pither, who was also a brilliant player and Caine Elisara, Captain of Netherlands Sevens. So we had no fewer than four international Sevens Captains in the team, from New Zealand, Fiji, Australia and Holland.

'We also had Freddie Asselin, a real flyer from Canada, who'd scored three tries against Fiji in the Commonwealth Games and who was also the highest scorer in that tournament. He is the player I'd wanted the previous year but he had injured himself falling down a rabbit hole in Tokyo! We also had

Craig De Goldi, who has subsequently played with us for years. At one time he became the most capped New Zealand Sevens player of all time - he's been capped 500 times!

'And we had a very unusual player in our team - a Dutchman. Well, he was a New Zealander who had been brought up in New Zealand but had gone to live in Holland. He had played for Holland at XVs and at Sevens. The reason that I recommended him in the Selection Committee was that he had gone to a school where basketball was the primary sport. He could pick up a rugby ball on the run with one hand. His handling was fantastic. His name is Caine Elisara and he was with an Italian Club at that time. He had come to China with us in May and on the plane back he said to me: "Alan, any chance of my being considered for the Middlesex Sevens?" And I said: "Well, the answer is yes, selection will be considered on merit. I'll talk to our other selectors because I think you're a wonderful Sevens player - even though you've not played for a major country!"

Penguins' Director of Sevens Bill Calcraft remembers: 'Yes, we had a little bit more time to get a side together, and we had a phenomenal team. Eric Rush was the pre-eminent rugby football sevens, tens and test player in the world at that time. Eric is an absolute gentleman so I just rang him up and I said

Penguins' Captain Waisale Serevi introduces RFU President Derek 'Budge' Rogers to the Penguins team before the final at Twickenham. Left to right: Caine Elisara, Freddie Asselin, Cameron Pither, Waisale Serevi and Budge Rogers.

"Why don't you come to the Middlesex Sevens with the Penguins and play with Serevi?" They had never played together. And of course he was quite keen. It's amazing how these things work out. And then we recruited Cameron Pither, the Captain of the Australian Sevens team and Qua Qua for the second year running. And we also had George Satala and Vilimoni Delasau, who is a super player. Delasau was considered at that time to be the best centre in the world. He started in the 2007 World Cup, but people didn't recognise him because of his long hair! Back in 2000 he was only 19 and he was unstoppable.

'I must say, though, that we owe a great deal of thanks to Richard and John Breen, our friends in Fiji, for their help in getting Waisale Serevi, Danny Qau Qau and George Satala out of Fiji during the military coup that just happened to coincide with the tournament! You see, the three of them were there at that time - it's the Fijian rugby season. So we had to get these guys out. Well, a military coup in Fiji is not a particularly dangerous exercise, but it does put a stop to people travelling around for a while. At the time the British Embassy was surrounded by the military, Parliament was closed down and surrounded by the military... but as Serevi himself said: "Yes, Bill - the Fijian Army all have guns, but they don't really want to shoot anybody. They just shoot in the ground!"

Sevens Final action: Cameron Pither on the charge. Saracens' Richard Hill tracks back.

Above left: Eric James Rush was the greatest New Zealand sevens player ever to grace the game.
In a distinguished career between 1988 and his 39th birthday in 2004, Rush played in more than 60 tournaments, with the highlights being two Commonwealth Games Gold Medals and the World Cup Sevens victory in 2001.
Rush also played in nine test matches for the All Blacks.
Above right: Vilimoni Waqatabu Delasau ('Delz') with his hair worn long! Delasau scored 85 tries for the Fiji Sevens team, and was named Player of the Year at the Fiji Rugby Awards after scoring 82 tries in the 1999 season. He also holds the world record for scoring the most tries in a sevens match (six) and also for scoring the most tries in a sevens tournament (16). He was first capped for Fiji at XVs in 2000.

'So I never got the impression that it was a hugely dangerous episode. But we had to get these players out while all of this is going on. So I spoke to Richard Breen, our Committee man in Fiji. He said: "Well, Billy, we have a bit of a problem here..."

'But the bottom line was that despite all this going on we *had* to get some Fijian players to the Twickenham Sevens in England and the authorities recognised that this was important. Rugby is top of the tree in Fiji. So they let them open the British High Commission for the players to go in and get their visas stamped, come out and get on a plane to England. Success!'

Alan: 'The team was, fundamentally, Fijian backs with New Zealand forwards.'

Bill: 'When the team got on the bus to leave for the stadium I sat down with Serevi. I asked him if everything was OK and whether there were any problems. Referring to the previous year he said with a smile: "No Bill. I am here for the whole day!"

'I then said: "How will we go today?" He replied, without a hint of arrogance: "We will win this for certain." There was absolutely no doubt in his mind. Of course, the year before he had been confident - but not certain.'

Craig Brown was also part of the build-up at Twickenham that day. He remembers: 'We had great players. They knew there was no point in getting uptight about all the expectations people had of them - they just had to do their own natural thing and keep it as relaxed as possible. There wasn't any shouting or getting upset beforehand. It was all very calm and collected.'

Alan: 'We won our matches comfortably, as the figures will show. We again met Saracens in the final, for the second year running, but this time we won in great style, beating them 47 - 19. It was a very happy occasion. Our President, Bob Weighill, enjoyed it all.'

Bill: 'So the years 1999 and 2000 were very high profile for the Penguins. We actually won £102,500 in prize money in those two years (the extra £2,500 had come from the fact that Eurobet, the bookmaker sponsor, had put up £2,500 for the team that scored the most tries in the tournament). So it was all very good for the Penguin RFC and very good for the Penguin RFC players!'

That evening the celebrations at the Lensbury Club were very special because, in addition to a few words from Alan, Eric Rush made a delightful speech, saying how proud he was to play alongside Waisale Serevi, '...having chased his tail for about thirteen years!'

Alan adds: 'Serevi was equally delighted to play on the same team as Eric Rush - even though he had once said to Bill Calcraft: "Fijians don't play with Kiwis!" So it all ended up very, very well.'

Above: Sevens Final action: Saimoni Rokini carries the ball supported by Craig De Goldi (left) and Cameron Pither (right).
Below: About to receive the Russell-Cargill Cup after beating Saracens by 47 points to 19 in the final tie - Waisale Serevi shakes hands with Derek Mann, President of the Middlesex Rugby Union and a Penguin Honorary Vice-President.

The full results were: Penguins beat Rotherham 54 - 7; Penguins beat Samurai 26 - 10; semi-final: Penguins beat Newcastle 38 - 12. Final: Penguins beat Saracens 47 - 19. Penguins won the Russell-Cargill Cup (back-to-back!).

Bill Calcraft has the last word: 'Well, we trained for a couple of days and it was good fun. All these guys got on fantastically well and they genuinely liked playing with the great Serevi paired with Eric Rush. We compared notes and I thought: How do you coach all that lot?! But I had my own little way of doing things - clearly, it was all just man-management and getting the right sort of structure together. But it was probably the greatest sevens squad ever assembled, and results proved that. We played fantastic rugby.'

Penguins squad: B. Calcraft (Director of Sevens and Team Manager), A. Wright (Chairman), C. Brown (Assistant Manager), R. Kinsey (Assistant Coach), A. Jarman (Liaison Manager), I. Bullerwell (Selector), C. Boynes (Physio).

W. Serevi (Fiji, Fiji Sevens, Captain), F. Asselin (Canada, Canada Sevens), C. De Goldi (New Zealand Sevens), V. Delasu (Fiji, Fiji Sevens), C. Elisara (Netherlands), C. Pither (Australia), D. Qau Qau (Fiji, Fiji Sevens), S. Rokini (Fiji, Fiji Sevens), E. Rush (New Zealand, New Zealand Sevens), G. Satala (Fiji, Fiji Sevens).

Below, left: Back-to-back glory at the Middlesex Sevens! Waisale Serevi holds aloft the Russell- Cargill Cup whilst Craig De Goldi and Eric Rush make their way up to the presentation area. Below, right: Barry Newcombe's newspaper report of the tournament from The Times.

Rugby Union

Penguins pull off diplomatic coup

By Barry Newcombe

WITHOUT the assistance of British Government representatives in Fiji the Penguins would have been hard pressed to produce a team with the competence and style to retain the Middlesex Sevens title at Twickenham.

The Penguins co-ordinator, Bill Calcraft, recognised that obtaining three visas to enter Britain for players based in Fiji might be difficult in the aftermath of a political coup, especially as only two were being issued each week. "We just made sure everybody knew how important it was and made sure we got to the right people," said Calcraft, who counted his final player into the squad only on Friday.

The response of the Fijian players was one of the key factors of the whole event, but it was Calcraft's clever mix of Pacific Island flair with the likes of New Zealand's Eric Rush which made the end product so compelling. Rush and the captain, Waisale Serevi, had never played sevens together but they were always in harmony and as the demands grew younger players such as Villimoni Delasu and the New Zealander, Craig de Goldi, began to make more impact.

In the 47-19 win over Saracens in the final, De Goldi scored the first two tries and Delasu the seventh and last after running 70 metres.

Serevi scored 60 points in four matches and is already planning a return to Twickenham in a year's time.

Saracens, too, looked strong, through Richard Hill's example in the close exchanges and the finshing of Thomas Castaignède and Darragh O'Mahony. But beating Northampton 28-26 in the semi-final was a huge effort and although they twice led in the final they were soon chasing the game.

Newcastle had looked strong in taking out London Irish and Leicester, with Gareth MacLure an impressive finisher. But the Penguins simply did not let them into their semi-final for long enough to make a sustained impact.

This old tournament, first played in 1926 when Wavell Wakefield was in the winning Harlequins seven, had been moved to the start of the season from the end and in hot weather drew a crowd of 23,000. Having been entertained so richly by the men from the South Seas, they are sure to want more of the same next year.

PENGUINS (squad): W Serevi (Fiji, capt), F Asselin (Canada), C de Goldi (New Zealand), V Delasu, C Elisara (both Fiji), C Pither (Australia), T QauQau, S Rokini (Fiji), E Rush (New Zealand), V Satala (Fiji). **Tries:** De Goldi 2, QauQau, Satala, Rokini, Rush, Delasu. **Conversions:** Serevi 6.
SARACENS: K Chesney, R-Hill, B Johnston, K Sorrell, N Walshe, B Hampson, D MacRae, D O'Mahony, R Haughton, T Castaignède. **Tries:** O'Mahony, pen try, Hill. **Conversions:** Castaignède 2.

Details: Sport 12

On 9th and 10th September the Penguins played in the Malaysian RU/COBRA International Invitational Tens Tournament in Kuala Lumpar - the first full Malaysian RU/COBRA Tournament to be held since 1996. The tournament was not held in 1998 due to the Commonwealth Games, and in 1999 COBRA were only able to stage a small tournament (mainly consisting of local teams) due to the Asian financial crisis.

Alan: 'In the Malaysian Tens we had our second Fijian Captain of 2000, Sailosi Nawavu. He had played in our winning team at Twickenham in the 1999 Middlesex Sevens - having been Captain of Fiji. Sailosi is delightful man, a qualified coach who has stayed an enthusiastic member of the Penguins (in 2009 he had his picture in *Rugby World* as he was coaching prisoners in Cape Town Prison as a HSBC Penguin Academy Coach accompanying the Lions Tour). All of these things link together! It's amazing how, particularly with us, we find over the decades people have stayed with us. There have been so many links.

'Sailosi is a great friend of the Club. There is a wonderful story about him. He was a diving coach, and he was diving once and lost his equipment and airline. When he came to the surface there had been a storm and his boat had disappeared. He swam for about 14 hours to an island and collapsed, but lived to tell the tale. He's a tough man. He's the only man I've seen, quite regularly in Sevens competitions, to get up under our kick-off and then throw the ball back with two hands - because he's so fast and so tall. Fijians are instinctive Sevens players and are nearly always well positioned so as to pick up unusual passes thrown backwards from kick-off. They understand that possession is everything, and certainly Sailosi is a great Sevens player.'

Bill Calcraft wrote the following note to the entire Penguins squad shortly after the end of the tournament: *We had a very good match against the Fiji side in our last pool match. Although losing 12 - 24 we certainly showed enough to suggest that if we took all our chances we could, perhaps, win a repeat in the final.*

We beat Samoa in the quarter-final and then got completely strangled by the Argentine national side. There must have been ten to twelve lineouts which degenerated into a catch-and-drive-type game. Hence there was no flow to the game and very little ball for us. It was a very niggly affair as it usually is against them. They won it fair and square, though, no question.

There was a lesson to be learnt here - I feel that had we got away from them early on they would have needed to respond with a more open game, and that would have suited us very much. Nevertheless, we regard it as a successful

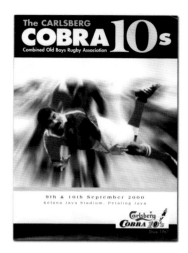

Programme for the Malaysian RU/COBRA 10s competition, 2000.

Sailosi Nawavu's visa application form for the 2001 Argentina Tour.

outing, given the strength of the semi-final teams. All you boys played very well as usual, although we were very disappointed and frustrated by the Argentina match.

The results were: Penguins beat China 61 - 0; Penguins beat USA 52 - 0; Penguins lost to Fiji 12 - 24. Quarter-final: Penguins beat Samoa 24 - 12. Semi-final: Penguins lost to Argentina 5 - 19.

Penguin International squad for the 2000 COBRA 10s:
Back row: Norman Langari, Alex Calcraft, Tom Soloman, Ben Peterson, David Townsend, Nick Humphries, Alan Wright, Saulo Rabaka, Bill Calcraft, Craig Brown.
Middle row: Stacey Miller, Adrian Donald, Dominic Byrne, Tom O'Brien, Sailosi Nawavu, Peter Playford.
On the ground: Brett Sheehan, Dan Qau Qau.

Alan Wright made the following observations in a memo to the Penguin Committee in April, 2000, when the invitation to play in the 2000 COBRA tournament first arrived: It is clear that the COBRA tournament takes place at the beginning of our professional season when the clubs will be very reluctant to release players. Accordingly, our best hope would be to have a minority of UK-based players - probably from Oxbridge (if it does not conflict with their tours) - plus nine or ten players from the Southern Hemisphere. This Southern Hemisphere slant with regard to selection during the UK rugby season has, of necessity, remained in place ever since.

Penguins squad: Craig Brown (Tour Manager, players), Alan Wright (CEO), Bill Calcraft (Coach), David Townsend (Liaison Officer), Alex Calcraft (Assistant Manager), Tony Jarman (Chairman of Selectors).

Sailosi Nawavu (Baravi Exiles and Fiji, Captain), Dominic Byrne (Manly and Australia Sevens), Adrian Donald (North Harbour), Nick Humphries (Oxford University and The New York Athletic Club RFC), Norman Langari (Baravi Exiles and Fiji), Stacy Miller (Bay of Plenty), Tim O'Brien (Manly and Australia U21), Ben Peterson (Manly and Australia U21), Peter Playford (Wests and Australia U21), Dan Qau Qau (Baravi Exiles and Fiji), Saula Rabaka (Baravi Exiles and Fiji Sevens), Brett Sheehan (Manly and Brisbane Broncos RL), Tom Solomon (Bay of Plenty).

Bob Weighill, a very dear friend of both Alan Wright and Peter Yarranton and a great President of the Club, passed away on Thursday, 27th October, 2000. Bob had served the Penguin RFC as President for 14 years (1986 - 2000) and was a great help to the Penguins before and during his tenure. He had a most distinguished career, both in the RAF and in rugby football. He Captained England and played for his country four times, and was Secretary of the RFU from 1973 - 1986, also serving as the Secretary to the International Rugby Board and the Five Nations Committee. He was a highly influential and respected administrator.

Bob was succeeded as Penguins' President by Sir Peter Yarranton, past President of the Rugby Union.

Sir Peter had not only been a Penguins player, but also a Member of the Penguins Committee for 20 years. He had played for Wasps, RAF, Combined Services and England, and was a past President of Wasps and the Rugby Union. In addition, he was a past Chairman of the National Sports Council.

Alan recalls: 'I had to use the good offices of my friend Lady Mary Yarranton to persuade her husband to become our new President! He had, unfortunately for the Club, just become Chairman of the Scarborough Cricket Week and felt that to take on office with the Penguins might be too much responsibility.'

However, Peter, loving the Penguins, quickly decided to trust Alan, who offered to keep Peter informed at all times of the Club's doings whilst he was President, and gracefully agreed to accept the office.

Air Commodore Bob Weighill

THE DAILY TELEGRAPH WEDNESDAY, NOVEMBER 1, 2000

Rugby playing pilot who taught the captain of Wales to fly Mustangs and in return learnt skills that brought him the England captaincy

AIR COMMODORE BOB WEIGHILL, who has died aged 80, enjoyed a notable career in the RAF but was more widely known for his services to rugby, both as a player (he once captained England) and as a highly influential administrator.

A robust No 8, Weighill was capped four times for England, making his debut against Scotland in 1947 in the first international played at Twickenham after the war; England won 24-5. A month later he was back at Twickenham, in the England side which narrowly beat the French.

At Murrayfield in 1948, however, the Scots took revenge, and when Weighill captained England against France in the Stade Colombes in Paris, the side went down 0-15. That proved to be his last game for England.

As an administrator, Weighill was secretary of the Rugby Football Union from 1973 to 1986, and thereafter served on on the International Rugby Board and the Five Nations Rugby Committee.

Weighill was very much a traditionalist; and in his early days as Secretary at Twickenham, when the sport was less commercially minded, the RFU telephone number was listed ex-directory. Yet he successfully guided the RFU into the era of sponsorship; and in his time the RFU's turnover increased tenfold, from £500,000 to £5 million per annum.

Robert Harold George Weighill was born at Heswall, Cheshire, on September 9 1920, and educated at Wirral Grammar School. As a young boy, he had been a keen soccer player, but once he took to rugger at school he never looked back.

He proved a fine all-round sportsman, and became the free-style swimming champion of Cheshire.

The Wirral school had only opened in 1931, with 100 first-formers. In its second year, there arrived a much older boy (born in 1916) called Harold Wilson, who was placed in solitary glory in the Sixth Form. He took the responsibility conferred by seniority extremely seriously, suggesting to the headmaster that there should be football at lunch time in order to prevent sexual mischief amongst the boys.

In 1948, when Weighill was captaining England at Rugby, the press asked Harold Wilson, by then President of the Board of Trade, whether he had any memories of his erstwhile schoolfellow. "He was a very intelligent boy," Wilson returned, "but not very good at rugger." Perhaps this was a joke; yet another contemporary recorded that Wilson "was not terribly good at sport, though he used to think he was".

Weighill joined the RAF in 1941, and the next year, after completing training as a pilot, joined No 2 Squadron, an Army Co-operation Command fighter-reconnaissance squadron equipped with Mustangs.

This aircraft had been built for the RAF in the United States by North American, having originated as a hasty sketch made in a London hotel room. Later, after pilots such as Weighill had demonstrated the Mustang's operational virtues, the USAAF adopted the aircraft as the P-51.

It was in the RAF that Weighill's rugby career began to take off. He owed much of his skill on

Weighill about to set off for the Lions tour of the Far East (1971)

the pitch to the Wales flanker and captain A M "Arthur" Rees, who had enlisted as a trainee pilot. "Arthur happily took my rugby in hand and taught me all the finer points and dodges of backrow play," Weighill remembered,

"while I taught him how to fly a Mustang. He undoubtedly got the best of the exchange."

Weighill, as always, was too modest. Rees became a squadron leader and rose to acting wing commander. After the war he

became Chief Constable of Stafford and Stoke-on-Trent.

Weighill's breakthrough in rugby came in December 1943. As a non-playing reserve for the RAF team facing the Army at Richmond Athletic Ground, he had joined two New Zealand pilot friends for a slap-up lunch before going on to watch the game. After lingering in a nearby pub, he got to the ground 10 minutes before kick-off — and was appalled to see two WAAF girls walking around the packed ground with a blackboard, on which a message had been scrawled ordering him to report to the dressing rooms.

There had been a late withdrawal, and Weighill was required to play. "For some peculiar reason," he recalled, "I played particularly well, we won, and I never looked back."

As a pilot, meanwhile, Weighill had been flying tactical reconnaissance missions over France and the Low Countries. In 1944, in the run-up to D-Day, he photographed the coastal defences in Normandy, before transferring to No 19 Squadron, another Mustang outfit, and attacking enemy positions in the Normandy battle area.

Later, from October 1944, Weighill operated with a large force of Mustang squadrons from Andrews Field (formerly Great Saling) in Essex, flying long-range daylight escort sorties in support of the heavy bombers attacking industrial Germany. He was awarded the DFC.

After the war he served (from 1948) as a squadron commander at the RAF College, Cranwell, and in 1952 was selected for a course at RAF Staff College. Three years

later he returned in command to No 2 Squadron, which had been re-equipped with Gloster Meteor jets, and simultaneously led No 138 fighter wing.

On the rugby pitch he captained the RAF between 1945 and 1952, and also turned out for Birkenhead Park, Waterloo, Harlequins, Leicester, Chesire and the Barbarians. In 1951 he captained the Combined Services.

After a neck injury had put paid to his playing career, he represented the RAF on the RFU Committee for many years, and served as an England selector (1959-64).

In the RAF, he had a spell on the Directing Staff at Imperial Defence College, then in 1961 was appointed station commander at RAF Cottesmore. His final postings were as Group Captain Operations, RAF Germany (1964-65), Assistant Commandant, RAF College of Air Warfare (1967-68), and Commandant RAF Halton (1968-73). He also served as an ADC to the Queen.

Weighill's love of rugby never waned. Recently he told an interviewer how, late at night before every rugby international at Twickenham, after he had completed his final checks, he would walk on to the pitch and stand on the centre spot.

"Slowly I would look around one of the great stadiums in any sport. It was always a thrilling moment. And then, without fail, I used to say a little prayer that everything would be OK the following day."

Bob Weighill married, in 1946, Beryl Hodgson, who died in 1981. They had two sons, one of whom predeceased him.

Air Commodore R.H.G. (Bob) Weighill - The fifth Penguin President

Air Commodore Robert Harold George Weighill CBE DFC (9th September, 1920 - 27th October, 2000). Educated at Wirral Grammar School. Served with Cheshire County Constabulary 1937 - 1941. Bob Weighill flew Mustangs during WW2. He was awarded the DFC. He has also served as an ADC to the Queen. In his rugby football career Bob Weighill played for Birkenhead Park, Waterloo, Harlequins and Leicester. He Captained the RAF XV from 1945 - 52 and Captained Combined Services in 1951. Bob was capped four times for England. He was one of the most able and knowledgeable administrators in the rugby world in the post-war era, being Secretary of the RFU from 1973 - 1986 and serving thereafter on the International Rugby Board, the Five Nations Committee and the British Lions Committee.

On 7th November Penguins lost 19 - 32 to Cambridge University. The Penguins were Managed by Ian Bullerwell and Tony Jarman, Captained by Craig Chalmers (Glasgow Caledonians, Scotland and the British & Irish Lions) and included Stu Forster (Leinster and New Zealand), Charlie Hodgson (Sale), Marcus Di Rollo (Edinburgh Reivers and Scotland), Wayne Proctor (Llanelli and Wales), and Alexander Mihajlovic (Bedford Athletic and Yugoslavia). Alan: 'This was the second time this year that we played Cambridge University - which was a most unusual situation. As a result of an invitation from them we began to play them in the autumn term prior to the Varsity Match, having previously played them in the spring term up until then. This short-term experiment did not continue because they already had the benefit of their great match against the Steele-Bodger XV in autumn.'

Above: Bob Weighill's Obituary from the Daily Telegraph of Wednesday, 1st November, 2000. Alan: 'Bob was a marvelous President. He was our longest-serving President and he and I had a wonderful working relationship. The Penguins greatly benefited from his knowlege and advice throughout all those years. He was much-loved and respected and a great gentleman.'

2001 CHRONICLE

31st January - Penguins lost to Oxford University 17 - 34 at Iffley Road, Oxford.

6th May - Penguins lost to Bedford Blues RFC 46 - 72 in The Bruce Willey Memorial Match at Goldington Road, Bedford.

29th May - Summer Tour to Germany (Captained by Mike Friday of England) and Argentina (Captained by Andre Fox of the Republic of South Africa).
2nd June - Penguins beat the German National XV 101 - 8 in Heidelberg.
3rd June - Grand Prix of Europe. Captained by Mike Friday (England). Penguins beat Comite Alpes Maritimes 35 - 0
Penguins beat Poland 33 - 14
Penguins beat Netherlands 36 - 0
Penguins beat Germany 57 - 7
Winners, Grand Prix of Europe Sevens

6th June - Penguins beat the Argentina Naval Selection 103 - 5 in Buenos Aires.
10th June - Penguins beat Combined Western Provinces 24 - 18 in Neuquén.

7th and 8th December - Thailand King's Cup International Tournament. Captained by Alan Bunting (New Zealand).
Penguins beat Thailand 57 - 7
Penguins beat Taiwan 57 - 0
Penguind beat Denmark 45 - 7
Penguins beat Netherlands 34 - 7
Penguins beat Germany 45 - 0
Penguins lost to Fiji 19 - 33
Finalists, Thai RU International Sevens

Bedford Blues v Penguins match programme.

Tony Jarman.

2001

The year began with the Penguins Committee, on the recommendation of Alan Wright, proposing a new office within the Penguin International RFC - that of Life President. Tony Mason became the first proud holder of this office.

Alan Wright: 'I was Hon. Secretary until Tony became ill in 1994. Then I was always hoping that he'd recover. Bob Weighill was the Club President at that time. I didn't want to say to Tony: "Stop being Chairman." So I switched from being Honorary Secretary to become Chief Executive, reorganised the Committee and utilised this new role to direct the Club.

'Then, in the end, I realised that Tony was not going to recover. I said to him: "You be Life President." Tony never wanted to be President, but I wanted him to have this honour during his lifetime. So, after talking to the Committee we agreed the new office and made him our first Life President.

Once again, the Penguins' year began with a match against University opposition, the Club losing to Oxford University by 17 points to 34 on the evening of Wednesday, 31st January.

Ian Bullerwell was the Penguin Team Manager, and the Club included three internationals in its starting XV: Luis Criscuolo (Argentina), Ngauku Ngauku (Western Samoa) and Caine Elisara (Holland) - although the squad had many players from Glasgow Rugby.

Sunday, 6th May brought another high scoring defeat - this time at the hands of Premiership One Club the Bedford Blues by 46 points to 72 in The Bruce Willey Memorial Match at Goldington Road, Bedford.

Bruce Willey was a former President of the Bedford Blues RFC who died prematurely of cancer in July, 1999. This match would be the first of two cancer charity fund-raising fixtures that Penguins would contest with the Blues.

Ian Bullerwell, long-serving Penguins Committee Man and the Penguins' Match Manager for this game, had served as President of the Bedford Blues between 1992 - 1998 and had been a close friend of Bruce Willey.

The Penguins squad for this match included six players from Worcester RFC and four from local rivals Bedford Athletic.

Penguins were suddenly and unexpectedly thrown into mourning once again when Tony Jarman, Alan's very close friend and the Penguins' Chairman of the Selection Committee and Media & Press Secretary, died suddenly in early May. Tony had been due to fly out to Germany and Argentina with the rest of the Penguin International squad at the end of that month.

On 29th May the Penguin International RFC set off on a *tours de force* - a two-centre, intercontinental tour encompassing Germany and Argentina. Alan explains: 'This was a significant year because this was the most ambitious rugby tour that maybe any Club, but certainly *this* Club, has ever undertaken. It was a lunatic idea of mine to play in two continents!

'It started with Bob Weighill advising me that Fritz Grunebaum, a man with whom he had been very close, had died of cancer. Fritz had come to England in the '30s and played for the Harlequins and loved rugby. He had then gone to the USA, where he'd been a very successful businessman, and when his wife died he founded a cancer hospital in Boston, USA, in her memory (the Karin Grunebaum Cancer Research Foundation). And then, a few years later, he himself died. But he'd married for a second time, and his new wife, Bobbie Grunebaum (a wonderful lady who arranged to have Fritz buried in his beloved Harlequins jersey), wanted to give Heidelberg, the city of his birth, a public park in his memory. But the red tape in local government in Germany defeated her, so she settled on giving the German Rugby Union an international rugby ground (the Fritz-Grunebaum-Sportpark) in Heidelberg, which had long been a big centre of German rugby (I'd actually played there myself about 50 years earlier on tour with Sidcup). She built them a small stand as well. Bobbie said to Bob Weighill that she thought her husband would have wanted this stand and ground to be inaugurated by a match between the German National XV and the Penguins.

'It so happens that it was also at this time that I had decided that I wanted us to return to Argentina, another country in which HSBC are closely involved, and a big rugby football nation. Craig and I talked, and came to the conclusion that we'd try and combine these two occasions - that is, go to Germany and then fly on to Argentina.

'I flew to Germany and met the Chairman of the German Rugby Union and said to him: "We're delighted to play in this match, but I'd like to mention to you in advance that we're going to have a very strong side because we're going on to play in Argentina." He said to me: "Don't worry, Alan - we intend to bring all of our professionals back from France. I'll make sure we turn out our very strongest side."

'We flew into Germany on a Thursday and played the German National side on the Saturday. We came to the conclusion at this time that they had failed to obtain the release of all their professional players from France as the score at the end of it was 101 points to 8 in our favour.

'We'd also received an invitation from the IRB via the German Rugby Union to play in the European Sevens which were also taking place in Heidelberg on the next day. This was because it was a non-qualifying year for the World Cup - so the IRB said they were happy to include us in the Sevens.

Bobbie Grunebaum holds a Penguin RFC shield surrounded by (from left to right) Julian Lamden, Hugh Thomas, Alan Wright, David Townsend and Derek Harris.

Deutcher Rugby-Verband plaque.

The Penguin squad before the match with Germany.

The Grand Prix of Europe Sevens Tournament Programme.

'On the Sunday (the day after defeating the German National XV) we played in the Sevens. Mike Friday, subsequently to become the England Sevens Manager, Captained our team. I had enough foresight to fly in about eight players specially for the Sevens, because I was unwilling to allow men to play for two days running. I considered this would be unfair to the clubs. We are always concerned for the players' welfare and our reputation with the clubs.

'I wanted to win these Sevens and didn't know how difficult it would be. In the end, we won comfortably. But a win is a win is a win, and to win the Grand Prix of Europe was very good news!

'This reminds me of something that one of our England players said to me on the evening before the German Sevens, which illustrated how conduct has changed beyond measure because of professionalism. He said: "Alan, would you mind if I have a beer with supper?" A beer! I was amazed (and pleased) with his discipline. I said: "Come on, it's OK by me!" Well, they knew we wanted to win!

Above left: Penguins' Captain Mike Friday and Alan Wright with the European Sevens Trophy.
Mike (former Blackheath, Harlequins and Wasps scrum-half and England Sevens Captain) is one of England's best-ever exponents of Sevens.
He became Assistant Coach of England Sevens between 2000 - '03, and Head Coach between 2004 - '06 (during these seven years England won the Hong Kong Sevens on no fewer than four occasions).
Mike resigned in 2006 in order to take up a business role in the City of London. He has recently been appointed Head Coach of the Kenya Sevens squad and he is also a leading rugby union TV pundit in the UK.

Above right:
The winning Penguins team.

'Well, we did win, and that evening they picked up their Winner's Cups and had a drink. Craig had a motor coach ticking over at the entrance to the ground and we all ran for it to make the journey to Frankfurt Airport so as to catch the plane. We had to rush like this on this Sunday night because there was no plane from Germany to Argentina on a Monday. And we were playing our first match in Argentina on the Wednesday. I didn't want to fly half-way around the world on a Tuesday and play on Wednesday afternoon!'

Craig Brown: 'One of my most enduring memories of that flight was seeing Mark Giacheri, our 6' 8" Italian international lock, squashed into a seat with 31" leg room. Of course, it was just the luck of the draw with ticket allocation - because we also had Darragh O'Mahony, the wee Saracens and Ireland winger, sitting in a seat by the exit that had enough leg room for someone who was eight feet tall. Fortunately I organised a change of seating before too many hours had gone by!'

Alan Wright takes up the story: 'We flew to Argentina, woke up in a very cold Buenos Aires at about six am, and the Argentinians, at the very last moment, had re-arranged the fixtures because of a change in their national holidays.

'Our first match was against the Argentinian Navy, and this was to be the first representative match they'd ever played. The Navy had three league club teams playing in Buenos Aires and believed they could put together a strong, competitive side.'

Craig Brown: 'We played them on an extremely muddy ground and it was "one-way traffic". I'm fairly certain that we won by well over 100 points. Except that they absolutely bulldozed us in the scrums! But that's what the Argentinians can do to you.'

Alan: 'I invited the British Ambassador, Sir Robin Christopher (who had kindly given us a reception the night before) to come to the game, accompanied by his wife, and they stayed on after the match. As I made my speech, in response to an Admiral of the Argentinian Navy making a delightful presentation, I invited the Ambassador to make his own speech, which he did, and the whole evening was very sociable and a great success.

'On the morning of 9th June we went back to Buenos Aires Airport to fly on to Neuquén. And I have to tell you that we appeared to be accompanied by a monk at the airport!

'Iain Sinclair, one of our Scottish players, had been found to be "arrogant" by Craig Brown in the "Players' Court" the night before (Craig, of course, is

Above: The Penguin International RFC Tour Party in Argentina.
Back row: S. Rabaka (Baravi Exiles), F. Fratti (Parma and Italy), D. Qua Qua (Baravi Exiles and Fiji), D. Clare (Connacht), R. Piovan (Parma and Italy), M. Oliver (London Irish), J. Brown (London Irish), C. Harrison (Rotherham).
Middle row: A. Dignan (Clontarf), F. Latuselu (Manly and Tonga), J. Winterbottom (Henley), M. Giacheri (Parma and Italy), G. Quinn (Lansdowne), S. Nawavu (Baravi Exiles and Fiji), B. Jackman (Sale).
Front row: N. Marval (Rosslyn Park), D. O'Mahoney (Saracens and Ireland), C. Brown (Tour Manager - Players), A. Fox (Bedford and Natal, Captain), A. Wright (Tour Manager), I. Sinclair (Edinburgh), D. Townsend (Liaison Manager), B. Breeze (Newport).
In transit: G. French (Parma), K. James (Neath), D. Moore (Clontarf), W. O'Kelly (Clontarf), M. Tamati (Parma).

This Argentinan Navy Pennant was presented to the Penguins after the first tour match.

Brother Sinkyio's Story - by Iain Sinclair

'After we had beaten the Argentinian Naval Selection side 103 - 5, I became good friends with Saula Rabaka from Fiji. Neither of us could speak the other's language and it caused great amusement to both of us that we were trying to communicate via various different means and methods. We both decided that we would have a beer or two together. He tended to go on 36-hour drinking benders, and I joined him for twelve hours of such a bout.

The following morning I woke up to find all the hair on my head was missing. I had no recollection of the previous evening's events. As it transpired, there was some photographic evidence from my own camera - I had, apparently, insisted that photographs were taken of myself and Sailosi removing each other's hair. Not just a close-shave, but all off - as smooth as a baby's bottom! So, the next morning I made my way gingerly downstairs for breakfast, only to be met in reception by Alan Wright and Craig Brown who could not contain their amusement at this Scotsman with a grey scalp taking breakfast in a rather sheepish fashion.

Later on that day I was handed the kit which I was to wear for the rest of the trip. It consisted of a monk's robe. This was my punishment for "arrogantly sporting a ridiculous haircut". And from that moment on I became "Brother Sinkyio from the Watsonians Missionary" (Watsonians being my rugby club).

I had to wear the robe until after we had played against the Combined Western Provinces.

So I was dressed in this outfit on the plane to Neuquén. When we touched down Brownie insisted that I get off first. There were some curious looks when I made my way down the steps off the plane and kissed the tarmac, and then got up and walked past the Argentinian liaison guys and the media! We all then made our way to the hotel.

The following morning I was made to sit at the front of the bus on the way to the match and to again adopt the role as the Penguins' Religious Representative. I would add that this all happened to coincide with the anniversary of the ending of the Falklands War. The players didn't think that much was going to happen, but by all accounts we had been told to sit tight on the way to the ground and not to incite anyone.

In fact people had got wind that a British representative team had come over, and on the way to the ground there was an occasional volley of stones aimed towards the bus. As we got closer the crowd did seem to get bigger, and hands started to bang on the side of the bus. So what started as something that was quite amusing and played-down became a little more tense as we got nearer to the ground. And as the bus eventually pulled up the crowd outside were visibly beginning to get quite quite agitated. There was some chanting and all the rest of it.

As players we just sort of sat tight. We just wanted to get off, get in the changing room and get changed.

And, once again, Brownie asked me to do the deed and take the first step off the bus.

As the bus doors opened, I stepped off in my robes, took a look around and immediately the assembled crowd fell silent. It parted like the Red Sea and created a wee corridor through which the boys had a safe passage through to the dressing rooms. I think all of us thought this was a good ruse!

Well, after getting changed I was last out of the changing rooms and onto the pitch. I was met with thunderous applause as I came out with my boots on. After about five minutes of play I was cautioned by the referee for dangerous play, and I think it was then that the crowd started to have their doubts about my background! After the match (which we won 24 - 18) I was asked to say a few words. So I launched into a bit of gobbledegook "Latin" - really to just preach the word of rugby from the brotherhood of the Watsonian Mission!'

the "Tour Judge" - and he is a very harsh - but fair - Judge!). Craig had brought with him on the tour a complete monk's outfit - cassock, sandals, etc - which Iain was obliged to wear for 48 hours. And this after having had his head shaved, too!

'As we got off the plane in Neuquén, there was quite a large party gathered at the foot of the disembarkation steps. And as we walked in to the terminal buildings the leader of the welcoming committee squeezed my arm and said to me (with a certain air of surprise as he knew we didn't come from a Catholic country): "Mr. Alan - you bring your own priest!"'

Alan continues: 'Now I come to our second match in Argentina, arranged by our Argentinian Committee member, Luis Criscuolo. He has played for Argentina at stand-off half, centre and at full-back, and he is a fine footballer (incidently - on one occasion he played for the Barbarians in the afternoon against the East Midlands in Northampton, and in the evening he played stand-off half for us against Cambridge University in Cambridge!). He had arranged these fixtures for us in Argentina (he had to rearrange the fixtures at the last minute because of a change in the Argentinian national holidays), and he had said to me: "Are you agreeable to fly out of Buenos Aires for the last match, because Neuquén are very keen to play the Penguins and have offered to pay your internal air fare, and host the squad in a hotel." I asked Luis who the match was to be against and he said "Oh - The Province. Well, I knew you wanted a strong fixture!" So. We flew 900-odd miles with the thought in our heads that we were playing one Argentinian Province.

'I then discovered, between the airport and the hotel, that we weren't playing just one Province - in fact we were playing a combined team from the seven strongest Western Provinces in Argentina. And the Provinces had also invited a couple of top Chilean players to play for them for good measure!'

Craig Brown remembers: 'It was only after the match that we found out that this team had been in camp for a about a week waiting for this game, and about four weeks before we'd got there they'd played Stade Français and beaten them!' Alan continues: 'They had made up their minds that they could continue their winning run and beat this English team. Well, I have to tell you that it wasn't an English team! We had twelve nationalities engaged in the match: Tongan, Fijian, Italian, French, English, Irish, Scottish, Welsh, New Zealander, South African, Australian and one Argentinian (because the day before the match the grandmother of our Irish tight-head prop died and he said he had to go home to the funeral).

'There is an interesting story about our search for a prop to take part in this tour. We had a crisis a couple of days before we left. So I 'phoned Bill Calcraft. I said, "Bill, I'm in terrible trouble, I can't find a versatile prop who can play at loose and tight-head for the Argentinian leg of this tour!"'

Bill Calcraft: 'I told Alan that I'd see if I could find one. I then rang my brother Alex in Australia, and when I got through he's walking down the street in

Iain Sinclair and Saula Rabaka - the photographic evidence.

Brother Sinkyio with Craig Brown in Argentina.

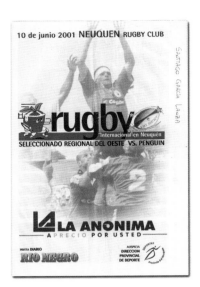

Programme for the final match of the Argentinian Tour - Penguins v Argentina Western Provinces.

Match action.

Presentation plaque from the Neuquén match.

Manly on his mobile. And I say: "Al - the Penguins are going off on this trip to Germany and then on to Argentina, and they need a prop." Right there and then he says: "Well, I'll tell you what - here comes Feki Latuselu walking down the street in Manly. He hasn't played for a while but he's the business." Feki walked right up to him while I'm on the 'phone, and Alec said: "This is Bill on the phone, do you fancy a tour? You've got to go to England, you've got to go to Germany, you've got to go to Argentina. Starting tomorrow morning." He says: "Fine!" And the deal is done! Before you know it he's over here!'

Alan: 'Later, when I was next on the 'phone to Bill's brother, I said: "What's this chap's name, Alex?" He told me it was Feki and that Feki played for Manly, and I said: "Is he an Australian?" Alec said to me: "He ******* well should be - he's been here long enough!"

'There is another funny story about Feki (who is, incidentally, a 6'6" Tongan and weighs something in the region of 22 stone). Well, because Feki was going to need a visa for Germany, I 'phoned the German Embassy (where I knew a very helpful lady) and I said to her: "We're just about to fly off on tour and we've got one more player who will need a visa. He's a Tongan." And she said to me: "Oh Alan - you make a yoke, ya? There's no such place as Tonga!"

'The ironic thing about this episode was that when we eventually got to Argentina we had a tight-head prop who had to go home. Craig said to Feki: "You'll have to play tight-head now." He said: "Oh no - I only play loose-head!"

'And that's why Craig went to San Isidro Rugby Club just a day before our match against the Combined Western Provinces to try to recruit a tight-head. And Craig arranged on the spot for S.G. Lanza (San Isidro RC and Argentina) to play for us the next day. You see, we knew how strong the Argentinians are up front and we couldn't afford to run the risk of breaking up in the front five in this great game!

'Anyway, the high-jinks were not over. On arrival we were taken to the hotel where we were going to stay and there was an enormous amount of food - a fantastic cold spread had been laid out, which was shortly to be followed by hot food. Craig whispered in my ear: "The kick-off's at 3.00!" So I said to El Presidente: "Excuse me, but we are kicking-off at 5.30, aren't we?" He said: "Oh no, Señor - we're kicking-off at 3.00pm." I said: "We can't do that, it's down in the itinerary as a 5.30 kick-off. Just switch the floodlights on." So he said: "Sénor - we don't have any floodlights." I'm afraid I had to say to him: "My players cannot possibly eat this beautiful lunch before playing. They'll eat some bread and cheese and a banana or an apple instead. We can't take all this wonderful food." It sounded a cruel thing to do, but...'

Craig Brown: 'We eventually got to the ground and the game started. There was a big crowd of roughly 5,000 people, right on the touch-lines. It was a very partisan and excitable crowd!' Alan: 'Yes - it looked like the largest crowd you've ever seen. I stood three rows back on a wooden box with David Townsend to see what was going on! It was a fantastic game. Fortunately the Argentinians had done us the courtesy of bringing in a referee from another country - a Uruguayan. Coincidentally, he had flown in on the same plane as us. The temperature of the spectators would have been enough to put the fear of God into any other referee. They were the wildest, most enthusiastic and partisan spectators we'd ever seen. When we took penalty kicks some of them fired guns in the air, others threw fireworks on to the field. They were not vindictive, you understand - it was just natural Latin enthusiasm and excitement!'

Craig: 'We went behind early on but managed to claw it back - the players really had to dig deep because it was a very hard, physical game. With about five minutes to go it was 18 - 18. Pippy, our little scrum-half from Italy, stood up and banged over two penalties and we won 24 - 18. It really was a tremendous victory.'

Alan: 'It was a wonderful win. Craig was, once again, our Tour Manager, Players, and he did a really splendid job on this difficult tour. He's a wonderful, natural leader and a great administrator and organiser. His cool-headed utilisation of substitution in this very tough game was absolutely first-class.

'This wonderful unbeaten tour was a great success both from a social and playing viewpoint. The last match of the tour was one of our greatest victories and it was particularly pleasing to maintain our record of having been invited back to every country we have visited.'

Penguins debió luchar hasta el cierre

NEUQUEN.- Con dos penales sobre la hora, el equipo británico Penguins venció ayer al seleccionado de rugby del Regional del Oeste 24 a 18 (parcial 10-8) en un emotivo encuentro, en el que un empate hubiese sido el resultado más justo. El partido se disputó en el predio del Neuquén RC y más allá de la derrota, la actuación del seleccionado anfitrión resultó brillante. Jugó, tackleó, fue fuerte en el scrum e incluso ganó en los lines a su favor y algunos del rival. Es que los dirigidos por Navessi mostraron gran concentración para plantarse ante un rival de la jerarquía del visitante.

Tras una igualdad en 18 y obre el cierre, el árbitro cobró un penal «de otro» planeta» para Penguins que terminó por amargarle la tarde a todos. Después, hubo otro que ya «selló» definitivamente el resultado.

Síntesis

SEL. DEL OESTE	18	24	PENGUINS
Rocusso; Díaz, Bustos, José Manson y Villanueva; Speroni y Carrasco; Correa, Mariano Olguín y Piergentili; Benítez y Santiago Olguín; Torcivia, Funes y Naveira.			Oliver; Breeze, Maruel, Mike y O'Mahony; Brown y Harrison; Satchel, Fox y Butcher; Giacheri y Winterbottow; Latsule, French y García Lanza.
DT: Navessi.			DT: Wright.

También ingresaron: Peralta, Capriolo, Juan Manson (SRO), Frati, Piosin, Clare, Rabaka y James (P). Tantos: PT, 4m. try de Oliver (P); 15m. penal de Speroni (SRO); 20m. try de José Manson, convertido por Speroni (SRO); y 27m. penal de Brown (P). ST, 7m. penal de Speroni (SRO); 10m. try de Oliver (P); 15m. try de José Manson (SRO); 31m. try de Breeze (P); y 40 y 41m. penales de Harrison (P). Arbitro: Carlos Sandoval (URBA). Cancha: Neuquén RC.

Gustavo Piergentili inicia el ataque del seleccionado del Oeste, sin que Jim Brown pueda detenerlo.

Above: Penguins v Argentina Western Provinces match - local newspaper reports.

Bedford Blues
Goldington Road
Bedford
MK40 3NF

31 July 2001

Dear Alan

This is one letter that is well overdue and for this I apologize. Since my return from Argentina my family and I have been continuously on the move. We have now settled in Bedford and the season is about to start with a pre-season tour to Scotland, where I will hopefully meet up with Iain Sinclair, a friend I made on the tour to Argentina and Germany.

I firstly would like to thank you personally for including me on the tour. It was a privilege to be on the tour and an honour to Captain it. I appreciate the level of planning and co-ordination that would have gone into such a tour. The team and I respect you for your enthusiasm towards the game and are forever grateful for what you do for the game of rugby.

I stand by my statement that : "you are the modern day Doc Craven", as it is with the same passion that you follow and approach the wonderful game.

Secondly thank you for the team photo and letter of thanks. The photo holds many happy memories, beaming faces, reminding me of new found friendships that I'm sure will be rekindled in the years to come. Thank you to your support team, namely Craig Brown and David Townsend. They were very supportive in every way and I think a major contribution to the success of the tour.

Last but not least HSBC bank. We were well looked after in every department. I think it is admirable that a large banking corporation like HSBC is prepared to back and share the philosophy and dreams of the Penguin club. Our mortgage for our new home in Bedford, we look to take through HSBC in some kind of reciprocation.

In closing I hope that this letter finds you in good health and spirits. I look forward to our next meeting wherever that may be.

Yours Sincerely

André

Letter from Penguins' Tour Captain Andre Fox to Alan Wright, thanking Alan, Craig Brown, David Townsend and the Club sponsors, HSBC, for inviting him to Captain the Penguin International Tour of the Argentine.

The statistics for both legs of this unbeaten intercontinental tour are as follows:

Penguins Sevens Squad to Grand Prix of Europe Sevens, Germany 2001:
Results: Pool games: Penguins beat Comite Alpes Maritimes 35 - 0. Quarter-final: Penguins beat Poland 33 - 14. Semi-final: Penguins beat Netherlands 36 - 0. Final: Penguins beat Germany 57 - 7. Penguins won the Grand Prix of Europe Sevens Tournament.

Penguins squad: Bill Calcraft (Director of Sevens), Alan Wright (CEO), Richard Kinsey (Tour Manager, Players). Mike Friday (Wasps and England Sevens, Captain), Ben Breeze (Newport), Hamish Innes (Cambridge University), Rory Jenkins (Wasps), Sailosi Nawavu (Baravi Exiles, Fiji Sevens and Fiji), Darren O'Leary (Gloucester), Darragh O'Mahony (Saracens and Ireland), Matt Oliver (London Irish), Dan Qua Qua (Baravi Exiles and Fiji), Saula Rabaka (Baravi Exiles and Fiji).

Penguins XV Tour squad to Germany and Argentina:
Results: Penguins beat Germany 101 - 8, Penguins beat Argentina Naval Selection 103 - 5, Penguins beat Combined Western Provinces of Argentina 24 - 18.

Penguins squad: Alan Wright (CEO and Tour Manager), Craig Brown (Tour Manager, Players), David Townsend (Liaison Officer).

Andre Fox (Bedford and Natal, Captain), Ben Breeze (Newport), James Brown (London Irish), Dave Clare (Connacht), Alan Dignan (Clontarf), Flilippo Fratti (Parma and Italy), Gary French (Parma), Mark Giacheri (Parma and Italy), Charlie Harrison (Rotherham), Bernard Jackman (Sale), Kevin James (Neath), Feki Latuselu (Manly and Tonga), Nick Marval (Rosslyn Park), David Moore (Clontarf), Sailosi Nawavu (Baravi Exiles and Fiji), Warren O'Kelly (Clontarf), Darragh O'Mahony (Saracens and Ireland), Matt Oliver (London Irish), Riccardo Piovan (Parma and Italy), Dan Qua Qua (Baravi Exiles and Fiji), Graham Quinn (Lansdowne), Saula Rabaka (Baravi Exiles and Fiji), Iain Sinclair (Edinburgh), Mike Tamati (Parma), James Winterbottom (Henley).

In December the Penguins played for the second time in the Thailand International Sevens and were defending their title of King's Cup holders, won two years previously in 1999 (the tournament that should have taken place in 2000 having been cancelled). The Club lost to the very fine Fiji Sevens team in the final, having beaten the National Sevens sides of Thailand, Taiwan, Denmark, Netherlands and Germany in the pool and knock-out stages.

With the 8th December being a full League Saturday in the UK and Ireland, the Club were able to select most of the Penguins squad from overseas players. The team came together and practised on 5th and 6th December - in sharp contrast to the preparation time of eventual tournament winners, Fiji.

As the Fijian Manager said in an interview after the tournament: 'We prepared the team over two months and they have worked very hard.'

Craig Brown recalls: 'I made Thailand our assembly centre so that we could afford to fly people in from all different directions. We ended up with a terrific team that included three men from New Zealand Sevens, three men from Fiji Sevens, two men up from Australia and two men down from the UK. It's interesting to note that one of the men from Australia was Wycliff Palu, who went on to become the Australian number eight. He was 18 years old at this time.

'We gathered together and went up to Chiang Mai, an ancient city in the north of Thailand. We had a couple of days there getting ready and training. It was nice and warm, and for a lot of the players it was the first time they had been in Thailand to experience a very different culture.

'There were teams from all around the world at the tournament itself, and the Penguins were one of the more fancied squads. We progressed comfortably enough through the pool games and the semis and what-not, playing mainly European teams.

'We met Fiji in the final. Now, the Fiji team was typical - you know, they all know how to play sevens and a number of them had also played for Fiji. Well, we had our three Fijians as well, remember. It was an interesting final, but the rub of the green didn't really go our way, and we also got rolled a little bit in the forwards. In the end the Fijians won easily enough. It was still a good effort by us, though. They ground it out. The Penguins did actually play some great sevens during the week. We thoroughly enjoyed the tournament.

Penguin squad for the Thailand International Sevens Competition:
Back row:
John Slater (Sydney University, Manly and Queensland), Saula Rabaka (Baravi Exiles, Nadi and Fiji), Alex Calcraft (Assistant Manager), Craig Brown (Tour Manager, Players), Charlie Baxter (Bay of Plenty and Wellington), Scott Waldrom (Wellington, Queensland and Australia Sevens), Howard Quigley (Coventry and Captain of England Students), Cliff Palu (Manly and Australia), Ian Bullerwell (Tour Manager).
Front row:
Craig Culpan (Watsonians and Bay of Plenty), Sailosi Nawavu (Baravi Exiles, Nadi, Fiji Sevens and Fiji), Alan Bunting (Bay of Plenty, Captain), John Kerr (Watsonians, Scotland 'A' and Scotland Sevens), Tim Walsh (Wests, Watsonians, Australia Sevens), Asiveni Latumailagi (Nadi, Fiji Sevens and Fiji).
In Transit: Bill Calcraft (Director of Sevens).

Wycliff Palu, the Australian number 8.

'We were very pleased with the performance of our squad. This was the second Thai International Sevens Tournament, and on each occasion one of our players has been nominated "Player of the Tournament". This year it was Charlie Baxter, but unfortunately he was badly injured and was unable to play in the final.

'The tournament, in addition to receiving national press coverage, was televised nationally in Thailand on both days.'

Penguins' results were: Pool games: Penguins beat Thailand 57 - 7, Penguins beat Taiwan 57 - 0, Penguins beat Denmark 45 - 7. Quarter-final: Penguins beat Netherlands 34 - 7. Semi-final: Penguins beat Germany 45 - 0. Final: Penguins lost to Fiji 19 - 33.

Penguins squad: Ian Bullerwell (Tour Manager), Craig Brown (Tour Manager, Players), Bill Calcraft (Director of Sevens), Alec Calcraft (PIRFC Representative in Australia).
Alan Bunting (Bay of Plenty, Captain), Charlie Baxter (Bay of Plenty and Wellington), Craig Culpan (Watsonians and Bay of Plenty), John Kerr (Watsonians, Scotland 'A' and Scotland Sevens), Asiveni Latumailagi (Nadi, Fiji Sevens and Fiji), Sailosi Nawavu (Baravi Exiles, Nadi, Fiji Sevens and Fiji), Cliff Palu (Manly and Australia), Howard Quigley (Coventry and Captain of England Students), Saula Rabaka (Baravi Exiles, Nadi and Fiji Sevens), John Slater (Sydney University, Manly and Queensland), Scott Waldrom (Wellington, Queensland and Australia Sevens), Tim Walsh (Wests, Watsonians, Australia Sevens).

Julian Lamden

Julian Captaining Old Freemen's RFC in 1979 - 80.

Julian Lamden joined the Penguins in 1992. He served the Penguins very well for two years having been appointed the Club's third Treasurer.
He also served on the PIRFC advisory board between 2005 - 2009.
Julian is a career banker and has over 30 years' experience in the City and the West End of London. A former Chairman of Partners at Coutts & Co., he is currently one of the Bank's three Principal Client Partners based in the Coutts Private Office.
Julian's rugby career started when he was a pupil at The City of London Freemen's School, where he played in the 1st XV.
Since then he has played for London Welsh U19s, Old Freemen's RFC 1st XV (Captain), and Combined London Old Boys.
Julian was also a Surrey County Trialist and played one game for the Penguins - versus the Commons & Lords RFC in 2009.

2002

On 30th January Penguins lost a close match 20 - 24 to Oxford University at Iffley Road, Oxford.

Just under a month later, on 27th February, Penguins beat Cambridge University 36 - 31 in another close and exciting match at Grange Road.

Both of these Penguin squads were managed and selected by Ian Bullerwell and Captained by Paul Volley of Wasps.

The next tournament for the Penguins was the Portuguese Rugby Federation Lisbon Sevens, which began on 8th June.

Alan remembers: 'We played in the Portugal International Sevens and our Captain was Waisale Serevi. Craig Brown managed the tour.

'We thought we had one the best teams that we'd selected for some years and we managed to lose the final to the Samurais! They were a very good side, Captained by our old friend Mike Friday, who had Captained our European Grand Prix-winning seven in Heidelberg only the year before. He handled his forwards very skillfully, and I would give him the praise for bringing down our great side. Well - you can't win them all, and that's one we didn't win.'

The Penguins' results in the Portuguese Rugby Federation Lisbon Sevens: Penguins beat Lousã 68 - 0, Penguins beat Belenenses 38 - 7, Penguins beat Marauders 35 - 12, Penguins beat Cascais 49 - 0.

Quarter-final: Penguins beat Euskarians 35 - 7. Semi-final: Penguins beat Marauders 47 - 0. Final: Penguins lost to Samurai 25 - 33.

2002 CHRONICLE

30th January - Penguins lost to Oxford University 20 - 24 at Iffley Road, Oxford.

27th February - Penguins beat Cambridge University 36 - 31 at Grange Road, Cambridge.

8th and 9th June - Portuguese Rugby Federation Lisbon Sevens. Captained by Waisale Serevi (Fiji). Penguins beat Lousã 68 - 0 Penguins beat Belenenses 38 - 7 Penguins beat Marauders 35 - 12 Penguins beat Cascais 49 - 0 Penguins beat Euskarians 35 - 7 Penguins beat Marauders 47 - 0 Penguins lost to Samurai 25 - 33 **Finalists, Portuguese Rugby Federation International Sevens**

June Tour - USA and Canada. Captained by Mark Denney (England). **15th June** - Penguins beat the NYAC Select XV 74 - 17 in New York. **19th June** - Penguins beat The Toronto Renegades (the combined clubs of Toronto) 32 - 7 in Toronto.

2nd October - Penguins beat Combined British Universities by 50 - 17 at Iffley Road, Oxford.

6th November - Penguins lost to Cambridge University 24 - 25 at Grange Road, Cambridge.

Above: Penguins squad for the Lisbon Sevens: Back row: Craig Brown (Tour Manager), Alan Wright (Chairman), David MacCallum (Gold Coast and Australia Sevens), Pat Sanderson (Harlequins and England Sevens), Peter Miller (Eastwood and Australia Sevens), Gregor Lawson (Heriot's FP and Scotland Sevens), Caine Elisara (Padova and Holland), John Kerr (Assistant Manager).
Front row: Bill Calcraft (Director of Sevens), Mark Meenan (Ebbw Vale and England Sevens), Tim O'Brien (Manly and Australia Sevens), Waisale Serevi (Mont de Marsan and Fiji), Conan Sharman (Edinburgh and Scotland Sevens), Shane Thompson (Montreal Barbarians and Canada).

The famous winged foot logo of the New York Athletic Club.

New York Athletic Club postcard showing the famous old building which overlooks Central Park.

This was the Penguins' first tour to Canada. According to Alan, the tour fulfilled an objective that the Club hadn't really thought about until they did it.
It meant that the Penguins had played from Chile and Argentina, the most southerly nations that play rugby football, then through the Americas and all the way up to Canada - the most northerly nation to play rugby.

In June the Penguins decided to go, for the second time, to the United States - where they were hosted by the New York Athletic Club. The tour began only four days after the Lisbon Sevens, and the Penguin party included several players who had also played in Portugal. Alan recalls: 'Bill Calcraft had heard that in the terrorist attack on Washington DC, in which one of the hijacked planes had crashed, a number of brave, unarmed men from the New York Athletic Club had been involved in the on-board fight to try to stop the terrorists succeeding.' This was the plane that crashed into a field near Shanksville, in Pennsylvania, after some of its passengers and flight crew attempted to retake control of the plane. The hijackers had redirected it toward Washington DC.

Bill Calcraft: 'I thought it would show our respect for the Americans if we were to go over there and play them. I put the idea to Nick Humphries, with whom I had been at Oxford University, and they invited us to come over and play. It was a short tour, and our players were all really keen to be invited! None of this "I'm saving myself for league games", etc! We were able to put a great team together. We stayed at the New York Athletic Club right by Central Park and we had a fantastic reception there.

'The match itself took place at the NYAC's own rugby ground on Travers Island, about thirty minutes' drive from the centre of New York. The Penguins had agreed that the NYAC Rugby Club could reinforce their team with players brought in from the Eastern Seaboard. It was a fast game, played in a very good spirit. The Penguins ran out convincing winners by 74 points to 17.'

Alan continues: 'We then went on to Canada and played the Toronto Renegades - an Eastern Canada Combined Toronto Clubs XV. It was a very, very happy tour. Gareth Rees, a past player for the Penguins and one of the Club's representatives in Canada, was kind enough to help us with the admin and arrange for us to stay at the Royal York Hotel in Toronto, which I believe is the biggest hotel in the Commonwealth. This very kind arrangement included the Club being charged at the same beneficial tariff rate as the Canadian national team.

'The match against the Toronto Renegades at the Oakville RFC ground was a very hard match, because they'd won three matches prior to our arrival and were very keen to beat us - but we came out on top. Due to the splendid work of the Penguin forwards, and some fine running by our backs, Penguins scored four tries in the second half, and we won the match 32 - 7. It was an extremely physical encounter and we were very pleased to run out winners.'

After the match in Canada, a traditional coaching session was arranged and some 120 boys, ladies and young men were coached by the touring party. In his traditional post-tour thank-you letter to the players, Craig Brown later wrote: *The Club was particularly pleased to continue its well-established tradition of providing coaching in countries where we tour. The training session at Sunny Brook Park had the biggest attendance ever in the 43-year history of the Club and was voted a great success by all those who took part. Simon Walker of HSBC and John Zimnoch worked together to arrange this, and of course, John Zimnoch has subsequently become a Manager of the King Penguins.*

The Penguins' players undoubtedly believed that this was one of the happiest tours the Club had ever undertaken, and they expressed this sentiment in the mass of unsolicited thank-you letters that Alan Wright received in the month or so after the tour ended.

Alan sums up: 'It was a very happy tour. And in a way, this tour fulfilled an objective that we'd never really thought about until we did it. In a nutshell, we'd now played from Chile - the most southerly nation playing rugby football, together with Argentina - through the Americas, up to Canada, the most northerly!'

The Penguins' results were: Penguins beat The New York Athletic Club Select XV 74 - 17, Penguins beat Toronto Renegades (Eastern Canada Combined Toronto Clubs) XV 32 - 7.

Penguins squad:

Craig Brown (Tour Manager, Players), Alan Wright (Chairman), Bill Calcraft (Tour Manager, USA), Ian Bullerwell (Tour Liaison Manager, USA), Hugh Thomas (Tour Liaison Manager, Canada). Mark Denney (Wasps, Captain), Chris Allen (Barnhall), Paul Beal (Redcar), Patrice Collazo (Gloucester), Russell Earnshaw (Rotherham), Caine Elisara (Padova, Vice-Captain), Charlie Harrison (Rotherham), Graeme Inglis (St. Mary's), Rory Jenkins (Wasps), Eion Keane (St. Mary's), Gregor Lawson (Heriot's FP), Dave MacCallum (Gold Coast), Mark Meenan (Ebbw Vale), Tim O'Brien (Manly), John O'Reilly (Leeds), Eric Peters (Rotherham and Scotland), Martin Ridley (Ebbw Vale), Peter Robertson (Edinburgh), Paul Rollerson (Bedford), Mike Tamati (Parma), Shane Thompson (Montreal Barbarians), Matt Volland (Bedford).

The 2002 Penguin International USA and Canada squad.
Back row: Ian Bullerwell (Tour Liaison Manager, New York), Caine Elisara (Padova, Vice-Captain), Chris Allen (Barnhall), Paul Beal (Redcar), Eric Peters (Rotherham and Scotland), Peter Robertson (Edinburgh), Dave MacCallum (Gold Coast), Mike Tamati (Parma), Paul Rollerson (Bedford), Eion Keane (St. Mary's), Patrice Collazo (Gloucester), Rory Jenkins (Wasps), Craig Brown (Tour Manager, Players), Alan Wright (Chairman), Hugh Thomas (Tour Liaison Manager, Toronto).

Front row: Martin Ridley (Ebbw Vale), Shane Thompson (Montreal Barbarians), John O'Reilly (Leeds), Mark Meenan (Ebbw Vale), Mark Denney (Wasps, Captain), Matt Volland (Bedford), Tim O'Brien (Manly), Russell Earnshaw (Rotherham), Gregor Lawson (Heriot's FP), Charlie Harrison (Rotherham), Graeme Inglis (St.Mary's). In transit: Bill Calcraft (Tour Manager, USA).

Robin Hutton

Robin was educated at The Judd School in Tonbridge and at Hull University. He played wing three-quarter for the school, and is a member of his local club, Tonbridge Juddians RFC. Robin, a brilliant accountant, is the Club's fifth Hon. Treasurer. He first joined the Penguins in August, 2002, assisting Julian Lamden. Robin took over the role of Hon. Treasurer from Tom Wacker in April, 2006. Since he accepted the role, the job has grown exponentially in size and significance year-by-year - and the Penguins are extremely fortunate to have such an excellent, charming, modest and very able man overseeing the Club's finances.

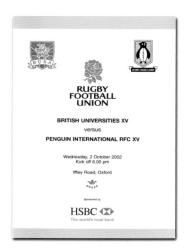

RUGBY
FOOTBALL
UNION

BRITISH UNIVERSITIES XV
versus
PENGUIN INTERNATIONAL RFC XV

Wednesday, 2 October 2002
Kick off 6.00 pm

Iffley Road, Oxford

Sponsored by

HSBC ⟨X⟩
The world's local bank

In the programme notes, Bob Reeves, Chairman of the Student RFU wrote of Derek: 'Derek is a true "rugby man". Players and officials alike have enjoyed his company and shared ideas on the game with him over a period of almost half a century. His knowledge and love of the game have shown no sign of abating, partly, perhaps, due to the unfailing support received from his wife, Ruth. He is known and respected throughout the world of rugby.'

Alan Wright decided to honour Derek Morgan's Presidency of the Rugby Football Union for 2002 - 03 by organising a very special match - The Penguin International RFC versus Combined British Universities at Iffley Road, Oxford, on 2nd October. The match was originally to be against English Students, but Derek particularly requested that the Penguins should play the Combined British Universities, thus reviving a selection that was often utilised immediately after WW2. Derek, of course, had served on the Penguin Committee for over 28 years, and had first played for the Club in 1968. He Captained the Penguin tour to Zambia in 1972. He had also been a principal officer of the Students Rugby Football Union.

This match was the first time in 30 years that British Universities had combined to field a representative team. The Penguins were Captained by Tim O'Brien, an Australian U21 international, and the backs were led by Howard Graham, of the British Army and England Sevens. It was a hugely entertaining game played to a very high standard, with good ball retention and strong tackling by both sides. The Penguins ran out convincing winners by 50 points to 17.

Outstanding players for Penguins included Stu Eru (Otago and Cambridge University) and Mike Friday (Rosslyn Park and England Sevens). Four tries were scored by the wings - Eddie McLaughlin with one, and Will Rubie with three.

Derek Morgan

Derek Morgan was educated at Durham University BDS. He is a member of the British Dental Association.

Captained the University Athletic Union team from 1958 - 1960. Derek played at all levels from club rugby with Newbridge RFC up to to International standard - gaining nine caps for England between 1959 - 1961.

When the RFU set up the Higher Education Panel in 1975 they brought together four organisations: British Colleges, British Polytechnics, London University and the University Athletic Union.

In 1976 Derek was invited to represent the panel on the RFU Committee and bring the four organisations together to form one rugby body. This was the precursor for all student sports organisations when BUSA (The British Universities Sports Association - now known as the British Universities and Colleges Sports, or BUCS) was formed.

The current Students Rugby Football Union developed from the Higher Education Panel and was made a full Constituent Body of the RFU in July, 2002 - the year that Derek resigned his position to become President of the RFU.

Derek has been a Selector and the Chairman of the RFU, an Honorary Team Manager of Tours for various England age grades, a British Lions Selector and, of course, President of the RFU from 2002 - 2003. And in 2002, the 'W.G.D. Morgan's Women's Championship Trophy' was established by BUCS for his services to Women's Student Rugby.

His most recent appointments include being on the Disciplinary Panel for the North of England and Chairman of Adult Rugby Northumberland RFU (2004 - 2007). He is currently the President and Honorary Treasurer of the Student Rugby Football Union, as well as sitting on the Penguin IRFC Committee.

Above: British Universities v Penguin International 2nd October, 2002.

Back row: William Parry (HSBC), Mike Friday (Rosslyn Park and England Sevens), Mark Lloyd (Orrell), Steve White-Cooper (Harlequins and England), Paul Beal (Redcar), Conrad Burke (Stellenbosch University), Will Rubie (Oxford University), Euan O'Connaire (Physio, Oxford University).

Middle row: Sir Alistair Mackechnie (PIRFC Committee), Derek Harris (PIRFC Committee), John Dick (Oxford University), Stu Eru (Cambridge University), Kevin Tkachuk (Oxford University and Canada), James Winterbottom (Henley), Steve Martin (Neath), Craig Brown (Watsonians, co-Match Manager), David MacCallum (Gold Coast and Australia Sevens), John Allen (Oxford University), David Townsend (PIRFC Committee).

Front row: Eddie McLaughlin (Rotoiti), Sam Reay (Orrell), Alan Wright (Chairman PIRFC and Co-Founder), Paul Newton (Orrell), Tony Mason (Life President PIRFC and Co-Founder), Derek Morgan (President RFU and PIRFC Committee), Tim O'Brien (Manly and Australia Sevens, Captain), Sir Peter Yarranton (PP RFU and President, PIRFC), Howard Graham (British Army and England Sevens), Ian Bullerwell (Honorary CEO, PIRFC and co-Match Manager), Ryan O'Neil (Harlequins), John Simmons (Te Puke Sports).

The Club was pleased, with the kind assistance of HSBC, to be able to field a strong, young team - including players from South Africa, Australia and New Zealand, to play in this prestigious fixture. But rather poignantly, this was the last time that Tony Mason was well enough to attend a Penguins match.

Match action.

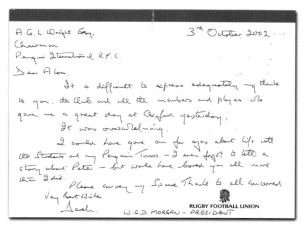

Derek Morgan's letter of thanks to Alan Wright and the rest of the Penguin International Committee. It was written the day after the match against the Combined British Universities XV at Oxford.

Army Sevens Captain Howard Graham holds aloft the Russell-Cargill Cup after winning the Middlesex Sevens Tournament at Twickenham in 2001. He has played for (and Captained) the Penguins many times since his first appearance for the Club in 2002. Alan Wright: 'Howard is a wonderful stand-off, and a great tactician and Captain of rugby in all its forms - sevens, tens and fifteens.'

Howard writes of the Penguins: 'Penguins IRFC - and specifically the opportunities they give to players from across the world in both playing and in introducing them to what I think of as "The Beautiful Game" - mean much to me. The combination of enjoyment and high-quality rugby is probably what draws players to want to turn out for the Club. You meet some great people in the world of rugby and the Penguins have always been a Club that has added to that community - both with their culture off the pitch and with their style on it. I hope to be involved with the Penguins for a very long time to come.'

On Wednesday, 6th November, Penguins travelled to Grange Road for the second time this year to play Cambridge University. In yet another close-run affair, the University managed to scrape home by one point, the final score being Cambridge 25, Penguins 24.

In an email sent to Craig Brown after the match, a disappointed Penguins Captain, Howard Graham, wrote: *...although a lot of the crowd said it was a superb game, we lost. And as I was skippering, I feel a bit responsible. While we were still up near the end of the game I could have had a shot at goal but decided to put it in the corner. Although I hate to lose I thought the match was played in the correct, open spirit, and that the team did well to cope with the power of the University front five. I'll watch the Varsity Match with interest* (just over a month later Cambridge University beat Oxford University by 15 points to 13).

The Penguins squad was again managed by Ian Bullerwell.

On Thursday, 17th October, Alan Wright arranged and hosted a Dinner at the Turf Club in Carlton Terrace, to celebrate PIRFC Committee Member Derek Morgan becoming the new President of the Rugby Union, and also in honour of the Club's principal sponsors, HSBC.

Among the many distinguished guests in attendance were: George Menzies (Oxford University Greyhounds and President of Edinburgh Academicals), Sir Peter Yarranton (Wasps, RAF and England. President, Penguin International RFC; Past President, Rugby Football Union; Past President, Wasps FC; Past Chairman, National Sports Council) and Richard Bennett (HSBC Group General Manager, Legal & Compliance; Patron (and future President), Penguin International RFC).

Howard Graham

Howard was born 1969 in Whitehaven, West Cumbria, in the heart of Rugby League country (his father was an RL International) and educated at St Bees School (where, in 1986, he was part of a team in which he says he achieved possibly his best-ever rugby moment when the School won the Rosslyn Park School Sevens - as St Bees had only 40 sixth form boys to select from).

Howard's first club was Egremont. He then travelled to Southern Suburbs in Sydney, NSW. He returned to RMA Sandhurst and joined 7th Parachute Regiment, RHA. Howard subsequently Captained England Sevens in 2002; played in the Army v Navy game 13 times at Twickenham; for Combined Services against many International teams and also skippered the British Army Teams of 2001 and 2004 when they won the Middlesex Sevens. Howard's nomadic life in the Army has meant that he has played at many clubs throughout the UK - from Boroughmuir to Harlequins to Armagh.

After 19 years in the Army and reaching the rank of Major, Howard took a coaching job at Coventry in 2008 to further his experience before taking up the Academy Coach job at Harlequins. Although he made his name on the Sevens pitch (which is also his first love) he joined the Harlequins Academy with 30 years' experience of playing and coaching in the XVs game.

2003

2003 was a very sad year which began with an invitation to play the Hong Kong RU for their 50th Anniversary in Hong Kong. Unfortunately there was a severe outbreak of SARS (Severe Acute Respiratory Syndrome) in the Far East and Craig Brown and Allen Payne, CEO of the HKRU, regretfully took the decision to cancel the tour on 25th April.

Craig Brown quickly busied himself trying to organise a replacement tour, and the Penguins were soon invited to participate in the 2003 Lisbon Sevens competition, due to take place in Portugal in early June, but the tournament was suddenly cancelled in May because of a lack of sponsorship. As Craig later said to the Selection Committee: 'That's one trip down to pestilence, one down to finances. So what next?!'

The annual Oxford University match was cancelled due to a frozen pitch, which meant that the Club's first fixture of the year took place on Sunday, 4th May, when Penguins, Managed by Ian Bullerwell, played the Bedford Blues in the Bruce Willey Memorial Match. The Penguins team included future England Captain Nick Easter, who was playing for Orrell at the time.

On 1st June the Club's year was tinged with great sadness with the death of Sir Peter Yarranton, a long-standing Penguin RFC player/Committee Member (Sir Peter had served on the Penguins Committee at the invitation of Tony Mason for over 25 years prior to becoming the Club's sixth President).

In addition to the great offices he held (which included being Chairman of the British Sports Council) he was a much-loved broadcaster, announcer and raconteur at the Middlesex Sevens.

Sir Peter was succeeded by Sir William Purves CBE, DSO (Scottish Rugby Union Committee), who became the seventh President of Penguins.

2003 CHRONICLE

Oxford University match cancelled due to frozen ground.

4th May Penguins played Bedford Blues

1st June *Death of Sir Peter Yarranton. Sir William Purves becomes the seventh President of the Penguins*

27th July *Death of Tony Mason.*

6th and 7th September *HSBC/COBRA International Tens, Malaysia. Captained by Dave Gorrie (New Zealand). Penguins beat Korea 39 - 0 Penguins beat Singapore 31 - 0 Penguins lost to New Zealand Legends 0 - 21 Penguins lost to Natal 0 - 12*

THE REGISTER

THE TIMES THURSDAY JUNE 5 2003

SIR PETER YARRANTON

Rugby player and official who became the hardworking head of the Sports Council

PICTURES: RFU

Yarranton played for London Wasps until he was 44, and went on to have great influence as a rugby administrator

There will be many who remember Peter Yarranton as a voice, rather than the company executive and leading sports official that he was. The thousands who flocked annually to the Middlesex seven-a-side rugby tournament at Twickenham throughout the 1960s and 1970s would have heard the amusing commentary that he gave over the PA system, in the era when rugby union was a more light-hearted affair than it is in the 21st century.

His contributions provided much entertainment, such as when Yarranton warned one spectator that he must return home immediately because a pile of quick-drying cement, which had been ordered for that day to resurface the drive, was about to be dumped in the road by the supplier.

An affable, energetic man, Yarranton was well suited to this extrovert role — though much of his life entailed lengthy, detailed committee meetings, which did not suit his temperament and background.

Nevertheless, he was constantly busy as an administrator, notably for the Sports Council, the quango financed with public money which he chaired for five years from 1989. In 1991, he was president of the Rugby Football Union (RFU) when the British Isles and France co-hosted the second World Cup, with the final, in which England lost to Australia, being staged at Twickenham.

Yarranton was a multifaceted man, who had done war service as a pilot, represented England at rugby, captained the RAF at swimming and water polo, worked in industrial relations and gave a lifelong support to Wasps, for whom he played until he was 44. His death occurred less than 24 hours after his beloved club had won the Zurich Premiership title.

Peter George Yarranton was brought up in West London, in a household where money was so short that, on occasions as a boy he was forced to wear dresses which had been handed down to him by relations. He was educated at Willesden Technical College and joined the RAF in 1942. He served in the Burma campaign and in South East Asia, flying more than 3,000 hours on operations. He left with the rank of flight-lieutenant to join Shell-Mex and BP, for whom he worked while playing for Wasps.

A tall lock, balding even as a young man, he won five England caps during the 1954-55 season. His fitness regime

in later years included a daily swim across the Thames from his Teddington home, while his ability to stand on his head was a source of fascination when he accompanied the England team to Fiji. They had not seen many visiting dignitaries perform such a feat.

Yarranton's business career went on to embrace work as a liaison officer with UK Industrial Relations and he subsequently became general manager of the Lensbury Club in Teddington. His administrative work for sport was immense and gradually became a dominant feature of his life. However, much of it, especially for charity, was unheralded and he was as assiduous in helping at grassroots as at international level. If he enjoyed long sociable evenings, they were only after he had completed long days of administration.

For nine years, as the Middlesex representative on the RFU committee, he advised the union on its public relations, and was president of the governing body when much of the rebuilding of Twickenham was agreed.

By this time Yarranton's interests had branched out to wider areas of

sport. He became chairman of the London and Southeast Region of the Sports Council in 1983, when the Greater London Council was being abolished, and negotiated behind the scenes to secure the future of many playing fields in the area.

In 1989 he was appointed chairman of the British Sports Council. He was not the automatic choice. Sebastian Coe, who had been vice-chairman, did not want the post, and Charles Palmer, the former chairman of the British Olympic Association, was not politically acceptable because he had been a leading figure in defying Margaret Thatcher's wish that no national team should go to the Moscow Games in 1980.

There were also criticisms that Yarranton was unsuited for such a prominent position in British sport. Unlike almost every other sport, the RFU still permitted teams to tour apartheid South Africa in contravention of the Gleneagles agreement. In the late 1980s rugby was also languishing in an age when players' preparations were barely beginning to catch up with what

was commonplace in other sports. It cannot have been easy for Yarranton to reconcile the amateurism of his own sport with the other activities that he was funding.

He worked ceaselessly for five years, although he found difficulty in driving through the separation of the Sports Council into UK and English bodies, with the other home countries often thwarting his ambitions.

Yarranton was also president of Ready, a charity for disabled children, and the Scarborough Cricket Festival. Among his other responsibilities was work as a governor of the Sports Aid Foundation, and he was on the board of trustees of the London Marathon. He was knighted in 1992.

In the past two years he had been troubled by respiratory problems and had suffered a stroke. He died in his sleep. He is survived by his wife, Mary, and by a son and a daughter.

Sir Peter Yarranton, sports administrator, was born on **September 30, 1924. He died on June 1, 2003, aged 78.**

Sir Peter Yarranton's obituary from The Times newspaper.

Tony Mason

Alan Wright, Tony's close friend and Penguins' co-founder, regarded Tony as the father of the Club.

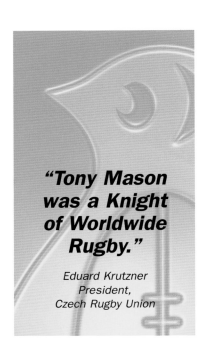

"Tony Mason was a Knight of Worldwide Rugby."

Eduard Krutzner
President,
Czech Rugby Union

Less than two months after Sir Peter Yarranton's death, the Penguins suffered perhaps the cruellest blow that fate has dealt the Club with the death of Penguins' co-founder and Life President Tony Mason on 27th July, 2003. He was 85 years old.

Tony was respected by generations of players from the home countries and throughout the Commonwealth, and indeed messages of condolence poured in from all over the world. His Memorial Service was attended by his wife, Doris, his son, Mike, Robert Horner, President of the Kent County Rugby Union and the Rugby Football Union, Alan Grimsdell, President of the Rugby Football Union 1986-87, Penguins' co-founder Alan Wright and many other friends from the world of rugby.

Just over a month later the following obituary appeared in the 2003 COBRA Tens programme. It was written by Alan, who, as well as being Tony's co-founder, had also been his close friend for 55 years:

Tony Mason was a true gentleman. His love of rugby union commenced as a small boy at Eltham College and continued with enormous enthusiasm for the rest of his life. His playing career started at Eltham College and prior to the War he played for Sidcup Rugby Football Club and for Kent County Rugby Union.

In the War he was commissioned in the Royal Engineers.

Tony was an exceptional leader and organiser and had a wonderful factual memory upon which he could draw instantaneously for the names of players stretching back many years. He was acknowledged worldwide as an extremely clever tactician and judge of rugby footballers. He was revered and respected by generations of players from the four home countries and throughout the world.

Alan: 'I would like to pay a tribute to my life-long friend by recording the compliment paid to Tony by our great friend Eduard Krutzner, the President of the Czech Rugby Union, who expressed his sincere condolences at the passing of this "Knight of Worldwide Rugby".'

Alan arranged for Tony's ashes to be scattered on the eastern touchline at Twickenham through the good offices of Robert Horner, past President of Kent County RU and RFU President at that time.

Penguins took part in the 31st Malaysian RU/COBRA International Tens on the 6th and 7th September. The tournament was held at the Petaling Jaya Commonwealth Stadium in Kuala Lumpur. This was the first MRU/COBRA Tens Tournament to take place since the year 2000, mainly due to the down-turn in Malaysia's economic climate.

For this, the Club's sixth COBRA Tens, Penguins were Captained by New Zealander Dave Gorrie (Tauranga Sports and Bay of Plenty), and coached by John McKittrick (coach of the Cook Islands and the USA), who had also coached North Harbour Rugby Club to success in the New Zealand National Sevens.

At the time, Alan Wright wrote of the tournament in his Tour report: *Our touring party was drawn from five nations, but included only two Englishmen because of a conflict with English League dates. This year we advanced into the quarter-finals, losing on the way to a very fine New Zealand Legends side who were, in turn, beaten in the final by the champion club of Fiji.*

In accordance with our tradition, on the morning prior to the tournament Craig Brown gathered the whole touring party together and the Penguins gave a coaching session to 100 Malaysian schoolboys. The session was a great success.

Our Malaysian Liaison Officer, Hang Kek Kang, arranged for me to be formally presented to the Deputy Prime Minister of Malaysia, who is shortly to assume the Premiership of the country. The organisers were particularly pleased to have the Deputy Prime Minister present for the first time, and perhaps the invitation came to the Penguins because we have been such strong supporters of the Tournament in recent years.

Craig Brown, who was managing the Tour, later wrote of the Tournament: *Obviously, going out of the Tournament in the quarter-finals was very disappointing and this showed on everybody's face at the end of the Natal game. However, Alan was particularly pleased to have met the Deputy PM and I hope this bodes well for COBRA and Malaysian Rugby in the future. Also, we were delighted with the coaching clinic for the youngsters from the local schools and hope that this could be encouraged more in the future.*

Penguins' results for the tournament were: Penguins beat Korea 39 - 0, Penguins beat Singapore 31 - 0, Penguins lost to New Zealand Legends 0 - 21. Quarter-final: Penguins lost to Natal 0 - 12.

Alan Wright: 'So 2003 was a pretty quiet time, really. We were coming to terms with the loss of Tony and Peter. In the end we only visited Malaysia (on 6th and 7th September) and were unable to make the semi-finals. It was one of our more difficult years in the Malaysian Tens. Sometimes injuries... no excuses... but if you get bad injuries in a squad of 14, particularly in the backs, it really finishes you off. We always enjoy going to Malaysia, though - they are our very good friends.'

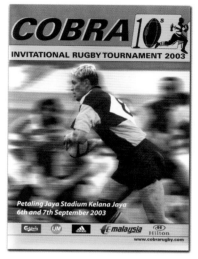

31st Malaysian Rugby Union/COBRA 10s Tournament 2003 Programme.

Presentation plaque given to the Penguins by the Korean XV.

HSBC advertisement celebrating the Club's involvement with the Bank.

Menu of the Turf Club Dinner which was held in honour of Robert Horner, President of the RFU.

Above: The Penguin International squad for the Malaysian RU/Cobra International Tens, 2003. Back row: John McKittrick (Tour Coach), Craig Brown (Tour Manager), Saula Roko (British Army), Alan Wright (Chairman), Akuila Tinasau (Baravi Exiles and Fiji Sevens), Caine Elisara (Treviso and Holland).

Middle row: Eric Peters (Connacht and Scotland), Nigel Watson (Mahurangi and North Harbour), Dean Jennings (Tauranga Sports and Bay of Plenty), Russell King (Silverdale and North Harbour), Rhys Lapidus (Bristol University), Vonivate Kunabilo (Baravi Exiles and Fiji U19), David Townsend (HSBC Liaison Manager).

Front row: Andy Dawling (British Army), Shane Thompson (Montreal Barbarians and Canada), Dave Gorrie (Tauranga Sports and Bay of Plenty, Captain), Aporosa Tunsau (Baravi Exiles and Nadi), Brendon Pascoe (Tauranga Sports and Southland), Hang Kek Kang (Liaison Officer).

On 4th December Alan Wright hosted a Dinner at the Turf Club, Carlton House Terrace, in honour of Robert Horner - an Honorary Vice-President of the Penguins, Past President of the Rugby Union, and also Past President of the Kent County Rugby Union, the Penguin IRFC's governing body. This special event was attended by many Senior Committee men and other ex-Presidents of the Kent Rugby Union. Mike Cordell (Hon. Secretary, Kent County Rugby Union) was elected Hon. Secretary of the Penguins (the second holder of this office) the same afternoon.

It was also in 2003 that Tom Wacker and Vincent Bramhall first joined the Penguins. Tom was the first CEO of the International Rugby Board in 1996 - 1997 and initially joined the Penguins as Membership Secretary, later to become Treasurer and then PIRFC Chairman. He was elected as a Director of the USA Rugby Union (Chairman of the Audit/Finance Committee) in 2006.

Vincent was first elected onto the PIRFC General Committee in 2005 as Hon. Secretary of the PIRFC Trust. He became the third PIRFC Secretary in 2011.

Tom and Vince have added their very considerable experience and expert knowledge to the PIRFC Committee.

Tom Wacker.

Tom Wacker

Born 11th August, 1943. Tom is American, but he also holds an Irish passport. Married with four children.

He has an AB in History and Geography and an MBA in International Business and Finance.

Tom has lived and worked in eleven countries. After two years at Exxon, Tom worked for 22 years in Commercial, Investment and Private banking. Then, between 1986 - 1991, Tom was at the Bank of Montreal, Royal Trust's international banking subsidiaries and the MD at a Texas-based office specialising in Hedge Funds and Private Equity. Currently a Director/Member of the Risk Committee of IFG Group plc, and a Non-Executive Director of Belmont Advisors UK.

Tom (a tight-head prop) first played rugby in 1963 at Indiana University. He then played for Baylor Medical School, Texas (1967 - 68), Old Blue RFC, New York (1968 - 69), Manila Nomads (1969), Taiwan Outsiders (1969 - 70), YCAC Yokohama (1971 - 73) and Hong Kong FC (1973 - 79), where he played once for the Colony. Played vets rugby for Dorking RFC, XLs and NOBs in Toronto, London Irish, Selkirk and Vagabonds. He became the first CEO of the IRB in 1996 - 1997.

Tom joined Penguins as Membership Secretary and has subsequently served as Treasurer and as Chairman.

Tom was also elected as a Director of the USA Rugby Union (Chairman of the Audit/Finance Committee) in 2006.

Vincent Bramhall

Born 14th September, 1946, in Warrington, England. Educated at Wade Deacon Grammar, Widnes; King Edward VI Grammar, Chelmsford and at Sheffield University. Married with two children.

Professional: Bachelor of Law 1969, Solicitor of the Supreme Court of England and Wales since 1972, Solicitor of the Supreme Court of Hong Kong since 1974. Hong Kong Notary Public since 1983.

Career: Solicitor in the City of London 1970 - 74. Solicitor with Hong Kong solicitors Johnson Stokes & Master, 1974 - 94. Partner of Johnson Stokes & Master, 1979 - 94 (Account Partner for major clients including HSBC and Swire Group).

Rugby: University of Sheffield; Hampstead RFC; Hong Kong FC (Colony Club Champions); Hong Kong FC 7s (Colony 7s Champions); Hong Kong FC Touring Team (Taiwan); Golden Oldies Tournament, Cape Town, 1998 and Toulouse, 2001.

From 2005 - 2011: Hon. Secretary of Penguin International Rugby Football Trust. Currently PIRFC Secretary and a member of the PIRFC Executive Committee.

2004 CHRONICLE

18th February - Penguins beat Oxford University 27 - 13 at Iffley Road, Oxford.

3rd March - Penguins beat Cambridge University 68 - 17 at Grange Road, Cambridge.

28th May - Penguins 45th Anniversary Grand Reunion Dinner at the Dorchester Hotel.

28th May - The Penguin International Rugby Football Trust formed.

Early June - Hong Kong Tour. Captained by Craig de Goldi (New Zealand).
10th June - Penguins beat Hong Kong 86 - 0.
13th June - Penguins beat Hong Kong Barbarians 73 - 17

Late June/July - Mexico Tour. Captained by Dave Gorrie (New Zealand).
26th June - Mexico Rugby Federation International Tens, Mexico City Captained by James Winterbottom (England).
Pool 1: Penguins beat Wallabies
Pool 2: Penguins beat Demonios
Semi-final: Penguins beat Miquizti
Final: Penguins beat McAllen (USA)
Winners of the Joaquin Perez Fernandez/Mexican Rugby Union International Tens 'Joaco' Cup
27th June - Penguins beat Mexico Select XV in Mexico City
30th June - Penguins beat Mexican Regions in Celaya
3rd July - Penguins beat Mexico Select in Acapulco

11th and 12th September - HSBC/COBRA International Tens, Malaysia. Captained by Howard Graham (England).
Penguins beat New Zealand Maoris 26 - 0
Penguins beat NS Wanderers (Malaysia) 31 - 7
Penguins lost to Marist St. Joseph (Manu Samoa) 0 - 17
Quarter-final - Penguins beat North Harbour (New Zealand) 17 - 7
Semi-final: Penguins lost to Ponsonby (New Zealand) 15 - 19
Semi-finalists, HSBC/COBRA International Tens

2004 was a hectic and successful year for the Penguins. The Club undertook three major international tours plus the two annual University matches, as a result of which more than 75 players pulled on the Club's famous white, black and gold colours during the course of the year.

The first notable event of the year, however, took place on 16th January. Alan wrote a letter to Sir William Purves, President of the Penguins, to inform him of a policy decision taken with regard to the annual University matches. In the letter he wrote:

We have now had regular fixtures with Oxford and Cambridge for 25 years. In passing, the original fixtures were Cambridge University Past and Present and Oxford University Past and Present, as for many years we were able to field teams for these matches with a large number of current internationals - and the Universities brought back their Blues who had won caps.

About a week ago I was contemplating the past and present positions, and decided I would request each Varsity's RFC to consider appointing a member to the Club's Committee, for the following reasons:

1. Together, we form part of the last bastion of amateur rugby in England.

2. It is becoming increasingly difficult to field good sides for these matches as they come in the middle of the League season, but we are keen to retain these fixtures, including bringing back Blues to play for us.

3. We would like to continue staying in touch with past Blues who might become good members of our touring parties - this has been our practice for many years and of course a very substantial number of Blues go on to play for Premiership clubs, and win caps.

I am delighted to record that both Universities have accepted this invitation, and the following appointments have been made:

i) Oxford University: Steve C. Hill, BA (Hons.) Director of Rugby.

Steve Hill coached Sidcup, Blackheath and Kent, and has been a very good friend to us, particularly on the day we played the President's Combined British Universities XV at Iffley Road in 2002. He is now coming as a Senior Coach on our Mexico tour.

ii) Cambridge University: Ian G. Peck, MA, MRICS, Treasurer.

Ian Peck is well known to Ian Bullerwell and takes a lively interest in Cambridge affairs. He has had a distinguished sporting career having been elected Captain of rugby and cricket at Cambridge University.

The Members of the Committee from whom I took soundings are delighted with the foregoing as it reinforces our long and happy relationship with both these great Universities.

The first of the annual University games was played against Oxford on Wednesday, 18th February in cool but dry conditions at Iffley Road. The match was a fiercely competitive contest with the score remaining close throughout. Both teams played attacking, entertaining rugby, with strong defence a feature. The scores were locked at 8 - 8 at half-time and at 13 - 13 with just under ten minutes to go. Through the attacking brilliance of right wing Neil Starling the Penguins scored two converted tries in the final five minutes, running out winners 27 - 13. Steve Hill, the newly appointed Penguin Committee Member and the Oxford University Coach, commented after the game: '...the annual Penguin/Varsity matches do not come any more combative than this one.'

The Penguins squad was managed and selected by Ian Bullerwell and Captained by David Gorrie of Monkstown. It also included Howard Graham (British Army) and Emile Wessells - a Namibian international playing for Esher.

The match against Cambridge University was played in fine conditions at Grange Road on Wednesday, 3rd March.

The Club was once again Managed by Ian Bullerwell and ably led by Dave Gorrie. The Penguins took control from the start thanks to some great individual performances. The Penguins' front row provided a solid platform, whilst behind them in the second row Henry Head was outstanding. He dominated the lineouts and popped up on several occasions in midfield, breaking the gain line and providing good ball for the backs.

The man of the match was undoubtedly Tim Walsh of Leeds and Australia Sevens, whose astute reading of the game, combined with his accurate kicking, kept Cambridge University on the back foot for the whole game. This match was one of the best recent performances by a Penguin team. The squad also included Joe Edwards of Ards and New Zealand Maoris and was only fully assembled some 90 minutes prior to kick-off! Penguins ran out winners by 68 points to 17. After the match both Phil Pask (a past Penguin Captain) and Tony Rodgers of Cambridge University RUFC complimented the Penguins on their wonderful performance.

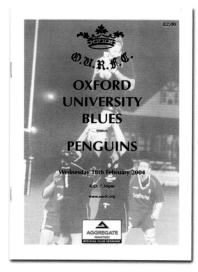

OURFC v Penguins match programme.

CURUFC v Penguins match programme.

Above: Tony Rodgers - the brilliant, long-serving Head Coach of Cambridge University RUFC.

Left: Cambridge University RUFC's Phil Pask's note to Alan, written after the Cambridge match.

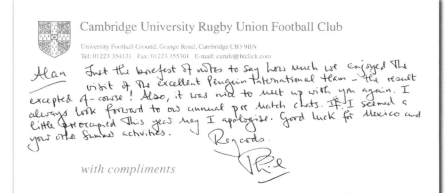

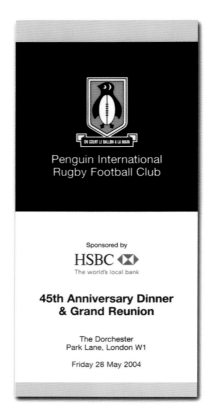

> *"Never mind coaching young men to play rugby, let's coach men to become coaches."*
>
> Craig Brown

Penguin International
Rugby Football Club

Sponsored by

HSBC ◁X▷
The world's local bank

45th Anniversary Dinner & Grand Reunion

The Dorchester
Park Lane, London W1

Friday 28 May 2004

PIRFC 45th Anniversary Dinner Menu & Guest List.

The early months of 2004 saw the beginning of the now world-famous *HSBC Penguin International Coaching Academy*. It all came about in this way:

In June 2003, at a policy meeting with HSBC, who at the time were represented by William Parry (Deputy Head of Group Marketing) and Richard Bennett, the Bank suggested that the Penguins applied their collective experience to the prospect of the beneficial extension of the Bank's investment in Rugby Union. Alan Wright and David Townsend represented the Club at this meeting, and a suggestion was made by the Bank of a Triangular Tournament in the Far East. David expressed a view that the tournament could not be arranged because of political difficulties, and Alan provided the observation that there were far too many new tournaments being proposed around the world. Alan then mentioned to the meeting that the Penguins had been holding ad hoc coaching programmes around the world since 1959, and suggested the formation of a structured coaching academy, adding that this would require only limited additional finance and that it could specialise in helping the game at grass roots level. He felt that as HSBC were 'The world's local bank' it would also fall in line with their policy of 'Education in the Community', and he proposed at this juncture that it be called the HSBC Penguin International Coaching Academy. It was agreed and minuted that the forthcoming tour of Mexico in 2004 would be an opportunity to implement the new Coaching Academy on a formal basis. Craig Brown, on being appointed the Club's Director of Rugby, immediately expanded the whole operation on the Mexican tour and cleverly made the observation 'Never mind coaching young men to play rugby, let's coach men to become coaches!' - which Alan likens to dropping pebbles into a pond and watching the ripples spread.

Since 2004, the HSBC Penguin International Coaching Academy has taken off under Craig's excellent leadership and advanced at a rapid pace, especially in Asia. In Malaysia alone, the Academy coached well over 600 men in some three years into passing their coaching exams and thus gaining their coaching certificates, in which they take great pride. Upon presentation of their certificate, each holder is requested to endeavour to introduce 40 young men into the game of rugby union. As Alan says: 'The Coaching Academy once again exemplifies that the planting of an acorn can lead to the growth of a mighty oak!'

Friday, 28th May brought with it the 45th Anniversary Dinner & Grand Reunion of the Penguins at The Dorchester in London. The evening started with a minute's silence in remembrance of Tony Mason and Sir Peter Yarranton, after which entertaining speeches were made by Peter Sutherland KCMG, Dudley Wood CBE, Ian Peck and Derek Harris.

Among the hundreds of guests that evening were H.E. Mr. Zha Peixin (Ambassador of the People's Republic of China), H.E. Mr. Juan-José Bremer (Ambassador of Mexico), H.E. Mr. Vikrom Koompirochana (Ambassador of Thailand), H.E. Mr. E. Boladuadua (High Commissioner for Fiji), H.E. Dato' Abd Aziz Mohammed (High Commissioner for Malaysia), H.E. The Hon. Russell Marshall (High Commissioner for New Zealand), Dr. Syd Millar (Chairman IRB), Robert Horner (President RFU) and The Right Hon. Sir Tasker Watkins VC, CBE, DL, President Welsh RU).

The HSBC Penguin International Coaching Academy is also supported by The Penguin International Rugby Football Trust - the charity side of the Penguins' organisation.

Alan: 'At the Grand Reunion Dinner I was taken by surprise by being presented with a splendidly engraved silver salver, together with a substantial cheque for the establishment of The Alan Wright Rugby Scholarship. Derek Harris had secretly arranged this with the Committee and Vice-Presidents (293 Committee Members and V-Ps had subscribed). On the spur of the moment, in expressing my thanks, I went on to say that I hoped the Scholarship could be awarded to youngsters from countries such as Fiji, Samoa, Malaysia, etc. The Penguin International Rugby Football Trust was subsequently charged with the responsibility of organising the Scholarship. So The Alan Wight Rugby Scholarship was formed and all of the money presented to me that evening was placed in the care of The Penguin International Rugby Football Trust.'

This magnificent silver salver was presented to Alan Wright by the Penguin International Committee at the Club's 45th Anniversary Grand Reunion Dinner in May.
The Committee also presented Alan with a cheque for £14,000 which was used to establish The Alan Wright Rugby Scholarship.
Alan writes: The Scholarship is a great success and we're anxious to try and utilise the Scholarship monies every year - but we want to use them with care and consideration.
We've had some very good candidates and it's still in its early stages - but it's working!

The HSBC Penguin International Coaching Academy

Founded by A.G.L. Wright and C. Brown.

Over the first 45 years of the Penguins' existence the Club had always endeavoured to provide coaching sessions to the local rugby population on the majority of its tours.

In moving the Club forward it was decided to formalise the coaching activities and in conjunction with HSBC the *HSBC Penguin International Coaching Academy* was formed in 2004.

Over time, Alan Wright and Craig Brown have developed the aims of the Academy.

These were to complement the touring sides by organising professional coaching sessions for rugby players in tour host countries. Coaching sessions were not to be limited to any particular aspect of the game - although the main areas of playing, coaching and refereeing have been the focus. The longer-term aim was to develop the Academy such that coaching-only trips were organised - and happily this objective has subsequently been achieved.

Next, the Academy would like to expand into other areas of the game such as injuries treatment (rehabilitation and prevention), rugby administration skills and other associated areas.

The first Academy coaching sessions were planned to coincide with both major tours in June and July 2004 - Hong Kong and Mexico respectively.

At present the senior Academy Officers are Craig Brown (Director of Academy) and Steve Hill (Director of Coaching).

Above and below:
2004 Hong Kong Tour Match
Programmes.

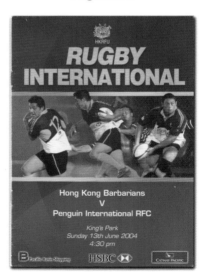

The Penguins' first tour of 2004 was to Hong Kong, and it took place between 7th and 14th June.

This tour should, of course, have taken place a year earlier, but had been deferred because of the outbreak of the SARS virus in the Far East. The SARS (Severe Acute Respiratory Syndrome) outbreak became a near pandemic between the months of November, 2002, and July, 2003, with 8,096 cases and 774 deaths. Within a matter of weeks SARS spread from the Guangdong province of China to infect individuals in some 37 countries around the world.

Craig Brown: 'So we rolled over the tour to 2004. It worked out quite well, actually. Both the Penguins and the Hong Kong Rugby Union wanted to put on a good show. We have a very strong relationship with the HKRU and we were very pleased and honoured to play them in these extremely prestigious 50th Anniversary fixtures.'

The tour consisted of two matches at King's Park on the artificial pitch of the Hong Kong Rugby Union. The first match, on Thursday, 10th June, was against the Hong Kong National XV, and the second match was against the Hong Kong Barbarians on Sunday, 13th June.

Craig: 'This was the first time we got a good selection contact in Japan - which was important (as well as Japanese players there are so many Australians and New Zealanders playing there). My friend and contact is Scotty Pierce, and it was Scotty that managed to land us our old friend Craig de Goldi and three other fine Japan-based players. We had a few men come up from Oz, I remember, along with George Ayoub, a leading Australian referee - a really nice chap.

'About a week before the tour began we still had some vacancies, so Bill Calcraft did some good work and managed to get in some excellent men from the Randwick and Manly Clubs in Australia.

The rest of the men came from the UK, including two England Sevens players - Andy Higgins and Phil Dowson, and also Ross Blake at scrum-half, a former Captain of Cambridge University.

'Funnily enough, we also had Sam Johnstone, a Kiwi prop who was playing for Henley RFC at the time. It just so happened that he was going on a two month tour of the Far East with his wife at the same time!'

Craig de Goldi (Kurita and New Zealand Sevens) Captained the Penguins team in both matches. Alan Wright continues: 'Craig Brown and I were very pleased to appoint Craig de Goldi as Captain. Not only is he an absolute genius on the field but he is such a well-balanced and pleasant man.'

The match against Hong Kong was played on a warm evening. Both teams set out to play open rugby, but the tourists' very large pack laid the foundation for a well-earned victory. Penguins won by 86 points to nil with Laurent Gomez scoring the first try of the tour, driving over from a rolling maul following a lineout. Hong Kong never gave up and continued to attack when in possession until the end of the match. Indeed, they came very close to scoring on a couple of occasions, but the Penguins' defence kept them at bay. Penguins' man of the match was Stu Wilson for his work in the tight and great support play in the loose.

The match against the Hong Kong Barbarians was played on a very warm afternoon in brilliant sunshine. The Barbarians began the stronger and made large gains by popping the ball close to the rucks and crashing through midfield. After about eight minutes they took a deserved lead. The Barbarians continued to match the Penguins for the next quarter of the match before the Penguins found their rhythm and started to put some phases together, with backs and forwards combining well. Once the Penguins had gained the lead about 20 minutes into the match they never looked back - completely dominating the Barbarians to win 73 - 17. Bedford's Arthur Brenton, Penguins' man of the match, chipped in with a brace of tries as well as contributing some great defending and brilliant support play.

Alan recalls: 'We played with great style. Spectators came up to me after the match to say that it was the best 15-a-side rugby football that they'd seen in Hong Kong for as long as they could remember.'

Craig adds with a smile: 'Bill Calcraft and I both played for about twenty minutes at the end of this match. It was great fun.'

Brian Stevenson, President of the Hong Kong Rugby Union said of the two matches: 'Our squad really appreciated the quality of the opposition the Penguins provided. We took quite a whacking in both games but we were pleased with the way our players stuck to their task. We have a new coach and he was not despondent with the results - he is confident the experience will have served our players well for the Asian Rugby Championship which will be played in Hong Kong in October of this year. Also, we very much appreciated the coaching, both on the playing side and also for our referees, which you provided. I think this is an excellent idea that you have introduced, and it is good to see the Penguins going from strength to strength. The visit of the

*Top and above:
July 2004 Hong Kong RFU
'Rugby Talk' Magazine
and the Penguins v HK Barbarians
match report that it carried.*

OPENING **KICKOFF**

Students scrum down for an end-of-session photograph, while (below) the HKRFU's Robbie McRobbie thanks coach Steve Hill.

The class of 2004

Students graduate with honours after test of ability

Students preparing for Hong Kong's first-ever Varsity Match revelled in the chance to learn from someone who knows all about such a fixture – Oxford University coach Steve Hill. About 30 players enjoyed an intensive clinic under the direction of Hill, who was in the SAR as part of the Penguin International RFC touring party.

"They did really well," said Hill after the 75-minute session with a mix of male and female players at King's Park. "Their skill level was higher than I thought it would be, and I think that comes from the amount of tag rugby they've played."

So what sort of workouts did he put them through? "We were looking at some basic skills, mainly handling, lines of running, trying to make sure that they have an understanding of how they should support the ball carrier. When you are new to the game, this is one of the most difficult areas to understand.

"When you're in a game the whole idea of time and space becomes quite difficult. So the aim in this session was to try to

get them to look for where the space is – if the space is close you attack there, if the space is wide, then you need to put two or three passes together to get there."

Hill pointed out he applied the same training routines to his squad at Oxford. "All the stuff that I did with the students here, I would do with our senior squad, which includes international and Super 12 players. The higher up you get, the more you go back to doing the basics, except of course the basics have to be much more precise and we do them under more pressure and in less time.

"All the moves and plays in rugby are designed to reach a situation where you

have two attackers against one defender. And if you can get players to understand that, then good."

Oxford University play their rivals Cambridge in the annual Varsity Match at Twickenham – and now the HKRFU is introducing its own fixture with Hong Kong University set to play Joint Universities on October 2 after its successful programme to introduce rugby to tertiary institutions. Hill was happy

to pass on his knowledge to the students as part of the coaching academy set up by the Penguins' main sponsor, HSBC. "One of the roles of the Penguins is to go to different countries where rugby is growing and spread the gospel of the game through playing and coaching," he said. "For example, I'm taking a squad to Mexico soon and we'll hold eight clinics – coaching players and, just as importantly, coaching the coaches.

"HSBC recognise this is a very important role, so they've established this coaching academy so that people like myself can come away and do this as part of the Penguins' tour. This is the first time the academy has been set up and run. From now on, when the Penguins tour, the academy will be part of the trip."

8 · July 2004 RUGBY TALK

More from the July 2004 Hong Kong RFU 'Rugby Talk' Magazine: An article about the new HSBC Penguin International Rugby Coaching Academy in action.

Penguins was a great climax for our season, and personally I am particularly pleased that it was the Penguins that were here to celebrate our 50th Anniversary with us. Much has happened since my plea for help to Tony and Alan in 1987 re our Hong Kong Sevens, and that, I think, has been good for both the Penguins and our Union.'

After the Hong Kong Barbarians match both of the teams and their officials travelled to the Hong Kong Football Club for the Tournament dinner. The post-match speeches thanked all those involved in organising the tour (especially those who had contributed from behind the scenes) as well as thanking all of the sponsors and supporters. In particular, Charlie Stewart-Cox of Cathay Pacific was presented with a Club shield by Craig Brown, and thanked for the role Cathay Pacific played in transporting the team to Hong Kong.

Craig: 'HSBC and Cathay Pacific were our joint sponsors and they really did us proud. Cathay Pacific arranged our flights. And I mustn't forget the Hong Kong Rugby Union, who looked after us extremely well!'

Alan adds: 'Of course, the HKRU are our great friends. We have lots of personal friendships, in particular with the man who telephoned Tony Mason at 4.30am our time in 1987, Brian Stevenson of the HKRU. Brian and I have been firm friends for over 25 years now, and he played very well for Penguins in our 50th Anniversary Match at Twickenham in 2009, alongside his namesake Jim Stevenson, President of the SRU!'

Craig: 'It was during this Tour that a few of the squad had a great day out at the races at Sha Tin Racecourse, courtesy of Brian Stevenson and Willie Purves of HSBC. In particular, I remember Willie arriving at King's Park in a Rolls Royce to pick up Alan Wright, Bill Calcraft and myself to drive us there. Bear in mind that it was nearly 30 degrees and I'd just been running around training for an hour. I'd had my shower and I was sitting in the back of this Roller between Alan and Bill in nothing but a pair of shorts sweating buckets. No wonder they were trying to edge as far away from me as possible. I did manage to pull on a shirt, tie and suit just before we got there, though!'

Following the formation of the HSBC Penguin International Coaching Academy earlier in the year, the Club's visit to Hong Kong was used to test the coaching ideas and formats that had been formulated and introduced. This resulted in three successfully run coaching clinics under the direction of the tour Academy Coaching Director Steve Hill, who at this time was Director of Rugby at Oxford University RFC.

The first session, with 25 elite Chinese players, was held on Tuesday, 8th June at King's Park. The entire Penguins squad was involved, and the session covered warm-ups, ball skills, positional development, decision-making and unit play.

The second session was held two hours prior to the Hong Kong versus Penguins match and involved 25 university students. The coaching included ball skills, decision-making, and attacking/defensive options. The session was so well received that it led to the Hong Kong Rugby Union staging their first university match later in the season, based on the annual Oxford v Cambridge Varsity match.

The final session, 'Coaching for Coaches', consisted of Steve Hill presenting a lecture and hosting a discussion on 'Breaking Down Flat Defences'. Twenty local coaches attended - most of them senior coaches in Hong Kong.

Below: The Penguin International RFC Hong Kong Touring Party, 2004. Back row: Steve Hill (Academy Coach), Craig Brown (Director of Rugby and Tour Manager, Players), Carlo di Ciacca (Edinburgh), Peter Jorgenson (Rotherham, Australia), Laurent Gomez (Harlequins), Phil Dowson (Newcastle, England Sevens), Chris Johnson (Bedford), Mark Giacheri (Coventry and Italy), Sam Johnstone (Henley), Ben Gulliver (Coventry), Mike Tamati (Botochini, New Zealand League Sevens), Arthur Brenton (Bedford), Ben Breeze (Newport Gwent Dragons and Wales Sevens), Dave Dillon (Blackrock), Blair Urlich (Mitsubishi, New Zealand Maoris), Flo Rossigneux (London Welsh), David Townsend (HSBC Liaison), Bill Calcraft (Tour Coach), Dave Peirce (Physio).
Front row: Raymond Rodan (Baravi Exiles, Fiji Sevens), Stu Wilson (Manly), Andrew Higgins (Bath), Gareth Smith (Randwick), Alan Wright (Chairman and Tour Manager), Craig de Goldi (Kurita and New Zealand Sevens, Captain), Sir William Purves (President PIRFC), George Ayoub (Referee - Australia), Joel Nasmith (Helensville), Ross Blake (Bath), Doug Tausili (Mitsubishi and Manu Samoa), Mark Sweeney (Randwick).

Peter Sutherland KCMG, SC

Peter Sutherland, an Irish international businessman, former Attorney General of Ireland, EU Commissioner, head of The World Trade Organisation and an Irish *People of the Year Award* winner, first became a Patron of the Penguins in 2004.
A great rugby man, Peter has Captained both University College Dublin RFC and Landsdowne RFC.
He often mentions that his one great regret in life is that he was never picked to play in the Irish front row!

The proposal of the 2004 Mexico Tour came from a meeting between Alan Wright and Sandy Flockhart (above) which took place in New York in 2002.

The Penguins played in a tens tournament and three XVs matches in Mexico.
Alan: 'In order to overcome the problem of professional players perhaps playing for two days running, we increased the size of our touring party so that we had a XVs team and a Xs team for the two days. As I have said before - we are always very concious of the players' welfare and of our reputation for not letting the Clubs down by over-playing their players.'

The official Penguin International 2004 Mexico Tour Programme.

The proposal of the Penguins touring Mexico in late June/early July arose from a meeting held in 2002 during the New York tour, when Alan Wright met with Sandy Flockhart (a former Watsonians player who was, at this time, a Director of HSBC in New York). The two men met for breakfast at the New York Athletic Club, together with another former Watsonian, Craig Brown. Later that morning Sandy Flockhart had to return to England on urgent business. Alan: 'And then, four months later and out of the blue, I received a very nice letter from Sandy, confirming to me that he'd been made Chief Executive of the Bank's new subsiduary in Mexico, where they have 1500 high street branches. And he thought that Mexico was ready to receive a Penguins tour to help them advance their rugby. This tour was formally approved by HSBC.'

Fortunately for the Club, Craig Brown acted as an 'advanced guard' for the tour. By chance he had been invited to Mexico for his cousin's wedding shortly before the tour took place, and he was able to undertake the pre-tour groundwork.

The tour gave most of the squad their first visit to Mexico and the chance to experience genuine Mexican culture first hand. One tens tournament and three XVs matched were organised.

On Thursday, 24 June, Sandy Flockhart hosted a dinner at the HSBC Office in Mexico City. It was attended by bank officers, invited guests and the Penguin touring party - 75 people in total. The evening was a great success with both Sandy and Alan Wright making speeches after a delicious, traditional Mexican meal.

The Tens Tournament was played on 26th June at Dos Rios, Mexico City, between nine teams. Apart from the Penguins, the other non-Mexican team was McAllen RFC, a visiting side from Texas. The tournament was arranged into three pools of three, with a series of round-robin games followed by semi-finals and finals. The Penguins met McAllen RFC in the final and ran out convincing winners of the Joaquin Perez Fernandez 'Joaco' Cup.

All-in-all, the day provided a good opportunity for the Penguin team to meet and observe the Mexican players in action, as well as meeting the various officials and supporters.

The first match of the XVs tour was played on Sunday, 27th June, again at Dos Rios, versus the Mexican National XV. It was a free-flowing game and both teams were very committed. The Mexican team was competitive in scrums, rucks and mauls and were well versed in the art of tackling - but the higher fitness levels and superior ability of the Penguins ensured a victory for the visitors. However, the Penguin players did comment on the impact of altitude and how it affected them occasionally during the game, especially during continuous play.

After the match the teams mingled around the tents at Dos Rios enjoying refreshments, swapping memorabilia and discussing rugby.

The second match was played at the University of Celaya on Wednesday, 30th June against a Mexican Regional Selection in fine and hot conditions. Five minutes prior to scheduled kick-off the field was unmarked, so a slight delay to the start of the match occurred whilst the groundsman was located! As with the match against Mexico three days earlier, the Penguins were comfortable victors, although the opposition forwards were very combative, and tackled strongly. After the match the Penguins were invited to a local hacienda, used by the local team as its base for post-match functions. Refreshments were provided, followed by formal speeches and presentations.

Next came Acapulco. With only a limited number of local players available, a reduced Sevens Tournament was held, followed by a XVs match between the Penguins and a Mexican select side. Due to the limited numbers involved, two scratch sides were formed and the two sides were mixed up. This traditional Penguins' coaching ploy proved a very popular idea with the Mexicans, who enjoyed playing alongside the Penguins and against some of their own team-mates.

Following the day's rugby activities, all concerned retired to a local beach on the Pacific Ocean for refreshments. This was a great setting to end the tour.

One of the Penguins' players in Mexico was Toronto Nomads RFC's Andy Prior, who had been invited to tour after playing against the Penguins in Toronto in 2002. He later wrote of the Mexico tour from a player's perspective: *As the lone Canadian on the tour, I met up with the group in Mexico City. I had barely put my bags down and I was off to a coaching session for some underprivileged children. I wasn't fully prepared for what I was about to see. As we arrived we saw the kids playing on a mix of sand and pavement. They knew only the basics of the game, but more than made up for it with enthusiasm.*

Our next two days consisted of coaching sessions for two local clubs and training sessions for us - to become accustomed to playing together. The coaching sessions had a mix of players from all skill levels. Some of these men had played for several years in Mexico and abroad, while others had just recently been introduced to the sport.

The Saturday consisted of the Tens Tournament which was won by the Penguins over an American squad. The tournament was a good lead-up to the XVs game against the Mexican team. While foreign-born players made up roughly half of the opposing team, they were all members of the twelve-team league in Mexico. The match was a hard-fought battle that resulted in a score that didn't reflect the effort and determination of the Mexico XV.

The following week involved two more coaching/training sessions, and a game against a Mexican Select team, mostly made up of players from Mexico's top club. While the score was closer, it proved to be a tough haul for the Mexican side.

Advertisement for the match against the Mexican Selection XV on 27th June at Dos Rios.

Local press report of the match against the Mexican Regions XV at the University of Celaya.

There was plenty of time for fun on the Mexico tour, too!

The most rewarding visit of the tour came as it concluded, with a trip down to the beach resort area Acapulco for three days. We were able to pay a visit to a local orphanage. With the help of HSBC and our fine tour kitty, we were able to bring the kids all kinds of toys. The kids were extremely excited and proceeded to show the predominately UK-based Penguins how baseball is played!

The final Saturday consisted of some friendly sevens team play with a couple of other clubs.

I'd like to thank Alan Wright and Craig Brown for putting this tour together, as well as HSBC for all their continuing support of the Penguin organisation. Finally, hats must come off to the Mexican players themselves for hosting us, and for playing with such heart.

The Penguins bring donated food and gifts to Huerfanos de la Guerra Sucia (Orphans of the Dirty War) at Penjamo, near Acapulco.

Of course, the principal aims of the Mexico tour were to promote goodwill and provide as many coaching sessions as possible. To this end, six coaching sessions were held, involving the participation of boys, girls and adults. The Mexican Rugby Federation subsequently confirmed how successful the tour was on a number of fronts - not least of which was the work of the HSBC Penguin International Rugby Coaching Academy.

Alan sums up: 'Craig arranged for the entire touring party to show kindness and interest to Mexican orphanages in the players' spare time. It gave the boys a lot of pleasure. We were glad to do it.'

Above: Penguin Internation squad to Mexico, 2004.

Back row: Paul Beal (Redcar), Neil Meikle (Ayr), Dave Bassett (Loughborough University), Ross Winney (Plymouth Albion University), Antonio da Cunha (Portugal), Graeme Inglis (St. Mary's, Vice-Captain), John Kilbride (St. Mary's, Vice-Captain, Tens team), Alan Maher (Lansdowne), James Jones (Loughborough University), James Winterbottom (Henley, Captain, Tens team), George Oommen (Dundee HSFP), Neil Wardingley (Rosslyn Park), John Swords (London Welsh), Ryan O'Mahoney (Oxford University), Peter Robertson (Nantes University), Jamie Astbury (Wasps), Andy Prior (Toronto Nomads), Henry Head (Richmond), Dylan Pugh (London Welsh), Ali Rowe (Watsonians).

Front row: Conan Sharman (Currie), Nopera Stewart (Ionstonians), Karl Cleere (Lansdowne), Dafydd Lewis (Cambridge University), Steve Hill (Tour Coach), Glen McLellan (Orkney), Craig Brown (Tour Manager), Dave Gorrie (Monkstown, Captain), Alan Wright (Chairman), Ben Dormer (Cambridge University), Andy Ireland (SRU Referee), Graham Barr (Oxford University), Karrelle Dixon (Oxford University).

For the weekend of 11th and 12th September the Penguins returned for their seventh trip to the Malaysian RU/COBRA International Tens in Malaysia.

The assembled squad included two New Zealanders; one each from Canada, the USA, England and Portugal; three South Africans and five Fijians. It was coached by John McKittrick of New Zealand and Sailosi Nawavu from Fiji. Graeme Halse, a prominent Auckland lawyer, also joined the Club for the first time as technical adviser. Graeme played for Auckland on a number of occasions.

Alan Wright: 'This tour was managed in an excellent and successful fashion by Craig Brown.'

Penguins were drawn in the hardest pool, with matches against the New Zealand Maoris, Marist St. Joseph (from Samoa, including most of the Samoan IRB Sevens team), and the local champions NS Wanderers - who had the Penguins' old friend Waisale Serevi as a guest player.

Federación Mexicana de Rugby A.C

28th September 2004

CRAIG BROWN
DIRECTOR OF RUGBY
PENGUIN INTERNATIONAL RUGBY FOOTBALL CLUB

PENGUIN TOUR TO MEXICO 2004

Dear Craig:

On behalf of Mexican rugby community, I am writing to express my sincere gratitude for your efforts in the planning, coaching and matches ,for your camaraderie and the extraordinary spirit of rugby displayed by Penguins R.F.C. .Your tour has been a successful and memorable occasion for all of us .

Mexico has just obtained affiliation to the International Rugby Board; your visit has helped us to enhance our efforts to develop our rugby; I believe thath with good management and some support from abroad, we have a lot to look forward to.
The Mexican team will participate in the LA Sevens Tournament in February, and hopefully we will participate in more international tournaments in the future.
Now the FMRU is more structured, and more people are involved in specialist areas.

I'd like to inform you that thanks to your contact , we're wellcoming a team from Bermuda, next summer. Also I want you to know that rugby has become something very important to the kids from Alianza , Jaimie Johnston (Harlequins, Bath, Bristol) and I coach them every wednesday, and we have more kids involved every time.
Also as consequence of your visit, I am also working with the Anglo Mexican Foundation (AMF) on a new project, developing their web page; I am dealing with sports in the UK, mainly rugby, Mexican and international . The AMF is the largest and most important British cultural institution in Mexico, linked with British institutions and companies, such as HSBC, British Airways, Hivisa Travels, EMI records, WEA, Pepe Jeans and some other. They have about 18,000 students per year and I think they are another great opportunity to promote rugby between students.
As you know, the potential in this country is extraordinary.

Letter from the FMRU to Craig Brown and Alan Wright, thanking them for organising the 2004 Penguins tour.

Tournament Programme for the 2004 COBRA Tens in Malaysia.

English Penguins to parade their multi-national players

PETALING JAYA: Penguins RFC are the team from England but their players are anything but all English.

With players of seven different nationalities assembling for the first time to play in the Cobra Invitational Rugby 10s, which begin at Petaling Jaya Stadium in Kelana Jaya today, Penguins are perhaps the only rugby club in the world to have such unique representation.

Penguins have made it clear that they are not here for a holiday.

Team manager Craig Brown said that they were looking to win the title for the third time. Incidentally, Brown was the captain of the Penguins team, who emerged as the champions in 1993 and 1994.

"We are certainly not here to make up the numbers. We come to do well here. We have four or five guys here who are capped players for their countries," he said.

There are five Fijians, three South Africans, two New Zealanders, an American, a Canadian and a Portuguese in the 14-member team. The lone English player is Howard Graham.

"I believe our club is unique in this way. We have a committee who source for players whenever we get an invitation to play," said Brown.

"And we only take players who have proven themselves at some level. We have won a lot of titles this way and we will continue doing so."

Penguins have been recognised as the most travelled rugby club in the world.

They have competed in 57 countries and in 2000, became the first European club to go to China to play against the Chinese national team.

Penguins will probably look at Fijian World Cuppers Tone Daunivicu and Saula Rabuka as their trump cards when the Cobra 10s get underway.

They have been drawn in Group D with Negri Sembilan Wanderers, Samoa's Marist St Joseph and New Zealand Maoris.

"This is not going to be an easy group to qualify from. St Marist will be very strong in defence because they have a player in Brian Lima," said Brown.

"New Zealand Maoris, being one of the top clubs in their country, will also be tough customers. NS Wanderers are the Malaysian champions with Waisele Serevi playing for them. But we are prepared for the challenges."

The top two teams from each of the four groups will qualify for the quarter-finals of the Cup competition. Penguins were beaten in the quarter-finals last year.

Penguins got down to their first training session yesterday.

Local press report on the composition of the Penguin International squad for the 2004 COBRA Tens.

Above: Line-out action from the pool stages.
Right: David Townsend, Craig Brown and Alan Wright mingle with a few of the Penguin contingent in the Petaling Jaya Stadium.

As with the previous year, there were no easy games and most contests finished with a close scoreline. The objective of day one was to qualify for the cup quarter-finals on day two, and Penguins achieved this with two wins from two in the opening games. A hard-fought final pool game was lost to the eventual champions, Marist St. Joseph.

The team progressed to the semi-finals with a convincing win over the North Harbour Mavericks from New Zealand. The semi-final kicked off during a thunderstorm and a torrential downpour, with Ponsonby from New Zealand leading by 14 points to nil after five minutes. The game was then stopped for 90 minutes due to the risk of lightning strikes. When the match recommenced Penguins showed great character and skill to take the lead 15 - 14 after three well-worked tries with only 16 seconds remaining (none of the tries could be converted - drop kicking was impossible due to the flooded pitch).

Alan remembers the occasion well: 'It was undoubtedly one of the most incredible turnarounds that I have ever seen and I cried out aloud "saved from the jaws of death!" However, with less than 30 seconds left to play, Ponsonby managed to get close the Penguin line - where, to everyone's amazement, a penalty try was awarded - meaning that Ponsonby snatched victory from the jaws of defeat! This was regarded generally as a very strange decision by the referee and of course it denied us a place in the final. In passing, we have always accepted refereeing decisions, good or bad, and we have certainly had some strange ones! We have been motivated by the ethos of "never complain, never explain" and this is a particularly apt policy when one is nearly always playing away.

'I will also say that we had a very good Captain in Howard Graham, who had Captained the British Army team. And we made the semi-final - which is a big achievement in the Malaysian Tens.'

The Penguins' results during the tournament were: Penguins beat New Zealand Maoris 26 - 0, Penguins beat NS Wanderers (Malaysia) 31 - 7, Penguins lost to Marist St. Joseph (Samoa) 0 - 17. Quarter-final: Penguins beat North Harbour Mavericks (New Zealand) 17 - 7. Semi-final: Penguins lost to Ponsonby (New Zealand) 15 - 19.

Two HSBC Penguin International Coaching Academy sessions were arranged by Craig Brown prior to the Penguins' arrival in Kuala Lumpur. The first took place at the COBRA Club grounds and involved 150 children aged from 10 to 14. The Penguin squad and the children participated in a mixture of skills and fun games.

The second session was held in Ipoh, north of Kuala Lumpur. Local teachers, coaches and local HSBC officers were present and videoed the session for further reference.

Both coaching sessions were very well received and the COBRA Club Coaching Coordinator said that the Academy would be welcome back at any time.

The Penguins had brought with them many HSBC Penguin International Rugby Coaching Academy T-shirts and badges and these were distributed to the students. During the COBRA Tens Tournament it was noticeable that many students were present in these T-shirts and badges, cheering on the team!

More action from the COBRA Tens pool stages.

Penguin International RFC squad for the Malaysian RU-COBRA International Tens, 2004.

Back row: Marc Daniels (Physio), Craig Brown (Tour Manager), John McKittrick (Coach), Haden Kose (Mahurangi, North Harbour Sevens and Development), Craig de Klerk (Villagers, Western Province and Golden Lions), Todd Clever (Reno, United States Eagles and United States Sevens), Johann Gerber (Villagers, Western Province and South Africa Sevens, Vice-Captain), Simione Saravanua (Baravi Exiles and Fiji Sevens), Jaco Hanekom (Shimlhas, Free State Cheetahs Sevens), Jone Daunivucu (Baravi Exiles and Fiji Sevens), Alan Wright (Chairman), David Townsend (Liaison Officer).

Front row: Hang Kek Kang (Liaison Officer), Antonio da Cunha (Belenenses, Portugal and Portugal Sevens), William Hafu (Silverdale and North Harbour U21), Shane Thompson (Montreal Barbarians, Canada and Canada Sevens), Howard Graham (British Army, England Sevens, Captain), Vonivate Kunabilo (Baravi Exiles, Nadronga and Fiji U19), Saula Rabaka (Baravi Exiles, Fiji and Fiji Sevens), Raymond Rodan (Baravi Exiles and Fiji Sevens), Sailosi Nawavu (Coach).

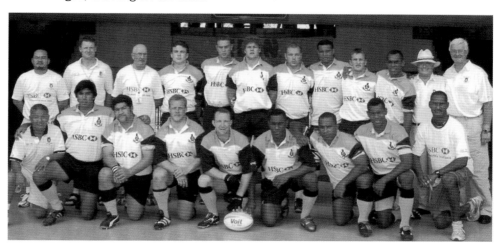

Thank-you letter to the Penguins from the President of COBRA.

Penguin International RFC Coaches - three of the best!

John McKittrick

John's area of expertise is in Sevens Rugby: North Harbour Sevens Coach, 1994 - 2010 (only three losses in eight years); Mahurangi Premiers (North Harbour) 2005 - 06; Penguin International RFC Coach at COBRA Tens, 2003 - 07 and 2010 - 11; USA Rugby National Men's Sevens Coach 2001 - 05; Technical Advisor to the USA Sevens Programme, 2004; Technical Adviser to the Cook Islands Sevens Programme, 2004; National Coach Cook Islands Rugby Union, 2001 - 04; IRB initiated training in Guam Sevens for South Pacific Games 2003; Cook Island Manchester Commonwealth Games Sevens Coach, 2002; North Harbour Colts Coach, 1993 - 95 (undefeated in 1994); North Harbour Development XV Coach, 1996, 2000, 2001 and North Harbour Tens Selector/Coach to Ballymore in 1996 - 97.

Steve Hill

Steve's Club playing career was with Chislehurst and Sidcup Grammar School 1st XV, Loughborough University 1st XV, Sidcup RFC 1st XV, Blackheath RFC 1st XV, Askeans RFC 1st XV and the Kuwait Nomads RFC 1st XV.

His representative playing career was as Captain of Kent County Championship XV; the Arabian Gulf Sevens team at Singapore and the Hong Kong Sevens in 1990 and as Captain of the Arabian Gulf XV.

Steve's Club coaching career includes: Level 5 RFU Coach; Head Coach at Kuwait Nomads; Coach at Sidcup RFC; Head Coach at Askeans RFC; Coach at Newbury RFC 1st XV 2006 - '07; Director of Rugby at Oxford University 1996 - 2010 and Director of Rugby at Richmond FC.

His representative coaching career includes: Head Coach of England Universities; Head Coach of England Students 2002 - '07; Head Coach of England Students Sevens; Head Coach of GB Students Sevens; Head Coach of Oxbridge XV. Coaching the Penguin International RFC: PIRFC XV v Hong Kong and Hong Kong Barbarians; PIRFC XV on tour to Mexico; PIRFC XV on tour to Malta; PIRFC XV at Sidcup RFC 125th Anniversary Celebrations Match; PIRFC XV on tour to Portugal; PIRFC at Hong Kong Tens... etc etc!

Grant McKelvey

Grant McKelvey is a dedicated, professional coach who has helped the HSBC Penguin Coaching Academy get to where it is today. Grant has led a number of Coaching Academy tours and has visited places such as Malaysia, Dubai and Malta. He is a meticulous planner and prepares exceptionally well for each coaching session. The feedback following any session Grant has led has always been extremely positive and the Penguins know he always leaves a legacy from each session he delivers. The Club was delighted when Grant accepted the post of Director of Player Development and he has provided significant input in the last few years in planning the Academy tours and in particular identifying suitable coaching resources to go on the trips.

Grant has played for Haddington, Watsonians, Edinburgh and Scotland and has also been the Edinburgh Rugby Development Manager for the SRU. He has also played for the Penguin International RFC as part of the successful team that toured Croatia in 1998. Grant is currently SRU Senior Regional Academy Manager.

2005

The annual match versus Oxford University was scheduled for the evening of Wednesday, 23rd February, 2005. Unfortunately, freezing conditions with snow led to the match being abandoned. This was the second time in four years that the fixture had to be cancelled due to inclement weather.

The match against Cambridge University was played on Wednesday, 3rd March on a cool, blustery and damp evening. A vocal crowd was entertained by adventurous rugby, although the first-half error count for both sides was high. The half-time score was level at 12 - 12. It was the more determined and better-organised Cambridge University team that dominated the second half, and they ran out eventual winners 24 - 43. Strong performances from Cambridge University players including Steff Thomas and Tom Kirkman ensured the Blues had the upper hand for long periods. For the Penguins, Ryan Pearcy had a strong game while Ricky Pellows ran well from half-back.

This match was the 50th appearance for Cambridge by Ben Dormer, who has toured twice with the Penguins in recent times. Ben has subsequently become the PIRFC Committee/Cambridge University Committee Officer and a Trustee of the Penguin International Rugby Football Trust.

The Match Manager for this game was Craig Brown, the Penguins were coached by Steve Hill and the Captain was Antonio da Cunha of CF Belenenses and Portugal. Another Portuguese International also played for the Penguins in this match, Miguel Morais (GD Direito and Portugal), along with Sam Alatini (Cambridge City and Tonga) and Rory Jenkins (ex-Harlequins).

The Annual PIRFC Committee Supper was held at The Peasant Gastropub in Clerkenwell. The Peasant is owned by Alan Wright's sons Greg and Patrick (who, incidentally, are both Penguin IRFC Vice-Presidents). 44 Committee Members and their guests attended.

Late April brought with it Penguins' second visit to Malta (the first had been 38 years earlier in 1967) following a suggestion from HSBC that the Club could perhaps assist with the expansion and popularity of rugby on the island.

During preparations for the tour, HSBC advised the Club that the Malta Rugby Union runs an international XVs tournament in the spring of each year which attracts teams from the UK and other European rugby nations to compete against local sides. Arrangements were quickly made to send a team to compete in this tournament - supported by qualified coaches to assist the local rugby community.

Alan remembers: 'In 2005 our sponsors were very keen for us to take a side to Malta where they have banking interests. And the Maltese Rugby Union

2005 CHRONICLE

Oxford University match abandoned - snow.

3rd March - Penguins lost to Cambridge University 24 - 43 at Grange Road, Cambridge.

27th April - 3rd May - Malta International Clubs Rugby Tournament. Captained by Gareth Taylor (Wales). Penguins beat La Vallette (Malta) Penguins beat Cymbran RFC (Wales) Penguins beat Bishop's Stortford RFC (England) Penguins beat Walcot RFC (England) Penguins beat Old Alleynian FC (54 - 0) **Winners, Malta RU International Clubs Rugby Tournament**

8th - 12th September - HSBC/COBRA International Tens, Malaysia. Captained by Howard Graham (England). Penguins beat Oriental Rongotai (New Zealand) 32 - 7 Penguins beat Northlink College (Republic of South Africa) 33 - 5 Penguins beat Chinese Taipei 50 - 7 Penguins beat Mendoza (Argentina) 19 - 5 Penguins lost to Marist St. Joseph (Samoa) 0 - 12 **Semi-finalists, Malaysia RU/ COBRA International Tens**

The annual Oxford University match fell victim to the February weather.

The Peasant, at 240 St. John Street, Clerkenwell, has quickly established itself as a favourite London venue for Penguin RFC International functions.

Malta International Clubs Rugby Tournament Souvenir Programme.

Penguins win a lineout against Maltese Club La Vallette during the pool match stages.

The HSBC Penguin International Coaching Academy had a large part to play in the Maltese Women's 7s team winning their first-ever international match.

were very keen too, because they particularly wanted to have our Coaching Academy help them. We took over a very good Touring/Coaching party - and the Tour culminated in our winning the Malta International Clubs Rugby Tournament.'

The Tour commenced with the team assembling for a training run at at the Crawley RFC ground near Gatwick Airport on Wednesday, 27th April, prior to departure later that same day.

The Tournament itself was very well organised. There were eight teams competing in two pools on day one. Day two consisted of the semi-finals and final. All matches were 15 minutes each way.

The Penguins squad was selected from both amateur and professional ranks and consisted of a number of Oxford and Cambridge University Blues, First and Second Division players from both Scotland and Ireland, one player from HSBC RFC, and two players from Sidcup RFC. The team was Captained superbly by Welshman Gareth Taylor who was a lock forward from the Cross Keys and Ebbw Vale Rugby Clubs.

Alan: 'We won every match and met the Old Alleynian FC in the final, which made me laugh! I mean, we'd gone all the way to Malta to play the Old Alleynians! I mention this because I was a Governor at Dulwich College for twenty years or so, and I'm also an Honorary Old Alleynian. It was a strange coincidence!

'The Tournament itself was a great success. And the locals ensured everyone enjoyed themselves with a post-tournament function held at the Black Bull in Paceville, St. Julian's. It was a very happy tour - in fact it embraced exactly the type of tour that we like to run. We wanted to help the local rugby community.'

The Penguin results were: Penguins beat La Vallette, Penguins beat Cymbran. Quarter-final: Penguins beat Bishop's Stortford. Semi-final: Penguins beat Walcot. Final: Penguins beat Old Alleynian FC (54 - 0).

Craig: 'We took along Grant McKelvey as our HSBC Penguin International Coaching Academy Coach. Grant is an ex-Watsonians player who also played for Scotland and who was, at the time, the Edinburgh Rugby Development Manager for the Scottish Rugby Union. We also took David Jack on this Tour, a Scottish Rugby Union referee. We did a lot of coaching work. We ran sessions for the local senior men's team, youth teams, children and the Malta National Women's team. Women's rugby is a reasonably new concept in Malta and at this time the number of players was small - they were concentrating on sevens. They also lack the numbers

to play a regular competition at home and the squad had, up until then, recorded no victories. Grant McKelvey introduced a wide range of skills and drills as well as working on the basics, organisation and team play. The women played an exhibition match as the curtain-raiser to the final of the Tournament, and it was evident they were very enthusiastic and had taken on board the ideas and skills presented to them.'

It is a matter of great pride to the Club that, only a fortnight after these HSBC Penguin International Coaching Academy training sessions, the Malta Women's XV travelled to Prague to play in a sevens tournament. They had a difficult start, playing the Czech Republic in the opening match. Nevertheless, Malta won the match 12 - 7 to record their first-ever win as a national team. Penguins were extremely pleased to receive feedback from the Malta Rugby Union, confirming that the work of the HSBC Penguin International Coaching Academy had a large part to play in that first success!

Penguins squad:

Craig Brown (Tour Manager), Alan Wright (President), Steve Hill (Coach), Grant McKelvey (Coach), David Jack (SRU Referee).

Gareth Taylor (Cross Keys, Captain), Samuel Adlen (Oxford University), Shaun Baxter (Oxford Harlequins), Paul Beal (Redcar), Padriag Brennan (Co. Carlow), Sean Brophy (Oxford University), David Cox (Co. Carlow), Ben Dormer (Cambridge University), Owen Edwards (Ballymena), Ferg Gladstone (Cambridge University), Henry Head (Ballymena), Euan Herkes (Haddington), Deri Hughes (Oxford University), Neil Meikle (Heriot's FP), Danny Mizen (Sidcup), Brendon Pascoe (Tauranga Sports), Mark Pusinelli (HSBC), Richard Roddis (Sidcup), Elliot Stephenson (Oxford Harlequins), Sam Stoop (Oxford Brookes), Ben Wheeler (Cambridge University), Scott Wight (Melrose), Huw Williams (Cambridge University), Andrew Wilson (Heriot's FP), Ian Wilson (Borders).

This is an Old Alleynian FC account of the Maltese Sevens final:
'The Penguins proved to be the ringers of the tournament by continuing with their enviable style of rugby. However many tackles we put in, the ball would be transported 50 yards further along the pitch courtesy of leg-speed, slick passing and great communication. They were big lads, too. We put up a fantastic fight, but by the end, it was more like a scene from a war movie - with twisted limbs writhing in various corners of a foreign field.
The OAs were by no means disgraced to lose to a team who have won the Middlesex Sevens twice, and which can count Waisale Serevi as a former Captain.'

Ben Dormer (above, left, alongside All Black Captain Todd Blackadder) playing for New Zealand Club side Glenmark RFC in 2001.

Benjamin Leif Dormer

Born Christchurch, New Zealand, 25th November, 1978. Education: MA (Politics) Cambridge University, BCom from Canterbury University, BA (Management) from Queensland University. Presently working in commercial property development.

Sporting: Cambridge University RUFC Triple-Blue (2002, 2003, 2004). Canterbury Crusaders Colts, Glenmark RFC, Australian Universities, Queensland Colts and the Barbarians. Ben has also played cricket for Cambridge University and the MCC.

He toured with the Penguin International RFC to Mexico in 2004 and Malta in 2005. Penguins Cambridge University Liaison/Selector. Oxbridge Fixtures Manager. Manager PIRFC Portugal Tour, 2010.

The Club was pleased when Ben accepted its invitation to become the youngest member on the PIRFC Committee as its Cambridge University Representative, and then again later, when he became a trustee of the Penguin International Rugby Football Trust.

In September, 2005, the Club made its eighth visit to the COBRA Tens. Armed with its previous experience, the Club was determined to do well. This required the selection of a very strong side, because over the previous few years the standard of competition had increased significantly - with many teams fielding players with IRB Sevens or Provincial Rugby experience.

Craig Brown: 'This was the year that they moved everybody! Usually everyone stays around the COBRA Club at Lorong Utara in Petaling Jaya, Selangor. But an arrangement had been made with another hotel called the Sunway Lagoon. It was a massive complex. You've never seen anything like it - Disney World was just a part of it. There were 30-meter-high pyramids, big sculptured lion heads, all that sort of thing. So that's where we stayed!'

The Penguins' team was Captained by Howard Graham of Harlequins, British Army and the England Sevens squad, and included Amasio Valence (star New Zealand Sevens player and the one-time record holder for the most IRB Sevens tournament appearances) as well as Fijian Sevens Captain Jone Danuvucu alongside his fellow Fiji Sevens players Jope Ledua, Raymond Rodan and Watisoni Gonewai. Craig Brown was very impressed with Gonewai and later said: 'Watisoni is seriously quick. You've never seen acceleration like it in your life!' The side also included Mike Davis from Canterbury who was recommended by Robbie Deans (ex-Coach of Canterbury Crusaders and current Head Coach of Australia).

As with previous years, the Penguins met for the first time upon arrival in Kuala Lumpur and had only three training runs prior to the Tournament. The team had very mobile forwards, very fast outside backs and extremely experienced half-backs/centres.

Craig: 'Howard Graham, who was our Captain for this tournament, is a very good coach, and I think he was keen to become part of the HSBC Penguins Coaching Academy at that time' (Howard has subsequently served as a coach at both Coventry and Harlequins and also at another English *club by invitation*, the White Hart Marauders).

Craig continues: 'I remember one brilliant "Player's Court" session on this tour which involved Howard Graham. Howard was a Major in the British Army, and it so happened that another player in our squad, Jope Ledua, was a Private in the Fijian Army. I was presiding over this particular "trial" as The Judge, and

Above and far right:
The HSBC Penguin International Coaching Academy's burgeoning reputation for excellence was already making headlines in the Malaysian press.

I reversed their ranks. So we had "Major Jope" putting "Private Graham" through his marching drills. It was outstanding! Jope had obviously been itching for a chance to get back at Officers for quite some time. It was so, so funny!'

Under the Captaincy of Howard Graham the Penguins gelled well, and the squad also performed very well on the day one of the Tournament. Three excellent victories were achieved (over Oriental Rongotai, Northlink College and Chinese Taipei) through a determined defence allied to pace and skill in attack out wide.

On day two the team had a good 19 points to 5 win in the quarter-finals over Mendoza, who fielded numerous Provincial and two international Argentinian players.

Semi-final opponents were defending champions Marist St. Joseph from Samoa, who included six of the Samoan IRB Sevens team in their line-up, plus two other Samoan XVs internationals. The Penguins defended well, and made Marist work hard for their two tries, but the famous Samoan defence held fast and the Penguins were unable to cross the Marist line. It was disappointing to lose, but the general consensus was that Marist St. Joseph deserved their win. But it *was* interesting to learn later on that the Samoans had been training together for six full weeks prior to the Tournament!

The PIRFC's results in the tournament were: Penguins beat Oriental Rongotai (New Zealand) 32 - 7, Penguins beat Northlink College (Republic of South Africa) 33 - 5, Penguins beat Chinese Taipei 50 - 7. Quarter-final: Penguins beat Mendoza (Argentina) 19 - 5. Semi-final: Penguins lost to Marist St. Joseph (Samoa) 0 - 12.

Alan Wright: 'In passing, I must say that I regard an appearance in a semi-final, or as finalists, or as winners of an international abbreviated tournament of any standing, to be an honour - and, as thus, they are recorded in the annual Penguin International fixture card.'

On the coaching front, following on from discussions at the 2004 COBRA Tens about how best to develop the game in Malaysia, the HSBC Penguin International Coaching Academy assembled a team of qualified coaches to lead a Level One Coaches' Course for school teachers. The course was based on the UK's Level One Course, although it was adapted to suit local conditions.

At first, only one course had been planned and facilitated in February, 2005. But following on from the tremendous success of that course, the Academy was invited back to run a further three courses over the year and to plan ahead

RUGBY

FOR THE ALBUM: Participants of the five-day rugby coaching course pose with the three facilitators and the organisers after the closing ceremony in Penang. — Pic: FARIZ ISWADI

Penguin lesson for northern teams

■ By K. Kandiah

RUGBY in the northern States got a boost after the conclusion of a Level One Coaching course at the Continental Hotel in George Town, Penang, recently.

The five-day course, organised by the Combined Old Boys Rugby Association (Cobra), was conducted by certified coaches from the HSBC Penguin Rugby Coaching Academy from the United Kingdom.

The third phase of the Cobra Schools Development Programme, conducted with the cooperation of the Malaysian Rugby Union (MRU) and the Education Ministry, was attended by 32 teachers from Perlis, Kedah and Penang.

The programme consists of four Level 1 Rugby coaching courses — the first for the central region was held in Kuala Lumpur (February), the second for the east coast region in Kuala Terengganu (May), while the fourth will be held in Malacca for the southern region (September).

The facilitators were Cobra resident coach-cum-course coordinator Tan Tai Fatt, Penguin director of rugby Craig Brown and Penguin coaches Anthony Robinson and Malcolm Chumbley.

Programme director Col. (rtd) Wong Hin Jee said the participants are supposed to create interest and awareness of the sport in their respective schools.

"The concept of this programme

SCHOOLS WATCH

SAHC emerge champions

SULTAN Abdul Hamid College (SAHC) stormed to a 21-8 win over SM Pokok Sena Sains (SAINA) to win the inaugural Kedah President's Shield Under-18 rugby competition at the SMDSO ground in Alor Star yesterday.

Though SAINA got off to a 3-0 lead through a penalty by Hafizuddin Yusof in the fifth minute, it was evident that SAHC were in full com-

is to promote, develop and create an awareness of the sport among the school children at the grassroots level, especially the Under-15 age-group children.

"It is nice to receive a certificate, frame and display it, but what is the point if your knowledge is not put into use or imparted to others, the whole idea of this effort is to develop rugby.

"I know it is hard to get funding for this sport as it would be tough fighting against other more popular sports, but if we put our heart and soul to it I am sure we can do it," he told the participants at the closing.

Present at the closing ceremony were Cobra vice president Lt Col

mand.

And it took them only four minutes after SAINA took the lead to get a try through Shafiq Hashim which Arif Saad converted to make it 7-3.

Thereafter, it was SAHC all the way and they got another seven points from a try by Nor Azmil Shaari which Arif Saad converted to give them a 14-3 lead at halftime.

(rtd) Tommy Pereira, Education Ministry Sports and Physical Education department's sports management division director Chua Hong Tam and Penang Rugby Association president Hassan Farouke.

Apart from the coaching course, Cobra also conducted a coaching clinic for the island state's school students at the Polo Ground, Jalan Sepoy Lines in George Town yesterday.

The clinic was conducted by HSBC Penguin Rugby Academy coaches, while the Penang-based teachers who had attended the course assisted in conducting the drills.

for a further two years of five to six courses per year (formal certificates are awarded to the participants upon successful completion of these courses).

As a part of the 2005 COBRA Tens Tournament, the Academy supplied two dedicated coaches to assist in the COBRA Schools Rugby Development Programme. Six sessions of general skills coaching were led by Grant McKelvey and Sailosi Nawavu at various schools around Kuala Lumpur. Average attendance was sixty children aged between 10 and 18. One general skills clinic was conducted by the Penguin squad in association with the Academy for 169 school children aged between 12 and 16. At the time this was a Club record for the number of players coached in one session at the time.

Following on from the great work undertaken by all the Academy Coaches and the players involved in coaching during 2005, the HSBC Penguin International Coaching Academy saw its reputation continue to grow - and this resulted in numerous requests from rugby unions and other interested parties (India, Malta, Malaysia, Mexico, Guam, Brazil, the USA, Canada, Bermuda and others) for visits (or revisits) of the Academy to roll out similar programmes.

Above: COBRA Tens, and General Schools' Coaching Programme Tour to Malaysia. Back row: Marc Daniels (Physio), Grant McKelvey (Academy Coach), Oliver Brown (Scotland Sevens), Haden Kose (North Harbour 'B'), Craig de Klerk (Western Province), Damian Hall (Bective Rangers), Jope Ledua (Fiji Sevens), Todd Clever (USA), Kini Nauvasi (Nadi), Craig Brown (Director of Rugby).

Front row: John McKittrick (Coach), Amasio Valence (New Zealand Sevens), Raymond Rodan (Fiji Sevens), Mike Davis (Canterbury), Howard Graham (England Sevens, Captain), Watisone Gonewai (Fiji Sevens), Willy Hafu (North Harbour Sevens), Jone Daunivucu (Fiji Sevens), Sailosi Nawavu (Academy Coach).

PENGUINS UNBEATEN

The Penguins' 'Glorious Year' began on a cold evening in March at Grange Road, Cambridge. The Penguins were quickly into their stride, and with Pat Howard directing operations from fly-half an ample supply of good ball from the forwards was put to good use. Cambridge University defended desperately, but it wasn't long before a break by Howard led to Ollie Montgomery scoring a try which was converted by Kieron Hallett. As the match progressed, the forwards became more and more dominant, and further tries came from Adam Slade and hooker Matt Baker. Unfortunately the temperature was well below freezing and conditions deteriorated to such an extent that certain areas of the pitch became dangerous. With the agreement of both Captains, referee Bruce Robertson called proceedings to a halt at half-time, Penguins leading Cambridge University 19 - 0.

The Penguins were Managed by Ian Bullerwell and Captained by Pat Howard (Queensland, ACT Brumbies, Leicester and Australia). Ben Dormer also played for the Club in this match, in a team which was mainly comprised of University and London Welsh players - including one of the Penguins' Committee, Florent Rossigneux.

Oxford University were next up on the fixture list - and with a cold snap passing over the country in the lead up to the match, a repeat of last year's cancellation was a possibility. However it was rain, and not frost, that persisted - and the game went ahead on a soft and muddy pitch. Both sides played an expansive game, and the crowd was treated to some excellent running rugby. Penguins, skippered by Gareth Taylor, scored eight tries and ran out convincing winners by 46 points to 5. The Penguins' tries were scored by Ben Breeze (three), Lee Hinton (two), Ian Warbrick, Matthew Baker and Steve Winn. The pack supplied quality ball and supported well, with loose forwards Flo Rossigneux, Jim O'Donovan and James Ball providing the link and the continuity.

The Penguins were Managed by Craig Brown and Captained by Gareth Taylor (Ebbw Vale and Wales 'A'. Among the other members of this strong squad were Steve Winn and Ben Breeze (both of Newport Gwent Dragons and Wales Sevens), and David MacCallum (Esher and Australia 'A').

Spring 2006 saw the creation of *The St. James, Caledonian & Penguin International Golfing Society*. Alan: 'At this time a lot of our Members wanted to play golf. I made the point that a new golfing society would find it very difficult to reserve days at any really good golf club because all the best courses are fully booked up with well-established societies that have been around for years. As I was already the founder of an Anglo-Scottish golfing society, I arranged for the Penguins to be incorporated into that.'

2006 CHRONICLE

March - Penguins beat Cambridge University 19 - 0 at Grange Road, Cambridge (match abandoned at half-time).

March - Penguins beat Oxford University 46 - 5 at Iffley Road, Oxford.

Spring - Incorporation of the Penguin International RFC into the Anglo-Scottish Mutual Golfing Society to form The St. James, Caledonian & Penguin International Golfing Society.

10th June - Paris University Club Centenary Year Celebration Match, Paris. Captained by Rod Moore (Australia). Penguins beat PUC 40 - 7

8th, 9th and 10th September - HSBC/COBRA International Tens, Malaysia. Captained by Uale Mai (Samoa).
Penguins beat Sandakan Eagles (Malaysia) 12 - 5
Penguins beat Australian Legends 15 - 10
Penguins beat Aoteroa Maori (New Zealand) 12 - 0
Penguins beat Northlink College (Republic of South Africa) 19 - 15
Penguins beat Te Hiku O Te Ika (New Zealand) 15 - 0
Penguins beat Natal Duikers (Republic of South Africa) 33 - 14
Winners, Malaysia RU - HSBC COBRA International Tens

15th and 16th September - Royal Kedah International Sevens, Alor Star. Captained by Uale Mai (Samoa).
Penguins beat Police United 77 - 0
Penguins beat RMN ORCA 77 - 3
Penguins beat ASAS 62 - 0
Penguins beat NS Wanderers (Malaysia) 46 - 5
Penguins beat COBRA (Malaysia) 33 - 7
Penguins beat Sandakan Eagles (Malaysia) 36 - 33
Winners, Royal Kedah International Sevens

Sir William Purves steps down as President. Alan Wright becomes the eighth President of the Penguins.

The Berkshire GC, Ascot.

'All Members of the Penguin International RFC are Honorary Members of the St. James, Caledonian & Penguin International Golfing Society. We play team golf twice a year at The Berkshire in Ascot and at Bruntsfield Links - one of Edinburgh's finest Golf Clubs.'

The St. James, Caledonian & Penguin International Golfing Society

This mutual Society has two annual fixtures at outstanding venues - The Berkshire Golf Club in Ascot and The Bruntsfield Links Golf Club in Edinburgh.

Team competitions are played and cups are presented to the winners in the morning and the afternoon.

Alan Wright is the President of the Society. In England the present Honorary Secretary is Tony Carpenter, and the present Honorary Secretary in Scotland is Richard Taylor.

PIRFC Advisory Board Member Dudley Ankerson (himself a former British Diplomat) kindly arranged for the Penguins to attend a reception at the British Embassy on the day before the PUC match.

Penguin Committee men in the Stade Charléty Stadium for the Paris University Club match. Left to right: Craig Brown, Alan Wright, Tom Wacker, Bill Calcraft and Hugh Thomas.

At the request of HSBC, Penguins were asked to arrange a high profile match in Paris, to coincide with the re-branding of CCF (Credit Commercial de France) to HSBC. A match with the Paris University Club Past and Present was duly arranged, and to add to the occasion, it was PUC's Centenary Year and the match against the Penguins became the Centenary Celebration Match. The Paris University Club ensured a competitive game by inviting a number of former players to play.

Having never played on the winning side in France, Club President Alan Wright was keen that the Penguins assemble a good side. The result was one of the strongest teams the Club has ever fielded, and certainly the strongest Penguin International XV since the game went professional.

Alan: 'One of the undoubted highlights of 2006 was the invitation from the Paris University Club to play a 'PUC Past and Present' side in Paris for their Centenary Celebration. This invitation came through Flo Rossigneux, one of our players and a Committee Member, whose brother is the President of the PUC. The two brothers played, unusually, and in the spirit of the occasion, for both teams. We had an outstanding side who played very well in probably 100 degrees of heat. Sadly it was so hot that I think it rather put off the spectators.'

The match took place on an extremely warm Paris morning on 10th June

Above: Lionel (left) and Florent Rossigneux have both played for the Paris University Club and Racing Club. Florent has also played for Stade Français, Wasps, Richmond and London Welsh. During the course of this match both men played for the Penguins and for Paris University.

and a number of Club officials and supporters made the trip to Paris to join the team for this great rugby occasion. The Penguins team included Australian test props Rod Moore and Matt Dunning, New Zealand Sevens star Craig De Goldi, Rob Henderson of Ireland and the British and Irish Lions, Duncan Hodge of Scotland, French National Sevens players Nic Le Roux, Rida Joauher and Kris Kopetsky, New Zealand Maoris Blair Urlich and Reece Robinson, Joel Nasmith from North Harbour, Arthur Brenton from Bedford and ACT Brumbies hooker James McCormack. The team was coached by former Scotland player and coach John Rutherford, and managed by Craig Brown.

The Paris University Club team included a number of players from the Top 14 and D2 Pro divisions in France who had links to PUC.

It was the hosts who held the early advantage with strong driving play and it was only determined Penguins defence that kept them out. As the match progressed the Penguin team found its feet and began to string together phases of play which gained territory. First-half tries by James McCormack and a truly out-standing solo effort from Craig De Goldi gave the Penguins a half-time lead of 14 - 0.

Both sides proceeded to play open, running rugby in the second half, despite the very hot conditions at Stade Charléty (the temperature reached 30 degrees Centigrade that morning). The Penguins built on their late first-half momentum and ran in four more tries to PUC's one. The final score of 40 points to 7 flattered the Penguins, as PUC were very competitive for most of the game but found themselves stretched at the end of multi-phased plays.

After the match the Penguins attended the French Rugby Cup Final as guests of PUC, and later that evening they were guests at the PUC party during their return trip from the match on the Seine by boat to central Paris.

The trip was very well organised by Lionel Rossigneux and other staff from PUC, and the possibility remains for further PUC/PIRFC fixtures in the future.

Officials and subs watch from the touchline.

Players from Penguins and Paris University Club take a breather in the 30°C heat.

Left: John Rutherford and the late Andy Ripley relax on the Seine on the way back from the French Cup Final. Andy Ripley always had a soft spot for the Penguins and often joined their tour parties in his latter years. He first played for the Penguins in 1984 and he was also an Honorary Vice-President of the Club.

Above: Penguins squad, Paris Tour 2006

A wonderful momento of a very special day - a framed Paris University Club playing jersey.

Back row: Craig Brown (Tour Manager), Claude Lalande (Liaison Officer), Steve Lawrie (Edinburgh and Scotland U21), Paul Neville (Garryowen and Ireland 'A'), Dave Gorrie (Lansdowne and Bay of Plenty), Arthur Brenton (Bedford), Rod Moore (Ulster and Australia, Captain), Peter Jorgensen (Edinburgh and Australia), Paul Laffin (Oxford University), Ben Breeze (Newport Gwent Dragons and Wales 'A', Vice-Captain), Reece Robinson (Mitsubishi and New Zealand Maori), Blair Urlich (Mitsubishi and New Zealand Maori), James McCormack (ACT Brumbies and Australia U21), Flo Rossigneux (London Welsh, French Barbarians), Joel Nasmith (Helensville and North Harbour), Alan Wright (CEO), Bill Calcraft (Committee).

Front row: Xavier Gousse (Physio), Craig De Goldi (Karita and New Zealand Sevens), Nicolas le Roux (Worcester and France Sevens), Rida Joauher (Montuban and France Sevens), Matt Dunning (NSW Waratahs and Australia), Ian Warbrick (Staines and Scotland Sevens), Kris Kopetsky (USBC and France Sevens), Mike Prendergast (Munster), Marc Camburn (Takapuna and New Zealand Sevens), Rob Henderson (Munster, Ireland and British and Irish Lions), Duncan Hodge (Edinburgh and Scotland), Tom Wacker (Chairman).

Insets: Top left: John Rutherford (Coach), top right: Henry Head (Richmond, Ballymena).

In September the Penguins returned to Kuala Lumpur for the ninth time as a participant in the COBRA Tens, and also accepted an invitation to play in the Royal Kedah Sevens for the first time.

Craig Brown: 'This was the first time we went on a Far-East tour rather than just to take part in a single tournament. The dates were good so we had back-to-back tournaments.'

As the Penguins were due to play Tens followed by Sevens the team had to be selected with enough size and speed to cover both tournaments. Coupled with this, the Club were very keen to select players from Samoa, as they had a number of world-class rugby players who would be available at this time.

As a result of selecting for this tour, a very strong link has subsequently been established with the Marist St. Joseph Club in Apia, and also with Brian Lima and his wife Sina, who manage the interests of a number of leading Samoan players.

For their part in organising the rest of the team the Penguins also owed a debt of gratitude to Richard Breen (for arranging for a number of talented Fijians to play in the squad), to John McKittrick (for his links in New Zealand), to Bill Calcraft (for his contacts at Manly) and to Penguins' Committee Member David Townsend - whose support during the two weeks of the tour (and his strong links to HSBC) were invaluable.

And many thanks were also due to the Penguins' special friend, Hang Kek Kang - the Liaison Officer whose magic touch resolved every problem.

The Penguins assembled in Kuala Lumpur on Monday, 4th September for the COBRA Tens. The team consisted of five New Zealanders, four Samoans, three Fijians, one South African and one Australian.

Craig: 'So we had this wonderful group. And John McKittrick and I got together and asked each other: 'Who are we going to make the Captain?'

'We had two outstanding candidates - Mesake Davu of Fiji and Uale Vala Mai of Samoa, both of whom were senior figures in their respective international squads. After much consideration we approached Uale Mai, only to discover that he wasn't really keen on being the Captain. So we chatted to him for a while and it transpired that he was a bit nervous of heading up all of the different nationalities - he's not a very outgoing kind of guy. But in the end he agreed to do it. And what a star he was!'

*Monsoon rain called
a temporary halt to proceedings.*

Over the next three days John McKittrick and Uale ran a number of training sessions to try and mould the players into a cohesive unit. As usual, the biggest challenge was to facilitate sufficient opportunities for the players to become used to playing with each other and to drill the defensive patterns and first-phase plays.

Craig continues: 'We had a few guys there who didn't drink, and we had a few guys there who probably drank too much, but we had a good mix. Everyone knew when it was "on" and when it was "off". John McKittrick did a great job with the coaching, but the thing that probably impressed me the most was watching Uale bond everyone together by means of his structured stretching exercises! Mostly he'd lead these. And he'd say: "For ten seconds we are stretching this..." and it might be a leg or the groin or whatever. But he'd get everyone to count the seconds off during each stretch. Well, by the end of the tour everyone there could count from one to ten in Samoan, Tongan, Fijian, Malaysian, English, Afrikaans and a couple of others that got thrown in as well. It really got everyone together!'

Although the Penguins were being billed as favourites in some sections of the media, Craig Brown and John McKittrick were under no illusions. There were many other good teams, and there is rarely an easy game in the COBRA Tens.

Each team had one match on Friday and two on Saturday to complete the pool play. As the tournament started the monsoon rain arrived and turned the field into what looked like a lake, resulting in one game being suspended for 45 minutes due to the threat of lightning strikes. The weather conditions evened up every contest and only a couple of games were won comfortably. The Penguins, through great defence, great team spirit, outstanding individual play by the likes of Mika Senio and Mesake Davu, plus the inspirational leadership of Uale Mai, ended by qualifying in first position.

Finals day broke fine and sunny, and the pitch was drying out well. The team again relied

*Wet but happy!
Left to right: Mika Senio, Willy Hafu
and Alapasa Cordtz.*

upon great spirit, great defence, and more brilliance - in particular from Mika Senio, Mesake Davu and Uale Mai - to win both the quarter and semi-finals in very closely fought encounters. It was testament to the reputation of Uale Mai that he was targeted by the opposition for some very close 'marking'!

78 ▶ SPORT

NEW STRAITS TIMES MONDAY, SEPTEMBER 11, 2006

> RUGBY

Penguins taste sweet success

■ **By Ranjini Thangaraju**
ranjini@nst.com.my

LAST year's runners-up Natal Duikers ended up as bridesmaid again after United Kingdom's Penguins thumped them 33-14 in the final of the 37th HSBC-COBRA Invitational Rugby 10s at the Petaling Jaya Stadium in Kelana Jaya yesterday.

However, for the hard-tackling Penguins, it was sweet success and made up for last year when defending champions Samoans Marist St Joseph beat them in the semi-finals.

The Samoans did not return to defend their title this year but loaned four of their players to the English side.

The Penguins also had three Fijians, five New Zealanders and an Australian to power them.

"We did not expect to take the lead. The plan was to secure the back and defend whenever we got the ball. No tackles were missed and we implemented pressure," said Penguins manager and former player Craig Brown.

The Penguins have won the Cup twice before this — in 1993 and 1994 — when Craig played in both editions.

The Penguins led 26-0 in the first half of the 30-minute match, scoring tries through Nasoni Rokodiau, Egeleni Fale, Alapasa Cordtz and Mika Senio.

Brett Sweeny converted three tries.

After the breather, the Penguins continued scoring with one more converted try by Nasoni to lead 33-0.

The South Africans got on the score sheet in the dying minutes through two converted tries from Darren Van Rooyen and Orkert Vermevlen, but it was a little too late. The Penguins sealed it 33-14.

Sandakan Eagles won the Plate final when they beat another local side, Cobra, 24-5.

The Bowl finals was won by British Army who beat Australian Legends 26-10.

In the schools' category, the Cup final was won by Bandar Penawar Sports School (BPSS) who outplayed SM Sains Sultan Mahmud of Terengganu 26-0.

Results (All Finals) — Cup: Penguins 33 Natal Duikers 14; **Plate:** Sandakan Eagles 24 Cobra 5, **Bowl:** British Army 26 Australian Legends 10.

Schools — Cup: BPSS 26 SESMA 0; **Plate:** SM Sains Johor 5 Royal Military College 10; **Bowl:** SM Tunku Anum 15 Kolej Yayasan Saad 7.

United Kingdom's Penguins celebrate after beating Natal Duikers 33-14 in the final of the 37th HSBC-COBRA Invitational 10s at the Petaling Jaya Stadium yesterday. Pic: HAIRUL ANUAR ABD RAHIM

So finally, after twelve long years, Penguins had made the COBRA Tens final again. The opposition would be the previous year's runners up, Natal Duikers - a very strong South African team which included a sprinkling of Natal and Super 14 players in their ranks.

Conditions were ideal for running rugby with clear skies overhead and firm, dry footing underneath. The Penguins started in tremendous fashion, scoring 19 unanswered points in the first four minutes, and went on to lead by 26 - 0 at half-time. Three-quarters of the way through the match the Penguins led 33 - 0, but Natal came back in the final five minutes to score twice - but it didn't matter. The final result was a glorious 33 - 14 victory to the Club.

Broad smiles covered the faces of the Penguins team, management and supporters when the referee blew for no-side. The win was based upon great team spirit, first-class contributions both on and off the field by all, great leadership by John McKittrick, Uale Mai and Mesake Davu, and a *Man of the Tournament* display by Mika Senio.

Craig Brown: 'It was a gutsy, team effort from everybody, but Mika Senio scored the tries that gave us that tournament.

'I remember in one game he was 60 meters from the line. He side-stepped and headed for the corner in a great big arcing run. We were all shouting: "Go Mika! Go Mika! Go Mika!" But the whole team did incredibly well to win that tournament.'

Local press report on the Penguins' magnificent win in the 2006 HSBC COBRA Tens.

The Hui Weng Choon Trophy.

Penguins' results in the tournament were: Penguins beat Sandakan Eagles (Malaysia) 12 - 5, Penguins beat Australian Legends 15 - 10, Penguins beat Aoteroa Maori (New Zealand) 12 - 0. Quarter-final: Penguins beat Northlink College (Republic of South Africa) 19 - 15. Semi-final: Penguins beat Te Hiku O te Ika (New Zealand) 15 - 0. Final: Penguins beat Natal Duikers (Republic of South Africa) 33 - 14. Penguins were the winners of the Hui Weng Choon Trophy.

This was the third time the Penguins had won the COBRA Tens. And, quite uniquely, it also meant that Craig Brown had also won the COBRA Tens three times in three different capacities as a member of the Penguins: Once as a Penguins player in 1993, once as the Penguins Captain in 1994 and now, once more in 2006, as the Penguins Team Manager.

This picture and above left: The HSBC Penguin International Coaching Academy in action.

The HSBC Penguin International Coaching Academy and the COBRA Club also coached well over 150 boys (at Under 14 and Under 16) in no fewer than eight different Malaysian schools during this, the first leg of the Tour. The consensus among the Coaches was that since the last Academy Coaching visit in September, 2005, there had been an obvious increase in the general understanding of the game at all age groups.

After the marvellous COBRA Tens victory, the team headed to the Island of Langkawi off the north-western coast of Malaysia to prepare for the Royal Kedah Sevens - and also for the Academy to run coaching sessions for even more local school children.

As Craig said at the time: 'Hang Kek Kang, our wonderful Liaison Officer, is from Langkawi, and this is the first time he's been back for several years. All of his family and friends are here. We are staying in a little place on the beach and we are here for four days. There's just enough grass to train for Sevens.'

Tomasi Neilumi takes a nap on the way to Langkawi.

So it was that the Penguins moved from tens to sevens mode in just four training runs prior to the Royal Kedah Sevens. The atmosphere was more relaxed than it had been in Kuala Lumpur, and the squad managed to get some rest - but intensity and concentration was forthcoming from all whenever it was required.

Craig: 'On Thursday we got the ferry from Langkawi over to the mainland. We played the next day, Friday - it was a two-day, Friday/Saturday tournament, because that is the Malaysian weekend.'

Day one of the Sevens pitted the Penguins against three local teams. The expectation was that the Club would win these matches fairly comfortably, and they did. Nevertheless, the team still had to apply itself and concentrate on playing careful sevens rugby to build for day two.

On the second day Penguins played the top three Malaysian Clubs who had all been successful against the two New Zealand teams in the tournament. The quarter and semi-finals were won comfortably enough, although the COBRA Club did make Penguins work very hard in the semi-final.

2006 Royal Kedah International Sevens Tournament Programme.

Craig remembers: 'On the second day the games got progressively harder, but we won them comfortably enough. Well, we had a wonderful team! The final was against Sandakan Eagles from Malaysia, who had included eight Fijians and Samoans to strengthen their squad. As a matter of fact one of them was a professional rugby league player from Sydney.'

The final was a close affair in which the Eagles scored first. Although the Penguins did manage to take the lead, it seemed that every time the Club managed to pull away the Eagles would bounce back. With four minutes remaining the Penguins led 36 - 19, only for the Eagles to again get back into the game by pulling back two tries. However the Penguin defence stood firm after this (despite some very tired legs in the hot conditions) and held out for a crowd-thrilling and heart-stopping 36 - 33 win.

Mesake Davu (with ball) ably supported by Marc Camburn.

For the Penguins Nasoni Roko, Brett Sweeney and Mika Senio topped the try scoring list, and Tomasi Neilumi, on his first trip outside Fiji, put on a magical side-stepping and running display. Marc Camburn was a great sevens exponent and a tireless worker, and Mesake Davu ensured an endless supply of restart ball, winning the aerial competition in spectacular fashion. Much credit must also go to the Captain, Uale Mai, who worked skillfully in the sweeper position, directing defensive operations from the back as well as leading many attacks.

The victorious Penguin International squad collect the Kedah Sevens Trophy in the Stadium Darul Aman.

Penguins' special coach John McKittrick and his wife, Lesley.

Craig: 'It was a close match in the end, and there wasn't much in it. But sometimes, matches are won or lost on a bounce of the ball or a referee's interpretation. But it was an outstanding achievement by the boys, and we won it!'

After the final, the Cup Championship Trophy was presented to the Penguins by the Sultan of Kedah (Patron of the Royal Kedah Sevens) who attended the second day of the tournament.

The Penguins results were: Penguins beat Police United 77 - 0, Penguins beat RMN ORCA 77 - 3, Penguins beat ASAS 62 - 0. Quarter-final: Penguins beat NS Wanderers (Malaysia) 46 - 5. Semi-final: Penguins beat COBRA (Malaysia) 33 - 7. Final: Penguins beat Sandakan Eagles (Malaysia) 36 - 33. Penguins won the Royal Kedah Sevens Cup Championship Trophy.

The general consensus after this tournament was that The Royal Kedah Sevens could only grow on the international stage now that it is to be held directly following the COBRA Tens.

Mika Senio holds the 2006 Royal Kedah International Sevens Trophy.

Above: The Trophy and the 2006 COBRA - Kedah Penguin International tour squad. Back row: Marc Daniels (Physiotherapist), Craig Brown (DoR), Ryan Barker (North Shore and North Harbour Sevens), Mesake Davu (Fiji and Fiji Sevens, Vice-Captain), Egelani Fale (Savaii Samoa and Samoa), Sam Paddison* (Mahurangi), Nasoni Rokobiau (Natisori and Fiji Sevens), Mika Senio (Marist St. Joseph, Samoa Sevens), Alapasa Cordtz (Marist St. Joseph and Samoa Sevens), David Townsend (Liaison), John McKittrick (Coach).

Front row: Yun Ting (Physio), Marc Camburn (Takapuna and New Zealand Sevens), Willy Hafu (Mahurangi and New Zealand U19), Brett Sweeney (North Shore and North Harbour), Tomasi Neilumi (Fiji Sevens squad), David Collis (Manly and Queensland), Johann Gerber* (Villagers and South Africa Sevens), Uale Vala Mai (Marist St. Joseph and Samoa Sevens, Captain).

* denotes COBRA Tens only.

Inset left to right: Jamie Dempsey (Academy Coach), Hang Kek Kang (Liaison Manager), Grant McKelvey (Academy Coach).

Alan Wright has the last word on what was undoubtedly a wonderful season for the Penguins in which the Club were unbeaten: 'Well, 2006 was a very special and a very successful year for us. Winning any International Tens or Sevens Tournament is very difficult these days, as many teams are able to attend these invitational events with the benefit of a lot of practice together. Which is something we've learnt to live without!

'Without doubt, the whole credit for this success lies with Craig Brown. I couldn't go because of illness - it was the first time I hadn't been able to go to Malaysia. We had our first Samoan Captain, Uale Vala Mai, who was a big star at that time in Samoan Sevens. So we won both the COBRA Tens (for the third time) and the new Royal Kedah Sevens in great style!'

It was on 17th August, 2006, that Sir William Purves retired from the Penguins Presidency to be succeeded by Alan Wright. Tom Wacker became PIRFC Chairman at the same time.

Craig Brown with the Royal Kedah International Sevens Trophy.

John Grove

John Grove is a Hong Kong-based businessman and his company, Grove Industries, is an international apparel, sourcing and manufacturing operation. He was first introduced to the Club in 2006 by Vincent Bramhall, PIRFC Secretary and an old friend of John's from their time together in Hong Kong. John was very impressed by the vision of the Club, particularly the work of the HSBC Penguin International Coaching Academy, and immediately became a Member.

John became a significant sponsor of the Penguins in 2007 by supplying - through Grove Industries - casual clothing for players in the HSBC Penguins teams and for coaches in the HSBC Penguin International Coaching Academy. He was most deservedly elected an Hon. Vice-President that same year.

Since then John has generously agreed to extend his support of the Club by making significant contributions to the expenses of the Club's playing and coaching tours around the world. He is a keen supporter and follows the team whenever his

John Grove and the framed PIRFC shirt which was recently awarded to John and his wife Thea by the Club in appreciation of all their much-valued support.

busy schedule allows him to. When the HSBC Penguins are in Hong Kong, John and wife Thea kindly host a 'Penguin Party' for the players, coaches, officials and members of the Club.

In recognition of John's generous sponsorship and support, the Club has recently inaugurated a 'John Grove Award'. The Award takes the form of an engraved tankard and it will be awarded annually to the 'Best and Fairest Player' in the HSBC Penguins team at the Hong Kong Tens. It will also be awarded to an HSBC Penguins player on any overseas tour in which John has been directly involved as a major sponsor.

Sir William Purves - the seventh Penguin President

Sir William 'Willie' Purves CBE, DSO, born 27 December 1931, was the first Group Chairman of HSBC Holdings following the creation of a holding company to act as parent to The Hongkong and Shanghai Banking Corporation and the Midland Bank, after the former's acquisition of Midland in 1992. Born in Kelso, Scotland, Willie attended Kelso High School before commencing training with the National Bank of Scotland (now The Royal Bank of Scotland). This was interrupted by National Service in Korea, during which time he was awarded the Distinguished Service Order (DSO) - 'a unique and never-to-be-repeated achievement for a National Service Officer.'

He returned to banking in 1954 and moved to Hong Kong to join HSBC, where he remained for the rest of his working life. In 1986, he became Chairman and CEO of HSBC, and was then appointed Chairman and CEO of HSBC Holdings in 1991, overseeing the purchase and integration of Midland Bank.

Retiring from HSBC in 1998, Willie played a large role in overseeing the transition from British to Chinese rule in the Territory's significant financial services sector. He was knighted in 1993 and awarded the Grand Bauhinia Medal by Hong Kong in 1999.

As a Borderer, it is only natural that Willie has had a lifetime's enthusiasm for rugby union football, in particular for seven-a-sides. For many years he was a member of the Organising Committee of the world-famous Hong Kong Sevens, and on his return to England he became a member of the Committee of the Scottish Rugby Union. Furthermore, he is Patron of the London Scottish FC and Chairman of Friends of Scottish Rugby.

Willie has been a steadfast member of the Penguin International RFC for over 25 years, first as a Vice-President, second as the Penguins' long-serving Patron, and third as the seventh President of the Club (2003 - '06).

He is highly regarded and universally respected as the most successful and distinguished Scottish banker of his era.

Sir William Purves and Alan Wright share a joke at the Hong Kong Sevens.

2007

Once again the Penguins' season began with a Varsity match - this time against Oxford University on 27th February. In difficult conditions both sides contrived to produce a very entertaining game. The Penguin XV, under the Captaincy of Howard Graham, took a while to settle down and soon found themselves 0 - 12 down. Oxford (who were, on this occasion, Captained by Joe Roff, the seasoned Australian International) were causing the Penguins' defence a lot of problems.

Aussie star Joe Roff caused the Penguins a lot of problems.

Gradually the more experienced Penguins' pack came to terms with the conditions and began to dominate in the tight. Eventually the pressure told and Penguins scored two tries. Matt Jones converted one of these and kicked a late penalty to see the Penguins go in at half-time with a three-point lead.

In the second half Penguins continued to dominate and scored a further two tries, one of which Matt Jones converted. The University scored another try at the death to make the final score Oxford University 19, Penguins 27.

The Penguins squad were managed by Ian Bullerwell, Captained by Howard Graham and included Matt Jones of the Ospreys and Wales as well as six other Ospreys players and seven players from the Bedford Blues.

On 7th March Penguins travelled to Grange Road to play Cambridge University. In a scintillating display of open, running rugby, Penguins totally overwhelmed a spirited Cambridge side.

Centre Brian Milne was outstanding, scoring three tries and making three others. The remaining 12 tries were scored by Lucio Fleming (three), Tim Holgate (two), Adam Barnard (two), Shaun Brady, Mauritz Botha, Karl Dickson, Ben Alexander and Joe Wheeler. The final score was Cambridge University 12, Penguins 93 - the highest score ever achieved by the Penguins in the UK. This was an astonishing win - especially as the score was 12 - 23 at half-time.

Once again the Penguins were managed by Ian Bullerwell. The full squad consisted of: Arthur Brenton (Bedford, Captain), Ben Alexander (Bedford), Adam Barnard (Northampton), Mauritz Botha (Bedford), Shaun Brady (Bedford), Simon Cross (Edinburgh), Karl Dickson (Bedford), Ayoola Erinle (Wasps), Lucio Fleming (Edinburgh), Kieran Hallett (Bedford), Tim Holgate (London Welsh), Simon Hunt (Ebbw Vale), Andrew Kelly (Edinburgh), Paul Kendall (Bedford), Toobs Koroinavlivou (British Army), Dan Lavery (Northampton), Richard List (Doncaster), Brian Milne (London Scottish), Ryan Peacy (Doncaster), Matt Price (Bedford), Scott Stumbles (Watsonians), Joe Wheeler (Nottingham).

2007 CHRONICLE

27th February - Penguins beat Oxford University 27 - 19 at Iffley Road, Oxford.

7th March - Penguins beat Cambridge University 93 - 12 at Grange Road, Cambridge.

28th and 29th March - Hong Kong Tens. Captained by Craig De Goldi (NZ). Penguins beat Chinese Agricultural University 57 - 5 Penguins beat Overseas Old Boys 55 - 0 Penguins beat HSBC New Zealand Legends 28 - 17 Penguins beat Aliens (New Zealand) 7 - 5 Penguins lost to Auckland Metro (New Zealand) 0 - 24 *Finalists, Hong Kong Tens*

7th April - Orkney RFC 40th Anniversary XVs Tournament. Captained by Paul Beal (England). Penguins beat 'West' Penguins beat 'East' Penguins beat President's XV Penguins beat Orkney 1st XV 17 - 0 *Winners, Orkney XVs*

26th June - Falklands Anniversary Match at the Twickenham Stoop. Captained by Howard Graham (England). Penguins drew with the Falklands Task Force XV 33 - 33.

1st and 2nd November - HSBC/COBRA International Tens, Malaysia. Captained by Scott Waldrom (New Zealand). Penguins beat Northlink (Republic of South Africa) 17 - 12 Penguins beat Oriental Rongotai (New Zealand) 45 - 0 Penguins beat Borneo Eagles (Malaysia) 24 - 5 Penguins lost to Natal Duikers (Republic of South Africa) 5 - 7 Penguins lost to Marist St. Joseph (Samoa) 12 - 21

8th and 9th November - COBRA Invitational Tens, Borneo. Captained by Scott Waldrom (New Zealand). Penguins beat Labuan (Malaysia) 88 - 0 Penguins beat Sabah Eagles (Malaysia) 43 - 0 Penguins beat ASAS (Malaysia) 62 - 0 Penguins beat COBRA (Malaysia) 24 - 0 Penguins beat Marist St. Joseph (Samoa) 12 - 5 Penguins lost to Sandakan Eagles (Malaysia) 15 - 24 *Finalists, COBRA Invitational Tens*

Frank Hadden.

On the 28th and 29th March the Penguins were very kindly invited to play in the GFI Hong Kong Football Club Tens for the first time. This Tournament is renowned around the world as being one of the strongest Tens competitions, so the Penguin International Committee tried to draw on its selection expertise to assemble a strong team capable of competing. Two players, Willy Hafu and Brett Sweeney, returned from the victorious COBRA Tens team of 2006 and were joined by a number of other top-class players and exciting youngsters. In addition, a major triumph for the Club was securing the coaching services of Frank Hadden (at that time Scotland Head Coach) and John Rutherford (the Scotland and British and Irish Lions international and former Scotland Backs Coach).

Frank Hadden

Frank Hadden was born in Dundee on 14 June, 1954. He was educated at Dundee High School and the University of Strathclyde (he played rugby union football for both schools). He then attended the Carnegie School of Physical Education in Leeds (now Leeds Metropolitan University) to pursue a teaching career.

While teaching at Guiseley School, he played rugby football for Headingley RFC at the same time that Ian McGeechan also played for the Club. Hadden also played for Dundee High School Former Pupils.

At one point he came very close to playing soccer - having trials with both Queens Park Rangers and Forfar Athletic, as well as being offered a contract by Raith Rovers FC.

Frank Hadden writes: *I have been coaching rugby for around 30 years, starting at Guiseley School in West Yorks followed by 17 years at Merchiston Castle School in Edinburgh. I worked with Scottish representative teams for 17 years from 1992, starting with the National U16s and culminating with the Full International side from 2005 - 2009. My first professional appointment was in 1997, when I worked as Assistant Coach to the Caledonian Reds in the inaugural year of pro rugby in Scotland.*

In 2000, Jim Telfer offered me the job as Head Coach of Edingburgh Rugby. In my first away game we lost by 80 points in Cardiff. Four years later we became the only Scottish side ever to qualify for the quarter-finals of the Heineken Cup. In many ways this was an even greater achievement than anything I did with Scotland. We qualified in style, playing an expansive 15-man game which was not normally associated with our country. Sadly we had to visit Toulouse in the quarter-final. My record with the National team was 17 wins from 41 matches, or 42% - which was on a par with Ian McGeechan (42%) and Jim Telfer (39%) and a vast improvement on my predecessor, Matt Williams, who won only three of his 17 games in charge.

In my time at the helm we beat all of the Six Nations countries at some stage, and won the Calcutta Cup twice, in 2006 and 2008. In 2007 we reached the quarter-finals of the Rugby World Cup, losing to Argentina by six points. Since 2009 I have spent four months coaching in Asia with the HSBC Penguin International Coaching Academy, working in tandem with the Asia 5 Nations.

Frank Hadden is a well-respected and much-loved coach worldwide and the Penguin International Coaching Academy is very proud that he has become a senior member of the organisation.

Alan: 'We were finalists in the Hong Kong Tens and, for the first time, we met Auckland Metro, an All Blacks team, and they defeated us narrowly in the final - quite deservedly. It must be said that Auckland Metro were a wonderful team. Many people ventured the opinion that the Penguins were the reigning Tens World Champions at this time - having been winners in Kuala Lumpur and now runners-up in Hong Kong. But Metro practise frequently - they can get together. I'd do the same thing if we had our team based in London! I congratulated the Metro manager, saying to him: "You thoroughly deserved to beat us because you played the match to perfection." It's the first time I've ever said that to anyone about rugby. They made not a single handling or positional mistake in the whole game! We tackled like demons, but we lost. They beat us fair and square.'

After the Hong Kong Tens final.

After the final, Craig Brown wrote: *The team did well although we fell at the final hurdle. I was proud of them and how they fronted up on the field. Frank Hadden said that he had not seen such a determined and gutsy performance since Scotland last beat England at Murrayfield in 2006.*

Alan: 'Although we were very disappointed to lose the final to Auckland Metro, it is a matter of great pride to the Penguins that we beat two other very strong Kiwi sides - that is, HSBC New Zealand Legends and the Aliens - in the quarter and semi-finals.'

The Penguins' results were: Penguins beat the Chinese Agricultural University 57 - 5, Penguins beat Overseas Old Boys 55 - 0. Quarter-final: Penguins beat HSBC New Zealand Legends 28 - 17. Semi-final: Penguins beat Aliens 7 - 5. Final: Penguins lost to Auckland Metro 0 - 24.

During the week of the Hong Kong Tens the playing team also held a coaching session at the Hong Kong Football Club for 60 local school children, after which the players presented each participant with an HSBC Penguins Coaching Academy T-Shirt and a PIRFC badge. The Academy also coached the People's Liberation Army in China. The coaches involved were Craig Brown, Stuart Mather, Dean Herewini and John McKittrick.

Many of the Penguins' touring party stayed over and attended the Hong Kong Sevens which took place immediately after the Hong Kong Tens competition. The Hong Kong Rugby Union and the PIRFC also took this opportunity to discuss the Club's future participation in the development of rugby in the region. This later resulted in four experienced coaches visiting Hong Kong for nine days in August.

The squad for the Hong Kong Tens. Back row: Frank Hadden (Coach), John Rutherford (Coach), Craig De Goldi (Karita and New Zealand Sevens, Captain), Frank Afeaki (North Harbour Marist and North Harbour Sevens), Reece Robinson (Mitsubishi and New Zealand Maori), Glen Varcoe (Clive and Hawkes Bay), Charlie O'Connell (Linwood and New Zealand U19), Kevin Brennan (Oxford University and England Sevens), Francis Bryant (Bush and Manawatu), Clark Laidlaw (Jed Forest and Scotland Sevens), Tom Tombleson (Oxford University and England Students), John Zimnoch (Press Officer), David Bell (Assistant Manager). Front row: Craig Brown (Manager), Brett Sweeney (North Shore and North Harbour Sevens), Phil Burleigh (New Brighton and Canterbury Development), Jovan Bowles (Natal and South Africa Sevens), Willy Hafu (OMBAC and New Zealand U19), Apo Satala (Heriot's FP and Fiji Sevens), Brad Fleming (Castres and New Zealand Sevens).

The Penguins help Orkney RFC
celebrate their 40th Anniversary.

Below:
The Penguins pose before kick off.
Below, far right:
The Orkney and Penguin players
together after the match.

Alan: 'This year we had a Scottish tour at the invitation of the Orkney Islands RFC - one of the most northerly places in Britain where rugby is played. They invited us to help celebrate their 40th Anniversary and we provided a team (Managed by our old friend, Scottish Committee member Iain Sinclair) which included two former Scottish internationals and a number of Oxford and Cambridge University Blues. Paul Beal, a Yorkshireman who has played a lot for the Penguins, was made Captain. We found it a delightful and very sociable visit and were pleased to to help celebrate rugby on this proud island.'

The Tournament took place on the 7th April, during the Easter weekend. There were six teams from Orkney plus two others - a President's XV (which was comprised of players from Cathiness, Shetland and Aberdeen) and the Penguins. The tournament format was two pools of four with matches of twelve and a half minutes each way. Each team played the other teams in their pool, and the two pool winners met in the final.

The weather was appalling and continual wind and rain prevented open rugby. Nevertheless, all of the teams participated with gusto and determination, running the ball whenever they could. In the end it was the Penguins and the Orkney 1st XV who won their respective pools and met in the final.

It was a tough match. At half-time the score was 0 - 0, but in the second half a wonderful solo effort (kick through/gather/touch down) from Neil Chisholm gave the Penguins the lead. Further tries from Craig Joiner and Hamish Murray looked set to seal the victory, but play was slowed up by Orkney with driving lineouts and impressive phase play. However the Penguins' defence - well organised by skipper Paul Beal - held firm until the final whistle was blown. This sound also signalled by far the quickest move of the day, as both teams sprinted to the shelter of the dressing rooms!

The PIRFC results were: Penguins beat 'West', Penguins beat 'East', Penguins beat President's XV. Final: Penguins beat Orkney 1st XV 17 - 0.

Alan: 'Well, it rained all the time, but socially the Tour was a big success. And just in passing - they had a player named Andy McGill who is a member of a farming family who are the only people that live on the island of Gairsay. Once or twice every week he would get in a canoe and paddle to the mainland to train or to play rugby for Orkney RFC. How fantastic! I'd never heard of such a thing. He was a very good player and Craig rightly invited him down to play for Penguins against Sidcup in their 125th Anniversary celebratory match in March, 2008.'

Penguins squad: Craig Brown (Director of Rugby), Iain Sinclair (Manager - Watsonians, Edinburgh and Scotland 'A'), Stuart Grimes (Watsonians, Border Reivers, Newcastle and Scotland, Coach).

Paul Beal (Redcar, Captain), Douglas Abbott (Oxford University), Alan Anderson (North Berwick), Neil Baggett (Warfdale), Kenneth Baillie (Glasgow Hawks and Scotland U21), Andrew Benger (Oxford University), Mark Blair (Currie, Ulster and Ireland 'A'), Craig Brown (Watsonians, Waikato and New Zealand Maori), Neil Chisolm (Currie), Winston Cowie (Oxford University and North Harbour Development), Stuart Eynon (Hamilton), Ian Hope (Dundee HSFP and Scottish Schools), Gareth Jacobs (Oxford University), Craig Joiner (Stewart's Melville, Leicester and Scotland), Daniel Moussa (Watsonians), Hamish Murray (Cambridge University and Canterbury), Alan Nash (Watsonians and Scotland U21), David Officer (Currie, Harlequins and Scotland 'A'), Daniel Rosen (Oxford University), Matthew Smith (Glasgow Hawks and Scottish Silver Thistles), Jon Williams (London New Zealand and Old Varstonians), Neil Young (Redcar).

Andy McGill's preferred mode of transport on Orkney RFC training nights and match days.

48   Thursday, April 5, 2007   - ORKNEY TODAY NEWSPAPER

SPORT

TITLE JOY FOR MO
Badminton singles tou

Penguins all set to fly north for Orkney RFC celebrations

RUGBY
by **ROBERT LESLIE**

THE man voted 'Most Travelled Rugby Tourist Ever' by sport magazine Rugby World in 2006, says he can't wait to make his fourth trip to the islands this weekend to help Orkney RFC celebrate its 40th anniversary.

Craig Brown, director of rugby with the Penguins International Rugby Club, the premier touring rugby club in the UK, is coming north with a Penguins side which will be one of eight teams taking part in a special tournament at Pickaquoy on Saturday afternoon to mark 40 years of ORFC.

Craig, recently returned from managing the Penguins side for the Hong Kong 10s, first trotted out onto an Orkney rugby pitch in May 1996 as a member of the Old Varstonians side which reached the semi-finals of ORFC's Zanussi Sevens.

They were whipped 40-0 by Orkney A on that occasion, but that didn't stop Craig returning to the county in August 1997, as part of the Scottish Classics side that took on Orkney during a charity weekend to raise funds for Sanday man Dugald McArthur, who was paralysed in a clash while playing rugby in Edinburgh the previous year.

Craig's third visit wasn't rugby related – he stayed with former ORFC chairman David Fairnie one New Year and played in the Ba'.

This time though Craig is back in full rugby mode, and says the Penguins can't wait to get to Orkney to play their part in the 40th Anniversary weekend.

Speaking from London on Tuesday night, he told Orkney Today: "We are very keen on this trip. A big part of what we do is grass roots rugby, so coming to Orkney is ideal and we were delighted to accept the invitation."

Scotland international and former Newcastle player, Stuart Grimes, is coach for

the weekend, but is still in contract to Border Reivers, and will not be able to play for that reason.

Also in the party is Craig Joiner, former Scottish internationalist and now with Stewart's Melville FP.

However, the prize for travelling the furthest to Orkney this weekend is likely to go to Jon Williams of London Kiwis.

Jon, who recently married an Irish woman, was also in Hong Kong playing in the Tens, but is currently on honeymoon in India. He is flying back to London on Friday and then up to Orkney via Glasgow especially to turn out for the Penguins on Saturday.

Craig added that sponsorship from HSBC was as important to the Penguins in their exploits as ORFC's backing from Highland Park was in theirs.

"They are the only reason we can survive really," he said.

■ 40th Anniversary feature **Pages 12–17**

The Orkney Today newspaper looks forward to the Penguins' arrival.

Match programme.

Army prop Steve Tretheway bursts through the Penguin defence.

Blazer badge of the organisers, the South Atlantic Medal Association. This match was arranged to commemorate the British Forces' liberation of the Islands in 1982. The Task Force XV was drawn from the units that took part in the conflict.

The Club's next match again took place in the UK - this time at the Twickenham Stoop on 26th June to take part in the Falklands Anniversary Charity Match. The match was part of the 25th Anniversary commemorating the ending of the war in the Falklands, and the Penguins were honoured to play the Falklands Task Force XV - effectively a 'Combined Services' team. It was in support of the South Atlantic Medal Association and was to help fund places on the Pilgrimage to the Falkland Islands in November.

The match had the support of the Prince of Wales, General Julian Thompson, and, of course, many leading rugby players. The crowd was entertained by the Bands of the Royal Marines, the Queen's Colour Squadron RAF, and a lone piper from the Scots Guards. And as part of the festivities surrounding the match, a team of coaches ran a coaching session for local schoolchildren. The sessions culminated in a small tournament with the finalists playing in a curtain-raiser before the main event.

Bill Calcraft: 'To be honest, the chances for Penguins to feature at a high level in the UK are pretty limited these days. But every now and again an opportunity still comes along to take part in a match in which the Penguins should play. A prime example, of course, being this match at the Twickenham Stoop.'

The Falkland Taskforce team started the brighter, and they quickly scored two well-worked tries through the midfield. The Forces team then led for the majority of the match. However, the Penguins never gave up, and with less than two minutes remaining, and down by twelve points, they managed to score two tries and a conversion to draw the match 33 - 33.

Alan: 'Yes - those last moments were very dramatic. We were 26 - 33 down with only one-and-a-half minutes left on the clock - and then we drew the match with a last-minute try and conversion!

'We have drawn very few matches in our history: Benfica in 1966, and again on tour in 1982 when we drew with Bermuda in Hamilton. And then there was this 33 - 33 draw with the "Combined Services". It was a good result in the end. We didn't really want to lose this match, but neither did we want to win it. It was the perfect result for this very special day.'

Penguin squad: Bill Calcraft (Match Manager), Joe Roff (Coach).

Howard Graham (Army, Captain), Felise Ahling (Barking), Ken Aseme (Blackheath), Graham Barr (Esher), Arthur Brenton (Bedford), Oliver Brown (Scotland Sevens), James Bucknall (Richmond), Simon Cater (Newbury), James Fleming (Exeter Chiefs), James Gaunt (Henley), Rory Greenslade-Jones (London Scottish), Nicky Griffiths (Worcester), Kieran Hallet (Loughborough University), Henry Head (Richmond), Chris Johnson (Bedford), Andrew le Chavalier (Henley), Matt Miles (Pertemp Bees), Brian Milne (London Scottish), Rod Moore (Calvisano and Australia), Jon Phillips (Bedford), Matt Price (Rugby), Jack Smales (Bath University and England Students), James Strong (London Welsh), Andy Wright (Loughborough University).

Matt Cornish (left) and Joe Roff. Matt Captained the Task Force XV and former Australian international Joe coached the Penguins squad.

In July the HSBC Penguin International Coaching Academy (represented by Craig Brown, Steve Hill, Tony Robinson and Kevin Brennan) conducted a range of coaching sessions and tutorials to clubs and schools in and around Toronto, Canada. The group was hosted by the Toronto Nomads RFC, one of the top Club sides in the city. All four coaches worked with members of the Nomads, including their senior squad, U18 squad, and women's team.

The Academy also worked with the Ontario U18 and U16 squads. These young players were really keen to learn, and pleasingly, there were about twenty other rugby coaches in attendance - so the Academy Coaches were able to share their ideas with them.

The hospitality the Academy Coaches received was tremendous. Many thanks were due to John Zimnoch, the Canadian Penguin Committee representative, and Jim Flynn from the Ontario Rugby Union for all the help and assistance they gave during the course of the trip.

The HSBC Penguin International Coaching Academy was again in action between 25th August and 2nd September - this time in Hong Kong.

Craig Brown led a team that consisted of John McIttrick, Dean Herewini and Stu Mather. The coaches taught IRB Level 2 courses, as well as working with 'The Naughty Boys' - a project run by the police for children who have gone off the rails and which uses rugby football as a conduit for steering them back on to the straight and narrow.

Coaching sessions were also held with all of the local first-division clubs. Ivan Torpey, Head of Performance of the Hong Kong Rugby Football Union said of the Academy Coaches: 'They were a first-class team and excellent ambassadors for the Penguin International Rugby Football Club both on and off the paddock. They brought with them, and shared, the true rugby spirit and ethos that makes our game so special.'

Letter from the HKRFU thanking the HSBC Penguin International Coaching Academy team for all their hard work in Hong Kong.

The Malaysian Schools Coaching Team. Left to right: Ben Fisher, a Penguins supporter, Abby Wills, Grant McKelvey, Jamie Baron and Zarin Akmal, the Penguins' driver.

Abby Wills - the Academy's first female coach and PIRFC's first lady Committee Member.

On 1st and 2nd November Penguins returned to play in the COBRA Tens in Kuala Lumpur as defending champions. The Club was then due to fly off to Borneo to play in the Borneo Tens for the first time on 8th and 9th November.

This Tour was a first for the Penguins insofar as three different elements of the Club would be active at the same time. Penguins entered a team in both the Tens Tournaments and also had grass-roots and Coach Education Coaching teams in action. The big rain that had greeted the 2006 COBRA Tens Tournament held off and a fast-moving tournament treated the crowd to some fast, end-to-end matches. The Penguins gelled well under the Captaincy of Scott Waldrom. Day one had no easy games, but the Club played very well - especially in the pool game against Oriental Rongotai. Penguins wore down the opposition and pulled away in the second half. Good team play and individual skills ensured the team had a successful opening day. All players started at least one match, and all contributed. Penguins finished top of the pool at the end of day one, with the prospect of a quarter-final match against the Natal Duikers the following afternoon.

On day two the team failed to finish off numerous scoring chances in the quarter-final and only led 5 - 0 at half-time. The Natal Duikers defended well and produced some good attacks. The second half was more of the same, with dogged defence denying the Penguins scoring opportunities. With two minutes left, the Duikers found a hole in the Penguin defence and went the length of the pitch to score. The resulting conversion was the difference between the two teams at full-time. It was a disappointing end to the Tournament after a promising start.

Penguins then played Marist St. Joseph from Samoa in the Plate semi-finals. The Samoans attacked from the beginning, and eventually wore down the Penguins' defence. The Penguins fought back and managed two well-worked tries, but the deficit was too large, and the clock eventually ran out for the team.

Abby Wills

Craig Brown writes: Abby Wills has been a sports fanatic from an early age and played just about any sport she could. Whilst studying at Bristol Polytechnic Abby played rugby - featuring at scrum-half in the local women's competition. Rugby was always her favourite sport and she watches every England match she can (she still tips England for every World Cup!). After being a supporter on a couple of Penguin tours she decided she should coach too. Abby enrolled herself in the Scottish Rugby Union's UKCC Level 1 course, held over two and a half days at the Sports Academy in Largs. She passed with flying colours and is now always working on increasing her skills level. Abby specialises in coaching the smaller children and she was the first woman to coach for the HSBC Penguin International Coaching Academy. Since those early days she has gone on to coach in Scotland, Malaysia, Hong Kong, South Africa, Rwanda and Cambodia. Abby is also the Penguins' Records and Reports Manager - which makes her the first woman to hold office on the PIRFC Committee. *Alan Wright:* 'I was also very pleased to propose to the PIRFC Committee that this great lady should become only the second female Honorary Vice-President of the Club (the first was Doris Mason) - and that the proposal was accepted.'

The Penguins' results were: Penguins beat Northlink (Republic of South Africa) 17 - 12, Penguins beat Oriental Rongotai (New Zealand) 45 - 0, Penguins beat Borneo Eagles (Malaysia) 24 - 5. Quarter-final: Penguins lost to Natal Duikers (Republic of South Africa) 5 - 7. Plate semi-final: Penguins lost to Marist St. Joseph (Samoa) 12 - 21.

As well as the team taking part in the COBRA Tens, four Academy coaches (Grant McKelvey, Ben Fisher, Jamie Baron and Abby Wills) carried out an extensive programme during Tens week, in which a large number of schools were visited.

In addition, a Coaching Education Programme, run by Craig Brown, Ivan Torpey (of the Hong Kong Rugby Union), Tony Robinson, Rick Hicks, Ian Minto, Jon Bates and Rob Drinkwater, made three trips to Kuala Lumpur during the course of the year. Run in association with COBRA, these visits were to deliver courses similar to the UK Level One course. Over 100 candidates passed.

The Penguins' first trip to Borneo centred around the Seventh Borneo Tens Tournament which was played at the Likas Stadium in Kota Kinabalu on the 8th and 9th of November. After a day of rest following the COBRA Tens, the Penguins got down to some serious training on the beach - with a combination of runs, sprint work, skills and team play.

Pre-tournament highlights included meeting a long green snake which jumped and glided from the third storey of the hotel when it was touched, and a torrential downpour that formed massive lakes in only twenty minutes.

Alan Wright: 'In the COBRA Malaysian Tens we were defeated in the quarter-final but here in the Borneo Tens we did much better and reached the final - after beating a very strong Marist St. Joseph side on the way. But we lost in the final to Sandakan Eagles, the champion Club of Borneo. They were an all-Fijian International team so it was certainly no disgrace. All-in-all it was a happy and successful year.'

Penguins' results in the Borneo Tens were: Penguins beat Labuan (Malaysia) 88 - 0, Penguins beat Sabah Eagles (Malaysia) 43 - 0, Penguins beat ASAS (Malaysia) 62 - 0. Quarter-final: Penguins beat COBRA (Malaysia) 24 - 0. Semi-final: Penguins beat Marist St. Joseph (Samoa) 12 - 5. Final: Penguins lost to Sandakan Eagles (Malaysia) 15 - 24.

The Penguins team also ran a coaching session for local school children during the course of the Borneo Tens Tournament. The field in Kota Kinabalu that was used for the coaching session was caught in the tropical downpour and became absolutely saturated. This led to many comical situations and some very muddy Penguins and children - indeed, the session warm-down consisted mainly of stomach puddle-surfing!

Above: The Penguin International RFC squad to Malaysia and Borneo:
Back Row: Yun Ting (Physiotherapist), Abby Wills (Academy Coach), Alan Wright (President), Matua Parkinson (Bay of Plenty, New Zealand Sevens), Scott Waldrom (New Zealand Sevens, New Zealand Maori - Captain), Mesake Davu (Fiji, Fiji Sevens), James Rodley (North Harbour, New Zealand Maori), Tony Penn (Hurricanes, New Zealand Maori), James Annabel (Taranaki), Frank Afeaki (North Harbour Sevens, New Zealand Sevens trialist), Ati Olive (Wellington 'B'), Ben Fisher (Academy Coach), John McKittrick (Coach).
Front Row: Jamie Baron (Academy Coach), Hang Kek Kang (Liaison Manager), Marc Camburn (New Zealand Sevens), Matt Hodgson (Bay of Plenty Development), Steve Alfeld (Canterbury), Mike Davis (Northland), Willy Hafu (New Zealand U19), Toby Arnold (Bay of Plenty), Grant McKelvey (Academy Head Coach), Craig Brown (Tour Manager).

Pre-tournament Borneo highlight - the Paradise flying snake!

High fives with the schoolchildren at the end of a wet HSBC Penguin Academy session in Kota Kinabalu.

2008 CHRONICLE

26th February - Penguins lost to Oxford University 24 - 25 at Iffley Road, Oxford.

5th March - Penguins beat Cambridge University 36 - 25 at Grange Road, Cambridge.

22nd March - Sidcup RFC 125th Anniversary Match. Penguins beat Sidcup RFC 48 - 24 at Crescent Farm, Sidcup.

26th and 27th March - Hong Kong Tens. Captained by Craig De Goldi (New Zealand). Penguins beat Marauders 83 - 0 Penguins beat Cardiff University 47 - 7 Penguins beat Borneo Eagles 36 - 0 Penguins beat Hong Kong Barbarians 21 - 0 Penguins beat Aliens 14 - 5 Penguins lost to Auckland Metro 0 - 38 *Finalists, Hong Kong Tens*

3rd May - Bedford Athletic RFC Centenary Match. Penguins beat Bedford Athletic RFC 67 - 43 at Wentworth Drive, Bedford.

6th and 7th June - Rome International Sevens, Italy. Captained by Marc Camburn (New Zealand). Penguins beat Unione Rugby Capitaliona 44 - 0 Penguins beat Mel's Exiles 37 - 0 Penguins beat British Army 19 - 5 Penguins beat White Hart Marauders 22 - 17 Penguins lost to Stellenbosch University (RSA) 17 - 22 *Semi-finalists, Rome International Sevens*

1st and 2nd November - HSBC/COBRA International Tens, Malaysia. Captained by Jordan Smiler (New Zealand). Penguins drew with NS Wanderers (Malaysia) 12 - 12 Penguins beat SA Mustangs (Republic of South Africa) 31 - 12 Penguins lost to Borneo Eagles (Malaysia) 14 - 22 Penguins beat Canterbury (New Zealand) 7 - 5 Penguins lost to North Harbour (New Zealand) 7 - 14 *Semi-finalists, Malaysia RU - HSBC/COBRA International Tens*

8th and 9th November - COBRA Invitational Tens, Borneo. Captained by Jordan Smiler (New Zealand). Penguins beat Borneo Development Team 53 - 0 Penguins beat Country Browns 48 - 0 Penguins beat Australian Legends 14 - 13 Penguins beat Datatelevu (Fiji) 31 - 7 Penguins beat COBRA (Malaysia) 24 - 0 Penguins beat Sandakan Eagles (Malaysia) 19 - 5 *Winners, Borneo Invitational Tens.*

2008

The Penguins began a very busy year on 26th February with a narrow, one-point loss to Oxford University at Iffley Road in the first of the two annual university matches. Both teams played a running game, treating the spectators to end-to-end action throughout the match. Six tries were scored in all. The Penguins were leading 19 - 17 at half time but lost the match 24 - 25.

The Penguins' Match Manager was Ian Bullerwell, and Brian Milne of the Sutton & Epsom RFC was the Captain of a squad which included several players each from the British Army, Rugby Lions and Henley Hawks.

Penguins fared rather better against Cambridge University on March 5th, beating the Light Blues 36 - 25 at Grange Road. The Penguin backs constantly threatened, with Bryan Milne making several telling breaks, while Howard Graham distributed the ball well. The forward exchanges were fairly even, especially at the start of each half, but the support running from the Penguins gave them an early lead which Cambridge struggled to peg back.

The Penguins were once again Managed by Ian Bullerwell, but Captained this time by their old friend, Howard Graham of the British Army. The team was made up mainly of players from the Rugby Lions, Bedford Blues and Sutton & Epsom.

On the 22nd March Penguins played in a very special match to celebrate Sidcup RFC's 125th Anniversary - thus echoing the Sidcup Centenary Match fixture which had taken place 25 years earlier almost to the day, on 20th March, 1983.

The Centenary Match Programme had been reprinted and inserted into the 2008 programme for the game and showed that the 1983 Penguins were Captained by Simon Halliday and featured an all-England back division which included Marcus Rose, Tony Swift, Nick Preston, Stuart Barnes and Derek Wyatt. On that occasion the Penguins won 44 - 22.

Four former Sidcup members who had played for Sidcup in the Centenary match were also present at this 125th Anniversary fixture, including Phil West, the current Sidcup President. Another Sidcup 'old boy' on the day was Steve Hill, Penguins' Match Manager and Coach. Steve played for Sidcup as a Colt and in the 1st XV, and also coached the Club. The Guest of Honour was Doris Mason, widow of Tony Mason who was, herself, a frequent tourist with the Penguins.

It was also on this occasion that Alan Wright first met Dick Tyson, the author of this book. Dick was at the match promoting his book *London's Oldest Rugby Clubs* (which was published in 2008), and was introduced to Alan by their mutual friends, Phil West and Ian Anderson (President and Chairman of Sidcup).

The Sidcup RFC Committee later wrote of the match: *The main event was a tough encounter for both teams with the Penguins dominating the first half and Sidcup competing commendably in the second half. Sidcup Rugby Football Club is rightly proud of its long association with the Penguin IRFC and we thank them for the distinction and privilege of their visit.*

Alan: 'We were honoured to include the Captains of Oxford and Cambridge Universities - Peter Clarke and Jon Dawson respectively - in our very talented squad for this important match. And in passing I must also mention a curious coincidence regarding this game - I have always been struck by similarity of the scores in these two Sidcup matches which took place 25 years apart: 44 - 22 and 48 - 24. On both occasions Penguins scored twice as many points as Sidcup. What odds would you have got against that happening?!'

Penguins squad: Steve Hill (Match Manager and Coach), Alan Wright (PIRFC President), Pete Stevenson and Emily Lintern (Physiotherapists).

Peter Clarke (Oxford University, Captain), Tom Bason (Blackheath), Bill Calcraft (Oxford University, Queensland and Australia), Winston Cowie (Oxford University), Matt Cross (Loughborough University), Ranako Daley (Blackheath), Kevin Davies (Oxford University), Jon Dawson (Cambridge University), Marcel Du Toit (Barnes), Tom Gregory (Oxford University), Toby Henry (Oxford University), Rob Hurrell (Henley Hawks), Ben Ibrahim (Blackheath), Chris Lewis (Cambridge University), Rick Lutton (Oxford University), Andy McGill (Orkney), Frankie Neal (Blackheath), Tristan Roberts (Cinderford), Euan Sadden (Oxford University), Sam Wardingly (Blackheath), James Wellwood (Cambridge University), Joe Wheeler (Cambridge University).

Top: Lineout action from the match.
Above: Penguins' Alan Wright and Sidcup's Phil West at the post-match presentations.

The two squads pose together after the match.

Penguin squad for the 2008 Hong Kong Tens Tournament.

Penguins supporters, left to right: Ian Ford, Vincent Bramhall and John Zimnoch.

Above: Match action. Below: Craig Brown and Craig De Goldi on the touchline.

Between 26th - 27th March the Penguins once again took part in the Hong Kong Tens - eager to improve on their second placing of the previous year.

Alan: '2008 was a very busy year for the Penguins. I went on all three tours (not a record, by the way - I've been on three tours before!). The first of these tours was to participate in the 2008 Hong Kong Tens. We reached the final for the second year running, losing once again to Auckland Metro, an All Blacks team. It is probably the best "abbreviated" Tens team that I've ever seen play. It was no disgrace to lose to them.'

The Penguins results were: Penguins beat Marauders 83 - 0, Penguins beat Cardiff University 47 - 7, Penguins beat Borneo Eagles 36 - 0. Quarter-final: Penguins beat Hill & Associates Hong Kong Barbarians 21 - 0. Semi-final: Penguins beat Aliens 14 - 5. Final: Penguins lost to Auckland Metro 0 - 38.

Penguins squad:

Craig Brown (Director of Rugby and Tour Manager), Alan Wright (President). Coaches: Hugh Campbell (former Scotland Coach) and Tony Hanks (Wasps and Waikato Coach). Jamie Baron and Hamish Lock (Assistant Managers).

Craig De Goldi (Karita and New Zealand Sevens, Captain), Frank Afeaki (North Harbour Marist, North Harbour 'B' and New Zealand Sevens Trialist), Asaeli Boko (Duru, Stallions, Nadi and Fiji Sevens), James Brown (HSOB, Canterbury U21 and Fiji U19), Nick Collins (Mitsubishi, Waikato Chiefs and New Zealand Sevens), Nathan Hohaia (Coastal, Taranaki and New Zealand Sevens Trialist), James Kamana (Fraser Tech, Waikato and New Zealand Sevens), Tim Mikkleson (University, Waikato and New Zealand Sevens), Tony Penn (Tukapa, Taranaki, Hurricanes and New Zealand Maori), Saula Rubaka (Natisori and Fiji Sevens), Jordan Smiler (Hautapu and Waikato), Blair Urlich (Mitsubishi, North Harbour, Auckland Blues and New Zealand Maori), Amasio Valence (Auckland Blues and New Zealand Sevens), Andrew Williams (Marist St. Joseph, Samoa U21 and Samoa), Josh York (East Coast Bays and North Harbour Sevens).

On 3rd May Penguins had the honour of taking part in a special match to celebrate the Centenary of Bedford Athletic RFC.

According to the Bedford Athletic RFC Committee: *The Centenary season ended with a superb celebration game against a Penguin International XV which featured players such as Scottish International Craig Joiner and Bedford Blues stalwarts Matt Allen and Jon Phillips. Although Bedford Athletic went down 67 - 43 in a match which yielded no fewer than 18 tries, it left the club in good heart for the season to come.*

Alan: 'We'd previously played Bedford Athletic RFC many years ago (1970) at the opening of their clubhouse. The stand-off half on that day was the current Secretary of the Barbarians, Geoff Windsor-Lewis - and our late President Peter Yarranton also played.'

Above: The match programme. Below: Pictures taken on the day and the Bedfordshire on Sunday match report. The black and white photograph features Tom Wacker, Alan Wright and Robin De Morgan

Penguins squad:

Craig Brown (Match Manager), Ian Bullerwell (Selector), Alan Wright PIRFC President), Robin De Morgan and Bill Calcraft (Committee).

Jon Phillips (Bedford Blues, Captain), Matt Allen (Bedford Blues), Arthur Brenton (Bedford Blues), Lawrence Coward (Bedford School), James Graham (Bedford Blues), James Hinkins (Bedford Blues), Craig Joiner (Edinburgh and Scotland), Ryan Owen (Bedford Blues), Harry Peck (Luton), Matt Price (Rugby Lions), Tommy Turner (Rugby Lions), Sam Viggers (Rugby Lions), Tristan Wati (Rugby Lions), John West (Sidcup), Jack Wrigglesworth (Bedford Blues).

Replacements: Marc Comb, John MacDonough, Roman Piotrowski, George Warner.

Ath frozen out by Penguins

FLYING PENGUIN: Even with a Penguin on his back Ollie Peck still manages to score

DIVING OVER: Scott Grant scores

CENTENARY MATCH	
BEDFORD ATH	41
INTERNATIONAL PENGUINS XV	67

BY SIMON HUTCHINSON

RUGBY fans were treated to a try fest as Bedford Athletic celebrated 100 years of existence yesterday afternoon.

The Ath capped off a splendid centenary year by scoring the first and the last of the 18 tries, but unfortunately the Penguins proved to be a little too strong for the hosts on the day.

Mourito Botha switched back to being an Ath boy for the day and he seemed to thoroughly enjoy going head to head with several Blues team mates who made up half of the Penguins starting line-up.

The crowd didn't have to wait long for the first try of the day and it came in the third minute courtesy of Ath's inside centre Phil Elphick who linked up marvellously with half back pairing Ollie Peck and Ashley Tapper who then converted.

From there the Penguins took charge running in three tries through Tommy Turner, Jack Wrigglesworth and Craig Joiner, Turner converting just one.

Ath responded with a converted try when flanker Scott Grant powered his way over. Joiner had popped him the ball but the Penguins kept ahead through the first of two tries by Jimmy Graham just two minutes later which was converted.

The hosts wouldn't lie down though and lively scrum half Peck added a try in the 31st minute.

Then the Penguins really stretched their legs running in five tries either side of half time without reply. Luton's Harry Peck got the ball rolling before Marc Comb, Matt Allen, Graham and then Comb again all scored with Turner converting three of them.

At 19-55 the Ath looked out of it, but they never gave in and in the 57th minute hooker Ollie Wills went over to score with John MacDonough responding immediately for the Penguins.

Botha capped off a good display with a converted try of his own before Roman Piotrowski touched down for the guests to make it 31-67.

The Ath finished on a high though running in two fine tries in the final five minutes. The superb Elphick scored a second when the Ath's forwards dazzled their opposites with a series of pick-and-go rucks, the centre scooping in the ball at the end to touch down in the corner.

As the 80 minutes ran out at Putnoe Woods the Ath completed an entertaining game with the final try courtesy of Grant who took in the ball following a quick tap penalty and dived through two Penguins to score and round off a splendid day of rugby.

P-P-P-PICK UP A PENGUIN: Line out action

Army Rugby Sevens - winners of the 2008 Roma Sevens despite losing to Penguins in the Pool stages.

The Penguins did win a handsome trophy at the 2008 Roma Sevens - the Corriere dello Sport Fair Play Prize.

One of the Penguins' greatest-ever victories - against the mighty New Zealand side Canterbury in the HSBC/COBRA Tens in Kuala Lumpur.

Alan: 'The next trip took place on 6th - 7th June and was our fourth visit to Italy, where we had previously won the Italian Rugby Union International Sevens on two occasions and were finalists on another occasion. However, this tournament was called *The Rome Sevens* and it was not under the auspices of the Italian Rugby Union as our previous three visits to Italy had been (the introduction had been made via our good friend and Italian Committee Member, Enzo Paolini). Because of our friendship with Italy we felt we should do them the honour of taking a strong side. Craig Brown arranged the Tour and David Harris was the Tour Manager.

'We had a very strange tournament. We won all of our pool matches, including comfortably defeating the British Army. We then won the quarter-final. We lost in the semi-final to Stellenbosch University from Cape Town (in my opinion the strongest university team in the world in a given year). And then the British Army team came through from second place in our pool to win the whole tournament, which was a great feat. Such are the vicissitudes of seven-a-sides!'

Penguins results were: Penguins beat Unione Rugby Capitaliona 44 - 0, Penguins beat Mel's Exiles 37 - 0, Penguins beat British Army 19 - 5. Quarter-final: Penguins beat White Hart Marauders 22 - 17. Semi-final: Penguins lost to Stellenbosch University (RSA) 17 - 22.

Penguins squad:
C. Brown (Director of Rugby), D . Harris (Tour Manager), J. McKittrick (Coach), Alan Wright (President). M. Camburn (North Harbour Sevens, New Zealand Sevens, Captain), F. Afeaki (North Harbour Sevens, New Zealand Sevens Training Squad), J. Blackwood (Edinburgh, Scotland Sevens), A. Boko (Crusaders, Fiji Sevens), S. Matelewana (Red Rock, Suva), L. Nabulliwaga (Suva, Fiji Sevens), B. Olesen (Waikato Sevens, New Zealand Sevens Training Squad), E. Rakikedike (Fiji Sevens), G. Rolls (Hawkes Bay Maori, Canterbury U21), R. Varty (Hong Kong Sevens, Hong Kong).

Next up in this very busy year was another 'double' tour - playing in the HSBC/COBRA Tens on 1st and 2nd November in Kuala Lumpur, and then on to the COBRA Borneo Tens on the 8th and 9th November in Sandakan.

Alan: 'At the end of the year we went to Malaysia where we were defeated in the semi-final. This defeat by North Harbour Rugby Union was by one try to two, but in the quarter-final we won one of our greatest victories ever. We defeated Canterbury Rugby Union, who the previous Saturday I'd watched on television here in England win the New Zealand Cup Final against Wellington. I really don't think anyone in the ground on the day gave us a chance. It was very close - I was holding my breath! The score was 7 - 5.

'I will re-emphasize here that Malaysia forms a very prominent part in Penguin history. Craig has made a very strong friendship with COBRA, and with the approval of our sponsors, HSBC, we have carried out a very large number of coaching programmes in Malaysia. Well over 600 men have now become qualified rugby coaches. So Malaysia holds a special place in the hearts of us all.'

The Penguins' COBRA Tens results were: Penguins drew with NS Wanderers (Malaysia) 12 - 12, Penguins beat SA Mustangs (Republic of South Africa) 31 - 12, Penguins lost to Borneo Eagles (Malaysia) 14 - 22. Quarter-final: Penguins beat Canterbury (New Zealand) 7 - 5. Semi-final: Penguins lost to North Harbour (New Zealand) 7 - 14.

Alan: 'A week later in Borneo we had a handsome victory in the Eighth Borneo COBRA Invitational Tens in Sandakan, beating three of the best Fijian teams (including the Fijian Club Champions) and also the Australian Legends on the way to winning the Cup. In the semi-final we beat COBRA, who had won the Malaysian Tens the week before.

'Mind you, some of these sides didn't show themselves as Fijian teams. For example, the team we beat in the final, the Sandakan Eagles - who we'd lost to the previous year - are top Fijian players who actually work and live in Borneo and who play for a Club that is very well sponsored.

'For the uninitiated, winning the Borneo Tens may sound like an everyday thing, but it was a triumph. All due to Craig. It just showed that, by having the players together for another week (which is unusual for us) they came up trumps.'

The Penguins' Borneo Tens results were: Penguins beat Borneo Development Team 53 - 0, Penguins beat Country Browns 48 - 0, Penguins beat Australian Legends 14 - 13. Quarter-final: Penguins beat Datatelevu (Fiji) 31 - 7. Semi-final: Penguins beat COBRA (Malaysia) 24 - 0. Final: Penguins beat Sandakan Eagles (Malaysia) 19 - 5. Penguins won the Eighth Borneo COBRA Invitational Tens.

Eighth Borneo COBRA Tens Winner's Trophy.

Local press reports of the Penguins' famous victory in the Eighth Borneo COBRA Invitational Tens in Sandakan.

The Penguins' squad for the COBRA Tens and the Borneo Tens tournaments in November, 2008.

Penguins squad:

Craig Brown (Tour Manager). John Walters and Dean Herewini (Coaches). Academy Coaches: Greg Cann, Doc McKelvey, Ben Fisher, Richard Breen, Peter Gallagher, Sailosi Nawavu.

Jordan Smiler (Hautapu and Waikato, Captain), Toby Arnold (Tauranga Sports and Bay of Plenty), James Brown (HSOB, Canterbury U21 and Fiji U19), Nathan Hohaia (Coastal, Taranaki Sevens and Taranaki), Josh Hohneck (Fraser Tech and Waikato), John Jackson (Nadi, Colonials and Fiji Barbarians), Kerian Koll (Christchurch and Canterbury U21), Lukas Quinn (Otorohunga and Waikato 'B'), Tua Saseve (North Harbour Marist and North Harbour 'B'), Adrian Smith (Massey and North Harbour 'B'), Henry Speight (Hamilton Old Boys and Waikato), Notise Tauafoa (Malie, Apia West, Samoa Sevens and Samoa), Aporosa Tunisau (Nadi, Colonials, Fiji Barbarians and Fiji), Chris Walker (Tukapa, Taranaki and New Zealand U21), Roger Warren (Marist St. Joseph's, Samoa Sevens and Samoa).

Above: The Penguins' Captain Jordan Smiler lives up to his name after a very successful Tour.

The HSBC Penguin International Coaching Academy also had a very busy and eventful year in 2008. Some of the many highlights included:

Guam in March: The Academy (represented by Lynn Evans) were invited by special request to Guam, where it undertook a range of coaching activities for coaches, clubs and schools.

Hong Kong in April: The Penguin Tens squad ran a session for youngsters and an experienced coaching team (Craig De Goldi, Steve Hill, Lynn Evans and Craig Brown) spent eight days in Hong Kong and China coaching and advising local youngsters and coaches, Hong Kong Academy players, women players, and HKRU Development Officers. A further trip to Guangzhou to coach the People's Liberation Army (China's strongest club) ended a very successful week.

Malaysia in May and November: The Academy (represented by Tony Robinson, Greg Cann, Doc McKelvey and Richard Hicks) continued its close relationship with the COBRA Club in Kuala Lumpur by running several coach educational courses.

Dublin in October: As part of the HSBC sponsorship of the British and Irish Lions Tour to South Africa the Academy ran a coaching programme in conjunction with an Irish Rugby Football Union Mini Rugby Tournament for 300 U12 - U14 boys with the help of Brian O'Driscoll and Jason Robinson. The Manager of this initiative was Scott Wacker and the Academy coaches involved were: Tony Robinson, Peter Gallagher, Dave Cockburn, Richard Hicks, Neil Young and Lynn Evans.

Malaysia and Borneo in November: For the HSBC/COBRA Tens and the COBRA Borneo Tens Rugby Fortnight, four Penguins coaches (Ben Fisher, Peter Gallagher, Richard Breen and Sailosi Nawavu) organised a number of coaching sessions across Malaysia including Penang, Sandakan, Kuala Lumpur and Taiping. Twenty schools and over 500 boys received coaching in the first week. Local coaches were also included in these sessions. In the second week the Coaching Academy held a three-day course for elite players and also ran sessions for local schools.

Dubai in December: The Academy, represented by Grant McKelvey and Lynn Evans, spent four days running coaching sessions for local school children from U8 to U17.

This page: Photographs of the HSBC Penguin International Rugby Academy sessions of November, 2008.

Penguins players participate in the HSBC Penguin International Academy coaching session for Hong Kong youngsters.

2009

The Penguins' Golden Jubilee year began with the annual floodlit Varsity match against Oxford University at Iffley Road on the evening of Wednesday, 4th February.

The match kicked off in very cold, wet and windy conditions (which soon became a raging gale) - but both teams tried to play running rugby. The Blues had the better of the early exchanges and at half-time were leading 0 - 15.

Penguins started the second half strongly, and Marty Veale, the Wasps' lock, scored two tries - one of which was converted to make the score 12 - 15. With 15 minutes left, both teams started using their bench - not so much for 'fresh legs' as for 'dry shirts'! In the final ten minutes Oxford scored twice more to make the final score 12 - 27. This was the first time that Oxford University had managed to beat the Penguins for two years in succession. The match also marked Penguin Committee member Steve Hill's last year as Oxford University RFC's coach. Steve left the Club shortly afterwards to become Head Coach at Richmond FC.

Penguins' Match Manager was Ian Bullerwell and the Club Captain was Howard Graham (British Army and Coventry). The Penguin squad was made up mainly of players from the Exeter Chiefs (including Steven Ward, Alan Miller, Ken Dowling and Ben Breeze) and one or two Scottish clubs.

The annual match against Cambridge University, which was due to take place on 3rd March, was cancelled due to a frozen pitch at Grange Road. This was the first time ever that the fixture had been called off.

Penguins accepted an invitation to play for the third time in the Hong Kong Tens. A very competitive squad was selected to try and go one better than the two previous years when the Club had fallen at the last hurdle as beaten Finalists. As with previous years the competition was held in late March.

Alan Wright: 'Of course, part of our strength now is being able to select from the southern hemisphere during the height of our league season - so the South Pacific was once again the main field for our Selectors.'

As is now normal practice for a Penguin tour, the team began by running a training session for local youngsters - much to everyone's enjoyment.

Penguins started the first day of the Tournament with an impressive win over the Wanchai Warriors, but found stiffer opposition in the remaining two pool games. The team was performing well but there was room for improvement.

Day two produced an interesting draw - a tough tie against the Aliens from New Zealand. Alan: 'The Aliens are the cream of the New Zealand professionals playing in Japan. They are a red-hot team. We've beaten them twice, but this time we got them in the quarter-final. It was cruel to meet them so early.'

The Aliens won by two tries to one in a match that could have gone either way and was easily good enough to have been the final. It was very disappointing, but the squad managed to get themselves up again for the Plate semi-final against the Borneo Eagles team, who had a number of high-profile Samoan and Fijians representing them. The Penguins controlled this match throughout and ran out convincing winners. Coach McKittrick singled out the Penguins' defence as the key to the win.

In the Plate final the team was up against the Wild Titans from Germany, who had a sprinkling of South Africans and Australians in their team. Penguins started well and ran in two tries to lead 12 - 0. The Titans rallied, and drew level to 12 - 12 at the break. However, the half-time team talk was very positive and the Penguins responded well, running in three converted tries in the second half to win 33 - 12 and lift the Plate. Sam Christie, Roger Warren, Fritz Lee, Alapasa Corstz, Roy Kinikinilau, Toby Arnold and James Afoa (Captain) all had strong performances in the Plate final.

The Penguins' results were: Penguins beat Wanchai Warriors (Hong Kong) 61 - 5, Penguins beat Wild Titans (Germany) 22 - 7, Penguins beat Hong Kong Barbarians 22 - 5. Quarter-final: Penguins lost to Aliens (New Zealand) 7 - 12. Plate semi-final: Penguins beat Borneo Eagles (Malaysia) 34 - 0.

Plate final: Penguins beat Wild Titans (Germany) 33 - 12. Penguins won the Hong Kong Tens Plate.

Penguins squad:

Craig Brown (Manager), John McKittrick (Coach), Jamie Baron (Assistant Manager), Peter Gallagher, Dean Herwini, Abby Wills, Fouina Sua, Jamie Baron (Academy Coaches).

James Afoa (Northcote, North Harbour, Captain), Toby Arnold (Tauranga Sports, Bay of Plenty), Ben Botica (Northcote, North Harbour Developement), Sam Christie (Fraser Tech, Waikato), Alapasa Cordtz (Marist St. Joseph, Samoa Sevens and Samoa), Chris Eves (Massey, North Harbour Development), Frank Halai (Marist St. Joseph, Waikato), John Jackson (Nadi, Fiji Barbarians), Josh Katene (Te Teko, Bay of Plenty), Roy Kinikinilau (Wellington, Hurricanes, New Zealand Sevens), Fritz Lee (Manurewa, Auckland U18, Counties-Manukau), Turuva Lumelume (Nadi, NS Warriors), Josh Sutherland (Marist St. Joseph, Waikato), Joao Uva (Belenenses, Portugal Sevens and Portugal), Roger Warren (Marist St. Joseph, Samoa Sevens and Samoa).

Penguin Intenational squad for the 2009 Hong Kong Tens.

Top: The Penguins' formidable front-row of James Afoa, John Jackson and Chris Eves.
Middle: The Academy kids join the players in the stadium.
Above: Academy Coaches Peter Gallagher and Dean Herewini.

Just over a month later, on the very warm evening of 29th May, the Penguin International Rugby Football Club celebrated its Golden Jubilee in great style at the Dorchester in Park Lane.

The Dorchester was packed with guests from all over the world for this joyful and historic occasion. Honoured guests included His Excellency Mr. Derek Leask, the High Commissioner for New Zealand, His Excellency Mr. Pio Bosco Tioisuva, the High Commissioner for Fiji, Group Captain Peter Norford, representing the High Commissioner for Australia, Brian Williams (President of the Rugby Football Union), Robert Horner (past President of the Rugby Football Union), Ed Crozier (Scottish Rugby Union Council), John Hussey (Irish Rugby Football Union and Chairman of the Celtic League), David Pickering (Chairman of the Welsh Rugby Union and a Member of the IRB Council) and Y.Bhg Dato'Krishnan Tan Boon Seng (President of the Combined Old Boys' Rugby Association (COBRA), Malaysia).

Pictures from the Penguin International RFC and HSBC Penguin International Coaching Academy 50th Anniversary Dinner and Grand Reunion at The Dorchester, London, on Friday, 29th May, 2009.
Above: A few of the hundreds of distinguished guests - Willie John McBride, Fergus Slattery, Tony Neary and Tony Mason's son, Michael Mason.
Below: Amongst the famous faces - Mark Evans, Sean Fitzpatrick, The Hon. Sir William McAlpine Bt., Terry Wogan and Peter Sutherland KCMG.

Alan Wright, Craig Brown, Peter Southerland KCMG (a Patron of the Penguins who played for University College Dublin, Lansdowne and the Irish Wolfhounds), Dudley Wood CBE (past Secretary of the Rugby Football Union and a player for Streatham/Croydon, Bedford and Oxford University) and the legendary Willie John McBride (Ballymena, Ulster, Ireland, British and Irish Lions, Rugby World Magazine's Heineken Rugby Personality of the Century and the Captain of the HSBC Lions Legends XV) all gave outstanding speeches to a spellbound audience.

The dinner itself was an huge success, and after a few days messages of thanks and congratulations began pouring in to Alan Wright from everyone lucky enough to have attended. They included letters from Lord Butler of Brockwell KG, GCB, CVO, Lord Green (Group Chairman, HSBC), Robert Horner and Dudley Wood (past President and past Secretary of the Rugby Football Union respectively), Jim Stevenson (President of the Scottish Rugby Union), John Hussey (Chairman of the Irish Rugby Union Management Committee) and many, many more.

Alan: 'In my heart I think that one of the good things I've contributed to the Penguins was starting up this Dinner in 1984 - and running it ever since. I remember saying to Tony at the time: "I'll underwrite the Penguins Grand Reunion Dinner financially, but only once every five years - otherwise it will become commonplace." I always managed to attract wonderful speakers - that was also important - and I do think that it's been held in high regard over the years in rugby union circles.'

Above: The speechmakers (left to right): Alan Wright, Craig Brown, Peter Sutherland, Dudley Wood and Willie John McBride.
Before the speeches began Stephen Herring had presented Alan with a beautiful, engraved Times World Atlas bound in crocodile leather on behalf of the Penguin Committee - all of whom had subscribed to the gift.

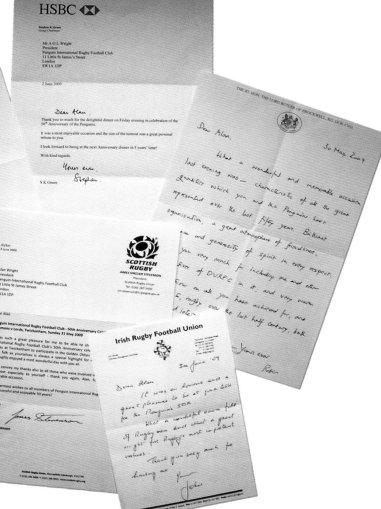

Just a few of the hundreds of thank-you letters. Those above are from: Stephen Green (HSBC), Robert Horner (RFU), Lord Butler of Brockwell, James Stevenson (Scottish Rugby) and John Hussey (Irish RFU).

This special joint Penguin International RFC/ Commons & Lords RFC tie was presented to all participants of this historic match. Alan Wright designed the tie and arranged for its production after a last-minute request from the Commons & Lords RFC.

Just 36 hours after the Jubilee Dinner and Grand Reunion the Penguins were greatly honoured to be playing a match at Twickenham Stadium, the headquarters of English rugby, against the Commons & Lords Rugby Football Club, at their invitation. The match was a celebration of the Commons & Lords RFC's 25th anniversary, as well as the Penguins' 50th anniversary.

Alan: 'The idea for this match was formed at a dinner in January, 2008, when Derek Wyatt MP, who is, of course, a long-standing Committee Member of both the Commons & Lords RFC and the Penguins, passed a note to me whilst a speech was being made. It read: *Parliament v Penguins - Twickenham. Yes or no?* So I crossed out the 'no' and passed it back to him! It took Derek until about

The Penguin International RFC squad for the match against the Commons & Lords RFC at Twickenham Stadium on Sunday, 31st May, 2009.
Back Row: Neil Young (Redcar RFC), Stu Eru (Newbold-on-Avon RFC and Manager of Cambridge University RUFC), Bill Calcraft (Manly, NSW, Oxford University and Australia), Brian Cusack (Lansdowne RFC, Bath RFC and Ireland 'A'), Tony Neary (Broughton Park RFC, Barbarians, North, England and British & Irish Lions), Keith Knowles (Penguin International RFC), Flo Rossigneux (Racing Metro, Bedford RFC, London Welsh RFC, Richmond FC, Wasps FC and French Barbarians, Head Coach at Rosslyn Park FC), Stuart Buchanan-Smith (London Scottish FC, Scottish Schools), Sandy Flockhart CBE, CEO HSBC (Watsonians RFC), Derek Wyatt MP (Oxford University, Barbarians, England - and who, incidentally, also played for the Commons & Lords RFC on the day!), Vincent Bramhall (Hong Kong FC), Scott Wacker (Penguin International RFC), Darragh McElligot (Clontarf RFC and Trinity College, Dublin), Gordon Dickson (Haddington RFC, Watsonians RFC, Gala RFC and Scotland).
Middle Row: Arwell Thomas (Swansea RFC, Wales), Julian Lamden (Penguin International RFC), Paul Heber (Penguin International RFC), Chris Horder (Reading RFC), John McKittrick (Tokoroa, Manager, North Harbour RFC), John Zimnoch (Toronto Nomads RFC), James Stewart (Penguin International RFC), John Kerr (Watsonians RFC, Scotland 'A', Scotland 7s), Keith Wallace (Haddington RFC, Scottish Rugby Council), Brian Stevenson CEO Royal Bank of Scotland (Hillhead/Jordanhill RFC, President, Hong Kong Rugby Union), Hamish Keith (Wasps FC and Scotland),
Front Row: Jamie Baron (Furness RFC), Ben Breeze (Bristol RFC, Exeter Chiefs RFC, Newport/Gwent Dragons, England 7s, Wales 7s, Wales 'A'), Iain Sinclair (Watsonians RFC, Scotland 'A'), Fergus Henderson (Watsonians RFC), Pete Gallagher (Watsonians RFC), Dave Cockburn (Boroughmuir RFC, Scotland 'B'), Peter Sutherland KCMG, Former Attorney General of Ireland (University College Dublin, Landsdowne RFC, Irish Wolfhounds), Alan Wright (Sidcup RFC - Captain), Tom Wacker (Old Blue NYC RFC, Manila Nomads RFC, Taiwan Outsiders RFC, YCAC Yokohama, Hong Kong FC, former CEO, IRB and Director, USA Rugby Union), Craig Brown (London Scottish FC, Watsonians RFC, Waikato RFC, NZ Maori - Vice-Captain), Jim Stevenson (Cambuslang, President Scottish RFU), Antonio da Cunha (Belenesse, Portugal 7s and Portugal), David Harris (Watsonians RFC).

February of 2009 to secure Twickenham Stadium, and by a happy coincidence it just happened to be the 25th Anniversary of the Commons & Lords RFC, too. Perfect! I did say to Derek when the speech was over: "It will have to be *Golden Oldies*. If it's not *Golden Oldies* you'll be having to hold a lot of by-elections!"'

It was a beautiful, hot and sunny early summer day, and the match was a very happy occasion, played in the true spirit of rugby. It was the first Penguins match ever to be played under Golden Oldies rules - the minimum age for the game being 35. The match itself was played in five periods - the first and last of which included the 'more mature' players of both sides, whilst the middle period gave some of the 'younger' squad members a run-out. And although nobody was counting, I can reveal that the first and last parts of the match were just shaded by The Commons & Lords RFC, whilst the Penguins prevailed in the middle section!

Alan: 'During the course of this match there was an occurence that perhaps deserves a place in the Guinness Book of Records! One of the Penguins team, John Zimnoch from Toronto, converted a try scored at the south end of the ground by our opponents. The ball had been placed on a kicking tee and the Commons & Lords kicker seemed undecided, so John just ran up *and converted it*!'

Top: Alan Wright and Humfrey Malins MP lead out the teams at HQ.
Above: Match action.
Below: 'The Governor' holds the match ball. As he himself later said of the weekend: 'All-in-all, this May weekend was a memory to treasure for all who took part.'

The Penguins squad, which consisted of nearly 40 players (some of whom flew in specially for the occasion) included such famous names as Jim Stevenson (Cambuslang RFC and President, Scottish Rugby Union), Brian Stevenson (Hillhead RFC and President, Hong Kong Rugby Union), as well as former internationals Hamish Keith of Wasps and Scotland (who had played alongside Alan Wright in the 1967 Twickenham match), Arwel Thomas (Swansea, Neath and Wales) Derek Wyatt (Bath and England) and Tony Neary (Broughton Park and England).

To top off the day, Alan Wright, 'The Governor' himself, Captained the Penguins and led them on to the pitch in this, his second playing appearance at 'Headquarters' - the first having been against Twickenham RFC nearly 42 years before, in September, 1967.

Players from both sides and their families and friends were generously entertained in the ERIC (English Rugby International's Club) Room by the Rugby Football Union, where the speeches and presentations were also made.

As Doris Mason later said of the occasion: 'Tony would have loved it!'

Credit for the the day being such a success must go not only to the instigator, PIRFC Committee Member Derek Wyatt, but also to another new PIRFC Committee Member, David Harris. David was responsible for the management and organisation of the Penguins' squad on the day.

The King Penguins, Penguins' 'Golden Oldies' Division, were founded in May by Alan Wright and Craig Brown.

As a direct result of needing to form a team consisting of over 35s to play in the Golden Jubilee celebrations at Twickenham on 31st May, the *Penguin International Golden Oldies Division* was founded by Alan Wright and Craig Brown (a few months later this section of the Club was rather imaginatively re-named 'The King Penguins' by Craig). John Zimnoch and David Harris, both of whom are long-standing Penguin International RFC Committee Members, have become the Penguin International Golden Oldies Division Match Managers.

John Zimnoch

Playing career: Archbishop Holgate's Grammar School 1st XV colours 1956 - 1964; York RUFC Life Member 1962 - present; Guisborough RUFC Founder Member (banned *sine die*) 1968 - 1973; Barclays Bank RFC Life Member Supporters Club 1969 - 1975; Balmy Beach RFC 1975 - 1979; Toronto Nomads RFC, Past President, Life Member 1979 - present; Golden Oldies, Toronto Tarts - Toronto Area Rugby Touring Side, Founder Member, Captain, Coach, President 1987; Penguin International RFC 2002. King Penguins Match Manager.

David Harris

Playing career: Watsonians 1978 - 1995. Watsonians Sevens 1978 - 2000. Watsonian Vets 1995 - present. Represented Tasmania at Age Group Levels in Australian Inter-State Cup. Scottish Legends XVs 2005 - present. As a Club Official: President Watsonians 2004 - 2006. Director of Youth Rugby Watsonians 2007 - 2009. President Watsonians 2010 - to present. King Penguins Match Manager.

John and David were the first King Penguin Match Managers for the Golden Anniversary match at Twickenham in 2009. John was invited to join the Penguin Committee after helping Craig to arrange a mammoth coaching programme in Toronto in 2002. David became a Committee Member in 2008, managing the Club's squads in Rome that year and at Twickenham in 2009 (Penguins have been fortunate throughout their history to have had so many Watsonian friends and players). It is pleasing to record that the King Penguins have already made their mark as a result of a fixture against the Australian Parliament in Sydney in 2010, and by playing in the Kowloon RFC International Tens in Hong Kong in 2011.

The Penguin International squad that played in the 2009 HSBC/COBRA Tens in Utara.

The Penguins' second overseas tour of 2009 saw the Club return to Kuala Lumpur for the eleventh time to play in the HSBC/COBRA Tens. The Penguins were Captained by New Zealand Maori prop forward Tony Penn and the tournament took place between 10th - 16th November.

This year, due to financial limitations, Penguins had decided to participate in only one tournament in the region as opposed to the two (Malaysia Tens and Borneo Tens) of previous years.

Due to the wordwide recession, it just so happened that the HSBC/COBRA Tens had attracted far fewer overseas teams than normal - which gave the Club the opportunity to lock horns with more Malaysian sides. In another change from previous years, the tournament was held at the COBRA fields at Utara, instead of at the PJ Stadium.

Nine of the team were on their first Penguins trip, including the Penguins' Coach - legendary New Zealand rugby union and rugby league star, Frano Botica. Not only that, but only two of the squad had played in the COBRA Tens before. Despite this, Penguins were favourites to win the competition. The Penguins had a steady build-up to the tournament with four training runs. In addition, the players also ran two coaching sessions for youngsters - the first for the RSC Club and the second for local school children.

After winning all of their pool games and scoring 211 points without conceding a point, NS Wanderers were beaten 24 - 12 in a far tougher quarter-final clash. In the semi-final, Penguins were beaten by their old rivals and the eventual winners of the tournament, the Borneo Eagles.

Penguins results: Penguins beat Kuching RFC (Malaysia) 95 - 0, Penguins beat ASAS (Malaysia) 73 - 0, Penguins beat Sabah Eagles (Malaysia) 43 - 0. Quarter-final: Penguins beat NS Wanderers (Malaysia) 24 - 12. Semi-final: Penguins lost to Borneo Eagles (Malaysia) 0 - 22.

Penguins squad:

Craig Brown (Tour Manager), Frano Botica (Coach), Ben Fisher and Neil Young (Academy Coaches), Hang Kek Kang (Liaison Officer), Marc Daniels and Lydia (Physiotherapists).

Tony Penn (Tukapa, Taranaki, Hurricanes and New Zealand Maori, Captain), Sam Christie (Fraser Tech, Waikato), Craig De Goldi (Karita, Bay of Plenty, New Zealand Sevens), Luke Hamilton (Western Sharks, Northland, New Zealand Sevens), Nathan Hohaia (Coastal, Taranaki), Jason Hooper (Narbonne, Taranaki, Hurricanes), Nick McLennan (Lincoln, Canterbury U21), Sean O'Connor (Marist, Manawatu), Reece Robinson (Marist, Manawatu, New Zealand Maori), Josh Sutherland (Marist, Waikato), Hua Tamariki (Marist, Southland), Nick Thomson (Taradale, Hawkes Bay, New Zealand Sevens), Ashee Tuala (Manurewa, Counties-Manukau), William Whetton (Northcote, North Harbour).

In 2009 the Pingvin Rugby Club of Sweden sent their U16 squad to England to play three matches. Alan Wright took this opportunity to welcome his friends in the Pingvin Rugby Club and watched the match which was played at Maidenhead. In order to celebrate the PIRFC's Golden Jubilee, the Pingvin Rugby Club presented the Penguins with a magnificent Pingvin flag.

Penguin International RFC will also play a special match against the Pingvin Rugby Club in 2012, when the Pingvins celebrate their Golden Jubilee.

Match action and coaching sessions at the 2009 HSBC/COBRA Tens.

The squad training sessions were taken by legendary New Zealand rugby union and rugby league star, Frano Botica, who had once played for Croatia against the Penguins in 1998.

HSBC Penguins

It was probably in late 2009 that the Penguins first began to be better known throughout the rugby press as *the HSBC Penguins* - a title that has no doubt come about in affectionate deference to their generous principal sponsors.

The Club's ninth President, Richard Bennett, is the longest-serving member of the Hong Kong Sevens Organising Committee and was the Worldwide Group Legal Advisor of HSBC.
He is pictured above at the 1995 HK7s with his son Johno, along with the great Willie 'O' - also known as Australian flanker Willie Ofahengaue.

At the end of 2009 Alan Wright decided to retire after 50 years of distinguished and selfless service to the Club. At the AGM in December the Committee accepted Alan's retirement from the position of President. Craig Brown, CEO, thanked Alan for all his years of service to the Club and, of course, for his friendship and guidance. In Craig's words: 'Alan's inspiration and dedication to the Penguins had built up a renowned sporting club, respected worldwide.'

Club Chairman Tom Wacker proposed Alan to be elected as the Penguins' second Life President, which Alan accepted. Alan continues to be involved in the Club in his role as Life President, part of the Executive Committee and also as a representative on the Advisory Board of the Club.

On 4th December, after being proposed by Alan Wright, Richard Bennett became the ninth President of the Penguin International Rugby Football Club after a unanimous decision taken by the Penguin Committee. Richard is an eminent international lawyer and was the first - and longest-serving - Patron of the Club.

Penguins' Life President Alan Wright and some of his guests in the East Stand at Twickenham enjoying a Calcutta Cup Match in the sunshine. Left to right: Dr. Robert Hancock, Alan Wright, Alisdair Hume, The Hon. Sir William McAlpine Bt, Stephen Herring, Robert Wallace and D. Robin Hutton.

The HSBC Penguin International Coaching Academy once again had a very busy and eventful year in 2009. Here are some of the highlights:

Kuala Lumpur, 4th - 7th May - Coaching educational trips were undertaken to Malaysia in partnership with COBRA. The courses run were equivalent Level 1 Coaching Courses and were run for local school teachers and other rugby coaches. The tutors were: Lynn Evans, Keith Green and Lee Adamson.

Jordan, May - HSBC Penguin Coaches spent a week in Jordan covering everything from grass-roots rugby development to the coaching of the national team. The Coaches were Gordon Henderson and Alexander Edmonstone - both Scottish Rugby Union Development Coaches.

South Africa, June - At the invitation of HSBC and the British and Irish Lions Committee (and with the agreement of the South Africa Rugby Board) the HSBC Penguins provided a grassroots coaching back-up programme to the British and Irish Lions tour in Johannesburg, Bloemfontein, Port Elizabeth, Durban, Cape Town, Nelspruit and East London. The Club considered it to be a supreme honour to have been invited by the Lions Committee to undertake this work.

The HSBC Penguin Coaches spent a total of two weeks, first coaching the Chinese national team in Guangzhou, then undertaking grassroots development activities in Macau, and finally travelling to Kuala Lumpur to offer coachind assistance to Pakistan at the Asian 5 Nations Division Two Tournament. The Coaches were: Chris

Lloyd (London Wasps) and Hugh Campbell (former Scotland and Glasgow coach).

Mongolia - HSBC Penguins spent a week in Mongolia covering a wide range of coaching activities from 'an introduction to the game' to coaching the national team. They also ran classroom activites on player/team development and planning. The Coaches were Frank Hadden (former Scotland National Team Head Coach), and Peter Gallagher (former Scottish Rugby Union professional coach).

Frank Hadden talks about his work with the Academy on the IRB's weekly TV programme, 'Total Rugby'.

Ruck and maul offer way to break free from shackles of gang culture

Michael Dakets, a convicted murderer serving his sentence at Nelson Mandela's former prison, is a new disciple of sport. Owen Slot meets him

Williams waits in the wings as Lions consider starring role

David Hands Rugby Correspondent Cape Town

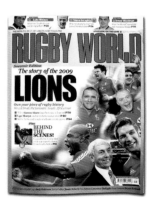

Above: The HSBC Penguin International Coaching Academy attracted a lot of media attention - from both the national and the rugby press - during the 2009 British and Irish Lions tour of South Africa.

Richard Bennett - the ninth Penguin President

Alan Wright proposed that Richard Bennett should succeed him in office, and this was approved unanimously by the Penguin Committee. Richard was officially confirmed as the ninth President of the Penguin International Rugby Football Club on 4th December, 2009.

Richard was educated at Temple Grove Preparatory School (by an unusual coincidence the Penguins' second President, Group Captain Sir Douglas Bader, also attended Temple Grove) and afterwards at Haileybury College.

Richard's career to date: 1976 - 1979: Assistant Solicitor with Stephenson Harwood;

1979 - 1988: Assistant Group Legal Adviser with the Hong Kong and Shanghai Banking Corporation;

1988 - 1992: Deputy Group Legal Adviser with the Hong Kong and Shanghai Banking Corporation;

1993 - 1997: Head of Legal and Compliance for Asia Pacific with the Hong Kong and Shanghai Banking Corporation;

1998 to date: Head of Legal and Compliance with HSBC Holdings plc.

Richard presently oversees more than 670 lawyers in 50 countries and is responsible for advising the HSBC Board on the Bank's legal and regulatory risks.

Richard's rugby career began when he played for Temple Grove School (where he Captained the 1st XV and led them to an unbeaten season in 1965) and Haileybury College. After leaving Haileybury he played for the Old Haileyburians & Imperial Service College RFC, Rosslyn Park FC and Kowloon RFC.

Richard was a co-founder of the Kowloon Tens (established in 1980). He was also a member of the IRB Hong Kong Sevens Committee for many years.

Wayfoong RFC, 1981. Richard Bennett is in the front row, third from the right and Sandy Flockart, an HSBC Director and a Patron of the Penguins, is second from the left. The photograph was taken before the Wayfoong v Hong Kong FC match of 1981 (the result was a 13 - 9 win to Wayfoong).

2010

2010 was another wonderful year with regard to results with only three matches lost out of 22 played.

In their annual match on Tuesday, 3rd February, HSBC Penguins (once again ably Captained by Howard Graham) beat Cambridge University by 39 points to 14 at Grange Road.

The HSBC Penguins squad was Managed by Ian Bullerwell and Ben Dormer and included in its ranks three Rugby Lions players, three players from Cambridge RUFC and four up-and-coming Saracens stars - including 18-year-old stand-off Owen Farrell (the son of dual-code England international Andy Farrell).

A Penguin Committee Dinner was held on 26th February at The Peasant in Clerkenwell, London. In the course of a witty and entertaining speech Alan Wright congratulated Richard Bennett on his appointment as the ninth President of the Penguins and made a presentation to him which included an autographed copy of Dick Tyson's book *London's Oldest Rugby Clubs*. In response, Richard thanked Alan for his inspirational and dedicated service to the Club over 51 years and presented him with a truly magnificent gift - a monogrammed leather case containing letters of tribute written by the officials of Rugby Unions from all around the world. The folder also included a letter written to Alan by Tom Wacker, the Chairman of the Penguins. In it Tom wrote:

Dear Alan - On behalf of the Penguin International Rugby Football Club, and its membership past and present, it is my honour to express our appreciation for your 51 years of service. Long ago, when you and Tony Mason founded the Penguins, I suspect you would have been very proud to know what would transpire. Throughout the Penguins' long history you have been involved in virtually every capacity, from washing the playing kit to now serving as Life President. You have also been incredibly generous in giving your valuable time, your unswerving commitment to detail, and, indeed, considerable financial resources for the benefit of the Club. I'm certain that our illustrious players, over the years, would join me in these sentiments.

You have always said that 'it's all about the players' - something that many rugby administrators often forget.

Tom Wacker and Alan Wright at the 2010 Committee Dinner.

Even though you have said you will be stepping back from day-to-day activities, all of us hope you will remain very much involved. You are the heart and soul of The Penguins.

From all of us, a heartfelt thank-you for everything!

Thomas J. Wacker, Chairman PIRFC.

2010 CHRONICLE

3rd February - Penguins beat Cambridge University 39 - 14 at Grange Road, Cambridge.

2nd March - Penguins lost to Oxford University 26 - 40 at Iffley Road, Oxford.

24th and 25th March - Hong Kong Tens. Captained by Nick Collins (New Zealand). Penguins beat
Hong Kong Football Club 47 - 0
Penguins beat
Cardiff University (Wales) 47 - 0
Penguins lost to Samurai 12 - 24
Quarter-final:
Penguins beat Borneo Eagles 6 - 5
Semi-final: Penguins lost to Aliens (New Zealand) 14 - 17
Semi-finalists, Hong Kong Tens

23rd - 31st May - Portugal. Captained by Marcus Di Rollo (Scotland). Penguins beat the Lisbon Regional XV 34 - 17.
Penguins beat Agronomia 30 - 17.

25th September - King Penguins v Australian Parliament in Sydney.

5th - 7th November - Singapore Cricket Club Sevens. Captained by Nafi Tuitavake (New Zealand).
Penguins beat Cottesloe (Australia) 31 - 0
Penguins beat Almaty (Kazakhstan) 40 - 5
Penguins beat Borneo Eagles 29 - 0
Penguins beat East Arnhem (Australia) 44 - 0
Penguins beat Ponsonby (New Zealand) 38 - 0
Penguins beat Horowhenua-Kapiti (New Zealand) 33 - 10
Penguins beat South African Vipers 19 - 14 (AET)
Winners,
Singapore Cricket Club Sevens

13th - 14th November - HSBC/COBRA International Tens, Malaysia. Captained by Shane Christie (New Zealand).
Penguins beat Sabah Eagles (Malaysia) 59 - 0
Penguins beat NNK (RSA) 47 - 5
Penguins beat Ponsonby (New Zealand) 12 - 0
Penguins beat Gungahlin Eagles (Australia) 30 - 0
Penguins beat Natal Duikers (RSA) 43 - 0
Penguins beat New Zealand Legends 21 - 7
Winners, HSBC/COBRA Tens

Left: The Home Unions' tributes to Alan Wright. Above: The PIRFC Committee Dinner, 26th February 2010.

At the end of February Karl Bryson, from the Manawatu Rugby Union in New Zealand, became the first recipient of the Penguin Award for the Best Performer, as voted for by the IRANZ staff coaches at the IRANZ course in Palmerston North, New Zealand. By special arrangement Karl was offered a place in the Penguins team to play in the Hong Kong Tens in March.

Craig De Goldi presents the Penguin Award for Best Performer to Karl Bryson at the end of the IRANZ Course in Palmerston. Craig said that Karl, whilst Captaining the IRANZ course team, was the top performer on and off the field, and that he would be a good ambassador for IRANZ, New Zealand and the Penguin International RFC.

On Tuesday, 2nd March, Oxford University beat HSBC Penguins 26 - 40 at Iffley Road in what was the 30th year of this plum annual fixture.

HSBC Penguins included Wasps' former Rugby League international Lee Smith at full-back in a very strong line-up. Quite by chance, the starting HSBC Penguins blindside flanker Stu Riding had transport difficulties, so Bill Calcraft (who was the 1987 Oxford University Captain, it will be remembered) pulled on the number 6 jersey for the visitors and started the match. Bill put in a most commendable first 20 minutes and was soon reunited with the Iffley Road turf - after an absence of some 20 years!

Despite Lee and Bill's best efforts Oxford University ran out deserved winners in an entertaining game that featured some fine attacking rugby from both sides. The match managers were, again, Ian Bullerwell and Ben Dormer.

Later in March the Club returned to Hong Kong for the fourth successive year to participate in the 2010 Hong Kong Football Club Tens. The HSBC Penguins' coaches for the tour were Steve Hill (Director of Rugby at Oxford University) and former Scotland Head Coach Frank Hadden. This was Frank's second time coaching the HSBC Penguins at the Hong Kong Tens. Three years earlier, in March, 2007, Frank had teamed up with former Scotland fly-half John Rutherford to form the HSBC Penguins' coaching team for the Club's first appearance at this tournament.

The squad arrived in Hong Kong on the evening of Sunday, 21st March. The following night the Club was hosted at a function by held by HSBC at the Bank's HQ. Sandy Flockhart welcomed the HSBC Penguins on behalf of the Bank, and Craig Brown replied for the Club. The evening was very relaxed and was a chance for the squad to mingle with HSBC staff and other guests, including many from the Hong Kong rugby community.

All Black John Kirwan with two Rwandan internationals at the HSBC Penguins/Sandy Bay RFC coaching session.

On the Tuesday evening, after the team's training run, HSBC Penguins players, along with former All Black star John Kirwan, ran a session for the Sandy Bay RFC youngsters. As in previous years, the players divided themselves up into groups and the Sandy Bay youngsters rotated around the various HSBC Penguin 'stations'. The Rwandan national team were also present, and they joined in the coaching.

The first two pool matches (which were played on Wednesday 24th March) were a testing challenge for the HSBC Penguins, and a lot of hard work was required to set up victories against Hong Kong FC and Cardiff University. But the

HSBC Penguins' coaches knew that the biggest challenge in the pool stages was yet to come - in the shape of the Samurai Rugby Club, who had selected a strong team which included many New Zealanders. Sure enough, Samurai caused problems by frequently getting over the gain-line and took the lead in the first half. HSBC Penguins rallied with two well-worked tries of their own, but ran out of time trying to close the deficit. It was very disappointing to lose the game, but the general consensus was that the Club had performed well and could only get better on day two.

The next day, in one of the most exciting matches of the tournament, HSBC Penguins met the the Borneo Eagles. In a thrilling final play, with the clock already showing full time, the Eagles strung a multi-phased attack together and touched down in the left-hand corner. The score was 6 - 5 with the conversion to come. Some watched, some could not. The kick sailed wide and the HSBC Penguins had held on to win the match.

The HSBC Penguins/Aliens clash was a very close affair featuring massive commitment, great skill and steely defence from both sides. HSBC Penguins had their chances but the last-ditch Alien defence held strong and the New Zealanders went through to the final courtesy of a penalty kick scored in the second half. It was a classic game of Tens with both sides scoring two converted tries apiece.

It was disappointing to bow out in the semis, after reaching the final in the previous three years, but the Club played well and upheld the reputation of the Penguin International RFC both on and off the field.

The results were: HSBC Penguins beat Hong Kong Football Club 47 - 0, HSBC Penguins beat Cardiff University 47 - 0, HSBC Penguins lost to Samurai 12 - 24. Quarter-final: HSBC Penguins beat Borneo Eagles 6 - 5. Semi-final: HSBC Penguins lost to Aliens 14 - 17.

The squad enjoyed the last three days of the Tour by watching the IRB Sevens and taking part in various fund-raising events. Indeed, six of the team acted as chaperones at the *Ladies' Long Lunch*, a charity event organised by The Christina Noble Foundation to raise money for underprivileged children.

HSBC Penguins squad:

Craig Brown (Manager), Coaches: Frank Hadden (former Scotland Head Coach), Steve Hill (Director of Rugby at Oxford University).

Nick Collins (Kamo, Northland, Chiefs, New Zealand Sevens, Captain), Beauden Barrett (Taranaki U18 and Sevens, New Zealand Sevens), James Brown (Fiji U19, Canterbury U21 and Development, Fiji Sevens), Karl Bryson (College Old Boys, Manawatu Sevens, Manawatu U20), Sam Clarke (East Coast Bays, Thames Valley), Ben Frame (Glenmark, Canterbury 'B'), Luke Hamilton (Coastal, Northland, North Harbour Sevens, New Zealand Sevens), Nathan Hohaia (Coastal, Taranaki Sevens, Taranaki), John Jackson (Otorohunga, Nadi, Nawaka

Sevens, Fiji Warriors), Mike Mayhew (Northcote, North Harbour), Reece Robinson (Marist St Joe's, Manawatu, Chiefs, New Zealand Maori), Orisi Seraki (Nasinu, Suva, Fiji Sevens), Jordan Smiler (Hautapu, Waikato Sevens, Waikato), Hua Tamariki (Marist St Joe's, Southland), Makota Tosa (Oxford University, NEC Green Rockets, Japan U23).

Agronomia v PIRFC match poster.

In May HSBC Penguins visited Portugal. The tour included two matches and three Coaching Academy sessions. This was the Club's third XVs tour to Portugal (the others were in 1975 and 1966 - when one of the opponents was Agronomia).

A strong squad was selected including Tour Captain Marcus Di Rollo, the former Scottish International. It was Coached by Steve Hill (now Director of Rugby at Richmond FC), John McKittrick (North Harbour) and Riccardo Franconi (Rugby Roma). The side was Managed by Ben Dormer with assistance from Craig Brown.

The first match was against a Lisbon Regional XV. The Lisbon team was based on emerging international young players based around Lisbon. In a highly entertaining, all-action encounter the HSBC Penguins won by 34 points to 17.

The second match was played in front of a large crowd against Agronomia Rugby Club to celebrate their 75th Anniversary. Penguins had no fewer than eleven nationalities on the field - Scots, English, Irish, French, Italian, South African, Albanian, Portuguese, Tongan, Australian and Kiwis. In another open, flowing game, the hosts took an early lead with two tries from the forwards. HSBC Penguins eventually found their rhythm and started to put together multi-phased attacks which eventually brought tries.

The victorious HSBC Penguins squad celebrate their win against Agronomia. During the course of the Portugal Tour the coaches (often assisted by the players) carried out several coaching clinics at the Agronomia and Belenenses Rugby Clubs, and also at the Escolinha de Rugby da Galiza children's project.

Reflecting just how strong Portuguese rugby has become, the result was far from certain until ten minutes from time - but HSBC Penguins then pulled away to win this very competitive match 30 – 17.

John Steele, a former first-class fly-half and a Heineken Cup-winning coach with Northampton in 2000, was appointed as the Chief Executive of the RFU on 6th September, 2010. John played for the Penguins against Cambridge University Past and Present in 1992.

Agronomia presentation plaque.

Following the great success of the PIRFC 50th Anniversary match against the Commons & Lords RFC at Twickenham in 2009, the Club formed The King Penguins - PIRFC's 'Social' team.

The King Penguins, brainchild of Alan Wright and Craig Brown, and currently managed by David Harris and John Zimnoch, played their very first match in September, 2010, having been granted the great honour of playing a fixture against the Australian Parliment XV in Australia.

HSBC Penguins returned to the Singapore Cricket Club Sevens over the weekend of 5th - 7th November for the third time (the Club had also played in the 1997 and '98 Tournaments). The squad was based on a core group of ITM Cup players from New Zealand, all of whom had a range of Sevens experience.

HSBC Penguins' Coaches John McKittrick and Rodney McIntosh prepared very carefully for the Tournament - John controlling the pre-match holistic planning and Rodney focusing on the physical preparation and recovery of the squad (the squad also played a major part in running the HSBC Youth Coaching Festival at the Padang on the Thursday before the SCC Sevens Tournament began).

The tournament favourites were the South African Vipers (the reigning SCC champions and the IRB Sevens second-ranked team in the world). The Vipers are the RSA National Sevens squad and had won the previous three SCC Sevens Tournaments. Also included in the 2010 Tournament were five other national sides, including Sri Lanka, Japan, Hong Kong and Kazakhstan.

On Friday, 5th November, the HSBC Penguins played in the first game of the Tournament against Cottesloe RFC from Perth in Australia. As expected, in their first full match together the HSBC Penguins struggled to find their rhythm and won more through individual endeavour and skill than classic Sevens team work.

The opponents on day two were Almaty RFC from Kazakhstan and the Borneo Eagles - both of whom were beaten comfortably.

On Sunday, 7th November, heavy overnight rain had saturated the playing surface - especially the bottom right-hand corner, which the team affectionately named 'The Swamp'. The Club adapted best to the conditions, and their pressure defence paid dividends. The first game of the top 16 round saw the Club easily beat Australian side East Arnhem.

In the quarter-final the HSBC Penguins came up against former champions Ponsonby RFC from New Zealand. In one of the most clinical games of the Tournament, the HSBC Penguins comprehensively outplayed their opponents and won by 38 unanswered points, setting up a semi-final with Horowhenua-Kapiti from New Zealand. Horowhenua-Kapiti scored first but the physical presence of the HSBC Penguins saw the Club emerge with a comfortable 33 - 10 victory.

This set up a classic encounter in the final between three-times winners South African Vipers and the Club. The South Africans totally dominated possession and field position in the first half, but the HSBC Penguins' resolute defence kept the South Africans at bay. And then, against the run of play, the Club scored when Nalu Tuigamala forced his way through a gap and ran a full 40 metres to score under the posts. The conversion gave HSBC Penguins a 7 - 0 lead at half-time.

HOLDERS TOPPLED

The Straits Times - 8 Nov 2010

Touring team Penguins upset 3-time defending champions Vipers 19-14

By ROYSTON SIM

TOURNAMENT newcomers HSBC Penguins pulled off a stunning victory to unseat defending champions SA Vipers 19-14 and clinch the Ablitt Cup yesterday.

The thrilling see-saw encounter provided a fitting finale for the Singapore Cricket Club (SCC) International Rugby Sevens at the Padang.

Winners for the previous three years, the Vipers were heavily favoured to win the 63rd edition of the tournament.

But they came up against an impenetrable iron wall in the Penguins, a touring club from Britain that last competed here in 1997. They came this year boasting New Zealand international Nafi Tuitavake and junior All Black Naly Tuigamala in their ranks.

Cheered on by about 4,500 fans, the Penguins drew first blood through a try by David Raikuna and subsequent conversion from Tuigamala.

The Vipers responded through a Bernardo Botha try and Branco du Preez conversion. Tuigamala then scored a try and conversion with less than three minutes to go, but with mere seconds left, Botha surged down the left flank to record a try. Du Preez kept his nerve to score a diffi-

However, the Penguins were not to be denied - Raikuna took advantage of a defensive lapse to score his second try.

He said: "It's such an amazing feeling, scoring the winning try for your team. I guess everyone wants to do that."

Penguins coach John McKitridge said defence won the day for his team.

"We placed a major emphasis on defensive strategies," he said. "If we got our defence right, out attack would take of itself, and so it proved."

Vipers coach Paul Treu agreed, saying: "They were clinical at the back. We conceded too many turnovers, and our support was just too slow."

In other finals, Australia's Sunnybank lifted the Plate after beating Malaysia's NS Wanderers 15-10. Sri Lanka SLRFU defeated Japan's Tamariya 19-12 to win the Bowl, and Southern Lions edged Casuarina Cougars 14-12 to lift the Jug.

Anglo-Chinese School (Independent) defeated Greenridge Secondary 34-0 to lift the Under-16 John Clark Trophy.

Tanglin Trust School trumped United World College 10-5 to clinch the U-19 Sithawalla Cup.

Meanwhile, organisers are looking to raise the standards of visiting teams for next year's tournament. Said Peter Hutton, chairman of the organising committee: "We are committed to improving every year and we are already getting inquiries from other world-class teams."

HSBC Penguins celebrating after beating the South Africans. The British team's emphasis on a strong defence paid off on a wet and slippery Padang pitch.
ST PHOTO: ALPHONSUS CHERN

The Straits Times press report.

Nalu Tuigamala.

The second half saw the South Africans change their pattern of play by using more width. This paid dividends and resulted in a converted try to level the scores within 90 seconds of the restart. The HSBC Penguins struck back with a converted try by winger David Raikuna. This set up a very tense final three minutes with the score favouring the HSBC Penguins at 14 - 7. After the final hooter the South Africans scored out wide on the left flank. The conversion sailed over to tie the game and send the match into 'sudden-death' extra time.

HSBC Penguins won the toss and chose to attack 'The Swamp' - pressuring the Vipers into an early turnover. From the resulting restart the Club attacked and were awarded a penalty close to the South Africans' goal posts. A quick tap saw David Raikuna burrow his way over through two defenders to ground the ball and end the contest. The entire HSBC Penguins team was absolutely delighted and the reserves all raced on to celebrate with their teammates.

It was a tremendous win for the HSBC Penguins in a very prestigious and high-profile Tournament, and it set up the Club very nicely for the beginning of the HSBC/COBRA Tens Tournament which was to start in just five days time.

The HSBC Penguins' results were: HSBC Penguins beat Cottesloe (Australia) 31 - 0, HSBC Penguins beat Almaty RFC (Kazakhstan) 40 - 5, HSBC Penguins beat Borneo Eagles 29 - 0, HSBC Penguins beat East Arnhem (Australia) 44 - 0. Quarter-final: HSBC Penguins beat Ponsonby (New Zealand) 38 - 0. Semi-final: HSBC Penguins beat Horowhenua-Kapiti (New Zealand) 33 - 10. Final: HSBC Penguins beat South Africa 19 - 14 (AET).

Roy Griffin.

Singapore Sevens press report from the UK's Rugby Times newspaper.

HSBC Penguins squad: Craig Brown (Tour Manager), Hang Kek Kang (Assistant Tour Manager), Coaches: John McKittrick (former coach of North Harbour 7s and Development XV, Cook Islands XV & 7s, USA 7s) and Rodney McIntosh (former coach of Hong Kong 7s). David Townsend (Liaison). Nafi Tuitavake (Massey, North Harbour, NZ U20, NZ 7s, Captain), Ben Botica (North Shore, North Harbour), Shane Christie (Nelson, Tasman, Tasman 7s), Villiame Fihaki (Patumahoe, Counties Manukau), Irwin Finau (Silverdale, North Harbour 'B', Auckland 7s), Roy Griffin (Kamo, Northland, Blues Development), Matthew Hodson (Tauranga Sports, Bay of Plenty 7s), Paulo Kinikinilau (Alhambra-Union, Horowhenua-Kapiti, Otago), Manu Leiataua (Mahurangi, North Harbour, Wellington 7s, Wellington 'B'), Johnny McNicholl (Sydenham, Canterbury 7s, U21, Crusaders Development), David Raikuna (Pukekohe, Counties Manukau XVs and Counties Manukau 7s), Nalu Tuigamala (East Coast Bays, North Harbour, North Harbour 7s, NZ U20).

It is interesting to note that Shane Christie and David Raikuna went on to play for NZ 7s after appearing in this match whilst Nalu Tuigamala and Matt Hodson were invited to participate in the NZ 7s trials.

Shane Christie.

After the Club's brilliant and victorious time in Singapore, the HSBC Penguins travelled north into Malaysia. Unfortunately, both SCC Sevens skipper Nafi Tuitavake and influential player Matt Hodson had to return to New Zealand. They were replaced by Phil Tuigamala and Nathan Hohaia. In addition, Paulisia Manu and Sam Hayes-Stevenson joined the twelve who had played in Singapore to make up the 14 players required for the HSBC/COBRA Tens.

Penguins set for tilt at Cobra 10s title despite losing two key players

The Star — 11 Nov 2010

PETALING JAYA: Three-time champions Penguins will be without two key stars when they head for the Cobra 10s at the MBPJ Stadium in Kelana Jaya this weekend.

Penguins, who won the Cobra 10s in 1993, 1994 and 2006, are in high spirits after winning the Singapore cricket Club's 7s tournament last Sunday.

Although their two star players – New Zealand 7s international Nafi Tuitavake and Junior All Blacks Nalu Tuigamala – have gone back,

Penguins are not perturbed as they have brought four new players for the Cobra challenge.

Team manager Craig Brown said yesterday that they would still have a strong team "as the players will still have time to get used to each other before the Cobra 10s begin".

"The two Kiwi players were the stars in our victory in Singapore, where we beat the Vipers 19-14 in the final. We are not setting any targets for the Cobra 10s but, like all other teams, we aim to win it

on Sunday," said Brown, who was a player with Penguins when they won in 1993 and 1994.

"It would be great if we can win two tournaments back-to-back.

"We have been regulars in the Cobra 10s and we always enjoy our trip here."

Brown, who said that the 7s was an easier game to play, felt that the team who settled down fastest during the two days in Kelana Jaya would have the edge.

The Penguins have been drawn

in Group B with Ponsonby of New Zealand, Northlink of South Africa and defending champions Borneo Eagles.

The preliminary round will feature four groups and the top two teams from each group will qualify for the quarter-finals on Sunday.

"It is a tough group for us but we'll take it one step at a time and see how it goes," said Brown.

The team stopped by in Port Dickson on Monday to conduct a coaching course for 120 childen

from schools in the district.

Brown said they would also make stops in Kota Tinggi, Batu Pahat and Mersing before heading here today.

"The coaching stints are part of our annual activities in this region. Our academy coaches also travel to other states to conduct clinics for schools and coaches," he said.

"We are happy to do this as it is our way to encourage and develop the game in other parts of the world."

Local press report of the forthcoming HSBC/COBRA Tens Tournament.

The following two nights were spent training and running a coaching session for over 130 local children in Port Dickson, Malaysia. The team greatly enjoyed running this coaching clinic and the laughter and smiles on the faces of the children during the session made it all worthwhile. The children and their coaches were presented with HSBC Penguin Coaching Academy T-shirts. Craig Brown later said that this was one of the best sessions run by any HSBC Penguins team, and credit was due to the players for the way they planned and executed the sessions.

As part of the build up to the HSBC/COBRA Tens, the team held a warm-up match against JLJ, the local Army-based side (HSBC Penguins were the first foreign team to play JLJ in Port Dickson). The game was a valuable exercise that helped transform the players from 'sevens mode' into 'tens mode'.

The Malaysian Police escort the team's motor coach to the ground.

Coach John McKittrick named Shane Christie as HSBC Penguins' Captain for the HSBC/COBRA Tens, based on his brilliant performance in Singapore.

Upon arrival in Kuala Lumpur, the team was hosted by Jon Addis of HSBC at the inaugural Rugby Legends dinner as presented by the COBRA Club. A very pleasant evening was had by all.

The next day the HSBC Penguins really began to get into tournament mode and the intensity in training reflected this. Many of the team had not played tens before, so a new experience awaited.

On day one of the Tournament a police escort ensured the HSBC Penguins' motor coach got to the stadium without delay, and the warm-up for the first match began under coach Rodney McIntosh.

The team did well during the day, running up two comfortable victories before facing top New Zealand Club Ponsonby in one of the feature matches of the day. Defence led the way, as it had in Singapore, and the team ran out 12 - 0 winners after a closely fought contest. Rolling subs meant everyone had ample playing time and all contributed to a great first day.

Day two dawned hot and sunny. First opponents were the Gungahlin Eagles, an Australian team from Canberra. The match was even for the first five minutes, with both defences coping well. However, the fitter HSBC Penguins team began to put the Australians under pressure. Eventually the vastly superior HSBC Penguins ten started to find the gaps and the tries came.

The semi-final was an interesting match. The Natal Duikers had a big side which included many representative players. The Club prepared for a very physical encounter but in the performance of the weekend, the HSBC Penguins were just too good with ball in hand and the game was all over by half-time - the Club leading 38 - 0 at the break. In the second half the players concentrated on conserving energy, and the final score was 43 - 0.

Doing well on the other side of the draw were the New Zealand Legends team, who had a number of representative players and had registered some impressive wins on day one. Most of the spectators were predicting a New Zealand Legends/HSBC Penguins final - which is exactly what happened.

Rodney McIntosh was again outstanding in preparing the team for the final, and the Club opened the scoring with a Viliame Fihaki try. Just before half-time Paulo Kinikinilau scored another and the Club was leading 14 - 0 at the break. Although the Legends scored soon after the resumption, sustained HSBC Penguins pressure saw Vice-Captain Nathan Hohaia score another try to put the final beyond the reach of the New Zealanders. The Club's victory was based on sound defence and the side conceded only twelve points throughout the entire tournament. The HSBC Penguins themselves scored a massive 212 points in the six matches.

This was the fourth time that the HSBC Penguins had won the HSBC/COBRA Tens title, and it was a marvellous end to a great two-week Tour. To win both of these tough and prestigious Tournaments back-to-back is a tremendous achievement which will be remembered by all in the Club for many years to come.

The HSBC Penguins' results were: HSBC Penguins beat Sabah Eagles (Malaysia) 59 - 0, HSBC Penguins beat NNK (Republic of South Africa) 47 - 5, HSBC Penguins beat Ponsonby (New Zealand) 12 - 0. Quarter-final: HSBC Penguins beat Gungahlin Eagles (Australia) 30 - 0. Semi-final: HSBC Penguins beat Natal Duikers (Republic of South Africa) 43 - 0. Final: HSBC Penguins beat New Zealand Legends 21 - 7.

HSBC Penguins were winners of the Hui Weng Choon Trophy.

THE STAR, MONDAY 15 NOVEMBER 2010 **SPORT** S57

Number one: Penguins players celebrating after being crowned the Cobra 10s champions at the Kelana Jaya Stadium yesterday. — AZMAN GHANI / The Star

Penguins rule again

English team beat Kiwis for fourth title

By S. RAMAGURU

KELANA JAYA: England's Penguins International RFC captured their fourth HSBC Cobra 10s rugby title after beating NZ Legends 21-7 in the final at the MBPJ Stadium here yesterday.

The Penguins were simply the better team in the two-day affair and deservedly took home the first prize money of US$5,000. NZ Legends received US$2,000.

The Penguins, champions in 1993, 1994 and 2006, came into the 41st edition of the tournament after winning the Singapore Cricket Club's 7s last weekend.

Their superior fitness gave them the edge over the other teams in the tournament and they were easy and worthy winners of all their matches, including the final.

Vili Eihaki, Paula Kinikinilau and Nathan Hohaia scored a try each and Ben Botica converted all three in the winover NZ Legends.

For the Kiwis, Charles O'Connel scored a try while Chris Noakes converted it.

The England-based Penguins were in equally devastating form in the semi-finals as they crushed South Africa's Natal Duikers 43-0 after virtually sewing up the game with a 37-0 lead at half time.

NZ Legends had a tougher time in the semi-finals, slogging to a 7-0 win over countrymen Ponsonby.

Malaysia's challenge in the main draw ended at the hands of Kiwi opponents in the quarter-finals, with defending champions Borneo Eagles losing 0-29 to Ponsonby and 2009 champion and last year's finalists Cobra Blacks going down 5-24 to NZ Legends.

Cobra Blacks, however, went to make the final of the Plate competition against Gungahlin Eagles of Australia.

The Cobra team were down 14-0 in the Plate semi-finals against Borneo Eagles but staged a late fightback to score three tries and two conversions for a 19-14 win.

But they faltered in the final against Gungahlin. The Malaysians held the lead at 15-12 with five minutes to go but allowed the Australians to hit back with a try and a conversion to win 19-15 and earn US$1,000.

Northlink won the Bowl final when they defeated Wainuiomata 31-0.

Results

■ CUP
Quarter-finals: Borneo Eagles 0 Ponsonby 29, NZ Legends 24 Cobra Blacks 5, Natal Duikers 3 SA Mustangs 0, Gungahlin Eagles 5 Penguins RFC 30.
Semi-finals: Ponsonby 0 NZ Legends 7, Natal Duikers 0 Penguins RFC 43.
Final: Penguins RFC 21 NZ Legends 7.
■ BOWL
Quarter-finals: Wainuiomata 7 Sabah Eagles 0, Sri Lankan Army 0 ASAS RFC 54, NS Wanderers 37 Royal Thai Navy 0, Cobra Stings 5 Northlink 43.
Semi-finals: Wainuiomata 15 ASAS RFC 12, NS Wanderers 7 Northlink 17.
Final: Wainuiomata 0 Northlink 31.
■ PLATE
Semi-finals: Borneo Eagles 14 Cobra Blacks 19, SA Mustangs 15 Gungahlin Eagles 26.
Final: Cobra Blacks 15 Gungahlin Eagles 19.

No way: NZ Legends player Luke Herden (centre) is tackled by Penguins players Pauliasi Manu (left) and Villiame Fihaki during the Cobra 10s final yesterday.

PENGU🐧NS

Singapore & Malaysia Tour 2010 - SCC Sevens, Singapore ★ **Tournament Winners** / COBRA Tens, Malaysia ★ **Tournament Winners**

A magnificent end to the playing year.

HSBC Penguins' squad:

Craig Brown (Manager), John McKittrick and Rodney McIntosh (Coaches), Hang Kek Kang (Liaison), David Townsend (Committee Member).

Shane Christie (Nelson, Tasman and Tasman Sevens, Captain), Ben Botica (North Shore, North Harbour), Villiame Fihaki (Patumahoe, Counties Manukau), Irwin Finau (Silverdale, North Harbour 'B' and Auckland Sevens), Roy Griffin (Kamo, Northland and Blues Development), Sam Hayes-Steveson (Burnside, Canterbury 'B' and Crusaders Development), Nathan Hohaia (Tukapa, Taranaki and Taranaki Sevens, Hurricanes Development, Vice-Captain), Paulo Kinikinilau (Alhambra-Union, Horowhenua-Kapiti and Otago), Manu Leiataua (Mahurangi, North Harbour, Wellington Sevens and Wellington 'B'), Paulisia Manu (University, Auckland), Johnny McNicholl (Sydenham, Canterbury Sevens U21 and Crusaders Development), David Raikuna (Pukekohe, Counties Manukau Sevens), Nalu Tuigamala (East Coast Bays, North Harbour, North Harbour Sevens and New Zealand U20), Phil Tuigamala (Northcote and North Harbour U20 Development).

On 17th December Rwanda's rugby players were visited by the HSBC Penguin International Coaching Academy (which included Penguins' CEO Craig Brown, former Scotland national coach Frank Hadden and Scottish Rugby Union referee development manager Colin Brett) for a week-long series of clinics - the first-ever visit to Rwanda by elite-level rugby coaches.

At the end of the week Frank Hadden said: 'In the last couple of years I've coached in nearly twenty countries and I'm amazed at the capacity of rugby to grow, and even thrive, in the most unlikely circumstances... It was fantastic to see all those enthusiastic and talented players coming together to enjoy the rivalry and camaraderie of the best team game in the world.'

Colin Brett also ran an introductory referees tutorial. This course was well attended and included all the current Rwandan referees plus a number of players who were keen to improve their understanding of the game.

Frank Hadden adds: 'At the end of the week there was a rugby sevens festival in our honour. It was fascinating watching the commitment, enthusiasm and no little skill of all the players.'

The Academy's coaching visit capped a remarkable year for Rwandan rugby that began with the Silverbacks travelling to Hong Kong for their first-ever overseas tour. They finished as Plate runners-up in the *inProjects Kowloon RugbyFest*, a tens tournament featuring 14 teams from around the world. South African rugby great Bob Skinstad was among the impressed spectators and immediately gave them an open invitation to play in the Cape Town Tens, the tournament he co-founded in 2009.

The Silverbacks also trained with the Aliens from New Zealand, and HSBC Penguins' coaches also put them through a first-level IRB coaching course - after which the team watched the Hong Kong Sevens courtesy of the HKRFU.

The result of all this activity is that rugby in Rwanda is booming, with youngsters taking up the sport in impressive numbers while more and more women players are also participating.

'The HSBC Penguin International Coaching Academy's visit generated huge excitement and gave the game another massive boost,' said Hong Kong-born rugby enthusiast, and Rwanda volunteer worker, Dave Hughes. 'We're extremely grateful to the Penguins and to Frank, Colin and Craig for giving their time, effort and expertise. Their trip to Rwanda - and the impact they made - will be remembered for a long, long time.'

And so ended a wonderful 2010 in which the HSBC Penguins won the two major Far East Rugby Tournaments in the course of one Tour. But if anything, 2011 would be prove to be even more successful...

SRU referee development manager Colin Brett takes charge of a sevens match during the HSBC Penguin Coaching Academy's visit to Rwanda.

HSBC Penguin Coaching Academy duo Colin Brett (grey shirt) and Frank Hadden (white shirt) make the trophy presentations after the sevens tournament which was held at the end of their visit to Rwanda.

Both photographs above are used courtesy of Two Up Front

2011 CHRONICLE

2nd March - Penguins beat Oxford University 43 - 10 at Iffley Road, Oxford.

9th March - Penguins beat Cambridge University 47 - 36 at Grange Road, Cambridge.

23rd March - Altus Kowloon Tens, Hong Kong. Captained by John Kerr (Scotland).
King Penguins drew with Playmore Phantoms 0 - 0
King Penguins beat DEA 14 - 12
King Penguins beat Pot Bellied Pigs 21 - 0
Quarter-final: King Penguins beat People's Liberation Army 14 - 0
Semi-final: King Penguins beat Rwanda Silverbacks 7 - 0
Final: King Penguins lost to Playmore Phantoms 7 - 21

24th and 25th March - Hong Kong Tens. Captained by Jordan Smiler (New Zealand).
Penguins beat Playmore Devil's Advocate 83 - 0
Penguins beat Hong Kong Chairman's X 21 - 7
Penguins beat Wild Titans (Germany) 17 - 7
Semi-final: Penguins lost to Asia Pacific Barbarians 10 - 17

4th - 5th June - London Tens Rugby Festival, London. Captained by Hugh Hogan (Ireland).
Penguins drew with Bootleggers 10 - 10
Penguins beat Wanchai Wanderers 48 - 5
Penguins beat Nice 44 - 0
Final: Penguins beat Bootleggers 36 - 7
Winners, London Tens Rugby Festival

4th - 6th November - Singapore Cricket Club Sevens. Captained by Willie Walker (New Zealand).
Penguins beat Casuarina Cougars (Australia) 33 - 7
Penguins beat Indonesian Harimau 57 - 0
Penguins beat COBRA (Malaysia) 12 - 10
Penguins beat French Pyrenees 38 - 7
Quarter-final: Penguins beat Japan Samurai 26 - 5
Semi-final: Penguins lost to Borneo Eagles 17 - 24

12th - 13th November - HSBC/COBRA International Tens, Malaysia. Captained by Willie Walker (New Zealand).
Penguins beat Shanghai Hairy Crabs (China) 58 - 0
Penguins beat Northlink (RSA) 45 - 0
Penguins beat COBRA (Malaysia) 19 - 17
Quarter-final: Penguins beat Ponsonby (New Zealand) 22 - 15
Semi-final: Penguins beat Borneo Eagles 17 - 15
Final: Penguins beat COBRA (Malaysia) 12 - 10
Winners, HSBC/COBRA Tens

2011 Yet another very successful year started with an HSBC Penguin International Coaching trip, when the Academy delivered coaching support as a part of the HSBC Dubai Festival which was held on February 18th and 19th. The festival was held for up to 2000 children aged 5 - 17 from across Dubai and the UAE, and also included two teams from Russia. The two HSBC Penguin International Academy Coaches (Gordon 'Sesh' Henderson and Ben Fisher) were there to offer a range of coaching on an open invitation basis at any time throughout the festival.

In the first of the annual Varsity matches, on Wednesday, 2nd March, HSBC Penguins (Captained by open-side flanker Tom George, also the Captain of Richmond FC) beat Oxford University 43 - 10 in an exciting game at Iffley Road - scoring no fewer than seven tries in the process.

HSBC Penguins played Cambridge University only seven days later at Grange Road, Cambridge, running out 47 - 36 winners after an immensely enjoyable, all-action display by both sides in which Penguins outscored the students by seven tries to six. HSBC Penguins were Captained on the night by Rosslyn Park scrum-half Graham Barr.

Steve Hill coached the HSBC Penguins on both occasions and Ben Dormer and Bill Calcraft were the Match Managers. The Cambridge match was also noteworthy in that it was the first outing for the Club since agreeing a new playing strip sponsorship deal with Tsunami. As Bill Calcraft said on the night: 'The new strip looks fantastic and it's great to be associated with a company that provides top sportswear.'

Tsunami's new Penguin International RFC playing strip.

Early Spring also brought with it a reorganisation of the PIRFC Management and Executive Committees. Three long-standing and hard-working Committee Members retired due to work commitments and relocation.

Tom Wacker retired as Chairman due to moving to the USA, but remained

the Club's Country Representative for the USA.

Mike Cordell retired as Club Secretary due to work and RFU commitments and joined the Club's Advisory Board. Mike continued in his dual roles as Secretary and RFU Council Member for the Kent Rugby Union.

Derek Morgan retired from the General Committee due to work and other rugby commitments, but joined the PIRFC Advisory Board.

The Club thanked all three for their invaluable contributions over the years, and looked forward to working with them again in their new roles.

Bill Calcraft and David Townsend were appointed Senior Vice-Presidents with a view to them working alongside President Richard Bennett. In addition, Vince Bramhall became acting Club Secretary.

HSBC Penguin Coaching Academy/IRB Trainers Doc McKelvey and Simon Jones visited Kuala Lumpur, Malaysia, between 6th - 12th March.

Their Courses included over 40 candidates, who were, for the most part, teachers from all over Malaysia. Doc and Simon ran a number of RFU CPD Courses which encompassed all aspects of play. All Courses went extremely well and were very popular with the candidates, and at the end Doc and Simon presented prizes and Penguin Course Certificates.

Newly appointed Senior Vice-President John Townsend and Club Secretary Vince Bramhall (seated) with Penguin International RFC CEO Craig Brown.

The HSBC Penguins' first overseas playing tour of 2011 took place between March 20th - 28th when the Club visited Hong Kong to take part in the Hong Kong Tens Tournament. The Club contingent that travelled to Hong Kong numbered about 90. It included a first team (under the guidance of former Scotland coach Frank Hadden), the Academy and a more social King Penguins selection who were to compete in the Kowloon RugbyFest.

In the week leading up to the Tournament itself, the HSBC Penguin International Coaching Academy - ably led by former Hong Kong national team prop forward Dean Herewini and including Foz Herewini, Abby Wills, Ben Breeze, the HSBC Penguins Tens squad and the King Penguins - ran clinics alongside the likes of All Blacks legends Jonah Lomu and John Kirwan together with Lawrence Dallaglio - the former British Lion and England Captain.

During the course of the week Herewini and the HSBC Penguin Coaching Academy completed a whirlwind tour of clinics for groups from Rwanda, South Africa, New Zealand, China and Hong Kong, with venues ranging from Sandy Bay and Sai Kung to Happy Valley and Hong Kong Football Club.

Dean Herewini explains: 'The HSBC Penguins players come to play in the Hong Kong Tens and watch the IRB Sevens, but when they leave, they often say that their best memory is that of coaching 120 kids!'

Above: The Academy in Hong Kong - including Foz Herewini, John Kirwan, Jonah Lomu, Dean Herewini and Abby Wills.
Below: Foz Herewini with Abby Wills and Lawrence Dallaglio.

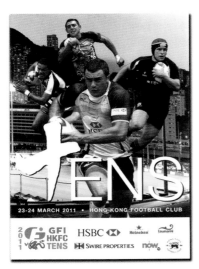

2011 Hong Kong Tens Tournament Programme.

On 23rd and 24th March the Club were ready for another crack at winning the Hong Kong Football Club Tens Tournament - their fifth attempt.

The team (Captained by New Zealander Jordan Smiler) had trained well in the run-up to the event: there had been the usual rustiness on day one as a result of the travel and the fact this was the first time the team had trained together, but Coaches McKittrick and Hadden set out the tactics for the Tournament and the HSBC Penguins worked well in adapting and refining the Coaches' ideas.

As usual, the HKFC Tens had attracted some great sides - there would be no easy games once the quarter-finals started. On day one the Club beat the Playmore team and the Hong Kong Chairman's X convincingly, and in the quarter-final on day two the Wild Titans from Germany were beaten by 17 points to 7.

In the semi-final HSBC Penguins came out of the blocks too slowly - allowing the Asia Pacific Barbarians (Captained by the brilliant Justin Marshall) to get a lead that could not be pulled back. Although the HSBC Penguins played very well and almost overtook them, the final score was 10 - 17 to the Barbarians.

The HSBC Penguins' results in the 2011 Hong Kong Football Club Tens were: HSBC Penguins beat Playmore Devil's Advocate 83 - 0, HSBC Penguins beat Hong Kong Chairman's X 21 - 7. Quarter-final: HSBC Penguins beat Wild Titans (Germany) 17 - 7. Semi-final: HSBC Penguins lost to Asia Pacific Barbarians 10 - 17.

HSBC Penguins squad for the HKFC Tens.
Back Row: John McKittrick (Coach - former Cook Islands, USA and North Harbour Sevens coach), Roelof Smit (Waterkloof, Blue Bulls Academy, Borland Craven week team), Sam Hayes-Stevenson (Takapuna, Canterbury B, Crusaders Development), Adam McGrevy (Rangataua, Bay of Plenty Sevens), Paulo Kinikinilau (Alhambra-Union, Otago), Takerei Norton (Linwood, Canterbury), Paula Ngauamo (Burnside, Canterbury, Crusaders Development, New Zealand U20), Matthew Graham (East Coast Bays, North Harbour Development, New Zealand U20), Andrew Higgins (Exeter, Bath, England Sevens & A), Jack McPhee (Glenfield, North Harbour XVs & Sevens, New Zealand Sevens), Sam Cottam (Christchurch, Canterbury U21 & B, Crusaders Development).
Front Row: Craig Brown (Manager), Joel McKenty (Kamo, Northland, Waikato, Chiefs Development, New Zealand U16), Rae Wilson (Wainuiomata, Wellington Sevens & XVs, New Zealand U20), Nasoni Roko (Waimanu, Natisori, Fiji Sevens & XVs), Jordan Smiler (Hautapu, Waikato Sevens & XVs - Captain), Ash Moeke (Mid Western, Northland, Auckland), Andrew Williams (Marist St Joseph, Savaii Samoa, Samoa), Frank Hadden (Coach - former Edinburgh and Scotland coach).
In transit: Hang Kek Kang (Assistant Manager) and Callum Wootten (Liaison Officer).

Match action from the 2011 Hong Kong Football Club Tens.

HSBC Penguin International Coaching Academy Coaches, left to right: Dene Herewini, Ben Fisher, Tony Robinson, Gary Henderson and Lynn Evans. An impressive array of first-class rugby knowledge and experience!

The Astonishing Growth
of the HSBC Penguin International Coaching Academy

Some of the Academy's earliest top-class coaches have already been featured in this book - John McKittrick, Steve Hill, Grant McKelvey, Frank Hadden and, of course, Academy co-founder Craig Brown.

But since its inception in 2004, the HSBC Penguin International Coaching Academy has grown as rapidly as its reputation for excellence.

More and more highly qualified coaches have subsequently joined the Academy's roster - here are a few of them:

Dean Herewini Dean is one of the Academy's most enthusiastic supporters. He has coached extensively in New Zealand, including stints at Hautapu RFC and Waikato, and in Hong Kong where he was player/coach at Valley RFC. He moved to Jakata in 2001 and was instrumental in setting up the Indonesian RU. More recently Dean has lived in Malaysia, where he coached the RSC Club and the Borneo Eagles. He has coached the Malaysian National team for the past three years.

Ben Fisher Ben, who played for Boroughmuir RFC, is the current Scottish Rugby Union Edinburgh, West & Midlothian Perfomance Development Manager.

Tony Robinson Tony is the RFU Coach Development Officer for London North and a Middlesex County RU Coach.

Gary Henderson Gary is the current RFU Head of Coach and Player Development.

Lynn Evans Lynn played for Oxford RFC and was one of the first people to attend the RFU Coaching Course at Lilleshall. He was Oxford University Head Coach 1981 - 1995. Aged 70, he is now a contributor for the RFU Coaching Website.

Since its inception in 2001 at Hong Kong's Indian Recreation Club by a number of Kowloon players, the Kowloon Tens RugbyFest has not only grown greatly in size, but is now an integral part of Hong Kong's week of 7s/10s rugby. It is a tournament that embodies the true spirit and camaraderie of the game - ensuring enjoyment for all whilst not taking things too seriously!

Photographs from the Kowloon Tens.
Top: Action from the final.
Middle: The playing squad.
Bottom: At the post-tournament HSBC Reception

As part of the Hong Kong tour, the King Penguins played in the Altus Kowloon Tens. Kowloon was the social team's third fixture - and in keeping with the great traditions of the Penguins, this made three games in three different countries!

Ably led by David Harris and John Kerr, the team, comprised of older heads plus a sprinkling of youth from Stellenbosch University, combined well and after a slow start produced their best rugby against old friends the Rwandan Silverbacks in the semi-final of the competition, winning by the narrow margin of 7 points to nil. The consensus was that the Penguins are coaching the Silverbacks too well! In the final against the Playmore Phantoms, King Penguins monopolised the ball for the first five minutes, playing excellent sevens possession rugby in their own 22. Unfortunately it was tens rugby that was required and before they knew it the King Penguins were two tries down, losing to the better team on the day.

The Kowloon hospitality was tremendous and an unexpected bonus at the tournament dinner was the surprise entertainment provided by MC John Bentley, ex-British Lion (and, as it happens, an ex-Penguin, too - having played for the Club in the 1989 Hong Kong Sevens).

The team also fulfilled their Penguin duty in giving to others by taking part in excellent coaching sessions for young schoolboys, in particular at the Hong Kong Football Club. Here they were ably assisted by the great John Kirwan and Lawrence Dallaglio. The players also volunteered their services to a charity fashion show as catwalk models - and so impressed the Society Ladies of Hong Kong that a repeat performance has been requested for next year!

Altus Kowloon Tens results:

Pool matches: King Penguins drew with Playmore Phantoms 0 - 0, King Penguins beat DEA 14 - 12, King Penguins beat Pot Bellied Pigs 21 - 0.

Quarter-final: King Penguins beat PLA 14 - 0

Semi-final: King Penguins beat Rwanda Silverbacks 7 - 0

Final: King Penguins lost to Playmore Phantoms 7 - 21

King Penguins at the Kowloon Tens:

Craig Brown (CEO), John Zimnoch (Team Manager), Yuill Irvine (Bagman).

John Kerr (Watsonians, Captain), Ben Breeze (Bristol), Ashley Cole (Mosman Whales), Gordon Dickson (Watsonians), Ross Ferry (Metropolitan Police), Marc Figgins (Old Varstonians), David Harris (Watsonians), Ian Hope (Dundee HSFP), Graeme Inglis (Mosman Whales), Nigel Jeynes (Wales), Paul Raeburn (Watsonians), Andrew Schorn (Stellenbosch), Tom Schorn (Stellenbosch), Iain Sinclair (Watsonians), Dawid Swart (Stellenbosch), Michael Tack (Stellenbosch), Keith Wallace (Haddington), Jon Williams (Old Varstonians).

The Rosslyn Park HSBC National School Sevens Tournament took place between 28th March - 1st April. This famous tournament now boasts 7,500 participants aged from 13 to 19, with both boys and girls taking part in the various different competitions during the week. Over 700 teams of all levels from across the UK as well as five international visiting teams from Denmark, Spain, Nigeria, Romania and Kenya played in the tournament, which was celebrating its 72nd year.

HSBC Penguin International Coaching Academy Coach Hugh Campbell joined HSBC Ambassador Jason Robinson and coaches from the HSBC RFC to run a number of specialist coaching sessions for the teams at the tournament.

Throughout the tournament teams would drop by to the designated coaching area for specific coaching including special skills and drills sessions, to help the teams advance in the tournament - and also to inspire the boys and girls involved in the tournament.

It had been a long time since the Penguins last made a visit to Sri Lanka - 1979, to be precise. On that occasion the Club was asked by the Rugby Union to field a side to represent the RU in order to celebrate the Sri Lankan Rugby Union's Centenary Season. The result was a Tour by a strong Penguins' squad, Captained by Irish international Mickey Quinn. The Penguins won all six matches played.

32 years later, former Scotland Coach Frank Hadden found himself leading the HSBC Asian RFU Rugby Coaching Tour's activity in and around Colombo between the 20th - 23rd April - the first week of the 2011 HSBC Asian 5 Nations.

After coaching HSBC staff at the historic Ceylonese Rugby and Football Club in Colombo on Wednesday, Frank enjoyed his first visit to an SOS Children's Village in Piliyandala on the Thursday before coaching a gathering of developing rugby schools on Friday.

Saturday, 4th June brought with it the beginning of the inaugural two-day London Tens Festival. The format consisted of 24 teams playing in Open, Social and Vet's Divisions. The first day's play took place in the Old Deer Park in Richmond and the final rounds on Sunday 5th were played at the Richmond Athletic Ground - home of Richmond FC, the Club of HSBC Penguins' Coach Steve Hill.

HSBC Penguins, Captained by Hugh Hogan of St. Mary's College, Dublin and comprised of players from London, Northampton, Bedford, Edinburgh, Lisbon and Dublin, took the overall Tens Champions title, winning the Open Cup Final against Bootleggers RFC from Oxford.

HSBC Penguin International Academy Coach Hugh Campbell and HSBC Ambassador Jason Robinson at the Rosslyn Park HSBC National Schools Sevens.

Frank Hadden coaching in Sri Lanka as part of the HSBC Penguin International Coaching Academy/HSBC Asian RFU Rugby Coaching Tour.

London Tens pre-tournament.
Top: Ben Gotting and HSBC Penguins' Coach Steve Hill.
Above: The pre-match team talk.

Winning the inaugural London Tens Festival was a terrific result for the Club in a competition that will surely go from strength to strength in years to come - and hopefully provide an annual opportunity to see the HSBC Penguins playing the abbreviated game in the UK.

The HSBC Penguins' tournament results were: HSBC Penguins drew with Bootleggers 10 - 10; HSBC Penguins beat Wanchai Wanderers 48 - 5; HSBC Penguins beat Nice 44 - 0. Final: HSBC Penguins beat Bootleggers 36 - 7. HSBC Penguins won the London Tens.

Above: The PIRFC Tens squad which won The London Tens Festival.
Back row, left to right: Steve Hill (Coach), Tim Little (Eastern Province and USA), Nigel Southcombe (Westcombe Park), Hugh Hogan (St. Mary's College, Dublin and Irish Amateurs, Captain), Aaron Johnstone (Canada), Tim Catling (Moseley), Chris Eves (Massey, North Harbour Development), Arthur Brenton (Coventry), Jason Welburn (Oxford Harlequins), Craig Brown (CEO).
Front row, left to right: Nigel Clarke (Manager), Phil Ellis (Blackheath), Graham Barr (Esher), Chris Lewis (Coventry), Xavier Andre (Henley), James Strong (London Welsh), Matt Price (Rugby Lions), Ben Gotting (London Scottish, England U21).
Left: More photographs from the London Tens Tournament.

Two Penguin International RFC stalwarts. Lynn Evans (right) receives an RFU Lifetime Achievement Award for Coaching from RFU Junior Vice-President Bob Reeves. Bob presented the trophy to Lynn during a ceremony at Heythrop Park in Oxfordshire.

The summer brought with it the very welcome news that PIRFC Honorary Vice-President R.A. Reeves had been elected as the Rugby Football Union Junior Vice-President. Bob played for Preston Grasshoppers RFC but retired from playing in his early twenties due to knee trouble. He moved to the City of Bristol to work at Bristol University over 30 years ago and coached University of Bristol RFC for more than 25 years, taking them to four finals at Twickenham. Bob also coached English Universities and England Students for many years and had three stints where he was involved in coaching the Bristol Rugby Club. Bob has also been a very helpful Penguins Selector in the past. He is presently Director of Sport, Exercise and Health at the University of Bristol.

Bob has been Chairman of the Students Rugby Football Union since 2001 and he has represented Students on the full RFU Committee since 1995. For most of this time Bob has worked alongside fellow Penguin Honorary Vice-

President and Student Rugby Football Union President Derek Morgan - who is himself an RFU Past President and a member of the PIRFC Advisory Board.

It is interesting to note that if all goes well, Bob should be the President of the Rugby Football Union in 2014 - the same year that Penguins celebrate their 55th Anniversary.

HSBC Penguin Academy Coaches pose with Louis Triay QC (centre) in Gibralta. Coaches, left to right: Dave Southern, Gary Henderson, Rob Clilverd and Mark Harrington.

Following a proposal made by PIRFC President Richard Bennett to PIRFC Life President Alan Wright some years back that Gibralta might be appreciative of rugby coaching support, Alan visited Gibralta and enlisted the services of Penguin Hon. Vice-President Louis Triay QC to assist in the organisation of such a visit. Louis arranged a meeting in his offices with officials of the Gibralta RFC, during which it was decided that the HSBC Penguin International Coaching Academy would provide a programme to this well-established and ambitious Club to assist all of their XVs.

PIRFC CEO Craig Brown then took over the organisation of the visit and arranged for four HSBC Penguin International Coaching Academy coaches (Rob Clilverd, Mark Harrington, Gary Henderson and Dave Southern) to travel to Gibraltar. The four men met up with Gibraltar Rugby Union Secretary Chad Thompson and other rugby officials for four days of official IRB courses and grass-roots coaching. The visit took place between 28th September - 2nd October.

In November the HSBC Penguins and the HSBC Penguin Coaching Academy set off on their second joint tour of grassroots coaching in Singapore and Malaysia, allied to competing in the Singapore Cricket Club Sevens in Singapore and HSBC/COBRA Tens in Kuala Lumpur.

This was the third year in a row that the HSBC Penguin Coaching Academy had visited Singapore, but the first time it had joined forces with the HSBC ARFU Rugby Coaching Tour - an exercise which reached 3000 children in 11 countries and territories in 2011. This built on the success of the two previous trips and the success of the SCC Sevens-winning HSBC Penguins team of 2010.

Ben Fisher and Sai Nawavu ran all of the sessions and were aided by Dean Herewini when his schedule of helping the Club's playing squad allowed.

The Singapore coaching sessions included: The NIE University, where 35 trainee teachers were given new ideas to help introduce the game when they move into schools in 2012; 'Rugby Fit International' training for 40 boys; Monfort

Frank Wagenstroom from Cape Town was the winner of the 2011 HSBC Penguin Rugby Award at the Investec International Rugby Academy High Performance Player course in June. Frank was selected by the course coaches, including Gary Gold and Dick Muir (current Springbok coaches), Murray Mexted (IRANZ MD) and Australian master coach, John Connolly. The award was presented by CEO Craig Brown at the course venue in Konka, north west of Johannesburg. Frank (a wing three-quarter) has represented South Africa at U18, U19 and U21 level (he was a member of the victorious South African U21 World Cup team), and as part of the Sharks Super 14 squad. He has also played in many Currie Cup games. Frank was a popular winner among the other 27 players on the course. As part of the prize, Frank was selected to take part in the November 2011 HSBC Penguins tour to the SCC Sevens and the HSBC/COBRA Tens in Kuala Lumpur.

Flying the flag! Penguin International RFC supporters and officials at the Singapore Cricket Club Sevens.

Secondary School training 25 boys aged between 14 and 16.

As well as coaching local rugby players, the Academy also conducted sessions at international schools as well - including the United World College and The Aussie International School. However, the biggest session of the week was at the SCC Festival itself where over 100 boys from a range of schools were invited down to participate in fun and coaching.

The last session of the week was at Centaurs RFC and had the added excitement of two HSBC Penguins players (Mat Luamanu and Josh Hohneck) coming along to help out.

All-in-all the HSBC Penguin International Coaching Academy carried out a total of nine sessions on this Singaporean leg of the tour which involved over 500 young players and students.

The PIRFC Singapore Cricket Club Sevens squad. Standing, L to R: John McKittrick (Coach), Andi (Liaison officer), Codey Rei, Vili Fihaki, Ray Niuia, Matt Vant Leven, Willie Walker (Captain), Andy Ritchie, Frank Wagenstroom, Carl Axtens, Phil Tuigamala, Craig Brown (Manager), Hot Rod McIntosh (Coach). Kneeling, L to R: Tua Saseve, Karl Bryson, Holly Moyes (Mascot), Ben Paltridge

The Australian Sevens outfit Casuarina Cougars were comfortably beaten on Friday night.

From a playing point of view, the first objective of the tour was to try and complete the first leg of 'the double' - by defending the SCC Sevens crown the Club won in 2010. HSBC Penguins' Coaches John McKittrick and Rod McIntosh instigated two training sessions per day and managed to arrange a practice match against the hosts, the SCC Sevens team.

The Club was drawn in Pool F as the top seed which meant a late start to matches. On the Friday night the team managed a respectable win over the Casuarina Cougars from Darwin. The second match on Saturday morning against Indonesian Harimau was similar to the first and the HSBC Penguins knew they would face a much stiffer challenge against their close friends from COBRA in the final pool match. Indeed, the COBRA match was a classic. Both sides were committed to defence but also looked to break the line when they could. The HSBC Penguins held a 12 - 0 lead with four minutes remaining in the match. But then a yellow card against the Club brought COBRA right back into the match. With only a minute to go COBRA had a conversion which would have drawn the match 12 - 12 but the kick hit the post. The final score was a 12 - 10 victory for the HSBC Penguins.

The first game on Sunday was a last-16 contest against the French Pyrenees. The Club started well and by half-time had a commanding 21 - 7 lead. A further three second-half tries saw the Club progress through to the last eight.

Next came the match against Samurai. The physical style of the Club saw them turn at the break 21 - 0 in front. Whilst the second half saw Samurai come back into the game, the HSBC Penguins ultimately ran out 26 - 5 winners.

The semi was against a Borneo Eagles team with plenty of Kiwi firepower in its ranks. From the kick-off HSBC Penguins scored out wide through HSBC Penguins Rugby Award-winner Frank Wagenstroom - but lapses in concentration in defence saw Borneo take a 7 - 12 lead into the break. Borneo came out all guns blazing in the second half and an early try saw them increase their lead to 7 - 17. The Club replied with another try to Wagenstroom to close to 12 - 17, but in the defining moment of the game, Phil Tuigamala chipped a kick ahead for what could have been a decisive try, but appeared to be tackled rather late. The ball bounced into the hands of a Borneo player who ran 80 metres to score. A late try to Tua Saseve narrowed the gap, but time had run out and the HSBC Penguins were eliminated.

Singapore Cricket Club Sevens Results (4th - 6th November)
HSBC Penguins beat Casuarina Cougars (Australia) 33 - 7; HSBC Penguins beat Indonesian Harimau 57 - 0; HSBC Penguins beat COBRA (Malaysia) 12 - 10; HSBC Penguins beat French Pyrenees 38 - 7.
Quarter-Final: HSBC Penguins beat Japanese Samurai 26 - 5
Semi-Final: HSBC Penguins lost to Borneo Eagles 17 - 24.

For the HSBC/COBRA Tens Malaysian leg of the tour, the Club was joined by HSBC Penguins Academy Coach Flo Rossigneux. The Coaching Academy group was now eight strong and included three Academy Coaches plus Martini Ip from the Hong Kong Ladies' team and Charlie French from the Hong Kong Mens' team.

During another very busy week, Academy coaching sessions included: Mersing, where over 100 boys from local secondary schools were coached; Pekan, where the Academy ran a session for 55 players from two boarding schools; Kuantan, where the Academy ran two sessions for over 100 boys from three boarding schools; Temoloh, where 55 boys had a two-hour session, and last

COBRA, Pyrenees Rugby Sevens and Samurai International RFC were all beaten on the way to the Singapore Cricket Club Sevens semi-final.

Flo Rossigneux and Dene Herewini in action with the Academy.

Boys from the Agathian's Shelter listen to Ben Fisher with Sailosi Nawavu looking on, at a Coaching Academy session near the COBRA rugby club in Petaling Jaya.

but not least, the Agathian's Shelter (a welfare home that cares for orphans and abandoned, neglected or abused children) where the Academy session was based around fun games and an introduction to rugby.

This proved to be yet another very successful Malaysian Coaching trip for the Academy, covering, as it did, a diverse range of development activities.

The consensus among the HSBC Penguin International Coaches was that there are some very talented young players in Malaysia - and hopefully, within the right structures, they will develop into potential international players of the future.

The Club's playing squad also arrived in Malaysia on Monday to begin their preparations for the HSBC/COBRA Tens Tournament which was to start on Saturday.

Tuesday was a busy day with two training runs and a session coaching the local rugby team. John McKittrick's main task was to switch the HSBC Penguins' playing style from sevens to tens mode. The squad concentrated on scrums and lineouts, as these aspects of the game feature much more in tens rugby.

The HSBC Penguins played the local side JLJ in a practice tens match on Wednesday morning. This was a very useful exercise as it enabled the lads to play a match together for the first time and gave the team some experience of local conditions (hot and wet!).

The team transferred to Kuala Lumpur on Wednesday afternoon and the rest of the week was spent training for the Tournament. By Saturday morning the

Penguin International RFC HSBC COBRA Tens team. Back row, L to R: John McKittrick (Coach), Matt Vant Leven, Ben Paltridge, Vili Fihaki, Andy Ritchie, Carl Axtens, Mat Luamanu, Tua Saseve, Josh Hohneck, Craig Brown (Manager), Rod McIntosh (Coach).
Front row, L to R: Frank Wagenstroom, Karl Bryson, Willie Walker (Captain), Ray Niuia, Phil Tuigamala. Inset: Malik (Liaison Officer), Codey Rei.

team was well prepared - but the day ahead would be a new challenge for most of them, as few had played in such hot and humid conditions.

The first match was against the Shanghai Hairy Crabs RFC. This was a relatively easy game to start the tournament with, which HSBC Penguins won 58 - 0. The match enabled all in the squad to get at least half a game and ease them into playing tens in the testing conditions.

The second match was against Northlink from South Africa - usually a strong team and regulars at the HSBC/COBRA Tens. Northlink had proved to be a troublesome opponent in the past, but after a hard-fought first spell HSBC Penguins eventually came away with a convincing 45 - 0 victory. Frank Wagenstroom dotted down no fewer than four tries playing against his fellow countrymen.

Prior to the last match of the day both the HSBC Penguins and COBRA teams lined up on the half-way line and joined with the crowd for a moment's silence as a mark of respect to their great friend Hang Kek Kang, who passed away on 12th September, 2011.

The COBRA and Penguin International RFC players and officials paying their respects to the memory of their late, great friend, Hang Kek Kang.

As expected, COBRA were always going to be the 'test match' in pool play. They took a 0 - 7 lead into the break, but a more direct pattern of play in the second half saw the HSBC Penguins take a close match by 19 points to 17.

The first game on Sunday was the quarter-final against Ponsonby from New Zealand. The game kicked off in very hot and humid conditions. Both teams were striving for a place in the semis, so the pace and physicality was intense. The Club scored first after some good ball control, showing they had the ability to build pressure and worry the opposition defence. Not to be outdone, the Auckland side struck back immediately, putting the Club under pressure. After half-time both teams re-focused and played some entertaining, attacking rugby. However, the bigger HSBC Penguins forwards eventually laid the platform for a solid win.

As had happened the previous week in Singapore, the HSBC Penguins found themselves up against Borneo Eagles in the semi-final. At the end of a very physical opening ten minutes the Club led 5 - 0. This time, however, control was maintained throughout the second spell and only a last-minute try by Borneo made the eventual 17 - 15 margin seem such a close one.

Near the end of the Club's semi a torrential downpour saw the playing surface become waterlogged and the COBRA v Canterbury semi was delayed by

Action from the HSBC/COBRA Tens.

an hour. When the match resumed COBRA ran out winners - so the final was a repeat of the last game of day one. Injuries to Codey Rei and Mat Luamanu saw the Club draft in Nafi Tuitavake and Ash Parker from Hong Kong Club Tradition RFC.

Vili Fihaki opened the scoring for the HSBC Penguins with a try from 40 metres after a lineout steal, but continual COBRA pressure saw them take a 5 - 10 lead into the break. Midway through the second spell Tua Saseve scored for the HSBC Penguins close to the posts and Karl Bryson converted - giving the Club a 12 - 10 lead. Back came COBRA with a continuous period of attack, camping on the HSBC Penguins' line. After surviving over three minutes of goal-line pressure the Club was awarded a drop-out 22. This was duly kicked dead and the referee blew the whistle for full-time.

The winning HSBC Penguins Tens squad celebrate their glorious back-to-back triumph in Malaysia.

This was the fifth time that the Club had won the HSBC/COBRA Tens title, and the second time HSBC Penguins had won back-to-back HSBC/COBRA Tens titles (the previous double having been in 1993-'94).

The emphasis on defence certainly paid dividends, with the opposition only managing to convert one out of the 11 tries they scored throughout the tournament as the HSBC Penguins scrambling defence pushed all tries conceded out wide. And when one considers that seven of the 14 HSBC Penguins players were affected by a stomach bug, the win was even more monumental!

HSBC COBRA Tens Results (12th and 13th November)

HSBC Penguins beat Shanghai Hairy Crabs (China) 58 - 0; HSBC Penguins beat Northlink (RSA) 45 - 0; HSBC Penguins beat COBRA (Malasia) 19 - 17.

Quarter-final: HSBC Penguins beat Ponsonby (New Zealand) 22 - 15.

Semi-final: HSBC Penguins beat Borneo Eagles (Malaysia) 17 - 15.

Final: HSBC Penguins beat COBRA (Malaysia) 12 - 10.

HSBC Penguins won the HSBC/COBRA Tens for the second year running.

It is with a sense of some satisfaction that this history of the PIRFC can be brought to a close by referring to the four great back-to-back triumphs that the Club has achieved in the last 53 years - namely: reaching (against all the odds) the semi-finals against the All Blacks in the Hong Kong Sevens of 1987 and 1988; the two extraordinary Middlesex Sevens triumphs of 1999 and 2000, and the magnificent 'Double Double' of winning the Malaysian COBRA Tens Tournaments of 1993 & 1994 and, more recently, 2010 & 2011.

And so ended a most successful year for the Club - a year which brought with it glorious wins against Oxford and Cambridge University XVs on consecutive Wednesdays in March, another great UK win in the inaugural London Tens Festival in June and the glorious 'double' triumph in the November HSBC/COBRA Tens - without doubt, the toughest and most prestigious tens tournament in the world. Penguins are very proud that this history book has ended at this pinnacle point!

When the Club's fame on the playing field is added to the wonderful, worldwide, runaway success that is the HSBC Penguin International Coaching Academy, it becomes clear that the Penguins' star is in the ascendancy - and still burning very brightly!

AFTERWORD

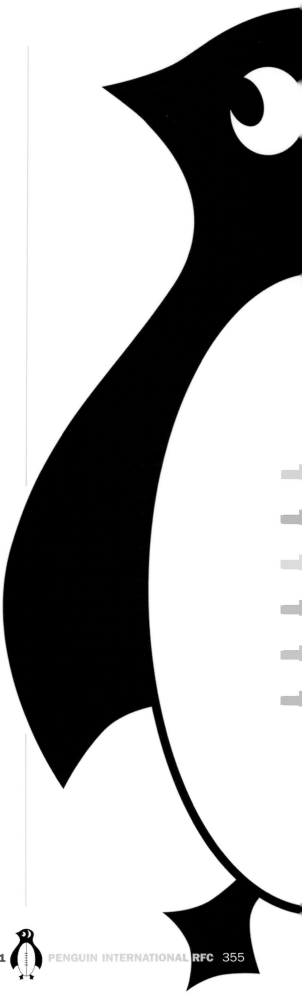

The Penguins, like all other *clubs by invitation*, have been swept along on a flood of change. The late Roy Fawden (a former President of Saracens and Chairman of London Senior Clubs) once said of the introduction of league rugby in England that he wondered what kind of monster he and others had helped to create. The monster, in the end, turned out to be professional rugby and English rugby is still trying to tame it.

Since the onset of league rugby and then professionalism, the Penguin Club has streamlined and modernised itself without losing its character. Alan Wright once said to me: 'What is crucial is that we have good people running the Club, team men who understand the need to evolve and to move with the times - but who are also concious of retaining rugby's historic values.' And it holds true that, for everybody involved with the Penguin International Rugby Football Club, rugby remains an amateur game - to be played for enjoyment and in the Corinthian spirit. The kind of rugby football which is built on friendship, skill, pride - and of putting the welfare of the players first. That is, a game without cynicism.

The Club likes to think that rugby union's governing bodies in the many countries and territories that the Penguins have visited over the years have recognised these qualities too - because at the end of every tour the Club has ever undertaken, it has been invited back to tour again.

As the Penguins enter their 54th year I think there is every hope that the Club will continue to prosper and afford enjoyment to succeeding generations of top rugby players from all over the world who may otherwise never get to know the joys of touring with an invitational side.

But there is now much more to the Club than just *playing* rugby union football, of course. Through the foundation of the Penguin International Rugby Football Trust and the HSBC Penguin International Coaching Academy, the Penguins will leave a lasting legacy - not only by spreading our wonderful code all over the world, but also by coaching young players in the game's skills and ethos, and, probably most importantly, by teaching men how to coach our great game.

I know I speak for every member of the Penguins when I say that this marvellous Club is extremely proud that the image of the Penguin which adorns its jersey has become a worldwide symbol of all that is good in the game.

Dick Tyson

September, 2012

PENGUIN INTERNATIONAL RFC HONOURS BOARD

PRESIDENTS

Field Marshall Sir Claude Auchinlech
GCB, CGIE, CSI, DSO, OBE, LLD.
1965 - 1981

Group Captain Sir Douglas Bader
CBE, DSO & BAR, DFC & BAR, FRAcS, DL.
1981 - 1982

Sir Robert Lawrence CBE, ERD (OA).
1983 - 1984

Douglas Harrison CBE
1984 - 1985

Air Commodore Bob Weighill CBE, DFC.
1986 - 2000

Sir Peter Yarranton
2000 - 2003

Sir William Purves CBE, DSO.
2003 - 2006

Alan Wright
2006 - 2009

Richard Bennett
2009 -

PATRONS

Alexander Flockhart CBE

Peter Sutherland KCMG

Andrew Thornhill QC

FOUNDERS
Tony Mason and Alan Wright

LIFE PRESIDENTS
Tony Mason 2001 - 2003
Alan Wright 2009 -

CHAIRMEN
Tony Mason 1959 - 2001
Alan Wright 2001 - 2006
Tom Wacker 2006 - 2010

DEPUTY CHAIRMEN
Craig Brown 2007 - 2009

CHIEF EXECUTIVE OFFICERS
Alan Wright 1999 - 2001
Ian Bullerwell 2001 - 2003
Craig Brown 2009 -

HON. SECRETARIES
Alan Wright 1959 - 2003
Mike Cordell 2003 - 2009
Vincent Bramhall 2010 -

HON. TREASURERS
John Morgan 1977 - 1995
Dennis Hearn 1995 - 1999
Julian Lamden 2000 - 2002
Tom Wacker 2003 - 2006
Robin Hutton 2006 -

SENIOR VICE-PRESIDENTS
Bill Calcraft and David Townsend 2011 -

HSBC PENGUIN INTERNATIONAL COACHING ACADEMY FOUNDERS
Alan Wright and Craig Brown

PENGUIN INTERNATIONAL RUGBY FOOTBALL TRUST FOUNDERS
Alan Wright and Andrew Thornhill QC

PENGUIN INTERNATIONAL RFC AND THE RUGBY FOOTBALL UNION

It is a source of great pride to the Penguins that, although the Club's fame is in the international field, over the years the Club has had more than its fair share of elite RFU personnel among its Presidents, Honorary Vice-Presidents and Vice-Presidents.

SIX PENGUINS WHO HAVE SERVED AS PRESIDENTS OF THE RFU:

Douglas Harrison - RFU President 1966 - 1967
(Penguin President 1986 - 1987)

Alan Grimsdell - RFU President 1986 - 1987 (Penguin Hon. V-P)

Captain Mike Peary - RFU President 1990 - 1991 (Penguin Hon. V-P)

Sir Peter Yarranton - RFU President 1991 - 1992
(Penguin President 2000 - 2003)

Derek Morgan - RFU President 2002 - 2003
(Penguin Hon. V-P & Advisory Board)

Robert Horner - RFU President 2003 - 2004 (Penguin Hon. V-P)

In addition to the gentlemen listed on the left, Bob Reeves (Penguin Hon. V-P) is currently (2012) the RFU Junior Vice-President, and is widely expected to serve as RFU President in 2014. Bob Weighill held the office of RFU Secretary between 1974 - 1986. It is a matter of interest that Bob first held the office of Penguin President (1986 - 2000) whilst still serving the RFU as Secretary - the first time that an RFU Secretary had ever held high office in a Club whilst still serving in the Union. Dudley Wood (Penguin Hon. V-P) held the office of RFU Secretary between 1986 - 1995, Derek Mann (Penguin Hon. V-P) was the Middlesex RU Member on the RFU Committee for many years and Mike Cordell (Penguin Past Hon. Sec.) is the RFU Council representative for Kent.

PENGUIN INTERNATIONAL RUGBY FOOTBALL CLUB

STATUS AND MEMBERSHIP

Penguin International RFC is an amateur rugby club, affiliated with the RFU. Membership of the Club is by invitation.

LIFE PRESIDENT

Alan G L Wright (Co-Founder of the Club and Patron of Penguin International Rugby Football Trust)

PATRONS

Alexander Flockhart CBE, Peter D Sutherland KCMG, Andrew R Thornhill QC (Chairman of the Trustees of Penguin International Rugby Football Trust)

CHARITY

The Club established Penguin International Rugby Football Trust, which is registered with the Charity Commission as an educational charity, to promote the training of youngsters in the skills of rugby and to provide scholarships, coaching and other assistance for that purpose.

GENERAL COMMITTEE

The Club's General Committee comprises the members of its Executive Committee, the members of the Coaching Advisory Board, certain members of the Management Advisory Board and the Trustees and Hon. Secretary of Penguin International Rugby Football Trust.

EXECUTIVE COMMITTEE

President **Richard E T Bennett**, Chief Executive **Craig S Brown**, Senior Vice-President **Bill Calcraft**, Senior Vice-President **David J Townsend**, Treasurer **Robin Hutton**, Club Secretary **Vincent E Bramhall**, Life President **Alan G L Wright** (ex officio)

COACHING ADVISORY BOARD

Head of Coaching and Trustee **Steve Hill** (RFU), Head of Coach Education **Gary Henderson** (RFU), Lead Coach Educator **Tony Robinson** (RFU), Head of Player Development **Grant McKelvey** (SRU), Lead Player Development Coach **Ben Fisher** (SRU)

MANAGEMENT ADVISORY BOARD

Dudley Ankerson, Jonathan Bremner (Hon. Secretary of Penguin International Rugby Football Trust), Ian Bullerwell (former International Referee), Mike Cordell (Hon. Secretary of Kent RFU and RFU Council representative for Kent), Robin DeMorgan (UK Reporter), Ben Dormer (Cambridge University Representative and Trustee), David Harris (King Penguins Manager), Derek Harris (International Ticket Manager and Trustee), Stephen Herring, Ian MacDonald, Derek Morgan (past RFU President 2008-09), Sir Alistair Mackechnie (Trustee), Paul Raeburn (Website Manager), Tim Stevens (Oxford University Representative), Dick Tyson (Historian and Information Secretary), Tom Wacker (Trustee), Ian Warbrick (Commercial Manager), Derek Wyatt, John Zimnoch (King Penguins Manager)

PENGUIN INTERNATIONAL RUGBY FOOTBALL CLUB COUNTRY REPRESENTATIVES

Argentina **Luis Criscuolo**
Australia **Bill Calcraft**
Canada **Gareth Rees & John Zimnoch**
Fiji **John Breen & Richard Breen**
France **Florent Rossigneux**

Hong Kong & Asia
Robbie McRobbie & David Townsend
Ireland **Brian Cusack**
Italy **Avv. Enzo Paolini**
New Zealand **John McKittrick & Gordon Tietjens**
Portugal **Antonio de Cunha**

Samoa **Faafouina Su'a**
Scotland **John Rutherford & Ian Sinclair**
South Africa **Paul Treu** (Coach, South Africa 7s)
USA **Tom Wacker**
Wales **Ben Breeze & Hugh Thomas**

PENGUIN INTERNATIONAL RUGBY FOOTBALL CLUB HONORARY V-Ps

A.A. Flockhart (Patron)
P.D. Sutherland KCMG (Patron)
A.R. Thornhill QC (Patron)
J. Addis
The Rt. Hon. Lord Blaker of Blackpool
KCMG PC
His Excellency, Mr. E.L. Boladuadua
Sir John Bond
J.R.P. Breen (Fiji)
J.R.W. Breen (Fiji)
Lord Butler of Brockwell KG GCB CVO
Prof. Hugh C. Burry (NZL)
Z.J. Cama
T.R. Carpenter
P. Cook
S. Fitzpatrick (New Zealand)
D. Flint CBE
G. Flowers (Australia)
M. Friday
S. Gmuender (Germany)
T. Grandage (India)
T. Gregory (Hong Kong)
A.A. Grimsdell
J.M. Grove (Hong Kong)
F. Hadden (Scotland)
D. Hearn
D. Hopley
R.W. Horner (Past President RFU)
A. Hosie (Scotland)
J.W.J. Hughes-Hallett

A. Hume (Scotland)
H.H. Tunka Imran (Malaysia)
A.R. Irvine (Scotland)
K-E. Jarlsborg (Sweden)
Professor B. Johnson
J.R. Kane (BER)
Rt. Hon. Neil Kinnock (Wales)
D. Kirk (New Zealand)
Air Chief Marshal Sir Michael Knight
KCB AFC FRAeS
K. Knowles
E. Krutzner (Czech Republic)
E.H. Lund (Denmark)
N. Mallett (Republic of South Africa)
D.C. Mann
R.W.D. Marques
Mrs. D. Mason
M. Mexted (New Zealand)
J. McKittrick (New Zealand)
N. Melville (CEO, USA Rugby)
H.M.P. Miles OBE
C. Morgan CVO OBE (Wales)
G. D. Morgan
G. Morgan
W.G.D. Morgan (Past President RFU)
K. Moyes (Singapore)
Dr. Chan Pen Mun (Singapore)
W. Osterling (Sweden)
P. Pask
I.G. Peck

D. Pickering (Wales)
Sir William Purves CBE DSO
M.A.M. Quinn (Ireland)
R. Quittenton
J.C.S. Rankin
I. Rawcliffe (Germany)
C. Rea (Scotland)
G. Rees (Canada)
R.A. Reeves
P. Ribeiro (Portugal)
I. Robertson (Scotland)
J. Rutherford (Scotland)
D.S. Sariputra (Thailand)
W. Serevi (Fiji)
F. Slattery (Ireland)
M.P. Smith (France)
M.R.P. Smith OBE
Air Chief Marshal Sir Peter Squire
GCB DFC AFC
J.S. Stevenson (Past President SRU)
T.B. Stevenson (President HKRFU)
B. Thomas (Wales)
G. Tietjens (New Zealand)
R. Wainwright (Scotland)
S.G.D. Walker
P.J. West
Ms A. Wills
D.E. Wood CBE
D. Wyatt

PENGUIN INTERNATIONAL RUGBY FOOTBALL CLUB BRITISH & IRISH LIONS

Paul Ackford (England)
Neil Back (England)
John Bentley (England)
Gareth Chilcott (England)
Maurice Coleclough (England)
Mike Gibson (Ireland)
Rob Henderson (Ireland)
David Irwin (Ireland)
Ken Kennedy Ireland)
Josh Lewsey (England)

Colin McFadyean (England)
Brian Moore (England)
Derek Morgan (England)
Tony Neary (England)
Charles Norris (Wales)
Phil Orr (Ireland)
John O'Shea (Wales)
Iain Paxton (Scotland)
David Powell (England)
Derek Quinnell (Wales)

Chris Rea (Scotland)
Mark Regan (England)
Andy Ripley (England)
Keith Savage (England)
Andrew Sheridan (England)
Fergus Slattery (Ireland)
Simon Taylor (Scotland)
Mike Teague (England)
Tony Underwood (England)
Jason White (Scotland)

In addition to the thirty players listed above, Martin Offiah, like John Bentley, played for the Great Britain Lions Rugby League Team.

PENGUIN INTERNATIONAL RFC PLAYING MEMBERSHIP, COACHING AND TOURS

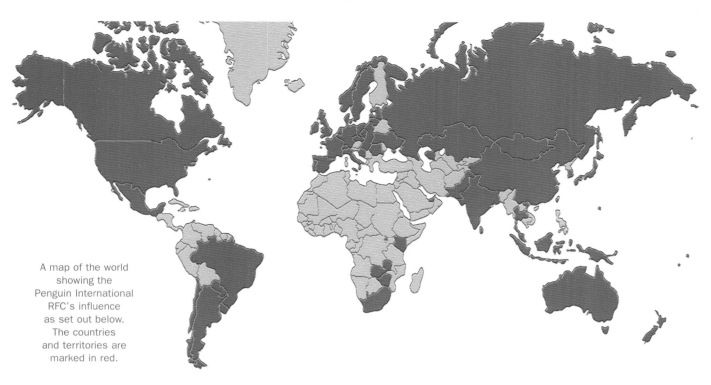

A map of the world showing the Penguin International RFC's influence as set out below. The countries and territories are marked in red.

INTERNATIONAL PLAYING MEMBERSHIP

THE PLAYING MEMBERSHIP OF THE CLUB HAS, TO DATE, BEEN DRAWN FROM NO FEWER THAN 32 COUNTRIES:

Argentina	Italy
Albania	Japan
Australia	Mexico
Bermuda	New Zealand
Canada	Portugal
Croatia	Romania
Czech Republic	Russia (CIS)
Denmark	Samoa
England	Scotland
Fiji	Sierra Leone
France	South Africa
Holland	Tonga
Hong Kong	USA
Hungary	Wales
Ireland	Zambia
Israel	Zimbabwe

PENGUIN INTERNATIONAL RFC TOURS

PENGUINS ARE THE WORLD'S PREMIER TOURING CLUB. PENGUINS ARE PROUD TO HAVE COACHED AND/OR PLAYED IN OR AGAINST TEAMS FROM 72 COUNTRIES/TERRITORIES (AS ABOVE):

Argentina	Holland	Paraguay
Australia	Hong Kong	Poland
Abu Dhabi	Hungary	Portugal
Belgium	India	Rhodesia
Bermuda	Indonesia	Romania
Borneo	Iran	Russia
Brazil	Ireland	Rwanda
Brunei Darussalam	Italy	Samoa
Cambodia	Japan	Scotland
Canada	Jersey	Singapore
Chile	Jordan	South Africa
China	Kenya	South Korea
Croatia	Kazakhstan	Spain
Czech Republic	Laos	Sri Lanka
Czechoslovakia	Latvia	Sweden
Denmark	Macau	Switzerland
Dubai	Malaysia	Taiwan
England	Malta	Thailand
Fiji	Mexico	Tonga
France	Mongolia	Uruguay
Germany	New Zealand	USA
Georgia	Norway	USSR
Gibraltar	Pakistan	Wales
Guam	Papua New Guinea	Zambia

PENGUIN INTERNATIONAL RUGBY FOOTBALL CLUB V-Ps

A

G.G. Able
John Adler
R. Albert (USA)
R. Aldridge
R.C.P. Allaway QC (RSA)
Peter A. Allen
I. Anderson
John H.F. Anderson
Dr. Dudley C. Ankerson
Miss Maria Appleby
Peter Ayling
Robin V. Azis

B

Claus-Peter Bach
Dr. Mark Bailey
Simon Bailey
Angus Bain
M.G. Baker
James Bannister
R. Barnard (ZWE)
Ashley Barnes
John Barton
Philip Barwick
Miss T.M. Bateman
Paul Beal
P. Bell
David Bell
Colin P. Bennett
Jonathon R.T. Bennett
Paul R.T. Bennett
Sir Christopher Benson JP
James R.F. Berkeley
Grahame J.F. Berkeley
P. Berry
Jasvinder Singh Bhatt
Alan D.H. Black
Alan Black
Peter Blacker
Godfrey Blott
R.J. Boissier
Roger Boissier CBE
Dr. Alberto Bonavolonta
R.A. Booth
Javier Bordaberry (URG)
Randall S. Bowen CBE
Chief Cons T.J. Brain
OPM PhD
Vincent E. Bramhall
Oliver Breech
Ben Breeze
Jonathon S.G. Bremner
(SCO)
Peter Brennan
Lt. Cdr. H.J. Brickwood RN
David M. Briggs
Philip Brooks
Alan Brown
Peter A. Brown
Craig Brown
P.C. Brown (SCO)
W. Brown
John B. Buchanan
Stuart Buchanan-Smith
(SCO)
Ian M. Bullerwell
Chris Buttery

C

Alec Calcraft (AUS)
Bill Calcraft (AUS)
J.R. Caldwell

J.D. Camps-Harris
V. Cannon
E.J. Carpenter
G.B. Carpenter
Carlo Casagrande
Clifford R. Catt
Graeme C. Cattermole
Dr. Chan Peng Mun Chan
(SGP)
Carl Chan
M.J. Chapman
Dominic Cheetham
David Chisnall
Jon Chivers
Stephen Christie-Miller
M.J. Christmas
Sir Robin Christopher
KBE CMG
Pioter Ciechowski
Roger I. Clarke
Frederick Clelland
Jonathon C. Clelland
David R. Coffer FRICS,
PRPAS
F. Conklin (USA)
Cliff J. Cook
Michael Coombes
Mike R. Cordell
W.I. Corlett
D.P. Coskie
W. Cotton
Ian Coull
Sir Robert Crawford CBE
Luis Criscuolo (ARG)
Dr. A. Cull
Gus Cunningham QPM, CPM
(HKG)
Brian Cusack (IRL)
Peter Cutfield

D

António da Cunha (PRT)
DR.M. Danaher
Marc J. Daniel
C.M. Daughton
Sir David Davies
Dr. I. Davies
K.M. Davies
Michael J. Davies (WAL)
M.H. Davies
K.F. Davison
DChristopher C.C. de Jong
Dr. Pedro de Noronha Pissara
(PRT)
David de Yong
DD.T.H. Deagle
M.J. Deagle
Paul Denman
Danny Desmond
P.E. Dickinson (BEL)
M. Dives
P. Dixon
J. Dobinson
Alan Dodd (AUS)
Ben Dormer
Michael Dormer
B. Driver
Ian Duncan (PRT)
H.A. Dutton
Clive Dytor MC, MA

E

John Eales
Major G.R. Edwards
John Edwards

L. Edwards
N.G.B. Edwards
P. Edwards
Steven Eldridge
B.K. Elliott
Stewart Eru
R. Escot (FRA)
R. Evans
J. Evans
N. Evans

F

David Fairnie
Angus Falconer
P. Falconer
Timothy Fattorini
P.J. Fegen
J.J. Fenwick
Charles Ferguson
R. Ferry (SCO)
J. Finch
A. Finlayson (WAL)
Ben Fisher (SCO)
Ian M. Fitzsimon
Ken Flaherty
Joe Flaherty
Jim Fleming (SCO)
Peter Floyd
BDS, MSc
J. Flynn (IRL)
P. Follet
Ian Ford
John Foster
R.W. Fowles
Andre Fox (RSA)
J.N.M. Frame (SCO)
Riccardo Franconi
Michael Franks
G.A. Franks
J.A. Franks
Michael French

G

Mrs. D. Gaffney
J. Gainsford (RSA)
Peter A.J. Gardner OBE
John Gatehouse
D.J. Gay
M. Gee
J. Giannotti
S.G. Gibbons
I. Gibson
Sunil Gidumal (HKG)
A. Gifford
M. Gimblett
A. Glasgow
D. Glynn-Jones
(WAL)
Duncan Goldie-Morrison
C.T. Gosling
Major Howard Graham
Andrew Greystoke
D. Griffiths

H

S. Hall
Rupert N. Hambro
Ross Hamilton
G. Hammond
(BMU)
Dr. Robert Hancock
Robert J. Hancocks
David Harris
Derek P.C. Harris

C. Harrison
Philip Harvey
C. Haworth
Lord Andrew Hay
Peter Hayman
G.M. Heald
Paul D. Heber
A.C. Hemming
Gary Henderson
Archie Hendrickses
(RSA)
Charles Hendry MP
George Henry
Stephen J. Herring
George Herring
Ray Hewllett
Steven Hilditch
(IRL)
Steve Hill
Norman Ho (HKG)
R. Holmes
Christopher B. Horder
R.W. Horner
Mrs. V. Howarth
Gill Howarth
Nick Howe
T.F. Howe
Ms. L.V. Hughes
David F. Hughes
(HKG)
Dr. David Hughes
John W. Hughes
P.E. Hughes
A.C. Humphries OBE
D.R. Hutton

I

Graeme Inglis (SCO)
J.A.M. Innes QC
Malcolm Innes
Yuill Irvine (SCO)

J

Y.A.M. Tunku Tan Ja'afar
Hugh Jackson
Mark Jackson
P.R.J. Jarman
N. Jeffrey
David G. Jenner
Timothy Jensen (SGP)
Gordon Johnson
R.F. Johnson
Camille Jojo (HKG)
Dennis Jones
Stephen Jones
Morgan Jones
W. Jones (WAL)

K

Graydon Karlson
David Keane (IRL)
Hamish G.J. Keith (SCO)
P. d'A. Keith-Roach
M. Kemp
Dr. Robert M. Kennard
John Kennedy
C. Kerr
John Kerr (SCO)
Dean King
Richard Kinsey
David Kneller
Alan W. Knight
Keith Knowles
Kevin Knowles

L

C. Laity (WAL)
Michael Lake
Julian G. Lamden
Alan Lammin (HKG)
G. Landau
Jonathon S. Langlois
M. Lavery
Andrew J. le Chevalier
Peter Legg
Robert Lester
C.H. Lewis
David Lewis
M.R.M. Lewis
D.E. Lines (BMU)
Tony Ling
J.A. Linton
R.G. Lloyd
R.H. Lloyd (HKG)
Hamish Lock
Mrs. J. Logan (BMU)
Tony Lowrie
W.W. Lowson
R.W.P. Luff
Marco Lupo (ITA)
R.M. Lyons
Graeme A. Lythe

M

Ian M. MacDonald
K. MacGarrow
David Mackay
Edward Mackay
Sir Alistair Mackechnie
Gordon MacKenzie
David Maguire
Terence F. Mahony
Kublai Malik
David Marques
A.C. Marriott
Jim Martin
Philip J. Martin
A.J. Mason
M.A. Mason
John Masterton
Jim Masywale (NZL)
Andrew W. McAlpine
The Hon. David McAlpine
Ian M. McAlpine OBE
The Hon. William McAlpine Bt
Colin McCallum
Lord John McCluskey QC
R.F. McCormick
Iain McCrone CBE
Alison McDougall
Richard McFarlane
John McGowan (HKG)
John McGregor
Grant McKelvey (SCO)
W. McMaster
Donald McNab
Robbie McRobbie (HKG)
W. Mehrens (USA)
George Menzies (SCO)
C.H.R. Meyer
James Middleton
David Millard (SCO)
Alan C. Mitchell (HKG)
Michael J. Moir (HKG)
Douglas L. Montgomery
Robin Morgan
David Morgan
M.B. Morley (USA)
Keith Morris

Jamie Moyes
Kenny Moyes (Keith)
Brian Murdock
Iain Murray

N

Sailosi Nawavo (FJI)
Tony J. Neary
Ben J. Neary
Dan J. Neary
Bruce Newbigging
M.J. Newsom
Alasdair Nicholls
Robert Nimmo
M. Norrie (NZL)
Nigel Northridge
John Norton
P. Nove QPM

O

Patrick O'Connor
Ms. Marianne Okland
Lee O'Leary
H.B. Olsen
S. O'Reilly
The Hon. Robert Orr-Ewing
E.H. Owen (WAL)

P

Bernardino Paganuzzi
Jaco Page
R.H.J. Painter
Avv. Enzo Paolini (ITA)
M.A.G. Parker
William Parry
Giles Payne
Keith Peckitt
David Peirce (AUS)
Nick Penny (SCO)
Col. (R) Tommy Pereira (MYS)
Geoffrey Perkins
Eric Peters (SCO)
Stephen Picton-Pegg
Stephen Piercy
D.J. Piper
P. Plume
Brent Pope (NZL)
Campbell Povey (UAE)
A.T.H. Powell
D.L. Powell
T.S.T. Powell
H. Prevezer
Mark Prevezer
Charles E.R. Prewer
L. Prideaux
Dr. Roy Pryce
Miss Annie Pryer

R

Paul Raeburn (SCO)
David F. Ramsay
D. Ravitch (USA)
B.T. Read
R.W. Redwood
C. Rees
D. Rees
David Reid
M.H. Revill
Bernard Reynolds
D. Rhys-Williams
Nigel Rich CBE
Clive Richards OBE DL
B. Richardson

P.J.R. Riddell
A. Roberts (WAL)
Peter D. Roberts
W.B. Robertson (NZL)
Tony Robinson
Tony Rodgers
Maurizio Rodighiero (ITA)
Peter Rogers (SPR)
Jonathon Rosenthal
Florent Rossigneux (FRA)
D. Rowland
M. Ruda
E. Rumsey
G. Russell
Richard Russell (HKG)

S

Major Abdullah Khir Saidi (MYS)
Vijay Sarda
Jonathon Saunders
E. Schwartz (USA)
M.L. Schwartz (USA)
K. J. F. Scotland (SCO)
Richard Seale
Paul Selway-Swift (HKG)
Andrew Seth
David Sexon
W. Shaw
Christopher Sheasby
Derek Shepherd
Jonathon Shipsides
Iain Sinclair
Tim Sketchley
David Skillen (SPR)
Peter Smith
Eric Smith
Frank Smith
G.G. Smith
L. Smith
J. Smyth
C. Stacey (ZMB)
Tim Stevens
C.J. Stewart
Richard Stonehouse
R. Storry-Deans
Martin G. Sturgis
Faafouina Su'a
G.A. Sullivan
R.S. Sutherland
Sir Peter Sutherland KCMG
K. Svoboda (CAN)
Sir James Swaffield CBE, RD, DL
Anthony Swift
C. Syer (MYS)

T

Dato Krishnan Tan
P. Tarrant
Nicholas Tatman
Jan Tauber (CZE)
WIlliam Taylor
P.W. Taylor
M.R.B. Telford
R.R. Templeman
D. Thomas
Hugh Thomas
Nick H. Thomlison
A.R. Thornhill QC
H. Thornhill
George Thornhill
David Townsend (AUS)
David J. Townsend (HKG)
W.J. Townson
Paul Treu

Louis W. Triay QC LLB
P. Trower
H. Turnbull
Mike Turner
Robin Turner
Dick Tyson

U

Robert Udwin

V

Richard Vander
Frank Vandermeer (AUS)
Edward Villiers
Christopher I. von Christierson

W

T.J. Wacker (USA)
Brody Wacker
Scott Wacker
Keith Wallace
R. Wallace
T. Walsh (AUS)
D.R. Walter FCA
John D. Walters
Iain Watson
James. J. Watson (NIR)
S.R.A. Weighill
L.V. Wheeler
F.R. White
P.A. Whitelaw (SCO)
James Whitston
R. Wildman
R.M. Wilkinson
Michael Williams
R.M. Williams
Brian T. Willis (MEX)
A. Wills
John R. Wills Williams
Keith Wilson
Norman A. Wilson (SGP)
Magnus Wilson-Webb
Michael Winfield
James Winterbottom
D.J. Wise OBE
Col (R) Charlie Hin Jee Wong (MYS)
Guy Woodford
Craig Wooten (HKG)
C. Wright
Patrick A.L. Wright
Gregory A.F. Wright
John R. Wright
Mr. Alan G.L. Wright
James Wyness

Y

Mrs. Anna Yallop
David Yallop
Lady Yarranton
Nigel Yates
Neil Young
David J. Young
Zain Yusoff

Z

Ivan Zenovic
Hans Zimnoch
John Zimnoch (CAN)
J.M.G. Zinzan (NZL)

PENGUIN IRFC INTERNATIONAL TOURS, TOURNAMENTS AND TOUR CAPTAINS

2011

Hong Kong FC 10s - Jordan Smiler (NZ)

Kowloon 10s - John Kerr (Sco)

Singapore CC 7s - Willie Walker (NZ)

Malaysia - HSBC/COBRA 10s - Willie Walker (NZ)

2010

Hong Kong FC 10s - Nick Collins (NZ)

Portugal - Marcus Di Rollo (Sco)

Australian Parliament (Sydney) - Craig Brown (NZ)

Singapore CC 7s - Nafi Tuitavake(NZ)

Malaysia - HSBC/COBRA 10s - Shane Christie (NZ)

2009

Hong Kong FC 10s - James Afoa (NZ)

Malaysia - HSBC/COBRA 10s - Tony Penn (NZ)

2008

Hong Kong FC 10s - Craig De Goldi (NZ)

Italy - Italian RU 7s - Marc Camburn (NZ)

Malaysia - HSBC/COBRA 10s - Jordan Smiler (NZ)

Borneo - Invitational 10s - Jordan Smiler (NZ)

2007

Hong Kong FC 10s - Craig De Goldi (NZ)

Scotland (Orkney Isles) - Paul Beal (Eng)

Malaysia - HSBC/COBRA 10s - Scott Waldrom (NZ)

Borneo - COBRA 10s - Scott Waldrom (NZ)

2006

France - Rod Moore (Aus)

Malaysia - HSBC/COBRA 10s - Uale Mai (Sam)

Royal Kedah 7s - Uale Mai (Sam)

2005

Malta - Gareth Taylor (Wal)

Malaysia - HSBC/COBRA 10s - Howard Graham (Eng)

2004

Hong Kong - Craig De Goldi (NZ)

Mexico - Dave Gorrie (NZ)

Mexico RF 10s - James Winterbottom (Eng)

Malaysia RU-COBRA 10s - Howard Graham (Eng)

2003

Malaysia RU-COBRA 10s - David Gorrie (NZ)

2002

Portuguese 7s - Waisale Serevi (Fiji)

USA & Canada - Mark Denney (Eng)

2001

Germany & Argentina - Andre Fox (RSA)

Germany (Grand Prix of Europe) - Mike Friday (Eng)

Thailand - King's Cup 7s Tournament - Alan Bunting (NZ)

2000

People's Republic of China - Brian Cusack (Ire)

Middlesex Charity 7s, Twickenham - Waisale Serevi (Fiji)

Malaysia RU-COBRA 10s - Sailosi Nawavu (Fiji)

1999

Middlesex Charity 7s, Twickenham - Waisale Serevi (Fiji)

Croatia - Richard Kinsey (Eng)

Czech Republic & Poland - Brian Cusack (Ire)

Thai RU 7s Tournament - Cameron Pither (Aus)

1998

Croatia - Richard Kinsey (Eng)

Brazil & Chile - Brent Pope (NZ)

Singapore CC 7s - Craig Brown (NZ)

1997

Czech Republic & Hungary - Brent Pope (NZ)

Singapore CC 7s - Nick Penny (Sco)

1996

Malaysia RU-COBRA 10s - Craig Brown (NZ)

1995

Uruguay 7s - Craig Brown (NZ)

Malaysia RU-COBRA 10s - John Kerr (Sco)

1994

Malaysia RU-COBRA 10s - Craig Brown (NZ)

Sweden & Denmark - Rob Wainwright (Sco)

Scandinavian Stockholm 10s - Rob Wainwright (Sco)

Nordic 7s (Copenhagen) - Rob Wainwright (Sco)

Italian RU 7s - Craig Brown (NZ)

1993

Malaysia RU-COBRA 10s - David Pickering (Wal)

Ireland - Eric Peters (Sco)

Italian RU 7s - Chris Sheasby (Eng)

Malaysia & Singapore - Peter Cook (Eng)

Dubai - Phil Pask (Eng)

1992

Ireland (Irish RFU/Aer Lingus 7s) - Colin Laity (Wal)

Indonesia, Singapore & Hong Kong - Peter Cook (Eng)

1991

Italian RU 7s - David Millard (Sco)

1990

India (British Airways Calcutta Cup Centenary) - Kevin Rafferty (Sco)

Belgium - Bill Calcraft (Aus)

1989

Kenya - Peter Steven (Sco)

1988

Hong Kong 7s - Bill Calcraft (Aus)

Wales - David Pickering (Wal)

Cambridge University Volvo 7s - Paul Turner (Wal)

1987

Hong Kong 7s - Bill Calcraft (Aus)

1986

Bermuda - Mickey Quinn (Ire)

1985

Jersey & Scotland - David Pickering (Wal)

1984

Brazil & Paraguay - Nick Martin (Eng)

1983

Kenya - Vince Cannon (Eng)

1982

Bermuda - John Cantrell (Ire)

1980

Argentina - Nick Martin (Eng)

1979

Sri Lanka - Mickey Quinn (Ire)

Jersey - Jacko Page (Eng)

1978

Bermuda - John Frame (Sco)

1977

USSR (Eastern European Inter-Nations Championship) - Bob Wilkinson (Eng)

1976

Scotland - Ian Mclauchlan (Sco)

1975

Portugal - Ally Black (Sco)

Ireland - Martyn Davies (Wal)

1974

Bermuda - Jim Flynn (Ire)

Jersey & Ireland - John Frame (Sco)

1973

Rhodesia and South Africa - Fergus Slattery (Ire)

1972

Zambia - Derek Morgan (Eng)

1970

USA (California) - Colin MacFadyean (Eng)

1969

Denmark and Germany - David Powell (Eng)

1968

Zambia - Bill Redwood (Eng)

1967

Malta - Tony Mason (Eng)

1966

Portugal - Joe Armstrong (Eng)

1965

Germany and Belgium - Archie Hendrickses (RSA)

1964

Belgium, Denmark & Sweden - Tony Mason (Eng)

1963

France & Switzerland - Niggie Mee (Eng)

1961

Denmark - Tony Mason (Eng)

1959

Denmark, Sweden & Holland - Tony Mason (Eng)

PENGUIN INTERNATIONAL RFC RECORD IN 7S AND 10S COMPETITIONS

2011 HSBC/COBRA 10s **Winners**

2011 Singapore Cricket Club 7s Semi-finalists

2011 London 10s **Winners**

2011 Hong Kong Football Club 10s Semi-finalists

2010 HSBC/COBRA 10s **Winners**

2010 Singapore Cricket Club 7s **Winners**

2010 Hong Kong Football Club 10s Semi-finalists

2009 HSBC/COBRA 10s Semi-finalists

2009 Hong Kong Football Club 10s **Plate Winners**

2008 8th Borneo Invitational 10s **Winners**

2008 HSBC/COBRA International 10s Semi-finalists

2008 Rome International 7s Semi-finalists

2008 Hong Kong 10s Finalists

2007 7th Borneo COBRA Invitational 10s Finalists

2007 Hong Kong 10s Finalists

2006 Royal Kedah International 7s **Winners**

2006 HSBC/COBRA International 10s **Winners**

2005 Malaysia RU-COBRA International 10s Semi-finalists

2005 Malta RU International 15s **Winners**

2004 Malaysia RU-COBRA International 10s Semi-finalists

2004 Mexican RU International 10s **Winners**

2002 Portuguese Rugby Federation International 7s Finalists

2001 Thai RU International 7s Finalists

2001 Grand Prix of Europe 7s, Germany, **Winners**

2000 Malaysian RU-COBRA International 10s Semi-finalists

2000 Middlesex Charity 7s **Winners**

1999 Middlesex Charity 7s **Winners**

1999 Thai RU International 7s **Winners**

1997 Singapore 7s Ablitt Plate **Winners**

1995 Malaysia RU-COBRA International 10s Semi-finalists

1994 Italian RU International 7s **Winners**

1994 Nordic 7s **Winners**

1994 Scandinavian 10s **Winners**

1994 Malaysia RU-COBRA International 10s **Winners**

1993 Italian RU International 7s **Winners**

1993 Malaysia RU-COBRA International 10s **Winners**

1992 Irish RFU Aer Lingus International 7s Semi-finalists

1991 Italian RU International 7s Finalists

1988 Cambridge University International 7s **Winners**

1988 Hong Kong 7s Semi-finalists

1987 Hong Kong 7s Semi-finalists

With regard to the abbreviated game, the Club was mentioned in the 2001 Middlesex Sevens Programme as

THE ACKNOWLEDGED MASTERS OF SEVENS

PENGUIN IRFC PLAYERS 1959-2011

PENGUINS WHO HAVE PLAYED FOR THEIR COUNTRY'S SENIOR INTERNATIONAL XVS OR VIIS TEAMS
AND/OR THE BRITISH AND IRISH LIONS ARE HIGHLIGHTED IN RED

A

D. Abbott (Oxford University)
R. Abell (Bath)
G. Abraham (Rosslyn Park)
J. Abrahams (Bedford)
P. Ackford (Rosslyn Park, Harlequins, England and British Lions)
B. Adam (London Welsh)
R. Adams (Heriot's FP, Edinburgh Accademicals and Scotland Students)
S. Adlen (Oxford University)
F. Afeaki (North Harbour Marist, North Harbour Sevens and New Zealand Sevens trialist)
J. Afoa (Northcote, North Harbour)
P. Agnew (CIYMS, Bangor, Ulster and Ireland)
G. Aherne (Lansdowne)
F. Ahling (Barking)
G. Ainscough (Leicester and England 'A')
D. Aitchison (Highland)
C. Aitkins (Loughborough University and England U21)
S. Alatini (Cambridge City and Tonga)
B. Alexander (Bedford)
J. Alexander (Harlequins)
D. Alexopolos (Wasps)
S. Alfeld (Canterbury and Crusaders)
T. Allchurch (Rosslyn Park and England 'B')
C. Allen (Barnhall)
C.J. Allen (Richmond and Scotland Trialist)
J. Allen (Oxford University, Leicester and Midlands)
M. Allen (Bedford Blues)
P. Allen (Bedford)
G. Allison (Oxford University)
P. Alston (Bedford Athletic)
K. Amos (Selkirk and South of Scotland)
M. Anayi (Rosslyn Park)
A. Anderson (North Berwick)
W.F. Anderson (Orrell and England)
R. Anderson (Esher)
X. Andre (Henley)
J. Annabel (Taranaki)
B. Anthony (Newbridge)
M. Appleson (London Scottish)
E. Aramaki (British Army)
P. Archer (Cambridge University)
A. Armstrong (Jordanhill, Sterling and Scotland 'B')
I. Armstrong (Wasps)
J. Armstrong (London Irish)
T. Arnold (Tauranga Sports, Bay of Plenty and New Zealand Sevens)
K. Aseme (Blackheath)
C. Ashby (Wasps and England)
R. Ashforth (Cambridge University)
F. Asselin (James Bay, Canada Sevens and Canada)
J. Astbury (Wasps)
C. Atkinson (Nottingham)
J. Attlee (Manchester University)
C. Axtens (Tauranga Sports, Bay of Plenty, New Zealand U20)

B

N. Back (Leicester, England and British Lions)
N. Baggett (Warfdale)
K. Baillie (Glasgow Hawks and Scotland U21)
J. Baker (Rugby)
C. Balding (Rugby)
C. Bale (Harlequins and Surrey)
J. Ball (Bedford)
T. Ball (Sidcup)
D. Bailey (Rugby)
L. Bailey (Southland and Kent)
M. Baker (London Welsh)
J. Ball (Bedford)
C. Barbor (Moseley)
R. Barker (North Shore and North Harbour Sevens)
B. Barley (Wakefield and England)
A. Barnard (Northampton)
I. Barnes (Hawick and Scotland)
S. Barnes (Oxford University, Bath and England)
S. Barnes (Northampton)
D. Barnett (Rosslyn Park)
G. Barr (Oxford University and Esher)
R. Barr (Moseley)
B. Barrett (Taranaki U18 and Sevens, Taranaki, Hurricans and New Zealand Sevens)
D. Barrett (Bristol University)
A. Barrie (Highland)
K. Barrie (Jed Forest)
C. Barrow (Bristol)
T. Bason (Blackheath)
S. Basra (Tabard)
D. Bassett (Loughborough University)
S. Bates (Wasps and England)
B. Battishall (Rosslyn Park)
J. Baxendale (Sale and England)
A. Baxter (St. Luke's College)
C. Baxter (Bay of Plenty, Wellington and New Zealand Sevens)
S. Baxter (Oxford Harlequins)
P. Beal (Bedford and Redcar)
A. Beales (Northampton)
D. Beard (London Welsh)
C. Beech (London Wasps)
L. Beech (Ospreys)
D. Bell (Watsonians and Scotland)
P. Bell (Bay of Plenty, Blackheath and England)
A. Benger (Oxford University)
B. Bengka-Coker (Old Elthamians, Rosslyn Park and Surrey)
A. Bennett (Orrell)
N. Bennett (Bedford, London Welsh and England)
J. Bentley (Sale, North of England, Yorkshire, England and British Lions)
J. Berthinussen
P. Berwin (Bedford and Russia)
E. Binham (Loughborough University and Northampton)
G. Birkett (Harlequins and Scotland)
R. Birkett (Wasps)
A. Bishop (Loughborough University)
D. Bishop (Rugby)
A. Black (Boroughmuir, British Police and Scotland 'B')
A. Black (Newport Gwent Dragons)
A.A. Black (Heriot's FP)
J. Blackwood (Watsonians, Edinburgh, Scotland Sevens)
D. Blaikie (Cambridge University)

M. Blair (Currie, Ulster and Ireland 'A')
R. Blake (Bath)
S. Blake-Knox (North of Ireland, Bangor and Ireland)
R. Blyth (Swansea and Wales)
A. Boko (Duru, Stallions, Nadi Crusaders and Fiji Sevens)
J. Bonney (London Scottish)
N. Booth (Oxford University)
M. Botha (Bedford)
B. Botica (Northcote, North Harbour and Blues Dev)
G. Botterman (Saracens, London Welsh and England Sub)
J. Bowles (Natal and South Africa Sevens)
J. Bowman (London Welsh)
P. Brady (Rosslyn Park and Harlequins)
S. Brady (Bedford)
J. Bradey (Wanderers and Leinster)
K. Bray (Oxford University, Harlequins and New South Wales)
B. Breeze (Newport Gwent Dragons, Exeter Chiefs, Wales 'A', Wales Sevens and England Sevens)
K. Brennan (Oxford University and England Sevens)
P. Brennan (Co. Carlow)
A. Brenton (Bedford)
D. Brewster (Stewart-Melville FP and Scotland 'B')
R. Bridge (Oxford University)
R. Britton (Rosslyn Park and Oxford University)
S. Bromley (Oxford University, Rugby, Northern Division and Harlequins)
B. Brookes (Blackheath)
J. Brooks (Bedford)
M. Brooks (Wasps and England U23)
S. Brophy (Oxford University)
R. Brotherston (Highland)
N. Broughton (Exeter University, Bedford, Worcester and Scotland)
A. Brown (Gala and Scotland)
C. Brown (Auckland University, Waikato University, London Scottish, Watsonians, Glasgow High, Kelvinside, Scottish Exiles, Waikato and New Zealand Maori)
J. Brown (London Irish)
J. Brown (Fiji U19, Canterbury U21 and Development, Fiji Sevens)
O. Brown (Boroughmuir and Scotland Sevens)
S. Brown (Harlequins)
G. Bruwer (Wanderers, Johannesberg and South African Barbarians)
F. Bryant (Bush and Manawatu)
Q. de Bruyn (Oxford University and Orange Free State)
K. Bryson (College Old Boys, Manawatu)
A. Buchanan-Smith (Loughborough University, London Scottish and Scotland)
S. Buchanan-Smith (London Scottish)
I. Buckett (Swansea, London Welsh and Wales)
T. Bucknall (Richmond and England)
P. Buckton (Liverpool)
M. Budd (Bridgend, Cardiff, Crawshay's Welsh and Wales 'B')
D. Budge (Stockwood Park)
W. Bullock (Coventry and England U21)
J. Bunyan (London Irish)
C. Burke (Stellenbosch University)
P. Burke (London Irish, Bristol, Cardiff and Ireland)
P. Burleigh (New Brighton, Canterbury Development, Bay of Plenty and Chiefs Dev)
P. Burnell (London Scottish and Scotland)
S. Burnhill (Roundhay, Loughborough and England U23)
D. Burns (Boroughmuir and Scotland Sevens)
S. Burns (Blackheath)

S. Burns (London Irish)
H.C. Bury (Guy's Hospital and New Zealand)
K. Bushell (Harlequins and England 'B')
D. Butcher (London Scottish)
R. Butland (Richmond, Bath)
M. Butterworth (Esher)
A. Bunting (Bay of Plenty, Chiefs and New Zealand Sevens)
A. Buzza (Loughborough University)
D. Byrne (Manly and Australia Sevens)

C

J. Cabemaikadavu (British Army)
B. Calcraft (Manly, New South Wales, Queensland, Oxford University, London Welsh, Barbarians and Australia)
S. Cater (Newbury)
G. Caldwell (Currie)
M. Camburn (Takapuna, North Harbour Sevens and New Zealand Sevens)
O. Campbell (Old Belvedere and Ireland)
S. Campbell (Glasgow)
F. Campion (St. Mary's Dublin)
D. Campton (Coventry)
M. Cannon (London Welsh)
V. Cannon (Northampton, Barbarians and England)
C. Cano (Bedford)
J. Cantrell (University College Dublin, Blackrock, Leinster and Ireland)
A.B. Carmichael (West of Scotland and Scotland)
C. Casagrande (Treviso and Italy)
D. Caskie (London Scottish)
J. Cassell (Saracens, England Sevens and England 'B')
T. Catling (Mosely)
N. Celliers (Oxford University)
M. Challander (Sydney University and Oxford University)
R. Challis (London Scottish and London Counties)
C. Chalmers (Melrose, Glasgow, Scotland and British Lions)
R. Cheval (Old Askeans)
G. Chilcott (Bath, England and British Lions)
N. Chisolm (Currie)
S. Christie (Nelson, Tasman, Tasman Sevens and New Zealand Sevens)
P. Clackin (Coventry)
D. Clare (Connacht)
A. Clark (Richmond, England Universities)
N. Clark (Bedford)
B. Clarke (Saracens, Bath and England)
N. Clarke (Bristol and England Universities)
P. Clarke (Oxford University)
S. Clarke (East Coast Bays, Thames Valley)
K. Cleere (Lansdowne)
A. Clement (Swansea and Wales)
R. Clegg (Bangor, Ulster and Ireland)
T. Clever (United States Eagles and United States Sevens)
F. Clough (Cambridge University, Orrell, Bedford, Wasps and England)
G. Coakley
D. Cockburn (Boroughmuir and Scotland 'B')
J. Cockle (London Irish)
T. Coker (Oxford University, Harlequins and Australia)
A. Cole (Mosman Whales)
M. Coleclough (Angouleme, Wasps, Swansea, England and British Lions)
P. Collazo (Gloucester, Toulan, Begles, Stade Francais and France)
N. Collins (Mitsubishi, Waikato Chiefs and New Zealand Sevens)
D. Collis (Manly and Queensland)
M. Comb
J. Connolly (Bedford)
R. Constable (Saracens and Australia)
D. Cook (Rotherham)
M. Cook (Moseley)
P. Cook (Nottingham, Midland and Northern Divisions, Barbarians)
P.W. Cook (Richmond and England)
P. Cooke (Blackheath)
M.J. Cooper (Moseley and England)
I. Corcoran (Gala, South of Scotland and Scotland)
A. Cordtz (Marist St. Joseph's, Samoa Sevens and Samoa)
M.C. Cormack (Auckland University and Blackheath)
M. Cornish (RAF)

C. Corrigan (Ealing)
S. Corstorphine (London Scottish and Hampshire)
R. Coskie (Manchester University)
S. Cottam (Christchurch and Crusaders Development)
S. Cottrell (Richmond, Otago University, Otago and New Zealand Universities)
M. Court (Banbury)
L. Coward (Bedford School)
W. Cowie (Oxford University and North Harbour Development)
D. Cox (Co. Carlow)
S. Crabbe (Bedford)
F.J.R. Craig (Richmond and Ireland Trialist)
R. Crane (Loughborough University)
B. Crawley (Saracens)
G. Cressman (Honorable Artillery Company)
L. Criscuolo (Walsall, Coventry, Barbarians and Argentina)
D. Cronin (Ilford Wanderers, Bath and Scotland)
N. Crooks (Gala and Scotland Sevens)
M. Cross (Loughborough University)
S. Cross (Edinburgh)
G. Crothers (North of Ireland and Ulster)
P. Cue (Bath)
A. Cruikshank (St. John's, Leatherhead and Trinity Hall)
J. Cullen (Richmond)
G. Culliton (Wanderers and Ireland)
C. Culpan (Watsonians, New Zealand U18 and Canada)
V. Cunningham (St. Mary's Dublin and Ireland)
D. Currie (Harlequins)
D. Curry (Rosslyn Park and England Students)
P. Curtis (Rosslyn Park, Harlequins, Sussex and England 'B')
B. Cusack (Bath, Richmond, Lansdowne and Ireland 'A')

D

R. Daley (Blackheath)
A. Dall (Heriots FP and Scotland)
G. Dall (Heriot's FP, Edinburgh, Scotland U19 and Scotland Sevens)
C. D'Arcy (Saracens and Middlesex)
M. D'Arcy (Terenure and Leinster)
A. Da Cunha (Belenenses, Portugal and Portugal Sevens)
J. Daunivucu (Bravi Exiles, Fiji Sevens and Fiji)
A. Davidson (Scottish Borders)
B. Davidson (Harlequins)
A. Davies (Rugby Lions)
B. Davies (Queensland 'B', Cambridge University and Australia U21)
H. Davies (Cardiff and England U19)
H. Davies (Neath and Wales)
H. Davies (Wasps and England)
K. Davies (Oxford University)
M. Davies (Swansea and Wales)
M. Davies (Neath and Wales 'B')
M. Davies (Rugby)
P. Davies (Llanelli)
S. Davies (Rosslyn Park and England Students)
R. Davies (Oxford University and Australia)
A. Davis (Bedford)
A.M. Davis (Harlequins and England)
E. Davis (Harlequins and England 'B')
M. Davis (Canterbury and Northland)
M. Davu (Fiji and Fiji Sevens)
A. Dawling (British Army)
J. Dawson (Cambridge University)
R. Dawson (London Welsh and Zimbabwe)
B. Daynes (Bedford)
P. Dean (St. Mary's College, Leinster and Ireland)
M. Deane (London Irish)
S. Dear (Harlequins)
D. Dearden (Glasgow)
S. Deer (Rosslyn Park)
C. De Klerk (Villagers, Western Province and Lions)
P. De Glanville (Durham University, Oxford University, Bath and England)
H. De Goede (Cardiff and Canada)
C. De Goldi (Karita, Bay of Plenty and New Zealand Sevens)
V. Delasu (Fiji, Fiji Sevens)
L. De Luca (Ealing, Rome and Wasps)
C. Dennehy (Ebbw Vale)
M. Denney (Cambridge University and Wasps)
J. Devenport (Wasps)
C. Di Ciacca (Edinburgh)

J. Dick (Oxford University)
L.G. Dick (Jordanhill and Scotland)
W. Dickinson (Richmond and England Trialist)
N. Dickonson (Rosslyn Park)
G. Dickson (Haddington, Gala and Scotland)
G. Dickson (Watsonians)
K. Dickson (Bedford)
N. Dickson (Boroughmuir)
A. Dignan (Clontarf)
G. Dilger (Lansdowne and Connacht)
D. Dillon (Blackrock)
M. Di Rollo (Watsonians, Edinburgh Reivers and Scotland)
I. Dixon (Bedford, London Scottish and Scottish Exiles)
K. Dixon (Oxford University)
P. Dixon (Harlequins)
A. Donald (Takapuna and North Harbour)
B. Donald (Northampton)
N. Donovan (London Irish and Western Australia)
B. Dormer (Cambridge University, Australian Universities, Glenmark and Barbarians)
J. Doubleday (Bristol)
K. Douglas (Harlequins)
Mark Douglas (Llanelli and Wales)
K. Dowling (Exeter Chiefs)
N. Downer (Lansdowne)
P. Dowson (Newcastle, England Sevens)
G. Drummond (Boroughmuir)
Q. Dunlop (West of Scotland and Scotland)
K. Dunn (Gloucester, Wasps)
M. Dunning (NSW Waratahs and Australia)
M. Duthie (Cambridge University and Rosslyn Park)
C. Du Plessis (Bedford)
F. Du Tout (Oxford University, Barnes and Western Province)
N.J. Dwyer (Lansdowne and Ireland Trialist)
D. Dye (Boroughmuir, Heriot's FP, Dunfirmline, Scottish Schools and Zambia)

E

C. Eagle (Silverdale, North Harbour, Bristol and London Welsh)
R. Earnshaw (Cambridge University, Rotherham and England Sevens)
W. East (Wasps)
N. Easter (Orrell, Harlequins and England)
M. Edison (Cambridge)
A. Edmunds (Neath and Wales)
D. Edwards (Wakefield)
J. Edwards (Ards and New Zealand Maoris)
O. Edwards (Ballymena)
C. Egan (St. Mary's, Dublin)
C. Elder (Wasps)
P. Elder (Wasps)
C. Elisara (Padova, Rovigo, Treviso, Stade Francaise and Holland)
R. Elliott (Bedford)
H. Ellis (Wasps)
P. Ellis (Cambridge and Blackheath)
J. Ellison (Cambridge University)
T. Elman (Old Emmanuel)
T. Elmer
J. Elphick (Bedford Athletic)
S. Emms (Llandovery)
A. Emyr (Swansea and Wales 'B')
P. Enevoldson (Oxford University)
T. Ensor (Wanderers and Ireland)
U. Erinley (Wasps)
S. Eru (Cambridge University, Otago University and Otago)
P. Essenhigh (Blackheath and Rosslyn Park)
T. Ewington (West Hartlepool, London Irish and Northern Suburbs)
C. Evans (Newbridge and Wales)
G. Evans (Coventry and England)
G. Evans (Newbridge and Gwent)
L. Evans (Treorchy, Bridgend, Swansea, Bedford, Barbarians and Wales)
S. Evans (Swansea and Wales 'B')
T. Evans (Ospreys)
C. Eves (Massey, North Harbour Developement)
J. Ewens (Rotherham)
I. Exeter (Blackheath)
T. Exeter (Moseley)
T. Exeter (London Scottish and Scotland 'B')
S. Eynon (Hamilton)

F

E. Fale (Savaii Samoa and Samoa)
M. Farrell (Old Alleynians)
O. Farrell (Saracens)
S. Fenn (London Scottish)
M. Ferguson (Stourbridge)
J. Ferris (Blackrock and Ireland Sevens)
R. Ferry (Metropolitan Police)
R. Field (Rugby Lions)
N. Fielden (Northampton)
M. Figgins (Old Varstonians)
V. Fihaki (Patumahoe, Counties-Manukau)
A. Findlayson (Cardiff, British Police, Barbarians and Wales)
R. Finn (University College Dublin and Ireland)
Colin Fisher (Waterloo and Scotland)
M. Fitzpatrick (Wanderers)
L. Fleming (Edinburgh)
R. Flannery (Ireland)
B. Fleming (Castres and New Zealand Sevens)
J. Fleming (Exeter Chiefs)
N. Fletcher (Leicester and Sale)
J. Flynn (Dublin Wanderers, Leinster and Ireland)
M. Fontaine (Northampton)
G. Forbes (Watsonians)
S. Ford (Bridgend)
A. Forster (Old Alleynians)
S. Forster (Leinster and New Zealand)
J. Foster (Bedford, Newport and Wales Sevens)
D. Foughy (London Welsh)
J. Fowler (Rosslyn Park and England Students)
A. Fox (Bedford and Natal)
B. Frame (Glenmark, Canterbury 'B')
J. Frame (Gala, Edinburgh 'A' and Scotland)
R. Francis (Neath)
D. Fraser (Harlequins)
J. Fraser (London Scottish, Surrey and Scotland Trialist)
S. Fraser (Highland and Scotland Trialist)
W. Fraser (Saracens)
F. Fratti (Parma and Italy)
M. Friday (Rosslyn Park, Wasps and England Sevens)
D. Flatman (Dulwich College, Saracens and England)
M. Freer (Nottingham)
G. French (Bath)
G. French (London Welsh)
G. French (Parma)
N. French (Wasps)
A. Fuller (Nottingham)
R. Fuller (Henley)

G

B. Gabriel (Leicester and Midlands Division)
J. Gadd (Glocester and England 'B')
D. Galbraith (Northcote Seniors)
M. Gallagher (Coventry)
P. Gallacher (Watsonians)
B. Gammell (Heriot's FP, Edinburgh Wanderers and Scotland)
I. Gardner (Caerphilly)
P. Garrett (Bedford and East Midlands)
J. Garth (Wanderers)
J. Gaunt (Henley)
K. Gay (Ebbw Vale)
N. Gaymond (Bristol, Bath, Somerset and British Universities)
S. Geary (Newbridge and Welsh Trialist)
I. George (London Welsh and England)
I. George (Northampton, Barbarians and England Bench)
T. George (Richmond)
J. Gerber (Villagers, Western Province and South Africa Sevens)
M. Giacheri (Randwick, NSW, Coventry, Parma and Italy)
M. Gibson (Cambridge University, Lansdowne, London Irish, Ireland and British Lions)
G. Gilbert (Richmond)
C. Gildea (Sundays Well and Munster)
P. Glackin (Rugby)
F. Gladstone (Cambridge University)
J. Glasson (Crusaders Colts)
J. Glasson (London Scottish)
B. Goff (Exeter University)

L. Gomez (Harlequins)
W. Gonewai (Fiji Sevens)
S. Goosen (Perthshire, Western Province)
D. Gorrie (Monkstown, Landsdowne, Tauranga Sports and Bay of Plenty)
S. Gorvett (Bristol)
J. Gossman (West of Scotland, Glasgow District and Scotland)
B. Gotting (London Scottish and England U21)
A. Grabham (Ebbw Vale)
M. Grace (Combined Australian Universities and Rosslyn Park)
D. Graham (Highland and Heriot's FP)
H. Graham (Coventry)
H. Graham (Marauders, Harlequins, British Army and England Sevens)
J. Graham (Bedford)
M. Graham (East Coast Bays, North Harbour Development and New Zealand U20)
P. Graham (Blackheath)
C. Gray (Edinburgh and Scotland)
C. Gray (Nottingham)
S. Gray (Bedford)
R. Greaves (Mosely and England Trialist)
C. Green (Treviso, Canterbury and New Zealand)
J. Green (Saracens)
P. Greenaway (Exeter University)
R. Greenslade-Jones (London Scottish)
N. Greenstock (Wasps)
M. Gregory (Saracens)
O. Gregory (Richmond)
T. Gregory (Nottingham University)
T. Gregory (Oxford University)
M. Griffin (Sydney University, AIS U21)
A. Griffiths (Moseley)
D. Griffiths (Cardiff)
D. Griffiths (Newport)
D. Griffiths (Wasps and Waterloo)
N. Griffiths (Ospreys and Worcester)
S. Griffiths (Glasgow Caledonians)
J. Grimmond (West Hartlepool and Manly)
D. Gill (Gala and Scotland)
C. Gubbins (Rugby)
B. Gulliver (Coventry)

H

M. Haag (Bath and England)
C. Hacking (Southland and Kent)
S. Hackney (Loughborough, English Students, Leicester and England 'A')
J. Hadfield (Henley)
W. Hafu (Silverdale, Mahurangi, North Harbour Sevens, OMBAC and New Zealand U19)
R. Hakin (Bath and Ireland)
F. Halai (Marist St. Josephs, Waikato)
D. Hall (Bective Rangers)
J. Hall (Bath and England)
J. Hall (Haileybury School and St. John's College)
J. Hall (Loughborough University)
M. Hall (Cardiff, Bridgend, Wales and British Lions)
M. Hall (Boroughmuir and Scotland U21)
K. Hallett (Bedford and Ireland U19)
S. Halliday (Oxford University, Bath, Harlequins and England)
L. Hamilton (Western Sharks, Coastal, Northland, North Harbour Sevens and New Zealand Sevens)
A.W. Hancock (Northampton and England)
J. Hanekom (Shimlhas, Free State Cheetahs Sevens)
D. Hankinson (Bedford)
R. Hannaford (Bristol and England)
R. Hannah (West of Scotland and Scotland)
Des Hanrahan
S. Harding (Bedford)
V.S.J. Harding (Saracens and England)
D. Hare (Leicester, North and England)
M. Harefoot (Bristol)
D. Harn (Old Freemens)
A. Harriman (Harlequins and England Sevens)
D. Harris (Watsonians)
H. Harris (Old Reigatians)
T. Harris (Rugby)
C. Harrison (Rotherham)
A. Harrower (Saracens)
V. Hartland (Bedford)
B. Harvey (Worcester)
D. Harvey (Wasps)

J.R.W. Harvey (Richmond and England Trialist)
F. Hawkins (Wasps and England Trialist)
P. Haycock (Terenure and Ireland 'B')
S. Hayes Stevenson (Takapuna and Crusaders Development)
P. Hayward (Gloucester and English Trialist)
H. Head (Richmond and Ballymena)
J. Heggadon (Saracens and Kent)
G. Hein (Oxford University and USA)
C. Henderson (Oxford University, London Scottish, Rosslyn Park and Scotland U21)
F. Henderson (Watsonians and Scotland U19 and U21)
R. Henderson (Munster, Wasps, Ireland and British Lions)
S. Henderson (Rosslyn Park and England U23)
A. Hendrickses (Streatham-Croydon, Rosslyn Park, Barbarians and England Trialist)
B. Hennessey (Watsonians)
N. Hennessy (Pontypridd)
R. Hennessey (London Irish)
J. Hennigan (Blackheath)
T. Henry (Oxford University)
K. Hepburn (Boroughmuir and Edinburgh District)
S. Hepher (Munster)
E. Herkes (Haddington)
P. Hewitt (Heriot's FP, Scottish Schools, Edinburgh and Scotland)
E. Hickie (Wasps)
A. Higgins (Bath, England Sevens and England A)
M. Higginson (Old Wesley)
D. Hilton (Glasgow Caledonians and Scotland)
J. Hinkins (Bedford)
J. Hinkins (Moseley)
L. Hinton (Newport Gwent Dragons)
J. Hoare (Beckenham)
D. Hodge (Edinburgh and Scotland)
S. Hodgkinson (Moseley, Nottingham and England)
C. Hodgson (Sale and England)
G. Hodgson (Neath and Wales)
M. Hodgson (Bay of Plenty Development)
H. Hogan (St Mary's College, Dublin and Irish Amateurs)
N. Hohaia (Costal, Taranaki and New Zealand Sevens Trialist)
J. Hohneck (Fraser Tech and Waikato)
A. Holder (Rosslyn Park and London Division)
T. Holgate (London Welsh)
Jerry Holland (Wanderers and Ireland)
T. Holloway (Newbury and Rugby)
G. Holmes (Wasps and England 'B')
J. Hooper (Narbonne, Taranaki, Hurricanes)
I. Hope (Dundee High School FP and Scottish Schools)
D. Hopley (Cambridge University, Wasps, England Sevens and England)
P. Hopley (Wasps)
C. Horder (Reading)
C. Horsman (Bath and Wales)
A.L. Horton (Blackheath and England)
J. Horton (Bath and England)
C. Howard (Loughborough University and Rugby)
P. Howard (Queensland, ACT Brumbies, Leicester and Australia)
S. Howard (Exeter, Cambridge University)
S. Howard (Rosslyn Park)
M. Howe (Bedford, England U23s)
D. Howells (London Welsh)
M. Howells (Aberavon and Barbarians)
A. Hughes (Newbridge)
D. Hughes (Oxford University)
D. Hughes (Newbridge and Wales)
D. Hughes (Stourbridge)
K. Hughes (London Welsh and Wales)
B. Hullin (Cardiff and Wales)
N. Humphries (Oxford University, New York Athletic Club and Manly)
S. Hunt (Ebbw Vale)
D. Hunter (Cambridge)
I. Hunter (Northampton and England)
M. Hunter (Glasgow High School FP and Glasgow)
D. Hurdle (Teachers RFC and Bermuda)
R. Hurrell (Henley)
A. Hurst (Wasps and England)
C. Hutchin (Coventry)
Neil Hutchins
M. Hutton (Richmond)
M. Hyde (Cambridge University and Australian Universities)
C. Hynd (Jed-Forest and Scotland U21)

I

B. Ibrahim (Blackheath)
P. Ince (Penzance)
G. Inglis (St. Mary's Dublin and Watsonians)
A. Innes (Cambridge University)
B. Innes (Coventry and England)
H. Innes (Cambridge University and Blackheath)
J. Ions (Wasps)
M. Ireland (Rosslyn Park)
M. Irish (Bristol and England Universities)
D. Irwin (Ulster, Ireland and British Lions)
L. Isaacs (Neath)
K. Izatt (Kiatoa and New Zealand Sevens)

J

B. Jackman (Sale, Leinster and Ireland)
J. Jackson (Otorohunga, Nadi, Nawaka Sevens,
Fiji Warriors)
L. Jackson (Wasps)
C.R. Jacobs (Northampton and England)
G. Jacobs (Oxford University)
T. Jacques (West Hartlepool, Northern Suburbs,
ACT Brumbies and Australia)
A. James (Wasps and Southland)
D. James (Oxford University and USA)
K. James (Neath and Wales Sevens)
K. James (Penzance)
L. James (Glamorgan Wanderers)
S. James (Richmond)
S. Jardine (South Glamorgan Institute, Pontypool
and England 'A')
S. Jardine (Stourbridge)
J. Jarrett (England Trialist)
J. Jeffrey (Kelso, Northumberland, English Universities,
British Universities and Scotland)
G. Jenion (Sale)
A. Jenkins (Bridgend and Cardiff)
D. Jenkins (Cambridge University, Harlequins and
England U21)
R. Jenkins (Wasps, Harlequins, South of England
and England 'A')
V. Jenkins (Bridgend)
J. Jenner (Bristol University)
D. Jennings (Tauranga Sports and Bay of Plenty)
T. Jensen (Oxford University, Blackheath and Wasps)
M. Jenson (West Hartlepool and Northern Suburbs)
M. Jermyn (Rosslyn Park and England Colts)
N. Jeynes
R. Joauher (Montuban and France Sevens)
G. John (Bridgend)
G. John (Llanelli, Wales 'B' and Wales Squad)
G. John (Cardiff and Wales 'B')
C. Johnson (London Scottish, Bedford and Rotherham)
A. Johnston (Currie)
N. Johnston (Queensland University)
A. Johnstone (Canada)
S. Johnstone (Henley)
C. Joiner (Melrose, Stewarts Melville FP, Leicester
and Scotland)
R.K.L. Jolliffe (Richmond and England Trialist)
A. Jones (Llandovery)
A. Jones (Neath)
B. Jones (Beckenham)
B. Jones (Northampton)
J. Jones (Loughborough)
K. Jones (Harlequins and Surrey)
L. Jones (Cardiff and Wales)
M. Jones (Ospreys and Wales)
N. Jones (Cambridge University)
R. Jones (Glamorgan Wanderers)
P. Jorgenson (Rotherham, Edinburgh, Penrith RL
and Australia)

K

J. Kamana (Fraser Tech, Waikato and New Zealand
Sevens)
A. Kardooni (Rugby, Wasps, Leicester, Bedford, Blackheath
and England 'A')
E. Katalu (Llanelli)
J. Katene (Te Teko, Bay of Plenty)

D. Kaye (Nottingham)
E. Keane (St. Mary's)
M. Kearney (Landsdowne)
R. Kearney (Wanderers, Leinster and Ireland)
R.R. Keddie (Watsonians, London Scottish and Scotland)
B. Keen (Moseley and England)
M. Keenan (London Irish, Auckland University, Auckland,
New Zealand Trialist and Western Samoa)
W. Kefford (Harlequins)
G.J. Keith (Wasps and Scotland)
H. Keith (Wasps and Scotland)
S. Keith (Selection Paloise, Wellington, Stade Francaise
and Croatia)
P. Keith-Roach (Rosslyn Park and England Trialist)
A. Kellock (Edinburgh, Glasgow and Scotland)
A. Kelly (Edinburgh)
P. Kendall (Cambridge University and Bedford)
M. Kendrick (Sale, Lancashire and England U23)
A. Kennedy (Rugby)
F. Kennedy (St. Mary's College, Leinster and
Ireland Trialist)
J. Kennedy (St. Mary's College Dublin)
K. Kennedy (London Irish, Ireland and British Lions)
T. Kennedy (St. Mary's College Dublin, Leinster
and Ireland)
L. Keri (Holland)
J. Kerr (Haddington, Watsonians, Scotland 'A'
and Scotland Sevens)
J. Keyter (Bristol, Harlequins and USA)
M. Keyworth (Swansea and England)
O. Kiely (St. Mary's Dublin, Shannon and Munster)
J. Kilbride (St. Mary's Dublin)
W. Kilford (Nottingham)
R. Kilpatrick (Jed Forest and Scotland 'B')
N. Killick (Harlequins and England U21)
R. King (Rosslyn Park)
R. King (Silverdale and North Harbour)
P. Kinikinilau (Alhambra-Union and Otago)
R. Kinikinilau (Wellington, Hurricanes, New Zealand
Sevens)
C. Kinnear (London Scottish)
R. Kinsey (Rugby Lions, Wasps, Queensland and
Barbarians)
D. Kirk (South Island Universities, Otago Colts,
Otago University, Aukland University, Aukland,
Oxford University and New Zealand)
I. Kirk (London Scottish and Anglo-Scots)
E. Kirton (Harlequins and New Zealand)
R. Knibbs (Bristol and England 'B')
K. Knowles
N. Knowles (Northampton)
A. Knox (Oxford University)
P. Kolakowski (Cambridge)
R. Koll (Christchurch and Canterbury U21)
K. Kopetsky (USBC and France Sevens)
T. Koroinavlivou (Army)
H. Kose (Mahurangi, North Harbour Sevens
and Development)
G. Kruis (Saracens)
V. Kunabilo (Bravi Exiles, Nadronga and Fiji U19)
R. Kurangi (Northern Ireland)

L

M. Lacy (British Army)
P. Laffin (Oxford University)
C. Laidlaw (Jed Forest and Scotland Sevens)
S. Laing (Edinburgh Reivers)
C. Laity (Neath, Barbarians and Wales 'A')
I. Lambie (Watsonians and Scotland)
J. Lamden (Old Freemen's)
N. Langari (Baravi Exiles and Fiji)
J. Lansbury (Sale, Barbarians and England Trialist)
S. Lanza (San Isidro and Argentina)
R. Lapidus (Bristol University)
A. Latumailagi (Nadi, Fiji Sevens and Fiji)
F. Latuselu (Manly and Tonga)
W. Lauder (Neath and Scotland)
D. Lavery (Northampton)
P. Lawlor (Bective Rangers, Leinster and Ireland)
K. Lawless (Clontarf)
G. Lawrie (Heriot's FP, Mussleburgh and Scotland U19)
S. Lawrie (Edinburgh and Scotland U21)
A. Lawson (Heriot's FP, Middlesex, Barbarians and
Scotland)
G. Lawson (Heriot's FP and Scotland Sevens)
M. Leadbetter (Broughton Park and England)
A. Le Chavalier (Henley, Wasps and Swansea)

J. Ledua (British Army and Fiji Sevens)
D. Lee (Edinburgh Reivers and Scotland)
F. Lee (Manurewa, Auckland U18, Counties-Manukau,
Chiefs and New Zealand Sevens)
D. Leek (London Scottish)
D. Leonard (Lansdowne and Munster)
N. Le Roux (Worcester and France Sevens)
C. Lewis (Cambridge University and Rosslyn Park)
D. Lewis (Cambridge University)
V.J. Lewis (Rosslyn Park and Surrey)
J. Lewsey (Bristol University, Bristol, Wasps, England
and British Lions)
T. Lewsey (London Welsh)
N. Ligairi (Baravi Exiles and Fiji)
S. Lincoln (Bedford)
S. Lineen (Boroughmuir and Scotland)
David Lines (Mariners)
C. Lion-Cachet (Oxford University and South African
Universities)
R. List (Doncaster)
C. Little (Glasgow Hawks and Glasgow Districts)
T. Little (Eastern Province and USA)
A. Llewellyn (Bedford)
P. Llewellyn (Swansea, Glamorgan, Barbarians and Wales)
J. Lloyd (Bridgend and Wales)
M. Lloyd (Orrell)
J. Lockwood (Saracens and Kent)
B. Lohan (Wimbledon)
S. Longstaff (Glasgow and Scotland)
M. Lovett (London Scottish and Scotland Trialist)
M. Luamanu (North Shore, North Harbour, Blues,
New Zealand U20)
J. Luke (South Glamorgan Institute)
T. Lumelume (Nadi and Warriors)
A. Lumsden (Bath)
R. Lutton (Oxford University and Belfast Harlequins)
A. Lynch (Redingensians)

M

P. Macauly (Thanet Wanderers and Kent)
D. MacCallum (Esher, Gold Coast and Australia Sevens)
D. Macer (Wasps)
C. MacDonald (Oxford University)
D. MacDonald (Oxford University, Toulouse and Scotland)
S. MacDonald (Rosslyn Park)
J. MacDonough
N.A. MacEwen (Highland and Scotland)
D. Mackay (Highland)
R. MacKay (Glasgow Warriors)
Gregor Mackenzie
G. Macklin (Cambridge University, England U23
and England Squad)
M. Madden (Llanelli)
A. Maher (Lansdowne)
U. Mai (Marist St. Joseph's, Samoa Sevens and Samoa)
N. Mallett (Western Province, Rovigo, Saint Claude,
Boulogne-Billancourt, Oxford University, Richmond
and Western Province)
C. Malone (Manly, AIS U21 and Australia U21)
D. Malone (Bedford)
N. Malone (Leicester and Ireland)
L. Mansell (Bedford and East Midlands)
M. Mansfield (Bedford)
C. Marr
N. Marsh (Oxford University Greyhounds)
S. Matelewana (Red Rock and Suva)
A. Martin (Bridgend)
A. Martin (Cambridge University)
A. Martin (Cardiff)
N. Martin (Harlequins, Bedford and England)
N. Martin (Oxford University)
S. Martin (Neath)
N. Marval (Rosslyn Park)
A. Mason (St. John's College, Cambridge University)
M. Mason (Harlequins)
M. Mason (Northampton and England Trialist)
M.A. Mason (Clifton and Kent)
T. Mason (Sidcup and Kent)
D. Mather (London Scottish and Western Province)
R. Mattheison (Edinburgh)
M. Mayhew (Northcote, North Harbour)
S. McCahill (Sunday's Well and Ireland)
S. McCallum (Jordanhill and Scotland Reserve)
M. McCarthy (Neath)
R. McClean (Gloucester)

J. McCormack (ACT Brumbies and Australia U21)
M. McCormack (Watsonians)
G. McClymont (Rosslyn Park and Petersham)
A. McDonald (Loughborough University)
D. McDonald (Oxford and South Africa)
D. McElligot (Clontarf and Trinity College, Dublin)
N.A. McEwan (Gala and Scotland)
C. McFadyean (Moseley, England and British Lions)
D. McGavin (Bedford and Scotland U21)
T. McGhee (Edinburgh)
G. McGilchrist (Watsonians and Scotland U21)
A. McGill (Orkney)
K. McGowan (Glamorgan Wanderers and Leinster)
R. McGrath (Wanderers, Connacht and Ireland)
A. McGrevy (Rangataua and Bay of Plenty Sevens)
H. McHardy (Harlequins)
A. McHarg (London Scottish and Scotland)
M. McHarg (London Scottish)
I. McIlroy (Glasgow Warriors and Scotland Sevens)
G. McKelvie (Watsonians and Scotland)
J. McKenty (Waikato, Chiefs Development and New Zealand U16)
G. McKenzie (Highland, Barbarians and Scotland U23)
E. McLaughlin (Rotoiti)
I. McLauchlan (Jordanhill, London Scottish and Scotland)
A. McLean (Worcester)
G. McLellan (Orkney)
Alf McLennan
N. McLennan (Lincoln, Canterbury U21)
A.W. McMaster (Ballymena and Ireland)
T. McNab (Glasgow HSFP and London Scottish)
J. McPhee (Glenfield, North Harbour and New Zealand Sevens)
A. McRobbie (Heriot's FP)
M. McWhite (Lansdowne and Irish Schoolboys)
P. Meadows (Heriot's FP and Devon)
C. Mee (Rugby)
N. Mee (Sidcup, Bedford Athletic and Harlequins)
M. Meenan (Ebbw Vale and England Sevens)
N. Meikle (Ayr and Heriot's FP)
N. Melville (Headingley and England)
A. Metcalfe (Wakefield)
M. Meyer (Thanet Wanderers and Northern Transvaal)
S. Miall (Newbury)
A. Mihajlovic (Bedford Athletic and Yugoslavia)
T. Mikkleson (University, Waikato and New Zealand Sevens)
M. Miles (Pertemp Bees)
D. Millard (London Scottish, Scotland 'B' and Scotland)
A. Miller (Exeter Chiefs)
C. Miller (Watsonians)
P. Miller (Eastwood and Australia Sevens)
S. Miller (Bay of Plenty)
B. Milne (London Scottish)
J. Minshull (Coventry)
A. Mitchell (London Scottish)
C. Mitchell (Ospreys)
S. Mitchell (Harlequins)
S. Mitchell (Wasps)
D. Mizen (Sidcup)
A. Moeke (Mid Western, Northland and Auckland)
J. Moloney (St. Mary's College, Dublin)
M. Moncrieff (Gala and Scotland Sevens)
O. Montgomery (Bedford)
B. Moore (Nottingham, Harlequins, England and British Lions)
D. Moore (Clontarf)
R. Moore (Ulster, Calvisano and Australia)
M. Morais (GD Direito and Portugal)
J. Moran
J. Moreland (Rosslyn Park)
C. Morgan (Cardiff)
D. Morgan (Newbridge, England and British Lions)
D. W. Morgan (Stewarts-Melville, Edinburgh District, Barbarians and Scotland)
D. Morgan (Cardiff HSOB)
R. Morgan (Coventry)
R. Moroney (Landsdowne, Munster and Ireland)
B. Morrisey (Terenure and Ireland Trialist)
J. Morrison (Loughborough University, Bristol, Bath and England 'B')
D. Moussa (Watsonians)
I. Murchie (West of Scotland)
A. Murdoch (Worcester)
J. Murphy (Greystones and Lansdowne)
N. Murphy (Sunday's Well)
C. Murray (Hawick and Scotland U21)
H. Murray (Cambridge University and Canterbury)
R. Mynott (Swansea and Welsh Students)

L. Nabulliwaga (Suva, Fiji Sevens)
A. Nash (Watsonians and Scotland U21)
J. Nasmith (Helensville and North Harbour)
K. Nauvasi (Nadi)
S. Nawavu (Baravi Exiles, Nadi, Fiji Sevens and Fiji)
J. Nayler (Orrell and Newcastle)
F. Neal (Blackheath)
I. Neary (Clifton)
T. Neary (Broughton Park, Barbarians, North, England and British Lions)
D. Neave (Watsonians and Edinburgh)
T. Neilumi (Fiji Sevens)
P. Neville (Garryowen and Ireland 'A')
C. Newby (North Shore, Highlanders, Otago, Leicester, New Zealand Sevens and New Zealand)
P. Newton (Orrell
P. Ngauamo (Canterbury, Crusaders Development and New Zealand U20)
N. Ngauku (Western Samoa)
A. Nichol (Heriot's FP)
B.F. Ninnes (Coventry and England)
R. Niuia (Massey, North Harbour U20, New Zealand U17)
J. Nolan (Bedford)
C.H. Norris (Cardiff, Wales and British Lions)
T. Norton (Linwood and Canterbury)
M. Nutt Oxford Harlequins

W. Oakes (Instonians and Ireland Trialist)
C. O'Brien (Trinity College and Irish Universities)
N. O'Brien (Cardiff)
T. O'Brien (Manly and Australia Sevens)
J. O'Callaghan (Cambridge University)
C. O'Connell (Linwood and New Zealand U19)
K. O'Connell (Sunday's Well, Munster and Ireland)
B. O'Conner (Oxford University)
S. O'Connor (Marist, Manawatu)
J. O'Donovan (Lansdowne)
M. Offiah (Rosslyn Park and Surrey, Widnes RL, Wigan RL, London Broncos RL, Wasps and Great Britain Lions RL)
D. Officer (Currie, Harlequins and Scotland 'A')
T. O'Gorman (Glamorgan Wanderers)
L. O'Keefe (Richmond)
W. O'Kelly (Clontarf)
D. O'Leary (Gloucester)
B. Olesen (Waikato Sevens - New Zealand Sevens Training Squad)
A. Olive (Wainuiomata, Wellington 'B' and Samoa)
M. Oliver (Exeter, London Irish and Rotherham)
A. Olver (Worcester)
J. Olver (Harlequins and England)
D. O'Mahoney (Cork Constitution, Bedford, Saracens, Munster and Ireland)
R. O'Mahoney (Oxford University)
R. O'Neil (Harlequins)
G. Oommen (Dundee)
J. O'Reilly (Leeds)
M. Ord (Moseley)
R. Orledge (Bath)
M. Ormesher (Bedford)
P. Orr (Old Wesley, Ireland and British Lions)
A. Orugboh (Wasps)
J. Orwin (Bedford and England)
J. O'Shea (Cardiff, Wales and British Lions)
H. Owen (Sidcup)
R. Owen (Bedford Blues)
A. Ozdemir (Exeter)

F. Packman (Northampton)
J. Packo (Little Munster)
S. Paddison (Mahurangi)
B. Page (Bedford and England Trialist)
Colin Page
J. Page (Northampton and England)
S. Page (London Welsh)
B. Paltridge (Auckland University and Blues U18)

W. Palu (Manly, Waratahs and Australia)
John Palmer (Bath and England)
R. Palmer (Collegians, Ulster and Ireland 'B')
G. Parker (Melrose and Scottish Southern Districts)
M. Parker (Exeter University)
F. Packman (Northampton)
J. Packo (Little Munster)
S. Paddison (Mahurangi)
B. Page (Bedford and England Trialist)
Colin Page
J. Page (Northampton and England)
S. Page (London Welsh)
W. Palu (Manly, Waratahs and Australia)
J. Palmer (Bath and England)
R. Palmer (Collegians, Ulster and Ireland 'B')
G. Parker (Melrose and Scottish Southern Districts)
M. Parker (Exeter University)
D. Parkinson (Richmond)
M. Parkinson (Bay of Plenty, New Zealand Sevens)
A. Parton (Henley)
B. Pascoe (Tauranga Sports and Southland)
P. Pask (Northampton and East Midlands)
J. Paton (Edinburgh Academicals)
D. Patterson (Selkirk, Watsonians, Glasgow Caledonians and Scotland)
W.M. Patterson (Wasps and England)
I. Pattison (West of Scotland and Glasgow)
I. Paxton (Scotland and British Lions)
C. Payne (West of Scotland, Northern and England)
R. Peacy (Doncaster)
G. Peacock (London Welsh)
R. Peacy (Doncaster)
G. Pearce (Northampton and England)
R. Pearcy (Penzance)
H. Peck (Luton)
H. Peck (Newcastle)
D. Peglar (Wasps and England 'B')
R. Pellows (Penzance)
T. Penn (Tukapa, Taranaki, Hurricans and New Zealand Maori)
N. Penny (Watsonians, Edinburgh and Scotland Sevens)
M. Percival (Blackheath)
W. Petch (Harlequins and Middlesex)
E. Peters (Cambridge University, Saracens, Rotherham, Connacht and Scotland)
B. Peterson (Manly and Australia U21)
D. Pickering (Neath and Wales)
A. Phillips (Bedford)
A. Phillips (Cardiff and Wales)
J. Phillips (Bedford and Peterborough)
S. Philpot (Coventry)
D. Pickering (Llanelli, Neath, Crawshay's Welsh, Barbarians and Wales)
R. Pierce (London Irish)
N. Pike (Rotherham)
M. Pini (Richmond, Australia and Italy)
R. Piotrowski
R. Piovan (Parma and Italy)
M. Pinnegar (Wasps)
C. Pither (Australia Sevens and Australia)
P. Playford (Wests, Waratahs and Australia U21)
N. Pomphrey (Bristol and England)
M. Poole (Leicester)
B. Pope (Canterbury, South Island, New Zealand Universities, Otago, New Zealand Barbarians, New Zealand XV, St. Mary's Dublin, Clontarf and Leinster)
D. Porte (Exeter)
R. Pow (Selkirk, South of Scotland and Scotland Sevens)
D. Powell (Northampton, England and British Lions)
M. Powell (Saracens)
R. Powell (Llanelli, Gloucestershire and England Trialist)
S. Powell (Neath)
T. Powell (Sidcup and Kent)
I. Power (Greystones and Leinster)
M. Prendergast (Munster)
B. Prescott (Glasgow)
N. Preston (Richmond and England)
M. Price (Rugby)
A. Prior (Toronto Nomads)
D. Proctor (Heriot's FP)
W. Proctor (Llanelli and Wales)
D. Prout (Northampton and England)
D. Pugh (London Welsh)
P. Purcell (Lansdowne and Ireland)
A. Purves (Melrose and Scottish Southern Districts)
M. Pusinelli (HSBC)

Q

D. Qau Qau (Baravi Exiles, Fiji Sevens and Fiji)
J. Quantrill (Rugby and England Students)
H. Quigley (Coventry and England Students)
G. Quinn (Lansdowne)
L. Quinn (Otorohunga and Waikato 'B')
M. Quinn (Lansdowne, Leinster and Ireland)
D. Quinnell (Llanelli, Wales and British Lions)

R

S. Rabaka (Baravi Exiles, Nadi and Fiji Sevens)
C. Raducanu (Boroughmuir and Romania)
P. Raeburn (Watsonians)
K. Rafferty (Heriot's FP and Edinburgh)
M. Rafter (Bristol, Gloucestershire and England)
D. Raikuna (Pukekohe, Counties Manukau and
New Zealand Sevens)
C. Rainbow (Rugby)
A. Raines (Wasps and Middlesex)
E. Rakikedike (Fiji Sevens)
C. Ralston (Rosslyn Park, Middlesex, South West Counties
and England U23s)
D. Ramsay (London Welsh)
W.H. Raybould (London Welsh and Wales)
A. Rayner (Wasps and Hertfordshire)
C.W.W. Rea (London Scottish, West of Scotland, Scotland
and British Lions)
H. Rea (North of Ireland, London Irish, Ulster and Ireland)
S. Reany (London Scottish and New Zealand Trialist)
S. Reay (Orrell)
J. Redrupp (Swansea, Newport and Wales U21)
B. Redwood (Bristol and England)
B.I. Rees (London Welsh and Wales)
A. Rees (Bath and England U16)
A. Rees (British Army)
A. Rees (Resolven)
C. Rees (London Welsh)
G. Rees (Aberavon)
G. Rees (Castaway Wanderers, Oxford University, British
Universities, London Welsh, Wasps, Harlequins and Canada)
P. Rees (Newport and Wales)
T. Rees (Newport and Wales)
M. Regan (Bristol, England and British Lions)
C. Rei (East Coast Bays, Taranaki Sevens, North Harbour,
New Zealand U20)
S. Reid (Leicester)
M. Rennel (Bedford)
M. Rennie (Rosslyn Park)
L. Renwick (London Scottish, Anglo Scots and Scotland)
A. Reuben (Bristol University and Birmingham/ Solihull)
R. Reynolds (Manly, New South Wales and Australia)
A. Richards (Wasps and England Trialist)
C. Richards (Jed Forest)
J. Richards (Newport)
C. Richardson (London Scottish and Scotland 'B')
D. Richardson (Wasps)
S. Riding (Barking)
M. Ridley (Ebbw Vale)
A. Ripley (Rosslyn Park, England and British Lions)
A. Ritchie (Mid Northern and Northland)
C. Ritchie (Rosslyn Park)
G. Roberts (Swansea and Wales)
M. Roberts (Ospreys)
T. Roberts (Cinderford)
G. Robertson (Northampton and England Trials)
I. Robertson (Watsonians and Scotland)
J. Robertson (Heriot's FP, Edinburgh and Scotland U21)
P. Robertson (Nantes University, London Scottish
and Edinburgh)
B. Robinson (Cambridge)
M. Robinson (Bath)
R. Robinson (Marist, Manawatu, Chiefs and
New Zealand Maori)
P. Roblin (Rosslyn Park)
R. Rodan (Baravi Exiles, Fiji Sevens)
R. Roddis (Sidcup)
T. Rodgers (Bedford and England Trialist)
J. Rodley (North Harbour, New Zealand Maori)
A. Rogers (Rosslyn Park)
D. Roke (Worcester)
S. Rokini (Suva, Fiji Sevens and Fiji)

N. Roko (Waimanu, Natisori and Fiji)
S. Roko (British Army)
N. Rokobiau (Natisori and Fiji Sevens)
P. Rollerson (Bedford)
E. Rollitt (Wasps)
G. Rolls (Hawkes Bay Maori, Canterbury U21)
K. Ronaki (Cambridge City)
E. Rosa (Richmond)
C. Rose (Richmond)
M. Rose (Cambridge University, Coventry, Rosslyn Park
and England)
D. Rosen (Oxford University)
G. Ross (Heriot's FP and Scotland)
G. Ross (Natal Sharks, Otago, Stade Francais and France 'A')
J. Ross (Bedford)
M. Ross (Wasps)
F. Rossigneux (Stade Français, Bedford, Wasps,
London Welsh and French Barbarians)
L. Rossigneux (Paris University Club and Racing Club)
P. Rouse (Dundee HSFP)
A. Rowe (Watsonians)
B. Rowell (Leicester and England)
P. Rowell (London Welsh)
M. Rowlands (Ebbw Vale)
M. Rowley (Pontypridd)
S. Rubaka (Natisori and Fiji Sevens)
W. Rubie (Oxford University)
E. Rush (Takapuna, Otahuhu, Auckland, North Harbour,
New Zealand Sevens and New Zealand)
B. Russell (Northampton)
M. Rust (Rugby)
B. Ryan (Cambridge University, Richmond, Newbury,
Nottingham, West Hartlepool and England U21)
M. Ryan (Lansdowne and Leinster)

S

E. Sadden (Oxford University)
P. Sampson (Wasps and England)
P. Sanderson (Harlequins, Worcester, England Sevens
and England)
S. Saravanua (Bravi Exiles and Fiji Sevens)
T. Saseve (North Harbour Marist, North Harbour 'B',
Hawkes Bay, New Zealand Sevens Trial and New Zealand U19)
A. Satala (Heriot's FP, British Army, Fiji Sevens and Fiji)
B. Satala (Fiji, Fiji Sevens)
K. Savage (Northampton, England and British Lions)
R. Sawtrick (Manchester University)
L. Sayer (Leicester)
T. Schorn (Stellenbosch University)
L. Scrace (Wasps)
D. Scully (Wakefield and England Sevens)
K. Seecharran (Bristol University and England Students)
M. Senio (Marist St. Joseph's, Samoa Sevens and Samoa)
F. Sequeira (Coventry, Walsall and Argentina Sevens)
O. Seraki (Nasinu, Suva, Fiji Sevens)
M. Serevi (Natulcake)
W. Serevi (Leicester, Mont de Marsan, Fiji Sevens and Fiji)
T. Seru (Gordon's)
R. Shackleton (Richmond and England)
I. Shand (Heriot's FP)
C. Sharman (Currie, Edinburgh and Scotland Sevens)
M. Sharp (Tabard)
M. Sharpe (Tabard and Bedford)
C. Sheasby (Harlequins and England)
B. Sheehan (Manly, Brisbane Broncos RL, NSW,
Western Force and Australia)
C. Shepherd (Otago Highlanders)
R. Shepherd (Edinburgh Academicals, Melrose,
South of Scotland, Scottish Students and Scotland)
A. Sheridan (Dulwich College, Sale, England and
British Lions)
B. Sherry (Terenure College and Ireland)
E. Shervington (Ospreys)
P. Shillingford (Moseley)
J. Shipsides (Wilmslow, Cambridge University, Cheshire
and England Trialist)
A. Short (London Scottish and Sussex)
S. Shortland (Wasps)
P. Shufflebottom (Wilmslow and Cheshire)
P. Sibley (Bath)
P. Simmonds (Bedford Athletic)
J. Simmons (Te Puke Sports)
D. Sims (Bedford)
D. Simms (Gloucester and Worcester)

K. Simms (Wasps and England)
N. Simms (Cambridge University)
C. Simpson (Bedford)
G. Simpson (Glagow HSFP and Scotland)
I. Sinclair (Waikato University, Old Varstonians,
Watsonians, Edinburgh Reivers and Scotland 'A')
M. Singer (Cambridge University and Neath)
D.M.B. Skinner (Rosslyn Park and Hertfordshire)
M. Skinner (Blackheath, Harlequins and England)
O. Slack (Cambridge University and Cambridge City)
A. Slade (Henley)
B. Slade (Invercargill Pirates)
J. Slater (Manly, Queensland, AIS U21 and Australia U21)
J.F. Slattery (Blackrock College, Ireland and British Lions)
L. Smith (Coventry)
J. Smales (Bath University and England Students)
J. Smiler (Hautapu and Waikato)
R. Smit (Waterkloof and Blue Bulls Academy)
A. Smith (Massey and North Harbour 'B')
B. Smith (Oxford University, Murraha, Ireland and
Australia)
G. Smith (Moseley)
G. Smith (Randwick)
L. Smith (Wasps)
M. Smith (Glasgow Hawks and Scottish Silver Thistles)
R. Smith (Boroughmuir)
S. Smith (Ballymena and Ulster)
S. Smith (Richmond)
W. Smith (Casali, Canterbury and New Zealand)
T. Smithers (Rosslyn Park)
S. Snoddy (Bangor and Ulster President's XV)
A. Snow (Heriot's Former Pupils, Edinburgh
and England Students)
D. Sole (Edinburgh Academicals, Bath and Scotland)
T. Solomon (Bay of Plenty)
N. Southcombe (Westcombe Park)
M. Sowerby (Wakefield)
C. Sparks (Terenure College and Ireland Reserve)
H. Speight (Hamilton Old Boys, Waikato and ACT Brumbies)
M. Speight (London Welsh, Waikato University, Waikato,
North Harbour, New Zealand Universities and New Zealand)
C. Spence (Gisborne)
G. Spencer (Rosslyn Park)
H. Spencer (Saracens)
L. Spratt (London New Zealand)
P. Stafford (Rosslyn Park and Oxford University)
M. Stanojevic (Bristol and Italy)
D. Stark (Ayr, Glasgow Hawks, Glasgow and Scotland)
N. Starling (Rotherham)
C. Starmer-Smith (Begles)
B. Steele (London Scottish and Scotland)
J. Steele (Northampton and England 'B')
W.C.C. Steele (Langholm, RAF, Bedford and Scotland)
M. Steffert (Northampton, Waikato University, Waikato
and New Zealand Universities)
I. Stent (Heriot's FP)
E. Stephenson (Oxford Harlequins)
D. Stevens (Blackheath)
P. Stevens (Heriot's FP and Scotland)
S. Stevens (Penzance & Newlyn and England)
B. Stewart (Edinburgh Academicals, Sale, Northampton,
Edinburgh and Scotland)
K. Stewart (Cross Keys and Cardiff)
N. Stewart (Ards, Ionstonians, Rugby Lions and Harlequins)
R. Stewart (Newport)
R. Stewart (Collegians, London Irish, Ulster and Ireland 'B')
P. Stiff (Bristol, South West Counties and England U23s)
D. Stoddart (Heriot's Former Pupils and Scotland U21)
R. Stone (West Hartlepool and Newcastle)
S. Stoop (Oxford Brookes)
P. Stringfield (Rosslyn Park, Middlesex and Waikato U23s)
J. Strong (London Welsh)
J. Stuart (Glasgow)
S. Stumbles (Watsonians)
R. Subbiani (Bedford and Welsh Students)
R. Sugden (Army)
S. Summers (Ely and Cambridge)
J. Sutherland (Marist St. Josephs, Waikato)
K. Svoboda (Oxford University and Canada)
T. Swan (Waterloo)
D. Swart (Stellenbosch University)
B. Sweeney (North Shore and North Harbour)
M. Sweeney (Randwick)
T. Swift (Swansea, Bath and England)
J. Swords (London Welsh)
A. Syme (Stirling County and New Zealand Universities)

T

M. Tack (Stellenbosch University)
H. Tamariki (Marist, Southland)
M. Tamiti (Parma, Botochini, New Zealand League Sevens)
H. Tarr (Oxford University Greyhounds)
J. Tate (Cardiff and Canada)
C. Tatham (Clifton)
N. Tauafoa (Malie, Apia West, Samoa Sevens and Samoa)
D. Tausili (Mitsubishi, Canterbury and Samoa)
B. Taylor (Northampton)
G. Taylor (Cross Keys)
G. Taylor (Ebbw Vale and Wales)
G. Taylor (Loughborough University and England U21)
J. Taylor (London Welsh and Wales)
M. Taylor (Wasps, Bay of Plenty and New Zealand)
P. Taylor (Rosslyn Park)
R. Taylor (Nottingham)
S. Taylor (Heriot's FP, Edinburgh, Stade Francais, Bath, Scotland and British Lions)
M. Teague (Gloucester, England and British Lions)
M. Thatcher (Wasps)
A. Thomas (Swansea, Neath, Bristol and Wales)
B. Thomas (Ebbw Vale)
E. Thomas (Neath and Wales 'A')
H. Thomas (Glamorgan Wanderers)
M. Thomas (Rosslyn Park and Wales Sevens)
O. Thomas (Bridgend)
S. Thomas (Coventry)
G. Thompson (Rosslyn Park and England U21)
J. Thompson (Cambridge University)
R. Thompson (Abertillery)
N. Thomson (Taradale, Hawkes Bay, New Zealand Sevens)
S. Thomson (Kelso)
S. Thompson (Montreal Barbarians, Canada Sevens and Canada)
W. Thompson (Bristol and England Universities)
C. Thorburn (London Scottish, Middlesex, Barbarians and Scotland Trialist)
J.D. Thorne (Bristol and England)
P.J. Thorne (Blackheath and England Trialist)
H. Thorneycroft (Northampton, Barbarians and England 'B')
P. Thornley (Leicester)
J. Thorp (Bedford Athletic)
B. Thynne (Rosslyn Park)
N. Timmins (Manly)
A. Tinasau (Baravi Exiles and Fiji Sevens)
D. Titcomb (Bristol)
K. Tkachuk (Oxford University, Glasgow and Canada)
K. Todd (Northampton)
T. Tombleson (Oxford University and England Students)
M. Tosa (Oxford University, NEC Green Rockets, Japan U23)
S. Townsend (Wakefield, Yorkshire and England U23)
M. Trapp (Harlequins, Auckland)
W. Treadwell (Wasps and England)
D. Trick (Bath and England)
K. Troup (London Scottish)
A. Tuala (Manurewa, Counties-Manukau, Chiefs Development)
S. Tubbs (Loughborough University and England U21)
I. Tucker (Sydney University, Oxford University and Blackheath)
P. Tuigamala (Western United, North Harbour Development and New Zealand Sevens trials)
N. Tuitavake (Massy, North Harbour, New Zealand U20 and New Zealand Sevens)
A. Tunisau (Nadi, Colonials, Fiji Barbarians and Fiji)
A. Tunningly (Saracens)
C. Turnbull (Heriot's FP)
J. Turner (Blackheath and Kent)
P. Turner (Newport Crawshay's Welsh, Barbarians and Wales)
T. Turner (Rugby)
A. Turtle (Trinity College, Dublin)

U

V. Ubogo (Oxford University, Bath and England)
J. Ufton (Wasps)
T. Underwood (Cambridge University, Leicester, Newcastle, England and British Lions)
M. Underwood (Northampton)
B. Urlich (Mitsubishi, North Harbour, Auckland Blues and New Zealand Maori)

J. Uva (Belenesse, Portugal Sevens and Portugal)
T. Uzas (Queensland University)

V

A. Valence (Auckland Blues and New Zealand Sevens)
M. Vant Leven (Fraser Tech, Waikato and Chiefs)
G. Varcoe (Clive and Hawkes Bay)
R. Varty (Hong Kong Sevens, Hong Kong)
M. Veale (Kubota Spears, Wasps, North Harbour, Northland)
R. Vickery (Somerset Police)
S. Vigars (Rosslyn Park)
S. Viggers (Rugby)
N. Vintner (Richmond)
M. Volland (Bedford)
P. Volley (Wasps, Castre Olympique, Harlequins and London Scottish)
M. Vunibaka (Leicester and Fiji Sevens)
C. Vyvyan (West Hartlepool and Sale)

W

R. Wainwright (Cambridge University, West Hartlepool, Army and Scotland)
F. Wagenstroom (Tygerburg, Sharks, Cheetahs, South Africa U18, U19 and U21)
M. Waite (Watsonians, Edinburgh and Scotland 'A')
T. Wakeford (Metropolitan Police)
S. Waldrom (Avalon, Tukapa, Wellington, Taranaki, Hurricanes, Waikato, New Zealand Sevens, New Zealand Maori and New Zealand)
A. Walker (Oxford University)
C. Walker (Tukapa, Taranaki and New Zealand U21)
W. Walker (North Shore, North Harbour, Gloucester, Blues and New Zealand Maori)
J. Wallace (Wasps)
K. Wallace (Haddington)
M. Wallwork (Bedford)
B. Walsh (London New Zealand)
T. Walsh (Wests, Watsonians, Leeds, Randwick and Australia Sevens)
S. Walters (AKA S. Thompson - Northampton and England)
I. Warbrick (London Scottish, Staines and Scotland Sevens)
J. Ward (Nottingham)
S. Ward (Exeter Chiefs)
N. Wardingley (Rosslyn Park)
S. Wardingly (Blackheath)
R. Wareham (Loughborough University and England U21)
P. Warfield (Rosslyn Park, Sussex and England)
G. Warne
R. Warren (Marist St. Joseph's, Samoa Sevens and Samoa)
T. Wati (Rugby Lions)
B. Watkins (Caerphilly)
C. Watkins (Ebbw Vale)
J. Watkins (Gloucester and England)
N. Watkins (Neath)
M. Watson (Wanderers, Johannesberg, Transvaal and South Africa Sevens)
N. Watson (Mahurangi and North Harbour)
A. Watt (GHK, Glasgow and Scotland)
D. Watt (Bristol and England)
W. Waugh (Randwick, Bath and Australia)
J. Webb (Bristol and England)
C. Webber (Bridgewater RFC)
M. Webber
G. Webster (Cambridge University)
M. Weedon (Bay of Plenty, Ponsonby, Auckland, Blagnac, Wasps and New Zealand U21)
N. Weir (London Scottish)
J. Welburn (Oxford Harlequins)
J. Wells (Leicester)
J. Wellwood (Cambridge University)
E. Wessells (Esher and Namibia)
J. West (Sidcup)
R. West (Gloucester)
J. Wharton (Beckenham)
B. Wheeler (Cambridge University)
J. Wheeler (Cambridge University, Leicester and Singapore)
J. Wheeler (Nottingham)
B. Whetstone (Bedford)

W. Whetton (Northcote, North Harbour)
A. White (St. Mary's College Dublin)
J. White (Bristol)
J. White (Cambridge University)
J. White (Aberdeen Wanderers, Watsonians, Clermont Auvergne, Sale, Glasgow, Scotland and British Lions)
M. White (Wasps)
S. White-Cooper (Harlequins and England)
P. Whitelaw (Heriot's FP and Edinburgh District)
M. Whiteley (Moseley and Midlands U21)
E. Whitely (Loughborough)
H. Whitford (Stade Francaise)
S. Wichary (London Scottish)
S. Wight (Melrose)
B. Wigley (Rugby)
R. Wilkes (Sale)
R. Wilkinson (Bedford and England)
A. Williams (Cardiff)
A. Williams (Marist St. Joseph's and Samoa)
F. Williams (London Welsh and Welsh Trialist)
G. Williams (Bedford Athletic)
G. Williams (Bridgend and Wales)
G. Williams (Harlequins)
H. Williams (Cambridge University)
J. Williams (Ebbw Vale)
J. Williams (London Kiwis and Old Varstonians)
M. Williams (Blackheath and Kent)
M. Williams (Ealing)
O. Williams (Glamorgan Wanderers, Bridgend, Cardiff and Wales)
P. Williams (Cardiff)
R. Williams (Harlequins)
A. Wilson (Heriot's FP)
B. Wilson (London New Zealand)
D. Wilson (Boroughmuir and Scotland 'B')
F. Wilson (Belfast HS and Ireland)
I. Wilson (Borders)
R. Wilson (Wainuiomata, Wellington and New Zealand U20)
R. Wilson (London Scottish)
S. Wilson (Manly)
S. Wilson (Wellington and New Zealand)
M. Wiltshire (Bridgend and Wales)
G. Windsor-Lewis (Oxford University and Wales)
S. Winn (Newport Gwent Dragons and Wales Sevens)
R. Winney (Plymouth)
J. Winterbottom (Henley and England Counties)
R. Winters (Harlequins)
M. Wintle (Llanelli)
R. Wintle (Bridgend and Wales)
R. Wintle (Caerphilly)
K. Wirachowski (Wasps and Canada)
T. Withers (Rugby)
T. Withers-Green (London Scottish)
S. Wolfe (Wasps)
M. Wood (Wasps)
A. Woodhouse (Loughborough University)
D. Wrench (Harlequins and England)
F.B. Wrench (Harlequins and England)
J. Wrigglesworth (Bedford Blues)
A. Wright (Loughborough College)
A.G.L. Wright (Sidcup)
C. Wright (Harlequins and London Counties)
I. Wright (Northampton and England)
I. Wright (St. Luke's College)
J. Wright (Harlequins and Herts)
M. Wright (Northampton and English Universities)
D. Wyatt (Bedford and England)
D. Wyer-Roberts (Bedford)
C. Wyles (Rosslyn Park)

Y

T. Yapp (Worcester and Exeter)
P. Yardley (Bridgend)
P. Yarranton (Wasps, RAF, Combined Services, Middlesex, Barbarians and England)
K. Yates (Bath, Wellington, Sale, Saracens and England)
J. York (East Coast Bays, North Harbour Sevens and North Harbour)
N. Young (Redcar)

Z

D. Zaltzman (Bedford, Saracens and Worcester)
J. Zimnoch (Toronto Nomads)

THE PLAYERS PENGUIN INTERNATIONAL RFC

INDEX

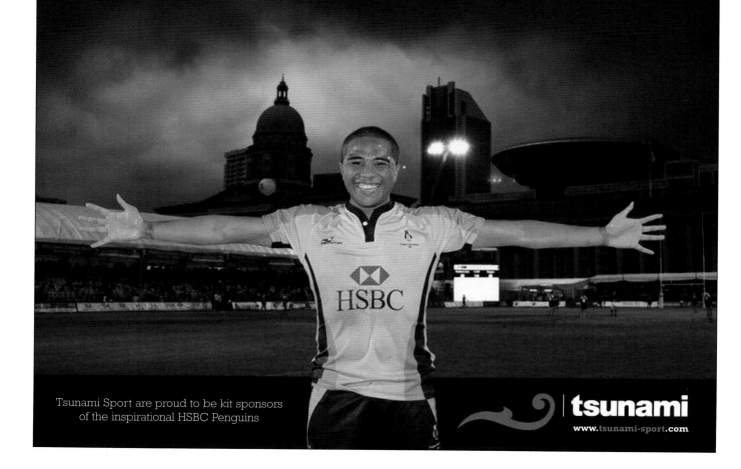

Don't just play.
inspire

Tsunami Sport are proud to be kit sponsors
of the inspirational HSBC Penguins

tsunami
www.tsunami-sport.com